D1431674

Cambridge Studies in the History and Theory of Politics

EDITORS

Maurice Cowling   G. R. Elton
J. R. Pole

DEMOCRACY AND RELIGION

For a list of other titles in this series see end of book

DEMOCRACY AND RELIGION

Gladstone and the Liberal Party, 1867–1875

J. P. PARRY

Fellow of Peterhouse, Cambridge

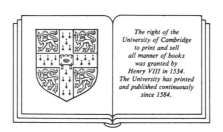

The right of the
University of Cambridge
to print and sell
all manner of books
was granted by
Henry VIII in 1534.
The University has printed
and published continuously
since 1584.

CAMBRIDGE UNIVERSITY PRESS

CAMBRIDGE

LONDON   NEW YORK   NEW ROCHELLE

MELBOURNE   SYDNEY

Published by the Press Syndicate of the University of Cambridge
The Pitt Building, Trumpington Street, Cambridge CB2 1RP
32 East 57th Street, New York, NY 10022, USA
10 Stamford Road, Oakleigh, Melbourne 3166, Australia

First published 1986

Printed in Great Britain at the University Press, Cambridge

British Library cataloguing in publication data

Parry, J. P.
Democracy and religion: Gladstone and the Liberal
Party, 1867–1875. – (Cambridge studies in the
history and theory of politics)
1. Liberal Party – History – 19th century
2. Great Britain – Church history – 19th century
I. Title
274.1'081   BR759

Library of Congress cataloguing in publication data

Parry, J. P. (Jonathan Philip), 1957–
Democracy and religion.
(Cambridge studies in the history and theory of politics)
Bibliography.
Includes index.
1. Great Britain – Politics and Government – 1837–1901.
2. Church and state – Great Britain – History – 19th century.
3. Gladstone, William Ewart, 1809–1898.
4. Liberal Party (Great Britain) – History – 19th century.
5. Great Britain – Church history – 19th century.
I. Title. II. Series.
DA550.P27 1986   941.081   86–6113

ISBN 0 521 30948 4

To my parents

Contents

List of tables	*page*	ix
Acknowledgments		x
Notes on text, index and footnotes		xii
Introduction		1

PART I

1 THE WHIG-LIBERALS: I   57
   Church and state   80
   The Church of Scotland   102

2 THE WHIG-LIBERALS: II   105
   Education   105
   Social reform   112
   The party system   116
   Protestantism and foreign policy   121
   Catholicism   125
   Ireland   128
   Perceptions of the Conservatives   137
   Perceptions of Gladstone   140
   Whig-liberals in parliament   144

3 GLADSTONE, HIGH CHURCHMEN AND LIBERAL CATHOLICS   150
   Introduction: the high-church mission   151
   Gladstone: Church and state   153
   Gladstone: education   164
   Gladstone and Liberal politics   167
   Gladstone: foreign policy   174
   Gladstone: Ireland   176
   Liberal high churchmen   181
   Liberal Catholics and Irish home rulers   193

4 THE RADICALS   199
   Nonconformists   200
   The radical MPs   229
   Working-men   232
   Morley, Harrison and positivism   239
   Academic liberals   249

PART II

5 SEARCHING FOR UNITY: THE IRISH CHURCH
   QUESTION, 1867–9   261
   Liberal disunity, 1867–8   261
   A fragile unity restored, 1868   267
   The apogee of unity: the Irish Church Act, 1869   280

6 EDUCATION, ESTABLISHMENT AND IRELAND,
   1869–71   289
   Irish disorder and the Vatican council, 1869–70   289
   The crisis over English and Irish education in the
      1870 session   295
   The arousal of provincial Liberalism, 1870–1   306
   First intimations of mortality, late 1871   321

7 THE RELIGIOUS PROBLEM INTENSIFIED, 1872–3   333
   The Manchester conference and English politics in 1872   333
   The Scottish Education Act   339
   Ireland in the 1872 session   343
   The framing, introduction and defeat of the Irish
      University Bill, 1872–3   353

8 THE FALL OF THE GOVERNMENT, 1873–4   369
   1873: a wasted session   369
   The 1874 election   381

9 DISUNITY EXPLICIT, 1874–5   411
   The 1874 session: ritualism and Scottish patronage   411
   Vaticanism and Gladstone's resignation, 1874–5   421

   Conclusion   429

   Bibliography   453
   Index   493

Tables

1 Distribution of the 115 radical and 151 non-radical MPs
  selected for the survey, by constituency   *page* 145
2 Conservative gains at the 1874 election   394
3 Party gains, 1874, and distribution of nonconformity, 1851   397

Acknowledgments

My thanks are due to the owners of manuscript material cited in the bibliography for permission to make use of their collections, and to a large number of archivists and librarians in the institutions listed there for making them available, and for their assistance in other ways. I have been especially demanding on the time of the staff of the University library, Cambridge (Mr Stephen Lees in particular), the Bodleian library, Oxford, the British library, the National libraries of Scotland and Ireland, the Public record office at Kew, and the libraries of Lambeth Palace and of Homerton college, Cambridge. Lord Blake kindly allowed me to see the papers of the 14th earl of Derby in his house. My thanks are also due to the managers of the Political Science Fund and to the Librarian of the Seeley library (both of the Cambridge History Faculty), for financial help. Mrs P. Stockham kindly typed the index. I am grateful to the Warden and Fellows of Merton college, Oxford, collectively, and to Dr Roger Highfield individually, for allowing me to spend a year researching there. I am greatly indebted to the Master and Fellows of Peterhouse for their support and encouragement.

It is a pleasure also to record my thanks to Dr David Bebbington, Dr Clyde Binfield, Mr David Cooper, Dr David Cornick, Mr Peter Ghosh, Mr Lawrence Goldman, Dr A. T. Harrison, Dr Boyd-Hilton, Dr T. A. Jenkins, Dr Alon Kadish, Professor R. B. Knox, Dr Ian Machin, Dr Edward Norman, Dr Agatha Ramm, Dr Alistair Reid, Professor Keith Robbins, Dr Miri Rubin, Dr Platon Tinios, Professor John Vincent and Dr D. G. Wright for assisting me with inquiries and for providing useful information and advice. Dr Peter Clarke, Mr Ian Harris, Dr Colin Matthew, Mr John Plowright and Mr Stephen Taylor read the whole typescript, and Dr Richard Brent, Dr David Cannadine and Dr Mark Kaplanoff read parts of it. I owe a particular debt both to them and to Professor Richard Shannon and Professor Paul Smith, who examined the Ph.D. thesis on which this book is based, for their helpful comments and bracing criticism. I am under a profound obligation to Professor Derek Beales, who supervised my thesis with unceasing judgment, tolerance, humour and patience, and Mr Maurice Cowling. They not only introduced me to the subject, but have provided stimulation and guidance over many years, which has gone far beyond the call of duty, and which has always been delivered in invigorating and harmonious counterpoint.

Note on text, index and footnotes

Text and index

Biographical details of the individuals discussed in this book are available in Part I (and, to some extent, in the index). Citations of the page numbers on which these details are given, are printed in bold-face type in the index entries for the individuals concerned in order to facilitate cross-referencing.

A number of individuals discussed had the same surnames. Where identity is not obvious from the context, the rule which has usually been followed is to refer to a politician by his surname, and to a cleric, academic or journalist by his surname and his initials or Christian name. For example, 'Bright' is John, not William; 'Lowe' is Robert, not E.C.; 'Russell' is Earl Russell, not G. W. E. Russell. Where ambiguities are still likely to arise, the part of the index entry which corresponds to the form generally used throughout the book is in bold-face type. Thus 'Grey' in the book can be seen, from the index, to refer to '**Grey**, Henry, 3rd Earl', and not to '**Grey**, Sir **George**', unless the context suggests otherwise.

Footnotes

Complete titles of works are given in the footnotes only when not listed in the bibliography. Full details of the great majority of the printed works which have been abbreviated here will be found in sections B4, B5 and C of the latter (see the list of the contents of the bibliography, on p. 453). Titles whose abbreviated forms consist entirely or mainly of proper names are nearly all listed in section B5, usually under the name in the abbreviated title, occasionally under that of the author.

Names in parenthesis usually indicate the person who said or wrote the material quoted or referred to in the text.

The following special abbreviations have been used throughout the notes:

Hansard   Hansard's *Parliamentary debates*, 3rd series.

Lathbury   *Correspondence on Church and religion of William Ewart Gladstone*, ed. D. C. Lathbury, 2 vols., London, 1910.

Matthew   *The Gladstone diaries*, ed. M. R. D. Foot and H. C. G. Matthew, 8 vols., Oxford, 1968–82.

PMP   *The prime ministers' papers series: W. E. Gladstone*, ed. J. Brooke and M. Sorensen, 4 vols., London, 1971–81.

Ramm   *The political correspondence of Mr Gladstone and Lord Granville 1868–1876*, ed. A. Ramm, 2 vols., London, 1952.

Introduction

The scholarly writing devoted to Victorian politics in the last twenty-five years has had one tendency in particular: to diminish our sense that ideological divisions underpinned political conflict at Westminster.[1] This tendency has been especially noticeable in discussing parliamentary reform on the one hand, and state intervention in social questions on the other. It is now widely recognised that, whatever groupings may have been thrown up at particular times, parties did not consistently possess agreed and opposing attitudes to such matters, let alone conflicting policies about them.[2] It has thus come to be seen as anachronistic to organise accounts of party politics between 1830 and 1890 around concepts of 'interventionism' or 'laissez-faire', 'collectivism' or 'individualism'. Much state intervention in these years was uncontroversial and inspired by *ad hoc* responses to problems. The wisdom of other measures was disputed, but not, usually, because of a doctrinaire opposition to the propriety of government interference in its citizens' affairs.[3] 'Interventionist' legislation was of many kinds: there were Factory and Licensing Acts; there were measures extending the state's role in the provision of education, abolishing the purchase system in the army, and redirecting the endowments of religious, educational or other corporate bodies. It was frequently the case that men who advocated one of these measures opposed others. In the last two decades, there has also been a growing realisation of the perils involved in attempting to explain politi-

---

[1] Much of the pioneering work was done by Hanham, *Elections and party management*, and Vincent, *Formation of the Liberal party*.

[2] Two of the most important works here are Smith, *Disraelian Conservatism and social reform*, and Cowling, *1867*.

[3] See the review by J. Harris in *Times Literary Supplement*, 11 November 1983, p. 1241; and Perkin, *The structured crowd*, ch. 4.

cal activity in 'class' terms, when classes were so ill-defined and politicians were so wary of appealing to class sentiment.[4]

Contributing to this change of emphasis, and at the same time feeding off it, has been the mode of historical writing adopted by the so-called 'high politics school'. This stresses the discreteness of each political situation, and the constraints on, and short-term aims of, individual politicians who were forced to work within it. A number of distinguished recent political biographies have similarly demonstrated that it is no longer possible to assume a simple connection between an individual's ideals and his political activity.[5] Politicians have come to be shown in a far more convincing light than before, as complex men creating and inhabiting an insular and sometimes devious world.

The combination of all these advances has been to emphasise the constantly shifting nature of values and priorities in high politics, and, accordingly, the difficulty of generalising successfully about political developments over any lengthy period of time. This has had particularly marked consequences for attempts to trace the influence of elaborated theory on the formulation of policy. It has come to be realised that bureaucratic constrictions on the one hand, and personal calculations of advantage on the other left little room for sophisticated beliefs or ideologies to affect discussions of almost any specific legislative measures. Historians, already aware of the danger of sailing the ship of 'ideas' too near to the rocky shoreline of political reality, have become further daunted as a result of the immense advances which have been made in the study of electoral politics; these have revealed the extent to which the local political experience was organised, not around detailed discussion of policy developments at Westminster, but through the prevailing power structures, among them, most obviously, those of landlords, employers and publicans.

All these developments have been beneficial to our understanding of nineteenth-century politics, and any new contribution to a branch of the subject must, to a large extent, incorporate the assumptions which have come to prevail among historians. This book certainly recognises that 'interventionism' and 'class' are tools of only limited utility to the historian of Victorian politics, and that the course of events was necessarily affected by the temperaments of leading politicians, their parliamentary tactics, the constrictions imposed by circumstances outside Westminster, and chance and timing. Nonetheless, the book is concerned with the relationship between beliefs and political action, and thus

---

[4] McCord, *North east England*, pp. 16–20; Nossiter, 'Middle class and nineteenth century politics', pp. 80–1.
[5] See e.g. Foster, *Churchill*; K. Bourne, *Palmerston: the early years 1784–1841* (London, 1982).

differs from the developing consensus described above in one sense. While rejecting the notion that elaborated theory can usually be assigned any very specific influence in the shaping of detailed policy, it asserts that prejudices, and 'ideas' in a less developed form ought not to be ignored by the political historian. It argues that a closer attention to the intellectual setting in which political activity took place is a necessary precondition for an understanding of the interest which politics evoked, the anxieties which it aroused, and the consequences of those anxieties for future developments. The book has attempted to establish the ideological context of politics after 1867 by concentrating primarily – although not exclusively – on arguments about religion. In doing so, it has resorted, if tentatively, to generalisation – in the belief that the detailed and the overarching must coexist if history is to be both convincing and comprehensible.

It concentrates on the discussion of religious policy within the Liberal party in the years after the passage of the Second Reform Act, years which encompassed Gladstone's assumption of the Liberal leadership, the turmoils of his first government, and his first resignation as leader. It embraces party policy concerning, and attitudes towards, a number of questions: the extension of civil liberty for all religious groups; the future of the Churches of England and Scotland; the disestablishment of the Anglican Church in Ireland; the conditions surrounding the provision of elementary, endowed, and university education in all parts of the kingdom; and the growth of ritualism inside the Church of England and of ultramontanism in the Roman Catholic Church. This is not to claim, of course, that no other policy questions were important: valuable works by Steele, Harrison and Offer have treated, respectively, the Irish land, licensing and local taxation issues in detail, while foreign and colonial policy was similarly controversial.[6] Nor have the specific questions which are discussed here lacked their historians: important accounts are available of the passage of the Irish Church Act, and of the disputes surrounding Irish policy generally, the Vatican council, English university tests, and ritualism.[7] Moreover, three books deserve especial mention for their contribution towards explaining the attitudes of individuals and groups to the issues discussed in Part I below.[8]

Nonetheless, this book aims to break new ground in a number of ways.

---

[6] Steele, *Irish land*; Harrison, *Drink and the Victorians*; Offer, *Property and politics*.

[7] Bell, *Disestablishment in Ireland*; Norman, *Catholic Church* and *Anti-Catholicism in Victorian England*; Matthew, 'Gladstone, Vaticanism'; Ward, *Victorian Oxford*; Harvie, *Lights of liberalism*; Marsh, *Victorian Church in decline*.

[8] Bebbington, *Nonconformist conscience*; Butler, *Gladstone: Church, state, and tractarianism*; Shannon, *Bulgarian agitation*. Many other works have, of course, been of considerable assistance in the writing of that section.

It seeks, unlike the works cited above, to provide an account of the political debate about religious policy as it developed over a number of years, in order to display the interconnections between each of the specific areas of contention. Political controversy arose not from discussion of policy *per se*, but because of the sensitivity – amounting almost to neurosis – afflicting sections of the party on so many of the issues: sensitivity which was caused by fear of the possible consequences of policy initiatives, if they were extended to their logical conclusions. By tracing the way in which debates on Church Establishments, English, Scottish and Irish education, Catholicism and ritualism all became heated as a result of the exploitation of fears for future developments in other spheres, we can begin to understand – in a way which would otherwise be impossible – the mentality of the majority of Liberals by 1874, after several years of such discussions. Especially important here was the Irish education question. The 1873 Irish University Bill has been all but neglected by historians.[9] The conjunction of this lack of interest with a similar absence of emphasis on the very considerable political consequences of the proposals which Disraeli had made in 1868 for Irish educational reform (see p. 267) have been decidedly unfortunate. It will not have been easy for most historians to understand Disraeli's contention, in 1874, that 'an attempt to deal with National Education in Ireland . . . has broken up two governments'.[10] By appreciating the context within which these religious debates proceeded, it is also possible to gain a new perspective on the 1874 election campaign, and on the party's defeat – which, in terms of seats lost, was unprecedented in scope, and which gave the Conservatives their first real victory for thirty-three years. The arguments used in the campaign are shown to have capitalised on the widespread concern for the religious future. An attempt is also made to link dissimilarities in the electoral behaviour of different regions to denominational distribution.

A second aim of the book is to restore perspective to accounts of the balance of forces within the Gladstonian Liberal party. In the past, attention has tended to concentrate on the radical wing – and, even then, the secular radical wing has been given more attention than it merits, and nonconformity less. In this work, the seminal importance of what in

---

[9] Hammond allocated it two pages out of a total of 740 on *Gladstone and the Irish nation*; G. M. Trevelyan, in *British history in the nineteenth century (1782–1901)* (London, 1922), did not mention it at all; E. Halévy and R. B. McCallum gave it one sentence in *Victorian years 1841–1895* (London, 1951); even Southgate, whose subject was whig attitudes to the development of the Liberal party, did not discuss whig criticism of the bill in his fifteen lines of treatment in *Passing of the whigs*, p. 348. The most useful modern analysis is offered in E. R. Norman's study of the political influence of the Catholic hierarchy: *Catholic Church*.

[10] To Hicks Beach, 17 December 1874, Hicks Beach, *St Aldwyn*, i, 47.

modern terminology would be called the Liberal 'centre-right' – the moderates and whigs, the propertied Anglican classes – is emphasised in all political calculations affecting the party. ('Right' and 'left' have, *faute de mieux*, been used to designate the wings of the party throughout the book, despite the anachronism which is entailed in so doing.) Conversely, Chamberlain is presented as exerting a less significant influence over the development of Liberalism, at least in the 1870s, than is customary.

The book's most important argument, however, is that politics, in the 1860s and 1870s, cannot be understood if it is treated merely as a secular activity. It is contended that, for most politicians, politics had a religious dimension; and that, for vast numbers of voters, it was conceived as an activity of significance mainly because religious issues were so prominent. It is argued, moreover, that, for both politicians and writers on the one hand and for voters on the other, the importance of religion was not appreciated primarily in terms of the secular consequences that might follow from extending its hold. Its potential contribution to the preservation of law and order, or the suppression of class consciousness did not go unnoticed; but the main consideration in men's minds was that religion offered an inspiring and awful conception of their place in the order of things.

The Victorian age was a moral age, and one task of politicians was held to be educative: to guide public opinion; to teach citizens, many of them newly enfranchised, the basic tenets of good political behaviour; and to establish the conditions in which spiritual progress could be generated.[11] In discussing religious questions, many politicians and writers were concerned, directly or indirectly, with what Mill – and others – called the 'moral regeneration of mankind'.[12] Victorian politicians were as ambitious, cunning, vain, self-deluding and inconstant as the general run of performers on the public stage have been, but none of this debarred them from having religious preconceptions. Indeed, few of them – even those who had rejected many elements of traditional Christian dogma as implausible – doubted that man's most important duty on earth was to discover a religious life in Christ. In addition to the impulse which this gave them to promote religious ends in public life, they were inspired to undertake the same work by a horror of the consequences which they anticipated from spiritual destitution: revolution and anarchy. Britain was prosperous, but warnings against complacency were frequent. It was widely held that man's enjoyment of material benefits was consequent upon the blessing of Providence, and dependent upon his right behaviour; and that the preservation of social stability,

---

[11] See below, e.g. p. 444. [12] *On liberty*, p. 114.

class harmony and civilised values was a gift not given to all nations, as the example of France and the United States showed.[13] The impulse to propagate belief in an effective religion was especially powerful in the 1860s and 1870s, because of the unprecedented interest in the nature of religion, as a result of the publicity given to scientific discovery and biblical criticism: in these decades more than any other, 'society' and the quality press were preoccupied with religious subjects.[14]

It was not, of course, the 'upper ten thousand' alone who were concerned about religion. Religious debates touched issues which were more relevant to, and more momentous for, most electors than almost any others which politicians were prepared to consider raising; and this was of considerable importance for the smooth working of a democratic system. The arousal of mass enthusiasm for the political process was by no means automatic; and it was unlikely that, once aroused, it would be maintained by discussions of dry administrative, social and diplomatic questions. Religion was, as we shall see, of crucial importance in defining the political outlook of voters, because it played such a central part in their lives.

According to the 1851 census, the number of those attending religious services on 30 March 1851 was the equivalent of 61 per cent of the population. This figure was inflated by the tendency of many to attend more than one service daily; but, on the other hand, it is generally recognised that the proportion of the electorate which attended places of worship was much higher than that of the population as a whole.[15] Church attendance was especially high in the villages. Contemporaries were worried by the numbers of those in the large towns who did not attend religious worship. However, as Chadwick and others have shown, Anglicans and nonconformists made immense efforts to match the great increase in the urban population throughout the nineteenth century by providing extra churches, chapels and ministers; and they succeeded remarkably well, at least until the mid 1880s. The mid-century decades saw the greatest increase in Anglican activity: between 1841 and 1870, 2,859 new and rebuilt churches were consecrated, compared with 1,004 in the previous thirty years.[16]

The Anglicans' activity in the towns was, in fact, a response to the appeal of Protestant nonconformity as much as anything. The major nonconformist sects, the evangelical sects, had benefited greatly from

---

[13] See below, e.g. pp. 127–8.
[14] See e.g. Hirst, *Morley*, i, 305; Ernle, *Whippingham to Westminster*, p. 163; Ward, 'Priesthood in Irish politics', p. 266.
[15] Chadwick, *Victorian Church*, i, 325, 365.
[16] *Ibid.*, ii, 227, 232; Gilbert, *Religion and society*, p. 130; K. S. Inglis, *Churches and the working classes in Victorian England* (London, 1963), p. 27.

the expansion in the urban population since 1780. During the forty years after 1800, the numbers of methodists, congregationalists and baptists all increased by between 300 and 400 per cent (the quakers, a non-evangelical sect, lost members in the same period). In the sixty years before 1820, the proportion of Protestant nonconformists in the population rose tenfold to about 30 per cent.[17] Workers in the developing industrial districts became attracted to sects which were not as clearly identified as was Anglicanism with the agricultural parishes and the power structure prevailing in them; and to sects which appeared to place less emphasis than did their rival on hierarchy, and to leave the individual freer to seek his own relationship with God. But the power of nonconformity was not limited by region, and only slightly by class. It was strong in small towns and large villages; merchants and manufacturers, skilled artisans, and unskilled labourers were all attracted to it.

In 1800, nonconformists suffered a number of political and social disadvantages, as we shall see. The most irritating were their liability to payment of rates to keep up the local Anglican church, the restrictions on their eligibility for political office, and the illegality of marriage and burial services conducted according to their own rites. Nonconformists' grievances were intensified by perception of their social position *vis-à-vis* powerful Anglican landowners. At national level, factory employers and artisans were able to forge a political alliance on the basis of a common dislike of aristocratic and agricultural privilege: this began to be effective from the late 1820s. At local level, there were also clashes between Anglicans and nonconformists – about patronage, for example, especially in local government.[18] But, throughout the mid-nineteenth century, rivalry between the Church and nonconformity, in towns and villages, was also institutionalised by two elements, both of which engendered a strong sense of community feeling. The first was the unprecedented devotion and religious commitment displayed by their respective congregations. The second was the remarkable network of organisations which offered material and spiritual support to the working-class members of each sect. Most important were the elementary and Sunday schools (75.4 per cent of working-class children between the ages of five and fifteen were enrolled in Sunday schools in 1851, and their importance continued to grow until the 1880s).[19] There were also clothing clubs; boys' and mothers' groups; societies aimed at providing

---

[17] Laqueur, *Religion and respectability*, p. 3; Gilbert, *Religion and society*, p. 41; N. Gash, *Aristocracy and people: Britain 1815–1865* (London, 1979), p. 63.
[18] Fraser, *Urban politics in Victorian England*, pp. 115–24.
[19] Laqueur, *Religion and respectability*, p. 44; Chadwick, *Victorian Church*, ii, 227–8, 257.

help against sickness and assistance with funeral expenses; and, later in the century, musical and sporting clubs.[20]

Nonconformists' political influence was increased by the extensions of the franchise in 1832 and 1867, both of which led to clamour for the satisfaction of a number of their grievances. This was one reason why politics in the years after the 1867 Reform Act was dominated by 'unmaterial issue[s]'.[21] But the activity of nonconformist leaders in those years was in fact merely one element in fomenting the divisions between Liberal politicians and intellectuals which form the subject of this book. For they were split as to the best mode in which to advance the 'moral regeneration' of man. Moreover, the exigencies of the political process dictated that politicians and political publicists would exaggerate the extent of these divisions in order to win support for their own positions in the country. The consequence, it is suggested, is that the Liberal party – which, albeit as a loose coalition, had been so successful in government since 1846 – split, with fatal consequences for its electoral prospects.

The differences between the most important sections of the party are traced at length in Part I of the book. Chapters 1 and 2 deal with Liberal defenders of Church Establishments, men who have been described throughout as 'whig-liberals' (because there are difficulties with using the word 'whig' to describe them, given that not all were connected with the 'Great grandmotherhood' of leading whig families). They deal, that is, with the members of the whig aristocracy and of the Anglican Liberal gentry; with politicians who, on the whole, were younger and more advanced politically than most representatives of these two groups; and with broad-church clergymen and lay intellectuals. The analysis in chapter 3 centres on Gladstone, the high churchman who had migrated from Peel's Conservative party; but it also embraces high churchmen outside parliament who were attracted to the Liberals by his importance in the party, the remnant of Peelite MPs, and Irish liberal Catholics and home rulers. Chapter 4 discusses the views of the nonconformist sects; of radical MPs who supported the disestablishment of the Church and other nonconformist policies; of representatives of working-men; of positivists; and of academic radicals. The party did not, of course, split in the same way over each religious issue. But, while it did not always divide neatly along quite the lines indicated by the organisation of the chapters, the broad differences between those analysed in chapters 1 and 2, and in chapters 3 and 4, were of great significance, as will become apparent.

---

[20] Laqueur, *Religion and respectability*, pp. 172–4; S. Yeo, *Religion and voluntary organisations in crisis* (London, 1976), chs. 3, 5 and 6.

[21] (Haslam Mills) Binfield, *So down to prayers*, p. 106.

The bones of contention discussed in the book did not remain as divisive in the decade after 1875: in the most direct sense, they therefore had little to do with the permanent division within the Liberal party in 1886 on the subject of Irish home rule. However, an attempt is made in the book's conclusion to link the quarrels of 1870–5 with the controversies which inspired the latter crisis. The proposal of home rule was divisive partly because it appeared to endanger the safety of the Protestant minority, but this was only one among many considerations. Gladstone's initiative in 1886 in fact raised questions which were fundamental to nineteenth-century Liberalism – questions affecting the rights of the individual *vis-à-vis* the state, the proper extent of the rule of law, the wisdom of the popular judgment, and the rectitude of a political crusade based on emotional communion with the 'people'. It is suggested here that such arguments were more influential in deciding men's responses to Gladstone's Home Rule Bill than were purely secular assessments of their class interests, or sophisticated calculations of the political advantages that a certain course might offer them personally. Furthermore, it is impossible fully to appreciate the appeal of these arguments about 'freedom', 'law', and the 'people', without an understanding of the more specifically religious quarrels of the 1870s, which used the same terms. If these terms are appreciated merely in a secular light, they might easily remain imprecise abstractions. By interpreting them in the light of the disputes of 1870–5, we can come closer to comprehending the dilemmas of the Liberal mind, a mind in which the religious and the mundane were inextricably intertwined.

An introductory account of Liberal politics between 1832 and 1868 is now necessary in order to explain the relationship between the various sections of the party discussed in Part I – in particular, between whig-liberals, nonconformists, Gladstone, the radicals of the 1860s, and Irish Catholics – and the contentiousness of the debates analysed in Part II. These being the sole purposes of the account, it is necessarily more schematic and abstract than a fuller version would be: detailed definitions of the range of opinion within each section, and more sophisticated treatments of the arguments adopted by individuals belonging to each, will be found in the chapters in Part I.

In 1867, during one of the brief spells of minority government which the Conservative party enjoyed in the mid-nineteenth century, Disraeli persuaded it to sanction a reform of the electoral system. One calculation prompting this move was the hope that it might thereby establish the political centrality of the Conservative leadership in the changed situation following Palmerston's death – demonstrating its ability to lead a consensus government of Conservative and Liberal opinion. By adopting this strategy, Disraeli hoped to win the grudging support of Palmerstonians who would prefer apparently statesmanlike and realistic Conservatives to unpredictable Liberal–radical guidance from Gladstone and Bright.[22] This strategy failed. It failed partly because cautious Liberals like Grey, Lowe and Grosvenor did not find Disraeli's pose of responsible statesmanship very convincing; but it failed mainly because the Liberal party was reunited in March 1868 in pursuit of an apparently radical and destructive policy: the disestablishment of the Anglican Church in Ireland.

Two instructive conclusions may be drawn from these events. Firstly, they help to explain what has frequently been regarded as a mystery: the acceptance of parliamentary reform by the bulk of the Conservative party in 1867. For backbenchers, as for the prime minister Derby (a Reformer in 1832), the question of parliamentary reform was one of detail and degree: unpredictable in effect, potentially dangerous, potentially beneficial; to be treated with suspicion, but nonetheless undogmatically. The alternative to accepting reform was recognised to be the return to power of the Liberals, under the leadership not of the easygoing Palmerston, but, probably, of Gladstone. This was a much graver threat, especially since Gladstone seemed to be moving towards a policy of Irish Church disestablishment. Conservatives believed that it was of the highest importance to resist the disestablishment of a Church in any part of the United Kingdom; indeed, Derby had left the whigs with the intention of resisting such a policy, when the latter had moved to strip the Irish Church of the surplus revenues from its endowments in the 1830s.[23]

Secondly, the events of 1867–8 shed revealing light on the mentality of even the most cautious wing of the Liberal party, those old whigs and their intellectual allies who are often grouped with the Conservatives as common defenders of a propertied order, and common antagonists of 'reform'. How, if their perspectives on the world were so similar to those of Conservatives, could whigs like Grey, Fitzwilliam and Bouverie, and Adullamites like Lowe and Laing, differ so diametrically from them on a question as central as disestablishment? In fact, Disraeli, in planning to effect a permanent disruption of the Liberal party, forgot the pull of religious arguments on the whig-liberal conscience – an example of his greatest weakness as a politician, his inability to treat religious questions with sufficient seriousness.

The reunification of the Liberal alliance in 1868 was the third occasion since 1832 on which agreement on a great political question had regrouped the loosely agreed segments of Liberalism into a united force.

---

[22] Cowling, *1867*, pp. 309–10.
[23] *Ibid.*, *passim*. See Machin, *Politics and the Churches*, pp. 37–8.

On both previous occasions, the primary cause of harmony had also been religious. In 1835, Liberals had come together on a ticket of appropriating those revenues of the Irish Church which they considered surplus to her requirements to the benefit of the Irish population generally; in 1859, they had supported Italian unification against papal and Austrian interests. The potency of religious arguments on the Liberal conscience was no accident: since 1832, the organisation of both parties in the localities had been intimately connected with denominational affiliation – with seminal effects on their *raison d'être* at national level.

Although the struggle for the 1832 Reform Act cannot be understood if considerable attention is not paid to economic considerations, it is probably true, as both the *Spectator* and Earl Russell subsequently remarked, that nonconformists were 'the life of the agitation' for the bill.[24] The existence, before 1828, of an exclusive connection between Church and state had resulted in discrimination against religious minorities at many points: at birth, marriage and burial, in education, and in the definition both of political privileges and of liability to taxation (for the upkeep of the Establishment). A great amount of recent work has established that religious affiliation was the primary cause of loyalty to party under the 1832 and 1867 electoral dispensations. Given the sudden need, after 1832, to extend political organisation throughout the country to thousands who had been only intermittently politicised, and given the fears and hopes for reform in religious affairs which were genuinely held by many and which were exacerbated by political rhetoric, it would have been astonishing if this had not been the case. Nonconformists were overwhelmingly Liberal, usually by ratios of between eight and twelve to one. The Liberals also retained a respectable Anglican vote, which usually ensured that they received a majority of parliamentary seats: the Conservative to Liberal ratio among Anglicans was usually between 2½ and 4 to 1.[25] The Conservatives' greatest electoral problem thus became their manifest identification with the Established Church.

Of course, other variables affected election results, the most important of which was the organisation of local political sentiment by individuals who were able to define the purpose of political activity for the

---

[24] *Spectator*, 28 June 1873, p. 817; Skeats and Miall, *Free Churches of England*, pp. 597–8.

[25] Machin, *Politics and the Churches*, p. 40; McDonald, 'Religion and voting in an English borough', pp. 232–3. See also Clarke, 'Electoral sociology of modern Britain'; Wald, *Crosses on the ballot*, ch. 7; Vincent, *Formation of the Liberal party*, pp. 66, 97, 106; Brent, 'Immediate impact of the second Reform Act'; Greenall, 'Popular Conservatism in Salford'; Lowe, 'Tory triumph of 1868', esp. p. 742; Abram, 'Social condition and political prospects', p. 436.

voters.[26] The most powerful of these local interests were landowners, employers, and religious leaders, while local newspaper editors and artisan orators played a subordinate but important role in arousing opinion. (In addition, there were, of course, publicans and other purchasers of votes who, although significant, are not relevant to this discussion since they were, presumably, not susceptible to the pull of religious argument.) In particular, Conservative landowners were often able to prevent religious leaders and ecclesiastically minded orators from arousing the denominational loyalties of voters.[27] This was most obvious in many county and small borough seats in Scotland, Wales and Ireland, until alternative structures of influence, founded on popular religious sympathies, broke down landowners' hegemony in the late 1850s and 1860s. It was this shift of the 1860s which restored to the Liberals the natural parliamentary majority which they had anticipated possessing in 1832, but which (except at the 1857 election, held after the Crimean victory) they had come close to losing between 1841 and 1859. They were still able to retain office throughout most of these two decades, partly as a result of the informal and then formal support given to them by those nominal (Liberal-)Conservatives who had split from the mass of their party in 1846, in support of Peel's repeal of the Corn Laws. Nonetheless, the decline in Liberal support since 1832 was evident. This, to a considerable extent, was the result of the sway of religious argument in the counties and small boroughs of England – which had swung against the Liberals in the 1830s largely in reaction to the threat to the Anglican Church Establishment.[28] The advocates of Reform in 1832 had not expected such a development: one of their main aims had been to increase the number of county seats, on the assumption that the independent propertied county voter would wish to prevent a return to *ancien régime* executive tyranny, and would thus vote Liberal. Because of the Conservative reaction, however, the Liberals had been driven back, more than they had hoped, upon borough support.[29]

In most medium- or large-sized English boroughs, Conservatives suffered from the predominance of the independently minded small businessman, shopkeeper or artisan, so often a nonconformist. They could hope to do well only in those boroughs where nonconformity was weak and where Conservative organisation was atypically well developed – and such conditions were found, in large towns, only in Lancashire and London. In Lancashire, Conservative strength, especially in those towns

---

[26] Vincent, *Formation of the Liberal party*, pp. 82–96.
[27] See e.g. Machin, *Politics and the Churches*, pp. 40–1.
[28] And then in 1841, also owing to fear for the survival of the Corn Laws.
[29] See the tables in M. Brock, *The Great Reform Act* (London, 1973), pp. 19–20, 310–11.

where the religious distribution favoured Anglicanism, was harnessed from the 1860s. This was effected both by the reintroduction of the Irish issue into national politics – which permitted the manipulation of anti-Catholicism in a region with a distinctively Catholic presence – and by the creation of a powerful factory culture. The latter gave tory employers, like Hornby in Blackburn and Lindsay in Wigan, the muscle to politicise a previously unorganised workforce by turning elections into carnivals celebrating occupational loyalties and a common Protestantism.[30] In London, in the same decade, Conservative organisation also became professional, and was also based on employer power and on the exploitation of the fears of religious radicalism which accompanied the rise to national political prominence of evangelical nonconformity. The extraordinary weakness of nonconformity in London enfeebled the Liberal capacity to respond to their opponents' newfound aggressiveness (which may also have been sharpened by hopes of gaining support from the expanding professional and clerical classes).[31]

But, given Liberal strength in the boroughs generally, the Conservatives could do little to remedy their minority position – until the nature of the electoral system, the role of religious issues in politics, and the structure of British industry changed. The only astute policy open to them was to try to work on the Anglican Liberal vote – and, especially, on the fears of the local Liberals with most political influence, among whom Anglicanism was disproportionately strong. It is no coincidence that the only two elections between 1832 and 1886 which the Conservatives conclusively won – indeed the only two at which they collected over 250 English seats while the Liberals held under 200 – followed the two periods of most intense speculation that nonconformist and Catholic pressure might force the incumbent Liberal government into radical religious reform. One was in 1841;[32] this book is concerned with the other, and with its causes and consequences. On both occasions, of course, the defence of 'property' in general was intimately linked with the Conservative reaction; but it was Church and Protestant interests which were most obviously at risk.

On the whole, therefore, the Liberal alliance was able to secure a parliamentary majority between 1832 and 1885. The Conservatives enjoyed two spells of majority government, from 1841 to 1846 and from

---

[30] Joyce, *Work, society and politics*, pp. 213–14, 217, 272–5; Greenall, 'Popular Conservatism in Salford'; Lowe, 'Tory triumph of 1868'.

[31] Baer, 'Social structure, voting behaviour'. I have added the reflections on the impact of nonconformist weakness.

[32] D. H. Close, 'The rise of the Conservatives in the age of reform', *Bulletin of the Institute of Historical Research*, xlv (1972), 89–103; (Stanley, 1847) Gash, *Reaction and reconstruction*, p. 133.

1874 to 1880, and four brief ones, in an imperilled minority. In parliament, British nonconformists and radicals, and Irish Catholics frequently pursued a course independent of the Liberal leadership; but, at grass-roots level in Britain, a force identifiable as the Liberal party was in existence from the 1830s, and the genuinely independent MP was a rarity.[33] But how was this Liberal force so successful in maintaining the commitment and enthusiasm of its voters?

One basic aim of nineteenth-century party politics was to channel public feeling about politics so that it harmonised with the efficient organisation of forces in the legislature, rather than disrupting it and thus weakening government. This involved the disciplining, firstly, of MPs at Westminster and, secondly, of those who were most influential in marshalling public opinion outside it. It was impossible to organise large numbers of these, as was necessary after 1832, without adopting and propagating arguments stressing common priorities and values, which could give direction to the attitudes of those who created public opinion, and unite them in sentiment.

A successful 'political language' had to be able to give meaning to people's participation in the political process;[34] it had to be intelligible; it had to appear more central to people's concerns, and less disruptive of their interests, than any other; yet at the same time it had to summon a fund of enthusiasm for the cause. Successful political languages, therefore, had to tackle questions of basic and general interest. Parties won support by appealing to emotions and prejudices, by employing persuasive slogans in order to unite people with similar dispositions. This did not require them constantly to legislate in order to advance their common interests, since to institute perpetual change risked offending more voters than it pleased. Indeed, one essential task of parties which sought office was to appear more competent and less irresponsible than their opponents. Not only did they have to avoid undue recourse to programmatic statements, for fear of alarming some voters (and of committing them to administratively unwise projects): commitment to other, uncontroversial, policies, while proving their competence, might well fail to rouse their supporters from a state of apathy. Governments did not yet campaign on policy programmes or manifestos – indeed, the

---

[33] D. E. D. Beales, 'Parliamentary parties and the "independent" member, 1810–1860', in *Ideas and institutions of Victorian Britain: essays in honour of George Kitson Clark*, ed. R. Robson (London, 1967), pp. 1–19; Gurowich, 'Continuation of war'.

[34] These reflections arise out of the findings of this book, but they also owe something to other reading, including G. S. Wood, 'Intellectual history and the social sciences', in *New directions in American intellectual history*, ed. J. Higham and P. K. Conkin (Baltimore, 1979), pp. 27–41, and Jones, *Languages of class*.

advocacy of detailed policy was likely to engender great enthusiasm only if it satisfied two requirements. It had to appear to bring nearer an inspiring and easily comprehensible goal, and it had to attack those outposts of the enemy's position which were most indefensible, and least likely to win voters' sympathy.

Such unity as the coalition of whigs, radicals and nonconformists (and, intermittently, Catholics) possessed was sustained, after 1846, by a number of sets of attitudes. There was a commitment to maintain and extend the free-trade system against sectional economic policies (a commitment which later in the century enabled a certain degree of unity even on temperate land reform); there was a belief in economy, in efficiency, in sober, undoctrinaire administration free from class bias, and (after 1860) in responsible and cautious diplomacy abroad (in contrast to showy imperialist adventurousness). At elections, and in order to maintain party unity at Westminster, these issued in a number of potent cries: 'peace, retrenchment and reform', 'economy', 'free trade', 'improvement' and 'progress'. Many of these were still immensely valuable cohesives in 1874, 1880 and 1886, and even, to some extent, in 1906. The Liberals claimed to be uniquely capable of delivering these goods. However, the Conservative party was not as sectional, irresponsible, reactionary and amateurish as the Liberals alleged, although until the 1870s and 1880s it was undeniably less interested, as a party, in promoting legislative reform, and less experienced in financial administration. Most influential in creating the Liberals' image of unchallengeable administrative competence was their tenure of power for all but four years between 1846 and 1874. During this period, the work of public servants like Chadwick and Simon, and the weight of pressure from philanthropic societies and individuals, ensured that action on administrative, educational and sanitary questions became recognised functions of government. Liberal ministers, especially George Grey, Morpeth, Cornwall Lewis, Cowper-Temple, Lowe, Forster, Bruce and, not least, the Peelite defectors from the Conservatives, naturally took the credit for dealing with these questions. Their activity made it easy to dismiss the Conservatives, by comparison, as a landed rump.[35]

The Liberals' appeal was, therefore, not solely religious; but it was in dealing with religious questions that the party's aims were most explicit and innovatory. Political language about secular issues sometimes degenerated into flaccidity, and the differences between the parties in practice were not always clear. Cohesion, loyalty, discipline and

---

[35] See e.g. O. MacDonagh, *Early Victorian government 1830–1870* (London, 1977); R. J. Lambert, *Sir John Simon 1816–1904 and English social administration* (London, 1963); and S. E. Finer, *The life and times of Sir Edwin Chadwick* (London, 1952).

enthusiasm could be secured most effectively, on both sides, by appeals to religious sentiment and aspirations.

The Liberals' language about religious matters was, of course, profoundly affected both by events abroad and by British history before 1832. Wherever it appeared in Europe and North America between the 1780s and 1914, the liberal movement took the form of an assault on the influence wielded by allegedly exclusive and corrupt régimes. These régimes were condemned because of their intimate alliance with particular religious agencies, the discrimination enforced between favoured and unfavoured religions, and the penalties imposed on the adherents of the unfavoured. Given the immense influence which religion was credited with possessing, this repression was thought to constitute one of the most basic reasons for the régimes' hold on authority. Any group which was isolated from the network of power established by those régimes – such as the band of whig politicians in Britain led, from the 1760s, by Rockingham, Fox and then Grey – was thus bound to sympathise with the complaints of those religious minorities which experienced discrimination. These opposition groups tended, in consequence, to win the latter's loyalty.[36] In Catholic continental countries where the association between Church and state under the old dispensation was even more pronounced, similar movements against entrenched régimes were almost necessarily led mainly by educated men whose religious ancestry was Protestant (like Cavour in Italy) or who had given much thought to religious questions and had become sceptics or liberal Catholics.

Because it inherited the whig tradition of opposition to George III and Pitt, the British Liberal party was united, after 1832, in support of a number of policies. It advocated the diminution of the exclusiveness of the Church–state connection, and the extension of the civil liberties enjoyed by religious minorities. It demanded an assault on clerical control of the education system at both primary and higher levels, and its replacement by a system which was both more open and more closely supervised by the impartial state. It also recommended offering as little assistance to clerical régimes abroad, when they offended liberal principles, as was diplomatically wise for British interests. Of course, many individual MPs unthinkingly supported particular policies because they were pressured by constituents or because party allegiance seemed to require it. Inevitably, also, some MPs wished to implement these policies more thoroughly than did others. Nonetheless, one can trace a shared disposition of mind among Liberals. This had originally been founded on the tolerance, and condemnation of government corruption, which had

---

[36] See J. A. Phillips, *Electoral behavior in unreformed England: plumpers, splitters, and straights* (Princeton, 1982), pp. 159–68, 286–305.

been the hallmark of the Foxite whigs; but these sentiments then became powerfully affected by a religious vision in the early nineteenth century, under the impact of the evangelical revival, and of the renewed effort which non-evangelical churchmen were stimulated into making in reaction to it. The first generation of whig politicians who were noticeably affected by this religious temper were those, like Howick, Althorp and Spring Rice, who reached maturity in the 1820s and 1830s; their associates in literature, the Church and education, who responded similarly, are usually termed 'Liberal Anglicans'.[37] The immense influence of the major 'Liberal Anglican' writers – such as Thomas Arnold and Thirlwall – further entrenched this sense of rectitude in the young whig-liberals of the 1840s and 1850s, who became so politically influential in the 1860s; and it is these men, and the survivors of the older generation, who form the subject-matter of chapters 1 and 2 below.

The disposition of mind which religiously minded whig-liberals shared, from the 1830s, was a Protestant one. It was founded on a belief that it was within man's capacity to work towards a state of spiritual and social harmony on earth, guided by Providence. But this state, they argued, could be promoted only by developing the sense of individual responsibility, and divinity, inherent in every human being; progress was dependent upon man being encouraged to exercise his free will in beneficent ways. Essential, therefore, was a religion which cultivated individual responsibility, which explained man's duty and which developed his inner spiritual life – without which he would fall prey to 'materialist' impulses and lose his sense of higher purpose. The existing exclusive connection between Church and state had given the impression that those who did not subscribe to Anglican doctrine could not possess such a spiritual life: it had also made Anglicans complacent and had repressed their own spiritual sense. Whig-liberals contended that the tone of Church activity must be raised, the shackles on spiritual discovery imposed by irrelevant dogma lifted, and education in essential religious truths promoted.

Whig-liberals shared these views with the majority of other Protestant Liberals, including most nonconformists and Anglican radicals of the type discussed in chapter 4. But, despite this, it was not always easy, between the 1830s and the 1860s, for the former to remain in political harness with the latter: a pragmatic difficulty and a temperamental divergence both obtruded. The pragmatic difficulty was that whig-liberals were conscious of the conservatism of the Anglican section

---

[37] Forbes, *Liberal Anglican idea*; Spring, 'Aristocracy, social structure and religion'; R. Brent, 'The emergence of Liberal Anglican politics: the whigs and the Church 1830–1841' (Oxford D.Phil., 1985), and his forthcoming book.

of the electorate, and the alarm which would have been created had the destruction of religious exclusiveness been more thorough and hurried than it was. After 1841, when the strength of the Conservative reaction had become apparent, whig-liberals were reluctant to associate with religious radicalism even to the extent that they had in the 1830s. The temperamental divergence arose because whig-liberals' interpretation of the ways in which spiritual awakening could best be propagated, and materialist passions defeated, often differed from that of nonconformists who advocated disestablishment, and doctrinaire radicals who wished to sweep away all entrenched and social obstructions to spiritual arousal and dignity. This led to disputes in discussion of specific policies, but there was also an underlying incompatibility: the emotionalism and enthusiasm which was central to the political and religious activity of many nonconformists profoundly disquieted whig-liberals, whose ideal was a purely rational Protestantism. Before 1867, although this divergence was sometimes apparent, its effect on practical politics was only limited. After 1867, its political implications could no longer be contained.

In the 1830s, the whig government had been inspired by the passage of the Reform Act to tackle a series of religious grievances. In 1833, following the policy long advocated by Lord Chancellor Brougham, they gave the first state grants to the religious societies which were promoting education in England – the National Society, associated with the Church, and the British and Foreign Schools Society, identified primarily with nonconformity. In 1839, Russell steered through a measure which increased the annual grants, made them dependent on satisfactory state inspection, permitted agencies outside the two societies to receive them, and established a government committee for educational affairs under the Privy Council, in order to superintend the system. Later, in 1846 and 1847, the whigs further increased the amount of the grants, enticed the Wesleyans and Catholics into accepting them, gave a great boost to teacher-training facilities, and imposed a lay committee on each school receiving a grant.[38]

Their most radical party initiative was taken with regard to the Irish Church – in which they attempted to interfere with ancient religious endowments and to redirect them for the benefit of the whole Irish population. According to the 1861 census, 12 per cent of the Irish people were members of the Irish branch of the Church of England and Ireland established by the Act of Union in 1800; 78 per cent were Roman Catholics,

---

[38] J. L. Alexander, 'Lord John Russell and the origins of the Committee of Council on Education', *Historical Journal*, xx (1977), 395–415; D. G. Paz, *The politics of working-class education in Britain, 1830–50* (Manchester, 1980).

and most of the rest Ulster Presbyterians. For the whigs, committed to a general lowering of the exclusive connection between Church and state, the injustice of Establishment was nowhere more obvious than in Ireland. All Liberals were united in the belief that, in the conditions obtaining in the nineteenth century – that is, when religious profession was divided – no sanctity was attached to Church Establishments, and that they should be judged by practical considerations. Whig-liberals believed that their continuation was justified if they were supported by a simple majority of the population, or if they conduced to the preservation of social stability and the effective ministration of the gospels – as opposed to being so unpopular as to threaten the one and render the other impossible. The Irish Church Establishment clearly failed both tests. The whigs' ideal would have been either formally to establish all three Irish sects or, as was more commonly suggested, to subsidise the non-established sects with money transferred from the existing Establishment. The Irish Church Temporalities Act of 1833 was an attempt to begin this process, by abolishing nearly half the bishoprics, by repealing the church cess, and by removing existing abuses in the Church – measures which, it was said, would save £150,000. The most controversial question was the destination of the expected surplus; this was left open to parliament's discretion by Clause 147 of the bill, but it was expected that the surplus would be appropriated either directly for the use of non-established sects, or for other educational and moral purposes. Intense Conservative opposition and splits among the whigs forced the abandonment of Clause 147; but the appropriation issue became the touchstone of division between the parties throughout the next five years, and the one on which the Liberals (minus those like Stanley and Graham who had defected to the Conservatives on the issue) reunited in order to return to government in 1835 – although in the end they did not get their way.[39]

The whigs placed considerable emphasis on other Irish legislation throughout the 1830s: in particular there was the Irish measure of which they remained most proud for the next half-century, the institution, in 1831, of the national system of Irish elementary education. This was aimed both at improving educational provision and at diminishing the power which the priests – who were perceived as narrow, bigoted and potentially disloyal to the Union – had gained from controlling what education there was. The national system was designed to diminish sectarian hatred by educating Protestants and Catholics together, both for secular subjects and for the reading of biblical passages; more controversial religious education might be given separately by the denomi-

---

[39] Akenson, *Church of Ireland*, pp. 159–94; Machin, *Politics and the Churches*, pp. 31–9, 53–63.

nations. The whigs were proud of this system because it seemed to improve the prospects of stability – and, in a subtle and non-coercive way, of Protestantism. Most whig-liberals believed their kind of rational Protestantism to be innately more persuasive than formalistic and superstitious faiths, if only it could be given fairer play than had previously been possible in a country where anti-Protestant hatreds were entrenched – as a result of the influence of an offensive missionary Establishment on the one hand, and of an unreasoning and authoritarian priesthood on the other. It was not that they expected the Irish to be swiftly converted to Protestantism. They did anticipate, however, that the tone of Catholic instruction would improve once it was in competition with Protestant teaching; and, moreover, that, as extreme Catholic dogmas came to appear more and more indefensible in comparison with Protestant doctrines, their place in the curriculum would steadily diminish.[40] Unfortunately for whig dreams, the reality of the national system was different, because Catholics were in such a majority in most of Ireland as to be able to gain effective control of the system, and it was the Protestant sects which proved reluctant to accept it until they became convinced that they could not afford to continue with their voluntary schools.[41] In 1845, when the Conservatives were in office, Peel extended the principle of this system to Irish university education, when he established the Queen's colleges in order to provide an undenominational education for middle-class students who did not wish to attend the essentially Protestant Trinity college, Dublin. In 1850, the whigs established the Queen's university as an examining and degree-giving board for the three colleges. There were now two university structures in Ireland, but neither – to the Catholics' irritation – offered them denominational education.

The whigs' relationship with provincial British nonconformity had been distant before 1830, in the manner of pre-Reform politics, but the bond between them had nonetheless grown strong, and had inspired the repeal of the Test and Corporation Acts (under a Tory administration) in 1828. When in government after 1830, the whigs satisfied further nonconformist grievances, for example by passing the Civil Registration and Marriage Acts in 1836, which instituted civil registration for births, marriages and deaths, and allowed nonconformist chapels to be licensed for weddings. The 1835 Municipal Corporations Act undertook a fundamental reform of local government, breaking down the Anglican hold on corporations far more effectively than the repeal of 1828, and establishing unshakable Liberal majorities in most large towns for the next fifty

---

[40] See below, pp. 133–4.
[41] Akenson, *Irish education experiment*, pp. 107–315.

years.[42] In 1836, the government also agreed to grant a charter allowing the undenominational London university to confer degrees. Later, in 1847, Russell began the next major step in the attack on constitutional exclusiveness in religious affairs by proposing the admission of jews to parliament – prompted by the election of Rothschild as a Liberal in the City of London at the recent election. This became a major question for the next decade, which on the whole followed party lines (although not entirely, since the interests involved were not Christian, and since Disraeli was sympathetic to the measure). It was finally settled by the Conservatives in 1858.

Whig-nonconformist agreement was more difficult, however, on questions affecting the Church of England itself. Hardly any whig-liberals believed that the Church should be disestablished; most maintained that it had an immensely useful spiritual purpose, and all recognised its practical value as an agent of social stability throughout the country. Whig-liberals did, however, wish to reform it. This was partly an offshoot of their general attack on the corruption of unreformed institutions, but it also stemmed, for most, from a concern that the spiritual message of Christianity was being obscured because churchmen were too intent upon enjoying the material advantages of endowment. Believing as they did in the stabilising, and yet the potentially moral, effects of Establishment, the whig-liberals' ideal was usually to break down the barriers between the Church and nonconformist congregations, hoping to persuade the latter to rejoin the Establishment or at least to identify with its function in a brotherly spirit. This accommodation, in their eyes, was to be achieved by emphasising the spiritual purpose of the Church more and by diminishing its doctrinal and organisational exclusiveness.[43] The latter involved questioning the necessity of traditional church dogma and practices, an especially congenial task given the widespread adoption by whig-liberals of scepticism as to the value of most religious dogma. They believed that much of it hid the basic truths of Christianity, on which rational believers might yet come to agree.

The first major issue on which whigs and nonconformists came into conflict after 1832 was that of church rates. Most whigs could see the pressing need to remove the nonconformist grievance; there was, however, an equally strong feeling that, since the Church was a national institution for the preservation of good order and sound religion, some payment from government funds for the upkeep of its fabric was as legitimate and necessary as was taxation for the secular purposes of govern-

---

[42] Fraser, *Urban politics in Victorian England*, pp. 115–22.
[43] See below, pp. 90–1.

ment.[44] Most whig churchmen, like Thirlwall, wished to preserve the abstract rights of the Church, while defusing the controversy by relieving nonconformists who disliked the rate from the obligation to pay.[45] Probably the major reason for whig reluctance to abolish church rates, however, was concern for the consequences for the government's popularity with the Anglican electorate (and with some conservative whig MPs), when, in the decade after 1832, the assumption was widespread that the attack on church rates was a preliminary to an attack on the Church Establishment itself. In 1837, the government proposed a compromise scheme, but it was withdrawn after extensive criticism from defenders and opponents of the rate.[46] In 1839 and again in 1849, it did not support private members' bills which proposed abolition.

Melbourne's government fell in 1841, and until the late 1850s the Liberals attempted little further radical religious reform. In or out of government, their electoral position was relatively weak, and any adoption of policy initiatives of this sort would have led to defeat in the Commons and a further loss of support in the country. Consequently, advanced nonconformist opinion, led by Miall and Baines, was irritated with the party leadership – as it had been since the mid 1830s. Many Irish Catholics, under O'Connell in the 1840s and G. H. Moore and Frederick Lucas in the 1850s, were similarly lukewarm. In neither case, however, was there yet a sustained cry from the constituencies for a radical political strategy, of the type that was to develop in the 1860s and 1870s. Most nonconformists, especially, were not yet disposed to follow a radical lead, and indeed the opportunity for them to do so was only gradually increasing.

Between 1780 and the 1830s, the leadership of political nonconformity had been dominated by unitarians. Many of the early unitarians were educated clergymen who had left the Church of England after parliament had rejected their plea of 1772 to abolish compulsory subscription to the Articles.[47] In the late eighteenth century, therefore, unitarians were more closely attuned to the Enlightened circles in which the parliamentary whigs moved than were the evangelical nonconformist bodies – the baptists, congregationalists and, later, the methodists – which took little organised part in politics and which drew most of their support from lower social classes than the unitarians. Prominent unitarians like William Smith, chairman of the most important nonconformist political pressure group, the Protestant Dissenting Deputies, between 1805 and

[44] (5th Earl Fitzwilliam) Machin, *Politics and the Churches*, p. 260.
[45] Norman, *Church and society*, p. 110.
[46] Machin, *Politics and the Churches*, pp. 59–61.
[47] U. Henriques, *Religious toleration in England 1787–1833* (London, 1961), pp. 32–55.

1832, broadly shared the moral vision of the whigs, working for civil liberty and moral reform, and against corruption, but not for disestablishment.[48] After the reform of parliament in 1832, two of the evangelical sects whose membership was growing so spectacularly, the baptists and congregationalists, made only a gradual impact in the Commons. However, they gained control of the (increasingly uninfluential) committee of Dissenting Deputies in 1836, when the unitarians seceded because of a quarrel about access to an endowment fund.[49] More importantly, through the agitations of individuals, they slowly became a powerful force in arousing and then radicalising provincial political nonconformity.

The first sign of this radicalisation had been the resistance to church-rate payment in the late 1830s; but it reached maturity with the activity of the mid 1840s. It was boosted by the Disruption of the Scottish Kirk in 1843, when the Free Church of Scotland was founded in defence of the right of congregations to resist ministers imposed on them by the Crown and other patrons, a right denied by the 1712 Act and, on appeal, by the House of Lords.[50] It was further fuelled by intense and successful opposition to the education clauses of the Factory Bill introduced by Peel's Conservative government in 1843, which gave the Church of England considerable influence in the direction of factory schools (which were to be established in a number of manufacturing industries). In 1844, Edward Miall, a congregationalist ex-minister and editor of the *Nonconformist*, which he had founded in 1841, launched the Anti-State Church Association, in order to work for the disestablishment of the Church of England. During the next four years, the Association (which changed its name to the Liberation Society in 1853) actively promoted three movements subordinate to its main aim: movements for the abolition of church rates, of the Maynooth grant, and of all state grants to elementary education. In all these it went against whig policy, in the last two diametrically, as, of course, it did in demanding disestablishment itself. These movements, in one respect, were clearly protests against taxation by the state for objects with which nonconformists did not think the state should be concerned. They were religious equivalents of the movement for free trade and economy in administration, and, like it, promoted by commercial men who disliked paying their dues. But behind them lay the consciousness of nearly two hundred years of state discrimination in favour of a religion which, by virtue of its privileged position, they believed had become too effete and corrupt to experience an intense

---

[48] See R. W. Davis, *Dissent in politics 1780–1830: the political life of William Smith, MP* (London, 1971).

[49] Machin, *Politics and the Churches*, pp. 56–7.   [50] *Ibid.*, pp. 112–47.

drive to save souls. Radical nonconformists contended that disestablishment would advance the evangelisation of the country, just as the spread of earnest religious education would be intensified if the missionary zeal of each of the religious denominations was stimulated.

The campaigns of 1845–7 culminated in the return of twenty-six alleged voluntaryists – opponents of the endowment by the state of religious teaching and of Churches – and sixty more sympathisers at the 1847 election.[51] But the campaigns did not alter the course of whig religious policy, and radical nonconformity made little further impact on Westminster politics for a decade. Even in 1847, in northern towns like Bradford, the nonconformists had desisted from running a voluntaryist candidate, whereas in Halifax and Leeds, in the eye of the intraparty storm, Charles Wood subsequently succeeded in reuniting the fragmented party on the free-trade issue.[52]

Radical nonconformity had many weaknesses. It had to battle against a strong residual feeling in congregationalists, less so in baptists, that evangelical nonconformists had nobler aims outside politics.[53] This feeling was even more strongly held by the largest single nonconformist denomination, the Wesleyans, hardly any of whom yet advocated disestablishment, and who were happy to receive state grants for education; Bunting, their leading figure, had tory sympathies.[54] Just as importantly, most of the nonconformists who *were* interested in politics were disposed to accept their place in the Liberal alliance, and to work for limited reform – pre-eminently the abolition of church rates – by pressuring individual MPs. Moderate nonconformists were gratified by the Liberals' commitment, firstly, in the 1830s, to the termination of slavery, and then to the achievement and extension of a free-trade system. They were similarly pleased, on the whole, by their Church policy: the Liberals refused to grant any more parliamentary aid for church building, passed several bills in the 1830s limiting the possibility of abuse in Church administration, and (especially under Palmerston) appointed liberal and evangelical bishops, like Bickersteth, Pelham and Villiers, who believed it important, in a way that tory bishops usually had not, to cultivate local nonconformist sects and to work with them.

The nonconformists' relationship with official Liberalism was thus ambivalent at many turns, as was also apparent in discussion of Palmerston's foreign policy. In the 1850s, some of them, especially those

---

[51] *Ibid.*, p. 192.

[52] A. Jowitt, 'Dissenters, voluntaryism and Liberal unity: the 1847 election', in *Nineteenth century Bradford elections*, ed. J. A. Jowitt and R. K. S. Taylor (Bradford, 1979), pp. 7–23; D. Fraser, 'Voluntaryism and West Riding politics in the mid-nineteenth century', *Northern History*, xiii (1977), 199–231.

[53] Machin, *Politics and the Churches*, p. 164.   [54] Hempton, *Methodism and politics*, p. 196.

small manufacturers who equated the recovery of domestic demand with low taxation and expenditure, advocated non-intervention abroad.[55] But not all nonconformists followed the Manchester school's stand against Palmerston at the 1857 election. Bright was never the official nonconformist spokesman; Cobden was an Anglican who did not sympathise with radical nonconformist educational and ecclesiastical positions.[56] Palmerston was always able to retain a grip on the bulk of the Liberal conscience. He established his credentials with the mass of the provincial Liberal party from 1847, by his advocacy of interventionism abroad on 'liberal' grounds, especially in 1848 and in the crusade against Russia and her dreams of an Orthodox empire in the Balkans in 1854; he subsequently reaffirmed his commitment to the movement against autocratic clericalism by actively supporting Italian unification in 1859, reuniting the Liberal party more effectively than since 1835; he then trimmed his sails to the more earnest and cost-conscious wind which blew up from the provinces in the 1860s. The tolerance of radical nonconformity towards official Liberalism in the mid 1850s was evident from the role that the electoral committee of the Liberation Society played in securing several county gains for the Liberals in the 1857 election.[57]

It was not until the late 1850s and early 1860s that a number of trends became apparent which signalled the possibility of an effective new departure in religious policy. The first was the emergence from the political shadows of the church-rate and university-tests questions. In fact, these had been increasingly exercising backbench Liberals for some time; most whig-liberals now sympathised with nonconformist grievances on both points. By the 1850s, payment of the church rate was no longer demanded of nonconformists in most sizeable towns, in order to prevent agitation – despite the fact that each parish was legally bound to keep its churches in repair. The spread of this practice came to make refusal to abolish the Church's abstract right to compulsory support ridiculous, and embarrassing to the defaulting parishes themselves.[58] Very few Liberal MPs opposed the private members' bills designed to do this, which were introduced by Trelawny and Clay throughout the 1850s. Such a bill gained a second reading in the Commons for the first time in 1855, and by 1858 its majority on the third reading was sixty-three. In the

---

[55] V. A. C. Gatrell, 'The commercial middle class in Manchester, c. 1820–1857' (Cambridge Ph.D., 1971).

[56] Machin, *Politics and the Churches*, p. 185; Gurowich, 'Continuation of war', p. 617; Gash, *Reaction and reconstruction*, pp. 105–6.

[57] Hamer, *Politics of electoral pressure*, p. 97; Vincent, *Formation of the Liberal party*, p. 72.

[58] Machin, *Politics and the Churches*, pp. 243–355 *passim*; Chadwick, *Victorian Church*, i, 146–58.

same year, it was taken to the Lords for the first time, where it was introduced by the duke of Somerset, but was heavily defeated. A revival in the Conservatives' strength in 1859 enabled them to defeat the bills in 1861–3 (by margins of ten or less). But Palmerston and Russell were now actively supporting the abolition bills, and so favourable was the parliamentary Liberal party as a whole to a quick settlement of the question that Liberation Society pressure, exerted after 1863 in order to force through abolition, needed to be applied against candidates in only ten constituencies.[59] The question was finally settled in 1868.

Individual whigs had proposed the abolition of university tests in the 1830s. At that time, Oxford refused to allow anyone who would not subscribe to the Thirty-nine Articles to matriculate; Cambridge allowed matriculation but imposed a similar test before granting the BA degree. In 1850, the Liberal government established a Royal Commission in order to inquire into the condition of Oxford university. Four years later, Aberdeen's government sanctioned a reform of the statutes and government of Oxford which opened up many formerly restricted fellowships, transferred revenues within the university according to need, and allowed the establishment of private halls, imposing no tests, for religious minorities. Whig-liberal and radical backbench pressure, tacitly supported by government whigs, forced the widening of the measure in order to abolish religious tests on matriculation and for the BA degree.[60] In 1856, another Act abolished tests in Cambridge for all non-theological degrees, but did not allow nonconformist MAs to participate in university government with their Anglican counterparts. These reforms merely intensified pressure for more; in 1860 and 1861, a nonconformist was Senior Wrangler at Cambridge but was debarred from fellowships, while many of the young men elected to open fellowships after 1854 were active promoters of the total abolition of tests for degrees, fellowships and participation in university government. In 1862, E. P. Bouverie, the son of a whig university reformer of the 1830s, introduced into the Commons the first of several proposals to abolish tests for admission to fellowships in Cambridge; in 1864, J. G. Dodson, another whig-liberal, proposed the abolition of tests for the Oxford MA and thus for many fellowships. In 1865 and 1866, similar bills passed their second reading in the Commons; in 1867 an Oxford bill was defeated in the Lords. In 1868 a joint Oxford and Cambridge bill passed the Commons, while by now two other Liberals, J. D. Coleridge and G. J. Goschen, had gained major reputations by their advocacy of the bills. Moreover, a number of links had been forged between noncon-

---

[59] Vincent, *Formation of the Liberal party*, p. 73.   [60] Ward, *Victorian Oxford*, pp. 180–209.

formists and young academic liberals in order to fight for complete abolition.[61]

What had also changed was the intellectual climate: in the two decades after 1845, an immense impetus had been given to the development of liberal theology and to freedom of discussion of doctrinal matters. By the mid 1860s, books as heterodox as Strauss's *Life of Jesus* (translated by George Eliot, and published in 1846), Feuerbach's *Essence of Christianity* (also translated by her: 1854), F. W. Newman's *The soul* (1849), Greg's *Creed of Christendom* (1851), the commentaries of Jowett and Stanley on the epistles of St Paul (both 1855), Buckle's *History of civilization in England* (1857–61), Mill's *On liberty* (1859), the collection of *Essays and reviews* (1860), Spencer's *First principles* (1862), and Seeley's *Ecce Homo* (1865), were among the tracts most widely discussed by those who meditated upon religious dogma. Similarly controversial, of course, were scientific works such as Chambers' *Vestiges of the natural history of creation* (1844) and Darwin's *Origin of species* (1859). Many young men graduated from the universities in the 1860s believing that the quest for moral, spiritual and all other forms of truth could be successful only if accompanied by candid examination of the claims of all existing institutions and dogmas. One of the most important indications of the interest in such matters was the marked expansion of the 'higher' journalism in the late 1850s and 1860s: the increased influence of a whole host of periodicals which discussed politics, religion, literature and science side by side, and which gave a great deal of space to broad churchmen and to less orthodox writers. Maurice, J. M. Ludlow, Llewelyn Davies and occasionally Fawcett wrote for *Macmillan's Magazine*, founded in 1859; Frederic Harrison, Huxley, Amberley, Spencer and the scientist Herschel were featured in the *Fortnightly Review*, founded in 1865 and edited, at first, by G. H. Lewes; John Tulloch and Stanley contributed to Alford's *Contemporary Review*, founded in 1866. *Fraser's Magazine*, one of those periodicals which was already established, published articles by J. F. Stephen, Goldwin Smith, F. W. Newman and Froude. Many leading whig MPs had held liberal theological views – at least in private – for years. But the widespread influence of these opinions in the literary world in the 1860s, and the close, even incestuous, relationship at this time between the literary, social and political worlds, now created a striking shift in political expectations. This can be seen by contrasting the extremely common acceptance of the new beliefs, with the political ostracism which had faced the heterodox Philosophical Radicals of the 1830s.[62]

[61] Harvie, *Lights of liberalism*, pp. 87–9.
[62] W. Thomas, *The Philosophic Radicals: nine studies in theory and practice 1817–1841* (Oxford, 1979), pp. 445–52.

Most significant, however, in permitting radical initiatives, was the newfound influence on the party of popular constituency pressure. The crucial development here was the success of the strategy of evangelical nonconformity in infiltrating borough constituency associations, and in spreading the gospel that moral regeneration could be promoted through political activity; and, associated with their success, the emergence of a respectable working-class political movement.

Evangelical nonconformity had been quietly extending its power in the constituencies for a dozen years before 1862, but it was in that year that mass political enthusiasm was first engendered, as a result of the celebration of the bicentenary of their ejection from the Church of England.[63] Political activism was then provoked and sustained by the preaching of a younger generation of evangelising ministers, who were to become national celebrities in the following fifteen years – Spurgeon and Maclaren for the baptists, Dale and Rogers for the congregationalists, George Dawson in his own church in Birmingham.[64] Political missions to spread the Liberation Society's message began in 1862, the most important of which was to heavily nonconformist Wales, naturally fertile territory for Liberationism once habits of deference to landlords in the counties and to Anglophile industrialists in the south could be broken.[65] In breaking them spectacularly in 1868, Welsh nonconformists sent a number of MPs to Westminster, including another immensely forceful speaker, Henry Richard, as, in effect, their leader. In England, the Wesleyans similarly became more involved in politics in the 1860s, and happier to participate in the aims of the Liberal alliance.

This enthusiasm was infectious. In 1865–6, donations to the Liberation Society nearly doubled to £7,556, and a special fund was launched in order to permit further political campaigns – a fund which spent £18,000 by 1871.[66] The movement was further aided by the expansion of the cheap press after the repeal of the paper duties in 1861. But it was probably helped most of all by its close connection with the parliamentary reform movement of the 1860s, led by Bright, which it infused with religious principle. By doing so, it gave a great impetus to the 'moralisation' of politics – to the demand for a zealous assault upon manifestations of evil, and for an injection of enthusiasm and passion into public life. It stimulated the dormant feelings of the Liberal middle classes against the iniquity of vested interests, and in favour of moral regeneration and the proclamation of the individual responsibility of the

[63] Machin, *Politics and the Churches*, p. 322.
[64] See below, p. 201.
[65] Jones, 'Liberation Society and Welsh politics'.
[66] Ingham, 'Disestablishment movement', p. 39.

independent citizen. It had a number of side-effects: it gave birth, for example, to a widespread temperance movement.[67] But, of profound importance, it also enabled Liberals to look on the working-man in a different and more religious light than before.

Many of the working-men who were most prominent in constituency politics had risen through the local political network provided by nonconformist organisation. Others, in the 1860s especially, were positivists, or had no connection with particular religious sects but were widely read in political economy and ethical religion.[68] Standard demands from politically active artisans were for the extension of unsectarian education and for other means of encouraging self-advancement, such as temperance. Their political ideology owed a lot to the arguments of the Chartists of the 1840s, but had been transformed by the passage of time, the improvement in the standard of living, and a further infusion of respectability and morality. This ideology maintained a crucial distinction between the idle – aristocrats and paupers alike – and the industrious and virtuous, those working to promote material and spiritual progress.[69] In theory, such an ideology could have profound practical implications; and academic radicals of the 1860s, like Mill, Fawcett and Goldwin Smith, who enjoyed a certain cachet among some of the more widely read artisan leaders, developed the ideology in precisely this way. They called for a thoroughgoing destruction of manifestations of privilege, which, they argued, in addition to offending those who did not enjoy them, blighted the prospects of moral regeneration for those who did. The republican movement of the late 1860s was one offshoot of this ideology.[70] Of course, many 1860s radicals, and many working-men, were led towards such arguments by the simple operation of class feeling, and by revulsion for high society and its ostentatiousness. But it is important to remember that the radicalism of many others was founded upon a reading of the bible.[71] Despite their differences, discussed in chapter 4, radical nonconformists, positivists, academic radicals and leading working-men shared much in common, and, in particular, an ethical vision: most of them hoped, by radicalising the Liberal conscience, and by using it to diminish privilege, to work towards an ideal state of material and spiritual class harmony.[72]

The whig-liberals within the party reacted to the changing pattern of Liberal politics in the 1860s with mixed feelings. On the one hand, they approved of the ethical earnestness, piety and respectability of the

---

[67] Harrison, *Drink and the Victorians.*
[68] See below, p. 232. [69] Jones, *Languages of class*, ch. 3.
[70] Royle, *Radicals, secularists and republicans*, pp. 198–206.
[71] See Laqueur, *Religion and respectability*, p. 244.
[72] See below, e.g. p. 206.

working-man – his cooperative groups and teetotal organisations. This respect was all the more marked because the generation of whig-liberals who rose to political and intellectual prominence in the 1860s – typified by Goschen, Harcourt, Grant Duff, Lubbock, Huxley and Seeley – had a much greater sympathy for 'the people', a more developed spiritual intensity, and, above all, a greater dislike of aristocratic decadence, than their predecessors. This was the generation who had been influenced by Christian socialism and by the experience of witnessing Chartism at a young age, and many of whom had been educated at the universities in the aftermath of the Oxford movement. But, on the other hand, as we shall see (p. 116), most whig-liberals of all ages were not complimentary either about some of the practical policies which were demanded by the representatives of provincial and academic radicalism, or about the populist tone of politics which they predicted would accompany the latter's arrival at the centre of Liberal politics.

This ambivalence is central to understanding the dilemma which beset so many politicians in the 1860s and 1870s. It was a dilemma which first became unmistakably apparent during the parliamentary reform crisis of 1866–7. The flexibility which most MPs (of both parties) displayed in discussing levels of enfranchisement was the result of a desire to see sober and responsible artisans exercising a right to vote, combined with a dislike of any reform which threatened to vulgarise politics. But it was not clear how to achieve one without the other.[73]

In order to appreciate their dilemma, it must be set in context. One of the most deeply held concerns of the 1860s, for the Liberal mind in particular, was with the apparent prevalence of 'materialism' in society. At one level, this was a response to the markedly increasing standard of living after 1850, and to the revolution in communications. These made former luxuries and even exotic imports widely available and increased the general awareness of the working-class's capacity for civilised leisure – as a result of the growth of the railway excursion and of the professionalisation of the music-hall.[74] But, at another level, it was a response to the consequences of widespread urbanisation, which was familiarising society with the degradation and drunkenness of many of the urban poor, and with the extent of infidelity in the slums. Another shock to the Liberal mind was the revival of ritualism in the Church of England and ultramontanism in the Church of Rome, both of which seemed to place an unhealthy emphasis on external forms and practices at the expense of a developed inner spiritual life.

[73] Cowling, *1867*, pp. 48–57.
[74] P. Bailey, *Leisure and class in Victorian England: rational recreation and the contest for control, 1830–1885* (London, 1978), chs. 3–7; W. H. Fraser, *The coming of the mass market, 1850–1914* (London, 1981).

Given these failings, the apparent rectitude of the 'respectable working-man' or 'artisan' was praised. There was also admiration for the Lancashire working-men's willingness to endure material sacrifices during the cotton famine of 1863, and their enthusiastic support, the famine notwithstanding, for the northern cause throughout the American civil war. If this admiration was restricted, at the time, mainly to those few who advocated the claims of the north – including some whig-liberals, such as Argyll, Houghton, Hughes and the *Spectator* – it was much more widespread once the war had been won.[75] Many Liberal MPs who entered the Commons in the late 1850s and 1860s were anxious, in consequence of all this, to see not only the extension of the franchise, but also a number of administrative and social improvements designed to help such men help themselves, most obviously by extending the education system, expanding savings facilities, reducing indirect taxation and enabling local agencies to tackle the housing problem more effectively.

But, at the same time, the extension of the franchise was perceived as dangerous precisely because of the fear that all classes in the newly expanded electorate were too materialistic to contribute to the preservation of good government. There was a widespread concern, for example, that aristocratic morals were too enervated to provide righteous leadership in the new democracy. This had a number of causes, among them the seclusion and cantankerousness of the queen after Prince Albert's death in 1861; the gossip about the libidinous behaviour of the prince of Wales, culminating in the popular response to the Mordaunt case in 1870;[76] and the concern at the fast lifestyles, especially the gambling, of young peers, which is so well depicted in Trollope (another manifestation of it can be seen in the publicity given to the bankruptcy cases of a number of peers – among them the duke of Newcastle and Lord de Mauley – in 1870).[77] But, if a benevolent aristocracy could not take the reins of government, they would be left to a provincial middle class and to a metropolitan plutocracy whose wealth was spiralling, but who were generally condemned in high literary and political society – by Matthew Arnold, George Eliot and Gladstone alike – for their cultural narrowness and lack of ethical and political vision. Both they and the new working-class electors – whose increasing propensity for strike action was alarming – were thought fatally susceptible to the most alarming manifestation of materialism: a desire to use

[75] See B. Jenkins, *Britain and the war for the union* (2 vols., Montreal, 1980), ii, 33–41, 209–34.
[76] P. Magnus, *King Edward the seventh* (London, 1964), pp. 107–9.
[77] F. M. L. Thompson, *English landed society in the nineteenth century* (London, 1963), p. 286.

their political power to press for a restructuring of the taxation system.[78] Since the material interests of these classes were likely to differ greatly in practice, to allow them to do this was considered to be potentially destructive of the political and social fabric. It was also feared that an inevitable consequence of the extension of the franchise would be the inflammation of political life by irresponsible demagogues.

Given this awareness of the evils of materialism, it was hardly surprising that the propagation of a spiritually intense and anti-formalistic religion was advocated with such passion and feeling by Liberals of all sorts in the 1860s and 1870s as the major hope for the moral and political reformation of society. For the nonconformists, and for religious-minded radicals, such a creed was required if class exclusiveness and privilege were to be banished and fair dealing established between men. But for whig-liberals, moral reform and the attack on corruption were necessary prerequisites for the re-establishment of legitimate authority, of the order which was an inseparable part of the proper Providential government of the world. They agreed that corruption, excessive formalism, and undue repression of national life and of individual enthusiasm threw the workings of the state out of joint; but they considered populism, demagogy and strike action to be equally destabilising.

These worries for whig-liberals were intensified by the reintroduction of the Irish Church question into political debate in the 1860s. They had no loyalty to the Irish Establishment in itself; but the reappearance of Irish matters in the new political climate operating after 1867 struck at what had always been the Achilles' heel of the whig-liberal conscience: its attitude towards Catholicism.

Whig policy towards the Irish Church and Irish education in the 1830s had been liberal, in some senses revolutionary, in tory eyes. That should not obscure the fact that one aim of policy in both areas had been to provide a fairer field on which a liberalising, undogmatic modern religion could fight against the Catholic priests' apparent monopoly of influence over young minds.[79] In the same way, the preservation of the Union was, and continued to be, justified on the grounds that it offered the best chance of modernising Ireland both in the spiritual sense, and economically – the two being seen to be intimately interdependent. The whigs always tried to portray their Irish policy not as following the whims of the Irish parliamentary leaders – although, this, of course, had been the impression they had left in the 1830s – but as pursuing a statesman-like course which, while satisfying legitimate grievances, also maintained firm order. This was why, for example, a Coercion Act

---

[78] See below, p. 85.   [79] See below, pp. 129–34.

accompanied the Irish Church Temporalities Act in 1833. But the whigs' belief in the beneficial long-term effects of the national and Queen's university systems had tended to make them regard any further major reform in religious matters, while desirable in the abstract, as of no pressing importance – given the damaging effects that disestablishment might have in promoting a cry for similar treatment of the English Church, or in creating a Conservative reaction. This explains both why innovations in Liberal policy in Ireland between 1846 and 1866 were so few, and yet why most, even of the older generation of whigs, joined, with deliberation but without demur and sometimes with enthusiasm, in the disestablishment movement in 1868.

The whig creed of religious toleration and civil liberty was designed for implementation against clerical régimes, in the belief that the removal of artificial restrictions was an essential preliminary to material and spiritual progress. Despite the Catholics' gratitude for Emancipation and the reforms of the 1830s, the whole emphasis of this policy conflicted with the attitudes of the Irish Catholic Church, and of many Irish MPs. Since whigs defined progress as progress away from clerical reaction, they identified the Roman Catholic Church as one of its major enemies, and as an institution which would try to abuse any rights which it was given. Whigs had pressed for Catholic Emancipation in the 1820s in order to avoid the political consequences which they foresaw arising from the repression of political life in Catholic Ireland,[80] and never subsequently reneged on the principle that Catholic participation in the public affairs of the Union was immensely beneficial to stability. But they made a distinction between this participation and organised political intervention on the part of the Roman Church; to the latter, whig attitudes varied. At times, individuals invoked the spirit of 1688 and protested; more frequently, the majority of whigs argued that the papacy's political influence was diminishing naturally and that manifestations of it were paper tigers. (Such a division was apparent within the party in response to the most famous of whig attacks on the pretensions of the Roman Catholic Church, Russell's Durham letter of November 1850, and the subsequent Ecclesiastical Titles Bill – to the introduction of which, Carlisle, Grey and Labouchère, for example, of the cabinet, were opposed.)[81]

But if, on the whole, the whig-liberals were tolerant towards manifestations of ultramontane power in themselves, they were far less tolerant in reacting to any policy which would actively encourage the Church in

---

[80] G. I. T. Machin, *The Catholic question in English politics 1820 to 1830* (Oxford, 1964).
[81] J. Prest, *Lord John Russell* (London, 1972), p. 323; Machin, *Politics and the Churches*, pp. 217–18.

its attempts to control the direction of Irish life. This problem was especially likely to arise in the educational sphere, since the Church was constantly demanding the reform of the national and Queen's systems in order to give more weight to denominational teaching.[82] Whig-liberals prided themselves on their refusal to countenance this, and one of their main concerns after 1868 was that the increased prominence given to Irish Catholicism in the Liberal alliance might increase its possibility.

Whig relations with Catholic MPs, then, were confused. But what increased their complexity was the rise of tractarianism in England from the 1830s. The Oxford movement was launched in 1833, in reaction to the whig threat to loosen the Church's hold over her endowments. Its leaders, such as Keble and Pusey, contended that the Church of England was a branch of the original Church Catholic, whose doctrine and, to some extent, organisation had been established by the time of the Early Fathers. They maintained that it was not the function of the state to interfere with that inheritance, which was a priceless security against the contemporary drift towards latitudinarianism and scepticism; nor was it its right to force any internal reform on the Church without the consent of Church leaders. At the same time, they insisted that it was the state's duty to exercise discretion, and judgment of spiritual worth and doctrinal orthodoxy, in nominating these leaders, through its control of episcopal appointments. The tractarians, and high churchmen who were broadly sympathetic to them (such as Samuel Wilberforce), were extremely active in demanding the revival of Convocation, the Church's own assembly, which had been allowed no influence in Church affairs since 1717; they hoped to see it become a check on erastian reform of the Church.

In addition to challenging whig Church policy at several points, the Oxford movement was an evangelising movement, arising out of the earlier evangelical revival and extending its stress on the importance of missions to the poor. It therefore encouraged two generations of earnest young men to enter the Church ministry; many of these, moreover, such as Mackonochie and Lowder, migrated to inner-city parishes. Both here and wherever else such men began to establish themselves in the late 1840s and 1850s, many tended to adopt practices and rites – such as the eastward position, auricular confession and the wearing of brightly coloured copes and chasubles – which had not been common practice in the Church within the previous century, and which appeared to bear a close resemblance to Romanist behaviour.[83] They defended these rites, and a love of striking decoration in churches, both as legitimate in them-

---

[82] Akenson, *Irish education experiment*, pp. 294–310; Norman, *Catholic Church*, chs. 2, 5 and 6.
[83] Marsh, *Victorian Church in decline*, pp. 112–14.

selves and as attractive and relevant aids to their parishioners, especially to working-men who were attempting to embrace the Christian faith. Nonetheless, the new ritualism caused immense hostility among broad churchmen and traditionalist evangelicals, a hostility which grew as the practices spread during the 1860s. But the growth of the Oxford movement itself had also created immense revulsion, because it appeared to be a stepping-stone towards Catholicism – an argument which gained some force after the secession to Rome of Newman in 1845, Manning in 1851, and a number of other high churchmen in the following twenty years.

This revulsion was not limited to one political party. But the Liberals were most embarrassed by the impact of the Oxford movement, because it intensified the ambivalence with which not only whig-liberals, but nonconformists, regarded all sacerdotal practices, Romanist and Anglo-catholic. Nonconformists were repelled by tractarianism and ritualism as fundamentally opposed to their doctrinal beliefs and emphasis on the individual's personal relationship with God. But they overlaid this feeling with a scarcely veiled approval of high churchmen's missionary zeal, their attack on erastian state control of Church affairs, and the disruptive influence which the revival of emphasis on the importance of traditional church doctrine would have on the attempt to keep together the Church Establishment in an age of theological ferment. However, as we shall see, whig-liberal hostility to what they saw as proto-Catholicism within the Church was exacerbated by precisely this awareness that the high churchmen's insistence on doctrinal purity and on the self-government of the Church would wreck their own vision of far-reaching Church reform and comprehension.

Between 1846 and 1851, indeed, Russell's government had made enemies of the leading tractarians and created the climate in which Manning and others seceded to Rome in 1851. It did this, firstly, by appointing a long string of broad and low churchmen to bishoprics, among them the controversial liberal theologian, Hampden.[84] Then, in 1850, the Judicial Committee of the Privy Council – a mixed court of laymen and bishops, which had been established by the whigs in 1833 as the court of appeal for ecclesiastical cases, but which had previously avoided controversy – pronounced what became known as the Gorham judgment. This reversed the verdict of the ecclesiastical Court of Arches, and maintained that an evangelical clergyman who preached unorthodox views on baptismal regeneration, and who had been presented to a parish by the whigs' lord chancellor, could not be debarred from institution to it by the opposition of his local bishop to his theo-

---

[84] Machin, *Politics and the Churches*, pp. 182–3, 198.

logical views.[85] The judgment appeared to high churchmen to be a blatant attempt to widen the boundaries of allowable Church doctrine – and, moreover, the first of a number pronounced by the Committee, as it came to be dominated not only by whigs on the lay side, but by Palmerstonian bishops like the future Archbishop Tait on the clerical. Within months of the judgment came Russell's Durham letter, the primary purpose of which was, in fact, to insult tractarians within the Church, whom it described as posing a far more serious threat to Protestantism than the ultramontanes.[86]

The letter also had a cutting political edge: it was intended to belittle the status of the band of leading Peelites – many of whom were high churchmen – who had left the Conservative party in 1846 and who were widely expected to seek an alliance with the Liberals. Their administrative talent would be a boon to any Liberal government; but, on the other hand, they posed a threat to Russell's continued tenure of the premiership. In fact, however, the Liberals were so weak that in 1852 they were forced to accept a coalition with the Peelites, under the leadership of the Peelite Aberdeen, as the only way in which to prevent a Conservative government. Relations between the two groups were not altogether happy between 1852 and 1858. The most important quarrel, as far as this book is concerned, broke out between Palmerston and Gladstone, after Gladstone's resignation, with most Peelites, from the former's government in 1855: it touched on many contentious points, but centred on the conduct of financial policy. In 1859, however, the prospect of the Conservative alternative brought the Peelites back into alliance with the Liberal coalition, under Palmerston; and their leading politicians now became established members of Liberal governments. Aberdeen, Graham, Herbert and Newcastle died in the early 1860s, but Gladstone – the most devout high churchman among them – did not, and, as he rose, apparently inexorably, to the leadership of the Liberal party by the late 1860s, his influence began to be exerted on the conduct of religious policy. Gladstone's effect on the development of the 'Liberal conscience' was at once restricting and radical. His perspective on religious questions did not quite coincide with that of whig-liberals, nonconformists, radicals or Catholics. But whig-liberals were right to suspect that their interests would be most likely, in the long run, to suffer from his intrusion into the higher echelons of Liberal politics.

Gladstone had been a high tory until the mid-1840s. His move into the Liberal party had been made possible by his realisation that the higher spiritual interests of the Church would suffer from Conservative attempts to bolster her privileged material position, at a time of wide-

[85] *Ibid.*, pp. 203–4.   [86] *Ibid.*, pp. 208–10; Acland, *Acland*, p. 165.

spread questioning of theological orthodoxy, and of increased nonconformist and Catholic activity at Westminster. He accordingly advocated the abandonment of those privileges wherever they jarred with prevailing political sentiment – and thus wherever they threatened to provoke a backlash from those who disliked the spiritual independence of the Church. Between 1852 and 1865, he invested a lot of energy in fighting English ecclesiastical battles, usually against the whig-liberals. It was during the premiership of Aberdeen that the first tractarian bishop, W. K. Hamilton, was appointed (1854), and that the crucial first steps were taken in allowing Convocation to become an effective force in the Church, by allowing it to sit for longer periods.[87] In 1857, when out of office, Gladstone bitterly attacked the Palmerston government's Divorce Bill for its erastian tendencies; this not only permitted divorce on grounds of adultery, but, until amended by high-church pressure, gave the local clergyman no choice but to solemnise the remarriage of divorced adulterers.[88] After 1859, when in government under Palmerston, Gladstone's relationship with him, stormy enough on matters of defence expenditure and taxation, was stormier still on religious issues – especially given the continued bias against high churchmen which was evident in Palmerston's episcopal appointments.[89]

Although in certain ways Gladstone remained extremely conservative – for example in his reluctance to sanction the abolition of university tests – in others he was coming to share the outlook of nonconformists. Both now tended to believe that the promotion of moral regeneration would be advanced most efficiently by increasing the freedom of competition between the various sects: each sect would expend its zeal on evangelising missions, and none would interfere through parliamentary legislation with the independence of any other.[90] Gladstone's support for evangelism, his admiration for popular religious and moral passion, and his assault on erastianism won him the general support of provincial nonconformity in the early 1860s; this was paralleled by the popular devotion which he gained through implementing generous reductions of direct and indirect taxation, as chancellor of the exchequer during seven prosperous years between 1859 and 1866.[91] In 1862 he began to support a measure frequently demanded by nonconformists, the Burials Bill; he was also now eager to settle the church-rate controversy (although not quite in the same way as they were);[92] and, from 1864, a series of private

[87] Machin, *Politics and the Churches*, p. 262.
[88] *Ibid.*, pp. 285–8.   [89] Steele, 'Gladstone and Palmerston', p. 131.
[90] See below, p. 162.   [91] Matthew, v, pp. xxix–xlvii.   [92] See below, p. 216.

meetings was arranged between him and leading nonconformists, such as Newman Hall, Allon, Binney and Baldwin Brown.[93] This mutual sympathy soon bore succulent political fruit – and the first major issue on which it did was that of the Irish Church.

Since his shift away from high toryism on the Maynooth issue in 1845, Gladstone, like whig-liberals, had been, in theory, amenable to the disestablishment of the Irish Church. Unlike them, however, he was not particularly committed to the policy of aiding all sects in Ireland with state money in place of Establishment; this implied that he did not share their belief in the state's duty to guide and corral religious practice and to channel enthusiasm into harmless areas. On the contrary, he had far more sympathy than did broad-church whigs with the theological dogmas and spiritual devotions of Irish Catholics. This was by no means total, because of his characteristically tractarian dislike of the effects of papal corruption in perverting the original doctrines and practices codified by the Early Fathers. But, notwithstanding this, he was willing to give Catholics full denominational rights in education – to give them as free a hand in their religious (and, ultimately, political) destiny as he wished to see maintained for Anglican churchmen.[94] It was therefore not surprising that the advent of Peelite influence on the Liberal party increased its attractiveness to Irish Catholics. This was apparent as early as 1853 when, after three Catholic ministers, Monsell, Keogh and Sadleir, had tendered their resignations in protest at Russell's public repetition of his virulently anti-papal arguments, the Peelite Aberdeen stated that he and others of his colleagues did not share Russell's views.[95] Not for a dozen more years, however, until Palmerston's influence had been removed from the political scene, could the Liberals pursue a distinctly pro-Catholic policy; indeed, before then, Irish Catholic opinion had been further alienated from the party by the latter's warm support for Italian unification.[96] But the Catholic Irish MPs joined enthusiastically with the Liberal party from the mid 1860s in its attack on the Irish Church.

The first steps in cementing this alliance were taken by O'Neill Daunt, who had been in contact with the Liberation Society since the 1850s.[97] In 1864, the National Association, a pressure group of lay and clerical Irish opinion, was launched – campaigning for the disestablishment of the Irish Church, and campaigning, from the beginning, in association with the Liberation Society.[98] In 1867, an agreement was reached between the two, by which Catholics agreed not to press for endowment for them-

[93] Machin, 'Gladstone and nonconformity', pp. 354–5.   [94] See below, pp. 179–80.
[95] Whyte, *Independent Irish party*, pp. 99–100.   [96] Hoppen, 'Tories, Catholics, and 1859'.
[97] Bell, *Disestablishment in Ireland*, p. 41.   [98] Norman, *Catholic Church*, pp. 135–89.

selves upon disestablishment; this would facilitate support for the policy from the body of anti-Catholic nonconformists in England, while strengthening the hand of the Liberation Society in its aim of presenting the measure as a preliminary to English disestablishment. A series of parliamentary motions on the state of the Irish Church was instituted in 1865, when Gladstone made his famous, but still ambiguous, announcement that he was not loyal to it as an Establishment. Most Liberal MPs supported the motions:[99] and the Liberation Society mounted a national campaign for Irish Church disestablishment with the money from its reserve fund. This coalition of interests imposed almost irresistible pressure for the move. But the irony, and the ultimate problem for the Liberal party, was that the Irish Catholic hierarchy, led by Cardinal Cullen, had not intended the main work of the Association to be the attainment either of this goal, or of land reform, another of its policies. Cullen's main interest had long been in securing endowment for Catholic education – advocacy of which would inevitably bring him into conflict with British Liberal opinion.[100]

Such were the relationships between the component sections of the party in 1868, and they offered much scope for conflict. So also did the problems to be tackled.

The most awesome, although also the most intangible, was the consequence of the passage of the 1867 Reform Act. This doubled the number of nonconformists in the Commons, and added significantly to their claim to represent electoral opinion. Inspired by this, and by the disestablishment of the Irish Church in 1869, they increasingly advocated the disestablishment of the Church of England; they used as their main statistical argument the findings of the 1851 census, which showed that 40 per cent of churchgoers in England, and 75 per cent in Wales attended nonconformist chapels. They claimed that in the intervening two decades, their position had strengthened considerably.

Allied to this problem, but posing more immediate difficulties, was the need for educational legislation. The university-tests question was still unsettled when Gladstone's government came to power. More importantly, there was a general consensus that the system of elementary and endowed education in England and Scotland urgently required improvement. The Newcastle, Taunton, Clarendon and Argyll Commissions had all reported in the 1860s to this effect, and had recommended more state intervention. There was especial concern about the availability of

---

[99] Bell, *Disestablishment in Ireland*, p. 43.
[100] See H. Senior, 'Paul Cullen: cardinal and politician', in *The view from the pulpit: Victorian ministers and society*, ed. P. T. Phillips (Toronto, 1978), pp. 273–97.

elementary education, and many Liberals had been proposing since the mid 1850s that the state should permit (or, increasingly, compel) local authorities to levy a rate in order to remedy deficiencies in the provision of schools by the voluntary religious agencies.[101] In addition to widespread concern at the lack of educational provision in secular subjects, there was considerable distrust of the aims of these agencies, especially the National Society (since over three-quarters of all elementary schools receiving state aid in 1870 were Anglican) – and much disquiet at the amount of state money which was going to support its teaching. By 1862, the annual educational grant had reached £840,000: in the same year, the Liberal government instituted the Revised Code, in an attempt to channel the grant towards schools which were deemed efficient in their teaching of secular subjects.[102] It was also claimed that Church interests were preventing the efficient redistribution of the endowments of secondary schools, most of which were tied to purposes specified by pious founders. In the 1860s, there was much Liberal pressure for state action in order to redirect these endowments more beneficially.

Until the mid 1860s, radical nonconformists – and Gladstone – opposed Liberal demands for rate-aid to elementary schools. They defended the voluntary system on the grounds that it encouraged individual zeal.[103] Both objected to rate-aid, in addition, because it would force taxpayers to subsidise an educational system which ran contrary to their most strongly held beliefs. The system which nonconformists resented supporting was the Anglican system. That by which Gladstone continued to be repelled all his life was the 'undenominationalism' which the whigs wanted to impose on the schools: that is, a 'common Christianity' of extracts from the bible, divorced from any instruction in the disputed dogmas of any sect. For Gladstone, such a scheme involved the perversion of Christian doctrine by state authority.

However, two leading nonconformist voluntaryists, Baines and Miall, announced in late 1867 that they could no longer refuse to admit the logic of rate-aid.[104] On the one hand, there was an increasing consensus, after the reports of the various educational Commissions, that the voluntary system was inadequate; on the other, nonconformist contributions towards education were proving insufficient to dent the massive preponderance of Church schools over unsectarian ones. In addition, one of the strongest demands from the aspiring newly enfranchised after 1867

---

[101] See e.g. Russell's motion, *Hansard*, cxl, 1955, 6 March 1856.
[102] J. Hurt, *Education in evolution: Church, state, society and popular education 1800–1870* (London, 1971), pp. 202–4.
[103] For Gladstone, see Shannon, *Gladstone*, p. 322.
[104] D. Fraser, 'Edward Baines', in *Pressure from without in early Victorian England*, ed. P. Hollis (London, 1974), pp. 201–2.

was for an extension of the unsectarian system. The ex-voluntaryists' declaration united the bulk of the Liberal party behind proposals for a rate system. Perhaps it convinced Gladstone too, because, slightly later in the same year, he made his first known public pronouncement in favour of an activist state-education policy.[105]

Once the need for rate-aid was accepted, however, the religious difficulty assumed even greater proportions. The proposal on which the whig-liberal centre of the party was agreed was that embodied in bills brought in by H. A. Bruce, W. E. Forster and a Conservative MP, Algernon Egerton, in 1867 and 1868. The 1867 bill gave ratepayers the power to establish local boards, in order to remedy any insufficiency of educational provision. These would administer new schools and determine by local arrangement how much religious instruction they would give; all existing schools which accepted rate-aid and instituted a conscience clause would retain control of religious instruction in their schools. The 1868 bill included provisions to force boards on recalcitrant localities. There were at least two other popular schemes, both associated with the more radical end of the party. One, adopted by the more anti-clerical whig-liberals, and by some nonconformists and radicals, desired the cessation of aid to voluntary denominational schools, and the establishment of a national rate-supported educational system on undenominational lines (in which religious instruction would be restricted to either the teaching, or the simple reading, of the bible). The National Education League was founded in 1869 and pressed for this system – together with educational compulsion – except that it proposed to give schools the option not to give religious instruction at all. This was a compromise forced on the League by the advocates of the third solution, which was that of other radicals and nonconformists: the restriction of rate-aid to the provision of secular education in the schools. Under this system, clergymen of the various denominations would come in at specified times and provide whatever religious instruction they wished to the children whose parents desired them to receive it.

Discussion of educational reform in England was to be greatly affected by anti-clerical pressure from Liberals. Such pressure was increased as a result of the Catholics' request for educational reform in Ireland, both at elementary and university level, requests which most Liberals considered unacceptable. The state of the national elementary system has already been touched upon (p. 20). The difficulties associated with the university question were more complex. In 1845 and 1850, as we saw, the British government had taken steps to establish a university system – the Queen's university and colleges – which was designed to provide

---

[105] Beales, 'Gladstone and his first ministry', p. 994.

Protestants and Catholics with a joint higher education in secular subjects. The provision of religious instruction was left to voluntary
agencies. The most successful of the three Queen's colleges was that at
Belfast, although it was heavily dominated by Ulster presbyterians (as
was the private university college, Magee college, Londonderry, which
was founded in 1863). The Catholic bishops repeatedly condemned the
Queen's colleges, and dissuaded Catholics from attending them (in
1869, Cullen claimed that only thirty-seven Catholics were studying for
arts degrees at them).[106] Instead, the hierarchy demanded endowment
for the denominational Catholic university on St Stephen's Green,
Dublin. (The other important Catholic-controlled institution of higher
education was the theological college at Maynooth, although this
received endowment from the state until 1869, as compensation for the
maintenance of an Established Church.) The bishops' hands were
strengthened by the existence of a lavishly endowed Protestant college,
Trinity college, Dublin. Trinity had been granted a charter in 1592, and
had been envisaged as part of a collegiate Dublin university. No other
colleges were affiliated, however, and the consequence was that the university structure was subordinated to the government of Trinity. Aspiring reformers of the Irish university system thus faced several problems.
The Catholic hierarchy demanded endowment for their own university.
Liberals who opposed the endowment of denominational education
argued that the proper policy was to abolish all theological tests in
Trinity and thus to extend the provision of mixed education. (Until
1793–4, Roman Catholics and Protestant nonconformists had in effect
been excluded from studying at Trinity; in the nineteenth century,
although allowed to matriculate and gain degrees, they were still
excluded from fellowships, professorships, and a role in university
government.) But, if tests were abolished, it would be necessary to
reform the government of Trinity (which had long been controlled by its
Protestant senior Fellows), in consideration of the non-Anglican element
in the college. The termination of the university's (the examining
board's) subjection to the college was also advocated on grounds of
efficiency.

The unbiassed discussion of Catholic educational grievances at
Westminster was threatened by two further elements. Firstly, Irish
political radicalism was reviving in the mid 1860s, as was apparent not
only from the formation of the National Association, but, more alarmingly, from the growing militancy of bands of Fenian insurgents. Fenianism had been founded by Irishmen in America in 1858, in order to work
for the overthrow of English rule in Ireland. In March 1867, there was an

---

[106] F. S. L. Lyons, *Ireland since the famine* (London, 1973 edn), p. 96.

attempted Fenian uprising in the major towns of southern Ireland; in the following autumn, two attacks in England, at Manchester and Clerkenwell, killed thirteen people and outraged public opinion. Although the Fenians themselves were less active subsequently, groups of peasants in rural Ireland were increasingly operating 'Ribbon conspiracies', resorting to violence against landlords and wealthy tenants. After 1870, moreover, the spirit of political radicalism was reborn among Irish MPs as well, as the newly founded home rule party won a number of by-election victories. Secondly, British MPs knew little about Ireland. They tended to discuss its problems in the light of their own, and to recommend solutions for Ireland for no reason other than that they considered them to be appropriate for Britain: a problem especially acute in the debates about education.

In politics generally after 1867, Liberals' tendency to adopt anti-clerical positions was also strengthened by dislike of manifestations of ultramontane power in Rome. Pius IX, attempting to shore up his position against the attacks of European liberals on his temporal power, and of liberal theologians on the spiritual authority of the Catholic faith, promulgated the Syllabus of Errors in December 1864, and then secured the Church's acceptance of the doctrine of papal infallibility at the Vatican council in the spring of 1870.[107] These judgments shocked British Protestants, and encouraged further suspicion of the designs of Cullen and the Irish Catholic priesthood, who were among the most loyal supporters of the pope's ultramontanism.

On top of this, there was unparalleled antipathy to the rapid growth of ritualism in the Church of England. In 1865, the Church Association, an evangelical group, was founded in order to take ritualists to court; the first case was instituted against Alexander Mackonochie, a vicar in Holborn. The Court of Arches upheld the legality of his practices in 1867, but the Judicial Committee reversed this in 1869, condemning all ceremonial not specified in the rubrics, such as the use of incense and altar lights, and genuflection. There was a further controversy in 1871 when, after the Court of Arches had confirmed the validity of wearing eucharistic vestments and the adoption by the celebrant of the eastward position during the prayer of consecration, the Judicial Committee condemned both, in what became known as the Purchas judgment (John Purchas, the offending ritualist, was a clergyman in Brighton).[108] Both Mackonochie and Purchas were suspended, but this did not deter ritualists from continuing with the practices; the process of prosecution

---

[107] See e.g. C. Butler, *The Vatican council 1869–1870: based on Bishop Ullathorne's letters* (London, 1962 edn).
[108] Benham and Davidson, *Tait*, ii, 92–100.

was expensive and tortuous, and so it was impossible to stamp them out. The situation called forth two conflicting movements.

One, by high churchmen such as Liddon and Pusey, was to press for the replacement of the Judicial Committee by a distinctly ecclesiastical tribunal, or, alternatively, by a completely secular one which they could therefore ignore. They were increasingly disquieted by the activities of the Judicial Committee, not only on ritual matters, but on doctrinal issues. In 1864, the Judicial Committee had overturned the judgment of the Court of Arches which had found two of the contributors to the controversial *Essays and reviews* guilty of heresy. The Committee had also ruled that the bishop of Cape Town had no right to deprive Bishop Colenso of his see, after he had published a critical treatment of the Pentateuch.[109] High churchmen continued to complain about the decisions of the Committee, despite its Bennett judgment of 1872. This, as a logical corollary of the Committee's extreme latitudinarianism on matters of dogma, tolerated the doctrine of the Real Presence – antagonising nonconformists even more than by its previous displays of religious breadth.

The other movement was begun by broad churchmen and evangelicals who wished to check the spread of sacerdotal practices. In 1867, the Conservative government established a Royal Commission on the Rubrics, in order to determine policy concerning the conduct of worship. When the Commission began to report, it added weight to the demands of many whig-liberals for ecclesiastical legislation. They called for measures which would speed up the operation of ecclesiastical courts, and thus provide a more effective remedy for parishioners oppressed by ritualist practices (some also wanted to institute local lay councils in order to make the clergy more accountable to parishioners). They also aimed to pass bills which would simplify and shorten services, in the hope of appealing to non-Anglicans and broadening the Establishment. Especially controversial in any reform of services was the place of the Athanasian Creed. This Creed was now widely believed to be an invention of the years after AD 600;[110] it was too precise in its descriptions of mysterious events for the modern mind; and its damnatory clauses appeared to promise consignment to eternal damnation for all who did not accept the Catholic dogmatic system. Although it had to be recited publicly thirteen times a year, it had only been revived from disuse by the influence of the Oxford movement. It was thus a prime candidate for removal from the prayer-book, or for demotion to optional status in the

---

[109] Chadwick, *Victorian Church*, ii, 75–97.
[110] E.g. (Ffoulkes) Marsh, *Victorian Church in decline*, p. 41.

conduct of services; in 1872, six thousand laymen signed Shaftesbury's petition against its continuance in its existing place in worship.

Apart from their effect on the discussion of education, these questions provoked great mutual bitterness from warring parties within the Church, which did not present onlookers with an edifying spectacle. This had a number of political consequences. On the one hand, the prosecution of ritualists led a number of them publicly to advocate disestablishment, and led other high churchmen to view its prospect with some equanimity. On the other, whigs regarded high-church fractiousness as deeply damaging to Church unity, as preventing accommodation with non-Churchmen, and as diminishing the Church's claim to represent the average feeling of the nation. They, therefore, as we saw, fervently supported measures to broaden the appeal of the Church. Their anxiety was intensified by two further developments – the effects of the 'scientific revolution' promoted by Darwin and Huxley, and the biblical criticism which had spread to England from Germany – in encouraging doubt in Christian tenets; and the growing nonconformist pressure for disestablishment of the Church of England after 1869. Nonconformists could exploit the disarray in the Church by using a number of arguments. They could point to the proto-Romanism in one section of the Church, and yet to the erastian repression of spiritual independence that broad churchmen were being tempted to adopt in reaction to it. They could ask whether the Establishment of the Church served any purpose when, under the impact of biblical and scientific criticism, and grave disagreement on theological questions, it could agree on little of substantive merit; whether the various sects, especially the high churchmen, would not be happier in different Free Churches; and whether the growth of materialism in society was likely to be checked by a Church which was so paralysed that it was not able even to reform itself. In 1871 and 1873, Edward Miall proposed the disestablishment of the Church of England in the Commons.

Nonconformist activity also called into question the propriety of maintaining the Church Establishment in Scotland. The vast majority of Scotsmen were presbyterians; of these, considerable numbers had seceded from the Establishment during the course of the eighteenth century, and most of the sects thus formed had coalesced as the United Presbyterian Church in 1847. This Church actively supported disestablishment of the Church of Scotland – unlike the other main nonconformist presbyterian body, the Free Church, founded in 1843, after the Disruption. In the decade after 1863, representatives of the United Presbyterians and Free Churchmen were discussing the prospect of union, which, since the two sects ministered to over 60 per cent of the Scottish population, would place the Established position of the Church of Scotland in grave jeopardy from any future political agitation. In an attempt to win back converts from the Free Churches, a movement for the abolition of patronage – the original bone of contention with the Free Church – began within the Establishment in the mid 1860s.

One of this book's major contentions is that it is possible to trace the operation of a broad distinction between two Liberal camps after 1867: between most whig-liberals on the one hand, and the Gladstonians, and most nonconformists and radicals, on the other. Both, it is asserted, believed that religion – understood as including education and the role of the Church – was the most important component in ensuring that society was well-ordered. But the first was more anxious than the second for the wise state to superintend the community's religious life, so that the success of anti-social forces could be checked. Whig-liberals wished to restrain demagogic politicians and ecclesiastics; they did not trust the unbridled passions of man; and they did not believe that it was desirable to sweep away all the securities for order which many radicals wished to destroy in the name of promoting individual responsibility – the Church Establishment, bible reading in the schools, and, later, the union with Ireland. The other camp distrusted the capacity of those in authority to regulate morality and promote spirituality without repression and formalism. They therefore tended, far more, to disapprove of the interference of the state with the evangelisation of society (while, broadly, accepting its capacity for day-to-day intervention in administrative affairs). They placed more faith in the ability of religious forces, in free competition, to raise the national standard of morals and spirituality; they thus tended to wish to promote the independence of the spiritual power from the temporal, so that the zeal and purity of the former might regenerate the plutocratic and effete 'governing classes'.

This was not a division between 'optimists' and 'pessimists': each camp merits both of these epithets, for both appreciated man's capacity for progress in the eyes of God, yet were suffused with awareness of the obstacles to realising that progress which derived from man's flawed nature, his sinfulness. Nor can the division be simply equated with any divergence of opinion about the merits of parliamentary reform in the 1860s – about which, as we saw, most whig-liberals had been ambivalent. Moreover, a number of those who were most active for parliamentary reform before 1867, including men who continued subsequently to press for administrative, trade-union, local government and land reform, were on the 'right' of the party on the religious and later on the home-rule issue.[111] Nonetheless, it is asserted that such a division does most to

---

[111] See below, pp. 58, 70.

explain the antagonism within the party by 1874, and, probably, should also be accorded most weight in accounting for the permanent division of 1886.

The rigidity of this division must not be overstressed: indeed there are individuals whom it is difficult to categorise in particular sections. There was in any case no hard-and-fast distinction between the two camps, because Liberals shared so many assumptions; there were many circumstances in which individuals from one camp could appreciate the wisdom of acting in a manner specified by the other. For example, nearly all asserted the unwisdom of opposing demands of public opinion, if they were consistently articulated, believing it to conduce to the breakdown of order. Equally, nearly all disliked ignorant displays of popular imperialism or jingoism, when they appeared from the late 1870s. Some politicians, moreover, did not take part in the debate recorded below: they were happy to drift with the tide, upholding the basic principles of the 'Liberal conscience' wherever others asserted them. A number did this simply for form's sake, whereas others believed in the innate progressiveness of the Liberal party – possessing that most comforting of political gifts, the certainty that the tenure of power by one's own party, at whatever cost, would advance the 'cause of right'. In the Liberal cabinet of 1868–74, this belief was held by Granville and Cardwell, and to a lesser extent by Childers, Kimberley and Lowe. The divergence between the two camps was in fact between two dispositions of mind: it sometimes amounted to no more than a dispute about the viability of particular means of influencing and harnessing public opinion – a force which all respected, but which all knew was malleable.

Nonetheless, there were real differences of outlook among those Liberals discussed in this book; and the most difficult problem for the historian is to decide how much weight they should be given in an explanation of political divergence. With politicians more than most, it is ambitious and perhaps naive to suggest that there was any connection between rhetoric, belief and manoeuvre. But Part I has been written on the assumption that aspirations, and in particular religious aspirations, influenced political behaviour at Westminster, and the political allegiance of Liberals outside parliament. The rest of this introduction has been written for those who are interested to discover the methodological foundations on which this half of the book has been based.

Part I attempts to reconstruct the different thought-worlds of representative and articulate sections of the Liberal party: articulate in the sense that they were represented in the newspaper and periodical press, and in the flood of books, pamphlets and speeches. To this end, the major periodicals have been examined, and a number of important newspapers consulted extensively – as have all other publications which could be traced and which appeared to bear on the subject-matter. This process of research could, of course, be continued indefinitely; but enough work on it has been done to convince the author that there was a public debate which revolved around the distinctions set out in Part I, and that it was a more important debate than any contemporary competitor. This debate took place, moreover, at three different levels of sophistication: not only among politicians, but among writers of texts on the one hand, and among the leaders of local opinion and politically interested voters themselves on the other. It should be borne in mind, therefore, that the arguments presented in Part I were formulated in different ways by each of these three groups.

Writers have been included in the analysis in Part I, on the assumption that Victorian political society was so intimately linked with the literary and cultural world that historians, classicists, theologians and even scientists, in writing and speaking as they did, were consciously making contributions to the political debate. It has also been assumed that the views which they expressed in public, in letters and in conversation were as likely to be influential in promoting or sabotaging political causes as were the views of backbench politicians. Trollope himself suggested this when he had journalists, city men, barristers, actors, painters, poets and novelists welcomed to the political salons in his novels, because they 'all had tongues of their own, and certain modes of expression, which might assist or injure the Palliser Coalition'.[112] One recent book has very perceptively traced the ramifications of this close connection between authors and contemporary political debates, in one field of scholarship.[113] In Part I, some of the most famous literary battles of the 1860s and 1870s – those between Froude and Freeman, Arnold and Harrison, Mill and Fitzjames Stephen – are set in a political context.

This is not to say that most writers were directly interested in promoting individual politicians' careers, or in assisting the victory of the Liberal party: but their productions, and informal contacts, helped to create a climate which encouraged voters to respond in one political direction rather than in another. Neither, of course, can all famous writers be fitted into one constricting model: this would be an absurd aim, given the infinite perversity of human nature, and, more particularly in the case of professional writers, the subtlety which is their claim to respect. Some writers were not interested in stating a public position about the religious dimension of politics; others were, but cannot be

---

[112] *The prime minister* (Oxford, 1973 edn), i, 98.
[113] Turner, *Greek heritage.*

classified within the categories adopted here, even though, in some cases, their political influence might be considerable in later decades, as with T. H. Green. Nonetheless, an impressive number of the most active writers of the 1860s and 1870s did set forth views on the subject, in the categories classified in this book. (Occasionally, evidence of writers' views has been taken from their later publications, but, except where a shift of opinion on their part is indicated in the text, this policy has been adopted only where the author believes that their views remained unchanged.)

These writers were usually sophisticated thinkers. They are treated below in a way which does disservice to the precision and complexity of the views which they spent so many years formulating; and intellectual historians may well consider this treatment to be unhelpfully simplistic. However, Part I is not an exercise in intellectual history, but an attempt to reconstruct a political climate. The significance of these writers for the elucidation of *political* debates is twofold. It is important to discover what they themselves thought about politics; but their ideas were all the more important for being disseminated to the reading public, and in particular to the leading figures in local politics – whose assumptions can often be traced in no other way. We know that this was an age of wide reading of theological and political works and periodicals; we know that individual whig peers whose papers have survived avidly read works from the theological schools that one would expect them to read. It has therefore been assumed below that other like-minded leaders of local public opinion did the same; and thus that the ideas developed in Part I, albeit in a readily intelligible form, percolated down to educated readers and informed their political judgment.

It is at the level of overtly political debate at Westminster that the most profound methodological problems are encountered. Even limiting our attention to those politicians who were interested in religious debates and took up coherent positions during them – which is to include a very large number – how can we guarantee that they were acting 'sincerely'?

One criticism frequently levelled against such politicians is their subordination of their aspirations for policy, and their ideals, to a calculation of short-term political prospects. All politicians knew that progress towards a desired end could be made only very hesitantly, and as a myriad of other political considerations dictated: the most important aim was, necessarily, to gain or retain office for their party. But it is not clear why this should be regarded as a hypocritical stance. It was on the whole legitimate for both Conservatives and Liberals to regard the tenure of power by their own party as preventing the institution of wrong-headed religious policy by their opponents. Furthermore, it was understood that one could make political advances only by working with the grain of public expectation: all upholders of the Liberal conscience saw public opinion as a force created by the exercise of free will on the part of God's creatures. To follow it – albeit with qualifications, especially in the case of the whig-liberals – was thus to fulfil God's purpose. Gladstone, as is well-known, believed that his function in politics was to try to promote God's ends, but only with such instruments as the world supplied; that is, by harnessing public opinion when possible.[114]

It is, however, the case that the religious attitudes of politicians sometimes developed in such a way as, *inter alia*, to promote their personal advancement. One might say this, for example, of Chamberlain, of Harcourt, and of Gladstone. As it happens, the present author believes that Gladstone, endowed as he was with a fund of self-deception, had a 'sincere' belief that the public interest would be best served by his continued tenure of power and his manipulation of the Liberal conscience in particular ways, while Chamberlain had fewer public ends, and Harcourt fell somewhere between the two. Disraeli, at all periods, and Chamberlain, in the 1880s, suffered politically, in relation to Gladstone, from imputations of hypocrisy or lack of principle. The most important conclusion for the historian to draw from this is not whether they were or were not 'sincere', but that they were less professional at their job than Gladstone: less skilled at appreciating the demands of their audience and at advocating their cause in a way which would succeed in moulding a half-formed public opinion to support that cause. The fact that Gladstone wove a spell over audiences, that he often refused to make a politically unwise move, that one of his major preoccupations after 1868 was to prevent the party from splitting, should not obscure the fact that he did wish the party to have a moral purpose, that he took risks for this end, and that he ultimately divided the party for it. In assessing political motivation, all estimates of the 'sincerity' of individuals are, in fact, purely arbitrary: a psychological study of their temperaments would be required in order to elucidate their political behaviour, and the materials for this are fortunately unavailable. (Such a study would, however, surely reveal that the determining consideration was, not an impulse as generalised and calculating as 'ambition', but the interaction of a number of personality traits to which the politician was in uncontrollable bondage, such as arrogance, gullibility, sensitivity, irascibility and insecurity.)

In this book, what is being assessed is not so much the motives of politicians in their use of arguments, as the arguments themselves – and their effect on those who were influenced by them. Political rhetoric was most significant when it struck a chord with a large number of people,

---

[114] Schreuder, 'Gladstone and the conscience of the state', p. 91.

when it upheld or attacked or reverenced something of central concern. If the number of unfamiliar names mentioned below should ever become bewildering, it should be remembered that this book is not attempting to particularise politics, and that individuals who articulate a point are relevant only to the extent that they represent opinion more generally. If politics is the art of survival in the open sea, this work is concerned not with the rowing-boat – for which the waves may well be too choppy unless it is blessed with a constitution of Gladstonian fortitude – but with the ocean-going liner. Inherent in the exploitation of these 'political languages' was, of course, rhetorical exaggeration. It was only by adopting the standard arts of persuasion used by all public performers that a political reaction could be attained. Public opinion would be persuaded that cherished interests were being threatened only by the constant repetition of readily intelligible illustration, and only if the importance of specific legislative proposals was continually inflated by presenting them as the significant thin end of an ideologically attractive or unattractive wedge.

Because political arguments had to be easily intelligible, and had to appeal to large numbers of people, they cannot be treated with the intellectual rigour which historians apply to the study of philosophical or theological texts. In order to attempt to explain the popularity of some of the political arguments deployed to most effect between 1867 and 1875, and set out in Part II of this book, those who were most influential in forming public opinion (politicians and writers) have been grouped, in Part I, into broad categories. This has been done, even though the individuals grouped in these categories differed, sometimes markedly, between themselves on individual points (such differences are indicated, as far as possible, in the relevant chapters). The reason for proceeding in this way is the author's belief that all those grouped in each section could set down their intellectual baggage within a generously defined ideological perimeter, and claim to stand for certain fundamental tenets and values which they considered it vital to promote, and against whose enemies they believed it vital to stand firm. These tenets and values were those which could give most meaning to the political participation of individuals, and which could thus be erected by political standard-bearers to greatest effect.

In contrast, members of a group might differ from each other on a particular set of proposals or details: but this was not usually politically significant in the long run. Most spectators of politics did not possess rigid opinions, on most practical questions of the day, which they were determined to express and to see embodied in legislation. If detail was of comparatively little interest to them, politicians, for their part, were wary of becoming committed to a course which was so narrowly defined as to maximise the chance of producing disagreement with other politicians, and an apathetic response from spectators. They knew that room for manoeuvre was necessary, given the number of imponderables which affected the course of affairs; to be tied to principle too closely earned a reputation for doctrinairism, the possession of which was usually fatal to prospects of advancement. Accommodation with other interests was necessary, if politicians were to remain members of a central party, rather than one which would lose votes through appearing exclusive.

In other words, the issues which became politically significant were those which politicians and writers could suggest affected very broad principles. It was not only voters who viewed politics in these simple terms, but the 'governing classes'. Peers, notables, journalists and academics were just as keen as anyone else to uphold cherished slogans and to reiterate what may appear to be cant phrases. The stuff of day-to-day politics, the detailed consideration of clauses of bills, was not, there-fore, usually of relevance in arousing opinion, in religious matters any more than in others. When clauses were controversial, it was because they touched issues which could be inflated into matters of broad prin-ciple – even though such controversy often bore little relationship to administrative reality. As will become apparent in Part II, there were great nationwide agitations over issues arising out of the preamble to the Irish Church Bill, of Clause 25 of the 1870 Education Act, and of the whole of the Public Worship Regulation Bill. But these provisions had almost no discernible practical consequences; while arguably the most paralysing difficulties of all stemmed from fears that the party leadership might pursue policies concerning Irish university education which it had no intention of pursuing. Disraeli's comment on Clause 25 could be applied more generally: 'we all go down to our constituents and say that the Constitution depends upon it, and we none of us know what it means'.[115]

To recapitulate, Part I has been organised on the assumption that it is legitimate in a work of *political* history to construct broad schools of argument by grouping together people who, despite individual differ-ences of opinion, would agree on the importance of maintaining certain propositions, which were politically controversial, against potential threats to them. If this appears a rather crude way of writing about the relations between views about religion and political reality, it is nonethe-less the only one that the present author has been able to justify to him-self. He has shared the widespread scepticism about the impact of developed beliefs on day-to-day political life, which has been propagated by the concentration of recent historical writing on specific events and

---

[115] Russell, *Lawson*, p. 106.

situations in nineteenth-century politics. But, if the contributions made by all these works are to be set in context, and a wide-ranging view of politics adopted (a view which sees it as an activity which sustained the social fabric), the relationship between men's ideals and aspirations on the one hand and political practice on the other has to be more systematically penetrated. This book proceeds from the assumption that, except when taxation and, more occasionally, property and foreign policy questions, became inflamed, it was only religious issues which *were* able to link the world with which the politically interested public was concerned to the high political world. It was religious issues which could most consistently inspire enthusiasm and ensure that the political system worked smoothly; they alone, moreover, were able to convey to the political nation a sense of higher purpose, an inspiration for a more devout spiritual life. As a result of their prominence, politics in the nineteenth century was disciplinary, educative and uplifting; but the consequences for political organisation itself were profound, because questions which touched spiritual nerves and which assaulted religious consciences inevitably outraged individuals and divided parties. But then, as even the anti-clerical Huxley said in 1889, 'the reproach made to the English people that "they care for nothing but religion and politics" is rather to their credit. In the long run these are the two things that ought to interest a man more than any others.'[116]

[116] To Knowles, 29 February 1889, Huxley, *Huxley*, iii, 107–8.

PART I

1

The whig-liberals: I

The 'whig-liberals' of this chapter and the next shared many of the
religious views generally attributed to mid-century continental liberals.
The latter viewed the Church as the willing ally of intolerant autocrats,
and saw clerics as opponents of free expression and as agents of corruption. In Britain, the triumph of whig principles had ensured that such
clerical pretensions had been checked, but it was seen to be the duty of
the liberal state to continue to check them, and to use its considerable
power to improve the moral and intellectual content of national religion.
The response of whig-liberals to developments in the party after 1867
was to welcome whatever efforts continued to be made towards this end.
At the same time, they tended increasingly to view Gladstone with
suspicion, as a zealous high churchman, a passionate demagogue, and an
inscrutable political thinker. Moreover, they disliked his tendency to
place more weight than Palmerston had done on the opinions of three
groups – English and Scottish nonconformists, Irish Catholics, and
demagogic radicals – whose power, it seemed, had been so much
strengthened by Disraeli's rather cavalier extension of the franchise in
1867.

Whig-liberals believed that national progress would be promoted by
the elevation of the individual moral character to a pitch which would
enable each man to appreciate his duty before God. Towards this end,
they advocated the rule of a wise, moral executive government, and the
use of state law to prevent the national level of morality falling through
man's desire to indulge his selfish interests. They condemned those who
wished to escape from that rule of law as 'materialists', as men who were
determined to live by the senses and for pleasure, and to gratify the baser
passions. In public affairs, they saw materialism to be especially
frightening among three classes of men: firstly, elements among the
working classes, newly enfranchised in 1867, and largely uneducated;
secondly, those politicians who did not wish to elevate the morality of

the common man, but who stimulated his baser side by offering exciting and irresponsible legislation and passionate demagogy; and, thirdly, ecclesiastics who were similarly divisive, sectional and rabble-rousing, and who gloried in party badges and in formalistic practices and doctrines. Only through the rule of law, then, could national life be wisely directed.

In the broadest sense, this response to politics after 1867 was shared by men who had often not agreed before then; those who had not been Palmerstonians began to stress arguments similar to those who had. Definitions of 'Liberalism' were perhaps drawn more rigorously than before, in order to emphasise Gladstone's apparent infringement of them, and distinctions between whig-liberals themselves often received less attention than hitherto.[1]

However, it is important not to treat 'whig-liberalism' as a coherent political force. There were disagreements between the individuals discussed here, occasionally vehement: some, for example, attached far more weight to Christian dogma than did others. On secular questions, the group included the most diehard anti-Reformers in 1867, as well as men like Tom Hughes (associated with the Reform League and with the trade-union movement) and Dicey and Brodrick (contributors to the optimistic *Essays on Reform* of 1867). One of the most significant divisions was between a more 'evangelical' strain – tending to emphasise the importance of state control in repressing certain anti-social forms of religious or class behaviour – and the 'latitudinarians', who usually asserted that the state functioned best by including and tolerating all sects and ideas. Another was between an 'emotional' and an 'intellectual' outlook. But even granted these differences of emphasis, the similarities are sufficient to justify inclusion in the same narrative. If these two chapters delineate an ideological perimeter within which 'whig-liberals' might stand, five of the points on the periphery, the most extreme manifestations of opinion which whig-liberals could display, may be represented by Clarendon; Shaftesbury; Froude, Huxley or Stephen; Arnold or Stanley; and Hutton. That is to say, to embrace, respectively, sceptical old whiggism; the purest form of evangelicalism sustainable, in 1865, by a non-Conservative; its secular, hard-nosed pessimistic Carlylean equivalent; tolerant optimistic latitudinarianism, hardly aware of sin, and infused with a Wordsworthian or Newmanite reverence for tradition and beauty; and latitudinarianism injected with a powerful belief in the

---

[1] See, for the connections drawn between the views of Grant Duff, Hartington, James, Matthew Arnold, Bruce and W. R. Greg: Grant Duff, *Notes from a diary, 1851–72*, ii, 15–16; *Out of the past*, i, 220; Russell, *Letters of Arnold*, i, 400; *Letters of Aberdare*, i, 14; Greg, *Enigmas of life*, pp. lxxiv–lxxv. For the approximation between the attitudes of Fitzjames Stephen and Carlyle after 1867, see Colaiaco, *Stephen*, p. 156.

spiritual awareness of the common man. Within this perimeter roamed numerous classes of old whigs, Liberal country gentry, Arnoldian educationalists, broad churchmen, Christian socialists, academic liberals and deist intellectuals. Many individuals discussed here cannot be dogmatically characterised, except, perhaps, as liberal evangelicals: 'evangelical and liberal' as the queen called her favourite clergymen,[2] and combining 'the opinions of the Broad Church with the fervour and warmth of the Evangelicals', as Cowper-Temple's wife described him.[3]

The figures treated below also adopted widely differing attitudes to the government of 1868–74, as will become apparent in Part II. Some were vehemently critical, others apathetic; many were diffident and silent lobby-fodder, but privately expressed occasional alarm. Office-holding at all levels made men more accommodating and less fractious. For example, Grant Duff, who held office under Gladstone until 1874, dissented from the pessimism expressed by W. R. Greg in some articles of 1874: but he later came to believe that Greg had been right.[4] In the case of a few, mainly office-holders, support for Gladstone extended even beyond 1886. Childers, for example, held liberal-evangelical religious opinions, but had become a faithful disciple of Gladstone's views on fiscal policy when financial secretary to the treasury under him in 1865–6. Childers' grasp of minutiae won him promotion to the cabinet in 1868, and his inability to break away from Gladstone's shadow kept him there even in 1886.[5]

But in the main, despite differences, these men shared enough of a common outlook to take a similar view of the nature of the Liberal party, as it developed in the twenty years after 1867. The bulk of these two chapters attempts to elucidate this outlook, and thus treats the men concerned *en bloc*, as far as is possible. However, at the end of the next chapter, some attempt will be made to distinguish between the responses, in practice, of different types of whig-liberal; while it is essential to indicate the very considerable distinctions between them, in introducing the individuals to be discussed, as must now be done.

Regency whiggery had embraced a good deal of Voltairean scepticism and hedonism, and perhaps some materialistic utilitarianism. One way of expressing this had been to cultivate a flippant and detached view of the world, often allied with a loose personal morality. In this latter sense,

---

[2] Gordon, *Charteris*, p. 392.
[3] Mount-Temple, *Memorials*, pp. 17, 61; see also, for similar examples, Bryce, *Studies in contemporary biography*, pp. 110–11 (on Tait); Leveson-Gower, *Years of content*, p. 26 (on F. Leveson-Gower); Creighton, *George Grey*, p. 134; and Mallet, *Northbrook*, pp. 254, 298–9.
[4] Greg, *Enigmas of life*, pp. lxxvi–lxxvii; see Grant Duff, 'Must we then believe Cassandra?'
[5] See e.g. diary, 25 January 1869, Brabourne papers, F27/3, p. 46.

at least, old whig values survived into the age of Palmerston, Clanricarde and the 2nd Baron Stanley of Alderley. They were also expressed, in a milder form, by some of the older whigs discussed in these chapters, like Somerset (a former cabinet minister), Clarendon (who was primarily interested in foreign affairs), and Westbury (an ex-lord chancellor whose influence on the Judicial Committee of the Privy Council, in leading it to pronounce liberal judgments on the *Essays and reviews* and Colenso cases, had been considerable). But, as was said of Westbury, although 'very loose in his life, he was naturally religious';[6] Clarendon, however flippant, had devout, simple and fixed Protestant beliefs.[7] Much the same, in fact, had applied to the general run of whigs of the previous generation, who had held a 'rational' religion of tolerance, virtue and charity. This might be Anglican, unitarian or deist, but its political consequence was support for civil liberty and for majority Establishments.[8]

For nearly all of the men discussed in these two chapters, this Enlightenment inheritance had been overlaid by others: by one or several of a set of influences which sprang from the same roots, from late eighteenth-century romanticism and from the evangelical revival. From these stemmed the Coleridgean model of the organic state, an evangelical impulse to duty, and an increased consciousness of the spiritual character of every human being. They created overlapping 'schools' of thought from the 1830s onwards: an evangelical or liberal-evangelical strain of country-house whiggery; an Arnoldian tradition of educational and ecclesiastical broad churchmanship; a Carlylean romanticism and organicism; and the Christian socialism of the 1840s. These schools were further affected by the – usually indirect – *spiritual* (as opposed to dogmatic) influence of the Oxford movement from the 1840s. If it is understood that at many points each of these traditions enriched the others, then the different strands may be treated separately, as is necessary for the purpose of analysis.

Country-house whiggery has not been given its due in the formation of the whig world-view, which has been interpreted primarily as a cosmopolitan one.[9] The most identifiable whig standard-bearers, in the period under discussion, were the products not of the London–Edinburgh circle of Enlightenment thinkers, but of the ring of country houses, nearly all in the north, in which lived the Greys – and their relatives the Woods (Halifax) and the Barings – the Fitzwilliams, the Dundases (Zetland), the

---

[6] According to Jowett: Abbott and Campbell, *Jowett*, ii, 54.
[7] Maxwell, *Clarendon*, i, 52–3, 126, 244, 314–16, ii, 369–70.
[8] Best, 'The whigs and the Church Establishment in the age of Grey and Holland', *History*, xlv (1960), 103–18.
[9] E.g. Mitchell, *Holland House*.

Cavendishes (Devonshire), the Howards (Carlisle) and the Leveson-Gowers (Sutherland). In the north of England alone, the heads of these families owned 273,000 acres in the 1870s; in addition, Fitzwilliam and Devonshire were major Irish landowners, and Sutherland and Zetland held vast estates in the Scottish Highlands. Other peers who were politically associated with this fraternity were also substantial landlords: Cleveland in Durham, Earl Fortescue in Devon, Lichfield in Staffordshire and Minto in Scotland. There were also the dukes of Westminster, in London and Cheshire, and of Bedford, in London, Bedfordshire, Cambridgeshire and Devon (Hastings Russell, the 9th duke of Bedford from 1872, was before then an influential backbench MP).[10]

The family links between these houses (and other important whig-liberal ones) were closer even than has generally been recognised. Devonshire's son, Hartington, was, from 1870, the unofficial political leader of whig-liberal opinion. His first cousins included the current duke of Sutherland, duchess of Westminster and duchess of Argyll, and the future duchess of Leinster and earl of Carlisle (son of a whig MP, C. W. G. Howard). Hartington's aunt was the sister-in-law of the 3rd Earl Grey and of his brother – the queen's private secretary – who, in turn, were the brothers-in-law of Viscount Halifax. Halifax's daughter married the brother of the 3rd earl of Zetland (succeeded 1873). Zetland's father was the first cousin of Earl Fitzwilliam, of three whig MPs – C. W. W. Fitzwilliam, F. Dundas and Sir John Ramsden – and of the wife of another Liberal MP, Edward Horsman. Ramsden married Somerset's daughter. Halifax was also intimately connected with the family of Hugh Childers, a cabinet Liberal from a Yorkshire evangelical family, who in turn was related to an important broad churchman who will appear later, W. H. Fremantle (who also came from an evangelical family; he was later to succeed his uncle as dean of Ripon). Earl Grey's brother Charles produced Grey's heir Albert, and two daughters: one married the young Liberal junior minister, the impecunious duke of St Albans; the other married the future 4th earl of Minto. The latter was the brother of A. R. D. Elliot (Albert Grey's future political henchman and Goschen's biographer), the son of the current earl of Minto, and the nephew of H. G. Elliot, ambassador at Constantinople. Three of Earl Grey's first cousins were Sir George Grey, Edward Ellice, an important whig MP, and Samuel Whitbread, the father of the namesake who will appear here, another whig MP; the latter's mother was the sister of Henry Brand, Liberal chief whip until his retirement in 1867. Sir George Grey's sister married into the Barings: George Grey's nephew was thus another important whig figure, the earl of Northbrook – another of whose

[10] *Bateman's great landowners.*

uncles was the evangelical bishop of Durham, Charles Baring, appointed by Palmerston, under the influence of Shaftesbury, in 1861. There was also a more distant connection between this group and the Harcourts – not only William Harcourt, the Commons leader of whig-liberal dissidence during the Gladstone government, but his grandfather and father, the erastian archbishop and canon residentiary of York respectively.

What is most important about these connections is not their existence, because others who were not so sympathetic ideologically were also linked, albeit not as closely. It is the noticeable strain of evangelicalism which ran through much of the group. This was not a rigid doctrinal Calvinism, but rather a sense of devout Protestant piety and duty, overlying entrenched whig latitudinarianism; a latitudinarianism reinforced by a close reading not only of Enlightenment thinkers, but of Arnold, Maurice, Carlyle, Thirlwall and Stanley. In some, evangelicalism was more profound than in others – in the Fitzwilliams, in Halifax and, most noticeably, in George Grey, who as a young man was nearly ordained, and who married a daughter of Bishop Ryder. But in nearly all cases it played a part and contributed to a new seriousness of tone in the whig aristocracy.[11] In most, it had been a valuable aid in establishing the relations with north-country nonconformity that had sustained the whig alliance since the 1830s. In some especially it found an outlet in philanthropic endeavour on a massive scale. This was pre-eminently true of Devonshire and Westminster, but also, for example, of Sutherland.[12] Such work in turn enabled them to forge links with the world of the high-minded bourgeoisie – the commercial evangelicals and nonconformist philanthropists. Indeed, the piety and humility of many of these peers was so intense that in some senses it is irrelevant to treat them as culturally distinct from the mass of the Liberal party. In being touched by religious revivalism, they had come to share many characteristics with the entrepreneurial Liberal middle class, just as their position as large landowners in the manufacturing heartland of England had allowed – indeed required – Devonshire, Fitzwilliam, Zetland, Sutherland, Cleveland and others to become great industrial magnates.[13]

In other ways, however, they were clearly set apart from the Liberal middle class. As nobility, they were intimately bound to the Church Establishment by the exercise of a great deal of private patronage: Fitzwilliam alone was patron of twenty-seven livings. By virtue of their landholdings, they had, particularly when other influences worked with them, a considerable weight in elections, an influence especially power-

[11] Spring, 'Aristocracy, social structure, and religion'.
[12] *Vanity Fair Album*, ii (1870).
[13] Cannadine, *Lords and landlords*, pp. 28–9; Spring, 'English landowners', pp. 30, 47.

ful in the cases of Devonshire and Fitzwilliam. These considerations added to their political weight and to their determination to defend the Church Establishment. But in many cases their political weight counted for a good deal beyond this. Fitzwilliam, Sutherland and Zetland hardly ever played a part in Westminster politics, and Devonshire, Minto, Cleveland and the duke of Westminster only occasionally – although the last, when in the Commons, had led the Adullamite criticism of the 1866 Reform Bill. But others were to be the most outspoken whig critics of the new directions taken by the Gladstonian Liberal party.

The most distinguished whig critic was, necessarily, ex-prime minister Russell, but his importance was retarded by his age (seventy-six in 1868) and his oncoming senility, which increased his liability to indecision, inconstancy, impetuousness and incoherence. Thus the intellectual centre of resistance came to be Earl Grey and his circle. Grey, the son of the prime minister, had not served in a Liberal cabinet since 1852, and might easily be dismissed as a doctrinaire. However, the weight of his family name and the strength of his intellect counted for something, while after 1867 the crossbench position which he adopted became more and more respectable, as considerable antagonism to the tone of the new politics became apparent. His criticism was increasingly viewed as genuinely disinterested, powerful and sensible, even by much more loyal Liberal newspapers;[14] while the extent of his power has always been understated. He was, in effect, the organising force behind the whig revolt of 1866;[15] his nephew, heir and political pupil, Albert Grey, in close touch with his uncle, played a similar and crucial role in planning the permanent split of 1886.[16] The informal 'Grey connection' included two of the most respected whig cabinet members of the 1846–66 governments, Sir George Grey, and Charles Wood, Viscount Halifax – who had embodied the 'Grey' qualities of 'good official efficiency with parliamentary ability sufficient for daily use'.[17] George Grey was, according to Granville, in effect prime minister for domestic affairs under Palmerston.[18] Earl Grey was not offered cabinet office by Gladstone in 1868; George Grey refused it in 1868 and 1872; Halifax refused it in 1868 and accepted it in 1870.

The Grey connection also included the queen. The queen's religious views were a crucial component in her growing dislike of Gladstone. Because she was not a sophisticated and precise thinker, the character of her opinions was such that she was able to communicate warmly with an especially large number of the groups treated in these two chapters; she

---

[14] *Spectator*, 15 November 1873, p. 1431.   [15] Cowling, *1867*, ch. 2, esp. p. 100.
[16] Cooke and Vincent, *The governing passion*, pp. 84–118.
[17] H. Grenfell, in Mallet, *Northbrook*, p. 228.   [18] *Ibid.*, p. 35.

was also thoroughly representative of the informed, intelligent, but unintellectual propertied Anglican Liberal in the country. Her private secretary until his death in 1870 was General Charles Grey, Earl Grey's brother, 'so full of faith but not fettered by bigotry'.[19] She respected the Grey connection's judgment and its solicitude for her: only Halifax of the 1868–74 cabinet won her full trust. The degree of political intimacy between the queen and Earl Grey survived his brother's death; not only had she tried to force the government of the day to adopt his policies both on Reform in 1866 and the Irish Church in 1869, but she sent her new private secretary to seek political advice from him in the constitutional crises of March 1873 and May 1886.[20] Other peers in the Grey circle included Earl Fortescue, an ex-junior minister who was related to George Grey and to the evangelical Harrowby family (now Conservative). Commoners included Edward Ellice and E. P. Bouverie, an ex-minister, son of a whig peer, and 'the leader of the old Whigs in the House of Commons'.[21]

The whig resistance to the government in the Lords was also led by the theist Somerset, another ex-cabinet minister displaced by Gladstone; by 1872, Granville saw him as the centre of a 'very formidable cave in the Lords'.[22] Together with the dozen or so named earlier, Lyveden, Minto, Overstone, Eversley, Strafford and Airlie were well-known whig peers who were not content to be Gladstonian lobby-fodder (although the Lords in fact rarely voted on religious questions of the sort which made this apparent). Gower and Fitzmaurice both dated the beginning of serious whig disaffection with the party in 1868;[23] Gladstone and Granville complained about the declining number of reliable Liberal supporters in the Lords in 1869;[24] Leinster, Norfolk, Bedford and Portsmouth all declined the Garter from Gladstone, while Zetland accepted it only on condition that he might remain free to dissent from government policy;[25] the duchess of Sutherland reluctantly accepted the post of mistress of the robes in 1870, as a personal honour from the

---

[19] Victoria, 2 April 1870, in Fulford, *Your dear letter*, p. 272.
[20] Monypenny and Buckle, *Disraeli*, iv, 456; Grey memorandum, 14–15 March 1873, Ponsonby file, Grey papers; Cooke and Vincent, *The governing passion*, p. 499, fn. 512.
[21] Dilke memoirs, Dilke papers, 43932, fo. 28.
[22] Ramm, ii, 308.
[23] Gower, *Reminiscences*, i, 278; Fitzmaurice, *Granville*, ii, 3.
[24] Guedalla, *Queen and Gladstone*, i, 197–9.
[25] Matthew, vii, lxxii, 166, 350; Norfolk to Gladstone, 29 August, 4 September 1870, Gladstone papers, 44428, fos. 68, 86; Bedford to Gladstone, 16 August 1872, *ibid.*, 44435, fo. 97; Zetland to Gladstone, 9 November 1872, *ibid.*, 44436, fo. 13; Gladstone to Zetland, 11 November 1872, *ibid.*, 44542, fo. 83; (Portsmouth) *Vanity Fair Album*, viii (1876). Westminster and Leicester were the only other non-official Liberal peers who accepted the Garter.

queen, in the hope that it did not involve being publicly linked with Gladstonian policies.[26]

Inside the cabinet, only one place was filled by a man in whom old whigs felt total confidence: Clarendon became foreign secretary in 1868, and, in the reshuffle following his death in 1870, Halifax was brought in as lord privy seal. Granville, as leader in the Lords, was not so reliable in their eyes: many found him too easy-going, clubbable and intimate with Gladstone.[27] In any case, he was hardly a typical whig: the son of a diplomat, he was married to a Catholic (Acton's mother), and had hardly any non-industrial wealth.

However, the old whigs were cheered by the staunch support of one influential journalist, Henry Reeve. Reeve was a cosmopolitan figure who had guided the foreign policy of the *Times* until 1855, when he began forty years as editor of the main whig house journal, the *Edinburgh Review*: Lecky considered him to be a man of immense political influence.[28] The old whigs were frequently aided by others, most notably Delane, the editor of the *Times*, who was endowed with whig contacts, Palmerstonian opinions, and the power to weaken any government of which he disapproved.[29] Finally, in this section may stand Sir Edward Strachey, as a representative of the older whig gentry. His religious views were typically liberal-evangelical; he was a friend of Carlyle and Maurice, and a renowned Oriental scholar. It was thus fitting that his son was to be a major interpreter of Liberal unionist thought to a later generation.[30]

Another important centre of Palmerstonian resistance to the government was much more evangelical than those so far discussed: the connection of the great philanthropist Shaftesbury. Nearly all rigid and pessimistic evangelicals were Conservative by 1865; Shaftesbury, although rigid and pessimistic, was no longer a party politician, but he had been closely associated, through marriage, with Melbourne and Palmerston. He could hardly be described as an instinctive religious liberal, but neither was he an inflexible conservative; he won the plaudits of the Christian socialists, he approved of Hampden's appointment to a bishopric in 1847, and he acknowledged the defects in the Irish (and even the English) Church Establishment.[31] He was closely related to a number

---

[26] G. W. E. Russell, *Portraits of the seventies*, p. 250.
[27] Laughton, *Reeve*, ii, 253; Reid, *Cabinet portraits*, p. 80; (Argyll) Jones, *Politics of reform*, p. 38.
[28] Ernle, *Whippingham to Westminster*, p. 112.
[29] Cook, *Delane*, pp. 100–1, 105, 161; Hamilton, *Parliamentary reminiscences*, pp. 24–5, 29.
[30] His son was John St Loe Strachey (1860–1927), educated at Balliol, editor of the Liberal unionist magazine, of the *Cornhill*, and then of the *Spectator* 1898–1925. For Edward, see J. St Loe Strachey, *Adventures of living*, pp. 34–5, 47–8.
[31] Kingsley, *Alton Locke*, p. 300; Machin, *Politics and the Churches*, p. 197; Finlayson, *Shaftesbury*, pp. 473–4.

of whig-liberal politicians, including Earl Cowper, his brother H. F. Cowper, and Shaftesbury's brother-in-law and Palmerston's stepson William Cowper-Temple, an important ex-minister (Shaftesbury's son Evelyn Ashley also became a Liberal MP in 1874). There were other staunch evangelicals among the Liberal MPs – such as Whalley and Thomas Chambers – while Shaftesbury had connections with the Grosvenors, not only through joint philanthropic effort with the duke of Westminster, but through religious sympathy with his evangelical uncle Lord Ebury – two of whose sons also sat as Liberal MPs.

It is sometimes assumed that whigs and tories rarely intermarried; yet it is striking, and significant, that the vast family networks traced so far already drifted off into Conservatism at several points. Closely related to both the Sutherlands and Devonshires were the Ellesmeres: one brother sat as Liberal MP for a Devonshire-influenced seat, while the other sat in Lancashire as an evangelical Conservative philanthropist. One branch of the Grosvenor family held the Wilton peerage, and was also Conservative. Harcourt's brother was a Conservative MP after 1878. Except for Northbrook's branch, most of the Baring family was Conservative: so were the Harrowbys and most Fremantles. Evangelicalism was a powerful force impelling this movement.

Most of those from the traditional Liberal aristocracy and gentry who were still willing to serve in Liberal governments after 1868 were of a slightly younger generation, and were usually more tolerant politically and more intense religiously than their elders. They therefore require separate treatment. The most important was Hartington, although he, shy, educated partly at home and partly on the racecourse, was comparatively unaffected by what his private secretary called the 'higher intellectual interests'.[32] The only other cabinet minister with strong whig claims was Kimberley, but just outside the cabinet, and accordingly freer to dissociate themselves from its conclusions, were three able and undoctrinaire whig administrators. Northbrook and Dufferin left English politics to rule India and Canada respectively in 1872; the third, Spencer, was viceroy of Ireland. Younger government ministers in the Lords included Lansdowne, Camperdown, St Albans, Earl Cowper and the earl of Morley, while outside the government stood a number of important peers, including not only Westminster, Lichfield and Portsmouth, but also the new, 3rd, Baron Stanley of Alderley.

Hartington and one or two others apart, what distinguished this generation was its receptiveness to the university teaching of the two decades after 1844, when the theological liberals asserted themselves and the Oxford movement, although still influential, was on the wane. Many,

---

[32] Esher, *Cloud-capp'd towers*, p. 99; G. W. E. Russell, *Portraits of the seventies*, pp. 84–98.

indeed, were in Oxford actually in the mid 1840s: at the same time as Westminster was at Balliol, Northbrook, Dufferin (an Ulster episcopalian with whig and tory antecedents) and Kimberley were at Christ Church together.[33] Also there then had been J. G. Dodson, an influential whig-liberal backbencher, and Chichester Fortescue, a cabinet member from the Commons who became associated with the whig peerage through his marriage to the ambitious hostess Lady Waldegrave. (Fortescue himself did not have standard whig-liberal views on the Irish question, because as an Irish MP he was forced to accommodate more and more to Catholic demands in an increasingly desperate attempt to keep his seat.) At Oxford, Kimberley and Fortescue both won firsts and Northbrook came close to one. All three, like Dufferin and Westminster, were high-minded, pious and earnest. Dufferin had a brief encounter with tractarianism, but most were liberal-evangelicals to different degrees, Fortescue being the most latitudinarian and Kimberley, until the mid 1860s, the most anti-Catholic.[34] Of the later generation, Hartington and Spencer were together at Cambridge, but most of the others were Oxford intellectuals – Cowper won a double first at Christ Church, while Lansdowne, Camperdown and the earl of Morley were clever young men who were lionised by Jowett at Balliol in the early 1860s.[35]

It would be misleading, of course, to present all these wealthy young aristocratic Liberals as spiritually intense to the exclusion of other pursuits: they were able to combine evangelical purpose with long-standing extra-marital liaisons, horse-breeding or elopement with Spanish Moslems.[36] Nonetheless, their intellectualism had important repercussions. (It also continued a whig tradition: George Grey and Halifax had won firsts at the Oriel of Whately and the Noetics in the early 1820s, while Devonshire had a double first from Cambridge.) University training in the 1840s and 1850s was to have a similar impact on those from within and outside the whig aristocracy; central in determining the impact it made on aristocrat and non-aristocrat alike was the influence of Arnold, Carlyle and, in a sense, the tractarians.

The theological liberalism of the 1820s and 1830s had owed most to Coleridge, to German theology and to the spiritual intensity infused by the evangelical revival. The concepts of organic national unity, of a national Church inspired by a regenerative mission, and of a civilising

---

[33] For Dufferin, see Harrison, 'Dufferin'.
[34] See e.g. Mallet, *Northbrook*, pp. 17, 254, 299; Lyall, *Dufferin*, i, 40; Cooke and Vincent, *Lord Carlingford's journal*, p. 5.
[35] Abbott and Campbell, *Jowett*, i, 334–7.
[36] Hartington, Westminster, Stanley of Alderley.

clerisy, soon became deeply entrenched in the liberal mind.[37] One of the
leading 'Liberal Anglicans' of the 1830s, Connop Thirlwall, the historian
and broad churchman, was still a significant figure in the early 1870s, as
bishop of St David's. In the 1840s and 1850s, the basic tenets of their
intellectual position were adopted extremely widely. In the process, and
in reacting to other intellectual trends, they took on a variety of subtly
altered forms. Two of the men most responsible for propagating these
ideas and for reshaping them – Thomas Arnold and Thomas Carlyle –
were very unalike and were politically influential in very different ways.

Thomas Arnold's influence as an educationalist has frequently been
discussed, and is now considered less ubiquitous than once it was.[38]
What is unquestioned is his importance in leading generations of
teachers to teach pupils to develop a personal spiritual relationship with
God. This had been the purpose of his reform of public-school education:
to attack corruption, to end formalistic doctrinal teaching, and to convey
the spiritual word of Christ in the hope of inspiring boys to work for the
regeneration of society.[39] A man as evangelical as Shaftesbury trusted
Rugby to teach his son 'duty', 'sterner stuff', 'serious responsibilities',
and a 'desire and a courage to live for the service of God'.[40] Arnold's
influence in this area spread far beyond Rugby, through the schools and
colleges colonised by his pupils and followers: in particular, through
Harrow, Marlborough and Brereton's middle-class schools, and Balliol
and University colleges, Oxford. In Oxford, moreover, there was already
a separate tradition of intellectual liberalism whose most influential
leaders by the 1860s were Jowett of Balliol and Liddell of Christ Church.
It may be too crude to see all these rivers flowing into each other –
especially as Arnold himself had been far less liberal than most of his
disciples[41] – but, by the 1860s, they seemed to have created a flood of
intense latitudinarianism, pouring into the Church, the schools, the universities, the press and politics. Most of the broad-church clergymen,
and the whig-liberal laymen, who appear in these two chapters and who
were at university between 1835 and 1855, were influenced either by
Arnold or by one of his disciples.

Arnold was succeeded as headmaster of Rugby by A. C. Tait and later
by Frederick Temple, both of whom had also been Fellows of Balliol and
were to be archbishops of Canterbury. A. P. Stanley, Arnold's favourite
pupil and biographer, and a more thoroughgoing broad churchman than
Tait (who retained evangelical deposits owing to a presbyterian upbring-

[37] For Coleridge, see Knights, *Idea of the clerisy*, ch. 2.
[38] Honey, *Tom Brown's universe*, pp. 1–46.   [39] Stanley, *Arnold*, pp. 94, 217.
[40] Mandler, 'Cain and Abel', p. 83.
[41] E.g. regarding church rates, jewish and unitarian relief: Stanley, *Arnold*, pp. 305, 331,
     402, 433–4.

ing) was a Fellow of University college, Oxford, and then professor of ecclesiastical history at Oxford; he was thus an important academic liberal for most of the twenty-five years before he was appointed dean of Westminster by Palmerston in 1864. Tait had further been an influential tutor at Balliol; he was a great ecclesiastical politician, but Gladstone doubted 'if he ever read a theological work in his life'.[42] Bishop Fraser of Manchester was a Fellow of Oriel for twenty years, and a leading proponent of educational reform. He was immensely influential in the development of Tom Hughes, the most famous interpreter of Arnold's Rugby; Hughes was a Christian socialist and then an important Liberal backbench MP from 1865. Fraser was also associated with Christian socialism and was a supporter of the trade-union movement.[43] Vaughan, headmaster of Harrow and later dean of Llandaff, and A. G. Butler, headmaster of Haileybury, were both Rugby men; the latter's brother, H. M. Butler, succeeded Vaughan at Harrow and was then Master of Trinity, Cambridge. Jex-Blake, another future headmaster of Rugby, was taught by both Tait and Stanley. Two other important Arnoldians were Arnold's son Matthew, poet, essayist and schools inspector, and J. L. Brereton (Rugby and University college, Oxford). The latter was a broad-church clergyman, and the founder of undenominational county schools in Devon and Norfolk, and of an undenominational college at Cambridge liberally supported by the duke of Devonshire. Three more influential teachers in the Arnoldian religious tradition were G. G. Bradley (Stanley's disciple, headmaster of Marlborough, Master of University college and then dean of Westminster), F. W. Farrar (also headmaster of Marlborough, dean of Canterbury, and author of *Eric, or little by little*) and Reginald Bosworth Smith (master at Harrow and important Orientalist). A fourth, influenced by Arnold in the 1820s and later a master at Rugby, was Bonamy Price, professor of political economy at Oxford after 1868.[44]

At Rugby, Price had a major effect on the intellectual development of the man whose defection from the Liberal party in the 1880s was to symbolise more than anyone's the cultural shifts away from Gladstonianism – George Joachim Goschen.[45] Goschen was the son of an immigrant banker, was educated at Rugby and Oriel, became a director of the Bank of England at twenty-seven and entered the cabinet in 1866 at thirty-four. Serving throughout Gladstone's first government, by the mid 1870s he was disillusioned with the drift of the party; his subsequent move

---

[42] G. W. E. Russell, *Portraits of the seventies*, p. 347.
[43] Phillips, 'Fraser', p. 111.
[44] For Arnold's spiritual influence on Price, see Stanley, *Arnold*, pp. 30–9, 187–93.
[45] Goschen, *Mental training*, p. 20.

towards unionism mirrored that of both the financial establishment and the broad-church intelligentsia. Among the whig-liberal products of Balliol were two of particular significance for this work, Goschen's close contemporaries and friends, G. C. Brodrick and W. H. Fremantle. Both were representative liberal evangelicals. Fremantle was the son of an evangelical Conservative (a friend and Oriel contemporary of Halifax's), married into the family of Eardley and Childers, and became a Fellow of All Souls' in 1854, Tait's chaplain in 1861 and rector of a mixed-class London parish in 1866, before returning to Balliol as a Fellow and tutor in 1883; in 1865, he and Brodrick jointly published a defence of the activities of the Judicial Committee, with a preface by Tait. Fremantle became a leading advocate of Church reform; Brodrick, failing to enter parliament, became an influential Liberal and later unionist journalist and university reformer. Between 1860 and 1873 he wrote sixteen hundred leading articles for the *Times*;[46] he became Warden of Merton college, Oxford in 1881. Goschen, Brodrick and Fremantle appeared in the 1860s to be rather radical university liberals, with very broad, often hazy theological views, impatient for parliamentary reform and for the abolition of university tests and church rates. They disliked the conservatism of most Anglican clergymen, and thus appeared to be strongly anti-clerical. They shared these views with other near contemporaries from Balliol, such as Grant Duff, a future Liberal junior minister, and A. V. Dicey, the jurist and historian.[47] They also shared them with other young whig-liberals like Sir John Lubbock, a wealthy baronet, banker, amateur scientist and pundit. But such men should not be confused with the academic liberals discussed in chapter 4, who were not broad-church defenders of a reformed Establishment, but rationalist radicals bent on the Establishment's destruction.

Two more figures should be mentioned in the context of Arnoldian Liberalism, both friends of Stanley. George Grove was a Christian socialist (who came to lose most of his faith in the 1880s and 1890s), and a man of wide cultural tastes, who edited *Macmillan's Magazine* (a house journal for Christian socialists and Oxford liberals) and married Bradley's sister. R. E. Prothero, a man from a later Balliol generation, wrote Stanley's *Life* when Grove was unable to do it and Bradley unable to complete it; with Reeve's aid, he was to become an important journalistic figure.[48] Another young broad churchman and Oxford intellectual, Mandell Creighton, was vicar in George Grey's Northumberland parish after 1875, where he began a distinguished ecclesiastical career.

---

[46] Brodrick, *Memories and impressions*, p. 130.
[47] For Dicey's religious views, see Rait, *Dicey*, pp. 227, 242, 298.
[48] Ernle, *Whippingham to Westminster*, pp. 111–12, 137, 161.

The Anglican clergymen best liked by the queen were serious yet liberal, and intolerant of the narrowness of both high and low: Stanley,[49] Tait (for whose appointment to Canterbury in 1868, in preference to Bishop Ellicott, she was responsible), Wellesley (the dean of Windsor), Kingsley and Llewelyn Davies. The latter two were broad churchmen with a pronounced evangelical, Carlylean and scientific strain. Kingsley was a friend of Froude and edited *Fraser's* for a time in 1867; his attempt to reconcile scientific discovery with the retention of a very strict code of individual responsibility appealed to Albert's modernising Germanic mind. With Stanley and Lyon Playfair (see p. 75), he was therefore made mainly responsible for the higher education of the prince of Wales. Stanley especially was instructed to guard the prince against high- or low-church views when at Oxford, and the prince did indeed develop 'whiggish' Palmerstonian leanings.[50] This combination of serious evangelicalism, latitudinarianism and awareness of the value of scientific discovery was shared by the queen's favourite Church of Scotland preachers, Macleod, Tulloch, Charteris and John Caird. In 1871, Gladstone thought that Macleod and Disraeli were 'about the two greatest flunkies in the country'.[51] Tulloch was one of Froude's successors as editor of *Fraser's* (between 1879 and 1881).

Except for those at the oldest end, the generation of churchmen and university graduates which has been treated here was influenced by one, or both, of two intellectual movements which profoundly affected the development of the whig-liberal mind: the Oxford movement and Christian socialism.

Regency whigs had viewed the common man with some disdain, and had a low view of the romantic poetry which invoked the latter's spiritual aspirations.[52] But after the 1820s, evangelicalism and the romanticism of Wordsworth, Coleridge and Scott made inroads into the whig mentality, inroads which the impact of the Oxford movement greatly deepened. Most of those who were at university between the late 1830s and the mid 1840s were affected by the movement, not usually doctrinally, since they retained their latitudinarianism,[53] but morally and spiritually. In many of them, the combination of education under such influences, and the economic climate and social unrest of the 1840s, created a belief in the decadence of materialistic society – especially aristocratic society – and in both the nobility and the degradation of the poor. These feelings – vaguely expressed as they were in most cases – lent a powerful impulse

[49] See Gathorne-Hardy, *Cranbrook*, i, 274.
[50] Lee, *Edward VII*, i, 77, 200–1; the only vote of his recorded in the House of Lords was in support of the Deceased Wife's Sister Bill.
[51] Ramm, ii, 283.
[52] Mitchell, *Holland House*, pp. 190–2.   [53] See Russell, 'Freddy Leveson', p. 172.

to their burgeoning Liberalism, creating the climate both for administrative reform, and for a renewed emphasis on the spiritual function of the party, as this generation and its successor grew to political maturity from the late 1850s. Whig-liberal Oxford graduates of these years included Granville, Stanley, Jowett, W. H. Gregory, Fraser, Froude, Hastings Russell,[54] Freddy Leveson-Gower, Temple, Bradley, Arnold, Brereton, Hughes and C. P. Fortescue, all born between 1815 and 1823; others of a similar age, not in Oxford, were to some extent affected.

It was also in this context that Christian socialism became a significant movement for half-a-dozen years from the late 1840s. What is important in this work is not its inner circle – although of these, Kingsley and Hughes will feature prominently throughout – but the wider influence of its basic tenets. The essence of Christian socialism was, as any reading of Kingsley's *Alton Locke* makes explicit, not the material reformation of society through legislation, but the regeneration of the individual soul, a far more radical proposition. The range of whig-liberals who were in some sense associated with the movement, especially with its practical work in education, philanthropy and the provision of open spaces for recreation, was large, including Cowper-Temple; Grant Duff, Seeley and Farrar (who taught at Maurice's Working-men's college); and Hutton and Townsend of the *Spectator* (see p. 76).[55] In so many ways, the radical and spiritually intense assumptions of the Christian socialists became commonplaces for Liberals twenty-five years later: as Hughes wrote in 1876, Kingsley's controversial sermons of 1849 'would scarcely cause surprise today if preached by the Archbishop of Canterbury [Tait] in the Chapel Royal'.[56] Indeed, two crusading radicals of the 1847–55 period, not fully Christian socialists, but imbued with an equally fervent feeling against corruption, appeared, in some ways, on the 'right' of the party by 1874. One, Horsman, whom we have met already, proposed a series of investigations and reforms in the late 1840s in order to eliminate abuses in the Church and to alter the episcopal salary structure.[57] The other, A. H. Layard, was the driving force behind the Administrative Reform Association of the mid 1850s. He was a Huguenot who had enjoyed a foreign education, in a class of Catholics. Their persecution of him as a Protestant, and their cowardice and submissiveness before the tyranny of their master left him with a keen perception of the repressiveness and lack of spirit embedded in the Catholic mentality, and a keen awareness

[54] A great friend of Jowett's: *Late duke of Bedford*, p. 72.
[55] Mount-Temple, *Memorials*, pp. 151, 181; Harvie, *Lights of liberalism*, p. 147.
[56] Hughes, *Kingsley*, i, 35.
[57] See e.g. *Hansard*, cviii, 348, 5 February 1850; and, for Christian socialist admiration of this work, Kingsley, *Alton Locke*, p. 194.

of the liberating function of nineteenth-century Liberalism.[58] He became an attaché to Stratford Canning at Constantinople; Canning encouraged him to excavate Nineveh, which brought him international fame and a springboard for a successful political career, in which he was able to preach the gospel of spiritual regeneration in a number of contexts.

In short, the mood of the late 1840s and 1850s infused a new spirituality and humanitarian fervour into the latitudinarian movement, whose flavour had previously been more exclusively intellectual. Between men affected by it and those who were even slightly older, a partial distinction may be drawn – which explains why Gladstone was so much more favourable to clergymen in the former camp than in the latter, promoting Temple and Fraser to the important bishoprics of Exeter and Manchester in 1869 and 1870. He considered them less aggressively erastian, more tolerant of doctrinal conservatism (if the conservatives did good missionary work), and more appreciative of spiritual intensity in whatever context it was manifested than the general run of latitudinarians. However, Matthew Arnold and Stanley from this same generation had a Wordsworthian reverence for beauty and even liked ritual, but did not excite Gladstone's warm approval, because they had lost a firm grasp on the essence of Christian dogma. Moreover, men of this age, and their juniors, often displayed another tendency which displeased him, because, as German Idealist thought and the administrative reform mentality became entrenched in the latitudinarian conscience, they increasingly stressed the importance of radical Church reform, in the hope of creating a community capable of inspiring and uniting the nation. In 1868, young men like Llewelyn Davies and the historian J. R. Seeley contributed to an influential publication, *Essays in Church reform* (edited by W. L. Clay); Fremantle and Llewelyn Davies were instrumental in the foundation of the National Church Reform Union in 1870. Nonetheless, whig-liberals affected by these moods of the 1840s and 1850s were, on the whole, disposed to approve of the Gladstonian Liberal party, and its spiritual aspirations, for a longer period after 1867 than were most other whig-liberals.

The 1840s and 1850s were also the period of Carlyle's greatest influence. The fact that Carlyle is remembered chiefly as an advocate of the 'strong state' should not blind us to the extent to which his concerns meshed with those of Thomas Arnold, Maurice and Kingsley: there was the same stress on the need for individual spiritual regeneration, and for the direction of aroused individual wills by enlightened and spiritually aware government. If Carlyle himself added anything to the Liberal Protestant tradition, it was his strong sense of presbyterian rectitude;

---

[58] Layard, *Autobiography*, i, 15–17.

this appeared to define the limits of acceptable behaviour with less tolerance than latitudinarianism, and his followers certainly tended to retain an evangelical rigidity of conscience even where the doctrinal substance had all but disappeared. Both he and his disciples were especially dismissive of popular political agitation, which they regarded as inherently undisciplined and open to demagogic influence. The political consequence was that Carlyleans were more hostile, earlier, to the development of the Gladstonian party after 1867 than were latitudinarians born after 1815, and as hostile as the older whigs.

The Carlylean influence can be seen in two contexts: in some hard-minded polemicists, and in many of the most famous of Victorian scientists. The first category includes such men as John Forster, biographer of Dickens, and the Scottish intellectual John Stuart Blackie (actually a pro-Establishment Free Churchman); but its two most distinguished exponents were J. A. Froude and James Fitzjames Stephen. Both came from evangelical families; both had become sceptical of the claims of Anglican dogma, while retaining faith in God – Froude after a sally into tractarianism which had left deep psychological scars. Stephen had been taught by Maurice at King's, London, and admired his piety.[59] Froude was already a distinguished historian of the sixteenth century; his books celebrated the superiority of Protestant forms of government, and passed lenient judgment upon the harsh measures which the Tudors had applied in order to enforce Protestant loyalties. Stephen was a barrister and, in the early 1870s, legal member of the Council in India. Both were influential journalists on the 'right' of the party: Froude edited *Fraser's Magazine*, and Stephen wrote frequently for the *Pall Mall Gazette*.

Many leading scientists shared Carlyle's emphasis on natural law and organic harmony, although their researches often led them to develop conclusions – especially about evolution – which Carlyle himself dismissed as 'materialist'.[60] The two men of whom this was most clearly true were T. H. Huxley and John Tyndall. Huxley had been a ship's surgeon and a lecturer and then professor at the Royal Institution; Tyndall was superintendent of the Institution. Both were self-made men – Tyndall, significantly, was from an Irish Protestant family – and both had been profoundly influenced by Carlyle in the 1840s. He had stimulated their interest in German theological ideas, and made them feel that 'without truckling to the ape and tiger of the mob, a man might hold the views of a radical'. Tyndall's dislike of the apparent increase of popular influence on government, and the accompanying decline of discipline and firm executive leadership, was even more marked than Huxley's. It led him,

[59] Colaiaco, *Stephen*, pp. 170–1.
[60] See Turner, 'Victorian scientific naturalism and Thomas Carlyle'.

together with Carlylean scientists like Sir Joseph Hooker of Kew Gardens who were *already* Conservatives, to support Carlyle, in the famous controversy of the mid 1860s, in defending Governor Eyre of Jamaica against charges of brutality in repressing an uprising.[61] Leading scientists met for discussions at the X-club, to which they invited sympathetic politicians like Lowe and Goschen.[62] The scientists were influential in university circles, which were linked to the whig world, especially through the duke of Devonshire – who was chancellor of London until 1856, and of Cambridge for thirty years after 1861 (playing an immensely important part in the expansion of science there). As will be seen below, whig-liberals were intensely concerned to reconcile scientific discoveries with religion, which they believed would be inevitable once enough responsible research had been conducted. Like Carlyle himself, many whig-liberals believed that the early publicity given to some materialist evolutionist theories was misleading, in that more thorough investigation would reveal the hand of God in the process more clearly.[63] This was especially the case with the duke of Argyll, another of the cabinet whig-liberals, and a 'tolerant' Carlylean.

Argyll was a Church of Scotland presbyterian who enjoyed a meteoric early career, reaching the cabinet at the age of twenty-nine, and retaining cabinet office in every Liberal government until his resignation in 1881. He was a Peelite with Palmerstonian sympathies and, although close to Gladstone, always distrusted his ecclesiastical views, on which they had clashed as early as 1848.[64] He was also a prolific amateur scientist, and, although his views were derided by some professionals,[65] they were undoubtedly similar to those of most whig-liberals in their emphasis on natural law, organicism and the 'unity of nature'. Argyll also deserves attention as a friend of the queen; his son, a Liberal MP, married her daughter in 1871. She approved of his liberal-evangelical presbyterian views, as she did in the cases of other prominent Church of Scotland laymen who were professional scientists, like Lyon Playfair and William Thomson (later Baron Kelvin). Playfair was a Liberal MP for a Scottish university seat after 1868, and was theologically and politically far more liberal than most Carlyleans, although his presbyterian feelings were roused by discussion of sacerdotalism in the Church:[66] he shared many traits with the younger academic liberals like Brodrick and Dicey.

[61] Eve and Creasey, *Tyndall*, pp. 223–4; Tyndall, 'Personal recollections of Thomas Carlyle', p. 6; Semmel, *Governor Eyre controversy*, pp. 124–5.
[62] Macleod, 'The X-club'.
[63] See Forbes, *Liberal Anglican idea*, p. 101.
[64] Gladstone, 'The duke of Argyll on presbytery'.
[65] Huxley, *Hooker*, ii, 114. [66] Reid, *Playfair*, p. 273.

Thomson was a devout non-sectarian churchgoer, happy with episcopalian or presbyterian services.[67]

In shifting back from the Carlyleans to the more tolerant atmosphere
of university liberalism, we reach, finally, two rather peripheral
examples of types of the whig-liberal conscience. The first stands at the
most liberal point of the perimeter, and is exemplified by the *Spectator*,
edited by R. H. Hutton, an Anglican converted from unitarianism.
Hutton's lifelong friend Bagehot, editor of the *Economist*, was a more
orthodox whig-liberal (and, in any case, the *Economist* did not discuss
theology, and did not often express political opinions except from the
viewpoint of market stability). But the *Spectator* continued after 1867 to
demonstrate a more developed conception of the spiritual nature of the
common man, and a higher regard for nonconformists and high churchmen, than all but a few whig-liberal MPs. These few included young
whigs like Samuel Whitbread, Frederick Cavendish and Lord Arthur
Russell – personal friends of Gladstone and Acton – and H. A. Bruce, the
south Wales industrial landowner who was home secretary between 1868
and 1873 (who might also be described as a Peelite).[68] Arthur Russell's
uncle, Earl Russell, occasionally approximated to this view, although it
did not sit well with his, more usual, trenchant anti-Gladstonianism and
anti-sacerdotalism. The latter's son, Viscount Amberley, was, however,
a different case, because he, like his Stanley of Alderley wife, sister-in-
law and brother-in-law (the future countess of Carlisle and Lyulph
Stanley), was a rationalist Liberal of the type discussed in chapter 4. The
only relatively orthodox member of this generation of the Stanley of
Alderley family was the eldest son and 3rd Baron, who became a Moslem
and, for connected reasons, a Conservative.

If 'Gladstonian' whigs form one point on the perimeter, 'utilitarians'
form another. The world-view developed below will place much stress on
the notion of politics as a moral pursuit, which at first sight might be
thought to conflict with the fact that two or three of those discussed are
renowned as utilitarians. This is especially so in the cases of Fitzjames
Stephen, W. R. Greg – a prolific essayist in the whig and Conservative
press – and Robert Lowe. In fact, however, there had always been an
element of utilitarianism in the whigs' practical attitude to politics,
deriving partly from Warburton and partly from sympathy with the

---

[67] Thompson, *Kelvin*, pp. 1087–9.
[68] Bruce, who entered parliament in 1852, is described as a Liberal-Conservative in W. D.
Jones and A. B. Erickson, *The Peelites 1846–1857* (Columbus, Ohio, 1972), p. 204. He was
a long-standing friend of Sir Robert Phillimore, the Gladstonian high churchman. He
seems to have had little fear of secular education or disestablishment (*Hansard*, ccii,
800–1, 23 June 1870; cvi, 500, 9 May 1871); but this is probably because he was aware
of the increasing force of the pressure from Welsh radicals for these policies.

Jacobinical assault on the high-tory doctrine of the state. This element, much attacked by Thomas Arnold in the 1830s,[69] was bound to appear when the whigs were engaged on breaking down the exclusive Church–state relationship; it was also apparent in Macaulay's famous 1839 rejoinder to Gladstone, when he argued that the only unquestioned function of the state was the preservation of body and goods, and that higher moral ends, valuable as they were, were to be justified only by their expediency at every point.[70] In practice, however, this belief almost never led to a commitment in favour of disestablishment; while the whole burden of the argument so far has been that the average Liberal MP of the 1860s was far more swayed by ethical considerations than his counterpart thirty years before. In the case of Stephen and Lowe, this argument should not be taken too far; nonetheless, they approved of the Church Establishment and of the state's attempt to advance moral ends where practicable – indeed for Stephen government 'must of necessity have a moral basis'. Lowe was not morally insensitive; he had a Balliol education and became a mild Idealist in religion, publicly opposing the tractarians in 1841.[71] As a leader-writer on the *Times*, he became closely associated with Delane's Palmerstonianism, before attracting attention as an Adullamite and opponent of concessions to Irish Catholics in the mid 1860s; he then won a place in Gladstone's 1868 cabinet as chancellor of the exchequer. After 1868, he represented London university in parliament (defeating Lubbock and Bagehot for the nomination). Greg came from a unitarian family but lapsed into deism, producing a famous statement of his ethical position in *The creed of Christendom* (1851). He was also Bagehot's brother-in-law. Few were more strident in defending the state's right to impose law in order to direct the community's attention away from sectional political and ecclesiastical influences which might check the course of progress. What the three shared – in common with Goschen, Brodrick, Grant Duff and the young university whig-liberals – was a greater emphasis on the role of the intellect in the direction of national affairs than many whig-liberals.

To persevere with the utilitarian influence, even the surviving Philosophical Radicals of the 1830s can be accommodated more easily with the whig-liberals than with the 1860s radicals discussed in chapter 4. J. A. Roebuck, for example, had been a doctrinaire utilitarian, but he had always been a member of the Church of England, and, while against

---

[69] Stanley, *Arnold*, pp. 318, 332.

[70] Macaulay, 'Church and state', *Edinburgh Review*, lxix (Apr. 1839), 273.

[71] R. Lowe, *The Articles construed by themselves*, and *Observations suggested by a few more words in support of No. 90* (both Oxford, 1841). For support for this interpretation of Lowe, see Bryce, *Studies in contemporary biography*, p. 304; for Lowe's support for Church reform, see Abbott and Campbell, *Letters of Jowett*, pp. 41–2.

the institution of Establishments on principle, had usually defended the existing Establishment on majority grounds. He now maintained that the Church had been much improved by a number of years of public agitation against its abuses, and that it was a force for good. He had always supported state intervention in education, believing that the 'chief duty of the State' was to 'prevent evil' and promote 'virtue and happiness'. He had once been an educational secularist, but had renounced this position through dislike of the sectionalism of nonconformist voluntaryists.[72] From the 1860s, he was an advocate of a government of the 'centre', in order to prevent control of politics by 'demagogues' trading on 'ignorance and vice'.[73] A number of other whig-liberal MPs can also be seen as developing from within the Benthamite tradition: Locke of Southwark, McCullagh Torrens, the biographer of Melbourne and housing reformer, and Horsman (the last, despite usually standing on the 'right' of the party, continued to advocate disestablishment).

Some of these men did not agree with all parts of the intellectual framework which is set out in this chapter and the next. Nonetheless, they accepted, in the main, the practical political conclusions which stemmed from it. The same can be said of a number of other MPs. Anglican industrialists, borough MPs of dubious morality, or well-heeled country gentlemen were not all whig-liberals in the sense of adopting every aspect of the 'higher thought' which is developed here. Some of them had probably not read even Arnold, Kingsley or Froude. They were, however, whig-liberals in the sense that they supported the Church Establishment, undenominational education, the abolition of university tests, and the extension of civil liberty in religion, and yet were hesitant about concessions to Catholicism in Ireland or to public pressure in Britain. Equally importantly, 'whig-liberalism' in practice approximated to the view of many mainstream Anglican Liberal voters, even if, again, such people did not read widely. The conception of the relationship of religion to politics developed in these chapters was a preeminently practical one, emphasising not complexities and formulae but character and morals. As such, it appealed to those for whom church-going was a social or tribal act: who instinctively believed but were sceptical of religious zealots as much as of freethinkers. This 'unconscious' broad churchmanship was a characteristic attitude among the 'middling classes';[74] and the disillusionment of a large portion of this constituency

---

[72] Leader, *Roebuck*, pp. 44, 56–7, 183–5, 328.
[73] *Ibid.*, p. 312.
[74] McLeod, *Class and religion in the late Victorian city*, pp. 155–8.

with the Gladstone government was to play a major role in destroying the healthy Liberal majorities of 1865 and 1868.

To sum up, the 'whig-liberal outlook' was expressed by men most of whom were born between 1815 and 1835 and thus particularly open to all the influences summarised above; but there were also some older whigs. A good half of the 1868–74 cabinet can be classed as whig-liberal. The old whigs were represented by Clarendon until his death in 1870, and thereafter by Halifax; the Liberal aristocracy by Hartington, Kimberley and Argyll; university, middle-class and financial Liberalism by Lowe and Goschen; middle-of-the-road Anglican Liberalism by Childers, Fortescue and, up to a point, Bruce. But, by virtue of their position, all had to be more open-minded than most whig-liberals. There were also junior ministers, including a number of semi-disaffected men in Dufferin, Northbrook, Layard, Grant Duff, Enfield and Knatchbull-Hugessen. There were ex-ministers in the Commons, such as George Grey, Brand, Horsman, Bouverie and Cowper-Temple; there were ambitious backbenchers who were whig-liberals, like Harcourt, Henry James, Dodson and Playfair; there were scores of other, less forceful, backbenchers.

What was also striking was the extent to which whig-liberalism was entrenched in the metropolis. It was, of course, to be found in the great 'society' houses of the whigs, and at court. But it was also influential in the scientific and university worlds (in addition to the men already mentioned, there was the latitudinarian divine and former headmaster of Cheltenham, Alfred Barry, now principal of King's college), in the ecclesiastical worlds of Tait at Lambeth and Stanley at Westminster Abbey, and in the City. The difference between the climate thus created, and that of nonconformist-dominated provincial politics, was marked – it also found expression in the peculiar conservatism of London MPs, which will be demonstrated later. It was also evident in the adverse reaction of much of the metropolitan press to Gladstone's government, about which he himself complained in 1871.[75] The *Pall Mall Gazette*, in particular, edited by the Palmerstonian Liberal Frederick Greenwood, and employing contributors like Fitzjames Stephen (and Tom Hughes), 'probably did more to write down Mr Gladstone's first Administration than any other journal of the day'.[76]

All these influences came together in one important institution, the London school board. This symbolised the traditional broadly anti-clerical, Protestant and tolerant Liberalism which found Gladstonian sectionalism and radical nonconformity unproductively disruptive

---

[75] *Times*, 4 September 1871, p. 12.
[76] Kebbel, *Beaconsfield*, pp. 25–6; for Hughes, see Russell, *Letters of Arnold*, ii, 25.

elements. It was associated with the undenominational approach to education, with the W. H. Smith–Samuel Morley compromise of 1871 (see p. 109). Its first chairman was the whiggish former Indian viceroy, Lord Lawrence, and the first board included Barry, Torrens, Huxley, the surgeon Elizabeth Garrett, the evangelical clergyman (and later bishop) Thorold, and the broad churchman William 'Hang Theology' Rogers. It also included a typical Shaftesburyite evangelical in John Macgregor, 'Rob Roy', the celebrated missionary canoeist and philanthropist, one of the least well-remembered of the Victorian heroes.[77] Some nonconformists of the type most sympathetic to whig-liberalism also sat on the board,[78] as did two evangelical liberal Conservatives, Smith and Sandon.

Church and state

The primary point of reference for whig-liberals in religious affairs – especially parliamentary whig-liberals – was anti-clericalism: a distrust of the power and conservatism of the Church. Although some individuals were content with this negative creed, the vast majority were not: in nearly all cases, their anti-clericalism had a positive and idealistic side. In some – especially in authors – this idealistic impulse was developed to a more intense pitch than in others, but, even where it was latent rather than constantly articulated, it had a profound influence in dictating their hopes and fears for the political future.

The life-work of Carlyle was once described as being to teach men that 'the only important fact is the state and structure of their soul, that the first and unique business is to reach that inner feeling'.[79] This impulse was at the root of the theological mission of whig-liberals; they demanded that man should attempt to surmount his failings and to work for moral ends, to 'start afresh in the race of duty'.[80] It was through indi-

---

[77] He was a Scottish-Irish presbyterian and a fervent anti-Catholic; his first cruise in the *Rob Roy* was in 1865. He steered it along the rivers and canals of Western Europe, through Scandinavia, and then, in his most famous journey, along the Jordan, Nile and Red Sea. The publicity engendered from sales of his books about these trips spawned the canoeing craze. He also gave talks of his experiences in order to promote philanthropic causes. Clothed in his canoeing dress, 'a red serge Norfolk jacket and light helmet with flowing puggaree', he would do several routines, of which the most requested were his imitations of camel noises, and his explicit recreation of a fight with a jackal which surprised him one night as he lay in his canoe reading the *Times*. He became a cult figure: the duchess of Sutherland sat in his canoe, and he inaugurated evangelical canoe missions around Tasmania and elsewhere: Hodder, *Macgregor, passim*.

[78] Samuel Morley, Reed, Rigg and McArthur's brother: see chapter 4. There was also a very small minority of secularists, including Picton and Chatfield Clarke: see chapter 4 also.

[79] (Taine) Forbes, *Liberal Anglican idea*, pp. 161–2.

[80] (Stanley) *ibid.*, p. 162; Froude, *Carlyle*, ii, 454.

vidual moral enthusiasm in the cause of 'duty' that the progress of the world was advanced. Only if man was able to overcome his passions and selfish concerns could the goal of harmony between interests be promoted. Such a state of harmony was envisaged by God, but society would approximate to it only through the exercise of individual free will. Human affairs were thus always in flux: their development was determined by the character of the pressure exerted by millions of individual wills. Change could be for good or for evil, depending on the state of men's souls; it therefore followed that the utilitarians' 'hazy conviction that society would be all right . . . when every man could do what he liked' must be rejected in favour of a call to perpetual struggle against sin.[81]

The more that individual wills were prevented from evil-doing, the more certain, it was contended, would progress be. The problem, however, was how far men – themselves potentially at the mercy of base motives – should use the power of the state (that is, of the nation considered as an organism) to regulate the wills and to repress the passions of other men. That individual rulers of the state could not assert their wills in direct opposition to prevailing opinion was agreed. But, although whig-liberals accepted that much freedom must be left to each individual will, they asserted that the state had a limited role, both in repressing passions on the one hand, and in developing spiritual awareness and harmony on the other. The more pessimistic – Shaftesbury and most Carlyleans – laid especial emphasis on the duty of a strong state to repress man's innate depravity by a rigorous imposition of law. They maintained that this did not involve interfering with 'true liberty', because 'true liberty' consisted in being governed by the law of God.[82] Many men, they argued, were 'utterly incapable' of fulfilling the moral law by themselves; restraint was necessary in order to prevent incalculable evil; indeed, in many ways, men had become morally weaker and less manly in the course of the nineteenth century.[83] But most whig-liberals, affected by the humanitarianism aroused in the 1840s, were more optimistic. They pointed to the increase in man's happiness since the primitive era, when he had been a slave to his 'own passions': his life had been 'one prolonged scene of selfishness and fear', because he could depend on no one. Civilisation had removed him from the grip of such passions.[84] This is not to say, however, that all were *bien-pensants*; ignorance and sin were still seen as the two great evils against which man in society must crusade.[85] Argyll, while seeing grounds for optimism under

---

[81] Hughes, *Tom Brown at Oxford*, p. 345.
[82] Froude, *English in Ireland*, i, 675–6; *Short studies*, ii, 338–9.
[83] Huxley, *Huxley*, iii, 224; Stephen, *Liberty, equality, fraternity*, p. 199.
[84] Lubbock, *Prehistoric times*, pp. 472, 484, 490–1.   [85] *Ibid.*, pp. 488–91.

proper conditions, knew that many men were incapable of the intelligence and discipline needed to enslave their passions.[86] He had learned from history a 'horror and hatred of unrestrained humanity, when let loose from the bonds of authority and of law'.[87] Even the most saintly whig-liberal insisted that the firm rule of law was necessary to control man's anti-social tendencies: 'Oh! by the supremacy of law may we all continue to be ruled, by law the passions of individuals restrained, and the liberty of speech and thought secured, and the peace and order of the whole community maintained!'[88]

Most whig-liberals would probably have agreed with Thirlwall that 'the general stream of tendency is toward good', despite the fearful dangers which would accrue through ignoring the call of duty.[89] It was the role of the statesman to lead progress towards the ideal, according to the best thought available,[90] and to try to steer nations away from the 'fearful calamities' which were consequent upon their abusing 'the advantages and blessings conferred upon them'.[91] Even the Carlylean pessimists believed that the state was capable of advancing 'peace, wealth, and the intellectual and moral development of its members'.[92] Each nation was a 'sacred work and instrument of God';[93] nations, like individuals, would progress to the extent that they adhered to the moral law.[94] Failure to do so would invite 'retribution' by an 'inexorable sequence of cause and effect'.[95]

Not all whig-liberals, of course, were devoted followers of party politics; but those who were naturally saw the Liberal party as the organ of government which best understood how to promote social and constitutional harmony and spiritual awareness. The party, it was asserted, knew that to eschew the dangerous and sectionalist extremism associated with either tory oligarchs or democratic radicals was the prerequisite for stability and progress. Between the 'dense mass of prejudice

---

[86] Argyll, *Reign of law*, pp. 434–5; 'Christian socialism', p. 704. See also Hughes, *Tom Brown's schooldays*, pp. 87, 165; Davies, *Social questions*, pp. 153–5.

[87] Argyll, *Argyll*, i, 84.

[88] Prothero, *Stanley*, ii, 542.

[89] Blackie, *What does history teach?*, pp. 4–5; Greg, *Enigmas of life*, pp. 5–6, 37–40; Thirlwall, *Letters to a friend*, p. 295; (Grey) Haultain, *Goldwin Smith's correspondence*, p. 132.

[90] Greg, *Enigmas of life*, pp. 37–43; *Literary and social judgments*, p. 281; (Jowett) Turner, *Greek heritage*, pp. 430–1; C. Fortescue, *Christian profession*, pp. 35–6; Caird, *The universal religion*, pp. 16–17.

[91] (Grey) Haultain, *Goldwin Smith's correspondence*, p. 132.

[92] Huxley, 'Administrative nihilism', p. 543.

[93] Davies, *National Church*, p. vii.

[94] Argyll, *Unseen foundations, passim*; 'Christian socialism'; Froude, *English in Ireland*, iii, 1; Paul, *Froude*, pp. 430–1. See also Akroyd, *On the present attitude of political parties*, pp. 25–6.

[95] Dufferin to Argyll, 19 March 1862, Dufferin papers; see also Grey, *Hansard*, cxcvii, 693, 29 June 1869.

and ignorance' of the tory-Anglican squirearchy on the one side, and the 'large popular masses easily excited' by 'crotchet-mongers' on the other, had long stood the whig aristocracy, those most representative of the 'intelligence, the property, and the highest honour and culture of the nation'.[96] The whigs believed that they had consistently acted to prevent the monarchy, the Church, or the Lords from destabilising British politics by disrupting the harmonious constitutional balance of powers.[97] Government at its best was defined, especially by those most conversant with German thought, as the 'representative and organ' of the national 'mind and will';[98] in maintaining this organic harmony between sectional interests, and in repressing sectionalism in the interests of the common good, government was seen to be following the path ordained by Providence.[99] Some perceived the Liberals, at their best, as capable of appreciating all sides of man, and thus of promoting his 'humanisation'.[100] Less 'humanitarian' and more 'intellectual' whig-liberals saw the party as being 'undisturbed and undistorted by the promptings of interest or prejudice ... complete[ly] independen[t] of all class interests, and ... relying for its success on the better feelings and higher intelligence of mankind'.[101]

There was a particular reason why whig-liberals were so keen to stress that temporal government was a 'Divine function',[102] or that man was truly free only if he were governed by 'just laws, laws which are in harmony with the will of the Maker and Master of the World'.[103] There was increasing alarm that Britain was on the verge of internal decay through sectional disharmony and rife materialism. Liberal Anglicans tended to believe that nations, like individuals, had grown only to die, and that Britain was at a late stage in the cycle.[104] But national decline was not inevitable, as Stanley had suggested in a prize essay of 1840, and Russell in his ambitiously titled Rectorial address at Aberdeen in 1864, 'The general aspect of the world'. It could be checked only by national religious regeneration: Froude had 'no expectation of any good coming to us either from politics or science, unless statesmen and philosophers

---

[96] Reeve, 'John Stuart Mill', p. 108; 'Plain whig principles', p. 257.

[97] Reeve, 'Plain whig principles', *passim*.

[98] Thirlwall, *Thirlwall*, p. 256; Arnold, *Culture and anarchy*, pp. 70, 97.

[99] Grey, Letter on the alarming state of public affairs, December 1871, Grey papers; Stodart Walker, *Letters of Blackie*, p. 185.

[100] Arnold, 'Future of Liberalism', pp. 139–44; Brodrick, *Political studies*, pp. 212–41.

[101] Lowe, 'A new Reform Bill', p. 441; see Grant Duff in 'A modern "symposium"', p. 810.

[102] Fremantle, *Church reform*, pp. 15–16; Hughes, 'National education', p. 238; *The old Church*, p. 223.

[103] Froude, *English in Ireland*, i, 675–6.

[104] Forbes, *Liberal Anglican idea*, p. 96; (Grey) Haultain, *Goldwin Smith's correspondence*, p. 132.

have some kind of faith in God'.[105] Somerset saw Christianity as 'the only solid security for the permanence of European civilisation'.[106]

Given these concerns, a great deal of whig-liberal attention was lavished on the causes of the decline of great nations. Layard's studies of the ancient sites of Nineveh and Babylon taught him that empires fell when love of wealth and display corrupted 'the manners of her people' and produced 'general profligacy and ... effeminate customs', and when the 'public weal' was 'sacrificed and made subservient to private interests'. Yet, while Assyria had fallen, the Hebrew kingdoms had survived adversity, inspired by the 'sublime ... moral lessons' of the Old Testament.[107] When he entered politics in the early 1850s, it was this conviction which provoked his attacks on the profligacy and inefficiency of the administrative system; it was no coincidence that his election agent presented him in 1852 as having discovered material of great interest to 'religious-minded men'.[108] He further developed this theme in a series of sub-Ruskinian articles on the history of art and architecture, which, *inter alia*, traced the decline of Italian painting from the thirteenth to the sixteenth century. He showed how the highest aspirations of the age of Dante, an age which combined a 'union of child-like faith with an earnest impatience of the vices and power of priestcraft', were expressed by painters whose 'first and paramount duty' was to teach 'the people', and who thus gave their paintings an 'ideal and spiritual treatment'. Later, art became the preserve of lackeys paid by a wealthy, proud society to deliver 'ornament for the delight of the eye'. Increasing realism in the representation of the human body and of light and shade left less to the 'imagination and the feelings'; by the sixteenth century nearly all painting depicted 'the ignoble actions and common emotions of humanity', a fitting parallel to men's 'cowardly resignation to priestly authority' in ecclesiastical affairs.[109]

Russell believed that the Roman empire fell because religion had been corrupted and could no longer prevent men 'giving entire rein to their passions'.[110] But another favourite example for whig-liberals was the development of the Byzantine empire, which Kingsley traced both in *Hypatia* and in *Alexandria and her schools*. He maintained that Hellenistic Alexandria had broken the 'spiritual, unseen, and everlasting laws of God', owing to the overweening pride of her intellectuals and the polish,

---

[105] *Short studies*, ii, 171.
[106] *Christian theology*, pp. 47–8.
[107] Layard, 'The influence of education', p. 86; *Discoveries*, pp. 539, 631–3.
[108] *Autobiography*, ii, 240.
[109] *Ibid.*, ii, 204; *idem*, 'Fresco-painting', esp. pp. 301, 309. See also 'Architecture' and 'German, Flemish, and Dutch art'.
[110] 'General aspect of the world', p. 142.

pedantry and spiritual deadness of her artists.[111] The same became true
of the later neo-Platonist movement, which in turn corrupted Eastern
Christianity into a formalistic religion of 'base fetish worship'. The
modern Orthodox Church had thus come to peddle an arid perverted
faith, whose celebration of celibacy had always prevented it both from
grappling successfully with the evils of human nature, and from understanding and being suffused by the spiritual intensity which sexual love
and family life instilled.[112]

In short, 'materialism' was characterised as the great evil to which all
nations were susceptible. This materialism was said to take two forms.
One was the growth of political sectionalism, the breakdown of
Providential class harmony as men pursued their individual economic
interests at the expense of the nation. The other was the perversion of
religion, as the moral dictates of the gospels were ignored in favour of
human dogmatic, superstitious and catechistical inventions – inventions
which suggested that formal obeisance to them would ensure salvation,
and thus did nothing to check sensualism and depravity. In the 1860s
and 1870s, whig-liberals feared that both these developments were only
too likely in Britain.

The standard complaint in the economic sphere was that the British
were becoming too concerned with wealth and pleasure, with 'doing as
they liked', and that they did not possess a sufficient sense of national
culture or communal pride to overcome this temptation. The French
example showed that, whether the fault lay in gorging oneself in
sensualism, in spending extravagantly, or in inventing exclusive
religions and moralities, society would collapse if everyone was able to
gratify the 'wishes of the flesh and of the current thoughts' as 'equally as
possible and as much as possible'.[113] Britain might well follow this path,
as the various manifestations of class feeling in the 1860s revealed: all
classes had become materialised, and conflict between them for sectional
gain was thus endemic. The statesman's primary task was to reverse this
process, to check the 'reckless self-indulgence' of *all* classes in order to
preserve the body politic.[114] Working-class propensity to strike, drink
and breed excessively; middle-class cultural narrowness and obsession
with profit; upper-class decadence and political apathy: all were
condemned.[115]

---

[111] *Alexandria*, pp. 3–4, 6–30, 64–6.
[112] *Ibid.*, pp. 136–9; Kingsley, *Kingsley*, i, 254–60. See also Layard, 'Architecture', pp. 299,
307; and Mount-Temple, *Memorials*, p. 37.
[113] Arnold, 'Literature and dogma', pp. 390–1.
[114] Arnold, 'Study of Celtic literature', p. 394; 'Future of Liberalism', p. 158; Froude, *Short
studies*, ii, 388–9. See also Greg, *Miscellaneous essays*, pp. 13–14.
[115] E.g. Arnold, *Culture and anarchy*; Greg, *Miscellaneous essays*, pp. 92–4; *Literary and social*

All classes must be taught the 'true philosophy of life', that honest work done well offered a greater reward than the pursuit of sordid acquisitions;[116] and the state must therefore encourage the propagation of practical and ethical religion. It was this which would lift men out of that very 'vulgarity' and obsession with individual salvation which was apparent in politics, economics and social life.[117] It was this which would 'moderate' the 'warfare between class and class', and 'introduce the principles of Christianity into men's social and civil relations'.[118]

The nature of this religion must now be established; but, before doing so, it may be as well to consider, since this aim was in many senses a radical one, whether it was not too visionary and too high-minded to have had widespread practical currency among whig-liberals or anyone else. These objections cannot, however, be sustained. The religion which they wished to promote was not impossibly pious, because it recognised the commonplace and everyday nature of sin. Its message was that man's duty was to fight as hard as he could against aristocratic snobbery, material degradation and sensual living alike, and towards a religion which was simple, manly and virtuous without being priggish or destructive of his daily business. The simplicity with which this goal could be portrayed, and the extraordinary degree to which the reading public was receptive to it, is best seen in the phenomenal success of the book which created the most convincing portrait of the classless, decent but flawed Englishman of the whig-liberals' hopes: *Tom Brown's schooldays* (1857), which went through fifty-two editions by 1892.[119]

Whig-liberals demanded that this religion be national in appeal and moral in essence, rather than sectional or exclusive. They waged war on the assumption that most 'dogmatic antipathies' were 'grounded in religion and morality'.[120] Christianity was not 'an intellectual faith in the doctrines of a metaphysical theology, but a living faith in the moral government of the world and a heroic conduct in life'.[121] The essence of religion, for latitudinarian and evangelical alike, was the promotion of 'moral duty', 'strenuousness in doing right and trying to do right'.[122]

---

judgments, pp. 280–303; 'The proletariat on a false scent'; Croskerry, 'Drunkenness, abstinence', pp. 400–2; Kingsley, *Alton Locke*, pp. 27, 135–8, 155–6, 175–7, 271–2, 313–14, 364, 378; Hughes, *The manliness of Christ*, p. 171; Hodder, *Shaftesbury*, ii, 262; Trollope, *The way we live now* (1875); Goschen, 'Intellectual interest'.

[116] Greg, *Literary and social judgments*, pp. 65–7; Froude, *Short studies*, i, 183–4.

[117] Abbott, 'The Church and the congregation', esp. pp. 189–91. See also Arnold, 'Literature and dogma', pp. 172–3, and 'Church of England'.

[118] Shannon, 'Seeley', p. 246; Stanley, *Arnold*, pp. 243, 502.

[119] J. Gathorne-Hardy, *The public school phenomenon, 597–1977* (London, 1977), p. 77.

[120] Brodrick, *Political studies*, p. 237.

[121] Blackie, *What does history teach?*, p. 92. See also Avebury, *Peace and happiness*, pp. 315–27.

[122] Thompson, *Kelvin*, ii, 1089; Froude, *Short studies*, ii, 161; Graves, *Grove*, p. 304; Shaftesbury, *National Education Union 1870*, p. 8.

Mastery of the individual conscience was the key to a proper relationship with God: as Argyll said, if the clergy knew how to direct that conscience for the best, 'they will, and must be, the greatest political reformers in the world'.[123]

In approaching questions of dogma, whig-liberals harked back to their theory of Providence. Since society was in constant motion, nothing should be artificially repressed by demanding allegiance to outdated forms: 'society and mankind, the children of the Supreme, will not stop growing for your dogmas'.[124] Nations and individuals could retain their spiritual freshness and 'goodness' only if 'religious liberty and freedom to search the truth' were secured.[125] If the Church was to remain a '*living* Church', she must allow a 'considerable variety of spiritual faiths'.[126] Unless man were given the liberty to interpret Christian doctrine in the way which most aided his spiritual journey into communion with God, he would fall off into formalistic religious practice.

All whig-liberals thus approved in principle of redrawing the boundaries of dogma so that wording relevant for a more primitive age would receive less emphasis than language which was fresh and inspiring to the modern mind.[127] Many, in fact, found it difficult, indeed counterproductive, to express their inner spiritual feelings in concrete language at all.[128] But whig-liberals differed considerably in their attitude towards dogma. It is possible to trace three broad schools of thought, and two of these were almost certainly unrepresentative of the majority feeling, certainly among Liberal public opinion. The first was theism or a more imprecise creed: Greg, Fitzjames Stephen and Huxley, for example, could not accept Christian dogma and the truth of the bible stories, but valued the ethical and moral teaching of the Sermon on the Mount. The second was that of Matthew Arnold, whose conception of religion was entirely ethical, and whose God was the 'eternal . . . which makes for righteousness'. Arnold's Romantic belief that the abandonment of dogma and the stress on holiness of life would itself be sufficient to sustain progress was, to a large extent, accepted by Stanley and by some younger university Liberals like Grant Duff, although Stanley's biographer thought that critics had underestimated his subject's awareness of the prevalence of sinfulness.[129] The first school (especially Stephen and

---

[123] Argyll, 'Christian socialism', p. 707.   [124] Kingsley, *Alton Locke*, p. 138.
[125] Russell, 'General aspect of the world', p. 146.
[126] *Spectator*, 27 April 1872, pp. 523–4.
[127] Hewett, ' . . . and Mr Fortescue', p. 163; Cartwright, *To the electors of Oxfordshire*.
[128] Thirlwall, *Thirlwall*, pp. 215–16; Jowett, *Sermons on faith*, p. vi; (Stanley) Bryce, *Studies in contemporary biography*, p. 80.
[129] Arnold, 'Literature and dogma', pp. 317–18, 339; 'Irish Catholicism and British Liberalism', pp. 334, 343; Begbie, *Albert Grey*, p. 86; Dowden, *Fragments from old letters*

Huxley) differed from the second in maintaining a more developed pessimism about man's spiritual receptivity, and a greater emphasis on the notion of duty in battling against sin.[130]

Both groups, especially the second, were attacked by majority whig-liberal opinion, the orthodox broad churchmen, evangelicals and Carlyleans. Orthodox broad churchmen valued the emphasis on righteousness and good conduct, and on the need to question and modernise theological dogma. But they did not believe that awe, enthusiasm and emotion would be permanently sustained in those who rejected the basic Christian doctrines – especially the Trinity, Incarnation and Resurrection, which enabled men to appreciate Christ's atonement for their sins, and to grasp the nature of their bond to a personal God. It was also usual to defend the notion of miracles, on the grounds that science was expanding man's conceptions and showing that concepts previously mysterious had not after all involved the breaking of natural laws.[131] Many in fact questioned the wisdom of biblical criticism when it appeared purely destructive, seeing it as aiming to undermine the moral lessons of the Old Testament and the miraculous nature of Christianity.[132] These complaints were even more persistent among the more rigid evangelicals and Carlyleans, who thought that to undervalue the conception of the atonement would dissolve the moral bonds of society by removing the sanctions for righteous behaviour.[133]

It was generally argued that scientific advances would consolidate the importance of ethical religion by stripping away irrelevant but divisive superstitions. Theology and science were, according to Stanley, hand-maidens: Lubbock maintained that 'men of science, and not the clergy only, are ministers of religion'.[134] The common assumption was that scientific discovery, if not dedicated *a priori* to 'materialistic' interpretations, would demonstrate the existence of a natural Providential harmony, and, by linking the Christian and everyday worlds in one explanation, would enable working-men to identify far more closely with

1869–92, pp. 44–5; Grant Duff, *Out of the past*, i, 148–50; *Letters of Aberdare*, i, 205–6; Prothero, *Stanley*, ii, 178–82.

[130] Colaiaco, *Stephen*, pp. 171–5, 181, 187–8.

[131] Tulloch, 'Arnold's "Literature and dogma"'; Davies, 'Mr Matthew Arnold's new religion of the bible'; (Tait) Marsh, *Victorian Church in decline*, pp. 60–3; Kingsley, *Alton Locke*, pp. 209–10, 367–71, 427.

[132] For whig-liberal complaints, especially at the *Essays and reviews* and Colenso cases, see Thirlwall, *Thirlwall*, pp. 228–42; (Tait) Marsh, *Victorian Church in decline*, p. 60, and *Times*, 7 November 1872, p. 6; Kingsley, *Kingsley*, i, 353–4, ii, 181, 183; Prothero, *Stanley*, ii, 103–4; Graham, *H. M. Butler*, pp. 343–4.

[133] Froude, *Calvinism*, pp. 8–9; Hodder, *Shaftesbury*, iii, 9–10, 162–5; Carlyle, 'Shooting Niagara', pp. 331–2. See Bell, *Disestablishment in Ireland*, p. 13.

[134] Stanley, 'Hopes of theology'; Avebury, *Pleasures of life*, i, 169–70, ii, 228. See also Hughes, *Fraser*, p. 194; Holland, *Devonshire*, i, 133; Somerset, *Christian theology*, p. 171.

Christianity.[135] This belief was shared even by Shaftesbury and the more rigid evangelicals;[136] their only concern was that, in the process of scientific discovery, man might give too much weight to the intellect, an amoral entity, to 'accept or reject at pleasure' any displeasing part of the Christian scheme. They argued that reason alone was incapable of proving the existence of moral principles or moral government; nor did it cultivate the conscience and courage necessary to effect a moral revolution, as Froude commented in his comparison of Erasmus and Luther.[137] But in fact the religious conception of very few latitudinarians allowed the intellect primacy over the moral conscience. Lubbock and Kingsley were typical in seeing no incompatibility between scientific research and awareness of man's sinfulness: science's 'stern yet salutary teaching' revealed that punishment for sin was a 'certainty'.[138]

In fact on most controversial points there was more agreement on the essentials than disputing whig-liberals sometimes maintained: they would attack what they saw as the extreme implications of one position, implications which its adherents would deny holding.[139] All but the most extreme shared similar assumptions. They believed that spiritual freshness and moral endeavour must be promoted at the expense of dogma and unthinking devotions. They contended that Church teaching must be open to new trends arising from man's biblical and scientific discoveries, and that the latter would be of great value, in so far as they harmonised with the real laws of the universe. They further tended to think that state influence could promote spiritual aspirations, could encourage the reception of new trends, and could help to regulate these trends in accordance with the will of God.

They saw this Church, in theory, as a national Church. Indeed, a great many whig-liberal intellectuals adopted the Coleridgean idea of the national Church as a Church which represented the minds and wills of the individuals who constituted the nation in just the same way that secular government did.[140] It would be misleading to suggest that in its highest form this conception was held by anyone involved in practical politics, given the political impracticability of achieving such a union of sects, when nonconformists did not wish for it. Nonetheless, most whig-

---

[135] Argyll, *Argyll*, i, 413; *Reign of law*, p. 432; Kingsley, *Alton Locke*, pp. 170–1, 419–20.

[136] Finlayson, *Shaftesbury*, pp. 517–18.

[137] Hodder, *Shaftesbury*, iii, 18–19; Froude, *Short studies*, i, 94, 98–9, 114–17, 124, 151–3.

[138] Lubbock, *Prehistoric times*, p. 489; Kingsley, *Science*, esp. pp. 15–16.

[139] For example, Greg and Stephen disliked the emphasis on muscular Christianity which they associated with Kingsley and Hughes, although Hughes denied that it involved anything other than training the body to subordinate the passions and to stand up for righteousness: Greg, *Literary and social judgments*, pp. 125–6; Livingston, 'Stephen', pp. 283–4; Hughes, *Tom Brown at Oxford*, p. 99.

[140] Thirlwall, *Thirlwall*, p. 256. See Shannon, 'Seeley'.

liberals wished to reduce differences between sects, not only by allowing nonconformists civil liberties which had previously been denied them, but also by transforming the organisation and broadening the doctrinal appeal of the Church Establishment so that it was more accessible to spiritually aware modern minds of all denominations. It would thus be uniquely well-equipped to teach a national morality.[141]

High-church opponents of these whig-liberal latitudinarians complained that they were erastians, actively wishing to use the power of the state to alter the Church's doctrine and organisation at will.[142] This, however, was only partly true. Some whig-liberals did believe that at the Reformation the Crown had in effect created a new Church and that its supremacy over it enabled it to effect major modifications of the Church's role at its pleasure.[143] But many others argued that the Church had a historic identity independent of the state, and that its present relationship with the temporal power was merely the result of a contract undertaken in order to promote morality and check evil. The Church, they contended, had rebelled from Rome in revulsion at her moral practices, not in order to reject her doctrines for new ones.[144] The state should therefore not concern itself with imposing one doctrine rather than another, a policy which was bound to create weakness and divisions.[145] Rather, the nationality of the Church would be increased by diminishing the power of any one school over it. Cowper-Temple probably represented prevailing opinion when he argued on the one hand that Christian energy was 'paralyzed by division', but at the same time that it was wrong to try to rectify this evil by force, by 'artificial unity . . . attained by mutual suppression of beliefs, or paring away of creeds'.[146] Freedom of thought and the operation of the individual conscience would, it was maintained, break down doctrinal exclusiveness and promote agreement between the sects. Some whigs, in fact, were so committed to freedom of thought under the beneficial supervision of the state that they believed that all religions tended to aid social stability and

---

[141] Shannon, 'Seeley', p. 245.

[142] For example, a high-church defector from a whig household defined the whigs' conception of the Church as 'practically a subdivision of the Home Department for the promotion of morals': G. W. E. Russell, *Social silhouettes*, p. 154.

[143] Froude, *History, passim*; see also Paul, *Froude*, pp. 136–7; *Pall Mall Gazette*, 11 September 1867, p. 1; Price, 'Church of England', pp. 161–8. Whigs like Westbury were concerned to uphold the doctrine of the Royal Supremacy when Gladstone proposed the disestablishment of the Irish Church in 1868.

[144] Prothero, 'Disestablishment', pp. 268–9; Arnold, 'St Paul and Protestantism', pp. 98–9.

[145] Arnold, 'St Paul and Protestantism', pp. 98–9; Reeve, 'The national Church', p. 265; Stanley, *Address at Sion college*; Tulloch, 'Dogmatic extremes', pp. 195–6; Avebury, *Pleasures of life*, ii, 220; Russell, 'General aspect of the world', p. 152.

[146] Mount-Temple, *Memorials*, pp. 183–4.

stress social obligations, and that doctrinal influences were sufficiently unimportant for all to be encouraged by state support.[147]

But whig-liberals agreed in working towards a national Church founded upon the essence of Protestantism; all religious divisions inspired by quarrels about this or that dogmatic excrescence were to be condemned. Fortunately, progress, if it worked for the best, would make these excrescences appear irrelevant, and would promote true spirituality in their stead;[148] it would break down 'the wall of partition between churchman and non-conformist', and transform the Church of England into the 'Church of the whole Protestant people'.[149]

There were, in whig-liberal eyes, two great dangers to the implementation of this ideal of a national religion. The first will have become evident from the introduction: the tendencies to spiritual deadness, materialism and political conservatism which they perceived in the Anglican Church Establishment. This had been a major preoccupation of each generation of Liberals; it continued to be so in the 1860s and 1870s. It even led some to contemplate disestablishment. But this was in nearly all cases only a fleeting thought, at most, as we shall see.

On this first danger, whig-liberals agreed with the rest of party opinion. On what they considered to be the second threat, other Liberals were in much less accord. This threat stemmed from the appeal of sectionalism, through the false god of dogma. It was not doctrine itself which was held to be offensive, but the argument that one particular caste of men had been the 'exclusive depositories' of truth. This conception, it was argued, not only prevented the effective imposition of national morality: it exacerbated the excited materialism of the common man by giving him dogmatic flags to brandish, and exercised his dangerously combative and exuberant nature. These party 'watchwords' would come to be slavishly followed by the ignorant, and would prevent any cooperation between sects.[150] Playfair defined ultramontanism as belief in the 'exclusive depository' principle, and Harcourt as 'priestly tyranny', whether by Romanist, Anglican or nonconformist.[151] Stanley, adopting this definition – as did Bismarck – listed the offenders as not only Roman Catholics, but also Anglo-catholics, English nonconformists, Scottish Free Churchmen, and 'philosophical or indifferent' politicians, such as the positivists. He classed on the other side of the fence all those who believed in a moral religion and in the supremacy of state

---

[147] Gregory, *Autobiography*, p. 167; Reeve, 'The national Church', p. 254.
[148] Avebury, *Pleasures of life*, ii, 228; Tulloch, 'Dogmatic extremes', pp. 189–90; Arnold, 'St Paul and Protestantism', p. 85.
[149] Somerset, *Christian theology*, pp. 178–9.
[150] Stanley, *Church of Scotland*, p. 168; *Essays on Church and state*, pp. 356, 358, 367.
[151] Reid, *Playfair*, p. 217; (Harcourt) *Times*, 9 December 1873, p. 12. See also Thomas Arnold's view: Stanley, *Arnold*, p. 535.

law, combined with toleration in matters of specific dogmatic import: Anglicans, presbyterians, Lutherans, Gallican Catholics and adherents of Oriental religions.[152]

The first set seemed determined to assert their authoritarianism and indulge in dogma-worship; this required them to escape from the control of law. State control of the Church was maintained not in order to restrict liberty, but to secure 'freedom of opinion'.[153] As Reeve put it, 'all Free Churches are by their nature theocracies . . . their authority is practically unlimited'.[154] Stanley saw the various Protestant and Catholic dissenters from the Establishment as sharing the same misconceptions, that, from the surviving deposits of early Christian writers, it was possible to create 'a complete, rigid, exact system of doctrine, ritual, and constitution', and that it was legitimate to impose this as a condition for joining a Church.[155] By evading the rule of law, they could preach immoral doctrine, doctrine which gratified the passions, and eschewed improvement and the goal of 'a purer, higher, and happier collective life'.[156] Jowett quoted with approval Plato's distrust of private worship and of 'individual enthusiasm'.[157] Prothero maintained that all non-Established Churches elevated the 'will and fancy of the individual' to a position of supremacy, and that this offered no guarantee for morality or social stability:[158] Greg characterised the history of Christianity as the invention of successive 'false doctrines' which could 'justify and canonize' the 'fierce passions and the wild desires of men', and thus excuse the 'devastation . . . over the social and moral world' that had been spread by those passions and desires.[159]

However, attitudes to the Protestant nonconformists – the members of the most conspicuous among Free Churches – were ambivalent. All whig-liberals agreed with Arnold that there was a 'waste of power' in not including them in the Establishment: their qualities were considerable.[160] The more evangelical whig-liberals voiced fewer criticisms of the nonconformist mentality, and emphasised more their joint adherence to the central tenets of an avowedly Protestant religion. Shaftesbury believed that the 'moral condition' of ecclesiastics must be deplorable if they refused to cooperate with nonconformity for the purpose of rescuing the working-man from ignorance and sin.[161] This respect was broadly

[152] Stanley, 'Christianity and ultramontanism', pp. 494–5.
[153] (Harcourt) *Times*, 9 December 1873, p. 12.
[154] Reeve, 'The national Church', p. 269.
[155] Stanley, 'The Church and dissent', pp. 200–1.
[156] Kingsley, *Kingsley*, i, 253–4; Brereton, *Newness of life*, pp. 15–17.
[157] Jowett, *Dialogues of Plato*, iv, 181–2. See also Arnold, *Culture and anarchy*, pp. 171–2.
[158] Prothero, 'Disestablishment', p. 262.
[159] Greg, *Literacy and social judgments*, pp. 410–11.
[160] Arnold, 'St Paul and Protestantism', p. 75.   [161] Hodder, *Shaftesbury*, ii, 280.

shared by latitudinarians: even Arnold, the most hostile, valued the Hebraistic qualities of 'self-conquest, self-devotion, the following not our individual will, but the will of God', which were found in noncon-formity.[162] Whig-liberals stressed, nonetheless, the error that non-conformists had made in withdrawing from the current of national life, which had protected their Calvinism from dilution by new theological influences,[163] and which had destroyed the chance of maintaining a national Church. The old whigs had long argued that nonconformist preachers were more excitable and intolerant than Anglicans, because they needed to stir up such passions in order to secure an adequate col-lection at the end of the service, off which to live.[164] But nonconformist distrust of the state's influence in religious affairs was seen as a particu-lar danger from the 1860s onwards, as militant organisations like the Liberation Society began to press harder for disestablishment of the Church. The extremism of young radical nonconformists was contrasted with the receptiveness of their forefathers to the whig arguments of the 1820s: Akroyd remembered how his father, although a nonconformist, had not pretended that he had insuperable doctrinal differences with the Church, and had favoured cooperation.[165] Hughes saw contemporary nonconformists as no less narrow, conservative and anti-social in their religious conceptions than ritualists. He was appalled at the pride that men like Spurgeon ('practically as infallible as the pope') and Dale took in the exclusiveness of their sects, and foresaw a decline to the standard of national morality prevalent in the United States, if such sectionalism were allowed to grow further.[166] But there was still a belief that the average nonconformist layman was less obsessed by differences with the Church than his political leaders, and that many of the former could still be encouraged to sympathise with a liberal and earnest Establishment.[167]

Other religions and philosophies which were accused of being danger-ously exclusive and potentially immoral included positivism (whig-liberals believed it to be impossible to define a powerful morality from

---

[162] *Culture and anarchy*, esp. pp. 11, 38, 132, 199.

[163] *Ibid.*, *passim*; Kingsley, *Alton Locke*, p. 12.

[164] H. Pearson, *The Smith of Smiths: being the life, wit and humour of Sydney Smith* (London, 1934), p. 277; P. Ziegler, *Melbourne: a biography of William Lamb, 2nd Viscount Melbourne* (London, 1978 edn), p. 31.

[165] Akroyd, *Church, state and nonconformists*, p. 10.

[166] Hughes, *The old Church*, pp. 117–18, 127–33, 174–5.

[167] Thirlwall, *A charge delivered 1869*, pp. 35–7; Halifax to Gladstone, 27 June 1868, Gladstone papers, 44184, fo. 200.

the behaviour of the mass of humanity)[168] and scientific 'materialism' – although the last was a matter of definition.[169]

But this attack on philosophies which might become 'materialistic' was directed above all at the ritualists and other radical high churchmen, who were often suspected of masterminding the whole attack on the conception of the moral Establishment. The Liberation Society was seen to be playing into the hands of sacerdotalists who would use the freedom gained by disestablishment to impose an anti-Protestant creed: it seemed willing to ally with 'the most sacerdotal, the most exclusive, the most superstitious of all the tendencies which the Church of England contains'.[170]

In whig-liberal eyes, high churchmen (with, of course, noble exceptions) were 'materialist', because the superstitious religion which they propagated appealed only to the senses.[171] They were unable to undertake the great role of a Christian ministry, to teach 'what is moral and what is not', because they mistakenly thought that the path to morality was through dogma. When priests were able to tell laymen that they could be 'in favour with God and man . . . while their enjoyments or occupations are in no way interfered with', religion became an 'instrument of evil' and 'a lie so palpable as to be worse than atheism itself'.[172] Tractarians were suffused with 'worldliness, pride of life, and self-indulgence', and motivated by vanity even when promoting good works.[173]

Allowing a priest to control one's intellectual and moral development

---

[168] Stephen, *Liberty, equality, fraternity*, esp. pp. 134, 221. See also Froude, *Carlyle*, ii, 372; Kingsley, *The limits of exact science*, p. 32; Davies, *Social questions*, pp. 1–62; Huxley, *Huxley*, iii, 222; Abbott and Campbell, *Jowett*, ii, 187.

[169] Huxley's arguments were interpreted in a materialistic way and scorned, although Huxley denied that he was a materialist: Froude, *Carlyle*, ii, 386; *Calvinism*, pp. 23–4; Thirlwall, *Thirlwall*, pp. 171, 228; Thirlwall, *Letters to a friend*, pp. 192, 223. On the same grounds, Blackie and Thomson attacked Tyndall's 1874 Belfast address (as president of the British Association): Thompson, *Kelvin*, ii, 649, 1092–9; Stodart-Walker, *Letters of Blackie*, p. 255. Tyndall himself did not see the problem in such stark terms: he certainly argued that human emotions, will and intellect might have evolved from matter, but also that matter was the 'living garment of God', bound up with spirit, and that its ultimate origins could not be elucidated: Turner, 'Victorian scientific naturalism and Thomas Carlyle', pp. 338–40; Tyndall, *Scientific use of the imagination*, pp. 33–6, 53; *Fragments of science*, ii, 41–2; *Sabbath*, pp. 44–6. He claimed to 'reverence' the bible, and his sentimental worship of nature and beauty was memorably satirised by Mallock: Tyndall, *Principal Forbes*, p. x; Eve and Creasey, *Tyndall*, p. 191; Mallock, *New republic*, pp. 219–20.

[170] Reeve, 'Plain whig principles', pp. 269–70; Stanley, 'The Church and dissent', pp. 205–6.

[171] Russell, *Essays*, p. 313; Davies, 'Erastianism *versus* ecclesiasticism', p. 161.

[172] Froude, *Calvinism*, pp. 17–18; Seeley, 'Church as a teacher of morality', pp. 247–50.

[173] Mount-Temple, *Memorials*, p. 27; Kingsley, *Alton Locke*, pp. 143, 374, 415–16. Froude clearly intended to smear modern high churchmen with the morals of Becket and the power-hungry mediaeval hierarchy: 'Becket', i, 548, vi, 679.

was presented as a denial of individual responsibility,[174] and as an encouragement to 'mental weakness'.[175] As Froude argued with respect to Catholicism, engaging a confessor who would clear away men's feelings of sinfulness was 'a contrivance to enable them to live for pleasure'.[176] Furthermore, it was claimed that superstition and confession promoted a 'valetudinarian and egotistic habit of mind'.[177] The publicity given to ritualists suggested that Christianity was for the weak, the dependent, and the effeminate.[178] High churchmen also struck a blow against the influence of the family by reviving the idea of an ascetic life 'apart from the conscientious performance of our duties to one another and to God'.[179] Both for these reasons and because they were obsessed with sacerdotal practices, high-church clergymen, it was suggested, were unable to understand the problems of ordinary men and thus influence their behaviour for good.[180]

Superstitious religion, it was argued, also obstructed the influx of 'knowledge and thought', because it provided 'crutches . . . for weak faith to rest upon'.[181] This was in turn counter-productive, because it turned genuinely inquiring minds away from Christianity in repugnance. The intellect must be harnessed on the side of faith, and this, whig-liberals stressed, would not be done by the 'revival of obsolete ceremonies', the 'mere loud reiteration of disputed dogmas', or a materialistic interpretation of the Eucharist.[182] By denying a living faith in favour of a system, high churchmen were promoting infidelity: the 'extravagant credulity' with which the 'sceptical' minds of tractarians accepted 'the wildest Popish legends' was 'only another side of . . . bottomless unbelief'.[183] It was thought that the growth of tractarianism and, especially, ritualism had exacerbated the materialist reaction against all forms of faith, because the organic balance had been disturbed. As in France, there threatened to be no middle ground between the 'spiritual cowards' dependent on sacerdotal guidance, and an intellectual elite contemptuous of it: 'atheism and superstition', revolution and counter-revolution, would be in perpetual symbiosis.[184] High-church activity was also seen as

---

[174] Argyll, *Presbytery examined*, pp. 258–67; Stephen, *J. F. Stephen*, pp. 222, 372–3; Hodder, *Shaftesbury*, ii, 406–7.

[175] Blackie, *Essays*, pp. 135–6.　　　　[176] Froude, *Short studies*, ii, 162.

[177] Davies, *Warnings against superstition*, p. 9.

[178] Davies, 'Erastianism *versus* ecclesiasticism', p. 164; Hughes, *Manliness of Christ*.

[179] Farrar, *The English clergy*, p. 11; Stanley, 'The Oxford school', pp. 333–4; Mount-Temple, *Memorials*, p. 37.

[180] Froude, *Short studies*, ii, 362–4.

[181] Davies, *Warnings against superstition*, p. 9.

[182] Tait, *Some thoughts 1866*, p. 9, and *Some thoughts 1876*, pp. 48–50.

[183] Thirlwall, *Letters literary*, p. 261 (on Newman); see Kingsley, *Alton Locke*, pp. 222–4.

[184] Froude, *Short studies*, iv, 252; *History*, xii, 534–7, 554; Stanley, 'The Church and dissent', pp. 222–3; Greg, *Literary and social judgments*, pp. 325–9.

militating against the promotion of national Church reform.[185] Grey felt that, if ritualists remained in the Church, 'a large number of far more valuable members' would be forced out; if they seceded, the Church might win some 'compensating accession from the best of the Dissenters'.[186]

Another source of complaint was that the clergy had decided that they might do 'whatever they like, whether their bishops, their congregations, or the nation at large like it or not'.[187] Their apparent determination to flout their congregations' wishes, especially on ritual matters, had, it was argued, opened up a great gulf between clergy and laity. Convocation, controlled by a minority 'priestly despotism' and 'uncongenial to the free play of thought and action', refused to bow to the supremacy of parliament and the lay courts: it was 'the chief obstacle to the harmonious working of the relations of Church and State'.[188]

What caused most alarm was the realisation that a 'considerable party' of high churchmen wished for disestablishment. The 'kind of liberty which they desire would be a grinding tyranny'.[189] They might introduce confession if they had the power.[190] At any event, the Church would become 'more *ecclesiastical* and less *political*'. Clergymen of 'ecclesiastical sympathies', rather than men like Tait and Thirlwall, would gain high office: and 'ecclesiastical energy' did not always follow 'the mind of Christ'. It was only by prolonged contact with the political and public world that bishops could be infused with 'courage, straightforwardness, and large-hearted consideration'.[191] A disestablished Church might employ 'weapons of excommunication against liberty of opinion'.[192] Its immense wealth would constitute a serious political threat.[193] Then again, the populism of high churchmen completely liberated from the constraints of law was worrying: upon the passage of disestablishment, with the 'sacerdotal tendencies' of the Church strengthened, it would foster 'that spurious religion which lives on popular prejudices, plays to popular passions, and relies for its power on superstition and fanati-

---

[185] (The queen): Buckle, *Letters of Victoria*, ii, 290–1, 302; Ponsonby, *Ponsonby*, p. 177.
[186] Grey to Halifax, 19 October 1867, Hickleton papers, A 4 55. See Earl Fortescue to Brereton, 19 December 1870, Brereton papers, F 27 70.
[187] Stanley, 'What is "disestablishment"?', p. 293.
[188] Hodder, *Shaftesbury*, ii, 403, 406–7; Stanley, 'The Oxford school', p. 332; Fremantle, 'Convocation, parliament, and the prayer-book'; C, Fortescue, in *Christian profession*, p. 47, had warned against the revival of a clerical Convocation.
[189] Thirlwall, *Letters literary*, p. 297; *A charge 1869*, p. 31.
[190] Hughes, *The old Church*, p. 73.
[191] Davies, 'Congregationalism and the Church', pp. 22–3, 25; see Abbott and Campbell, *Jowett*, i, 413, 442, 444.
[192] Prothero, 'Disestablishment', pp. 264, 272; Elliot, *Goschen*, i, 193.
[193] Hughes, *The old Church*, p. 61.

cism'.[194] The most alarming foreboding was the power, exclusiveness, and lawlessness of that most populist of all Churches, the Irish Catholic.[195] Alternatively, upon the achievement of disestablishment, different parties in the Church might break off into 'numberless independent sections', and the high churchmen might merge with the Church of Rome – as the latter was thought to be hoping.[196]

These concerns had hardly been voiced before 1867. But they spread markedly after 1870, as the political influence of radical nonconformity grew, as 'materialism' in secular affairs became more apparent, and as ritualists became more open in their calls for disestablishment – and, after 1874, as Gladstone became more equivocal on the subject. Of course, few whig-liberals were committed to the Establishment as a matter of rigid principle, and in the first flush of the reformed parliament, a number had believed that disestablishment was almost inevitable, in line with the theory that society was in constant flux.[197] One or two advanced whig-liberals like Huxley or Lubbock were not at all anxious for the survival of the Establishment unless it concentrated less on 'the iteration of abstract propositions in theology' and more on the preaching of 'an ideal of true, just, and pure living';[198] some evangelicals were so unhappy about the growth of ritualism and at the lack of missionary fervour in the Church that they occasionally questioned the practical utility of the Establishment.[199] But in the 1870s, there was a discernible shift of opinion. At one level, this was because those (usually younger) whig-liberals who had tended to be more critical of the Establishment in its existing state, and most concerned with elevating the level of spirituality in the Church, became happier with the tone and effectiveness of its preaching. This was the consequence of the increasingly obvious effect on parish life of half a century of effort, by all the Church parties, to improve the training of clergymen and their conscientiousness in the performance of their duties. At another level, this shift was caused by alarm that the groups listed by Stanley as ultramontane were precisely those who, in the 1860s and 1870s, were gaining ground both politically and – in the case of ritualists, freethinkers and pro-disestablishment Scottish Free Churchmen – numerically. Whig-liberals of middle-of-the-

---

[194] Prothero, 'Disestablishment', p. 262. Llewelyn Davies also distrusted the influence of 'votes of synods or congregations' in Church affairs, because they would give 'little chance . . . for a Thirlwall or a Stanley . . . to come to the top': 'Congregationalism and the Church', pp. 28, 31.

[195] Davies, 'Congregationalism and the Church', p. 26.

[196] Thirlwall, *Letters literary*, p. 393; *A charge*, p. 40.

[197] (Vaughan and Alford) Bell, *Disestablishment in Ireland*, pp. 22–3; Thirlwall, *Letters literary*, p. 285; (Tait) Marsh, *Victorian Church in decline*, p. 138.

[198] Huxley, 'Administrative nihilism', pp. 540–1.

[199] Hodder, *Shaftesbury*, iii, 5, 246; (Cowper-Temple) Walling, *Diaries of Bright*, p. 341.

road views – Spencer, for example – might still believe that society would one day (but not yet) be civilised enough to prosper without the aid of a Church Establishment.[200] But the effect of the changed religious climate was that, in the fifteen years after 1870, the feelings of the bulk of whig-liberals on the subject of disestablishment became very bitter.

The Establishment was seen as performing an 'immense' temporal service, by keeping men 'good Christians and therefore good citizens' and thus assisting the civil power in preserving 'the security of persons and property'.[201] Its influence was believed to be crucial if crime, class feeling, 'material interests' and 'extravagant political panaceas' were not to take root in the lower classes.[202] It alone conveyed a sense of the 'intimate relations' between Christianity and 'human interests and social duties', without which religion would become individualistic and promote selfishness.[203] Disestablishment would constitute an 'unparalleled national calamity'. It would 'prelude the downfall of much that is greatest in England'; it would reduce Britain to 'a second or third-rate power in Europe' and shake British rule in India; and it would foreshadow the 'decadence and the degradation that overtook the Romans after the great military mission had been fulfilled'.[204] As early as 1868, Argyll warned Gladstone that 'the whole idea of a Free Church is . . . specially feared and detested by a great section of the Liberal party'.[205]

From the 1860s onwards, most whig-liberals saw Church reform as imperative, in order to strike at the ritualists and at the pockets of entrenched conservatism within the Church, and in order to placate non-conformists and to reassert Church nationality.[206] Depending on whether the laity intervened and worked towards a practical religion emphasising 'forgetfulness of self', Froude anticipated in 1868 that the choice for Britain would lie between a 'future of moral progress which will rival or eclipse our material splendour', and 'revolution'.[207] It was recognised that the independence of one part of the Church might have to be curtailed, in order to preserve the spiritual character of the larger part.[208] Since the 1830s, whigs had preached the idea that the state had

---

[200] Gordon, *Spencer*, p. 124.

[201] Akroyd, *Church, state and nonconformists*, p. 4; Albert to Earl Grey, 12 November 1874, Grey papers; Earl Fortescue to vicar of Barnstaple, 30 June 1885, Fortescue papers, FZ 42.

[202] Hughes, *The old Church*, p. 127; Prothero, 'Disestablishment', pp. 263, 280.

[203] Creighton, *Creighton*, i, 349.

[204] Akroyd, *Church, state and nonconformists*, p. 11; Blackie, *What does history teach?*, p. 81; Prothero, 'Disestablishment', p. 258; (Tennyson) Grogan, *Bosworth Smith*, p. 213.

[205] Argyll to Gladstone, 30 November 1868, Gladstone papers, 44100, fo. 275.

[206] Reeve, 'Plain whig principles', pp. 269–71; Jex-Blake, 'Church reform'; Abbott and Campbell, *Letters of Jowett*, p. 189.

[207] Froude, *Short studies*, ii, 179, 391–2.

[208] Stanley, 'Christianity and ultramontanism', p. 497; Russell, *Essays*, p. 344.

the power, indeed the duty, to reform the terms on which the Church held its endowments, in order to ensure that they continued to serve the spiritual needs of society, which were constantly changing.

The prevailing whig-liberal feeling was that it was most important to use state power in three ways: to widen the boundaries of permissible doctrine; to diminish clerical influence in Church government and organisation; and to prevent unpopular innovations in ritual and devotional practice. In all three areas, the state would act to harmonise religious practice with the intellectual and spiritual drift of 'national life'.[209]

There was much pressure, firstly, for the widening of the Church's formularies and regulations in order to appeal to Protestant nonconformists.[210] Arnold and Stanley wished to see them welcomed into the Establishment on their own terms, retaining their prayer book and church discipline.[211] Even if most others – especially MPs aware of the need not to alienate radical nonconformists – did not go so far, there was much talk of the 'hand of brotherhood' reinforcing the 'bonds of a common faith'.[212] This was as strongly expressed by evangelicals, who proclaimed a willingness to sacrifice external privileges in order to attain a union of solid Protestants 'in Christ' – a task made easier by evangelical dislike of the badges of episcopacy, and of ritualistic excess, on which they felt reform should concentrate.[213]

Much interest was expressed by both evangelicals and whigs in relaxing the Act of Uniformity and the rules of subscription to the Thirty-nine Articles:[214] these would be loosened for the benefit of 'Protestants' – not for 'imaginary things called "Catholic truth" or "Catholic practice"', which were merely excuses for 'acts or beliefs of individual self-will'.[215] Whig-liberals presented 'obsolete' rubrics and formularies as divisive, especially the Athanasian Creed and its 'damnatory clauses'. Grey, like many others, thought that the Creed's retention in its present place in

[209] Stanley, 'What is "disestablishment"?', p. 297; Arnold, 'St Paul and Protestantism', pp. 104, 118; *Culture and anarchy*, pp. 13–14.

[210] Hughes, *The old Church*, pp. 16–18, 30–1, 51; Fremantle, *Progress; Lay power in parishes*, p. 39; Jex-Blake, 'Church reform', p. 417.

[211] Arnold, *Culture and anarchy*, pp. 23–8, 32, 166; Stanley, 'The Church and dissent', p. 207.

[212] (Tait) *Times*, 7 November 1872, p. 6; Fraser to Gladstone, 8 January 1870, Hughes, *Fraser*, pp. 170–2.

[213] Hodder, *Macgregor*, p. 99; Shaftesbury to Disraeli, 11 July 1873, Disraeli papers, B/XXI/S/144. For this, see also (the queen) Ponsonby, *Ponsonby*, p. 177; Horsman, *Five speeches*.

[214] Machin, *Politics and the Churches*, p. 333.

[215] Hughes, *The old Church*, pp. 30–1; Fraser, *Charge delivered 1872*, p. 73; Fremantle, 'Convocation, parliament, and the prayer-book', p. 461; Argyll, 'Disestablishment', p. 254.

worship would be 'suicidal' for the Church;[216] Stanley wished to omit it
from the prayer-book; more moderate solutions included the proposal of
an explanatory note, and optional use.[217] Shaftesbury opposed the compulsory use of the Creed in 1871–2, because it prevented cooperation
between Protestants, although he personally considered its message
'sublime and true'.[218]

Whig-liberals were anxious for the reform of Church government and
organisation, which, again, might facilitate cooperation with nonconformists.[219] It would also diminish clerical power, and especially that of
Convocation, which acted 'most perniciously', and made the Church
appear 'an Episcopal Sect with a strong sacerdotal bias'. The purpose of
reform would be to adapt the law to 'the actual convictions and desires
of a Protestant nation'.[220] The real danger to the Church was the 'growing estrangement' between clergy and laity, which had been exacerbated
by the high-church revival;[221] and if the existence of Convocation was to
be sanctioned at all, it must be far more representative of laymen.[222]
Church reformers wished to increase the power of laymen in other ways,
by the reform and democratisation of patronage, the admission of lay
preachers into Church services, and the institution of lay parochial councils of Anglicans and (in the case of radicals like Fremantle) nonconformists and non-Christians as well.[223] The National Church Reform Union
and other societies held mass meetings to advocate these proposals, and
were addressed by Temple, Barry, Stanley and Hughes, among others.
Hughes also spoke at meetings of the Church Defence Institution, a primarily Conservative body (although Tait was its president): his appearances there contributed to his unpopularity in radical Liberal circles.[224]
A number of Church reform bills were introduced into parliament: one
of the most popular was that of the Conservative evangelical Sandon

[216] Grey memorandum for Mr Stephens of Longhaughton, 26 October 1872, Grey papers;
see also Hughes, *The old Church*, pp. 109–10, 163.
[217] Stanley, *Athanasian Creed*; Prothero, *Stanley*, ii, 222–4. For the latter, see Hughes, *Fraser*,
pp. 202–5; Kingsley, *Kingsley*, ii, 395–7.
[218] Hodder, *Shaftesbury*, iii, 301, 309; Finlayson, *Shaftesbury*, p. 525.
[219] Brodrick, *Political studies*, p. 240.
[220] Fremantle, 'Convocation, parliament, and the prayer-book', esp. pp. 451, 461.
[221] Denison to Granville, 3 May 1869, Granville papers, 30/29/75, fo. 134.
[222] C. Fortescue, *Christian profession*, p. 47; Reeve, 'Plain whig principles', pp. 270–1;
Finlayson, *Shaftesbury*, p. 523; *Spectator*, 4 May 1872, p. 554.
[223] Nettleship, 'Fremantle', p. 568.
[224] Fremantle, *Church reform*, pp. 108–10; Fremantle to Tait, 20 May 1873, Tait papers, 92,
fo. 127; *Nonconformist*, 28 February 1872, pp. 209–10; Mack and Armytage, *Hughes*, p. 199;
Hughes, *The old Church*, pp. 24–32; Fremantle to Sandon, 11 March 1872, Harrowby
papers, 39.

which proposed the establishment of parochial councils with lay representation.[225]

In the fight against clerical exclusiveness, a valuable arm of the state was the Judicial Committee of the Privy Council, whose secretary was Reeve. Brodrick and Fremantle published a volume of the Committee's judgments in ecclesiastical causes, at Tait's suggestion, in order to show 'how wisely that maligned tribunal had ever held the balance even between extreme opinions on either side, always leaning in the direction of liberty'.[226] Russell, Stanley and Westbury all saw the Committee as performing a valuable function in preserving Church nationality, because of its unwillingness to pronounce doctrinal variations to be illegal. The Church was right to tolerate 'opposite and contradictory opinions', because there was only a slight legal basis for most dogma.[227] There was much opposition to the high-church demand either for a purely clerical court, or for an entirely secular Committee which clergymen might be able to ignore more easily.[228] Some evangelicals, however, disliked the liberality of the Committee in both broad and high directions.

The Judicial Committee was to prove far more restrictive in pronouncing on ritual innovations, in which it was also strongly supported by whig-liberals. With only a few exceptions,[229] even the most confessedly 'tolerant' were determined that licence in such areas must not be afforded to the clergy, and that the law must be unambiguous wherever parliament wished to act: ritualists were 'defying the convictions and common sense of their fellow-countrymen, and casting a slur upon the Reformation'.[230] Ritualism was seen to be threatening the comprehensiveness of the Church, preventing nonconformists from sympathising with its work, and likely to induce in parishioners a state of mind which might then easily become trapped in 'the network of Roman Catholic claims'.[231] Whig-liberals would therefore support legislation, not in order to restrict the extent of allowable ritual beyond that traditionally accepted by the Church, but in order to define more clearly the state of

---

[225] Fremantle, *Church reform*, pp. 20–2; Graham, *H. M. Butler*, pp. 341–2; Butler, *H. M. Butler*, p. 4; Earl Fortescue to Brereton, 1 March 1871, Brereton papers, F 5 71.

[226] Brodrick, *Memories and impressions*, p. 249.

[227] Prothero, *Stanley*, i, 386–7; Russell, *Essays*, pp. 304–6; Nash, *Westbury*, ii, 66–82, 102–4, 293–4.

[228] (Brodrick leading article) *Times*, 8 May 1873; (Tait) Brodrick and Fremantle, *Judicial Committee*, pp. xiii–xx; J. Jackson, *The parochial system: a charge* (London, 1871), p. 76; Nash, *Westbury*, ii, 66–82.

[229] Such as Maurice and Stanley: Marsh, *Victorian Church in decline*, pp. 118, 126–7.

[230] Fremantle, 'Convocation, parliament and the prayer-book', pp. 427–9; Grey to Halifax, 19 October 1867, Hickleton papers, A 4 55.

[231] Marsh, *Victorian Church in decline*, pp. 116–17; *Spectator*, 20 December 1873, p. 1610; Northbrook to Dufferin, 17 May 1874, Dufferin papers; Thirlwall, *Thirlwall*, p. 212.

the law and the procedure for enforcement, so that it could be exercised against the licentious.[232]

The Church of Scotland

The whig-liberal friends of the Church of Scotland had, not surprisingly, a conception of its role very similar to that sketched above for the English Church. They believed that its Establishment should be maintained because it was 'the formal and guaranteed homage of the State to the national Presbyterianism of her people', the 'most powerful' influence on Scottish national character.[233] Stanley thought it an ideal Church because it stressed the elements of Scottish religious life which were 'above and beyond all institutions and all parties'.[234] But, as Argyll emphasised, neither was it tied in erastian shackles: it was the product of a popular revolt against the views of sovereign and parliament alike. It consisted of the 'whole body of the believing people', and therefore enjoyed internal self-government in spiritual matters, while avoiding clerical exclusiveness.[235]

There was, however, a more profound division of opinion than in England between 'latitudinarians' and 'evangelicals', although again many were able to combine elements of both views. On the one hand were the intellectuals like Tulloch, pioneers of liberal theology; on the other, there was the bulk of presbyterian opinion, represented by Argyll. Men like Macleod straddled the two schools. However, all could agree in criticising the seceding presbyterian sects and the episcopalians, on the grounds that both had abandoned nationality and tolerance. Scottish episcopalians were condemned as illiberal and sacerdotalist (the queen, for example, disliked the strength of tractarianism in the Episcopal Church);[236] but so also were radical Free Churchmen.[237] The latter seemed to extol 'the claims of priesthood' in a new form. They asserted a principle which allowed them total licence: they had fallen into the trap of 'materialism' and 'fanaticism' by claiming the 'direct sanction of God' for their 'own opinions', by enunciating as God's 'holy truths the most trivial of our conceits', and by following 'as the impulse of His Spirit, the most earthly of our own passions'. They could not raise 'public or private character', because they had no lofty ideals.[238] In contrast, the Establish-

---

[232] See e.g. *Times*, 9 January 1874, p. 9.

[233] Argyll, *Some words of warning*, pp. 3–5.

[234] *Church of Scotland*, pp. 168–9.

[235] Argyll, *Argyll*, i, 169–70, ii, 452–3.

[236] Drummond and Bulloch, *Church in Victorian Scotland*, p. 213; (the queen) Fulford, *Your dear letter*, p. 231; Disraeli to Cairns, 13, 16 March 1868, Cairns papers, 30/51/1, fos. 7, 9.

[237] (The queen) Oliphant, *Tulloch*, p. 235; Stanley, *Church of Scotland*, pp. 69–70.

[238] Argyll, *Presbytery examined*, pp. xiv, 157–64, 183, 211–14, 218–19, 289–93; see also Stoddart, *Blackie*, ii, 125–6.

ment had, after a long struggle, secured the right balance between independence and licence.[239]

However, the supporters of Establishment were themselves divided over the proposal to abolish patronage, which was mooted from the 1860s in the hope of winning Free Churchmen away from the arms of the more radical and disestablishmentarian United Presbyterians, and back into communion with the Establishment. Argyll was a leading advocate of patronage abolition, hoping to see it facilitate reunion within the Establishment on the basis of 'spiritual independence'. As a zealous presbyterian and an ex-Peelite, Argyll diverged from the English whig tradition by believing that, if those within Establishments could not agree on essential propositions, it was best for them to be disestablished and disendowed: the state should not give financial support indiscriminately to different theological schools, offending individuals' consciences by making them support other men's creeds. In believing that a non-erastian Establishment of believing presbyterians might be attained through the abolition of patronage,[240] he disagreed with Scottish theological liberals. Some of these baulked at patronage abolition, on the grounds that association with narrow Calvinist Free Churchmen, and concession of control over appointments to public opinion, might retard the influx of modern theology into the Church.[241] Others supported abolition, but believed that ministers should in future be chosen by all parishioners, irrespective of denomination. Argyll regarded this plan as destructive of the Church's character and wished the choice to be vested only in communicants.[242]

The aggressiveness of the seceding Churches raised a further fear among whig-liberals, that security for religious teaching in schools would be surrendered in order to satisfy the seceders' sectional ideas. Established Churchmen tended to support compulsory bible-reading and teaching, and most Church of Scotland laymen advocated teaching according to 'use and wont', that is, of the shorter catechism as well.[243] Even those, like Tulloch, who saw 'use and wont' as controversially 'sectarian', wanted compulsory bible-reading, and were reluctant to accept the idea that each locality could have the power to cease religious

---

[239] Argyll, *Presbytery examined*, pp. 318–29.
[240] Argyll, *Argyll*, i, 171–2, 175, 302–3; *Presbytery examined*, pp. 221–2; *Hansard*, clxxxviii, 401, 24 June 1867, cxcvii, 210, 18 June 1869.
[241] Macleod, *Macleod*, ii, 310–11; (Tulloch) Fleming, *Church of Scotland*, pp. 193, 201.
[242] The broad plan was supported by whigs like Minto (to Ellice, 21 December 1870, Ellice papers, 15014, fo. 108), by Stanley and by a number of men in the Commons: see below, pp. 419–20.
[243] Fleming, *Church of Scotland*, p. 241.

teaching in its schools.[244] There was near unity in opposition to the principle of secular education, which was felt to be illogical in a country where the vast majority of the population, whatever their differences on the subject of Establishments, upheld presbyterian tenets.[245]

One word of warning is, however, necessary in discussing Scottish opinion. Agreement on presbyterianism, and awareness of national identity, forced Scottish Liberalism to develop differently from its southern counterpart in the 1880s, and the political distinctions which are apparent in analysing English opinion do not apply so strongly in Scotland. Although the bulk of Church of Scotland opinion was 'conservative' on the questions of Establishment and religious teaching, so indeed, in practice, was much Free Church and United Presbyterian sentiment. At the same time, the prevalence of presbyterianism made the prospect of disestablishment seem slightly less threatening than in England. Moreover, many Church of Scotland Liberals were inherently more tolerant of the development of the party towards populism and home rule in the 1880s than the supporters of Establishment in England; this was partly because of the nature of presbyterian church government, and partly because of the increasing potency of the cry of Scottish home rule. On the other hand, the strength of anti-Catholic feeling cut across denominational boundaries and was especially strong in the south and west, nearest to Ulster; many Scotsmen, irrespective of sect, were therefore to oppose home rule.

---

[244] He accepted it only on the understanding that in practice the old traditions would win out: Oliphant, *Tulloch*, pp. 264–6.

[245] See e.g. (Brodrick leading article) *Times*, 8 May 1872; Thompson, *Kelvin*, ii, 1091.

2

The whig-liberals: II

Education

The spread of education was central to whig-liberals' hopes for spiritual regeneration and social stability. After 1867, their assessment of the chances of securing a proper spiritual education for every child dictated, more precisely than did any other consideration, the degree of optimism with which they regarded the political future.

Although whig-liberals were agreed that education must propagate true religion and a sense of social and moral obligation, a broad distinction may be drawn between the priorities of the more latitudinarian and more evangelical schools. The former asserted the doctrine that the 'minority of the minority', the clerisy, must moralise the masses through education. It must 'cultivate the imagination' of the working-man, in order to make him appreciate the importance of correct ethical and social behaviour. If he was to be prevented from engaging in strike action or in other 'materialistic' habits, he must understand the tenets of morality and of political economy alike: he must become tolerant, and his aesthetic faculties must be developed.[1] This sort of education, it was believed, was needed as urgently by the 'materialistic' and 'utilitarian' business classes, which, unlike their counterparts in Germany, possessed neither cultural breadth (and the tolerance that stemmed from it),[2] nor sound economic principles,[3] nor a proper grounding in the

---

[1] See e.g. Layard, 'Italian painting', pp. 119–20; Goschen, *Cultivation of the imagination*, p. 8. Bruce recommended the learning by rote of passages of English literature, 'supplying thus a store of pleasing and useful subjects for the thoughts [of working-men, especially of] those who are to pass so large a portion of their lives in the monotony and darkness of the mine': *Lectures and addresses*, p. 18.

[2] Goschen, *Cultivation of the imagination*; Playfair, *Aspects of modern study*, p. 16; Arnold, *Culture and anarchy*, pp. 48–66; Lowe, *Primary and classical education*, pp. 31–2; *Middle class and primary education*, pp. 4–5.

[3] Grant Duff feared the growth of 'anti-social' doctrines like protectionism: 'Changes most wanted', p. 157.

natural sciences – and thus a reverence for the wisdom and power of the 'Creator'.[4] More emphasis was thus needed on modern languages, history and the sciences.

The evangelical wing distrusted the operation of the intellect if deployed outside its proper sphere, and was therefore alarmed by attempts to excite it unduly, especially in the education of the lower orders. This wing contended that the stimulation of the intellect, if unaccompanied by a firm foundation in moral behaviour, merely trained the 'wits' and encouraged boys to turn to 'rascalism', to 'fraud and sensationalism'. They held it to be irresponsible to encourage a man to feel discontented with his station in life; they believed that a faulty education might well lead him to be seduced by the 'latest popular chimera' or 'fetish worshipping superstition', peddled by demagogues, Fenians, trade unionists, socialists, or religious faddists and fanatics. Emphasis merely on intellectual cramming, they argued, did not encourage a sense of individual moral responsibility, of intense perception of the difference between right and wrong.[5] Froude and Kingsley propagated the notion of craftsmanship as the basis of a moral education: a man could not 'stand on [his] feet and walk alone' until he could fulfil a worthwhile role in the community, and do his duty.[6]

In practice, however, there was a broad consensus, stressing the primacy of moral training. Even if their language differed, Arnold and Huxley both saw the proper role of working-class education as being to impose moral principles, political good sense, 'love of liberty' and 'reverence for order'.[7]

Central to this effort, at both elementary and secondary levels, was the teaching of religion, as a 'divine cure, for the bondage and misery' of the human condition, and as a vital security for the preservation of community order.[8] But here again a distinction must be made. Some were instinctively attached to the instruction provided by the Established Church, and thus wished to defend the voluntary schools within the framework of a state system. Others were more anti-clerical, and considered that the state should play a more active part not only in edu-

[4] Lubbock, *Addresses*, pp. 44–69, 90–1; Price, *What is education?*; Layard, 'Influence of education upon character', pp. 90–1.

[5] Froude, *Short studies*, ii, 367–75, 452–7, 462, 466; Hodder, *Shaftesbury*, iii, 453; Kingsley, *Alexandria*, pp. 50–1; for the queen, see Cooke and Vincent, *The governing passion*, p. 455.

[6] Kingsley, *Alexandria*, pp. 50–1; Froude, *Short studies*, ii, 367, 441, 464.

[7] Arnold might see the process as a '*harmonious* perfection' of 'all sides of our humanity' (*Culture and anarchy*, p. 11); Huxley might picture it as the fashioning of a 'clear, cold' intellect 'in smooth working order', and a spirit 'full of life and fire', eager to 'love all beauty' and to 'hate all vileness': 'A liberal education', p. 370. See also Butler, *Public schools*, pp. 12–13; Seeley, 'Ethics and religion', pp. 505–11.

[8] Arnold, 'Irish Catholicism and British Liberalism', p. 330; Prothero, 'Disestablishment', pp. 263–4; Kingsley, *God's feast*, pp. 10–11.

cation but also in supplying a common religion which all sects could embrace. Those in the first group were more opposed to the drift of the provincial Liberal party towards a radical educational policy in the early 1870s than the second.

The first included most whig landowners, who had played an important role in preserving Anglican schools in their localities and, after 1870, intensified their efforts in the hope of preventing the need for school boards.[9] The same was obviously true of the clergymen: Temple, Fraser and Barry all hoped that Anglican effort after 1870 would provide enough education to avoid too much recourse to state interference. But, being on the liberal wing of the Church, they were like whig landowners in ultimately accepting both the help that school boards might give, and the undenominational religious teaching that they offered.[10] Despite this, a lot of whig-liberals were soon to develop increasing distaste for the board-school system, because of the centralisation and high rates which it imposed, together with the apparently incessant diminution in the degree of religious teaching which it produced. They complained that high rates for board-school teaching hit the middle-class Anglican ratepayer especially hard. If he wished to give his children a proper religious education in voluntary schools, he had to pay their fees as well; but he might then find them less well taught in secular subjects than children of a lower social class who had been educated in high-spending board schools subsidised by his own rates. This complaint was voiced especially frequently after the expansion of the board-school curriculum effected by the Liberals' New Code of 1882.[11] Already by 1874, 'right-wing' Liberal concern for the future of denominational schools was, as we shall see, an important cause of the election defeat of that year.

More advanced whig-liberals, however, viewed the Church's educational influence with suspicion, either on the grounds that she was hostile to scientific, historical and literary teaching,[12] or from a belief that the clergy did not inspire pupils. They charged that clergymen pandered to the baser interests and party temperament of their flocks, instilled 'bitterness . . . and ill-will', and prevented the possibility of a national compulsory system without which the imposition of morality

[9] E.g. Fitzwilliam, *Times*, 21 February 1902, p. 8.

[10] Sandford, *Exeter episcopate of Temple*, pp. 87–94; Barry, *True education*, p. 12; 'The new school boards', pp. 287–8; Fraser, *National Education Union 1873*; Hughes, *Fraser*, pp. 184–8; Cruickshank, *Church and state*, pp. 51–2.

[11] Earl Fortescue to Brereton, 20 March 1872, Brereton papers, F 4 72; Fortescue, *Rate-and-tax-aided education*; *Public schools for the middle classes*; Brereton, 'Middle schools', p. 876; Torrens, *Twenty years*, pp. 370–8; Finlayson, *Shaftesbury*, p. 490.

[12] Stoddart, *Blackie*, i, 229; Huxley, *Huxley*, iii, 10.

was impossible.[13] A lot of whig-liberals, especially in parliament, did not regard denominational schools with great favour. Many, including even Shaftesbury,[14] disliked the increase in the government grant to denominational schools in June 1870, while a large number were prepared to support the repeal of Clause 25 of the 1870 Act for the same reasons.

In fact, however, it was not impossible for even these two schools of thought to find common ground. Lord Henley was a typical whiggish MP in hoping after 1870 that in his area recourse to a school board would not be necessary, and in then coming round to the idea that board schools were most efficient in extending educational provision. He was thus prepared to surrender voluntary Anglican instruction, as long as a broad agreement on *religious* teaching under state control was secured.[15] Underlying this willingness to compromise was the belief that denominational *exclusiveness* was wrong, but that as long as some degree of religion was taught children would benefit, especially since at a young age their understanding was not sufficiently developed to cope with theological distinctions.

For whig-liberals, then, two considerations were of the essence – considerations which they shared with Forster, the architect of the 1870 Act (who was an archetypal whig-liberal, although he is discussed in chapter 4). Firstly, that the religion taught should be broad enough to placate different sects and teach the 'common Christianity' which was the essence of faith.[16] This was a religion in which there would 'lurk no seed for wars, no standing-ground for the Sacerdotal element, no fair pretexts or gorgeous disguises for the low bad passions of humanity'.[17] All could agree that the bible should form the basis of educational teaching. For broad churchmen, it revealed 'Christian truth free from sectarian dogma',[18] and displayed Christ's behaviour as the perfect example for mankind to follow, if it wished to develop its 'hidden possibilities'.[19] Men like Huxley wanted it taught because it set forth an 'ethical ideal' which could 'govern and guide conduct'.[20] Froude thought that accepting the moral example of the bible was more important – and safer – than accepting it as literal truth.[21] Shaftesbury, of course, regarded it as the 'eternal rock' of evangelical teaching; and saw the sects' failure to unite in agreeing to enforce its teaching as a national crime.[22] The London school

[13] *Letters of Aberdare*, i, 244–5; Kingsley, *Kingsley*, ii, 299–302; Russell, *Essays*, p. 344.
[14] Finlayson, *Shaftesbury*, pp. 488–9.   [15] *Northampton Mercury*, 7 February 1874.
[16] (Stanley) *Globe*, 27 February 1873, p. 4.   [17] Greg, 'Rocks ahead', pp. 358–9.
[18] Arnold, 'Literature and dogma', *passim*.
[19] Caird, *Christian manliness*, p. 30; see also Seeley, *Ecce Homo*.
[20] Huxley, *Huxley*, ii, 26–33, iii, 336; Bibby, *Huxley on education*, pp. 108–17.
[21] *Short studies*, ii, 375.
[22] Hodder, *Shaftesbury*, ii, 114; Shaftesbury, *National Education Union 1870*, pp. 3–4.

board imposed compulsory bible-reading in its schools, on a joint motion brought by the Conservative W. H. Smith, and by the evangelical nonconformist Samuel Morley: the vote was thirty-eight to three in its favour.[23] Nearly all whig-liberals supported Cowper-Temple's famous amendment to the 1870 Act preventing the teaching of particular catechisms and formularies in state schools. Although many were happy with that, others wanted to strike a further blow against denominational teaching by *restricting* religious education to bible-teaching or even bible-reading.

Secondly, whig-liberals generally agreed in protesting stridently against the proposals of nonconformists and secularists to remove religious teaching from schools.[24] Kingsley and Russell, who had been members of the National Education League, condemned its move towards secularism after 1871. Hughes joined the National Education Union (the body, dominated by Anglicans, which was founded in 1869 in order to defend the place of religious teaching and voluntary schools in an extended educational system) over the same question.[25] It is possible to trace interesting minor deviations in Forster's public position on educational policy, but he never wavered in opposition to secularism.[26] Shaftesbury saw 'the whole of the future history of this vast empire . . . wrapped up in the issue', because, if secularism in education were enforced, the idea of individual responsibility to God would be toppled by that of gratification of man's desires.[27] Not only did secularism remove the guarantee that all children would receive a spiritual education; both Shaftesbury and Russell saw that one of its great dangers was that it gave high churchmen the chance to impose sectional views and dogmas in the classroom in the hours allocated to teaching by the various sects – Shaftesbury believed that this was why Gladstone favoured it.[28] (Lowe and one or two other Benthamites, for example Horsman, were in favour of secularism in rate-founded schools, although not dogmatically. One powerful reason for this, certainly in Lowe's case, was that it would encourage people to use, and to give money to, volun-

---

[23] Philpott, *London at school*, pp. 25–6; (Brodrick leading article) *Times*, 24 June 1871.
[24] (Harcourt) Garvin, *Chamberlain*, i, 142; Kingsley to Dilke, 28 February 1871, Dilke papers, 43909, fo. 194; Argyll to Gladstone, 20 April 1870, Gladstone papers, 44101, fo. 227; Thompson, *Kelvin*, ii, 1091; Earl Fortescue to Brereton, 29 December 1871, Brereton papers, F 11 71; Price, 'University tests'; Graham, *H. M. Butler*, p. 347; Shaftesbury, *National Education Union 1870*, p. 6; Greg, 'Rocks ahead', p. 347; *Spectator*, 27 January 1872, pp. 101–2.
[25] Akroyd, Cowper-Temple, Westminster, Zetland, Lord Lawrence and most Liberal bishops were also among the members of the NEU.
[26] Temmel, 'Liberal versus Liberal', p. 618.
[27] *National Education Union 1870*, p. 8.
[28] *Ibid.*, pp. 4–5, 8; Hodder, *Shaftesbury*, iii, 267; Russell, *Essays*, p. 344.

tary schools teaching religion. Thus, by discouraging the expansion of the state system, it would minimise the need for tax- and rate-aid to education.)[29]

The major vehicle for the inculcation of moral and unsectarian education beyond elementary level was the vast network of public schools, whose story is a familiar one. Much effort was also expended on promoting unsectarian middle-class education, on the principle, advocated by Matthew Arnold and others, that the established middle classes, Anglican and nonconformist, would benefit from being educated together: they might then work jointly to defend their social position, rather than engaging in damaging sectional and political quarrels.[30] This idea inspired Brereton's establishment of private county schools for farmers' sons, and of a private college in Cambridge – which was intended to crown his system by taking middle-class boys at sixteen and offering a university education which hard-pressed ratepayers could afford. He wished to reconcile the Church and nonconformity, and the aristocracy and the middle classes. He saw a liberalisation of middle-class education to be necessary because the professions, commerce and the Church were all staffed by men whose minds were cramped and narrow.[31] His schools taught the 'common Christianity' of the New Testament in order to bring the sects together.[32]

As was noted in the introduction, whig-liberals were happy to use the power of the state to reform the exclusive structure both of existing endowed schools, and of the universities. Hardly any wished to see endowments which had been 'bequeathed by the people's friends in old times, just to educate poor scholars', now being appropriated for a few 'aristocrats' to 'go on rolling in riches'.[33] The only MPs who opposed the work of the Endowed Schools Commission after 1869 were those with vested interests to protect – or, occasionally, clergymen, when individual schemes threatened to place control of schools in anti-clerical hands.[34] Lowe in theory wished to *abolish* all educational endowments of this sort

---

[29] Marcham, 'Educating our masters', p. 187. See Horsman, *Hansard*, ccii, 914, 24 June 1870.

[30] Earl Fortescue, *Public schools for the middle classes*, p. 92.

[31] Brereton, *County education*, p. 1; 'Cavendish college', pp. 362–6, 374–5; see also Honey, *Tom Brown's universe*, p. 101.

[32] Brereton, 'Middle schools', pp. 873–4; *County education*, p. 12; 'Cavendish college', pp. 371–2.

[33] Kingsley, *Alton Locke*, pp. 49, 134, 137–8. See Cartwright diary, 13 May 1873, Cartwright papers, 6/10.

[34] For London MPs' dislike of the Emanuel Hospital scheme, see below, p. 146; for Tait's opposition to the 1873 scheme which gave substantial control of King Edward VI's school, Birmingham, to the Birmingham Town Council, see Marsh, *Victorian Church in decline*, pp. 69–70.

on the grounds that they checked effort, but knew this to be impracticable.[35]

Latitudinarians also pressed for reforms in university education, since they were of the opinion that in that field, also, the Church's exclusiveness was hindering the task of national cooperation. They called, firstly, for the abolition of university tests, which discriminated against nonconformists and the growing number of avowed freethinkers.[36] They argued that universities should not be 'clerical seminaries', but should be open to all classes and sects in order to encourage the propagation of the highest ideas. From these reformed institutions could be trained a future national leadership, emerging from diverse sectional backgrounds but united in possessing an uncommonly developed understanding of the need to guide national progress in accordance with the truth, and a determination to resist 'the transient will of the majority'.[37] Hesitation on the issue was apparent only from Shaftesburyite evangelicals (because of the impulse it might give to freethinking),[38] and, less markedly, liberal clergymen.[39] Some men, like Brodrick, wished to go further and abolish clerical fellowships, in order to rid the colleges of their 'dogmatic immobility'.[40] This was a more controversial question for whig-liberals, and a number of laymen, as well as the liberal clerics, argued that they ought not to be abolished, since abolition would drive clergymen out of the mainstream of national life and away from all contact with improving culture.[41] But there was a general hope that, if clerical exclusiveness were diminished, 'professional and manufacturing men' would be encouraged to attend Oxford and Cambridge, making them 'the highest national school of Arts and Sciences as well as of Letters'. Mercantile men must be drawn into the universities in order to 'temper' their 'vulgarity' and to enlist the 'love of wealth' as the 'ally' of academic culture rather than as its 'arch-enemy'. The universities thus had a 'noble mission . . . the revival, it may be, of a taste for plain living and high thinking in English society'.[42] Playfair also urged the reform of the older English universities

---

[35] Sylvester, *Lowe*, pp. 147–9.

[36] See Ward, *Victorian Oxford*, p. 243; Harvie, *Lights of liberalism*, p. 76.

[37] Elliot, *Goschen*, i, 63; (Jowett) Coleridge, *Coleridge*, ii, 57; Liddell to H. W. Acland, 1870?, H. W. Acland papers, d 69, fo. 91; (Ellice) Cardwell to Gladstone, 15 January 1868, Gladstone papers, 44118, fo. 251; (Grey) *Hansard*, cciii, 228, 14 July 1870; Price, 'University tests', p. 143. For a list of whig-liberal activists on the university tests question in 1864, see Harvie, *Lights of liberalism*, pp. 246–56. For T. H. Green's similar views (quoted), see *ibid.*, p. 145.

[38] Finlayson, *Shaftesbury*, p. 475.

[39] Tait did not think retention of the test crucial: Marsh, *Victorian Church in decline*, p. 84.

[40] Brodrick, *Influence of the older English universities*, pp. 8, 11.

[41] Playfair, 'Universities and universities', p. 210; see, for Tait and Bradley, Marsh, *Victorian Church in decline*, pp. 86–8.

[42] Brodrick, *Influence of the older English universities*, pp. 17–19.

so that they might build 'technical knowledge on the basis of liberal culture', as the German and Scottish universities did, and might resume their 'old function of being the great liberalising power of the professions'.[43] This cultivating process could be facilitated by spreading university culture into the provinces: the University Extension movement was therefore warmly supported by, among others, Jowett, Lubbock and Goschen.[44]

Social reform

No area of Victorian domestic policy has been tackled as exhaustively as that concerning 'social questions'. Although this emphasis may have exaggerated their political significance, much of the work has been valuable in qualifying the popular nostrum that politicians believed in, and actively sought to create, a 'minimalist' state. There were doctrinaires, of course, but these were very few; politicians had to respond to problems and deal with them pragmatically, which often involved legislation. It is possible to draw distinctions between the attitudes of different whig-liberals on social questions, but the task is fraught with difficulty and confusion,[45] and the distinctions usually of little relevance in understanding the party divisions of the 1880s.

It is true that in 1882, a few whig-liberals helped to found the Liberty and Property Defence League (LPDL), in order to protest against what they saw as the spectre of socialism, and thus developed a rigid opposition to 'interventionism'.[46] In discussing the preceding period, however, what is striking is whig-liberals' interest in practical questions of government. In some cases, this interest was merely with administration:

---

[43] Playfair, 'Universities and universities', p. 207; *Universities in their relation*, p. 12.

[44] Abbott and Campbell, *Jowett*, i, 377, ii, 57–61; Hutchinson, *Avebury*, ii, 37–8; Goschen, *Mental training*.

[45] To give three examples: Carlyle greatly influenced Stephen in his dislike of *laissez-faire*, and approved of Stephen's works; but they took a different view of *Ginx's baby*, the work of the nonconformist philanthropist Edward Jenkins, which aimed to uncover the social cost and absurdity of English *laissez-faire*. Carlyle was impressed; Stephen found it as sentimental as he did Dickens: Froude, *Carlyle*, ii, 398–9; Stephen, *J. F. Stephen*, pp. 155, 345. Again, Kingsley strongly supported the movement for sanitary reform (Turner, 'Rainfall, plagues', pp. 50–2), and attacked the Manchester school and Greg (Kingsley, *Kingsley*, i, 312, 314). But Kingsley emphasised the primary importance, not of legislation, but of voluntary example; while Greg, in fact, advocated central government interference in many areas. Both criticised equally the lack of fibre in the new radical middle class, and their resulting fear of a firm administration of the law, especially for murder. Kingsley, *Kingsley*, ii, 83; Greg, *Enigmas of life*, pp. 7–10. Again, Argyll criticised both the evils of centralised government, and unbridled political economy: *Unseen foundations*, pp. xi, 546–8.

[46] Earl Fortescue, Torrens and Brereton were members. See Bristow, 'Liberty and Property Defence League'.

in others, it was with substantial measures of land, local government, or humanitarian reform. But all believed that government had the capacity for wise administration, and were anxious that it should use this beneficially. When Greg argued that useful action was possible in a number of areas – in the housing, feeding and education of the poor, in sewerage, in drainage, in London government, in the prevention of crime, in poor law, rating, railway, army and navy and legal reform – he only rarely specified precisely what action would be desirable, but announced that a wise executive would select proper policies.[47] His own vagueness did not prevent him contrasting, as did the *Edinburgh*, the comfort, prosperity, aestheticism, soberness and cleanliness of the poor and middle classes in Germany with the standards prevailing in England. While arguing that Germanic centralisation was taken too far, he thought that it had enabled her to avoid the British vices – vices of overcrowding, and supine administration of the poor law and criminal codes – which had encouraged disease and alcoholism, pauperism and crime.[48] Froude's *History* had also displayed the social advantages of an active state, if its activity did not develop into a pauperising paternalism.[49]

Whig-liberal approval of a specific 'social policy' depended, above all, on its moral effect: on whether it encouraged or attacked 'materialism'. If whig-liberals had an abstract conception of 'the state' (and many did not), it was a 'minimalist' one only in contrast to alternatives – socialism, for example – about which there was certainly concern, but not yet obsession. Socialism was merely one form of 'materialism'; and alarm about it was most commonly expressed by pointing to the example of the Commune, which was seen primarily as the logical end-point of more fundamental and entrenched French 'materialist' habits – political and religious.[50] The maintenance of a national Church Establishment, and the creation of a national undenominational educational system, stood at the centre of the domestic political ideology of the majority of whig-liberals: both displayed a commitment to what, in secular terminology, would be called a 'strong state'. A natural corollary of this was a similar crusade against 'materialism' and degradation in the 'social' sphere: in so far as this necessitated 'interventionism', it was demanded. There was no paradox involved in arguing that the function of 'interventionism' was to set man morally and spiritually free: that, for example, the improve-

---

[47] Greg, *Miscellaneous essays*, pp. 122–43; *Political problems*, pp. 244–51; 'Cost of party government'.
[48] Greg, *Literary and social judgments*, pp. 57–74; *Enigmas of life*, pp. 7–10; Croskerry, 'Drunkenness, abstinence', pp. 398–9.
[49] *History*, i, 31–78; see also *Short studies*, i, 209, ii, 308–47.
[50] See below, p. 128.

ment of working-class dwellings would advance not only the 'physical comfort [of working-men] but their moral regeneration'.[51]

Viewed in this context, the attitudes of whig-liberals clearly had a common basis. The prime concern of the 'Christian socialists', for example, was not compulsory state philanthropy, but the need to arouse a 'sense of duty' to others, to 'realis[e] the kingdom of God and his righteousness'.[52] Men must recognise that 'the physical and intellectual improvement of every human being' was 'a duty no less sacred than his spiritual welfare', and that 'the morals, health, lives of thousands are at stake, from the negligence and superstition of those whom God has sent to teach men their duty to Him and each other'.[53] But Christian socialists were extremely anxious to denigrate those who sought to 'raise men by only making it easier to them to get what their appetites crave'.[54] They hoped that in a state properly infused with Christianity, 'the chivalrous and kindly gentleman' would have multiplied 'in such enormous numbers . . . that legislation against evil would presently cease to be needed'.[55]

It followed from their common assumptions that whig-liberals should 'endeavour to be perpetually ameliorating those laws and institutions which, being human, cannot be perfect, but which, according to the progress of society and the change of circumstances must be continually in need of emendation and extension'.[56] The ideal of whig government had been conscientious departmental administration, each department pursuing specific pragmatic objectives in association with parliament without overpowering ideological direction from the leadership.[57] Carlyleans, ex-Manchester school radicals like Greg, and academic liberals like Jowett all defended intervention by the state in social questions, since it was 'the corporate reason of the community'. They believed that interference was necessary in order to help men to help themselves, and in order to repress manifestations of evil. The difficulty came in deciding, in each case, according to pragmatic considerations, how far wayward and anti-social behaviour was to be tolerated in the interests of personal freedom.[58]

The real distinction, therefore, was made between legislation that promoted pauperism and that which encouraged individual responsibility.[59]

[51] Croskerry, 'Drunkenness, abstinence'.
[52] Davies, *Social questions*, pp. 199ff, esp. pp. 252–3, 270–1.
[53] Kingsley, *Kingsley*, i, 415, 417.　　　　[54] Davies, *Order and growth*, pp. 130–1.
[55] Begbie, *Albert Grey*, p. 95.
[56] (Palmerston, 1856) Steele, 'Gladstone and Palmerston', p. 121; see also Vincent, *Formation of the Liberal party*, pp. 146–8.
[57] Southgate, *Passing of the whigs*, pp. 210–12.
[58] Huxley, 'Administrative nihilism', pp. 530–8. Abbott and Campbell, *Jowett*, ii, 253.
[59] E.g. Argyll, 'Christian socialism', pp. 699–705.

At the root of this was an increasing identification (interesting, given the disillusionment with the Liberal party noticeable in so many suburban constituencies after the 1860s) with the plight of the lower middle-class ratepayer – with the thrifty family man, the fundholder, shopkeeper, clergyman and clerk, whose positions seemed to be threatened by a bureaucracy concerned to gratify the whims of the irresponsible masses.[60] From 1868, concern at the growth of demoralising pauperism, and the burden of local taxation, was marked, and not only within the ranks of the LPDL.[61] In the early 1880s, Shaftesbury was led to support the idea of national insurance: this idea, whatever its later connotations, was prompted by an evangelical drive to relieve the provident from the burden of maintaining the improvident, and to encourage the latter to help themselves.[62]

There was, as the *Edinburgh* perceived in 1873, a growing recognition that a 'wise State' might intervene constructively, might 'act with advantage, without any undue interference with individual liberty'.[63] (For example, it argued that the state should encourage the working-man to save and plan ahead, by allowing consols to be sold at post offices and by reforming stamp duty and share regulations; and that the evil of drunkenness would be diminished by a number of private and legislative initiatives.)[64] Of course, there were disagreements about the extent to which legislative interference was valuable. Carlyleans and evangelicals, broadly speaking, opposed latitudinarians and intellectuals in advocat-

---

[60] Greg, *Miscellaneous essays*, pp. 21–3.

[61] Argyll, 'Christian socialism', p. 696; *Unseen foundations*, pp. 134–49, 562. For Goschen in January 1868, see Vincent, *Journals of Lord Stanley*, pp. 327–8. See also Dodson, 'The Church, the land and the Liberals'.

[62] Shaftesbury approved of the proposal of William Blackley, the evangelical and Germanophile Hampshire rector, which shared common parentage with some of the German national insurance schemes. Blackley argued that 'our National Improvidence is a hindrance to our true approach to [God] as a nation': Blackley, *Thrift*, p. 129. The nation was heading for 'ruin' because of the demoralisation of the lower classes, who were failing in man's 'universally admitted duty' to provide for his own old age. Pauperism was evil in itself and fostered 'immeasurable social discords' – discords between the demoralised and the thrifty, and between the thrifty (made insecure by high rates) and the rich: *ibid.*, pp. 45–7, 57, 131–8. The 'struggling industrious ratepayer' was being asked to pay to support the declining years of drunken labourers and their widows and children, when those labourers had spent their youth 'continually and brutally drinking, and living almost like savages'. The labourer of twenty, with no dependants, was able to lead a riotous, sensual and irresponsible life in the knowledge that the provident would later care for him: *ibid.*, pp. 50–1. Blackley therefore recommended that, between the ages of seventeen and twenty-one, the labourer should be forced to contribute £10 to a National Friendly Society, with which he could be supported in old age. This scheme would cost the state nothing and would greatly reduce the rates: *ibid.*, pp. 51–7.

[63] Seebohm, 'Savings of the people', p. 114; Croskerry, 'Drunkenness, abstinence', p. 398. See also *Economist*, 6 April 1872, p. 414.

[64] Seebohm, 'Savings of the people', pp. 109–14; Croskerry, 'Drunkenness, abstinence'.

ing temperance legislation; the latter disliked the compulsion which it entailed.[65] The same dislike of interference for its own sake, interference which seemed to strike a blow at the independence of communities or of deserving citizens, was at the root of a very popular whig-liberal cry against the Gladstone government, orchestrated by Harcourt. He and allies like Cowper-Temple, Fawcett, Westminster and Russell, exploited a series of issues after 1870 – popular access to commons, parks, and the Thames Embankment, personal freedom to eschew the ballot in voting, the iniquity of introducing a royal warrant in order to enforce the abolition of army purchase, and some of the clauses of the Licensing and Local Government Bills. He alleged that Gladstone's was 'a grand-maternal Government which ties nightcaps on a grown-up nation by Act of Parliament'.[66]

To conclude, two things bear emphasising. Firstly, whig-liberals considered the extension of education to be the most important social reform of all, in helping men 'to help themselves'.[67] Secondly, despite all these disagreements on the merits of specific policies – which, of course, were mirrored in all other sections of the party – they were anxious to reiterate that a wise administration was bound to promote physical and moral regeneration better than a government which was influenced by sectional 'materialistic' pressures and by inflammatory demagogues. For Shaftesbury, and for many others, 'Democracy' must be prevented because it implied the overthrow of administration by unbiassed experts – which had benefited the higher physical and spiritual interests of the people – in favour of a materialistic and demagogic chaos.[68] For the same reason, a self-styled 'Christian Socialist' opposed the extension of the county franchise in the 1880s.[69]

The party system

There were frequent complaints after 1867 that parliamentary concentration on constructive matters, necessary as it was, would be threatened by the totally different expectations of the mass electorate, unless that electorate were well-disciplined. A 'vast . . . field of social amelioration' required harvesting, and a 'much more energetic system of government' was needed, but there were two difficulties. The first was that the numerical preponderance of the wage class in the new electorate might disturb the ability of the executive to govern impartially between classes.

---

[65] Harrison, *Drink and the Victorians*, pp. 288–90, 294–6. See Gardiner, *Harcourt*, i, 209–10; Mount-Temple, *Memorials*, pp. 88–9.

[66] Gardiner, *Harcourt*, i, 240.   [67] Seebohm, 'Savings of the people', p. 119.

[68] Finlayson, *Shaftesbury*, pp. 485–6.   [69] Begbie, *Albert Grey*, pp. 69, 156.

The second was that the dry and tedious debates on 'most urgent social and administrative reform' which were so necessary might be set aside in favour of more exciting political fun and games – sectional cries capable of gratifying clamouring enthusiasts. This seemed to bode extremely ill for the future survival of moral politics, especially as the sorts of initiatives usually mooted in order to appease the sectionalists were religious or financial ones.[70]

Expressions to this effect were not, it must be stressed, usually reactions to failings of the first Gladstone government. In accordance with the traditional view of the party's talents, there continued to be a widespread confidence in the Liberals' superior capacity to promote administrative reform. Of course, there were individual complaints at specific measures, as we shall see, but, on the whole, Liberals approved of the government's attitude to administrative and social questions.[71]

Notwithstanding this, in the decade after the 1867 Reform Act was passed, it came to be widely accepted (among non-office-holders) that it had threatened traditional governing principles – described by Reeve as government by 'the best', by those most representative of the 'intelligence, the property, and the highest honour and culture of the nation'.[72] It was seen to be essential to ensure that the state continued to be ruled by a class 'released from the necessity of manual labour', in order that 'refinement' and 'enlarged views' might be propagated.[73] Lowe, Stephen, Bagehot and others saw no merit in the dominance of the ignorant, which they believed had been encouraged by the 1867 Act,[74] and which it was thought would be further guaranteed by a new extension of the county franchise.[75] Some thought that the passage of the secret ballot in 1872 accentuated these problems, while itself being irresistible because of the strength of popular support for it.[76] Hartington was one who did not

---

[70] Grey to Halifax, 26 October 1867, Hickleton papers, A 4 55; Froude, *Short studies*, ii, 343–4; Greg, *Political problems*, p. 242; Halifax to Charles Grey, 13 January 1868, Charles Grey papers; Reeve, 'Claims of whig government', pp. 582–5; Trelawny diary, 8 April 1872, Trelawny papers, d 419, p. 11; (Stephen) Roach, 'Liberalism and the Victorian intelligentsia', p. 62.

[71] See e.g. Reeve, 'Claims of whig government'; *Times*, 14 October 1873, p. 9; Brodrick to Dufferin, 14 January 1874, Dufferin papers; *Economist*, 17 January 1874, p. 68.

[72] Reeve, 'John Stuart Mill', p. 108.

[73] Somerset, *Monarchy and democracy*, pp. 148–9.

[74] Martin, *Sherbrooke*, ii, 510; Bagehot, *Biographical studies*, p. 311; Roach, 'Liberalism and the Victorian intelligentsia', p. 72. See Dicey on the effect of the 1867 Act in hindering the reform of the Poor Law: Harvie, *Lights of liberalism*, p. 196.

[75] Greg, *Miscellaneous essays*, pp. 168–71; Earl Fortescue, *Our next leap in the dark*; Begbie, *Albert Grey*, p. 69.

[76] For the complaints of the *Spectator*, Shaftesbury and Grey at its corrupting effects on public life, see *Spectator*, 20 April 1872, p. 488; Finlayson, *Shaftesbury*, p. 476; Haultain, *Goldwin Smith's correspondence*, pp. 131–2. See also Kinzer, 'The un-Englishness of the

enjoy canvassing or the hustings: besides the unpleasantness involved in the process, 'almost all the gentlemen being on the other side, the society is not agreeable'.[77] In early 1869, he described the electors in his new Radnor seat as a 'set of ignorant idiots'.[78]

Under the new system, it was increasingly complained, most votes could be acquired by demagogues, wire-pullers, fanatics, priests and union agitators.[79] This view was expressed most vividly by Carlyle and his disciples, and by the old whigs.[80] But it came to be felt just as strongly by the younger liberal intellectuals.[81] Indeed, as early as 1860, Brodrick had written in the *Saturday Review* attacking the drift that characterised governments which seemed to have become frightened by 'democratic' politicians, and to have ignored the overridingly important attribute without which society could not properly function – the 'individual will'.[82] In fact, none of these feelings were new to the Liberal conscience after 1867. The Christian socialists had had them in the 1840s, when they had urged the working-man to eschew demands for franchise reform in favour of social reform and concentration on the inner life;[83] half the cabinet, and probably half the party, had had them in 1866.[84] Many, indeed, had complained at Palmerston for holding up the course of franchise reform, and thus unnaturally radicalising the pressure for it.[85]

The real source of objection after 1867 was the willingness of the parliamentary party to be pushed in directions to which it had proved resistant before. These concerns were to some extent a reaction simply to the phenomenon of popular political activity, and they thus became especially potent after the agitation of 1876 against the Bulgarian atrocities, and that of 1879–80 at Midlothian. Another element greatly adding to whig-liberal concern in the late 1870s was the institution of the caucus system.[86] In 1877, Bagehot complained how 'any gust of popular excitement' ran through constituencies 'instantly'; in 1882, Reeve condemned politicians for acting always to obey 'every gust of the popular

secret ballot', for a significant connection between anti-Catholic and anti-ballot rhetoric.
[77] Hartington to Granville, 13 September 1868, Granville papers, 30/29/22A/4.
[78] Hartington to Devonshire, 26 January 1869, Chatsworth papers 340, fo. 408.
[79] Greg, 'Priests, parliament and electors', pp. 284, 287; Froude, *English in Ireland*, iii, 1–4.
[80] Carlyle, 'Shooting Niagara', p. 321. Blackie thought that the 1867 Act would destroy the 'just influence of the middle and upper classes' and hand power to demagogues: Blackie and Jones, *Democracy*, pp. 12–17, 41. See also Stephen, *Liberty, equality, fraternity*, p. 212.
[81] See Harvie, *Lights of liberalism*, and Roach, 'Liberalism and the Victorian intelligentsia'.
[82] *Political studies*, pp. 133–8.
[83] Hughes, *Kingsley*, i, 10–12.
[84] Smith, *Second Reform Bill*, pp. 61–6, 82–3, 108–11, 255–6.
[85] Grey to Halifax, 26 October 1867, Hickleton papers, A 4 55; (Grant Duff) Harvie, *Lights of liberalism*, p. 121.
[86] Brodrick, *Political studies*, p. 276.

will'.[87] In 1878, Lowe argued that the new political dispensation was ensuring the quick extinction of the agent of the 'most beneficial laws' passed since 1832, the 'moderate Liberal party'.[88] By 1882, Grant Duff had also realised that demagogues and 'loathsome' commercial men had 'vulgarised' the whole political system.[89] But already in 1871, Grey pointed to the vacillations in official policy towards staffing the army before and after the Franco-Prussian war scare, and discerned an unedifying desire merely to follow gusts of popular passion – cheese-paring one day, war-mongering the next.[90] In 1870, Halifax thought that a government influenced primarily by common sense would retain the army purchase system.[91] In 1873, Argyll – a member of the cabinet – considered the 'policy of looking out for a "Cry" before a Dissolution . . . odious if not immoral'.[92]

The political effects of the extended franchise threatened to be especially alarming in financial and religious policy. Grey maintained that the weakened executive was no longer able to withhold demands for tax reductions and defence cuts, even when they were against the national interest.[93] There was a feeling of insecurity lest a redistributive taxation policy be pursued;[94] Kimberley and the *Edinburgh* criticised Gladstone for not tackling the question of local taxation, and implicitly ascribed this to its espousal by the landed interest.[95] Goschen in effect terminated his Liberal career in 1877 when he attacked the idea of further reductions in the county franchise – on the grounds that governments had already, on two occasions since 1867, given in to pressure to tax the higher salaried classes less favourably than the poor.[96]

Behind the concern over the caucus in the late 1870s also lay dislike of the standard nonconformist demands, for disestablishment and secular education. In politics, as in religion, there was a general distrust of the influence of 'large bodies of men, especially large parties of men' who were, 'by the very reason of their moving in masses and parties, likely to be mistaken'.[97] Nonconformists' influence over the party after 1867 was, as we shall see, much criticised. The most famous intellectual attack on

---

[87] Bagehot, *Biographical studies*, p. 316; Reeve, 'A whig retort', p. 281.

[88] 'A modern "symposium" ', pp. 183–4.

[89] Rendel, *Personal papers*, p. 228.

[90] Grey, Letter on the alarming state of public affairs, December 1871, Grey papers.

[91] Halifax to Dalhousie, 4 March 1870, Dalhousie papers, GD 45/14/689/174.

[92] Argyll to Dufferin, 18 August 1873, Dufferin papers. See also Shaftesbury on the 1874 election, in Finlayson, *Shaftesbury*, p. 559.

[93] Grey, Letter on the alarming state of public affairs, December 1871, Grey papers.

[94] Lowe, *Speeches and letters on reform*, p. 8; Lubbock, *Addresses*, pp. 103–18.

[95] Drus, *Journal of Kimberley*, pp. 35, 43; Dodson, 'The Church, the land and the Liberals'.

[96] *Hansard*, ccxxxv, 563–6, 29 June 1877; Elliot, *Goschen*, i, 163; Goschen, *Cultivation of the imagination*, pp. 37–8. See also Greg, *Miscellaneous essays*, p. 172.

[97] Stanley, *Church of Scotland*, p. 168; *Essays on Church and state*, pp. 356, 358, 367.

it came from Matthew Arnold, for whom nonconformists combined the low tone endemic in commercial life with unsound views on Church and state: they had no conception of the ends of a moral polity, and it was a matter of grave concern that they were gaining increased power within the party. They must learn to 'value and found a public and national culture';[98] this would not be done by insisting on disestablishment and voluntary education, nor by obsession with sectional trivia, nor by Gladstone's Irish policy. In 1869, Arnold saw it as his 'true business' to 'sap . . . intellectually' the nonconformists who had prevented the application of concurrent endowment on the Irish Church Bill, and also to sap the House of Commons 'so far as it is ruled by the Protestant Dissenters'.[99]

Only two remedies for these problems presented themselves after 1867, and the likelihood of success in them influenced the degree of pessimism as to the future. The first was, naturally, the extension of education, the only chance, according to Lowe in 1871, of taming the 'monster within whose claws' the 'narrow-minded and ignorant' radical and nonconformist reformers had placed the country.[100] Hartington and Brodrick continued to insist that the natural leaders of public opinion must continue to define policy initiatives for the grass-roots to follow, and must act responsibly.[101] The second remedy was a political one. It was maintained that the Liberal party must reassert what, in the mid seventies, Reeve and Brodrick both called its 'whig principles': principles of firm, impartial government, of anti-sectionalism in politics and Church affairs, of the rule of law, and of confidence in political economy and in the supremacy of expert opinion.[102] It was argued that the most moderate Liberals and Conservatives – emphatically not Disraeli – must cooperate, and eschew demagogy, unpredictability and fanaticism, in favour of constitutional government and stability, wise reformist administration, the defence of the nationality of the Church Establishment, the bible in schools, the monarchy and the rule of law.[103] This was not (at least usually) a call for a 'middle party' – which would leave radicals, nonconformists and Irish nationalists in charge of an advanced one – but for a 'middle government', representing the most central views of both parties.[104]

---

[98] *Culture and anarchy*, p. 207.
[99] Russell, *Letters of Arnold*, ii, 17–18.   [100] Martin, *Sherbrooke*, ii, 462–3.
[101] Hartington, *Address 1879*, pp. 9–10; Brodrick, 'Progress of democracy', pp. 923–4.
[102] Reeve, 'Past and future of the whig party'; 'Plain whig principles'; Brodrick, *Political studies*, pp. 212–56.
[103] Grey, Letter on the alarming state of public affairs, December 1871, Grey papers; Akroyd, *On the present attitude of political parties*; *Economist*, 6 April 1872, p. 414; Greg, *Enigmas of life*, pp. xlvii–xlviii.
[104] *Economist*, 17 January 1874, p. 62. See Drus, *Journal of Kimberley*, p. 1.

After 1867, disillusioned Liberal ministers came to argue that 'no man of honorable feeling or of any refinement will go into political life'. The political system, party organisation, the lack of individual responsibility and of scope for statesmanlike independence in politics, the premium placed on demagogy and flattery of sectional forces in the electorate, was – as Layard and Knatchbull-Hugessen maintained after 1870 – unappealing and ungentlemanly.[105] Layard was forced out of domestic politics in 1869, after an unhappy series of disputes with Ayrton at the Treasury, while he was first commissioner of works; Layard thought that Ayrton's lack of artistic interests, and parsimony, typified the new Liberalism.[106] Knatchbull-Hugessen and Grant Duff stayed at under-secretary level until 1874 and received no promotion thereafter; Grant Duff went to Madras in 1881. Dufferin and Normanby also left Britain for colonial appointments: Dufferin announced in 1871 that he was tired of domestic politics.[107] As Layard wrote to Gregory (who had been appointed to the governorship of Ceylon) in 1873, colonial governorship provided an 'independent position' in which one was able 'to mould things after one's own fashion': in English political life a man could no longer 'have his own way – whether in office or out of it'. His abilities would go unrecognised if they 'do not run him in the accepted groove', or if he did not accept being 'trammelled by . . . constituents or . . . colleagues'.[108]

These men were disappointed politicians. But their feelings were more widely shared: Bagehot, for example, came to have 'no sympathy with the *enthusiasms* of the Liberal party' after 1867.[109] Gladstone's greatest enthusiasms, of course, were the Bulgarian agitation and home rule, and it was particularly easy for whig-liberals to distrust the attitudes to Empire, to British power, to Catholicism and to the Orthodox Church that appeared to lie behind them.

Protestantism and foreign policy

The truths of a Christianity based not on dogma but on ethics and morals were, in theory, universally applicable; indeed it was not unknown for whig-liberals to suggest that it was the duty of the British to promote the

---

[105] Layard to Gregory, 15 August 1870, 21 February 1871, Layard papers, 38949, fos. 61, 83. See Hugessen to Granville, 22 February 1872, Granville papers, 30/29/73, fo. 495, and to Dufferin, 7 September 1872, Dufferin papers.
[106] Layard to Gregory, 5 March 1870, Layard papers, 38949, fo. 22. See Port, 'Contrast in styles'.
[107] Lyall, *Dufferin*, i, 150.
[108] Layard to Gregory, 6 February 1873, Layard papers, 38949, fo. 118.
[109] According to Hutton, and Bagehot himself: Stevas, *Bagehot*, v, 39.

conversion of the world to the Christian religion.[110] Conversion, of course, was the function of Macgregor's canoeing trips: he thought it 'strange and unfriendly to live with men for days, and not to impart one word to them about the great eternity in which they and we shall meet again most surely'.[111] Such feelings created a disposition – no more – in favour of an active foreign policy, as long as it was undertaken in order to promote Christian ends.[112] Demands for these policies were made most vociferously in the 1880s. It is true that there were already whig-liberal complaints at the foreign policy of the first Gladstone government, especially the reduction of troop numbers in the colonies, and the influence of commercial values on the conduct of foreign relations.[113] The *Pall Mall Gazette* headed a large number of Liberals who criticised the failure to strike a more aggressive tone during the Black Sea crisis of 1870 or the Alabama affair of 1871–2, and this line was shared in the cabinet, especially by the 'Pall Mallish' Goschen.[114] But there was as yet no serious challenge from within the party to a foreign policy dominated by principles of economy; and, in any case, conduct of foreign policy was invariably affected by so many considerations of national interest that discussion of it was not very susceptible to the application of abstract principle.

Nonetheless, attitudes to the East merit attention here, since the Bulgarian agitation of 1876 inspired a long-running argument within the party which had profound consequences for the future of Liberal politics. As Shannon showed, the bulk of whig-liberals were apathetic or hostile to the agitation.[115] Probably the most important determinant of their response was dislike of the prospect that the sober formulation of foreign policy (in which British interests were clearly at risk) would be prevented by frenzied and ignorant popular clamour – clamour, moreover, which

---

[110] Hodder, *Shaftesbury*, iii, 109; Caird, *Universal religion*, pp. 5, 7, 18; Davies, *Order and growth*, pp. 44–6; Kingsley, *Alexandria*, p. 66.

[111] Hodder, *Macgregor*, p. 332.

[112] Grogan, *Bosworth Smith*, pp. 154–5. See, on India, Stanley, *An Indian statesman*, pp. 7–15; *England and India*, pp. 12–13, 17; Hodder, *Shaftesbury*, iii, 59, 370; Greg, *Miscellaneous essays*, p. 43; Grey, 'South Africa', p. 953. Thomas Hughes promoted a settlement in Tennessee in order to spread Rugby's values to the United States: Briggs, *Victorian people*, p. 174. See Shannon, 'Seeley', p. 240.

[113] Froude, *Short studies*, ii, 328–9; Layard to Gregory, 12 September 1870, Layard papers, 38949, fo. 62; Russell, *Recollections*, p. 334; Buckle, *Letters of Victoria*, i, 584–5.

[114] Ramm, i, 161; Elliot, *Goschen*, i, 134–6; Kimberley to Gladstone, 26 February 1873, Gladstone papers, 44225, fo. 17; Layard to Gregory, 20 November 1870, 13 June 1872, Layard papers, 38949, fos. 67, 106; *Spectator*, 29 June 1872, p. 809.

[115] *Bulgarian agitation.*

was fuelled by 'various small ecclesiastical influences'.[116] However, there were other, more explicitly religious, considerations.

The whig-liberal conscience had always been sensitive to instances of apparent repression of liberty abroad. By the 1870s, it was, on the whole, far more sensitive than in the 1850s, and so support of the Ottoman empire could only be ventured cautiously and defensively, with much emphasis that the empire could not survive permanently – although similar arguments had in fact also been used twenty years previously.[117] Moreover, many whig-liberals actually joined the Bulgarian agitation, including not only conscience-stricken peers like Argyll, Russell and Westminster, but also Carlyle – and Froude, whose magazine argued that Britain's strategic interests would not be affected by a Russian conquest of Constantinople.[118] Because of these countervailing pressures, the views displayed below are less representative of the whole whig-liberal spectrum than those set out in other sections.

From the 1860s, there had developed considerable interest in Ottoman society and culture. It was connected with the expansion of archaeology promoted by Layard,[119] and with the impulse towards accurate evocation of the bible stories, which prompted the endeavours of the Palestine Exploration Fund. Frequent visits to the area were necessary, in order to confirm facts and silence doubts as to the bible's truthfulness, and to illuminate its message by bringing its context to life. Grove, Stanley, Reeve, Archbishop Thomson of York, Russell, Shaftesbury and Layard were involved with the Fund (as also were some high churchmen).[120] Shaftesbury, Layard and Macgregor were also advocates of the plan to find the jews a home in Palestine safe from Russian persecution. They, like Kingsley, Argyll, Stanley and Strachey, admired the jews' moral qualities and intense family loyalty, and the practical bent of their religion.[121]

Orientalism might take many forms. Stanley of Alderley, diplomat, traveller and linguist, became a Moslem, while Somerset's rakish son

---

[116] See e.g. Prothero, *Stanley*, ii, 486, 502; Brodrick, *Political studies*, pp. 246ff; *Memories and impressions*, p. 159.

[117] Hodder, *Shaftesbury*, iii, 389–93; Layard to Gregory, 2 December 1875, 30 November 1876, Layard papers, 38949, fos. 148, 161; Shaftesbury, *Hansard*, cxxxi, 591, 10 March 1854; Kingsley, *Alexandria*, pp. xiv–xix.

[118] Anon., 'Russia and Turkey'.

[119] See e.g. Hutchinson, *Avebury*, i, 138–41.

[120] See Stanley, *Sinai and Palestine in connection with their history* (London, 1856), and his 'Introduction' to *The recovery of Jerusalem*; Macgregor, *Rob Roy on the Jordan*, pp. 152–4; Tibawi, *British interests in Palestine*, pp. 183–205.

[121] Hodder, *Shaftesbury*, iii, 443–4, 509; Hodder, *Macgregor*, pp. 403–6; Layard, 'Turks and Greeks', p. 551; Kingsley, *Kingsley*, i, 258, 353–4; Argyll, *Unseen foundations*, p. 113; Stanley, *Lectures on the history of the Jewish Church* (3 vols., London, 1863–76); Strachey, *Jewish history and politics*; Warren, *The land of promise*.

dabbled in Islam and emigrated to Tangier.[122] Macgregor published a book on Turkish music; Edwin Arnold and G. A. Sala of the *Daily Telegraph* were committed Turcophiles,[123] as were Reginald Bosworth Smith and successive ambassadors to Constantinople, H. G. Elliot and Layard. Many others, like Dufferin, were 'rather friendly than otherwise to the Turk';[124] thus hinting at Palmerston's belief that the Turks were a 'highly improving and civilised race'.[125]

It was still possible to assert this, not because most whig-liberals still anticipated the conversion of the Ottoman empire to Christianity,[126] but because Islam could be defended, in itself, as a less developed form of Protestantism. It refused to tolerate idolatry and sacerdotalism; it was a practical, moralising religion, intimately linked with the civil power, encouraging philanthropy to the poor, sick, orphans and animals, and crusading against gambling and alcoholism.[127] Some felt that it had become corrupted and materialistic,[128] but the most common attitude was appreciation of the social and spiritual benefits which it provided.[129]

It was certainly seen as more acceptable than the threat – strategic, political, and religious – posed by Russia. Russia's potential influence in the Balkans was conceived to be so great because of her ability to win friends by developing the rhetoric of Orthodox solidarity, by wearing the 'party badge' which for the Greeks and other materialist Orthodox churchmen did duty for all spiritual commitment.[130] There was widespread whig-liberal dislike of the debasement, barbarism and immorality of the Orthodox Church, and of its sophistry.[131] In the 1850s, Layard and Kingsley, in particular, had alleged that its failure to understand the principles of political liberty, of moral government, and of the importance of family values in preserving political stability, had led inexorably to the decline of Byzantium. The corrupt, intriguing tyranny which it

---

[122] J. Colville, *Strange inheritance* (Wilton, 1983).

[123] Koss, *Political press in Britain*, pp. 200–3; Shannon, *Bulgarian agitation*, pp. 153–4.

[124] To Argyll, 21 November 1870, Dufferin papers.

[125] Bagehot, *Biographical studies*, p. 342.

[126] For this, see Shaftesbury, *Hansard*, cxxxi, 591, 10 March 1854; Layard, 'Turks and Greeks', pp. 545–56; Macgregor, *Rob Roy on the Jordan*, pp. 88–106.

[127] Bosworth Smith, *Mohammed and Mohammedanism*; Macgregor, *Rob Roy on the Jordan*, pp. 33–4. See also Layard, 'Turks and Greeks', pp. 542, 545; and the contribution of lapsed Jesuit and Arabist W. G. Palgrave to *Fraser's*, collected in *Essays on Eastern questions*, esp. pp. 1, 65–6.

[128] Kingsley, *Alexandria*, pp. xv–xix, 147–65.

[129] Palgrave, *Essays on Eastern questions*, pp. 66, 68. See (1845) Layard, *Autobiography*, ii, 90–1; Grogan, *Bosworth Smith*, p. 137; Kingsley, *Alexandria*, p. 170; Layard to Gregory, 13 August 1876, Layard papers, 38949, fo. 157.

[130] See Grant Duff, 'Russia', pp. 82–5; Vickers, 'The future of Turkey'; Palgrave, *Essays on Eastern questions*, pp. 177–9.

[131] E.g. Gregory, *Autobiography*, pp. 216, 268, 367–8; (the queen) *PMP*, iii, 239. See also Somerset, *Monarchy and democracy*, p. 183. Stanley was more tolerant: *Eastern Church*; Prothero, *Stanley*, i, 533.

became had been deservedly overthrown by 'Mohammedan invaders, strong by living trust in that living God, whom the Christians . . . were denying and blaspheming in every action of their lives'.[132] Even if there was now less willingness than before to defend the Ottoman empire, Russia was still regarded with much suspicion; and those Western high churchmen who were calling for reunion with the Orthodox Church were criticised for playing into her hands.[133]

Catholicism

The Orthodox Church was seen by some as an influential remnant of superstitious religion, providing an indication of the continued power of clericalist régimes for evil. But such feelings were held with much greater intensity in the case of the Roman Catholic Church, which was perceived as the most entrenched enemy of the liberal conscience.

Paradoxically, whig-liberals tended to be more tolerant of Catholicism, in one sense, than high churchmen: in their willingness to accept the doctrine of the temporal power of the papacy. Argyll, Stanley and Gregory all articulated a defence of the idea: 'spiritual jurisdiction of a central government over the visible Church was in itself no evil thing', because it established a 'great central fortress of law and order, resisting wild theories and destructive innovations'. The responsibilities of this position checked the pope's freedom of manoeuvre: he would accordingly be 'much more mischievous' in asserting his spiritual power, the real evil, once they were removed.[134]

But this argument was often deployed in order to contrast the high-church view of the Reformation, as merely 'a miserable contest' about the temporal power, with the proper view – the view which saw it as a 'cleansing of Faith from the leprosy of Superstition' and as the destruction of a system which was 'burying souls in delusion and deceit'.[135] The mediaeval Church, it was asserted, had at one stage provided men with protection against tyrannical behaviour, and had encouraged reverence and spiritual endeavour; but corruption and formalism had then entered into its soul.[136] Late mediaeval and modern-day Catholicism was condemned in the same terms as ritualism and Anglican sacerdotalism.[137]

---

[132] Layard, 'Turks and Greeks', pp. 537, 544; Kingsley's remarkable preface to *Hypatia*, pp. 9–10.

[133] H. E. J. Stanley (Stanley of Alderley), *The East and the West*, pp. 256–63.

[134] Argyll, *Presbytery examined*, p. 231; Gregory, *Autobiography*, p. 167; Prothero, *Stanley*, ii, 383.

[135] Argyll, *Presbytery examined*, pp. 228–9; see also Argyll to Gladstone, 12 October 1867, Gladstone papers, 44100, fo. 166.

[136] Forbes, *Liberal Anglican idea*, pp. 85, 104, 174; Kingsley, *Alton Locke*, p. 176.

[137] Froude, *Short studies*, i, 60–1, ii, 162; see also Price, 'Catholicity', p. 184; Oliphant, *Tulloch*, pp. 222–3; (Tennyson) Fuller-Maitland, *Reminiscences of Arthur Coleridge*, p. 166.

These attitudes inevitably affected whig-liberals' views towards foreign and Irish policy. They claimed to be tolerant of individual professions of Catholicism;[138] moreover, many whigs were reluctant to support political attacks on the Catholic Church, whether in 1850,[139] 1870,[140] or 1874.[141] In addition, whig-liberals would often advocate measures designed to extend the principle of civil liberty to Catholics.[142] Behind this lay a general assumption that, if progress flowed smoothly, men would become more spiritually aware, and the practical influence of Catholic dogma would inevitably decline.[143]

On the other hand, tolerance was tested by the apparent aggressiveness of the papacy, not so much in the doctrinal sphere, as in the political: it seemed to need to subvert civil liberty in order to enforce otherwise unconvincing doctrine. Wherever this aggressiveness manifested itself, whig-liberals considered that it should be checked. It was for this reason that Reeve maintained in 1873 that 'the opposition of civil liberty to clericalism is in all parts of Europe the great principle of the age';[144] it was for this reason that Layard was convinced in 1875 that 'a great struggle must arise sooner or later between the civil power and the Pope'.[145] It was this that made 'most of us live in great fear and horror of Romanism'.[146]

Despite protestations of toleration, Liberal policy abroad, especially on the Italian question, had often traded on the rhetoric of opposition to clerical exclusiveness in Catholic countries.[147] This ambivalence between advocating the use of state power to attack the intolerant, and reasserting principles of tolerance itself, was especially evident in whig-liberal attitudes to Germany. The more evangelical argued that Germany would be Britain's ally in the struggle against clericalism. Froude contended that it was because the Germans alone, by 1870, retained their 'faith in the living reality' that they were set fair for a

---

[138] Granville to Ripon, 27 August 1874, Ripon papers, 43521, fo. 125; Kimberley to Ripon, 22 August 1874, *ibid.*, 43522, fo. 251; (Houghton) Pope-Hennessy, *Milnes*, p. 238.

[139] Southgate, *Passing of the whigs*, p. 225.

[140] Matthew, 'Gladstone, Vaticanism', p. 429; Holland, *Devonshire*, i, 135; (Houghton) Pope-Hennessy, *Milnes*, p. 212.

[141] See below, p. 425.

[142] As when Cleveland and Trelawny proposed bills, in 1872 and 1873, to pay for the provision of a Catholic chaplain in prisons with a steady Catholic population: *Hansard*, ccx, 1798, ccxi, 360.

[143] Thirlwall, *Irish Church*, p. 9.

[144] Reeve, 'Claims of whig government', p. 575.

[145] Layard to Gregory, 8 May 1875, Layard papers, 38949, fo. 141. See also Shannon, 'Seeley', p. 252.

[146] Davies, *The Irish Church question*, p. 10.

[147] McIntire, *England against the papacy*; Layard, *Savonarola*, pp. 3, 14–15; Lewis, *Letters*, p. 389.

glorious future.[148] The queen, emboldened by her family connections, suggested that the Protestant Churches of Europe should unite in order to protest against 'sacerdotal tyranny' on the one hand and unbelief on the other.[149] She, Russell, Jowett and many others broadly approved of the *Kulturkampf*.[150] Similarly, Arnold and Stanley were glad to see German state power engaged in 'enlightening and purifying' the 'religious element in society', by bringing it more into accord with civilised feelings.[151] Others liked Bismarck's 'erastianism . . . in theory' but found his repression of religious liberties 'disagreeable' in practice;[152] the most tolerant whig-liberals accepted that the principle of the 'supremacy of the law' was a good one, but only if the laws in question were just and moral, which they believed they were not in this case.[153]

In the early 1870s, papal aggressiveness was causing concern in Spain, especially to Layard, after he became ambassador there; from 1874, he was alarmed at the control that Cánovas and the 'retrograde party' were winning over King Alfonso XII. The proposed educational reforms of 1875, for example, were 'perfectly monstrous as opposed to civil and religious liberty': Spain was 'really at the mercy of the Pope', whereas Alfonso should have been trying to win the support of the prosperous liberal respectable middle classes.[154] It was recent events in France, however, which provided the most graphic illustration of the tendency of all forms of 'materialism' to feed off each other. Many whigs, like Clarendon and Reeve, were traditionally attached to France, because she offered the best security for the maintenance of the balance of power; they were therefore appalled at her decline, and especially at the events of 1870–1. They argued that French history showed that clerical despotism led naturally to class hatred, violence and revolution (this, of course, had

---

[148] *Short studies*, ii, 366–7.

[149] After the 1870 war, she told Kaiser Wilhelm I that she hoped that Britain would support him in any future struggle with Catholic France; she was appalled at the suggestion of some English high churchmen that the Church of England should instead join forces with the Greek Orthodox Church: Fulford, *Darling child*, pp. 104, 114, 115; Bentley, *Ritualism and politics*, pp. 41–2; Ponsonby, *Ponsonby*, p. 177.

[150] Fulford, *Darling child*, p. 34; Walpole, *Russell*, ii, 446–7; Abbott and Campbell, *Jowett*, ii, 89.

[151] Arnold, 'Higher schools and universities', esp. p. 96; (Stanley) *Spectator*, 31 January 1874, pp. 134–5.

[152] Reid, *Houghton*, ii, 285. See also Thirlwall, *Letters literary*, p. 372.

[153] *Spectator*, 31 January 1874, pp. 134–5; see Reeve and Geffcken, 'Bismarck and the Church of Rome'.

[154] Layard to Gregory, 8 May, 2 December 1875, 10 May, 30 November 1876, Layard papers, 38949, fos. 141, 148, 153, 161. By 1875, Layard was becoming so heated in his views on Spain that he lost the support of Disraeli and the queen. He was arguing that 'the only way of dealing with Spaniards is to treat them as Palmerston did and let them know that we have a fleet of which we can make use if necessary': Waterfield, *Layard*, p. 345.

been the whig explanation for the events of 1789).[155] The 'narrow-minded' and 'ignorant' clergy were still giving a 'materialist' education in the nineteenth century: this had antagonised the thinking classes, who had reacted into atheism and subversion.[156] 'Passion for luxury and material enjoyment' was rife among the citizens; this issued in a 'greedy illimitable . . . thirst for territory', and in a widespread peasant selfishness, governed by the 'interests and passions' and ignorant of 'public objects'.[157] Over-centralisation had enervated individual responsibility: when government collapsed, owing to the alienation of the educated, and (in 1870) to the relative military inefficiency engendered by Frenchmen's lack of 'mutual sympathy', they were unable to live in social harmony. Peasants would not produce; the communes advocated extreme doctrines of self-government; each man wished to 'make his own will prevail, and to erect his doctrines and judgment into an absolute standard of the right and wise'. The subsequent decay of the rule of law was 'the most awful spectacle that the world has witnessed since the invasion of the barbarians'.[158] This, needless to say, was a pregnant warning to the British, who might also become religiously 'excitable', anti-social and prey to the dangers of over-centralisation.[159]

Ireland

Whig-liberals were almost unanimous in arguing that, if the union with Ireland was to be maintained, 'firm' executive government must be upheld, and 'Irish ideas' on policy questions ignored.

The assertion that government must be 'firm' became a shibboleth as the years passed, usually recited in disapproval of Gladstone's leniency on Irish coercion, but also in hostility to his perceived over-dependence on priestly support.[160] Agreement on this phrase hid a partial division of opinion. Froude's *English in Ireland*, and Greg's warm review of it, argued that the Irishman respected only, and could be ruled only by, a strong leader, like Cromwell.[161] Most whig-liberals followed the *Edinburgh* in disliking this emphasis on unrepresentative government, pointing to the benefits that Europe had gained from the replacement of despotism by

[155] Russell, 'General aspect of the world', p. 145; (Horsman) *Hansard*, cxxxii, 949, 27 April 1854.

[156] Reeve, 'France', pp. 17–18.

[157] Reeve, 'France'; Hodder, *Shaftesbury*, ii, 316; Greg, *Great duel*, pp. 9, 52.

[158] Reeve, 'France', and 'Communal France'; Greg, *Great duel*, pp. 50, 53–7.

[159] E.g. Blackie, *What does history teach?*, p. 53; Hodder, *Shaftesbury*, iii, 466–7.

[160] E.g. Davies, *National Church*, pp. x, xiii; Russell, *Recollections*, pp. 335–6, 393–401; Sherbrooke, 'Legislation for Ireland', pp. 686–8.

[161] See *English in Ireland*, *passim*; Froude, *Beaconsfield*, p. 207; Paul, *Froude*, p. 215; Greg, 'Froude's *English in Ireland*'; 'Realities of Irish life', p. 76.

the representative system. They maintained that a policy of repression had merely strengthened the hands of 'designing ecclesiastics' who wished to keep Catholics in ignorance and away from a modernising education. At the same time, the magazine showered much praise on Froude's views of the Irish and their history, and agreed especially with his account of the immoral concessionary politics of the eighteenth century: to govern on 'Irish ideas' was to govern in 'utter disregard of human and divine laws'. It hoped that a wise representative executive system would emerge, if middle-class education were modernised.[162]

Whig-liberals tended to argue that government should not be based on 'Irish ideas', because they were the ideas of the priests, the demagogues and the ignorant peasants.[163] All difficulties could ultimately be traced back to Ireland's peculiarly 'degraded' and 'unenlightened' version of Catholicism:[164] the priests were hostile to emigration, consolidation of farms and mixed education; they encouraged early marriages and over-population; their 'sacerdotal pretensions' gave them additional power over the 'poor ignorant' people.[165] The confessional system perpetuated terrorist activity, since the priests absolved murder; the public was cowed into complicity by threats of violence, and agitators thus escaped the 'sanction of all laws human and divine'.[166] 'Rabid newspapers' and political demagogues stimulated 'every bad passion . . . among an excitable and ignorant population'.[167] It was hardly surprising, whig-liberals maintained, that Catholic Ireland was less industrious, civilised and economically developed than the Protestant sector.[168]

In contrast, they argued, a wise state – in addition to encouraging scientific and technical education[169] – would invest capital in Irish industry, mines and ports, and would promote emigration[170] and the consoli-

---

[162] Croskerry, 'Trench's "Ierne" '; 'Froude's *English in Ireland*'; 'Froude's "Irish parliament and Irish rebellion" '. See also Brodrick, *Political studies*, p. 355.

[163] Brodrick, *Political studies*, p. 355; Froude, *English in Ireland*, iii, 577, 585; Dunn, *Froude*, ii, 363; (Horsman) *Hansard*, ccxiv, 1418, 6 March 1873.

[164] Greg, 'Ireland once more', p. 263.

[165] Greg, *Political problems*, p. 236; 'Priests, parliament and electors', pp. 290–2; 'The truth about Ireland', p. 284; Countess Grey to Ellice, 19 January 1868, Ellice papers, 15026, fo. 20; see also Clarendon to Granville, 26 November 1869, Granville papers, 30/29/55, fo. 83. For the queen, who found the Irish 'really shocking, abominable people', see *Letters of Aberdare*, i, 278; and the queen to Northcote, 2 October 1867, Iddesleigh papers, 50013, fo. 7. For Gladstone's irritation at her '*bigoted*' anti-Irish feeling, see Phillimore diary, 7 September 1875, Phillimore papers.

[166] Reeve, 'England and Ireland', p. 283.

[167] Greg, 'The truth about Ireland', pp. 287–8; Somerset to Dufferin, 30 January 1870, Dufferin papers.

[168] (Brodrick leading article) *Times*, 7 November 1872; (Tait) *Hansard*, cxcvi, 1717, 14 June 1869.

[169] Playfair, *On primary and technical education*, pp. 45–7.

[170] Lyall, *Dufferin*, i, 160; Torrens, *Imperial and colonial partnership*, pp. 5–6, and *Remonstrance against no-popery*, pp. 22–3; Horsman, *Manchester Guardian*, 3 January 1867, p. 3.

dation of the land. This would assist greatly in creating the 'middle-class' which was the 'social and political want of wants'.[171] But, if the 'wisdom of Parliament' would help to cure Irish disorders,[172] legislation could do only so much: the real need was for the 'merciful interposition of Divine Providence'.[173] The main function of the state must thus be to preserve order and to maintain a religious and educational system, in order to mitigate the growth of anti-social tendencies in Ireland.

In tackling religious questions, it was obvious even to Froude that the state must in practice allow religious liberty. But whig-liberals anticipated that Catholicism would be improved by exposure to intellectual movements. Religious liberty 'cannot but undermine sensibly the superstition which is the great antagonist of Protestantism, as it is of civilization itself'.[174] As Palmerston had said, the political consequences of Catholic practice might be greatly ameliorated by the spread of education: 'the most ignorant Catholic nations are the most bigoted, and ... the most enlightened are the most charitable and tolerant'.[175] In particular, it was hoped, by the steady influence of education, to create a middle class independent of priestly dictation in religious, political and cultural matters.[176] At the same time, British policy must 'endeavour to satisfy and retain on our side' the 'Saxon and Protestant' Irishmen who were 'friendly to the British connexion, and not in the pursuit of claptrap liberality eternally to alienate our friends without in the slightest degree conciliating our enemies'.[177]

Nearly all were prepared to accept, by 1868, that radical reform of the Irish Church was necessary. The whigs had long opposed the exclusiveness of the Irish Protestant Establishment: they argued in the 1860s, as in the 1830s, that it was absurd to force the religion of one-eighth of the Irish population onto the rest. Principles of toleration demanded that a Church should be maintained only when it was a '*National* Church': when it met the wishes of the majority of the population, when it chimed with the national 'mind and will'. Dufferin defined the Irish Establishment as a 'haughty priesthood identified in all its social interests with a military aristocracy'; Thirlwall saw it claiming 'infallibility' similar to the pope's, in imposing itself on Catholics; Maurice as 'anti-national' and reliant on

[171] Torrens, *Twenty years*, pp. 69–70; Croskerry, 'The Irish Roman Catholic laity'.
[172] Croskerry, 'Irish university education', p. 196.
[173] (Dufferin) *Hansard*, clxxxii, 383, 16 March 1866.
[174] (Brodrick leading article) *Times*, 15 May 1869 (about Spain).
[175] Ashley, *Palmerston*, i, 486.
[176] Croskerry, 'The Irish Roman Catholic laity', pp. 491–6.
[177] Lowe, 'What shall we do for Ireland?', pp. 263–4. See Roebuck, *Hansard*, cxci, 712, 2 April 1868.

purely materialist influences – money and temporal authority. On these grounds, the Irish Church was a monstrosity, unless it was doing good missionary work, which it clearly was not fit to do; the state must therefore intervene.[178]

Furthermore, it was seen to be politically counter-productive to maintain this exclusiveness. It was commonly argued that Catholicism was far more influential in Ireland for being challenged by such a blatantly unfair imposition. It drove intelligent Catholic laymen into the hands of the priesthood, whereas nothing would diminish priestly power more than allowing the laity 'free association with energetic, self-reliant, and honest men and women of other creeds'. Thirlwall, Dufferin and the *Economist* thought that to disestablish the Church offered more chance of rousing the 'peaceful spiritual aggression' needed to promote Protestantism than any measure passed since 1832. Many alarmist whigs considered that it was impossible to persuade Catholics that British administration was as fair as its defenders claimed unless something were done. Even Grey, hardly the most radical of whig-liberals, called for action on the Church question in the mid 1860s, because he feared that the situation was endangering the 'very existence of the empire' – and that the democratic United States would launch an attack to support the Fenians, in order to divert attention from its own domestic problems.[179] Thus in 1868, the most anti-Gladstonian whig-liberals welcomed disestablishment as a 'real instalment of justice to Ireland'; very few, apart from some of the clergymen, questioned that great benefits would stem from it.[180]

On the other hand, the policy involved political risks: dangers that it would promote an attack on Church endowments in England, remove state sanctions for social stability in Ireland, or upset Irish Protestant opinion without satisfying the Catholics. The vast majority of whig-liberals therefore coupled support for the principle of disestablishment

---

[178] Harcourt, *Irish Church*; Gardiner, *Harcourt*, i, 178–80; Akroyd, *Church, state and nonconformists*, p. 10; (Frederick Cavendish) Bailey, *Diary of Lady F. Cavendish*, ii, 45; (Charles Grey) Fair, *Interparty conferences*, p. 17; Martin, *Sherbrooke*, ii, 349; (Dufferin) *Hansard*, cxciii, 37, 26 June 1868; Thirlwall, *Thirlwall*, pp. 256–7; *A charge 1869*, p. 18; Maurice, 'The Irish Church Establishment', pp. 54–65.

[179] (Brodrick leading article) *Times*, 23 May 1869; Gower, *Reminiscences*, i, 304; Lyall, *Dufferin*, i, 169–70; Harrison, 'Dufferin', pp. 227–8; *Economist*, 24 July 1869, p. 865; Thirlwall, *Letters literary*, pp. 293, 295; Grey to Halifax, 31 December 1867, 16 January 1868, Hickleton papers, A 4 55; (for similar fears) *Pall Mall Gazette*, 12 March 1868, p. 1.

[180] *Pall Mall Gazette*, 25 November 1868, p. 1; even Shaftesbury abstained on the second reading in 1869: Finlayson, *Shaftesbury*, pp. 473–4. Tait argued half-heartedly against disestablishment in 1868 but could see little alternative; Stanley wished for the Irish Church's connection with the Church of England to be maintained, and wanted all three Irish Churches to be endowed; Temple and Thirlwall favoured disestablishment: Marsh, *Victorian Church in decline*, pp. 24–5; Stanley, *The three Irish Churches*.

with advocacy of 'concurrent endowment' or 'levelling up': treating all sects fairly, by endowing them all. Only the most evangelical and anti-Catholic whig-liberals (like Froude or Shaftesbury), or those most aware of the advantages of religious freedom, like Argyll in Scotland, dissented in principle.[181] Some others, however, did not press for concurrent endowment in public, realising that it was not feasible in the climate of 1868–9 – given that the Irish Catholic priests were unwilling to accept payment, and that nonconformists in England were agitating the new electors against it. But it was still advocated a very great deal in public and private. The general hope expressed that some form of it would be possible[182] was often justified by describing it as the 'policy of all our great statesmen . . . since the time of Pitt', and of the whig party in particular.[183] It was proposed in a number of different forms – the most common being that Catholic and presbyterian ministers might take some of the Established Church's houses and surrounding land.[184] Another idea was frequently canvassed, although less universally: that legal links with the Church of England and with the Crown should be maintained, in order to ensure that the disestablished Protestant sects did not become narrow and out of touch with national culture, or assertive and threatening to social order. The queen, churchmen of the Arnold–Stanley type, and old whigs like Russell, Westbury and Reeve were especially keen on this.[185]

It was argued that concurrent endowment, on the one hand, would mitigate the anti-social tendencies of the Catholic religion; the provision of better facilities would open cultural doors and thus increase the liberality and independence of the laity.[186] The Roman and presbyterian

---

[181] Hodder, *Shaftesbury*, iii, 250; Argyll to Gladstone, 12 October 1867, Gladstone papers, 44100, fo. 166; see also Grant Duff, *Some brief comments*, pp. 281, 284.

[182] E.g. Dasent, *Delane*, ii, 224, 237–8; Gregory, *Autobiography*, pp. 62, 168, 255; Tennyson, *Tennyson*, ii, 57; Arnold, *Culture and anarchy*, p. 168; (C. Fortescue) *Hansard*, clxxxvii, 171, 7 May 1867; (Dufferin) Bell, *Disestablishment in Ireland*, p. 68.

[183] Oliphant, *Tulloch*, pp. 241–2; (Brodrick leading article) *Times*, 1 April 1868; see also Stanley, *The three Irish Churches*, p. 44; Russell, *Recollections*, pp. 352–61; (Greg) *Pall Mall Gazette*, 14 September 1868, pp. 3–4; Thirlwall, *Letters to a friend*, p. 169.

[184] Some thought that the priests themselves should be paid, but this was often regarded both with distaste, and as politically impossible, given the opposition of the Catholic hierarchy. Russell, *Letter to Fortescue*, pp. 74–8, and *Recollections*, pp. 359–61; Halifax to Grey, 28 December 1867, 1, 15 January 1868, Grey papers. One suggestion was to allow the Irish Church all the post-Reformation endowments and the Catholic Church all the pre-Reformation ones: see e.g. Charles Grey to Grey, 25 March 1869, *ibid.*; Lake to Tait, 27 March 1869, Tait papers, 87, fo. 96.

[185] (The queen) *PMP*, iv, 5; Stanley, 'Reconstruction of the Irish Church', pp. 502–3; Argyll to Gladstone, 12 September 1868, Gladstone papers, 44100, fo. 225; Reeve to Cairns, 23 July [1868], Cairns papers, 30/51/17, fo. 51; Davies, *The Irish Church question*, pp. 20–1; (*Times*) Bell, *Disestablishment in Ireland*, p. 111. See, on the voluntary principle, Grey, *Hansard*, cxcvii, 693, 29 June 1869.

[186] C. Fortescue, *Christian profession*, pp. 43–4.

Churches in Ireland might thus be brought into 'contact with the main current of the national life': Irish Catholics, like English nonconformists, would be made 'larger-minded and more complete men'.[187] George Grey, Thirlwall and Lowe agreed that there was nothing irreligious in contributing to 'erroneous' doctrine, if to do so promoted 'religious comfort and ministration for the people'.[188] The state would also benefit, it was said, if priests were given financial security and removed from dependence on their flocks for aid. As it was, the priest 'dare not appear as loyal or as peacable as he really is', because of the need to gratify prejudiced and ignorant sentiment: he was also forced to obey the ultramontane hierarchy and the pope, who pulled the purse-strings.[189]

On the other hand, whig-liberals suggested that this policy would ensure that the beneficial Protestant flame was kept alive. Enough money must be left to the Protestant clergyman to enable him also not to be dependent on the parishioners' support, or the Church would become a 'narrow, proselytising, and exclusive sect'.[190] If a liberal religion were retained in Ireland, then, once 'freedom of trade' operated between all religions and educational establishments, the most just and enlightened could not but make headway.[191] Greg argued that the Protestant clergyman was not hated by the peasants – who cared little for religious distinctions – except when their priests had inflamed them.[192] Russell was certain that *not* conceding concurrent endowment would 'manifestly check civilisation, and arrest the progress of society in the rural parts of Ireland'.[193]

It was appreciated that Irish Church disestablishment, even with concurrent endowment, would not on its own check the aggressiveness of the Catholic hierarchy, which wished for temporal and spiritual ascendancy through control of education. It was seen to be vital to oppose this by the retention of state authority over the educational system:[194] if the Catholic clergy secured a monopoly, they would be 'complete and unassailable masters of Ireland'.[195] Reeve asserted, in discussing Irish

---

[187] Arnold, *Culture and anarchy*, p. 34.

[188] Creighton, *George Grey*, pp. 51–2; Lowe, 'What shall we do for Ireland?', pp. 279–80; Thirlwall, *A charge 1869*, p. 28.

[189] Trollope, 'The new cabinet', p. 541; Price, 'Mr Gladstone and disestablishment', p. 245; Lowe, 'What shall we do for Ireland?', p. 280; Stanley, *The three Irish Churches*, p. 45; Russell, *Recollections*, p. 361.

[190] Stanley, *The three Irish Churches*, p. 52.

[191] (Brodrick leading article) *Times*, 7 November 1872; Kingsley, *Kingsley*, ii, 295; Russell, *Letter to Fortescue*, pp. 69–70.

[192] Greg, 'Ireland once more', pp. 260–2.   [193] *Letter to Fortescue*, p. 66.

[194] Brodrick, *Political studies*, p. 356; (*Times*) Bell, *Disestablishment in Ireland*, pp. 48–9.

[195] Clarendon to Gladstone, 8 September 1869, Clarendon papers, 501, fo. 45; see also Greg, 'Ireland once more', pp. 264–71; Reeve, 'Claims of whig government', pp. 574–6; and Russell, *Recollections*, pp. 396–9. Russell saw the hierarchy as wishing to serve 'high treason' as the 'daily food of the Irish mind': *Essays*, pp. 320–1.

education, 'the fundamental principle of the Reformation', that 'civil rights, conceded to all and enjoyed by all in complete equality, are not to be overridden by the dictates of any Church or sect, still less by the authority of a foreign Power'.[196]

It was a whig-liberal commonplace to support the mixed national education system, which aimed 'to bring up all sects and races together, so as to accustom and train them to live in peace and harmony like brethren': this was the 'main civilising and elevating influence in the country', 'England's best gift to Ireland'.[197] They also argued that the Queen's colleges embodied an important principle, in encouraging the brightest young men of all sects to study together. They maintained that religious tests in Trinity college, Dublin should be abolished in order to facilitate this same process: the aim should be to make both institutions comprehensive and national.[198] Most whig-liberals believed that the abolition of tests would remove all imputations that the system discriminated against Catholics, and that the Catholic laity would thereafter be happy to attend the existing colleges. No further reform in university education would therefore be required.[199] A much smaller group, however, argued that, whether or not it would solve any Catholic grievance, it was advisable to endow a Catholic university, if by doing so it would bring Catholic culture into harmony with national life. If the endowed university were under lay control and out of the 'hands of the priests' who had made it a 'hole-and-corner' affair, the education that it would give would be free from 'sacerdotal despotism' and 'dogmatic pretensions'. This was the argument of Chichester Fortescue, of Grey and Russell, and above all of Matthew Arnold (in his case, it arose from his belief that an idealised undogmatic reverential religion could be created from Catholicism).[200]

Most whig-liberals, however, felt that it was 'false and insidious' to endow denominationalism, especially since the Irish liberal Catholic middle class was a broken reed at present and would not be courageous

---

[196] Reeve, 'Claims of whig government', pp. 576–7.

[197] Greg, 'Ireland once more', p. 264; Argyll to Gladstone, 16 September 1866, 16, 21 December 1867, Gladstone papers, 44100, fos. 132, 176, 178; (Horsman) *Hansard*, cxc, 1462–4, 12 March 1868.

[198] Croskerry, 'Irish university education'; Reeve, 'Claims of whig government', pp. 572, 574–5.

[199] Clarendon to Granville, n.d., Granville papers, 30/29/18/6; Greg, 'Froude's *English in Ireland*'. Kimberley and Lowe did not see the organisation of the university system as a grievance: Wodehouse to Gladstone, 12 February 1866, Gladstone papers, 44224, fo. 31; Carnarvon diary, 1 May 1868, Carnarvon papers, 60900; Lowe, 'What shall we do for Ireland?', p. 284.

[200] Fortescue to Clermont, 25 November 1872, Strachie papers, 338, 236b; (Grey) *Hansard*, ccxv, 1849, 13 May 1873; Arnold, 'Higher schools and universities', pp. 96–8; 'Irish Catholicism and British Liberalism', p. 334.

enough to assert its independence of the priests. Endowment of education would therefore sacrifice the laity to the priests, unlike concurrent endowment of the Churches.[201] Furthermore, a great many whig-liberals were disquieted, not merely by *endowment* of denominational education, but by any suggestion that the state should encourage it. Argyll warned Gladstone in 1867 that, while the party would 'go heartily in any place for still further liberalising the old Protestant universities . . . they will not go unitedly into any scheme for lending State countenance or support to purely "sectarian" Education'.[202] This feeling was even more marked in the political climate prevailing after 1870: only a few, like Chichester Fortescue and Hutton of the *Spectator* disagreed, believing that Irish national rights should be respected.[203] Gladstone's Irish university plan of 1873 shook the confidence of so many whig-liberals because, even though it did not directly endow denominational education, it not only extended the opportunities for such an education, but appeared to allow the denominationalists ultimately to control the university system, and therefore its endowments. This upset both the proponents of the majority whig-liberal view, and those who, like Hartington (the chief secretary for Ireland at the time), were prepared to consider the idea of endowing a denominational university as long as it was in liberal hands. (There was also a great deal of opposition, especially from Argyll and Playfair, to the idea of Lowe and Gladstone, embodied in the 1873 bill, that teaching and examining functions should be separated. The latter believed that a single examining board was more reliable as a degree-giving body than were teaching institutions, which might lower their examining standard in order to get pupils.)[204]

At the root of the attitude of many sceptical whig-liberals was the belief that no religious concession would solve the Irish problem. Clarendon did not believe that any such initiative would cure 'the dirty,

---

[201] Croskerry, 'Trench's "Ierne"', pp. 519–22; (Lowe) *Hansard*, cxc, 1499–1502, 12 March 1868.

[202] Argyll to Gladstone, 24 December 1867, Gladstone papers, 44100, fo. 182.

[203] E.g. Harcourt opposed attempts to encourage denominational education in Ireland: *Times*, 4 January 1870, p. 9. See, for *Spectator*, 13 January 1872, pp. 38–9. But its support for teaching according to the wishes of the Irish people should not lead us to think that it approved of Gladstone's desire for definiteness in the formulation of Church doctrine and for denominational education *per se*; it explicitly rejected it: 18 May 1872, pp. 618–19.

[204] Lowe argued that the examining board ought to be neutral, and unconnected with any religion or institution. This was strongly opposed by defenders of the four Scottish universities, who believed that the examination system was useful only in facilitating the teaching of a systematic curriculum, and thought that Lowe's scheme made cramming for examination success of more importance than a search for cultural improvement. Lowe, *Hansard*, ccxxxv, 1890–3, 26 July 1877; Sylvester, *Lowe and education*, pp. 180, 184; Playfair, *On teaching universities and examining boards*; Argyll to Gladstone, 4 November 1872, Gladstone papers, 44102, fo. 186.

drunken, turbulent habits of the Irish'.[205] Many – including Kimberley, who was atypical in eventually supporting home rule – agreed with him at this time that it was a 'dream' that the Irish would be contented by any remedial legislation. It was said that the Irish loved to trade on their grievances, and that they would invent new ones upon the granting of every concession: the process would culminate in home rule.[206] And if concessions were to be made, the Catholic hierarchy was the last group to which whig-liberals wished to make them.

The prevailing Palmerstonian attitude to Ireland had been inactivity, on the grounds that no reform would pacify agitators who were controlled by papal influence.[207] Brand, Palmerston's chief whip, had regarded Irish Catholics as 'the natural enemies of a Liberal Government';[208] Horsman, as chief secretary, had found 'nothing to do . . . worth doing'.[209] Therefore, from the beginning of Gladstone's government there was a strong tendency – articulated in early 1868 by one of his prospective cabinet ministers – to 'refuse to follow Mr Gladstone in his confessions of wrong and injustice towards a people who are saved by our agency alone from the most fearful and ruinous calamities': the 'total wreck of all property and credit; a desperate civil war . . . and ultimate subjection to some foreign Power'.[210] In December 1869, Lowe repeated his view: Gladstone's talk of a 'great debt' being due from England to Ireland was 'as exactly as possible the reverse of that of his party, who are not at all in a penitential mood, who are conscious of fair and honest intentions with regard to Ireland and consider that they have been met with insolence and ingratitude'.[211] There was much political mileage to be gained from maintaining, as Harcourt did in 1873, that 'one of his objects in life was to break the alliance between the Liberal Party of Great Britain and the Roman Catholics of Ireland'.[212] This sentiment, again,

[205] Clarendon to Granville, 25 August [1868], Granville papers, 30/29/29.
[206] Clarendon to Gladstone, 21 April 1870, Gladstone papers, 44134, fo. 188; see also Clarendon to Odo Russell, 1 March 1870, Clarendon papers, FO 361, i, 335. For Kimberley, see Kimberley to Clarendon, 1 October 1869, Clarendon papers, 499, fo. 163; Drus, *Journal of Kimberley*, pp. 9–10. In February 1870, he thought that Gladstone was under a 'happy delusion that his policy will produce a speedy change in the temper of the Irish towards this country': *ibid.*, pp. 11–12. Charles Grey thought that Irish grievances were 'rather sentimental, than such as can be removed by Acts of Parliament'; accordingly he recommended sentimental remedies, such as occasional royal residence in Ireland: Charles Grey to the queen, 23 December 1868, Charles Grey papers. So did Dufferin, to Gladstone, 9 February 1872, Gladstone papers, 44151, fo. 126.
[207] (1864) Ashley, *Palmerston*, ii, 443.
[208] Vincent, *Formation of the Liberal party*, p. 51.
[209] Torrens, *Twenty years*, pp. 34–5.
[210] Lowe, 'What shall we do for Ireland?', pp. 285–6.
[211] Lowe to Granville, 21 December 1869, Granville papers, 30/29/66.
[212] Fortescue to Gladstone, 30 November 1873, Gladstone papers, 44123, fo. 65.

was probably held within the cabinet: in 1867, Argyll had been eagerly anticipating the settlement of the Irish Church issue, because its obstinate survival as a political difficulty had had a 'fatal influence in allying English Liberalism with progress towards the most illiberal of all systems'.[213]

Perceptions of the Conservatives

It was in religious discussions that the Liberals had always been most clearly distinguishable from the Conservatives. Yet, since both parties were open to the same intellectual trends, and forced to work in the same political climate, accommodation was not impossible. By the late 1860s, important elements in the Conservative party were happy (rather than reluctantly forced) to work within the religious *status quo* established by previous Liberal reforms.

This was most true of Lord Stanley, after 1869 the 15th earl of Derby. Derby was a mainstream liberal evangelical trapped in the party by an inheritance which, after his father's death, he intermittently determined to renounce. The prospect of his leading a coalition of whigs and Conservatives was frequently dangled before his eyes, with the effect merely of mesmerising him and shipwrecking his career through inconstancy. In Derby, the broad-church froth of the Rugby-educated 1850s intellectual was set on top of the mild evangelicalism of Lancashire industrial capital; his disparagement of religious controversy and his advocacy of social and sanitary reform fitted him 'to be a perpetual President of a Social Science Association'.[214] It was his misfortune to be a Conservative politician while despising those who united 'strong convictions with very narrow intelligence';[215] he was, consequently, unpopular with his party on Church questions.[216]

As important in redefining the response of the Conservative party after 1867 was a group of men, representing urban seats, who were more popular with the mainstream of the party than Derby, because of their more entrenched evangelical feeling, yet who were also capable of appealing to disaffected 'right-wing' Liberals. These were men like W. H. Smith and Viscount Sandon – who had been Palmerstonian Liberals but had defected – or R. A. Cross, a Rugby-educated barrister. Cross, Sandon and the Liverpool shipowner Samuel Graves, a like-minded figure, all represented staunchly Protestant Lancashire constituencies; Smith won a famous victory in Westminster in 1868.

---

[213] Argyll to Gladstone, 21 December 1867, *ibid.*, 44100, fo. 178.
[214] Anon., *Political portraits*, p. 105.
[215] 'University education and teaching', p. 174.
[216] Johnson, *Diary of Gathorne Hardy*, p. 281.

Of course, like all Conservatives, these were firmer in their defence of the principle of Establishment than Liberals: Smith was a Wesleyan convert to Anglicanism who left the Liberal party on the prospect of Irish Church disestablishment.[217] The younger high-church Conservatives were similarly far more attached to the Establishment than Liberal high churchmen (as Northcote demonstrated to Gladstone).[218] In fact, the bulk of the Conservatives instinctively regarded Establishments as essential aids to the maintenance of order and the safeguarding of religious truth against infidelity. Whig-liberals, equally instinctively, distrusted this point of view, however much they shared it in practice. It was only slowly after 1869, therefore, that they came to realise that, with nearly all the major questions of civil liberty settled, and with nonconformists more vocal in support of an unacceptable policy of disestablishment, there was rather less difference between them and many of the Conservatives than they had always assumed. This realisation was also promoted by the campaigns of Derby, Smith, Sandon, Graves, Adderley, Gabriel Goldney, Russell Gurney and other Conservative MPs for administrative, social and local taxation reform in place of excited religious agitations: to promote that 'sober earnest work which has been left alone and laid aside only too long'.[219]

Even when this process of accommodation was under way, Liberals continued to regard the mass of Conservatives as the 'stupid party', incapable of appreciating the intellectual movements which it was necessary to ride in order to harness the forces of beneficial progress.[220] Most Conservatives were rigid evangelicals or old-fashioned high churchmen. This meant, of course, that there were occasionally differences within the party on religious questions, but, more importantly, backbenchers from both camps often united to press for a more thorough defence of Anglican interests than was politically possible – to the considerable embarrassment of the leadership. Frequent problems of this nature enabled Liberals to repeat their standard complaint, that Conservatives as a party made the fatal error of wishing to 'arrest the progress of society', and that they would insist on defending practices which had outlived their usefulness. This was to seek to check change by arbitrary fiat, rather than to continue the 'gradual but steady inroad on

[217] Maxwell, *Smith*, i, 19, 78–9, 113, 139.
[218] Northcote to Gladstone, 24 July, 4 August 1865, Gladstone papers, 44217, fos. 94, 100. The same may be said of Adderley, an ex-evangelical touched by tractarianism, and was also true, of course, of Salisbury and Carnarvon.
[219] (Cross, 1871) Smith, *Disraelian Conservatism and social reform*, p. 155; see also p. 162.
[220] Colaiaco, *Stephen*, p. 193; Begbie, *Albert Grey*, p. 43.

mischievous traditions' which was the basis of the Liberal claim to efficient government.[221]

This general reluctance to believe that the Conservatives could conduct affairs of state was reinforced by the prejudices inevitably arising from institutionalised party warfare; this was a handicap to changing one's affiliation which many, especially active politicians or guardians of the whig tradition, would not try to surmount unless under grave provocation. But arguably the most important consideration in delaying association with Conservatives after 1867 was the whig-liberals' genuine belief that Disraeli was an utterly irresponsible politician, and that the Conservatives in power would pursue a combination of blind reaction, and unpredictable and unprincipled opportunism – in comparison with which the most advanced Liberal radicalism was almost tolerable. No one knew if Disraeli would be 'Tory or Radical';[222] he could accept almost any change because he had no strong opinions;[223] he was 'dangerous and untrustworthy'.[224] His conduct in 1867, far from showing that the Conservatives could govern, displayed to many whig-liberals that they could not, since it revealed that, lacking principle and expertise in government, they would outbid their opponents and pass whatever measures would enable them to retain power.[225] His foreign policy of the late 1870s was usually criticised as being showy and irresponsible, and thus as diverging from Palmerstonianism as much as from Gladstonianism. His manifest lack of interest in religion, and his cynical exploitation of Church patronage for attempted political gain, revolted many of the more devout Liberals.[226] Trollope satirised Disraeli's religious irresponsibility in *Phineas redux* in 1873, by making his Disraelian character adopt the cry of English Church disestablishment in order to outwit the Liberals.[227]

In the sense that mattered most, in cultivating an image capable of permanently winning over moderate Liberal opinion, Disraeli was a failure (as the 1880 election result was to prove). Despite the reaction against Gladstone evidenced by many by-election losses between 1871 and 1873, whig-liberals still had little faith in the stability afforded by a Conservative government in the early 1870s.[228] Dufferin considered in 1873 that 'the time is hardly ripe for them, nor indeed is likely to ripen

---

[221] *Economist*, 29 March 1873, p. 371; see Forbes, *Liberal Anglican idea*, p. 104.

[222] Thirlwall, *Letters to a friend*, p. 159; Hardcastle, 'Mr Disraeli's "Glasgow speeches"'.

[223] *Times*, 20 November 1871, p. 9; *Economist*, 6 April 1872, p. 414; see Disraeli's own quotation in Trevelyan, *Trevelyan*, p. 76.

[224] *Spectator*, 6 April 1872, p. 426; Grant Duff, *Out of the past*, i, 199–211.

[225] Thirlwall, *Letters literary*, pp. 290–1; Finlayson, *Shaftesbury*, pp. 468–72.

[226] Blake, *Disraeli*, pp. 503–5, 564; Kebbel, *Beaconsfield*, pp. 42, 51–2; Finlayson, *Shaftesbury*, p. 472.

[227] *Phineas redux* (Oxford, 1973 edn), ch. 5.   [228] *Times*, 20 November 1871, p. 9.

as long as Dizzy lives'.[229] There was therefore a neat paradox. On the one hand, whig-liberals could not conceive of allying with such a man and such a party; but on the other, given the growing fear of religious radicalism, the public rhetoric of the Conservative party came increasingly, after 1870, to express the views of moderate Liberals in the country – and, in practice, in parliament. Conservatives were speaking for such Liberals when they stressed the centrality of religion in education, the importance of defending the Established Church and the Union, the need to assert British power abroad, and the desirability of checking rate increases and of promoting worthwhile sober legislation at home.

Perceptions of Gladstone

Given all the strands in the whig-liberal conscience, there was bound to be an ambivalence about Gladstone. On the one hand, he was seen as an effective parliamentary leader, a man who raised the moral tone of politics, and an efficient administrator in the Liberal tradition. On the other, it had to be recognised that he was a high churchman, whose language was mysterious and opaque, whose mental processes were unpredictable, whose temper was erratic, whose political impulsiveness was legendary, and whose demagogic abilities were frightening.

Since one major aim of this book is to chart the whig-liberal reaction to Gladstonianism, it is necessary here only to set the scene. At this point, of course, any attempt at generalisation is bound to fail, since individuals' attitudes varied so much according to situation and temperament. Some were anxious to stress Gladstone's achievements in secular politics, especially in finance; indeed, for many candidates in 1874, it was all that they could stress in attempting to quieten fears for the future. Many continued to believe until the mid 1880s that, whatever his faults, he was better able to unite the party and thus strengthen the power of moderates within it than any alternative.[230] Many backbenchers and peers, moreover, did not see it as their business to express opinions on general politics at all, however much they disagreed with specific Gladstonian policies.[231]

In tracing reasons for individual whig-liberals' distrust of Gladstone, then, one is merely trying to suggest how a cast of mind might slowly become more widely shared after 1868. What was really in dispute was the extent to which Gladstone's faults – his ecclesiasticism, populism

---

[229] To Knatchbull-Hugessen, 15 March 1873, Dufferin papers.
[230] Gardiner, *Harcourt*, i, 179; Hamer, *Liberal politics in the age of Gladstone and Rosebery*, pp. 76–7; (Goschen) Acland, *Acland*, p. 346.
[231] For Bedford, see Coleridge, *Coleridge*, ii, 367.

and impulsiveness – might lead him to channel party enthusiasm in uncongenial directions. What was at issue was not what had happened – which was constrained by many pressures, not least whig-liberal strength on the backbenches – but what might happen: but since policy was so often dictated by practical considerations, fear and exaggeration usually constituted the essential ingredients for the manufacture of political division.

Whigs had always tended to distrust Peelites,[232] and especially those with tractarian proclivities, as the episode of the Durham letter indicated.[233] This distrust centred, of course, on Gladstone himself. As Stanley wrote in 1865, 'between him and the Whig party there is a fundamental difference'.[234]

Much of this feeling stemmed from the latter's incomprehension of his religious perspective.[235] Whig-liberals made references to 'numerous political personages who were liberals in State, but not in Church'.[236] Fitzmaurice explained the 'slow but steady reduction in numbers' on the Liberal benches in the Lords after 1868, in terms of the concern with which supporters of Russell or the 'jaunty Erastianism' of Palmerston viewed the plans of a child of the Oxford movement.[237]

Gladstone's high churchmanship was often associated with political unpredictability and radicalism: his 'church principles' made it impossible to guarantee that he would maintain a 'straight course' in politics.[238] There were complaints that he was an 'impulsive . . . Jesuitical' man, a 'Puseyite Radical', a 'passionate, impulsive, unreasoning instrument'.[239] Bouverie saw him in the round: 'that d----d Gladstone – Tory as he was

---

[232] Reeve, *Greville memoirs*, vii, 249; Southgate, *Passing of the whigs*, p. 294.

[233] Machin, *Politics and the Churches*, pp. 208–10, 216–18; see also Gardiner, *Harcourt*, i, 64, and Acland, *Acland*, p. 165.

[234] Vincent, *Journals of Lord Stanley*, i, 229; see also Shannon, *Gladstone*, pp. 533–4; Hewett, '. . . *and Mr Fortescue*', p. 164.

[235] After a conversation with Gladstone on the efficacy of continual prayer, and after attempting to read the '*awfully stiff*' tract of Döllinger's that he had sent her, Lady Waldegrave confided to Lady Strachey: 'There must be, I think, a *considerable* screw loose somewhere': Hewett, *Waldegrave*, p. 240. See (Delane) Tollemache, *Talks with Mr Gladstone*, p. 186.

[236] (Grant Duff) Greg, *Enigmas of life*, p. lxxiv. When Somerset declined to join the Gladstone government in 1868, the whig *Vanity Fair Album* wrote that the loss of his influence would be sorely felt, because he was a true Liberal, 'not only in matters of State, but, what is more important, in Church matters'; and that his decision would leave the cabinet 'much more amenable to the uncontrolled will of the Premier': Mallock and Ramsden, *Somerset*, pp. 323–4.

[237] Fitzmaurice, *Granville*, ii, 2–3.

[238] Lady Russell notes, 14 November 1865, Russell papers, 30/22/15G, fo. 81.

[239] Honey, *Tom Brown's universe*, p. 97; Earl Fortescue to Brereton, 21 February 1874, Brereton papers, F 13 74; Earl Fortescue, *Our next leap in the dark*, p. v; (Grey) Hewett, '. . . *and Mr Fortescue*', p. 106; Elcho to Ellice, 25 March 1866, Ellice papers, 15013, fo. 25; (Emily Eden) Maxwell, *Clarendon*, ii, 224.

– High Churchman as he is, and revolutionist as he will be'.[240] It was the 'curious *ecclesiastical* form and colouring' over all his opinions, his 'peculiar mental and moral constitution', his 'Tory half-poetical associations' and his 'High Church proclivities' that were held to be responsible for his political irrationality, his unwillingness to give a firm lead: he tried to refashion Liberalism with tools of 'quivering sensibility', the 'imagination' and the 'sympathies'. Those MPs who were willing to follow him everywhere were, like the ritualist congregations, 'weaker spirits' subjected to the 'fatal and degrading' control of 'sensualists'.[241]

Different classes of whig-liberal saw this at different times. Clarendon told Granville in 1860 that Gladstone's 'insatiable desire for popularity' and his 'fervent imagination' would lead him to wish to 'subvert the institutions and the classes that stand in the way of his ambition'.[242] Price prophesied in 1864 that Gladstone could not provide mature and steady leadership of the nation, because he could not 'command his own intellect', a consequence of his 'enthusiasm', 'impressionableness', and 'want of intuition';[243] Bagehot, Carlisle, Palmerston and Cornewall Lewis had said much the same in the early 1860s.[244] There was much whig concern, especially between 1866 and 1868, about Gladstone's temper and unpredictability, and his apparent willingness to discard the views of the majority of the parliamentary party in order to gratify the clamour of the masses.[245]

In 1868, few Liberal MPs were yet as virulent as Bouverie, who maintained in 1866 that Gladstone was 'an impossibility as a *Liberal* leader – after all the real dividing line is upon Church and religious questions, – and has been for 200 years and on these he is a violent Tory'.[246] It is likely that few were as pessimistic as Shaftesbury, who had foreseen Gladstone succumbing to 'every pressure, except the pressure of a Constitutional and Conservative Policy . . . Thus we have before us democracy, popery, infidelity, with no spirit of resistance in the country, no strong feelings, no decided principles, a great love of ease, and a great fear of anything that may disturb that ease' – inevitably leading to 'the greatest social,

---

[240] Bouverie to Ellice, 4 April 1866, Ellice papers, 15005, fo. 23.

[241] Greg, 'Mr Gladstone's *Apologia*', pp. 130–4.

[242] Reeve, *Greville memoirs*, viii, 297; see also Kennedy, *Manchester*, pp. 97, 142, 194, and Mitford, *Stanleys of Alderley*, pp. 278, 421–2.

[243] Price, 'Political temper of the nation', pp. 155–7.

[244] Bagehot, *Biographical studies*, pp. 102–3, 110, 112; Lascelles, *Journals of Carlisle*, p. 342; (Lewis) Jennings, 'Mr Gladstone and Ireland', p. 258; Grant Duff, *Out of the past*, ii, 13; (Palmerston) Tankerville to Disraeli, 1 December 1868, Disraeli papers, B/XXI/T/54.

[245] Halifax to Grey, 5 April 1866, Hickleton papers, A 4 55; Denison to Halifax, 26 March 1866, *ibid.*, A 4 131; *Pall Mall Gazette*, 25 November 1868, p. 1.

[246] Bouverie to Ellice, 18 December 1866, Ellice papers, 15005, fo. 44.

political and religious revolution that England has yet endured'.[247] Most university liberals probably did not yet think, what Brodrick was later to think, that Gladstone, linchpin of 'the strange alliance between Radicalism and Ritualism', was neither a 'sound Liberal or a far-sighted statesman' – although they were already disillusioned to some extent by his delaying tactics over university reform.[248] Neither is it clear how many Derby grouped in the 'Whig' category when he wrote in 1870 that they looked forward to Gladstone's 'disappearance from public life as a relief; they follow, but fear and dislike him. Granville, Lowe, and Childers more accurately represent their ideas.'[249] Tulloch, however, was probably not untypical as early as 1871 – at least in private commentary – in arguing that Gladstone's attitude was 'very unlike that of a statesman. He seems to think it not so much his business to guide the country as to be led by it.'[250] One indication of feeling, moreover, was that leading whig peers were very reluctant to subscribe to election campaigns, even in 1868;[251] another, that whig backbenchers refused Gladstone's offer of peerages and baronetcies in 1869 and 1870;[252] and a third, the marked reluctance to accept the Garter from him.[253]

By the mid seventies, as will become apparent from Part II, a climate had certainly been created in which it was commonplace to argue that Gladstone's religion was inherently destabilising, and that it had led him to consort with equally unpredictable political allies. By then, it was widely believed, as Henry Reeve had said as early as 1868, that it had never been

more essential to defend the supremacy of the Crown and the Law in Ecclesiastical affairs . . . Catholics, High Churchmen, and Dissenters, are for the first time combined in the hatred of a Church governed and supported by law; and it is my deliberate conviction and firm belief that Gladstone shares their opinion on this point, and desires nothing so much as to destroy the control of the State over the Church, or, as he would say, to set her free from secular bondage . . . I believe such a course to be utterly at variance with liberal principles, with Whig principles, and with the very essence of the English Reformation.[254]

---

[247] Hodder, *Shaftesbury*, iii, 171–2, 185, 201.
[248] Brodrick, *Memories and impressions*, pp. 214, 238–9; see also Morrison to Grey, 26 August 1872, Grey papers.
[249] Derby diary, 9 April 1870, 15th earl of Derby papers.
[250] Oliphant, *Tulloch*, p. 263; see Trollope, *Phineas redux*, i, 80, and Henry Taylor, *Autobiography 1800–1875* (2 vols., London, 1885), ii, 280.
[251] Vincent, *Formation of the Liberal party*, p. 9; see below, p. 275.
[252] (Ellice's peerage) Delane to Ellice, 29 November 1869, Ellice papers, 15011, fo. 142; Lennox to Disraeli, 2 April [1870], Disraeli papers, B/XX/Lx/337; (Crawford's baronetcy) *Vanity Fair Album*, v (1873).
[253] See above, p. 64.
[254] Reeve to Clarendon, 9 August 1868, Clarendon papers, 496, fo. 252.

Whig-liberals in parliament

The number of Liberal MPs who sat through at least one session in the parliament of 1868–74 was 424. Each remaining chapter in Part I includes an analysis of the behaviour of different sections of Liberal MPs on religious questions, an analysis based on a study of twenty parliamentary divisions (which are discussed in detail in Part II). Those MPs who failed to register a vote in six of these divisions were excluded from the analysis: a total of eighty-six (of whom fourteen, nearly all whig-liberals, sat for British seats throughout the parliament).[255] A further thirty-four MPs were members of the government for sufficiently long to disqualify them from analysis.

Treatment of the attitudes of the 304 remaining MPs is divided among the chapters as follows: thirty-eight Irish MPs, and ten who are classed as 'Peelites', are covered in chapter 3; radicals and nonconformists are discussed in chapter 4; the rest appear below. Adding all nonconformist MPs to those others defined as radical – that is, who voted or paired for disestablishment in England, or for the 1870 motion for secular education, or who abstained on disestablishment motions while giving other indications of radical feeling on religious questions – establishes a total of 139 MPs, leaving 117 whig-liberals. However, 12 of the 139 were non-radical nonconformists, and the voting records of 12 others, Anglicans, were such as to place their radicalism in question.

If the ten Peelites are added, temporarily, to the 117 whig-liberals and 24 intermediate cases, it is illuminating to contrast the type of seat which they possessed with that held by the radicals. The figures in Table 1 show that in a number of categories of seat (especially those English borough seats of intermediate size), representation was divided fairly evenly between radicals and non-radicals. However, they also reveal that religious radicalism was almost a prerequisite for holding a large urban seat, and religious conservatism almost essential for an MP for a small English borough or for a county anywhere. The most interesting exceptions to these rules were provided by the recently radicalised Welsh counties (which form a striking contrast to their 'unemancipated' Scottish counterparts), and by the large urban seats in the south of England. The former were overwhelmingly radical; the representation of the latter was divided evenly between the two classes of MP. A crucial determinant in the latter case, of course, was the weakness of nonconformity: only 37 per cent of those Londoners (including inhabitants of

---

[255] Except for Bright and Childers, there were Ronald Gower, Lorne, W. O. Stanley, R. W. Grosvenor, H. B. W. Brand, Locke King, Wells, Montagu Chambers, two Rothschilds, Sir Robert Peel (the prime minister's son) and Tomline.

Table 1 *Distribution of the 115 radical and 151 non-radical MPs selected for the survey, by constituency*

	Radicals	Non-radicals
English boroughs		
Electorate over 5,000		
London	7	8
south[a]	6	10
north[a]	32	11
Electorate 2,000–5,000		
south	10	12
north	13	10
Electorate under 2,000		
south	9	25
north	1	11
English counties		
south	2	18
north	4	13
Wales		
boroughs	7	5
counties	7	1
Scotland		
boroughs	12	12
counties	5	15
Total	115	151

[a] 'South' and 'north' are defined, as throughout the book, by a line drawn straight between the Severn and Wash, and then distorted in order to follow county boundaries. The electorates are those recorded for 1868.

Middlesex) who attended Protestant religious services at the time of the 1851 census, went to nonconformist chapels. This was the same figure as for the six most south-easterly counties, but lower than the total for the south altogether (42 per cent), and far lower than that for the north (52 per cent).[256] Chamberlain admitted in 1872 that he was unable to organise London to participate in the Education League's campaign.[257] The relative conservatism of London Liberal politics is also evident from the behaviour of its MPs. In addition to the eight non-radicals among them who were covered in the survey, there were two who attended only sporadically. Taking these ten together, they included two jews, an

[256] Figures have been computed from *1851 census: religious worship: England and Wales*.
[257] Read, *English provinces*, p. 170.

Anglican director of the Bank of England, several evangelicals, an old ex-radical utilitarian, and a Protestant utilitarian whig. Even their radical colleagues could be swayed by religious argument towards conservatism, most notoriously over the Emanuel Hospital case (see p. 380), where four of these, in addition to five of the non-radicals, voted against the commissioners' scheme of reform. The London MPs, moreover, were also vocal against the government on other questions concerning local government, such as the Thames Embankment and Epping Forest issues; on both of these they were playing the game of W. H. Smith of Westminster, who was taking the lead in organising London political opinion for the Conservatives, in pursuit of the substantial metropolitan gains of 1874.

By no means all the 141 whig-liberals and intermediates can be said to be ideologically aware Arnoldian Liberal Anglicans. A number of the 12 Anglican[258] intermediates were anti-Catholic evangelicals who supported or abstained on disestablishment motions, such as Whalley, the Scotsman A. F. Kinnaird, and Thomas Chambers. Included in the 141 were also a number of unambitious and conservative Anglican industrialists who were heavyweights in their own towns – men like the Basses, Lancaster in Wigan, Bölckow in Middlesborough or Henderson in Durham. These might be evangelicals, utilitarians, or men of no developed religious views, but were usually content to display orthodox Protestantism with no appearance of reflection. This judgment may be undeserved, however, since some of their number were articulate, and spoke and wrote within the whig-liberal tradition – such as Akroyd of Halifax.

Most of the 117 purest whig-liberals were either, on the one hand, nobles or country gentlemen – 39 were related at one step to peers, either themselves or through marriage, and another 29 had no occupation listed in *Dod* and were usually substantial landowners – or, on the other hand, borough MPs. The latter were often evangelicals (especially in Scotland), and often lawyers (such as the evangelicals Dickinson and Monk, or the more latitudinarian Harcourt, Hughes and James); among them were a number of ex-unitarians, such as Amory, Bowring and Bonham-Carter.

What is striking about the MPs analysed is how strongly they expressed their views against the government's religious policy. Of the 141, 34 voted against the government in divisions which displayed their anti-Catholicism, either on the Irish University Bill (on which abstentions without pair have been deemed sufficient for inclusion), on the O'Keeffe case, or in support of a motion of 1870 to establish an inquiry

---

[258] Or Church of Scotland presbyterians, or Scottish episcopalians.

into convents (see pp. 365, 371 and 294 respectively). On matters affecting English and Scottish education, the 24 intermediates were usually as advanced as the radicals. Seventeen voted for Jacob Bright's undenominational amendment to the 1870 Education Act, only 4 supported the retention of Clause 25 of the Act by 1873, and 17 opposed the government on the selected amendments on the University Tests Bill (see pp. 306, 379 and 308).

Discounting these, and concentrating on the 117 purer whig-liberals, the range of dissidence is still remarkable testimony to the anti-clericalism which Liberal supporters of the Church Establishment could summon up. Twenty-nine voted for Jacob Bright's undenominational amendment of 1870, 35 for Anderson's amendment (of similar scope, given the different circumstances) to the 1872 Scottish Education Bill (see p. 341), 47 supported one or the other, and only 50 of the rest voted against either. Whig-liberals were slightly more reluctant to associate with the nonconformist campaign for abolition of Clause 25: 30 opposed this clause by 1873, and 24 more did not support it in 1872 or 1873. By 1874, a further 11 whig-liberals had changed from support or abstention to opposing the clause. On the two selected amendments on the 1871 University Tests Bill, the level of dissension was remarkable: only 24 supported the government on both (or supported on one and abstained on one), 45 were opposed on both (or opposed and abstained), 11 supported one and opposed on one, and 37 abstained on both.

On the other hand, a number of these men opposed the government in another sense, in attempting to impose guarantees for religion where the government itself was reluctant to do so. This can best be seen by examining the votes on two questions: on that of the destination of the surplus remaining after the disendowment of the Irish Church; and on the Conservative amendment to the 1872 Scottish Education Bill, which demanded that religion be taught in all schools (see pp. 286 and 342). Both were important divisions on which defeat would severely dent the government's credibility. Although, in both cases, the number of those who voted with the Conservatives reached only single figures, a substantial proportion of the 117 abstained, 32 per cent and 30 per cent respectively, whereas the corresponding figures for the 115 radicals were 8 per cent and 16 per cent respectively.[259] Eleven MPs can further be classified on the far 'right', because of their positive votes against the government on these issues, or because of their opposition to the Burials Bill or

---

[259] These figures are doubly striking in the 1872 case, since they measure abstention on *both* divisions concerning the question: on the first, the Conservatives scored a surprise victory, and the Liberals mounted a major and successful offensive to defeat the proposal on the second.

(excluding London MPs) to the commissioners' scheme for Emanuel Hospital.[260]

What is perhaps most remarkable is that, as a result of rebellions in anti-Catholic or anti-clerical directions, or to the 'right' of government positions, only a handful of these 117 MPs were throughout loyal to the government. Only 15 whig-liberals never voted against the government in the 20 divisions, and 8 of these 15 abstained either on the division on the Irish Church surplus in 1869, or on so many others as to devalue the importance of their loyalty. Apart from two friends of Gladstone (George Cavendish and Arthur Russell), the 7 most loyal kept a low profile, and were uninfluential at Westminster. The conclusion must be that, in opposing government policy on denominational education or university tests, whig-liberals did not consider that they were behaving badly; they saw themselves as upholding the Liberal tradition.

*   *   *

Whether one examines the attitudes of MPs or of whig-liberal writers outside parliament, it is important to realise that their reaction to the course of British politics after 1867 might take a number of forms. Firstly, there were those whiggish country gentlemen, plutocrats, evangelicals and Carlyleans who were very concerned to defend the Church Establishment and Protestant teaching in the schools, and who consequently disliked the anti-clerical attacks on the 1870 Education Act. They were likely to be the most worried about the likelihood of the party drifting towards disestablishment, secular education and home rule. They, moreover, were most representative of the average Anglican Liberal voter, and most likely to be sympathetic to the Conservatives in 1874.

Then there was average whig-liberal opinion in the Commons, worried, but not yet obsessively so, that the party was going too fast by 1874, and more worried by 1880 that the democratic juggernaut was out of control. These were men who prided themselves on being anti-clerical, and who still believed in 1874 that the Liberal party was the natural ruling party. Nevertheless, they were as opposed to the prospect of disestablishment, secular education, home rule and the caucus as the first group, and, although claiming to be tolerant of religious error, were still susceptible to anti-Catholic arguments, especially on education. Hartington was a typical representative of this group: in 1875, he was anti-clerical enough to appeal to nonconformist MPs who would not accept a denominationalist as party leader; in 1872, he threatened to resign rather than to support Gladstone's Irish University Bill.

---

[260] Akroyd, Brocklehurst, Nicholson, Sir W. Russell, Talbot and Torrens, plus Jardine, Maitland, Maxwell, McCombie and Pender of Scottish MPs.

There was also a more advanced component. These were men of a semi-radical disposition who were at this time happy with the liberating, uplifting tone of the Liberal party and of Gladstone, who were warm friends of the common man, and who wished that the government would go further in attacking entrenched orthodoxy and in infusing spiritual feeling. Here one can include some young academic liberals – Brodrick, Dicey and Fremantle – and some 'spiritual' whigs – Hutton, Lubbock, Playfair, Arthur Russell, Whitbread and Frederick Cavendish (and in a restricted, episcopal, sense, Temple and Fraser). These tended to believe, far more than the first group, that all religions were to be valued, and were thus far less concerned about nonconformist and Catholic activity; some would even be prepared to accept disestablishment in England, assuming that it would advance spirituality.

All these three groups were further alienated from the Conservative party by their distrust of Disraeli. Yet only a few, nearly all in the last group, were to remain with Gladstone after 1886. The difference between the most radical of whig-liberals and the average nonconformist or radical discussed in chapter 4 was clear-cut. It was most obvious in discussing disestablishment and, more intangibly, the role that the popular judgment was to play in defining the character of the Liberal party.[261] Defence of the English Church Establishment had become the *raison d'être* for most whig-liberals, in and out of parliament, by 1874, even for most of those who had counted themselves as radicals before 1867.[262] Behind this stance lay, in the case of those who set forth an intellectual position, abstract support for the use of state law to control the wayward, passionate, sinful individual. This led them naturally into Liberal unionism after 1886, as we shall see. The assumptions about politics in practice which stemmed from that intellectual position had become a commonplace by the mid seventies, not only among intellectuals, but also, more importantly, among those leading Anglican Liberals who did not articulate the position coherently.[263] They were nostrums, however, which were not shared by many of those discussed in the next two chapters. For the latter, the path to national moral regeneration could be discovered only by individual activity; they believed that state control, at least in the sphere of religion and morals, was to be deprecated in all cases where it threatened the independence of the individual conscience.

---

[261] See e.g. the dispute, in 1878, between two men who might at first sight be grouped together as academic liberals, Goldwin Smith and Brodrick: Smith, 'Whigs and Liberals'; Brodrick, *Political studies*, pp. 242–56.

[262] Wright, 'Liberal versus Liberal, 1874', p. 598.

[263] See e.g. the perfect correspondence between the views set out throughout these two chapters, and those in the books of John Vickers, especially *Tinker Aesop and his little lessons for the age*, pp. iii–iv, 221–34, 256–60.

3

Gladstone, high churchmen
and liberal Catholics

Differences between them notwithstanding, whig-liberals developed a conception of 'Liberalism' that was primarily anti-clerical, and that valued 'Protestantism', the alliance of religion with the state, and the use of law in order to control 'enthusiasm'. At a similar level of generalisation, Gladstone and most Liberal high churchmen, nonconformists and religious radicals shared a different conception of 'liberty'. For them, the overriding political and religious problem was the corruption inherent in the exercise of authority. They directed allegations of 'materialism', not at the 'enthusiasts', but at the wealthy and complacent, the men whose influence on state and Church had failed to trigger mass spiritual awakening. They therefore tended to assert that the power of the state over the individual should be rigorously checked; and that the religious agencies, the engines of spiritual regeneration, should be untrammelled by temporal rulers who wished to use them to impose 'erastian' or 'ultramontane' perversions in a misconceived attempt to improve national morality. The groups discussed in chapters 3 and 4 believed that the spiritual power, if independent, would play a vital part in regenerating society – that it would infuse 'enthusiasm' and 'direction' where apathy and flaccidity were rife. They therefore demanded 'free play' for all religions, in order that the most effective would win out. Different groups believed that this open contest would produce different victors. High churchmen hoped that it would popularise the notion of the universal Church catholic; radical nonconformists considered that it would lead to an extension of the congregational system; positivists anticipated the triumph of the scientific Church; and academic liberals expected that rationalism would conquer. With the partial exception of the last, these groups also viewed one aim of politics to be the harnessing of public 'enthusiasm' in support of moral and spiritual ends.

Introduction: the high-church mission

In 1870, Henry Parry Liddon, the most famous high-church preacher of his generation, delivered a series of sermons in St James's, Piccadilly, on *Some elements of religion*. In these sermons, he defined religion as the 'sacred bond' by which the soul was enabled to 'know and love and serve its Highest and Invisible Object', to lose itself in a 'greater, wiser, better' Being. The great evils which frustrated this achievement were 'the invading forces of temptation' and 'insurrectionary outbreaks of lawless passions': sin was 'the great fact' against which 'every Christian life' was always struggling, and with which religion must deal.

He argued that religion could succeed in giving support in man's fight against sin only if it gave an account of God which convinced the mind, while offering emotional and moral succour to the soul. It must therefore be based on the authoritative creed of the early Christians, aided by whatever symbols were necessary, in worship, in order to convince the soul of the reality of the Christian message. 'The religion which has no fixed doctrines, or scarcely any; no code of absolute truth, to be taught and suffered for at all costs; no word of heart-searching warning, and yet of tenderest consolation for sinners – is not really a religion at all' – because it was not persuasive or sympathetic, and so could not deal with the 'great heart-sores of humanity'. It was Liddon's complaint that modern thinkers had lost their belief in an unshakable doctrinal system, and so were unable to provide this religion.[1]

This was a standard argument of high churchmen. Moreover, one of the most controversial doctrines which they defended was the notion of the Real Presence in the Eucharist, which they saw as lending especial force to the role of the sacraments in leading repentant man to be received into the body of Christ. Christ, it was maintained, would thus strengthen those who came to Him against temptation, and would elevate them above the 'seducing pleasures of sense', providing a 'foretaste of heavenly sweetness, of blissful calm, of spiritual joy'.[2] This reception of the sacrament was seen to be most exhilarating when it was perceived as a communal activity; in being gathered into Christ, all the discordant elements of humanity could thus be envisaged as blending into 'one holy unison of truth'.[3] The Church was at its most inspiring as a world-wide community, fighting against the 'common enemy' of sin,

---

[1] *Some elements of religion*, esp. pp. 20–6, 48, 118–19, 129, 161–5.
[2] Pusey, *The Presence of Christ in the Holy Eucharist*, pp. 68–74.
[3] Pusey, *The doctrine of the Real Presence*, pp. 719, 721.

and attempting to restore harmony by 'binding us up in one holy fellowship' and 'Christian brotherhood'.[4]

Through its activity, high churchmen believed that men of all classes, not least the 'neglected poor', were to be wrested from 'the principalities and powers of evil'.[5] They stressed that Christians must remain constantly aware of the 'value of each separate life', the 'priceless dignity' of the 'individual soul . . . in the eye of its Maker'. For there was no inequality before God: each man must 'work out his salvation with fear and trembling', and the 'spiritual rules' which determined his fate knew no leniency on class grounds. The poor, indeed, were best fitted to understand the nature of the 'suffering' required to follow the path of Christ, and least able to indulge in the 'tyranny of self-indulgence' which was the greatest obstacle to a proper relationship with God. It was thus they who could most easily appreciate the essence of Christianity; and 'the day will come when the God-fearing peasants of Devonshire or of Yorkshire will rise in judgment against the cultured irreligion of the centres of our modern civilisation', which in its scrambling for material pleasures and gains 'has forgotten almost or altogether the Eternal Home beyond'.[6]

The core of the high-church view was thus its conception of the evangelistic crusade of the universal Church catholic for the repression of sin and for the deliverance of mankind into God's hands. The consequence of this crusade would be the creation of a society in which millions of souls would work together, irrespective of social distinction, to serve Christ's purposes. One setback to the realisation of this vision was the division, in previous centuries, of the Church into many branches; the adherents of each now held to widely different tenets. But this, it was argued, would not prevent evangelism, especially if different sects were willing to work in harmony. The possibility of eventual Christian reunion could best be kept alive, it was maintained, if the traditional doctrines of the Church, in allegiance to which alone unity was possible, were defended from their attackers – from freethinkers, or from latitudinarians or intolerant Protestants who had the same ideal of unity, but who believed, conceitedly and in vain, that unity could be founded on the human inventions of the nineteenth century.

---

[4] Liddon, *Some elements of religion*, pp. 166–7; Pusey, *The Church the converter of the heathen*, pp. 15, 35, 81.
[5] Pusey, *Councils of the Church*, pp. 3–5.
[6] Liddon, *Some elements of religion*, pp. 125–6, 200–3. See also Pusey, *'Blessed are the meek'*.

Gladstone: Church and state

Gladstone had begun his public career as an evangelical; in the six years after 1832, he slowly added to his evangelicalism a conception of the Church of England as a branch of the historic Church catholic, an independent society with its own doctrines and organisation. One excellent recent study has demonstrated that his most famous early statement of his religious views, *The state in its relations with the Church* (1838), was written only shortly after his acceptance of the latter idea; and that within four years of its publication he was already coming to realise that it was incompatible with his earlier position – the high-tory position that state authority remained an invaluable aid in promoting the regeneration of society.[7] *The state in its relations with the Church* was not, therefore, a considered statement of a settled view, but an unsuccessful attempt to reconcile two traditions of thought. In the next few years, Gladstone's increasing participation in high-level politics, and his extensive reading of tractarian accounts of the catholicity and independence of the Church, led him to modify the practical position set out in it. He had assumed that the Church must be intimately associated with the state, not in order, superfluously, to add the weight of civil sanction to the authority of religious doctrine, but in order to infuse the state with the spiritual principles necessary for its evangelising task.[8] From the 1840s, however, he came to realise that the retention of state power over the Church was likely to damage the latter's capacity for zealous missionary work, and that this must therefore be promoted in other ways. But this shift of position did not alter two ingrained beliefs. His commitment to the Christian dogmatic system never subsequently wavered; nor did his assumption that to aid man's journey towards salvation should be one essential facet of political activity. Politics and religion remained indissolubly linked in his mind. On the one hand, unless faith in Christian doctrine was preserved, the future of politics, he considered, was extremely bleak;[9] on the other, he saw the effective defence of the Church to depend on the maintenance of right political relations.

Central to Gladstone's conception both of Christian doctrine and of political relations was the idea of man's sinfulness, 'the great fact in the world'.[10] The Church's 'historical charter' imposed a 'rule of conduct' which was framed with the aim of combating sin;[11] in following this, man

---

[7] Butler, *Gladstone: Church, state, and tractarianism.*
[8] *State in its relations with the Church,* i, 63, 112, 159–60, 330–1.
[9] (1864) Acland, *Acland,* p. 229.
[10] Peterson, 'Gladstone's review of "Robert Elsmere" ', p. 451; Tollemache, *Talks with Mr Gladstone,* p. 96.
[11] *Letter to the bishop of Aberdeen,* pp. 26–7; Tollemache, *Talks with Mr Gladstone,* p. 95.

would battle with doubt and temptation, in order eventually to find 'complete repose in God'.[12]

Gladstone therefore maintained that, if society was to be well-regulated, man must be taught to recognise and obey 'higher authority', wherever 'the evidence of its title is clear'.[13] To uphold the 'integrity' of Christian dogma was 'perhaps the noblest of all tasks which it is given to the human mind to pursue', because it constituted the 'guardianship of the great fountain of human hope, happiness and virtue'.[14] Much remained mysterious and incapable of elucidation by the human mind; and man should not attempt to question what he did not understand. The exercise of 'private judgment' was to be condemned where it led man to invent a religion of his own; this was more offensive than 'rank unbelief'.[15] It was dangerous to leave the path along which Providence steered the mind of man 'in the orbit appointed for the consummation of his destiny';[16] it was impossible to correct 'the Christian Faith by the light of a modern speculation'.[17]

In other words, Gladstone objected vehemently to all neologian religious conceptions. He argued that heterodox thinkers could expect progress to accompany loss of doctrine only because they were complacent intellectuals, and therefore largely unaware of the 'subtlety, intensity, and virulence' of sin in the world. They had not suffered either materially or spiritually; they had borne 'a smaller share than others of the common curse and burden'. 'A deep and definite idea of sin' was the essential accompaniment to firm Christian belief.[18] Progress could not be seen as 'the great fact' in the world, unless it was defined as 'progress in the human being as he stands in his account with God'.[19] Somerset's 'quack remedy' should be dismissed along with the 'childish or anile superstition . . . indolence . . . wantonness of mind' of modern university youth who dabbled in irresponsible speculation.[20] German philosophy had 'added but little to the stock of our knowledge of the mind and nature of men, if indeed it has added anything'.[21] All rationalising arguments were based on an 'insufferable arrogance': that modern sceptics were

---

[12] *Later gleanings*, p. 116; Gladstone to A. P. de Lisle, 10 October 1873, Gladstone papers, 44542, fo. 194.

[13] (1866) Russell, *MacColl*, p. 246.

[14] *Church of England and ritualism*, p. 52.

[15] Russell, *MacColl*, p. 246; Tollemache, *Talks with Mr Gladstone*, pp. 154–5; Morley, *Gladstone*, iii, 357–8, 520–1.

[16] 'On the influence of authority', p. 22.

[17] (1864) Johnston, *Liddon*, p. 91.   [18] *Later gleanings*, pp. 114, 116.

[19] Peterson, 'Gladstone's review of "Robert Elsmere"', pp. 455, 458.

[20] Matthew, viii, 131, 133; 'On the influence of authority', pp. 21–2; Gladstone to Pembroke, 4 July, 13 September, 19 October 1873, Gladstone papers, 44439, fo. 114, 44440, fos. 60, 229.

[21] (1873) Matthew, viii, 287.

immeasurably superior to former generations of believers, and were able to appreciate truths hidden from them.[22] (Gladstone regarded positivism as similarly wrong-headed, although his condemnation was slightly less fervent, on account of positivists' recognition of the potency of the Christian message – a recognition which will be discussed in chapter 4).[23]

In response to this assault from unorthodox religious thinkers (including the more aggressive latitudinarians), Gladstone considered it necessary to guard jealously all the baggage of the Christian faith, even parts which were not of the essence. The Athanasian Creed, for example, must be defended because the vast majority of its opponents were 'not firm in adhesion to dogma and the truth'; they would interpret any victory gained on the issue of the Creed as 'a practical negation of the title or duty of the Church to proclaim the "damnatory" message', an interpretation which would lead to a *certain* schism' in the Church.[24] It was also necessary to defend the prayer-book and to refuse to relax the terms of subscription for individuals.[25]

Despite holding these views, Gladstone, at least in the period under discussion, should not be regarded simply as a conservative high churchman. Indeed, he criticised many tractarians for placing too much stress on the role of authority in religion.[26] For him, the 'right idea' of the Christian religion was 'authority addressing itself to freedom and reason, and taking its stand on history (or tradition)'.[27] This idea was threatened by two symptoms of the same 'deplorable characteristic . . . first the sacrifice of liberty in the name of religion, and secondly and to a great extent by way of reaction the sacrifice of religion in the name of liberty'.[28] The balance by which man's spiritual and intellectual liberties were both secured against the oppression of powerful individuals in Church and state was precarious; once rulers indulged an ambition to extend their authority too far in one direction, a reaction might follow in another. Various human despots had pretensions to tear up the seamless garment of the Christian faith, and refashion it. They came in many guises: as popes, as sultans, as erastians, as latitudinarians, as rationalists. All aimed to hold fast by spurious and arbitrary versions of the Christian message and to enforce that view on those under their sway. Man's freedom to think and search for God must be guaranteed

---

[22] *Address at Liverpool Collegiate Institution*, p. 27.
[23] Morley, *Gladstone*, iii, 358; see Figgis and Laurence, *Acton's correspondence*, pp. 210–11.
[24] Notes, 8 June 1873, Gladstone papers, 44761, fo. 144.
[25] *Church of England and ritualism*, p. 80; (1871) Bailey, *Diary of Lady F. Cavendish*, ii, 100.
[26] *Gleanings*, vii, 232–4.
[27] Gladstone to Helen, 13 October 1874, Glynne–Gladstone papers, 27/13.
[28] Gladstone to J. M. Capes, 18 January 1872, Gladstone papers, 44541, fo. 47.

against the might of reactionary rulers; but, equally, religious doctrine must be guarded against the onslaught of intolerant liberals.

On the one hand, this explains Gladstone's distrust of ultramontanism, which he viewed as denying man's mental freedom and moral conscience by subordinating the individual to the whims of the pope.[29] The papacy, like a temporal despotism, had taken the centralisation of power to excess.[30] It claimed the right to define the areas of its legitimate influence, and thus almost destroyed individual capacity for the exercise of free will.[31] It sanctioned 'violence and change' in received doctrines, in order to gratify one man's thirst for power.[32] The pope tried to define doctrine too rigidly. To elevate transubstantiation into a dogma, when it necessitated assuming the 'change, annihilation, disappearance' of matter, about which man could know nothing, was a piece of human folly. Unless divine authority had revealed the true nature of the composition of this matter, all assumptions about it must remain metaphysical speculations.[33] By its arbitrary decrees, the papacy was also exposing the whole 'principle of belief' to great danger, and acting as 'the most effective . . . ally of the great unbelieving movement which now lays waste the world'; the reasons for, and elucidations of, matters of faith which it gave invariably had a 'rationalizing character'.[34]

The pope thus violated the rule that Gladstone increasingly upheld as essential for the proper regulation of authority; that, in order to limit men's opportunities for oppressive behaviour, through the misuse of power, temporal and spiritual government should be as distinct as was viable. In 1874, Gladstone claimed that the pope had destroyed the barrier set up by Christ between 'the two provinces of the civil rule and the Church'. Christ had nowhere argued that the 'spiritual authority' was to control 'the authority which is alone responsible for external peace, order, and safety among civilised communities of men'.[35] Gladstone therefore strongly objected to papal interference in Irish and British affairs – which he discerned in the opposition to the 1873 Irish University Bill.[36] But he also contended that the pope's retention of claims to temporal authority made him more liable to attack from foreign powers, and more open to criticism from Italian Catholics who would otherwise support him. Gladstone thus wished to see the pope's tem-

---

[29] Gladstone to Manning, 16 November 1869, *ibid.*, 44249, fo. 116.

[30] *Vatican decrees*, pp. 14–15.

[31] Gladstone to Emly, 11 October 1874, Gladstone papers, 44152, fo. 251; 'Count Montalembert', pp. 149–50.

[32] *Vatican decrees*, pp. 6–17; *Gleanings*, iii, 105.

[33] *PMP*, i, 154; Lathbury, ii, 386–9.

[34] Gladstone to Helen, 13 October 1874, Glynne–Gladstone papers, 27/13; Lathbury, ii, 386.

[35] *Vatican decrees*, p. 19.   [36] *Ibid.*, p. 27.

poral power destroyed, not because he disapproved of Catholicism, but because it would free the pope 'much more . . . to exercise his great and real powers'.[37]

Just as Gladstone objected to the spiritual power controlling the temporal, so he worked ceaselessly to prevent the reverse. For him, ultramontanism and erastianism were twin corruptions: indeed Gladstone blamed the erastian excesses of the Liberal government of 1846–52 on the provocation supplied by the tractarian secessions to Rome.[38] *The state in its relations with the Church* was 'anti-Erastian from beginning to the end', and, for that reason, he had no retrospective regrets about publishing it, long after he had come to disagree with its positive recommendations.[39] He always considered that to argue that the governors of a state had the power to determine the limits of the Church's doctrine would be to bow to the 'tyranny' of those who found 'their whole religion upon private opinion'. All union was 'spurious' if it involved, as many broad churchmen seemed to want it to involve, merely 'coincidence in a set of opinions arbitrarily chosen'. Whigs and their allies wished to constitute the Establishment as a 'vague agreement upon undefined fundamentals'.[40] The idea that the civil power was 'the ultimate authority in matter of religious truth' was not only 'a very ugly monster', but was 'by far the worst of all forms of false religion, indeed that which is not worthy to be called even a false religion'.[41] Erastianism was an 'ultra-pagan principle', the 'parent and protector of scepticism', and a 'debased offspring of the human mind'.[42] Gladstone left correspondents in no doubt that he would prefer disestablishment to any such mutilation of creeds at the hands of the state;[43] he held in boundless contempt what he considered to be the foolhardy fantasies, indulged by latitudinarians, of national union achieved through concessions in matters of dogma.[44]

It was fear of precisely this mutilation that altered Gladstone's attitude to the state's connection with the Church – although even in *The state in its relations with the Church*, he had contended that ecclesiastical and civil society were constituted differently, and that the Church might with

---

[37] Lathbury, ii, 32–44, esp. p. 43.
[38] Butler, *Gladstone: Church, state, and tractarianism*, p. 142.
[39] *PMP*, i, 145–6, 253.
[40] *Church principles*, pp. 500–4; *State in its relations with the Church*, i, 119–20.
[41] Gladstone to Northcote, 28 July 1865, Gladstone papers, 44217, fo. 98.
[42] Gladstone to Northcote, 10 February 1852, Iddesleigh papers, 50014, fo. 27; (1866) Johnston, *Liddon*, p. 87; Gladstone to Manning, 22 January 1874, Gladstone papers, 44250, fo. 145.
[43] Gladstone to Northcote, 9 August 1865, Gladstone papers, 44217, fo. 102; and to Coleridge, 29 March 1870, *ibid.*, 44538, fo. 112.
[44] Lathbury, i, 157, ii, 169; *Church of England and ritualism*, p. 80.

ease 'resign her privileges and act in her free capacity' at any time.[45] In the 1840s, he became belatedly aware that, after the repeal of the Test and Corporation Acts and the passage of Catholic Emancipation and of the Reform Act, it was now an 'utter . . . impossibility to uphold a consistent religious profession in the State'. There was great danger in persevering in the policy advocated by the clergy and the Conservative party, the policy of continuing blithely to impose Anglicanism as the state religion.[46] The result of still insisting that the state should assert a definition of religious truth would be 'the greatest of civil calamities – the mutilation, under the seal of civil authority, of the Christian religion itself'.[47] The Church could appear representative of the whole nation only by widening her doctrinal boundaries and transforming her organisation, in an attempt to embrace non-Anglicans.

This, of course, was exactly the development which the more aggressive latitudinarians wished to promote. Gladstone was particularly upset by the Judicial Committee's liberal interpretations of dogma, especially in the Gorham judgment, which drove his friends Manning and Hope Scott to Rome:[48] he thought that it presaged a drive to empty the Church's creeds of all their force, in response to the whim of public opinion.[49] To give an essentially civil court authority over ecclesiastical jurisdiction was a 'plain and a gross violation' of the principle of the Reformation statute guaranteeing the spiritual power proper authority in this area.[50] For the same reason, he condemned instances of parliamentary interference with the Church's independence, such as the 1857 Divorce Act, and all attempts to repress ritual by legislation. All such proscriptions horrified him, 'unless they are founded on principles of great breadth and depth';[51] he wished to refer the problems to the authority of the bishops and the sanction of Convocation, whose revival in the 1850s he had warmly welcomed.

Gladstone's object thus became to 'keep religion entire', in order to secure 'to the individual man his refuge'.[52] This was a political aim: if the Church was to remain 'a body able to take her trial before God and the world upon the performance of her work as His organ for the recovery of our country', this involved fighting and defeating those 'who will have the Church keep all [her] gold that it may be the price and the pledge of her slavery'.[53] The 'permanent duty of securing the Church . . . in her

---

[45] Butler, *Gladstone: Church, state, and tractarianism*, p. 85.
[46] (1848) Lathbury, i, 81–2.   [47] *Letter to the bishop of Aberdeen*, pp. 16–17.
[48] *Remarks on the Royal Supremacy*, p. 81.   [49] (1852) Lathbury, i, 88.
[50] *Remarks on the Royal Supremacy*, pp. 72–3.
[51] Gladstone to Hervey, 25 February 1872, Gladstone papers, 44541, fo. 80.
[52] Butler, *Gladstone: Church, state, and tractarianism*, p. 119.
[53] (1845) Lathbury, ii, 265–6.

spiritual office should be the first principle of action: and if temporal sacrifices can promote this purpose, they should be made . . . freely'. External temporal privileges that might, if politically essential, have to be surrendered, included church rates, and the existing colonial Church and English university structures. In 1865, he wrote to his son that 'if I have lived to any purpose at all' it had been 'in great part' to promote that process.[54] In return for losing these privileges, the Church, and all other religious sects, were to be guaranteed freedom from state interference in their spiritual concerns. The Church's claim to respect would be, not the bludgeoning authority that it had gained from association with government, but the authority of the Christian system, which men would be free to accept or deny.

Consequently, Gladstone advocated the admission to parliament of the jews, and later of the atheist Bradlaugh, in order to challenge the assumption that parliament was fit to legislate on questions involving 'the distinctive tenets of the Church' or the 'maintenance of the integrity of her doctrine and discipline'.[55] If the jews were not admitted to parliament, it would feel able to work to propagate an invented, undogmatic Christianity, 'void of definite, substantive, historical meaning . . . endangering the verities of the Christian faith'.[56] If Bradlaugh was not allowed to take his seat, parliament would be defining deism as an acceptable religion, which was 'disparaging in the very highest degree to the Christian Faith'.[57]

Gladstone therefore came to believe that the state must always 'leave the domain of religious conscience free'; the politician's 'chief duty' in religious matters was to safeguard the 'freedom' of the various branches of the Christian Churches, when attacked.[58] This was the surest way in which to defend the Church's traditions. It also offered the best hope that all sects would be able to fulfil their highest function, their evangelising function – and thus that public opinion would be maintained in an aware and elevated condition. This in turn was essential, because acceptance of Christianity was the 'one central hope of our poor wayward race';[59] and, more specifically, because without it there was no guarantee that correct political relationships would be preserved. If politics was to be 'reinfused' with religious sentiment, it was no longer activity in parliament which was required (as Gladstone had once thought), so much as the 'converting and baptising' of the masses.[60] The 'individual convic-

---

[54] *Ibid.*, ii, 169–73.   [55] *Substance of a speech*, pp. 14–16.

[56] *Ibid.*, pp. 17–18.

[57] (1881) Lathbury, i, 177; Morley, *Gladstone*, iii, 14.

[58] *Vatican decrees*, p. 29; (1870) Matthew, vii, 310.

[59] Russell, 'Mr Gladstone's theology', p. 779.   [60] (1841) *PMP*, ii, 135–7.

tions' of the rulers and people must be reformed by 'religious agency addressed to the private conscience'.[61]

The Church Establishment would obviously be an important tool in this evangelising mission, if it was unfettered. Although Gladstone came close to disparaging the connection of Church and state in England on many occasions in the latter part of his life, he never overtly attacked it. He would go so far as to say only, in 1869, that, assuming that the existing Establishment was to end, the voluntary system would be the 'best and safest of the alternatives before us, as the most likely to keep in a state of freshness the heart and conscience of man'.[62] The Establishment was the 'spiritual nurse' of the people, and played an irreplaceable role in the provision of education; it was obviously sensible not to disturb it if it continued to do its work, and if it was able to retain control of its own affairs.[63] In 1872, he thought disestablishment unlikely to occur; in 1874, although Disraeli, Tait and the queen had brought it immeasurably closer, he still aimed 'to avert, not to precipitate it'.[64]

He contended that the Church Establishment would be best fitted for her work if – like the state – she combined strong and zealous leadership with active popular consent.

As far as strong leadership was concerned, Gladstone was convinced that, where the bishop's authority in his diocese was weak, the Church's strength and vigour would fail.[65] In his episcopal appointments, he was careful to try to balance the claims of conflicting ecclesiastical parties, largely in order to strengthen the bishops' authority. It was they who must continue, as they had done for eighteen hundred years, to superintend the safeguarding of Christian doctrine, and to enforce discipline.[66] Most importantly of all, the bishops must have the power to propose, and quash, legislation on ecclesiastical matters: unless this were given, the Church could not be independent, but would be a puppet of the temporal power, 'dependent mainly on sufferance and good feeling'.[67] After the revival of Convocation as the Church's own parliament – for which Gladstone, of course, had worked assiduously – he was determined not to proceed with an ecclesiastical matter in parliament unless Convocation had initiated and approved the legislation.[68] As for Church ritual, he believed that it could be an aid in involving the laity more in church services, in heightening spiritual awareness, and in con-

---

[61] (1845) *ibid.*, ii, 277.   [62] Machin, *Politics and the Churches*, p. 382.
[63] *Speeches 1868*, p. 53.
[64] (1872) Matthew, viii, 264; (1874) Lathbury, i, 396.
[65] (1847) *ibid.*, i, 76.
[66] *Ibid.*, i, 109, 112–13. See W. G. F. Phillimore, 'Mr Gladstone', p. 1023.
[67] *Letter to the bishop of Aberdeen*, pp. 43–7, 53–5.
[68] (1874) Buckle, *Letters of Victoria*, ii, 307.

version. He thought that ritual innovations had assumed too prominent and formal a part in some places, and had detracted from the goal of encouraging spiritual awareness; but he maintained that this was only in reaction to the vulgarity and 'debasement' of former church services. His major concern was to stress the absurdity of using the powers of the legislature in order to repress these local variations, especially since they so manifestly did not affect the fundamentals of Christianity. The proper object of concern should be, not ritual, but the lack of zeal in worship which had made the ritualists experiment with new means of heightening interest and involvement.[69]

In 1872, Gladstone maintained that the revival of Convocation had thrown the Church back on her own 'moral strength'.[70] He contended that there had been a great improvement in the attitude of the clergy, who had become far more assiduous in promoting education, improving standards of worship, and crusading against sin – although there was much more work still to be done.[71] A lot of this, he said, was due to high-church influence, to the influx into the Church of men who combined an awareness of the historic role of the Church, with the ability to preach evangelical sermons defining a rule of conduct – which party evangelicals themselves were often unable to do.[72] Some, he believed, was the result of a new spiritual reverence and devotion growing up within the latitudinarian school, evident in men like Temple (whose views on the role of private judgment Gladstone continued to deprecate).[73]

This increase in vigour was also very welcome to Gladstone because, in his eyes, it strengthened public support for the Church Establishment. From the 1840s, he thought that 'strength with the people' would be the 'only effectual defence of the Church in the House of Commons . . . As the Church grows out of doors, she will be more felt indoors.'[74] Whereas the whig-liberals seemed to wish to broaden the Church's appeal by widening doctrinal boundaries and reforming its organisation, Gladstone hoped to see it reconciled to public opinion as a result of its

---

[69] *Church of England and ritualism*, pp. 5–49; (1865) Lathbury, i, 378–9; Matthew, viii, 135, 7 April 1872.

[70] Gladstone to Döllinger, 29 April, 6 September 1872, Gladstone papers, 44140, fos. 286, 289.

[71] (1875) 'Is the Church of England worth preserving?', in *Church of England and ritualism*; (1871) Matthew, viii, 36.

[72] Gladstone to Döllinger, 21 April 1874, Gladstone papers, 44140, fo. 293; Tollemache, *Talks with Mr Gladstone*, p. 95; 'New parliament and its work', pp. 550–4.

[73] (1865) Acland, *Acland*, p. 253 (on Temple's 'character'); (1874) Buckle, *Letters of Victoria*, ii, 308 (on his 'wisdom and gentleness'); Temple, 'The education of the world', pp. 44–5, Hawarden copy; Jelf, *Supremacy of scripture*, p. 9, Hawarden copy.

[74] (1846) Lathbury, ii, 273.

increased zeal and fervour. If religious bodies concentrated on moral and spiritual work, public opinion would respect them all.[75]

One of Gladstone's most strongly held hopes was to see harmony, and consciousness of shared aims, realised between the Established and non-Established sects. This would allow evangelism to proceed unchecked by strife, and politics to be liberated from freethinking and nonconformist attacks on the Church Establishment. If the Church acted as a force for moral good, not as a privileged political Establishment, radical nonconformists would be unlikely to win enough support to force through disestablishment, and would probably be less likely to wish for it: thousands had been driven into dissent in the eighteenth century in reaction to the growth of erastianism, which had loosened discipline within the Church, had 'almost paganized doctrine' and had been 'never enthusiastic except against enthusiasm'.[76] Moreover, disestablishment would do less damage, if Christian energy – Anglican and nonconformist – was galvanised in this way.

To Gladstone's mind, two means of advancing accommodation with nonconformists in a 'safe way' would be to rely on 'the person of our Saviour' as a spiritual guide, and on 'real historic study' as a philosophical guide.[77] He thought that, if the sects could agree to promote these, then by their friendly competition, independent of state control, the evangelism which he had once hoped would be encouraged by the state would be attainable by other means.

It was by stressing the personal life of Christ as a standard of 'consummate and divine perfection' that, in the eyes of Gladstone – and of nonconformists – Christianity was able to preach a more effective spiritual message than other religions. Only by emphasis on a person could the message be brought home to men of all social classes, and only by this means could moral behaviour 'towards all men alike, independently of station or race, or even life or creed' be sanctioned. Through Christ's personal example, one could deepen a sense of the 'brotherhood of man'.[78] Christianity could appeal to the 'masses of mankind' only if it were 'filled full with human and genial warmth, in close sympathy with every true instinct and need of man, regardful of the just titles of every faculty of his nature'.[79] Christ's personal example was 'a vitality, an earnestness, an eloquence, a power'.[80] Christ had shown that it was by being 'elevated and enthusiastic', not by being tranquil and reasoned, that man would eventually reach a secure haven 'exempt from pertur-

[75] *Letter to the bishop of Aberdeen*, p. 19.   [76] (1847) Lathbury, ii, 3.
[77] Gladstone to Baldwin Brown, 28 January 1871, Gladstone papers, 44539, fo. 146.
[78] 'On the influence of authority', pp. 13–14, 21.
[79] 'Valedictory address "On the place of ancient Greece"', pp. 74–5.
[80] *Ecce Homo*, p. 122.

bation and unsteadiness'.[81] Gladstone's growing admiration for nonconformist endeavour was founded upon a perception of their evangelising
zeal,[82] and of their moral preaching, which, he thought, stressed that
'rule of conduct' for whose absence he berated Anglican evangelicals. In
1879 the baptist Alexander Maclaren published a book of sermons
emphasising the need for a strong personal relationship with God, and
for constant prayer and consultation; the book suggested that this alone
would conquer self-will, laxity in devotion, and a misleading belief that
the temporal tasks of the active, powerful and prosperous were more
important than those of ordinary men. Gladstone scored nearly every
other page of his copy.[83]

Nor did Gladstone ever lose his belief that a better understanding
between Christians would also be attained by relying on the traditions
and history of the Church in its widest sense (that is, not just on critical
examination of the Scriptures or of specific dogmas). Men must be
brought to study the Church's 'place and function in Christendom'; and
to be overawed by the inheritance which they must guard.[84] He considered that the Church of England was one of the few branches of the
universal Church which had retained the essence of the Christian
message in a pure enough form to serve as a basis for its eventual
reunion. (He also admired the Old Catholic movement on the continent,
for attempting to assert ancient catholic truth against the modern inventions of the papacy: he hoped that it too was opening a 'new door for
Christian union', and that it might even 'react . . . beneficially upon the
mass of the Roman Church'.)[85] Gladstone believed that scholarship into
the development of the early Church afforded an invaluable spiritual and
philosophical guide; he thus warmly welcomed the increasing amount of
nonconformist research into the creeds and the Early Fathers, as a
counterweight to the narrow Calvinism preached by previous nonconformist generations.[86]

In these two areas, Gladstone had evidence that the nonconformists
were increasingly coming to share his preoccupations. They seemed to
share it also in a third sense, in believing that parliament should not
interfere with the internal government of the Church; and so, it
appeared, did growing numbers of working-men. In 1865, Gladstone was
greatly cheered to see the *Daily Telegraph*, 'the advanced popular paper of

---

[81] *Ibid.*, p. 164.
[82] Bebbington, 'Gladstone and the nonconformists', pp. 374–5.
[83] Maclaren, *Week-day evening addresses*, Hawarden copy.
[84] (1878) Acland, *Acland*, p. 323; *Church of England and ritualism*, p. 79.
[85] Gladstone to Döllinger, 14 December 1874, Gladstone papers, 44140, fo. 317; Gladstone to Helen, 13 October 1874, Glynne–Gladstone papers, 27/13.
[86] Gladstone to Baldwin Brown, 28 January 1871, Gladstone papers, 44539, fo. 146.

the day, with a vast circulation', declare 'strongly in favour of free speech for Convocation'; it encouraged him to think that 'Erastianism . . . is at length decaying, and will soon be like to die'.[87] That nonconformists could be an effective ally against the erastian whigs who wished to tamper with internal Church doctrine and discipline had first become evident to Gladstone as a result of his own nonconformist ancestry (through his mother) – Scottish episcopalianism.[88] As early as 1844, he had maintained that he did not want the episcopalians' 'free expression' of historic principle to be restrained by an acceptance of the 'servitude' consequent upon an increased parliamentary grant.[89] It was also in 1844 that he first praised the zeal and earnestness of the Free Church seceders from the presbyterian Establishment;[90] he said in 1872 that, although not 'on the side of Scottish Presbyterianism' as a doctrinal historic creed, he had 'all my life been with it as against the Erastian system'.[91]

Gladstone: education

Gladstone also had some sympathy with nonconformists' views about educational policy. But his perspective in approaching the question was very different from theirs.

Since, for Gladstone, human progress was to be defined as progress in man's relationship with God, it followed that the primary aim of education must be religious. At university level, this implied, firstly, that the study of theology was essential. He believed that the older universities had a seminal role in determining the future direction of the 'national mind';[92] and that, unless theological scholarship were promoted, the rationalisers and sceptics would win the argument. The future of the human race depended 'in the main upon the great question of belief';[93] and the 'general want of study and learning' in the Church was alarming.[94] He maintained, secondly, that the secular arm of education should explain the 'mysteries' of human character, in order to help Christianity in restoring 'the order of our moral nature'. Unless human knowledge was regarded as a whole, and its various branches retained exact definitions of 'their proper provinces, and of their mutual relations', chaos would ensue. By harmonising old knowledge and new discoveries, the mediaeval university system had insured against the destabilising

[87] (1865) Lathbury, i, 143.
[88] S. G. Checkland, *The Gladstones: a family biography 1764–1851* (Cambridge, 1971), pp. 40–6.
[89] (1844) Lathbury, ii, 255–6; see Innes, *Chapters of reminiscence*, pp. 81–91, for his defence of voluntaryism as a result of his work for Trinity college, Glenalmond.
[90] *Gleanings*, iii, 36–8; see (1848) 'Duke of Argyll on presbytery', p. 80.
[91] Lathbury, i, 168.   [92] Morley, *Gladstone*, iii, 471, 486–7.
[93] Lathbury, ii, 220.
[94] Gladstone to H. W. Acland, 18 March 1863, Gladstone papers, 44091, fo. 55.

excesses of youthful radicalism, and guaranteed that the 'acquired wealth of mankind' was not forsaken. This was why he considered classics to be an essential branch of study: the lives of the ancient Greeks afforded the opportunity to investigate human nature in its 'largest, strongest, simplest' forms.[95]

In 1854, Gladstone was primarily responsible for the Act which reorganised the government of Oxford university and thus reinvigorated its teaching. But he could do little to prevent the spread of freethinking there: in 1865, he complained that the 'rationalizing movement' in the university had grown with 'fearful rapidity'.[96] While Döllinger and his friends had converted the German universities into bastions of 'stout and enduring resistance' by safeguarding eternal truths, Oxford, the 'eldest daughter' of the Church of England, was in the grip of young reformers who aimed to 'destroy' the established educational system there.[97] Gladstone saw reformers like Brodrick to be indulging in fantasy when they hoped to revive 'a taste for plain living and high thinking in English society', by cultivating the imagination, pinning faith in Idealism and eschewing specific doctrinal content: there was 'but one hope' of achieving such an end, and it was far removed from Brodrick's vision.[98]

The reformers aimed to liberalise the university and encourage nonconformists to go there, by enthroning 'what is barbarously called undenominationalism'; by minimising the influence of the Anglican clergy in university government; by asserting that no more 'denominational' colleges should be established;[99] and by abolishing clerical fellowships (which would create 'an undue and unnatural predominance of the lay element', and would remove the guarantees provided by the clerical presence, that teaching would be maintained 'at the highest possible moral level').[100] Rather than see 'its religion regulated in the manner which would please Bishop Colenso', Gladstone would wish Oxford to be 'level with the ground'.[101]

Gladstone naturally also condemned whig-liberal attempts to impose undenominational teaching at elementary level. An undenominational system was, for him, a 'moral monster', and the movement towards it a 'gross error'; it was 'glaringly partial' and he would 'never be a party to it'.[102]

---

[95] 'Address, 1860'.
[96] Gladstone to Northcote, 9 August 1865, Gladstone papers, 44217, fo. 102.
[97] *Gleanings*, vi, 213; Gladstone to H. W. Acland, 18 March 1863, Gladstone papers, 44091, fo. 55; (1870) Matthew, vii, 309–10.
[98] Brodrick, *Influence of the older English universities*, p. 17, Hawarden copy.
[99] (1870) Matthew, vii, 309–10.   [100] (1880) Lathbury, i, 223–4.
[101] (1865) Harvie, *Lights of liberalism*, pp. 90–1.
[102] *The Church of to-day*, 2 November 1894, copy in diary, Phillimore papers; Gladstone to Bright, 27 January 1874, Bright papers, 43385, fo. 247.

In line with his theory that to safeguard the Church's freedom was 'the chief duty of politicians in their direct relations with religion', Gladstone proposed to outflank the educational reformers by articulating a diametrically opposed principle. Just as individual religious sects should be given freedom to organise themselves and to propagate their message without hindrance, so all teaching was henceforth to be 'free and various'.[103] In universities, this meant that each sect was to be free to establish denominational colleges: throughout his later life, he wished to see the introduction and extension of nonconformist and Roman Catholic colleges at Oxford.[104] This in turn, he anticipated, would allow the Anglican colleges to retain their full identity; 90 per cent of parents of English university students were Anglicans, and they must be allowed 'full security for the rearing of those children in the principles and practices of their religion'.[105]

The same applied in primary education. Until the late 1860s, he was a staunch defender of voluntary schools, because he did not believe that a rating system would tap the religious zeal which transformed 'mere instruction' into 'education': the former 'only touches the understanding of man', while the latter 'acts upon his heart, purifies his sentiments, elevates his thoughts, and raises him to the standard of a Christian life'.[106] In 1869, he was still unenthusiastic for the institution of a national system, even when it was clear that the Liberals would be proposing one.[107] But, significantly, he had demanded in 1867 that secular schools should be entitled to rate-aid, as well as those teaching religion, if such a system were to be introduced – an eventuality for which the Bruce–Forster bill of that year had not provided.[108] In and after 1870, his enthusiasm for voluntaryism enabled him to recognise the merit of the 'secular solution' proposed by radical nonconformists: in principle, he had no objections to seeing this solution implemented (although circumstances made it politically impracticable).[109] As we shall see, whig-liberal pressure for undenominational education proved too strong for Gladstone to overbear in 1870, and on several occasions afterwards he made clear his dislike of the concessions forced on him then, especially

---

[103] (1870) Matthew, vii, 309–10.
[104] (1892) Tollemache, *Talks with Mr Gladstone*, p. 51; (1863) Harvie, *Lights of liberalism*, p. 83.
[105] (1866) Newman Hall, *Autobiography*, p. 268.
[106] *Hansard*, cxli, 948–9, 11 April 1856.
[107] (20 March) Bailey, *Diary of Lady F. Cavendish*, ii, 67.
[108] *Hansard*, clxxxviii, 1364, 10 July 1867.
[109] See e.g. Gladstone to Bright, 27 January 1874, Bright papers, 43385, fo. 247; Gladstone, 'Mr Forster and Ireland', p. 453; (Forster) Selby, 'Manning and the 1870 Education Bill', p. 208.

the Cowper-Temple clause – which he called an 'absurdity'.[110] But the clause nonetheless allowed some doctrinal teaching, and he was in practice happy to accept both the Act, and subsequent Conservative legislation bolstering the position of voluntary schools, rather than to excite the Liberal party towards further action on the education question – action which would almost inevitably take an anti-clerical direction.

Gladstone and Liberal politics

By the mid 1860s, Gladstone had come to appreciate the contributions to Christian practice made by nonconformists.[111] His fellow high churchman G. W. E. Russell was correct in describing him, in later years, as 'in sympathy and temper if not in formal theory, a Free Churchman'.[112] This sympathy was founded on his insistence that individual liberty of opinion must be secured against potential interference by temporal or ecclesiastical authority. His political views were increasingly shaped by a similar concern. Central to this was his belief that, if religious faith were not widespread, political misgovernment was certain and anarchy likely; and that misgovernment would also result if political liberty were denied to the working-man. He argued this on the grounds that, if faith were not widespread, and liberty not secured for all, there would be no chance of checking the manifestations of sinfulness which constantly and inevitably threatened to prevent responsible government.

For Gladstone, the operation of sin in politics was most debilitating at the centre of power. 'Ideals in politics' were 'never realised', because the political world afforded too many opportunities for 'the natural man. Self-seeking, pride, domination, power – all these passions are gratified in politics.'[113]

But, although the possession of power allowed much scope for oppression and corruption, Gladstone's answer was not simply to reduce the role of government to a minimum, since anarchy must be prevented, and society maintained in a healthy state of regulation.[114] In economic and foreign affairs, corrupt influences had to be held in check, through, on the one hand, a free-trade policy, and, on the other, the application of 'Canningite' principles of national independence and the maintenance of the international balance of power. The implementation of both sets of policies required constant effort because of the likely interference of

---

[110] (1870) Hodder, *Shaftesbury*, iii, 267; Raleigh, *Annals of the Church of Scotland*, p. xxiv; MacColl, *Education question*, p. 34. See below, pp. 302–4.
[111] Bebbington, 'Gladstone and the nonconformists'; (1870) Matthew, vii, 362.
[112] 'Mr Gladstone's theology', pp. 790–1.
[113] Morley, *Gladstone*, iii, 474–5; Gladstone, 'County franchise and Mr Lowe', p. 560.
[114] Matthew, 'Disraeli, Gladstone, and mid-Victorian budgets'.

vested interests. The same watchfulness was required in other departments of administration (for this reason, while Gladstone had a predis-
position against state intervention in the social sphere, he was keen to lay
down no 'invariable rule' in case action was required against abuses).[115]
But such policies could be instituted only if the executive was sufficiently
responsible, and of this there was no guarantee. From the mid sixties
onwards, for example, Gladstone would often maintain that the real
threat in politics was the growth of a plutocracy – the increasing susceptibility of the classes represented in parliament to an enervating love of
ease and wealth.[116] In the 1870s, success and above all wealth seemed to
him the most effective passports to a parliamentary seat. Sectional
interests, moreover, were 'ever wakeful, ever nimble', awaiting their
political chance, and frequently taking it.[117] In 1856, in order to check
their freedom of action, he called for a return to Peel's notion of executive
government, and to a 'policy of peace abroad, of economy, of financial
equilibrium, of steady resistance to abuses, and promotion of practical
improvements at home; with a disinclination to questions of organic
change gratuitously raised'.[118]

In the mid fifties, however, neither party wished, in Gladstone's eyes,
to follow such a policy. After his resignation in 1855, he considered
Palmerston's foreign policy bombastic and spendthrift, while criticising
the Conservatives' fondness for high defence expenditure.[119] He alleged
that recourse to war prevented the pursuit of economy, encouraged the
manipulation of speculators, and detracted from the incomes of the mass
of mankind 'who can but just ward off hunger, cold, and nakedness'.[120]
He criticised Palmerston as a 'most demoralising and a most destructive
minister', 'by far the worst . . . this country has had during our time'.[121]
Moreover, the 'strength of the Executive' had been greatly impaired
since Peel's fall, damaging the efficiency of the government process. The
lack of disciplined support in the country for any government
encouraged ministers to cast around the House for votes.[122]

In addition, he considered both parties' attitudes to the Church to be
dangerously subversive of the interests of true religion. 'One large

---

[115] Tollemache, *Talks with Mr Gladstone*, p. 160; Gladstone, *Wedgwood*, p. 13.
[116] Purcell, *De Lisle*, ii, 79; Gladstone, 'County franchise and Mr Lowe', pp. 554, 558–9;
Gladstone to Houghton, 13 September 1871, Gladstone papers, 44540, fo. 107;
Tollemache, *Talks with Mr Gladstone*, pp. 166–7; (1874) Matthew, viii, 491. See also, on
the moral advantages of poverty: 'A modern "symposium" ', pp. 188–9; (1844) *Gleanings*,
v, 119.
[117] 'County franchise and Mr Lowe', pp. 555–6, 560.
[118] Parker, *Graham*, ii, 296.   [119] 'New parliament and its work', p. 581.
[120] (1859) *Gleanings*, ii, 144.
[121] (1856) Stanmore, *Herbert*, ii, 67; (1858) Parker, *Graham*, ii, 338.
[122] (1856) Matthew, v, 112–13.

portion of the political world' was 'disposed to tamper with the purity and integrity' of Christian faith in the 'vain idea of making the whole nation become Churchmen'; 'another portion . . . perhaps yet more seriously endangers the same priceless treasure by clinging with obstinacy to all the temporal incidents of national Establishment'.[123] In 1865, Gladstone wrote that there were elements in 'both political parties' which tended to sap the foundations of belief, and that it was a 'chief remaining hope of my public life' to arrest this process.[124] There was no hope of achieving this through the Conservatives, whose bigoted defence of all the outward temporal signs of Establishment at any cost to the Church's inner spiritual and dogmatic life was, in Gladstone's eyes, 'treason to the Church'.[125] There was some hope of attaining it through the Liberals. This was because the whigs and their allies, although always recruiting new support – in 1875, he accused Forster of being an Arnoldian Liberal 'in the sense of forty years back'[126] – were not the only influence in the party, and because the other constituents of the coalition – nonconformists, radicals, Irish Catholics – might provide willing ears for his views.

His drift towards the Liberals, consummated on the Italian question in 1859, was impelled by many considerations. He was ambitious and realised that the Liberals had a natural majority and that the Conservatives did not, hardly a promising situation for an 'executive' politician, since a government which was in a minority in parliament was open to any sectional wind that blew.[127] He saw the Conservatives as irresponsible and willing to bribe sections of the House, mainly owing to Disraeli's lack of principle: Gladstone believed that, in 1846, in 1852 and in 1859 (and later, notoriously, in 1867 and in 1876–8), Disraeli ruthlessly and recklessly demoralised and shamed the executive system, and in doing so destroyed the idea that the Conservatives were a disinterested party.[128] Gladstone realised that the separate existence of the Peelites as a third party made majority government difficult and so

---

[123] (1865) Lathbury, ii, 169.
[124] Gladstone to Northcote, 22 July 1865, Gladstone papers, 44217, fo. 92.
[125] (1865) Lathbury, ii, 170. Of course, Conservative feeling against Gladstone on ecclesiastical grounds was equally strong: Vincent, *Journals of Lord Stanley*, p. 155.
[126] Fitzmaurice, *Granville*, ii, 148.
[127] (1857) *PMP*, iii, 221; Gladstone to Lyttelton, 20 August 1866, Glynne–Gladstone papers, G36.
[128] Rendel, *Personal papers*, pp. 83, 100, 108; Gladstone to W. H. Gladstone, 11 October 1868, 7 November 1869, Glynne–Gladstone papers, 36/2; *PMP*, iii, 271; Morley, *Gladstone*, iii, 475. Gladstone's most succinct comments on Disraeli's political morals were the two exclamation marks appended in the margin of his copy of an 1879 pamphlet whose author, addressing Disraeli, argued that 'during a long life, your political career has been untarnished by a single act of inconsistency, meanness, or duplicity': Carter, *Beaconsfield*, British Library copy, p. 8.

weakened the executive, intensifying the threat of organic constitutional change.[129] Moreover, he probably desired to use the Italian question to attack the pope's temporal power.

Most importantly, however, he wished to reforge the bond between politics and public opinion; one of his most heartfelt complaints about the Conservative party was that Derby was unwilling to do this.[130] In the 1860s and 1870s, this wish developed into a fully fledged mission to maintain the utility and impartiality of executive government by harnessing popular morality in its defence.

Gladstone was not unusual among nineteenth-century politicians in arguing that 'selfishness and passion' were the 'great disabling causes' which prevented men from judging 'rightly and patriotically of public questions'. Where he was more unusual was in stressing increasingly that the least potentially selfish were those classes 'which are lower, larger, less opulent, and, after allowing fully for trades unions, less organised'.[131] This doctrine became fully developed only in the context of the mid seventies: Acland found in 1878 that the 'burden' of Gladstone's 'song' was 'always the deterioration of the Governing Classes in comparison with the poor'; and that he maintained that God's teaching went 'very deep' in showing that the poor were 'better and wiser than the rich'.[132] It is important not to ascribe *fixed* 'populist' views to Gladstone from too early a date. In the period under review, his most populist phases – especially in 1866–7 and in the years after the humiliations of 1874–5, but also after the Lords' expression of antagonism to his ballot and army-purchase proposals in 1871 – all constituted reactions to political snubs from the whig-liberal and Conservative establishments: vengefulness was a potent Gladstonian characteristic. Nonetheless, it is instructive to analyse the viewpoint to which he was tending.

He was coming to argue that it was only by harnessing the superior morality of the poor that the activity of the British executive could be kept from sinking into the morass of vested-interest legislation. Corruption bred discontent: a ruling party must minimise both by constant activity in politics, 'to invigorate the institutions of the land, to strengthen the national cohesion, to increase the sum total of the public energies, to establish confidence between class and class, to train the people for the habitual hereditary discharge of public duty'. Vested interests made 'a night of it' whenever the public slept.[133] There was always a danger that the poor man, concerned with survival and the

---

[129] (April 1856) *PMP*, iii, 203.   [130] Ramm, 'Gladstone as politician', p. 112.
[131] 'County franchise and Mr Lowe', p. 542.   [132] Acland, *Acland*, p. 323.
[133] 'County franchise and Mr Lowe', p. 560.

basics of life, might, unless agitated into political awareness, vote merely in order 'to please the employer or the landlord'. It was therefore necessary to keep 'the national pulse in a state of habitual and healthy animation'.[134]

Gladstone wished to emphasise that the purpose of extending the franchise was not to equip the poor themselves to govern. He maintained that the working-man, like Gladstone himself, respected, indeed adored, the natural aristocracy, as long as it performed its social duty; and that there was no prospect, in the ordinary run of events, of any sort of social revolution.[135] The 'natural condition' of a 'healthy society' was that the 'leisured class' should rule, and, were this system to be displaced, a 'rot' would have entered into 'the structure of society'.[136] But, while the natural leaders, the propertied classes, would assume political command, the pressure for the maintenance of moral government would come from the common man. The economising Gladstonian Liberal party, devoid of class bias, was to reforge the bonds between the mass of electors, poor, incapable of taking policy decisions, but made moral through suffering, and the competent executive.

In other words, a neat balance would operate, which would minimise the opportunities for political corruption, for any class. The mass of the electorate would ensure that the propertied classes governed well and morally, while those who were trained in the practice of government would prevent the course of politics being perverted, by mass pressure, into undesirable channels – by avoiding the irresponsible exploitation of issues which would encourage manifestations of naked class feeling.

It was less likely that the masses would press for such a perversion by themselves, than that they might be tempted to do so by untrustworthy radical demagogues. Gladstone had no time for political radicalism in the accepted sense of the term.[137] He did not believe that the constitution was perfectible;[138] he had a lifelong distrust of those politicians who used half-baked ideas to arouse grievances and dissatisfactions, and thus to water the 'seeds of organic change': he had a fundamental aversion to great changes in the distribution of power or the operation of government.[139] In the 1850s, he called the idea of a secret ballot 'trash'.[140] He also disliked radical pressure for extensive redistribution of taxation or

---

[134] 'A modern "symposium"', p. 185.
[135] 'County franchise and Mr Lowe', pp. 547–8, 550.
[136] 'Notes and queries on the Irish demand', p. 177.
[137] Raleigh, *Annals of the Church of Scotland*, pp. xxiv–xxv; Hamilton, *Gladstone*, p. 46.
[138] H. L. E. Bulwer, Lord Dalling, *Sir Robert Peel: an historical sketch* (London, 1874), p. 100, Hawarden copy.
[139] 'Prospects political and financial', p. 268; Tollemache, *Talks with Mr Gladstone*, p. 78; see also *PMP*, ii, 10–17.
[140] (1856) Parker, *Graham*, ii, 295.

for state disbursements to the individual. In his view, popular pressure should be used to lower taxes, rather than to engineer the redistribution of wealth through the tax structure, or through other government legislation.[141] Indeed, in the decade after 1855, Gladstone came to see in Cobden and Bright the leaders of a popular radical movement articulating the interests of poor taxpayers who were anxious to press on government for tax reductions and for a cheap foreign policy:[142] in this way, the working-man would be able to retain enough of his money to raise himself into 'moral, Christian, and domestic habits'. As long as his comfort was 'tolerable', he would be far more suspicious of demagogic politicians who preached class war, far less hostile to the Church, and far 'better able to receive the consolations and to bear the discipline of religion'.[143]

Gladstone hoped that the electorate, instead of pressing for sectional gain, would pronounce on broad issues on which moral considerations dictated a course – while leaving government responsible for detailed policy. By the late 1870s, he was confident that it had done this. Reviewing its achievements over the previous half-century, he listed two Reform Acts, the abolition of slavery, corn-law repeal, cheap postage, tax relief, the abolition of church rates, Irish Church disestablishment and the 1870 Land Act. Such triumphs were not the triumphs of intellectual liberalism;[144] they arose from the popular belief in the 'brotherhood of man'. The 'nation, not the classes', had the best understanding of moral politics, because intellectuals were 'trained in pursuits which do not train nor touch the emotions and the affections, nor human sympathies, nor the deeper interests of life, nor the great human brotherhood'.[145] It therefore followed that 'the popular judgment, on a certain number of important questions, is more just than that of the higher order'.[146] The classes newly enfranchised in 1867 had been able to avoid the temptation of gratifying class interests, had 'desired, upon the whole, to act in the spirit of the olden time', and had 'greatly invigorated the action of the system'.[147]

In short, from the 1860s, Gladstone intended the Liberal party to excite popular enthusiasm behind moral causes, and thus to give legitimacy and strength to a revitalised executive government. To him, the most dangerous political threat was, far from being the advent of

---

[141] Matthew, v, xxix–xxxvii. See the *Corrected report of the speech at Greenwich*, pp. 30–1.

[142] Matthew, 'Disraeli, Gladstone, and mid-Victorian budgets', pp. 629–30; Matthew, v, xxxvii.

[143] *Times*, 15 September 1865, p. 7; 'Rejoinder on authority', p. 926.

[144] 'A modern "symposium"', p. 187.

[145] *PMP*, i, 113, iv, 86.

[146] 'County franchise and Mr Lowe', p. 545.

[147] *Ibid.*, p. 549. He had predicted this in 1866: *Hansard*, clxxxii, 58, 1135–9, 12 March, 12 April 1866.

democracy, the likelihood of a plutocracy, and of enervated leadership. If the new electors were guided correctly, and not by demagogues anxious to divide politics along class lines, they might be persuaded to sanction a series of responsible policies. They might help to safeguard the independence of religious interests from state interference: by 1868 he had reached the seminal conclusion that 'it is *chiefly* by retaining the confidence of the Liberal party that any good is to be done to the Church in its highest interests'.[148] They might press on government for the relief of taxation. They might constitute a moral force agitating against a missionary expansionist foreign policy, and against heavy expenditure in aid of vested interests.

This conception of the Liberal party was in some ways a radical one. But in essence it involved the harnessing of unfamiliar forces for traditional ends. Gladstone's aims were conservative: to preserve the political balance between the propertied and the masses; to maintain low expenditure and low taxation; to re-establish the authority of central executive government; to safeguard the doctrinal heritage of the Church of England from attack; to secure stability and the rule of law in Ireland; most importantly, to demonstrate to the enlarged electorate that its proper function was the age-old one of checking corruption and extravagance in government, rather than the disreputable one of using its voting muscle to press for sectional gain. What he said of religion, in 1888, has a more general application: 'I don't believe in any new systems. I cling to the old. The great traditions are what attract me'. He had no social – as opposed to religious – vision; he believed that Providence shaped the development of his career; he saw his political function as being to watch the drift of public opinion, adopting commitments at times when political flux threw up materials which he felt were capable of being fashioned in accordance with his conception of good or elevating government.[149]

It is because he had few distinct aims beyond the maintenance of sound government and the promotion of moral endeavour that he cut such an ambiguous political figure. He tapped the language of enthusiasm, of zeal, of veneration of popular morality; it formed the basis of his oratorical appeal. Its practical consequences were never as marked. In 1866–7, his parliamentary reform proposals were less adventurous than his exhilarating phrases of 1864. In 1870, he let slip to nonconformists his willingness to accept educational secularism, but for the next few years he actively defended the system of state grants to denominational schools. He applauded nonconformist endeavour, and gave

---

[148] Lathbury, i, 157.
[149] Shannon, *Gladstone*, p. 101; Vincent, *Formation of the Liberal party*, p. 214; *PMP*, i, 136; Hamer, 'Gladstone', pp. 43–5.

many hints of his unhappiness with the conditions of Establishment, but he mounted staunch defences of it in the early 1870s, and would not declare even for Welsh and Scottish disestablishment until 1889.

This ambiguity was, of course, the basis of Gladstone's political success. One can, if one wishes, see it as machiavellian, hypocritical or self-deceiving. But the essence of political activity, for Gladstone, was not the passage of legislation; it did not, therefore, matter that legislation was to be carried only by 'the ripeness of the public mind',[150] rather than immediately after it was first requested by a minority. Gladstone's goal in politics was, instead, the encouragement and maintenance of a self-questioning, evangelised and ever-alert political society, which was capable, when necessary, of a 'virtuous passion'.

The crux of Gladstone's relationship with the late Victorian Liberal party was that, while himself believing that the arousal of public opinion was beneficial (which distinguished him from most whig-liberals), he nearly always turned the flank of his radicals' assaults, when they identified certain targets as embodying political privilege to an unacceptable degree. Instead of rousing opinion to overthrow these institutions – of which the Church Establishment was under the greatest threat – he roused it in different directions, in favour of crusades which involved the material interests of the British voter, for better or worse, far less. The two most important of these crusades – both of which he fuelled within months of the launch of a major nonconformist campaign for the disestablishment of the Church of England – concerned Bulgaria in 1876 and Ireland in 1886.[151]

Gladstone: foreign policy

As is well known, Gladstone saw the only guarantee of peace in Europe to reside, not in isolationism, but in the maintenance of checks and balances through a system of international law and 'Public Right'.[152] One of the leading principles of such a system would be that no country was to 'regulate the affairs of neighbouring countries for its own convenience'. This was 'lawless and revolutionary . . . an unblushing assertion of the law of the strongest'.[153] To impose a rule on a people who did not consent to it was a policy to which he maintained, in theory at least, a steadfast opposition. It was the basis of his dislike of Palmerston's foreign policy, never better expressed than in his attack on the latter's

[150] (About licensing, 1869) Harrison, *Drink and the Victorians*, p. 260.
[151] (Rogers) Dale, *Dale*, p. 736.
[152] 'Germany, France, and England', p. 593; see Schreuder, 'Gladstone', pp. 96–100.
[153] 'Paths of honour', p. 602.

doctrine of *Civis Romanus sum*: Britain was not a 'universal schoolmaster' uplifted 'high above the standing-ground of all other nations'; the British had no 'mission to be the censors of vice and folly, of abuse and imperfection, among the other countries of the world'.[154]

One root of this belief was an argument of a religious nature. No government, he maintained, must override the authority of that branch of the Church catholic which held sway in any nation. It was wrong to condemn the version of religious truth held by any other man: all should be 'jealous for the honour of whatever we have and hold as positive truth'.[155] Men in any nation 'ought not to depart, except upon serious and humble examination, as well as clear conviction, from the religion they have been brought up to profess, even though non-Christian; for it is the school of character and belief, in which Providence has placed them'.[156] This was the 'clear and simple and indestructible basis of Churchmanship', which prevented Gladstone and all like-minded high churchmen from ever even considering secession to Rome.[157]

After Gladstone left office in 1855, he complained that these principles were being wrecked by Palmerston's Turkish policy, which was founded on 'the spirit of Protestant propagandism', and whose proponents displayed a 'wonderful union of bigoted tempers with latitudinarian opinions'.[158] He refused to accept Palmerston's argument that Turkey was 'one of the most progressive countries of Europe', and that the enemy of civilisation in the East was Russia. The imposition of Turkish rule on the Eastern Christians had been a triumph of might over right, a 'great savage incursion of brute force' invading 'some of the fairest countries of the world'.[159]

Gladstone's defence of the Eastern Christians, and therefore, to some extent, of Russia, owed a lot to his philhellenism,[160] but it also owed much to his sympathy with historic Eastern Christianity.[161] He regarded the Orthodox clergy as the focus of Greek national life during the long years of Ottoman occupation and degradation;[162] he kissed the hands of an Orthodox bishop in the Ionian Islands in 1858 – an act which was to dog him politically for years to come.[163] He defended the structure of Russian government, because of the informal harmony between it and its Orthodox subjects. In 1856, he argued that, although it was 'absolute', there was probably 'no single state in Europe, the organization of which

---

[154] *Hansard*, cxii, 587, 27 June 1850.   [155] (1876) Morley, *Gladstone*, iii, 542.
[156] 'Influence of authority', pp. 18–19.
[157] (1884) Lathbury, ii, 187.   [158] 'War and peace', p. 141.
[159] 'Past and present administrations', pp. 555–6.
[160] *Gleanings*, iv, 263–5; 'War and peace', p. 155.
[161] Matthew, 'Gladstone, Vaticanism'.
[162] *PMP*, iii, 239; *Gleanings*, iv, 270–1.   [163] Shannon, *Gladstone*, p. 368.

is better adapted to the wants, or more agreeable to the wishes, of the people';[164] in 1874, he told Queen Victoria of the 'great benefits' which Alexander II had 'conferred upon his people';[165] in 1880, he maintained that the 'uncalculating enthusiasm' of the common people of Russia for the plight of their Orthodox brothers had impelled a 'reluctant' Russian leadership to defend them in 1876.[166] Nor did he display any antipathy to Russia on account of her treatment of the jews, whose plight appears not to have interested him.[167] Russia was the 'natural head of Eastern Christendom', and thus also 'head and front of by far the most formidable antagonism to the Papacy that Christendom . . . supplies'. Historically, the papacy had allied with the Moslems in order to assert its 'unsleeping ambitions', and to try to drive the Eastern Christians back to Rome by persecution.[168] Gladstone perceived that Russia herself might develop conquering, as opposed to protective, designs; he suggested that the threat both of this, and of 'Papal aggression', could best be repelled by the institution of a quasi-federal structure of government within the Ottoman empire, which would give self-government to the Eastern Christians.[169] Gladstone's dream in 1856, and presumably thereafter, was to see 'the noble spectacle of a Christian empire with Constantinople for its capital, a friendly neighbour, and yet a wholesome check upon Russia in the interest of Europe'.[170]

In viewing Eastern affairs, therefore, Gladstone's hostility was not to Islam's political implications, as such. He wished to see Islam reign supreme wherever 'it has more of natural foundation and support'. There was no reason why, on home ground, Moslems should be unable to attain 'the ends of political society, as they understand them'.[171] But in arguing for self-determination on the basis of nationality and religious belief, Gladstone was adopting a policy which, when applied to Ireland, whig-liberals were to regard as revolutionary.

Gladstone: Ireland

At Southport in December 1867, Gladstone enunciated the principle that the Irish would have a legitimate grievance, as long as it could be said that Ireland was governed 'according to the traditions, the views and the

---

[164] 'War and peace', p. 142.   [165] Matthew, viii, 492.
[166] 'Russia and England', p. 541.   [167] Alderman, *Jewish community*, pp. 39–40.
[168] 'War and peace', pp. 141–2; *Gleanings*, iv, 266–7, 297–8; Ramm, ii, 337–8, 445–6; Matthew, viii, 194–5; Morley, *Gladstone*, iii, 478.
[169] 'Past and present administrations', pp. 558–60; *Hansard*, cl, 61–3, 4 May 1858; 'Paths of honour', p. 600; *Gleanings*, iv, 301; (1869) Matthew, vii, 151.
[170] 'War and peace', p. 155.   [171] 'Aggression on Egypt', p. 160.

ideas' of England or Scotland, rather than according to Irish ideas.[172] This assertion, the first of many such, fixed the orientation of Gladstone's Irish policy. Nonetheless, it was made over a decade before his first visit to Ireland, and, according to one of his closest supporters, even longer before he first perceived that Ireland should be treated as a separate nation.[173] In fact, his Irish religious policy between 1868 and 1874 cannot be understood if it is conceived as being concerned primarily with satisfying Irish national opinion. More importantly, it asserted general principles which Gladstone hoped might be beneficial, in securing the independence of the Church of England and of English religious education from parliamentary interference. And more importantly still, his aim throughout was to improve the position of the lay liberal Catholics in Ireland, in relation to the ultramontanes. His Irish policy was thus a branch of both his English Church policy, and his papal policy.

It is an error – understandable, perhaps, in the light of the *Vatican decrees* controversy – to view Gladstone as an evangelical anti-Catholic reluctantly overcoming his scruples to give Ireland justice. It is true that he regarded the pope with vehement and unshakable hostility, because he was aiming to interfere in the temporal affairs of another country; and that he saw the priests as papal instruments, especially when they opposed his university policy in 1873. Indeed, he eventually came to view the concession of home rule as a means of defeating papal designs: in 1886, he thought that, once the Irish had a legitimate structure of government to which they would consent, they would not tolerate foreign interference, from the pope, the Fenians in America, or anyone else.[174] He was already arguing in 1868 that ultramontanism could be attacked only if the British state allowed the Catholics as much say in their concerns as it gave to British Protestants in theirs.[175]

But Gladstone insisted that as *spiritual* agents, the Catholic priests were not to be viewed in the same light: they were God's vicars. The pope was a bishop of the Church, whose spiritual power Gladstone was determined not to assault.[176] He considered that the legitimate spiritual authority of Irish bishops and priests over their flocks was as great as that of English clerics.[177] The internal organisation of Irish Catholicism was entirely a matter for the Irish: Gladstone hoped to see them, as he hoped to see other Christians, 'zealous in upholding the laws and rules of their

[172] *Times*, 20 December 1867, p. 6.
[173] G. W. E. Russell, *Prime ministers*, pp. 246–7.
[174] See below, pp. 445–6. [175] *Speeches 1868*, pp. 60–2.
[176] See Gladstone to Manning, 10 September 1866, Gladstone papers, 44248, fo. 308.
[177] See Gladstone to Acton, 25 January 1866, *ibid.*, 44093, fo. 45.

own religious communions'.[178] If, at various times, Gladstone considered the priests to be subject to the pope's authority, he always denied that this state of affairs was inevitable. In 1891, he told Morley that Döllinger had 'the erroneous view that Irish catholicism is ultramontane, which it certainly is not'.[179]

In the 1830s, Gladstone had supported the Establishment of the Church of Ireland solely because he saw it to be the national representative of the historic Church catholic: it was a badge of truth. He rejected the whigs' arguments on the subject – that it was desirable on material grounds for the state to encourage Protestantism in Ireland in some way or other, and to give the Catholics money in order to pacify them – as immoral and deeply offensive to the latter.[180] Once he had decided that state support of a truthful religion was counter-productive, unless the Establishment concerned was a force for spiritual good or was politically uncontroversial, he could logically conclude that the Irish Establishment was indefensible.[181] Once it was viewed, not as a branch of the Church catholic, but as a foreign graft, dependent on state aid, the Church of Ireland looked absurd. It 'utterly neglected its people'; it was not favourable to religion 'in any sense of the word', because it was a narrow, intolerant low-church invention with no understanding of historic Christianity: it could not plead 'the seal and signature of ecclesiastical descent'.[182] It was neither the 'Church of the Nation' nor the 'Church of the poor';[183] the Catholic Church was both. Any attempts to effect a repair of the Church Establishment in order to prop up the Protestant mission were 'wretched compromises';[184] again, he differed from whig (and, in 1868, Conservative) opinion in disliking proposals to remodel the organisation of the Irish Church by force from without, in an attempt to make it less offensive. Compared with that, the Church would be 'nobler' as 'a religious communion, as a spiritual body', if disestablished.[185]

Gladstone's early views about the relationship of Church and state had proved unworkable because of their implications not only for the welfare of the Church of England, but for the stable government of Ireland. He came to perceive that Irish resentment against the Establish-

[178] (1875) Lathbury, i, 172.   [179] Morley, *Gladstone*, iii, 467.

[180] *Gleanings*, vii, 109, 112.   [181] *Ibid.*, p. 121.

[182] Rendel, *Personal papers*, p. 58; (1865) Lathbury, i, 153–4; G. W. E. Russell, 'Mr Gladstone's theology', p. 780. Argyll thought that it was practically the only religious body of which Gladstone was accustomed to speak with a real 'personal bitterness of dislike': Argyll, *Argyll*, i, 481–2, and, for corroboration of this, see Ashwell and Wilberforce, *Wilberforce*, iii, 241.

[183] *Speeches 1868*, pp. iv–v.

[184] *PMP*, i, 51.   [185] *Speeches 1868*, pp. 14, 30–3.

ment, and the English, was so strong because of the 'cruel and inveterate and but half-atoned injustice' to which the eighteenth-century erastian mind had subjected Ireland: full atonement was now necessary.[186]

However, when he voted for the increase in the grant to Maynooth in 1845, he did not do so because he had come uncritically to adopt the idea that the state should aid all religious sects. He did so because he could no longer defend the high-tory alternative.[187] He now accepted that it was not evil to endow religions with state money, and that in some cases it might be necessary. But he had not accepted indiscriminate endowment as a general principle, appreciating that it had disadvantages whenever it checked voluntary effort.[188] He had only limited sympathy for the attempts of Peel and the whigs to solve the Catholic problem with money and by extending undenominational education. While preferring them to any available alternative policies,[189] he remained sceptical of the benefits to be gained from Peel's two Irish measures of 1845, the consolidation of the Maynooth grant – designed to produce 'a higher class of teachers' who would mitigate the 'feelings of the Irish priesthood' – and the establishment of three 'godless' university colleges, the Queen's colleges, at which Protestants and Catholics might pursue a joint professional education. The cabinet 'deluded themselves I thought with visionary hopes of improvement, of controul [*sic*], of conciliation, all of which by the means proposed are entirely beyond reasonable expectation'. The Irish people would always wish to be educated 'according to the discipline of their Church'.[190] At the end of his career, he mocked Peel's fantasies, and called his Irish policies a 'black page' in his career.[191]

From the mid 1860s onwards, when he was in a position to address the problem, Gladstone emphasised the need to secure the consent of the Catholic population to any proposed educational scheme. In England, he pointed out, parents regarded it as a basic right that they could send their children to schools and colleges 'where the inculcation of the religion to which they belong forms an essential and fundamental part of the instruction that is given': to disallow this would create a 'great grievance'.[192] It was no duty of the state to limit Irish Catholics' 'civil

---

[186] (1845) Lathbury, ii, 265–6.
[187] In fact, he had reached this conclusion by 1841–2: Butler, *Gladstone: Church, state, and tractarianism*, p. 106; Lathbury, i, 51–2.
[188] See *PMP*, ii, 275, 280–4, also pp. 236–7, 247 on the foolhardiness of acting to overthrow a Conservative government, a result which a vote against the Maynooth policy would have assisted.
[189] On the Irish Colleges Bill, see (1853) Lathbury, ii, 135–6.
[190] *PMP*, ii, 232–4.
[191] Tollemache, *Talks with Mr Gladstone*, p. 127; Hamilton, *Gladstone*, p. 130.
[192] *Times*, 20 December 1867, p. 6.

privileges' on educational matters, even if they would 'lay their freedom as far as they possess it at the feet of their Bishops'.[193]

Gladstone's plan of 1873 for Irish university reform will be discussed in detail in chapter 7. It was essentially a liberal Catholic plan. It aimed to retain Trinity, Dublin, as a fundamentally Protestant college (but with tests abolished), and to supplement the Queen's colleges by introducing denominational Catholic colleges into the national university system: all colleges would be affiliated to a central examining board. The aim of this was twofold: to satisfy the grievance that Catholic youths could not secure a degree from a college which provided instruction in their own religion; and to ensure that the teaching in the Catholic denominational colleges was in constant competition with that in Trinity and the Queen's colleges. Competition in the same set of examinations would, Gladstone argued, raise standards in the Catholic colleges towards the level attained in the other institutions. (This part of the bill resembled Gladstone's 1858 plan to demote the four traditional Scottish universities to collegiate status under an examining board, in order to separate examination from teaching and thus stimulate the latter; memories of this plan were largely responsible for losing him the chancellorship of Edinburgh university, which he contested with John Inglis in 1868.)[194] While the examining board was to be endowed by the state, the colleges were not.

The decision not to endow the colleges indicates an important general rule; Gladstone had acted in the same way in opposing concurrent endowment for the Irish Churches in 1869. His general prejudices were in favour of refusing endowment to denominational teaching, partly because of the impetus to healthy self-regulating competition thus afforded, and partly for the allied reason that he believed it to be irresponsible and ineffective to try to solve the Irish grievance by bribing the people with public money, rather than by training them in habits of self-government. In the case of Irish Church endowment in 1867–8, he was probably also swayed to some extent by nonconformist opposition to the idea; but what made up his mind was the dislike of it expressed by the Irish Catholics themselves – given that the measure was aimed at settling their grievances.[195]

Motivating his university plan was a hope that it would enable the Catholic clergy and laity to develop away from ultramontane influence. The scheme gave the state no opportunity to dictate a theology or

[193] Gladstone to J. M. Capes, 18 January 1872, Gladstone papers, 44541, fo. 47.
[194] *Hansard*, cli, 738–42, 1 July 1858; *Lancet*, 6 June 1868, pp. 727–8, Glynne–Gladstone papers, 104/2; *Scotsman* cutting, 20 May 1868, Gladstone papers, 44415, fo. 89; Omond, *Lord Advocates*, pp. 220–1.
[195] Machin, *Politics and the Churches*, p. 358.

morality to Irish students; but the competition engendered by the proposed plan would also ensure that the clergy provided good teaching, and that they did not merely act as servants of the pope (Gladstone believed that the pope aimed to remove the clergy, in every country, 'from the general, open, atmosphere of human life and thought').[196] By refusing to endow Irish denominational education, and by making it reliant on voluntary support, the plan further gave the laity the chance to escape from the control of the priests if they so wished in future, instead of fixing them in a submissive relationship.[197] This self-regulating system thus secured independent denominational teaching, but would allow Irish Catholicism, priestly and lay, to 'follow in Döllinger's steps, throw off the Papal tyranny and gradually reform itself'.[198] This, in theory, was a brilliant scheme; and in 1897, Gladstone could think of no measure for which he was 'more desirous to claim my full responsibility' than the 1873 bill.[199]

As for the policy of home rule for Ireland, Gladstone was converted to it in the mid 1880s, but, as in so many other areas, his general line of thought had pointed him clearly in such a direction from much earlier: in 1871 he admitted that he favoured extensive Irish local-government reform. From this date, he was already distinguishing between a federal scheme which would encourage internal self-government, subordinated to the imperial parliament, and independence; when he condemned home rule in 1871, he was attacking the latter, not the former.[200] One of his aims in 1886, moreover, was to remove the influence of both interfering priests, and political agitators, and to restore 'the natural condition of a healthy society . . . that governing functions should be discharged in the main by the leisured class'.[201]

Liberal high churchmen

Gladstone's vision, and his mode of arriving at his political views, were unique. None of the men discussed in the next chapter copied his political outlook, however much they agreed with certain of his sentiments:

---

[196] *Gleanings*, vi, 213.
[197] *Hansard*, ccxiv, 1857–8, 11 March 1873.
[198] These were not Gladstone's words, but those of his niece (1871): Bailey, *Diary of Lady F. Cavendish*, ii, 112.
[199] *PMP*, i, 98.
[200] See below, pp. 325–6; Matthew, viii, 68; Russell, *Recollections*, p. 391, Hawarden copy.
[201] 'Notes and queries on the Irish demand', pp. 177–8. An intention of his Irish land legislation of 1870 was also to bolster landed influence in society, and to cure the 'paralysis' in Irish class relations: Gladstone to Argyll, 5 January 1870, Gladstone papers, 44538, fo. 41.

nor was there a simple affinity between his attitudes and those of Liberal
high churchmen.

This latter group has received little attention from political historians,
although its existence is evident. In 1883, W. R. W. Stephens regarded it
as far more common than it had been in the 1840s for politicians to
combine 'High Churchmanship' with 'advanced Liberal opinions in
politics';[202] a Conservative author later complained that his own party
had been unwise enough to alienate 'a strong High Church Radical party
which, adroitly used by Mr Gladstone, had not a little to do with the
Radical majority at the election of 1868, with the destruction of the Irish
Church, and with many, if not most, of the innovations which have been
made since'.[203]

Of course, many prominent high churchmen were either Conservatives, or were at least suspicious of the Liberal party; they tended in this
direction for three reasons. Firstly, many, especially of the older generation, remained instinctive supporters of the sanctity of the Church–
state relationship: such men included G. A. Denison, Christopher
Wordsworth, and T. T. Carter, and are not discussed here. Secondly,
many others, who *are* discussed, were again usually older men, who had
developed intellectually before the rise of tractarianism. They were not
as fixed in their views about Church and state as the first group, but
nor did they see the need to break with tory concepts as publicly as
Gladstone, or to define their political allegiance as rigorously as he did.
Their overriding political antagonism continued to be the erastianism of
the whigs of the 1830s and 1840s, and this made them suspicious of the
Liberal party:[204] but, while remaining strictly outside party politics,
nearly all approved of Gladstone's political activity at least as much as
they disapproved of it. In this category fell four of Gladstone's bishops,
Durnford and Moberly, whom he promoted from ecclesiastical obscurity
to be bishops of Chichester and Salisbury, and Wilberforce and E. H.
Browne, whom he elevated, in succession, from other bishoprics to that
of Winchester; Wilberforce, of course, was one of Gladstone's closest
ecclesiastical acquaintances. One can also group with them three other
important figures, the civil servant and ex-journalist Lord Blachford,
E. B. Pusey and Dean Hook. Pusey was the leading Oxford high churchman between Newman's secession and his own death in 1882; Hook
became famous as one of the first high churchmen successfully to

---

[202] Stephens, *Hatherley*, ii, 6.
[203] Saintsbury, *Earl of Derby*, p. 216. In 1884, when a leading high churchman upbraided the
Conservatives for failing the cause of 'dogmatic truth', he was reminded that they had
been hamstrung in this task by the determination of so many like-minded men to follow
Gladstone: Beauchamp to Woodard, in Heeney, *Mission to the middle classes*, p. 137.
[204] See Stephens, *Hook*, i, 419.

penetrate the industrial heartlands of nonconformity, as vicar of Leeds from 1837. Pusey was too distrustful of the reforming mentality to be a thorough Gladstonian; but in 1872, at the age of seventy-four, Hook described Gladstone as the 'greatest and I believe the best among the Great and good men of his age'.[205]

Thirdly, some of the younger generation discussed here, like King and E. S. Talbot, came to be alienated by the nonconformist ethos of, or, especially, by the strong freethinking element within, the late Victorian Liberal party.[206] Such men found the threats of Liberal radicals increasingly alarming because, from the mid 1880s onwards, the disestablishment campaign was directed far more towards criticism of the Church's extensive endowments than before, while erastianism now seemed to pose less of a threat to the independence of the Church – as a result of the political influence enjoyed by Gladstone and Salisbury. Disestablishment thus lost whatever attractions it had possessed in the eyes of most Liberal high churchmen.[207]

These qualifications notwithstanding, two broad groups of high churchmen, most of whom were distinctly Liberal, can be isolated, in addition to the older men mentioned already. These were the political and religious associates of Gladstone's own generation, and those, appreciably younger, who modelled their politics on him and thus adhered most closely to his views. Both were more affected by specifically tractarian conceptions than the older men.

In the latter compartment falls Liddon, the first vice-principal of Cuddesdon theological college (between 1854 and 1859), and then an important figure in Oxford: in 1870, Gladstone appointed him professor of exegesis there, and canon of St Paul's. There were also, for example, Malcolm MacColl, who came from a Scottish episcopalian family, ministered in inner London and became a prominent publicist and a friend of Gladstone's; W. R. W. Stephens, another clergyman, Hook's son-in-law and the nephew of Hook's great friend the Liberal politician Hatherley, and biographer of both; A. J. Butler, a staunch Gladstonian in politics and religion, translator of Dante, and future professor of Italian at University college, London; and E. C. Lowe, Woodard's lieutenant in

---

[205] Hook to Selborne, 2 October 1872, Selborne papers, 1865, fo. 33.

[206] See (King) *Dictionary of national biography*; (Talbot) *ibid.*, and Stephenson, *Talbot*, p. 7, for apparently conflicting, but on this reasoning, consistent views as to his politics. Scott Holland, although a Gladstonian, was irritated in 1897 both by Harcourt's erastianism and by the selfishness of nonconformist Liberal capitalists: Paget, *Scott Holland*, p. 211.

[207] Bell, *Disestablishment in Ireland*, p. 262. Acland found the Liberals' cry for 'undenominational' education in the 1890s 'horrid': Acland, *Acland*, p. 399. For an example of earlier alienation from the extremism of the Liberal party overcoming admiration for Gladstone, see A. P. Forbes to Gladstone, 3 August 1873, Gladstone papers, 44154, fo. 321. See also (1879) Johnston, *Liddon*, p. 229.

his high-church denominational middle-class school movement and, like MacColl, offered Church preferment by Gladstone.[208] Even younger was a more coherent group of churchmen, all of whom were personal friends of Gladstone in years to come, and nearly all of whom were radicals and Oxford men: G. W. E. Russell, raconteur and future Liberal MP; his close friend and contemporary, the future bishop Charles Gore; the Oxford academic Scott Holland; Gladstone's nephews Arthur Lyttelton and (by marriage) E. S. Talbot, the first heads of Selwyn and Keble colleges respectively, and both future bishops; and W. G. F. Phillimore, son of a close friend of Gladstone's, and a future judge. These were all active in *Lux Mundi* or wrote in an influential volume, *Essays in aid of Church reform*, edited by Gore and published in 1898. As well as these men, one can include a large number of the young ritualist clergymen who were colonising inner London, like Stanton of St Alban's, Holborn (Mackonochie's church), and Stewart Headlam of Drury Lane and Bethnal Green.

Those from Gladstone's own generation were not quite as radical politically as most of these men, or as Gladstone himself. This was true even of his close friends Sir Robert Phillimore – an ex-Peelite MP and, as Dean of Arches after 1867, the man who presided over the ecclesiastical court against whose tolerance on ritual questions the Judicial Committee was reacting – and T. D. Acland, Peelite and then Liberal MP. It was true, in varying degrees, of churchmen whom he admired, including R. W. Church, tractarian, Fellow of Oriel until 1852 and dean of St Paul's after 1871; W. K. Hamilton, the first tractarian bishop, and father of Gladstone's future private secretary; John Mackarness, a Liberal whom Gladstone promoted to fill Wilberforce's see, Oxford, in 1870; and J. R. Woodford, appointed to the see of Ely in 1873.

Five other men are less easy to categorise, although all showed sympathy with high-church positions. E. A. Freeman, the mediaeval historian, had been attracted to the Oxford movement by its historical conceptions rather than by its doctrinal emphases, and was a friend of his fellow-historian Church (and of academic liberals, although he was older and more orthodox than they were). The other four were leading Liberal politicians. Ripon was a former Christian socialist and radical, who was on a journey towards the Roman Church, into which he was received in 1874; he was lord president of the council, with charge of education, in the 1868 cabinet. He was known as Earl de Grey between 1859 and 1871. W. P. Wood (Lord Hatherley from 1868), Roundell Palmer (Lord Selborne from 1872) and J. D. Coleridge were all lawyers. The first two were, in succession, lord chancellors in Gladstone's government, and

---

[208] See Honey, *Tom Brown's universe*, pp. 47–103.

the third was a law officer in it before becoming a judge in 1873. Hatherley had been a radical Liberal in the 1840s and was the most high church; Coleridge and Palmer were ex-tractarians, but Coleridge had lost much of his belief, and his position increasingly resembled the reverent latitudinarianism of his Balliol contemporary Matthew Arnold. Palmer was always, and increasingly, 'a good deal more Protestant' than Gladstone.[209] In this respect, he resembled a number of the small band of Peelite MPs discussed below; half of them, including Palmer himself, were more and more indistinguishable from the most conservative type of whig-liberal. So were most surviving 'Peelite' peers, such as the earl of Dudley.

Finally, one ought to mention high churchmen who were, strictly speaking, Conservatives, but who had some admiration for Gladstone: William Bright, who had taught at Gladstone's foundation, Trinity college, Glenalmond, and was now professor of ecclesiastical history at Oxford; Robert Gregory, a vicar in Lambeth, canon of St Paul's, and educational activist on behalf of the National Society, under whom Gladstone sent his son Stephen to serve as a curate; Alexander Forbes, the Scottish episcopalian bishop of Brechin; and Edward King, principal of Cuddesdon until he was appointed regius professor of moral and pastoral theology at Oxford by Gladstone in 1873.

In this circle, then, in its widest sense, there were three cabinet ministers; six men whom Gladstone appointed to bishoprics between 1869 and 1873; five Oxford professors after 1873 (Pusey and Bright from before Gladstone's time, and Liddon, King and J. B. Mozley, Church's friend, appointed regius professor of divinity in 1871); and, after 1871, the dean (Church) and the canons (Liddon and Gregory) of St Paul's. Opponents might also detect high-church cells in the Woodard schools; Trinity, Glenalmond; Cuddesdon; Keble college, Oxford (founded on the initiative of Liddon and Pusey in 1870); and the ritualist churches of inner London.

The most important political fact about these men was the impression of unity given to anti-high churchmen, who feared that they would succeed in manipulating the Liberal alliance. For example, the hostile response to the Gladstone government's preferment of high churchmen to important ecclesiastical posts, particularly to bishoprics, to Oxford theological professorships and to stalls in St Paul's, was heightened by the awareness that Gladstone and his high-church lord chancellors were responsible for them: it was easy to allege the operation of a conspiracy of like minds.[210] In one sense, and a very important one in whig-liberal eyes, there *was* substantial agreement between high churchmen.

---

[209] (1856) Selborne, *Memorials I*, ii, 312.   [210] See below, pp. 373, 376.

Although many of the older generation questioned the wisdom of ritual innovations, and some even condemned them,[211] there was a general disposition (except among those with 'Protestant' tendencies, like Palmer and Blachford) to oppose the repression of ritualism by the state – as both immoral in itself and deeply threatening to the independence of the Church and the future of Catholic doctrine.[212] But, from the brief account just given, it may already be apparent that, in discussing general politics, there was little unity, and that the number of genuine political radicals among the high churchmen was in fact rather limited: as we can now see in more detail.

One of the best routes to understanding the political vision of radical and semi-radical high churchmen is to examine the history written by Freeman and Church. This displayed only a limited belief in the idea of political progress which was so central to most whig-liberals' world-view. For Freeman, man's political nature was 'essentially the same under every change of outward circumstances': justice, liberty and democracy had always been attainable, and indeed the régimes in ancient Athens and in Anglo-Saxon England had approximated to those ideals. But man's tendency to corruption always endangered the survival of these principles – as the Norman Conquest and the Tudor and Stuart despotisms had proved. Recent improvements in the law, the constitution and the franchise had been 'only the casting aside of innovations which have crept in in modern and evil times'.[213] For Church, all successful reforms and 'victories of truth' on the part of the 'good and brave' were likely to be only temporary, 'just enough in their own day to stop instant ruin'. Evil would be 'kept in check for a while only to return, perhaps, the stronger' – until the Second Coming, when it would be banished for ever.[214]

---

[211] Hook, Hatherley and Wilberforce criticised the ritualists as extremists, tending to materialism, whose activities were counter-productive: Stephens, *Hook*, ii, 276–9; Stephens, *Hatherley*, ii, 148; Ashwell and Wilberforce, *Wilberforce*, iii, 183–200. Church, like MacColl and Liddon, thought that their use of ritual was of great benefit in drawing out the spirituality of the poor: Church, 'Ritualism', pp. 204–6; MacColl, 'Rationale of ritualism'; Liddon, *Some elements of religion*, pp. 118–19. Moberly and Durnford were by and large tolerant: Stephens, *Durnford*, pp. 127–8; Moberly, *Charge 1873*, pp. 29–43. Pusey felt the whole question to be of secondary importance: Liddon, *Pusey*, iv, 211–16, 224–5.

[212] Hook to Harrowby, 17 July 1868, Harrowby papers, 37, fo. 288; Ashwell and Wilberforce, *Wilberforce*, iii, 183–200; Hutton, *Gregory*, pp. 117–18; Prestige, *Gore*, p. 24. Pusey and the high-church reformers of the 1890s were both happy for the local congregation to be consulted on the propriety of any innovation: Liddon, *Pusey*, iv, 216; Gore, *Essays in aid of Church reform*, pp. 19–21.

[213] *Historical Essays*, ii, 165, iv, 253; *Growth of English constitution*, pp. vii–viii, 20–1, 56; *Norman Conquest*, i, 2.

[214] *St Anselm*, pp. 345–6.

Church and Freeman argued that the struggle against tyranny and corruption must nonetheless continue. But they maintained that it was the intolerance of authoritarian individuals in positions of power which had promoted evil, not theological dogma.[215] Church and Freeman denounced the temporal claims and dogmatic innovations of the papacy; but they maintained that the pope's taste for temporal power constituted a reaction to the arbitrary incursions, in the dark ages, of the civil power into exclusively spiritual concerns.[216] Nor were the corruptions of the late mediaeval papacy unique, as so many modern liberals claimed: they provided merely one more example of the 'usual course of successful power in human hands'.[217] Froude's failure to understand this was at the root of Freeman's objection to his history. Froude's work, Freeman maintained, displayed a contempt for historical Christianity and a defence of the temporal power's repression of the Church in the sixteenth century, in the name of 'progressive intelligence';[218] but, in Freeman's eyes, the Reformation was a sham, which put 'one intolerant system in the stead of another'. Froude believed in the 'infallibility of Henry VIII', and saw the 'highest embodiment of stern English common sense' realised in a policy of 'boiling, burning, racking, or embowelling'.[219] Freeman and Church believed, instead, that mediaeval historical figures must be viewed in their own context, not judged by nineteenth-century standards: Anselm and Becket, for example, were working to sustain the rule of law against anarchy, or against the tyranny of the temporal power.[220]

Older, semi-theocratic high churchmen did not fully share the commitment to liberty which underpinned these arguments. Pusey, for example, had a higher view of the legitimate authority of the pope and the General Councils of the Church.[221] But those high churchmen who did hold this commitment were, consequently, able to sympathise with many of Gladstone's aims. Freeman deprecated conquest and valued the independence of nations with culturally distinct identities. He argued that small nations, united in religion, and with a sense of political community, were best able to operate a democracy, to agree on the moral ends of political activity.[222] Such conceptions explain his obsession with Swiss cantonal politics; in his election campaign of 1868, when address-

---

[215] 'Froude's *Reign of Elizabeth*', pp. 677–8; 'Froude's *History of England – Vol. XII*'.
[216] Church, *Beginning of the middle ages*, pp. 134–8.
[217] Church, *St Anselm*, p. 341.
[218] 'Mr Froude's final volumes', pp. 116–18.
[219] *Historical Essays*, iv, 289; 'Froude's *Reign of Elizabeth*', pp. 80–2; 'Froude's *History of England – Vol. XII*', pp. 221–3.
[220] Freeman, *Historical Essays*, i, 82; 'Mr Froude's "Becket"', pp. 832, 484, 213–19; Church, *St Anselm*, pp. 202–5.
[221] *Is healthful reunion impossible?*, pp. 3–4, 341.
[222] 'Eastern Church', pp. 328–33; *Unity of history*, pp. 57–8; *Historical Essays*, ii, 322–3, 391.

ing the labourers of Somerset, he would 'launch . . . out into an eloquent description of Landesgemeinde of Uri'.[223]

Freeman recommended the institution of federal government in the Balkans, which would preserve the independence of the constituent states, and yet would secure the area against attack.[224] He contended that a structure of this kind would resemble the highest ecclesiastical ideal of all, the principle – of independent national branches retaining full intercommunion with each other – on which the Eastern Church, the 'truest representative on earth of the old days of Fathers and of Councils', was organised.[225] His hatred of Islam was passionate even by high-church standards: he believed that Europe's 'one abiding duty' had ever been to fight the 'barbarism' to her East, and that the fall of Constantinople in 1453 had marked 'the darkest day in the history of Christendom'.[226] Islam was 'aggressive' and 'missionary'; it was propagated by the sword. Civil rights were denied to non-believers, who received neither the protection of the law, nor any share in making it.[227]

It was, of course, as Shannon has shown, high churchmen – including some of the more conservative spirits – who provided, together with nonconformists, most of the enthusiasm which stoked the Bulgarian agitation of 1876.[228] G. W. E. Russell and Freeman even saw Disraeli's effort to check the Christians' campaign for self-government as another example of the age-old unsavoury alliance between the 'Turk and the Jew', against Christian civilisation and the 'Christian Creed'.[229]

The more radical high churchmen were also especially conscious of the need to seek communion with the poor:[230] they saw the Church as 'the poor man's home where he can retire for a season from the tyranny and the turmoil of the world around him, and be reminded that there is indeed an invisible world above and behind this material scene of weariness and pain'.[231] As Headlam put it, the clergy should exist not to teach

---

[223] Bryce, *Studies in contemporary biography*, p. 282.

[224] *History of federal government*, pp. 554–5; Stephens, *Freeman*, i, 282–3.

[225] 'Eastern Church', pp. 322–8. See also Church, *Gifts of civilisation*, pp. 234–9, 253.

[226] *Chief periods of European history*, pp. 4–6, 168–9.

[227] *Ottoman power*, pp. 61, 75. See Church, *Beginning of the middle ages*, pp. 24–6, and, less stridently, Stephens, *Christianity and Islam*, pp. 167–8.

[228] Among the participants were, for example, Liddon, Pusey, MacColl, Selborne, Freeman, Church, Blachford, G. W. E. Russell, William Bright, Phillimore, Scott Holland, and E. S. Talbot: Shannon, *Bulgarian agitation*, pp. 171–80, 188–90, 220. See also Selborne, *Memorials II*, i, 190, 459–60; MacColl, 'Some current fallacies'; Stephenson, *Talbot*, p. 33.

[229] Freeman, *Ottoman power*, pp. xviii–xx; Russell, *One look back*, p. 183. Freeman developed this view in 1891, in refusing to condemn Russia's treatment of her jews: 'if any nation chooses to wallop its own jews, 'tis no concern of any other nation': Stephens, *Freeman*, ii, 428.

[230] See e.g. Russell, *MacColl*, p. 103.

[231] MacColl, 'Rationale of ritualism', p. 191.

a religion which would 'make you forget the evils around you', but to 'get men to live as brethren'. This required the working up of 'a strong discontent with the circumstances around you', with the 'awful inequalities' in society.[232] It was a 'sin against the Brotherhood' to endure circumstances which hindered the 'mental, moral, or physical growth' of the mass of mankind.[233] Gore criticised those in the Church who accepted the prevailing hierarchies of society, the 'notorious and grinding injustice' of the industrial system, and the bias of the legal system.[234] A number of younger high churchmen, especially the active ritualists like Mackonochie and Stanton, favoured disestablishment; and, although hatred of erastian interference with their liberty of action was clearly central in prompting their attitude, they also argued that the Establishment was unable to communicate sufficiently warmly with the poor.[235]

A number of the older men also shared Gladstone's intense sympathy for the poor and belief in the 'common level of Christian brotherhood':[236] Hatherley described himself as a *'philo-deme'*.[237] Associated with this was a distrust of the traditional governing classes. For example, Hatherley claimed that Palmerston's administration had 'enervated the conscience of the House';[238] and he and Coleridge, both of whom regarded themselves as having risen in the social scale by a lifetime of hard intellectual work, scorned what they saw as the indolence, insolence and ignorance of upper-class society. In one impassioned outburst during the American Civil War, Coleridge alleged that the aristocracy was 'destroying our glorious England', by attempting to corrupt the working-man into 'base, tuft-hunting, subserviency'.[239]

In short, the young radicals among the high churchmen especially appreciated the tone of the Gladstonian Liberal party. So did some of the politicians and tractarian clerics who were Gladstone's age or slightly younger, although in a number of cases with reservations about the

---

[232] *Priestcraft and progress*, pp. 25, 64.
[233] (Headlam, 1875) Norman, *Church and society*, p. 179; for commitment to the cause of the 'brotherhood of man', see G. W. E. Russell, *Stanton*, pp. 42–3; MacColl, *Damnatory clauses*, pp. 151–2, 159; E. F. Russell, *Mackonochie*, pp. 18–20.
[234] Gore, *Christianity applied to the life*, p. 22.
[235] G. W. E. Russell, *Stanton*, p. 108.
[236] Church, *Gifts of civilisation*, pp. 234–9; Stephens, *Freeman*, ii, 212; Acland, *Acland*, p. 317, on the 'geniality and Christian earnestness' of the Labourers' Union in 1874. Church joined a committee of thirty clergymen, mostly high church, in order to work for closer Anglican sympathy with the trade-union movement in the late 1870s; Marsh, *Victorian Church in decline*, pp. 91–2.
[237] Stephens, *Hatherley*, ii, 134.
[238] To Selborne, 6 April 1868, Selborne papers, 1863, fo. 52.
[239] Coleridge, *Coleridge*, i, 237, 259–60; ii, 22, 264–5; Stephens, *Hatherley*, i, 96, ii, 20–3. See also Marindin, *Blachford*, p. 358; Acland to Derby, 10 January 1871, 15th earl of Derby papers.

activities of the party's radical wing. These reservations did not prevent them from supporting most of his crusades with vigour. The first example of this had been when Phillimore, Acland, Church, E. C. Lowe, MacColl and Liddon (and the schoolboys G. W. E. Russell and Gore) all keenly supported Gladstone's Irish Church resolutions of 1868, because they promised justice to the Irish Catholics, and rejected erastianism and Establishmentarianism. As Coleridge said, they demonstrated the importance of not indolently expecting Establishments to do their own work, but of applying 'unceasing energy and untiring effort', without which 'nothing really great was ever yet wrought upon the stage of human affairs'.[240] Disraeli was certainly conscious of the appeal of the Irish Church question to high churchmen in 1868;[241] MacColl claimed that the Conservative William Bright was converted to Gladstonianism in that year.[242]

However, the semi-theocrats, and others among the older generation of Liberal high churchmen, tended not to approve of the manner of Gladstone's espousal of the issue. Some criticised him on the grounds that it was an unnecessarily sudden and drastic political move;[243] others because the scheme transferred Church endowments to secular uses.[244] This disapproval set the tone of their response to Liberal politics after 1867. They were likely to regard any political move which threatened the Church's privileges with suspicion and even hostility. Some, like Pusey, Blachford and Hamilton, disliked the abolition of university tests for this reason;[245] similarly, most could not share the enthusiasm of some of the younger men for secular education – an enthusiasm which arose from a vehement animosity to undenominationalism. (Undenominationalism was, of course, disliked nearly as strongly by the older men, but they put their faith in the National Society and in voluntary provision of denominational education.)[246] Of course, some older men were more amenable

---

[240] Phillimore to Gladstone, 12 April 1868, Gladstone papers, 44278, fo. 7; Acland, *Acland*, p. 267; Church, *Church*, p. 180; (E. C. Lowe) Gladstone to Selborne, 26 May 1873, Gladstone papers, 44542, fo. 121; Russell, *MacColl*, pp. 25, 268–9; Johnston, *Liddon*, pp. 128–30; G. W. E. Russell, *Portraits of the seventies*, p. 48; Prestige, *Gore*, p. 9; (Coleridge) *Hansard*, cxci, 852, 3 April 1868.

[241] Bell, *Disestablishment in Ireland*, p. 94.   [242] Russell, *MacColl*, p. 27.

[243] Moberly, *Moberly*, p. 202; Hamilton to Gladstone, 25 August 1868, Gladstone papers, 44181, fo. 369; Ashwell and Wilberforce, *Wilberforce*, iii, 241.

[244] Ashwell and Wilberforce, *Wilberforce*, iii, 281. Browne and Hook thought it logical for the Roman Catholic Church to be Established instead of the Anglican one: Browne, *A speech not spoken*, p. 18; Kitchin, *Browne*, p. 383; Stephens, *Hook*, ii, 258–60, 444–6.

[245] See (Pusey) Selborne, *Memorials II*, i, 105; Hamilton to Phillimore, 30 April 1868, Phillimore papers; Marindin, *Blachford*, pp. 272–3, 331–2.

[246] G. W. E. Russell and MacColl supported secularism in 1902: Russell, *Prime ministers*, p. 263; *MacColl*, pp. 226–8. For Headlam's position, see *The place of the bible in secular education*. For animosity to undenominationalism, see MacColl, *Education question*, p. 22; Acland to C. T. D. Acland, 30 April 1874, Acland papers, 19/13.

to radical arguments than others. Hook, in fact, had proposed a secular scheme in 1846, thinking that the state must aid the promotion of education, but that it was unfair to nonconformists to spend some of their taxes in subsidising instruction in Christian doctrine – while it was monstrous to impose the teaching of a mutilated creed.[247] Hook and Hatherley were similarly more willing than most of their generation to welcome disestablishment. They had always argued that disestablishment would be good for the Church: Hook had tended to think that it would be bad for the state, and so had disliked it (although by 1868 he expected it, and without alarm); Hatherley was confident that there was enough spirituality in the nation to survive it.[248] But, in the main, and excepting active politicians, committed and continuing support for Gladstone was the prerogative of those high churchmen born after 1820. Of course, there were many such Liberal high churchmen up and down the country.

Some among the remnant of Peelite Liberal MPs resembled those older high churchmen discussed above, in being able to appreciate Gladstone's aims, and yet being instinctively unhappy whenever the party threatened to attack the temporal privileges of the Church.

By 1868, there was, of course, no longer a recognised group of Peelite MPs. Omitting Gladstone and Cardwell, who were in the cabinet (Cardwell did not have distinctively high-church views, and indeed was rather 'Protestant'), only five men who sat as Liberals after 1868, and who had been Conservative MPs before 1846, are discussed here.[249] In addition, there were two more high-church Peelites who had first been elected in 1847, Roundell Palmer and John Walter, proprietor of the *Times*. Three MPs of a later generation have also been classed with these seven, for the purpose of analysis: Gladstone's nephew, C. G. Lyttelton, who was twenty-six in 1868 (his father, Lord Lyttelton, was a nominal tory); C. S. Parker, Cardwell's nephew, future biographer of Peel and Graham, and friend both of Gladstone and academic liberals (but,

---

[247] Stephens, *Hook*, i, 114, ii, 210, 242–3; Hook, *The efficient education of the people.* (He had envisaged separate schools, one of which, aided by the state, would teach secular subjects, but would not be allowed to teach from the bible. The sects would provide religious instruction in their own voluntary schools on Sundays, Wednesdays and Fridays.)

[248] Stephens, *Hook*, i, 221, 269; Machin, *Politics and the Churches*, p. 368; Stephens, *Hatherley*, i, 216–19, 230, ii, 91.

[249] T. D. Acland, E. Antrobus, Lord Ernest Bruce, Sir John Hanmer and W. B. Hughes. Two others who had sat as Conservatives, W. H. Gregory (an Irishman of the Clanricarde connection) and the maverick F. J. Tollemache, have been classified as whig-liberal and radical respectively. Two sporadic attenders (and thus disqualified from the survey) were also 'Peelites', although also mavericks: Tomline and Sir Robert Peel.

despite the latter, a staunch defender of the Establishment and of religious teaching in schools);[250] and Lord Charles Bruce, the younger brother of one of the original Peelite MPs.

None of these ten were radical. All except Lyttelton voted against at least one of the Bright/Anderson amendments to prevent dogmatic teaching in the schools; none voted for both selected amendments on the University Tests Bill; and none voted against Clause 25 of the Education Act in either 1872 or 1873. Five supported the mention of Convocation in the Act of Uniformity Amendment Bill, and none opposed it.

These votes do not, however, distinguish between those who not only shared Gladstone's views on religion and education, but were happy with his general politics; and those who opposed religious radicalism from a perspective very similar to the most conservative of whig-liberals. The second category was usually more 'Protestant', or at least less happy to support movements to disengage the Church from its temporal privileges. It included Antrobus (who had opposed the abolition of church rates in 1868) and Walter (who rebelled against Gladstone on both the ecclesiastical bills of 1874): both were to secede to the Conservatives, in effect, shortly after 1874.[251] It might also include Palmer and Ernest Bruce, who did not support Gladstone's 1868 Irish Church resolutions. Palmer was hostile to Gladstone's conduct on the 1874 bills (although Bruce was not); and, had he not become lord chancellor in 1872, he would probably have left the party far sooner than he did (between 1868 and 1872, he sat for a close borough belonging to the whig Lord Zetland). In addition, Knatchbull-Hugessen (discussed in chapters 1 and 2, because his complaints were similar to those of disgruntled whig-liberal junior ministers) was also, in fact a 'Protestant' and 'right-wing' high churchman.[252]

The other Peelites were content to vote with the government – unless when forced against it by constituency pressure, as Parker (MP for Perthshire) was when he voted for the Conservative amendment, on the 1872 Scottish Education Bill, which aimed to force schools to teach religion. Of those still active in politics in 1886, Lyttelton became a unionist (his brothers and sisters were much divided on the issue), but Acland and Parker remained Gladstonians. So did Coleridge, and Sir Arthur

[250] *Hansard*, ccciv, 333–6, 30 March 1886; *Questions for a reformed parliament*, pp. 185, 196.
[251] For Walter, see *The history of 'The Times': volume II: the tradition established 1841–1884* (London, 1939), 9, 36–7, 412.
[252] He had been a Peelite at university. Although he disliked the 1874 Public Worship Regulation Bill, he opposed disestablishment because it would enable the Church to become 'priest-ridden', and would destroy her 'breadth and liberality of spirit': *Speech at Sandwich*, p. 15. He defected to the Conservatives soon after receiving a peerage from Gladstone in 1880.

Gordon, the high-church son of the Peelite prime minister Aberdeen – in both cases with reservations, but nonetheless publicly, and out of reverence for Gladstone.

Liberal Catholics and Irish home rulers

Gladstone and his high-church allies supported the efforts of Irish liberal Catholics to develop a distinctively national, rather than ultramontane, religious culture. Liberal Catholic control of education, especially higher education, was perceived to be the most important precondition of such a development; and Gladstone's Irish university plan was ultimately based on the proposal of the most prominent Irish liberal Catholic politician, the convert and junior minister William Monsell.[253] Monsell in turn recognised that his plan was likely to gain support from Gladstonians concerned with the future of denominationalism in *England*, and with the need to counter both 'Tory' and 'latitudinarian' views on *English* university policy.[254]

Gladstone seems to have believed that Monsell and the other leading Irish liberal Catholics, O'Hagan (his Irish lord chancellor) and Sir Rowland Blennerhassett, MP, represented – together with other moderate Irish MPs such as Corrigan and the quaker Pim – a sizeable body of Irish opinion. He saw Irish liberal Catholicism as a variation of the German Old Catholic movement, and thus as potentially influential in checking ultramontanism. He also had particular faith in the political ability of one (non-Irish) liberal Catholic: Lord Acton, an especially virulent opponent of papal pretensions.[255] Acton had been profoundly influenced by Döllinger (one of the leading German Old Catholics), and from 1858 established a series of ill-fated anti-ultramontane periodicals. As he became more liberal in the 1860s, these began to advocate Gladstonianism in politics as well.[256]

Acton's distrust of political authority, as repressive of individual liberty and the individual moral conscience, became more explicit throughout the 1870s and 1880s; he welcomed successive Reform Acts, on the grounds that it was 'easier to find people fit to govern themselves

---

[253] See Monsell, 'University education in Ireland'.

[254] Monsell to O'Hagan, 26 December [1865], Teeling/O'Hagan papers, 17871 (2).

[255] For his respect for Acton's political powers, see Gladstone to Acton, 2, 27 November 1868, Gladstone papers, 44093, fos. 76, 80.

[256] On the *Chronicle* and *North British Review*, see Acton to Gladstone, 11 February 1868, 23 January 1869, *ibid.*, fos. 70, 83; Wetherell to Gladstone, 4 February 1868, 14 October 1869, *ibid.*, 44414, fo. 73, 44422, fo. 185. Wetherell, who edited them, was a Catholic convert, ex-Peelite and staunch Gladstonian, of a nervous and cantankerous disposition.

than people fit to govern others'.[257] The drift of his opinions led him to enunciate, in 1887, his famous dictum about power. It followed from this that great men were 'almost always bad men'. Indeed, Christianity had often been perverted into an 'appalling edifice of intolerance, tyranny, cruelty'; and in 1888, he criticised even Gladstone for unduly venerating the moral power of Christian dogma in preceding centuries.[258] But in the main, of course, he revered Gladstone's politics. In 1880, he described Gladstone's political vision as unique, because it combined sympathy for tradition and institutions on the one hand, with a belief that men of the employer class 'ought not to be the political masters' of their employees, and that solicitude was always due to those who had 'the heaviest stake in the country'. For those people, 'misgovernment means not mortified pride or stinted luxury, but want and pain, and degradation and risk to their own lives and to their children's souls'.[259]

Moreover, he maintained that, in the last resort, 'the poor have a claim on the wealth of the rich, so far that they may be relieved from the immoral, demoralizing effects of poverty'.[260] This was not a call to a redistributive policy *per se*; but it displayed his awareness of the constant need to struggle against human degradation, in so far as it interfered with the pursuit of liberty. This awareness might take a radical form: he saw the 'distribution of wealth' to be, with religion and education, one of the three levers which state influence might operate in order to give 'indirect help' in fighting the battle of life.[261] The fact that Acton – and other devout late Victorian Gladstonian Liberals – believed that the exercise of state power could be evil in its more 'direct' manifestations,[262] did not prevent them from arguing that incumbent upon man was the moral duty of relieving the degrading consequences of poverty. It did not require a great shift from this position for a Liberal survivor from the Gladstonian era to applaud the 1909 People's Budget.

Acton, like Freeman, believed that individual liberty and political justice were not modern inventions; they had always been attainable, but 'constant and invariable forces' were perpetually attempting to undermine them, and succeeding in doing so.[263] The Roman empire, for example, had confused 'tyranny and authority', 'lawlessness and freedom', and had thus encouraged 'all the errors' of political society, including 'Communism' and 'Utilitarianism';[264] a polity organised on such a

---

257 Himmelfarb, *Acton*, p. 172.
258 *Ibid.*, pp. 161, 166–7.
259 *Letters of Acton to Mary Gladstone*, pp. 49–50.
260 Himmelfarb, *Acton*, p. 178.
261 'History of freedom in antiquity', p. 245.
262 See Himmelfarb, *Acton*, p. 183.
263 *Ibid.*, p. 239; Acton, 'History of freedom in antiquity', p. 247.
264 'History of freedom in antiquity', p. 258.

basis was indefensible. A powerful state might pass more 'useful legis-lation' than a libertarian one, or increase a nation's capacity for self-defence; but the only test of value was not its capacity to promote temporal interests, but its behaviour 'before God'. It must obey the 'voice of God', the voice of 'self-reliance and self-denial'. The preservation of freedom was necessary in order to allow all 'children of God' to pursue life's 'highest objects'. Given 'all the evil there is in man',[265] he could not safely be entrusted with power over others. The rule of 'class over class' was wrong at all times: the domination of the 'ignorant by the wise' must be condemned along with that 'of the poor by the rich'.[266] This was why, with Freeman, Acton believed that it was better to be the citizen of 'a humble commonwealth in the Alps' than of a 'superb autocracy';[267] this was why he and his fellow-Gladstonians were so enthused by the notion of Irish home rule, irrespective of the social or political consequences.

Acton may – or may not – have had influence elsewhere, but he had little in Ireland, where the strength of liberal Catholicism was deceptive. It appeared considerable, in the years around 1870, because of the wide-spread invocation of a Catholic educational grievance: the impossibility of Catholic students attending a denominational college which was allowed to award them a university degree. But this was not the demand of a large, articulate and aspiring Irish middle class; it was the cry of the bishops, of the National Association, and therefore, to a considerable extent, of mass electoral opinion.[268] In the words of Bishop Moriarty of Kerry, the refusal of the British state to endow denominational Catholic educational institutions, and thus to permit them to compete fairly with other colleges and schools, constituted a far worse slight than the existence of the Church Establishment, because it 'keeps us down and keeps up the Protestants'.[269]

It became apparent after 1870 that the vast majority of Irish Catholic laymen would follow whatever leadership their bishops gave on edu-cational matters: that they were happy to accept that ecclesiastical authority was the safest bulwark against attacks on the faith. Typical of such men was J. A. Dease, a liberal, and a Commissioner of National Education, who nonetheless 'always felt that in the long run Rome is the safest guide', and repeatedly insisted that the bishops' demands that the Church should control education were perfectly reasonable, and that

---

[265] *Ibid.*, pp. 264–5; Gooch, *History and historians*, p. 367.
[266] 'History of freedom in antiquity', p. 248.
[267] *Ibid.*, p. 264.
[268] Norman, *Catholic Church*, pp. 190–281.
[269] Moriarty to Monsell, 2 March 1868, Gladstone papers, 44152, fo. 98.

Catholic laymen were not being bullied into supporting them.[270] Spencer's private secretary was soon lamenting that there were hardly any 'free-thinking Catholics of the continental type' in Ireland.[271] The views of English anti-Catholics seemed to be corroborated: liberal Catholicism was a phantom, and Irishmen would adopt whatever line their bishops forced on them on any political matter. As Manning told Gladstone in 1870: 'if you desire to know how the Catholics of England or Ireland are affected on any question involving either religion or Ecclesiastical questions, no man will mislead you more than Lord Acton'.[272]

Matters were complicated further by the bishops' willingness, in turn, to adopt the catchcries of the home-rule party, which achieved startling success in Irish by-elections after 1870. This success was owing to the manipulation of three issues in particular: denominational education, the detention of Fenian convicts, and tenant-right.[273]

The educational policy of the home-rule party was strongly pro-denominational. This, however, was not, originally, exclusively for Catholic consumption: indeed, many of the early leaders – Isaac Butt, Mitchell Henry and John Martin, for example – were Protestants. Home rulers demanded security for denominational education for both sects, opposing the compromises which Englishmen seemed to wish to impose on them, and arguing that undenominationalism led to the growth of infidelity, which would affect Protestantism and Catholicism alike.[274] After disestablishment had removed one prop of Irish Protestants, many of them were anxious not to see Trinity enfeebled as well, as Butt pointed out: no real university could 'survive the destruction of that religious life with which all her traditions are inseparably interwoven'.[275]

More importantly, large numbers of Irish Catholic voters keenly supported the home rulers' calls for an endowed denominational education system. (The denominational cry was also a potent influence on English Catholics, but in the context of English politics – especially school-board politics – it tended, by 1874, to encourage them to vote Conservative.) By 1872, these calls were swinging by-elections in favour of home-rule candidates throughout Catholic Ireland – with the further consequence that, as the movement roused mass Catholic support, Protestant sympathy for home rule inevitably waned.

---

[270] Wetherell to Acton, n.d. 1867, Acton papers, 8119, box 8; J. A. Dease to Portarlington, 4 February 1873, Disraeli papers, B/XXI/P/410a; H. Y. Thompson memorandum, 15 November 1872, Granville papers, 30/29/69, fo. 194, pp. 15–16.
[271] Granville papers, 30/29/69, fo. 194, p. 18.
[272] 11 November 1870, Gladstone papers, 44249, fo. 237.
[273] See Thornley, *Butt*, p. 176.
[274] Butt, *Problem of Irish education*, p. 71.   [275] *Ibid.*, pp. vii, 2–6, 37–8, 45.

Gladstone had no intention of satisfying the demand for educational endowment, because it would destroy the religious policy that he wished to pursue in England, and would break up his party. Butt led the Irish opposition to his 1873 University Bill on two main principles: the unfairness of its treatment of Catholic denominational institutions, which he alleged could not possibly compete with the lavishly endowed undenominational colleges; and the biassed system of university government which it proposed. There would, he said, be an unrepresentatively large number of Protestants on the governing body; moreover, the Catholics selected for it by the British administration would be liberal Catholics of the sort that Englishmen appreciated, 'the very last to whom the free choice of the Irish nation would entrust the control over national education'.[276] Butt wished instead to see Trinity and an endowed Roman Catholic college established as two independent denominational institutions, under the same examining board. The board would administer examinations in uncontroversial subjects; the other subjects would be taught entirely according to the wishes of the individual colleges, which would award their own divinity degrees.[277]

The secession of the Irish MPs on the 1873 Irish University Bill was obviously an important cause of the government's defeat on the measure, but its impact was slightly blunted by the fact that Irish MPs had been very lax in giving support even before then – primarily from indifference rather than from ideological disfavour of proceedings at Westminster. As a result, the government's majority, nominally over 110, was, in effect, halved by 1870, even before the spate of by-election losses on both sides of the Irish Sea.[278] Only thirty-eight Irish MPs even qualified for inclusion in our survey – thirteen Protestants and twenty-five Catholics – and these tended to vote only on those religious issues which had interest for their constituents. On other matters, their voting displays no pattern. Six Protestants and five Catholics supported the English Church Establishment; four and three respectively opposed it. Four Protestants and six Catholics supported the government on its university-tests policy; two Protestants and six Catholics opposed it. Where Irish interests were affected, voting was more straightforward. Only one man – the Protestant Agar-Ellis – dared to vote for Bouverie's motion on the O'Keeffe affair (see p. 371); only one – the Ulsterman McClure – voted for the repeal of Clause 25 of the 1870 Education Act, while thirty-two of the thirty-eight MPs voted for it, treating it as a test of the denominational principle. Three times as many Protestants supported the government on the Westmeath (coercion) Bill as opposed it;

[276] *Ibid.*, pp. 78, 83.
[277] *Ibid.*, pp. 52–3, 58–61.
[278] Ramm, 'Cabinet government', p. 741.

five times as many Catholics opposed it as supported it. In general, however, there were more Protestants who saw the necessity of voting in support of Catholic grievances on controversial questions than there were Catholics who were willing to support the government. This was most obvious on the Irish University Bill, which five of the Protestants in the survey supported and seven opposed; three Catholics voted with the government, as against twenty with Disraeli. Broadly speaking, six of the Protestants were loyal to the government on religious questions, while four generally voted on the Catholic/nationalist ticket; only five of the Catholics could be said to be genuine supporters of the government, and two of these opposed the 1873 bill.

Gladstone's reaction to the Irish MPs' rejection of his 1873 bill was to blame the bishops and the pope. He had not yet come to detect, emerging from the nationalist leaders, the authentic voice of Ireland. In the 1880s, however, he was not so preoccupied by the need to defend denominationalism in England, nor by the impact of ultramontanism on his ability to do so. He became more responsive to the demands of mass Catholic opinion; in doing this, rather than concentrating on specific questions of religious liberty, he was bound to affront propertied liberal Catholics. It is instructive to note that, of the latter, Blennerhassett and Monsell remained staunch unionists, and that O'Hagan (who died in 1885) would probably have joined them.[279] The only leading liberal Catholics to support Gladstone's home-rule policy were Englishmen like Acton and Camoys, who could afford to view Ireland from afar, with detachment, and with an interest merely in implementing long-held but utterly abstract principles, the principles of the Gladstonians, 'that the ends of liberty are the true ends of politics'.[280]

---

[279] Macknight, *Ulster as it is*, ii, 120.
[280] (Acton, 1886) *Letters of Acton to Mary Gladstone*, pp. 216, lxii.

4

The radicals

Popular enthusiasm for the Liberal party derived its greatest impetus from nonconformist commitment – and this was reflected in the eagerness with which Anglican MPs sitting for large urban constituencies upheld the sects' grievances. Any analysis of the basis of mid and late Victorian radicalism must therefore devote considerable attention to the nonconformist contribution. But another religious tradition also helped to define the outlook of urban constituency Liberalism: that which rejected institutional Christianity in favour of freethinking and ethical inspiration. This in turn brought leading working-men into contact with two classes of intellectuals, those positivists who were the disciples of the Frenchman Comte, and rationalist academic agnostics. In this chapter, nonconformists, urban radical MPs, spokesmen of the working-men, positivists and academic liberals are discussed in turn. The perspective of each group was different from that of the others, and most were also divided within themselves; but this discussion is intended primarily to display the extent to which they shared common values.

The academic liberals apart, all these groups, however diverse in outlook, were undoubtedly attracted by Gladstone, in much the same way as he was attracted by most of them. The cry which, with occasional difficulties, sustained Liberal unity at popular level was, simply, that of 'Gladstone'; the mass of the Liberal party supported him in 1886 despite lukewarmness on the issue of home rule itself. Thus the connections between the bulk of the party and its leader, informal as they were, were powerful, and it is suggested here that, enthusiasm for participation in politics and for tax reduction apart, much of this power was supplied by a moral vision. It is impossible to be certain to what extent this vision was possessed by the rank-and-file; some, no doubt, were driven towards political activity entirely by temporal considerations. But thousands who did possess it – and they included many of the most important figures in Liberal borough politics – wished to see the creation of a commonwealth of religious men: a commonwealth in which spiritual fervour would be unchecked by material temptation, in which privilege and exclusiveness would be destroyed if they interfered with the interests of the commonwealth, and in which idleness would be vanquished and industriousness rewarded. In practice, the most consistently articulated goal of Liberal radicalism in the period under discussion was for the disestablishment of the Church of England. There was a genuine belief that the passage of disestablishment would lead not only to religious harmony but to class harmony as well. It was in pursuit of this harmony that popular Liberalism was geared, thus explaining why a degree of political solidarity which has almost defied the belief of many twentieth-century historians was attainable between working-men, great industrialists, and Oxbridge intellectuals.

Nonconformists

Very few nonconformists of any denomination were unaffected by the surge of enthusiasm within the Liberal party in the 1860s. Despite all the qualifications which must later be made to the notion that nonconformity constituted a united political force, its response to the political situation after 1867 was discernibly more radical than that of most whig-liberals. This was hardly surprising, since agitations for the abolition of church rates and university tests had been two major causes of the popular activity of the 1860s, and since the combination of the reintroduction of the Irish Church issue and the extension of the franchise raised widespread hopes that further major steps towards religious equality would be taken.

Enthusiasm was greatest in the sects with the most lower-middle and working-class support; and it was particularly evident here among baptists and congregationalists, rather than among Wesleyans (who had a large popular following, but were also especially prone to bouts of evangelical anti-Catholicism and anti-sacerdotalism, which tempered their affection for Gladstone). It was less marked among the non-evangelical and more intellectual unitarians, or among quakers and jews. Notwithstanding this broad division, a few in the first category, especially educated or wealthy congregationalists, sympathised with the political outlook of unitarians; while other congregationalists had affinities with anti-Catholic Wesleyans. But baptists and congregationalists still comprised the major force in radical political nonconformity, and require most attention.

Despite their differences concerning the doctrine of baptism, congregationalists and baptists shared similar views about church government. Baptists had a lower social status, on the whole, than congregationalists, and, of all dissenting sects, were the least affected, in the 1870s, by the impact of biblical criticism.[1] Both had been much invigorated by the evangelical revival, and the two sects enjoyed much friendlier relations than they did with all other dissenting groups;[2] a number of leading nonconformists, like J. J. Colman, the mustard manufacturing MP, hoped that they would sink their differences and unite.[3] They may therefore profitably be considered together.

In the 1860s and 1870s, the teaching of both sects was enlivened by the influence of a number of intense preachers, emphasising spirituality, zeal and scholarship in the history of Christianity on the one hand, and political activity on the other. Two of the leading congregationalists were R. W. Dale of Carr's Lane Chapel, Birmingham, and James Guinness Rogers of Clapham; two of the baptists were Alexander Maclaren of Union Chapel, Manchester, and John Clifford of Praed Street, Paddington. Dale was the most anxious to advocate political involvement, owing partly to Maurice's influence,[4] and largely to that of a charismatic preacher, George Dawson, who belonged to no sect, but whose vision that class harmony might be achieved through activity in municipal government became a very potent one in Birmingham.[5] But the most profound political influence on all these men, and, in a sense, the founder of nineteenth-century radical political nonconformity, was Edward Miall, a former congregationalist minister, editor of the *Nonconformist* from 1841, and MP for Rochdale between 1852 and 1857 and for Bradford between 1869 and 1874. In the two decades after the mid 1840s, his was the greatest inspiration driving evangelical nonconformists into political action. Dale, Maclaren and Rogers all admired him greatly, and followed him in attempting to counteract the political quietude of the evangelical sects.[6] Miall also inspired a host of men who became nonconformist MPs, the most politically vigorous of whom were Henry Richard, the leader of Welsh nonconformity, and the baptist and Bradford worsted-spinner Alfred Illingworth, who became treasurer and later chairman of the Liberation Society. Under the influence of radical baptists and congregationalists such as these, political nonconformity, whose outlook had previously been defined by the interests of whiggish unitarians, became relatively less concerned with promoting civil liberties (which were now mostly secure anyway), and relatively more with evangelism –

[1] Bebbington, 'Baptist MPs in the nineteenth century', p. 4.
[2] (Birrell) Waller, *Democracy and sectarianism*, p. 15.
[3] Colman, *Colman*, pp. 134–5.
[4] Kenyon, 'Dale', p. 202.
[5] Hennock, *Fit and proper persons*, pp. 75–6, 155.
[6] Binfield, *So down to prayers*, p. 103; Hennock, *Fit and proper persons*, pp. 157–8.

and thus with the defence of doctrine and denominational independence. This change was certainly apparent by the early 1860s.

The fundamental aspiration of these radicals was for the re-Christianisation of society. One of the most emotional statements to this effect was the peroration of Dale's speech, *The politics of nonconformity*, delivered at Manchester in November 1871 – in which he asserted that nonconformists were active in politics 'not because we wish to make the political life of England less religious, but because we wish to make it more religious'.[7] He was subsequently to say that 'the Christian ideal of civil society' would never be realised until all those who held political and judicial office recognised the 'social and political order of the nation as a Divine institution, and discharge their official duties as ministers of God'.[8] Samuel Morley, the immensely wealthy hosiery manufacturer, philanthropist and MP, was 'a Nonconformist because I believe that the action of political parties has depressed and hindered the action of that which is essentially spiritual'.

Central to such beliefs was the assumption that 'to rely on the legislative enforcement of any Church system [is] to wither up all that is fresh and vital in our religious communities'.[9] Radical nonconformists believed that the world could not be brought under the rule of Christ by Establishments: their forefathers had seceded from the Church of England in defence of the hallowed relationship of the 'regenerate soul' to God, without human authority of any sort intervening.[10] Establishments were thought to formalise religious practice, repress religious expression, and blunt man's sense of individual responsibility for his own salvation. The argument that political and legal sanction was necessary in order to impose good Christian behaviour was dismissed as absurd.[11] Nonconformists maintained that the Church of England's determination to remain national at all costs required her to blur her doctrinal edges, and destroyed her ability to define and propagate religious truth. She thus departed from the nonconformist ideal, which saw a Church as 'a congregation of faithful men', determined to maintain adequate spiritual fare for all her members.[12] A national Church – the achievement of the Reformation – was in many ways a retrogression. It destroyed the mediaeval idea of a 'Church co-extensive with the Christian name': a Church ruled by a power whose authority derived from 'beyond this world', and which possessed 'a unity of spirit unexpressed in formularies or organizations, reigning in all the

---

[7] *Politics of nonconformity*, p. 32.
[8] Hennock, *Fit and proper persons*, pp. 162–3.
[9] Hodder, *Morley*, p. 455.
[10] Dale, 'Arnold and the nonconformists', pp. 547–8.
[11] Maclaren, *Religious equality*, pp. 15–17.   [12] Dale, *Dale*, pp. 103–4.

provinces of man's social, political, and national life'. This unity of spirit could be achieved only by allowing 'entire freedom' to 'the movement of His energy in individual human hearts'. The mediaeval Church had not been hidebound by dogma, but had encouraged the 'energetic action of individual men'; monks had been 'nonconformists' in that they had brought 'new ideas into the Church, and leavened it with their own independent life'. Any attempt to impose 'human orders' as 'essential bases of communion' was bound to create schism. The Church of England, in its Reformed state, was founded upon a 'miserably narrow, shallow, and selfish assertion of the right of a class to represent Christ in legislating for the Church'; it refused to concede that the 'weary heart of humanity' would be lightened if granted spiritual freedom.[13] Only by the propagation of a spiritual Christianity would 'the awful burden of sins and sorrows' which weighed down the mass of humanity be lifted, and the 'growing evils around us' be tackled.[14]

The core of this belief was thus emotional and not intellectual. It was spiritual fervour in a 'quickened Church' which would convert the poor to Christ, not the 'sharpest dialectics of a passionless understanding': nor could unbelief be challenged by relying on an intellectual defence of the faith.[15] 'Silence of the *mind*', the conquest of self-will, was necessary 'for a noble and devout life'.[16]

This distrust of the powers of the intellect was perfectly compatible with the belief – which Dale shared with Gladstone – that the most fundamental idea in any religion was the 'personal and experimental life of the human soul with God'.[17] Congregationalism could be kept vital and intense only if each individual were left free to give a 'fresh account' of the 'unique life' of Christ and his supreme spiritual example – a freshness which, Dale alleged, was often lacking in Anglican evangelicals, who had the 'poorest, meanest, narrowest conceptions of moral duty, and are almost destitute of moral strength'.[18] Dale argued that, if the spiritual essence, which had been hidden under the dry formalism imbibed by their ancestors, was to be rediscovered, nonconformists needed to devote more attention to theological scholarship: they lacked an awareness of the spiritual traditions in the Church.[19] A deeper account of Christian truths than Calvinist dogma had offered was necessary: an account

[13] Anon., 'The genius of nonconformity', pp. 129–31, 142.
[14] Clifford, *Jesus Christ and modern social life*, p. 8. See Rogers, 'Congregationalism of the future', p. 531.
[15] Maclaren, '*Time for thee to work*', pp. 13–17.
[16] Maclaren, *Week-day evening addresses*, pp. 8, 153–4; see also Clifford, *A New Testament Church*, p. 7.
[17] Dale, *Evangelical revival*, Hawarden copy, p. 10; Gladstone, *Gleanings*, vii, 223.
[18] Dale, *Evangelical revival*, pp. 48, 267–78.
[19] Dale, 'Anglicanism and Romanism', p. 334; and *Holy Spirit in relation to ministry*, p. 25.

which was capable of 'regulat[ing]' and 'control[ling]' man's religious outlook, and of ending 'speculation'.[20] Dale therefore considered that the one thing most 'essential to the spiritual vigour of a Christian Church' was 'systematic instruction in religious truth', because unless the truths of the gospel were properly inculcated it was often impossible to arouse sufficient 'spiritual ardour' in the congregation. A prerequisite for the re-Christianising of society was therefore that 'intense interest in religious doctrine which distinguished the heroic men who belonged to the times of the Commonwealth'.[21]

The Established Church was not, it was contended, a true Protestant Church, because it attempted to unite on 'ethical' rather than on 'spiritual' principles.[22] It was unable to propagate any sort of refreshing dogma. There was no possibility of promoting spiritual discovery merely by interpreting stringent articles with a new vagueness, in the hope of satisfying a restless mind.[23] The Church's attitude to dogmatic interpretations was 'inimical to ordinary convictions of the sacredness of truth and of the sanctity of conscience'.[24] Its discipline was paralysed, its constituency was the 'careless and irreligious'.[25] Broad churchmen, it was alleged, wanted the Church to embrace 'as many heretics as can possibly be gathered within its fold by subtle and dexterous interpretations of its legal position and creed'. Nonconformists were presented as having always prided themselves on their determination to exclude those who sought false unity at the expense of the believer's right 'to be true and faithful to his own experiences'. Broad churchmen, it was said, assumed not that *dogma* was true, but that one theory of *Church organisation* must be defended above all else.[26]

The determination of the Establishment to remain national was 'repressing and hindering' her essential spiritual function, to 'teach her own views of the truth'.[27] Bishops gave off only 'vagueness and uncertainty'.[28] It was quite wrong that 'vital questions of Church doctrine, ritual, and discipline' should be judged in civil law courts. Laws for 'Church societies' were 'the proper work of their members'.[29]

The existence of an Establishment was thought, therefore, to give too

---

[20] Dale, *Evangelical revival*, pp. 18–26, 267; *Protestantism*, pp. 25–30.
[21] Dale, *Dale*, pp. 107–8.
[22] Dale, 'Arnold and the nonconformists', esp. p. 548.
[23] Anon., 'The genius of nonconformity', pp. 147–8.
[24] Allon, 'Why nonconformists desire disestablishment', p. 390.
[25] Maclaren, *Religious equality*, p. 19.
[26] Crosskey, 'Nonconformist programme', pp. 360–1. See Dale, *Dale*, pp. 163–4, 169 (on *Essays and reviews*), and p. 215 (on Dean Stanley).
[27] Rogers, *Bennett judgment*, p. 15; *Ritualistic movement*, p. 10.
[28] Rogers, 'Social aspects of disestablishment', p. 443.
[29] Allon, 'Why nonconformists desire disestablishment', pp. 379, 385–6.

much latitude – in the sense of allowing the intellect to refashion Christian truth arbitrarily rather than leading it to grapple with truth and duty. But in the proper sense of allowing each individual spiritual freedom, it was considered that it did not give enough. The authority which the Establishment gave to clerics and the temporal power over individual Church members was believed to stultify religious profession by permitting men to force invented practices on unsympathetic members. The episcopalian Establishment legitimised 'priestcraft and kingcraft', just as it had in the seventeenth century when nonconformists had seceded. It manipulated 'true and beautiful' Christian principles into tools for the dominance of 'the restricting, misguiding, and depraving influence [of] the sacerdotal spirit'.[30] (Similar criticisms, taken even further, could be applied to Islam – that the closeness of the Church–state relationship enforced an 'abiding despotism', the imposition of 'the theology and morality of the Law'.)[31] Ritualism, 'bastard Popery', was, of course, one form of spiritual repression which aroused a great deal of nonconformist antagonism[32] – although some, like Dale, considered it an insignificant matter when compared with the general evil of sacerdotalism, which was believed to be an unwarrantable interference with the individual's relationship with God, and a reminder of the 'destructive tyranny' that the Catholics had imposed on Europe.[33] At any rate, nonconformists agreed in viewing with suspicion the revival in modern times of a high-church tradition which sought to establish 'a new priestly despotism'.[34]

Disestablishment would, it was thought, help to defeat such tyrannical aspirations. If the Church were set free from parliamentary control, laymen would take a revived interest in Church work, and a great step forward could be taken in the 'evangelising of England'.[35] They would check sacerdotal practices and assert the original Christian idea, the 'congregational polity', which alone was able to preserve truth and freshness, because it acknowledged 'no authority but Christ's'.[36] Disestablish-

---

[30] Miall, *Miall*, p. 303.

[31] These were the words, not of a nonconformist, but of E. A. Freeman, who, interestingly, was allowed space in Allon's *British Quarterly Review* to write on 'Mahomet': pp. 132–3. He contributed many other articles in the mid 1870s on the Eastern question: Peel, *Letters to Allon*, p. 75.

[32] (*Baptist Handbook*, 1871) Binfield, *So down to prayers*, p. 14; Rogers, *Bennett judgment*, pp. 25–7; 'Forster's defence of the Church', p. 530; H. Richard and J. Carvell Williams, *Disestablishment*, pp. 85–7; Miall, *Bearing of religious equality*, p. 7; Clifford, *Jesus Christ and modern social life*, p. 6.

[33] Dale, *Evangelical revival*, pp. 9–10; *Protestantism*, pp. 11–12, 99–101. For detestation of sacerdotalism, see also Williamson, *Maclaren*, pp. 53–4; Clifford, *A New Testament Church*, pp. 10–11.

[34] Anon., 'Parties in the Episcopal Church', p. 382.

[35] Maclaren, *Religious equality*, p. 17.   [36] Clifford, *A New Testament Church*, p. 12.

ment would remove the 'one obstacle to hearty cooperation' between Anglican and nonconformist evangelicals, and together they would be able to 'withstand the fierce onslaught' of crypto-popery.[37] If the Church were disestablished and able to 'fulfil [her] true mission', she would probably absorb a lot of nonconformity, and, with its help, would 'triumph' over evil.[38] 'Brotherly fellowship' would create a 'community of . . . Christian men and citizens'.[39] Disestablishment would bring nearer 'the Divine ideal of national and religious life . . . when the nation shall be religious because the individuals are Christian'.[40] Christian purity would 'bind together in mutual respect and confidence all ranks and conditions of men'; it would become obvious that 'the true prosperity of States does not lie in mere material wealth, but in the fidelity of its people and its rulers to the laws of eternal righteousness'.[41]

Nonconformists argued that this contrasted with the present position, not only in terms of religious zeal, but in social terms as well. Establishment split the nation, creating 'alienation' and the 'deepest crack that runs through English life', setting 'class against class'.[42] Fuelling the nonconformist desire for disestablishment was a vision of a meritocratic society in which the industry of self-made commercial and professional men, shopkeepers and artisans would be rewarded; as the editor of *The Baptist* put it in 1870, 'it is only in the absence of a State religion that social position is regulated by personal merit'.[43] Nonconformist industrialists like Illingworth or Morley supported trade-union activity in their workplaces and elsewhere – Morley, for example, gave a lot of money to Joseph Arch's Agricultural Labourers' Union. There is no reason to doubt their protestations of love for, and brotherhood with, their workers, and the religious inspiration behind these sentiments. In large- and small-scale Liberal firms, for example in the West Riding, religion certainly constituted a close bond of sympathy between employer and employee.[44] In 1868, one general principle of Miall's election campaign was the importance of securing equality before the law for all classes – in the sphere of property and trade-union legislation as much as in religious affairs. He argued that the legislature should view 'man as man', as dignified and spiritually aware, rather than as an interest either worth, or not worth, conciliating by bribes.[45]

[37] Anon., 'Parties in the Episcopal Church', p. 389.
[38] (1864) Colman, *Colman*, p. 147; (1868) Miall, *Miall*, p. 288.
[39] Clifford, *A New Testament Church*, pp. 5–7.
[40] Maclaren, *Religious equality*, p. 21.   [41] Dale, *Politics of nonconformity*, pp. 31–2.
[42] Maclaren, *Religious equality*, pp. 5–12.   [43] Hurst, 'Liberal versus Liberal', pp. 701–2.
[44] Joyce, *Work, society and politics*, pp. 141–2, 166–8; Horn, *Arch*, pp. 105–6; Phillips, 'Religion and society in the cloth region of Wiltshire', pp. 100–1.
[45] Miall, *Miall*, pp. 284–5.

Nonconformists insisted, in the main, that pauperism subsidised by the state – that is, by the poor, struggling but virtuous taxpayer – was to be condemned: it involved shielding both paupers, and the privileged rich, from their spiritual mission. For Clifford, relief of poverty by government was to 'lift . . . a man up by dropping him into a deeper abyss';[46] for Illingworth, the royal family was 'only a set of outdoor paupers'.[47] 'Great things' were 'not to be expected from the easy and self-indulgent, but from the self-denying, the earnest, the tempted, the tried, the harassed'.[48] The argument that the Church Establishment provided a social service by giving soup and blankets to the poor did not help its case for survival: 'life, warmth, disinterested affection, self-sacrifice, gentleness – these go much further to commend the grace of God to the poor than any costly provision of means at other people's expense'.[49]

However, many nonconformists, like many of those discussed in chapter 3, experienced an ambivalence between dislike of pauperism and concern for the poor: Dale, for example, was 'repelled' by the 'moral austerity' of a strict supporter of laissez-faire like Bright.[50] Radical nonconformists, like Gladstonian churchmen, believed that the rich and powerful were more susceptible to materialistic temptations than the poor, and constantly warned of the perils which accompanied indulgence in luxury – a relevant warning, given the rise of a powerful plutocratic class of successful nonconformist businessmen, many of whom were in parliament by the 1860s. Nonconformists, they warned, must not forsake their responsibilities. The poor man 'receives his wages at the end of the week, and does not get them unless his work is done; while the wealthy man receives his wages first, and is bound, as a matter of honour, to earn them afterwards'. The Christian faith was 'confessedly revolutionary', because it maintained that the profits of merchants, manufacturers, and tradesmen were 'all His'.[51] By omitting to set aside time for regular prayer, the active and powerful would lose 'the joy and the strength of . . . Divine protection'. God did not judge men by the 'apparent magnitude of their work'; 'beauty' could dwell in the most 'obscure life'.[52]

Nonconformists thus believed in the moral capacity of the popular judgment, as was especially evident in their view of foreign relations. They had little confidence in the ability of governments to avoid wars,

---

[46] Clifford, *Jesus Christ and modern social life*, p. 35.
[47] Bebbington, *Nonconformist conscience*, pp. 19–20.
[48] Wilson, *Dawson*, p. 110.
[49] Miall, *Bearing of religious equality*, p. 13; Rogers, *Bennett judgment*, p. 12.
[50] Kenyon, 'Dale', p. 205.
[51] Dale, *Evangelical revival*, pp. 282–5.
[52] Maclaren, *Week-day evening addresses*, pp. 21–4, 34, 69–70.

because they had little respect for the morals of politicians; their advocacy of pressure-group politics stemmed from an assumption that it was perpetually necessary to guard against unprincipled behaviour on the part of those in authority.[53] Diplomats, cunning and lying, were also seen as irresponsible: they constituted a state-subsidised 'forcing-house of demoralization'.[54] The 'war system . . . had its basis in what is called society'.[55] Radical nonconformists usually distrusted calls for war or imperial expansion, even on religious grounds.[56] Instead, they were confident that the common man's feelings of brotherhood with his fellows would assist the cause of peace. In the fight to preserve international concord, Samuel Morley relied 'more on electric telegraphs, steam navigation, cheap postage, international exhibitions, peace congresses – anything that brings PEOPLES together, as distinguished from their rulers – than all the armies in the world'.[57] Free-trade policies would, it was argued, have a similar effect, breaking down the 'narrow selfishness' of nations, encouraging the sharing of the world's resources without jealousy, furthering close and constant intercourse between nations, and thus promoting 'universal brotherhood'. At the same time, by allowing all classes at home free and equal access to the fruits of Providence, free trade would, it was suggested, forestall domestic class antagonism.[58]

To sum up, despite their hostility to sacerdotalism, and although their inspiration was different from Gladstone's, many of the practical opinions set forth by nonconformists coincided with his, and with those of his high-church followers. Dale and Maclaren had great respect for the devotion and learning of Anglican high churchmen.[59] High-church enthusiasm for the conversion of the poor was much admired: nonconformists were happy to attribute the revival of zeal in the Church of

---

[53] Hamer, *Politics of electoral pressure*, p. 33.
[54] (Miall) Summerton, 'Dissenting attitudes to peace and war', p. 159.
[55] (Illingworth) *ibid.*, p. 160.
[56] See the comment of Wilfrid Lawson, the Anglican radical and sympathiser with nonconformist demands, when an Anglican evangelical defended the Ashantee War with the argument that it was a war against the 'strongholds of Satan': 'if we were to attack all the strongholds of Satan, we should require Supplementary Estimates': Russell, *Lawson*, p. 33.
[57] Hodder, *Morley*, p. 451.
[58] Illingworth, *Fifty years of politics*, p. 39; Summerton, 'Dissenting attitudes to peace and war', pp. 158–9.
[59] See e.g. Dale, 'Anglicanism and Romanism', p. 333; Maclaren, *Religious equality*, p. 13. Dale's interpretation of the Eucharist, for example, held that real spiritual refreshment might be gained by receiving the bread, because it was charged with a spiritual message from Christ: it transferred the duties and responsibilities of Christian brotherhood and fellowship. It was thus far more than the merely 'technical' operation in which many Protestants believed; and he had no objection to being called a 'High Churchman': 'Doctrine of the Real Presence', pp. 377–90; Dale, *Dale*, pp. 355–67.

England to the influence of the Oxford movement and to Newman.[60] Dale and Rogers both warmly supported the efforts of churchmen to Christianise the industrial masses: their 'holiness' and 'zeal' had bound nonconformists to them 'by a thousand ties of affection, admiration, and confidence'.[61] Moreover, radical high churchmen were praised for not tolerating any longer 'the Erastian conditions of the Establishment'.[62] When Stanley alleged in January 1873 that high churchmen and nonconformists were in political alliance, the *Nonconformist* replied that this was not the case in the long term, because they differed fundamentally about sacerdotalism. However it affirmed that both certainly agreed 'in looking upon a Christian Church as an institution aiming at spiritual ends and governed by spiritual laws – capable of existence without the support of the secular power, and requiring, as the first condition of its existence, freedom from restraints imposed by the jealousy or the craft of statesmen, rather than in the interest of truth and godliness'.[63] Perhaps the *British Quarterly Review*, the leading nonconformist periodical (edited by the congregationalist minister Henry Allon), summed up nonconformist attitudes to high churchmen most neatly, in being confident that 'Protestantism' would triumph once zeal had been awakened among all evangelicals by disestablishment, while at the same time deploring Anglican attempts to repress Anglo-catholicism within the Church.[64] The Church should be allowed to keep her 'ancient creeds' intact from parliamentary interference;[65] the doctrine of religious equality meant that all sects were to be protected 'from molestation in doing their work'.[66] High churchmen should be given freedom to develop their conceptions; but disestablishment would be doubly beneficial, in that it would terminate state sanction of their speculations and practices, and in that, by establishing a perfect competition between sects, it would enable public opinion to refuse to tolerate any high-church activity which was not genuinely spiritual. By force of public pressure, high churchmen would thus find the 'spirit' which was 'working within them' – and which, since it had a 'definite meaning and purpose', was 'destined to become a power' – naturally channelled into harmony with God's will.[67]

Like Gladstone, Dale argued that to guarantee freedom from temporal interference for all sects was also the only safe ground on which to

---

[60] E.g. Allon, 'Why nonconformists desire disestablishment', pp. 389–90.
[61] Dale, *Dale*, p. 102; Rogers, 'Forster's defence of the Church', p. 524.
[62] Allon, 'Why nonconformists desire disestablishment', pp. 389–90.
[63] *Nonconformist*, 22 January 1873, p. 82.
[64] Anon., 'Parties in the Episcopal Church', pp. 389–90.
[65] Dale, *Politics of nonconformity*, pp. 30–1.
[66] Miall, *Bearing of religious equality*, p. 8.
[67] Anon., 'The genius of nonconformity', pp. 136–7.

oppose the 'lofty claims' which the ultramontane papacy made regarding its right to a voice in temporal affairs.[68] The *British Quarterly Review* used the same argument to refute Stanley's proposition (pp. 91–2) that Protestant nonconformists, and all Free Churchmen, were 'ultramontane'.[69] The *Review* also distinguished between the 'pernicious tyranny' and 'paralyzing and degrading ecclesiasticism' of ultramontanism, and the Old Catholic movement; the latter, as long as it rejected Roman presumptions and developed 'Evangelical principles', was to be applauded for its attempts to arouse 'Catholic sentiment' through 'fellowship and unity', while retaining 'apostolic . . . faith and purity'.[70]

In discussing education, the nonconformists' major principle had always been that a man's money should not be appropriated for the teaching of religious principles of which he disapproved. In the 1840s, this argument had led many nonconformists to advocate voluntaryism, rather than to support the teaching of Anglican doctrine; in the early 1870s, it also created a movement in favour of state secularism. Dale, Rogers, Clifford and others all upheld the secular idea in the early 1870s, contending that it would avoid the perils of the broad churchmen's undenominationalism, which was 'eating the very life out of so many'.[71] Maclaren found it to be incapable of instilling a 'hearty love' of truth, and a 'hearty hatred for its denial and contradiction'.[72] Clifford was sure that government could provide only 'colourless, soul-less teaching'; it was therefore 'a folly' and 'a wrong' to look to the state to impart religious education. Central government was a 'machine mostly working with as little humanity as possible'; the Churches must be left to provide intense and morally regenerating religious teaching[73] – and if they did so privately, strife between them would 'pass away'.[74] In parliament, the crusade for secularism was headed by Henry Richard for the Welshmen, and by the baptist MPs – all four of whom supported it,[75] probably because of that sect's unusually prolonged resistance to liberal theological arguments.[76]

But although, as a policy, secularism obviously had parallels with disestablishment, it was not necessary to support the former in order to be

---

[68] Dale, *Protestantism*, p. 97.
[69] Anon., 'Ultramontanism and civil allegiance', p. 472.
[70] Anon., 'Mr Gladstone's retirement from the Liberal leadership', pp. 497–8; 'Catholicism and papal infallibility', esp. p. 103.
[71] Dale, *Evangelical revival*, p. 264; Rogers, *Autobiography*, p. 41.
[72] '*Time for thee to work*', pp. 20–2.
[73] Clifford, *Jesus Christ and modern social life*, pp. 40–1.
[74] Illingworth, *Fifty years of politics*, p. 43.
[75] Plus Winterbotham, another MP disqualified from the survey by entering government.
[76] For this, see McLeod, *Class and religion in the late Victorian city*, p. 226; Bebbington, 'Gladstone and the baptists', pp. 234–5.

strongly in favour of the latter; for example, six of the eleven congregationalist MPs who voted for disestablishment, did not support the
secularist motion of 1870. In early 1870, even Richard made a distinction
between accepting secularism, if there was no satisfactory alternative,
and actively promoting a campaign for it, which he did not wish to do.[77]
Most nonconformists had been associated with the British and Foreign
Schools Society, which provided undenominational teaching; and they
continued to regard this as an acceptable compromise. After 1870, most
of them defined the main evils against which agitation was necessary to
be the rate-subsidised denominational teaching allowed by Clause 25 of
the Education Act – which none of the seventeen baptist and congregationalist MPs in the survey defended when it became a contentious
issue in 1872 and 1873 – and the failure to make school boards compulsory everywhere. The outcry against Clause 25, on the part of
'undenominationalist' nonconformists, in fact resulted from a general
dislike of the advantages still retained by the denominationalists,
especially in rural areas, where the Church in effect retained control of
education. These battles were fought in school-board elections throughout the country, but very few nonconformist candidates stood on an
explicitly secularist platform.

Although secularism was touted quite widely by radical nonconformists between 1871 and 1873, it was, on the whole, not because of its
inherent merits as an educational policy, and only partly as a corollary of
the argument for disestablishment. It was advocated mainly because of
the deep-seated concern for the future of *Irish* education. Those who
despised undenominationalism believed that to abolish all state grants
for religious teaching was the only principled alternative to a policy of
general denominational endowment, in Ireland as well as in Britain. In
Ireland, this would involve subsidising the 'deadly error' of Catholicism,
a policy which would constitute a 'death-blow to Protestantism'.[78] Similar considerations motivated nonconformists' hostility to a concurrent
endowment solution to the Irish Church problem in 1868–9; Rogers,
Henry Richard and others subsequently claimed that their trust in
Gladstone had been founded on his refusal to allow that solution.[79] But
the logical consequence of radical nonconformists' arguments in favour
of secularism was that religious education, if supported purely by voluntary effort, should be encouraged, and should be free from temporal
interference; and that those who were most active and zealous in the

---

[77] This attitude was widely shared by Welsh radicals: Hargest, 'Welsh Educational
Alliance', pp. 184–5, 189.
[78] Miall, *Richard*, p. 179; Winterbotham, *Letter to my constituents*, pp. 13, 36.
[79] *Report of the Manchester conference 1872*, pp. 135, 174–80, 196 (Rogers, Richard, Stitt);
Rogers, 'Mr Gladstone and the nonconformists', p. 35.

voluntary teaching of religion would justly reap the greatest reward, measured by numbers of adherents. In the Irish context, the Catholic priests would be the clear victors of this open contest; and, indeed, a number of radicals publicly argued in 1873 that Irish Catholics should be allowed to receive privately financed denominational education as part of a state-administered secular system. Richard, for example, maintained that it was hypocritical for the state to act in religion in the way that the whig-liberals desired – to allow one type of sect to teach its views but not the Catholics. This was the 'principle which forms the very basis of religious persecution, because it endows the State with the right and power to decide what is truth and what is error in religion, and to distribute its favours accordingly'.[80] As another MP said, 'perfect religious equality all round' meant refusing to 'patronise the Protestants at the expense of the Catholics, or the Catholics at the expense of the Protestants'.[81]

From this position, it was possible for radical nonconformists to accept home rule without difficulty: indeed Illingworth later claimed that he had publicly declared for it as early as 1868.[82] Guinness Rogers made a fundamental distinction between allowing an Irish parliament to endow a Catholic university – a purely domestic matter in which the British had no right to interfere – and agreeing that an imperial parliament should do the same, when it was a policy opposed to the wishes of nonconformists in that parliament.[83]

The foregoing account has concentrated on the attitudes of those radical nonconformists whose views about politics and ecclesiastical organisation dovetailed most neatly with those of the Gladstonian high churchmen. Such men had little in common with whig-liberal latitudinarians in the discussion either of political or of ecclesiastical affairs. However, not all baptists and congregationalists were able to view public questions in the clear-cut terms set out so far: their opinions coincided more with those of the whig-liberals. This was most obvious with some evangelical ministers, such as the most popular nonconformist preacher of his day, the baptist Spurgeon, and some liberal evangelicals, such as the congregationalist intellectual Stoughton, a historian and a favourite preacher with middle-class audiences. It was also true of a number of other congregationalists who distrusted populist politics, like Thomas Binney, Eustace Conder and to some extent Newman Hall. They

---

[80] *Hansard*, ccxvii, 561, 17 July 1873; see also Illingworth, *Fifty years of politics*, pp. 41–3.
[81] (R. M. Carter) *Leeds Mercury*, 3 February 1874, p. 5.
[82] *Fifty years of politics*, pp. 30–1, 40.
[83] Rogers, 'The middle class and the new Liberalism', pp. 718–19.

approximated to whig-liberals in two respects in particular. They were less convinced than were radical nonconformists that it was necessary to abolish the guarantees for the propagation of religion which were secured by the Establishment and by religious teaching in state schools; and they placed more emphasis than their radical co-religionists on the sacerdotal and Catholic threat in Britain and Ireland. It was not that they were more anti-sacerdotalist than the radicals, but that the sacerdotalist problem seemed to occupy relatively more of their thoughts.[84]

Calls for disestablishment played a far less prominent role in their political argument – Spurgeon, for example, was to withdraw from the Liberation Society[85] – and even when they did attack the Establishment, it was primarily on anti-sacerdotalist grounds.[86] All were fervent anti-sacerdotalists, and many were members of the Evangelical Alliance.[87] While favouring disestablishment in principle, they were unwilling to agitate for it in practice, believing that such agitation was a destructive cry which would encourage freethinking, and destroy the practical good which religious cooperation could do.[88] Stoughton declared: 'I am first a Christian, next an Englishman, and last a Dissenter.'[89] He welcomed Cowper-Temple's 1871 bill to allow nonconformists to preach in Anglican chapels, and in 1876 he organised a conference of churchmen and nonconformists, chaired by Tait, in order to discuss cooperation against infidelity.[90] Similarly, Newman Hall's links with Church of England ministers were so strong that he was often asked why he did not join them.[91]

Their position was in fact similar to that of many nonconformist laymen. In 1868, it was often commented that many laymen were suspicious and reluctant now that an act of disestablishment was actually threatened: it might involve 'some revolutionary thing'. Some disliked Irish Church disestablishment because it might encourage Romanism; others – like Newman Hall himself – supported it because the removal of a just grievance would destroy papal influence over the Irish and facilitate Protestant missionary activity.[92] It was these men who

---

[84] Newman Hall, *Autobiography*, pp. 361, 369–70.
[85] *Dictionary of national biography*.
[86] (Spurgeon) *Nonconformist*, 29 January 1873, p. 108; (Conder) Binfield, *So down to prayers*, p. 76; (Binney and Stoughton) Skeats and Miall, *History of the Free Churches of England*, p. 623.
[87] Stoughton, *Recollections*, pp. 85–6; Ray, *Spurgeon*, p. 417.
[88] See the comment of Rogers, 'Social aspects of disestablishment', p. 447; Stoughton, *Religion in England 1800–50*, pp. 411–12.
[89] Lewis, *Stoughton*, p. 83.
[90] Stoughton, *Recollections*, pp. 182–3, 259–65.
[91] Newman Hall, *Autobiography*, pp. 366–7.
[92] Allon to Gladstone, 5 May 1868, Gladstone papers, 44095, fo. 310; Carvell Williams, *Protestant nonconformists*, p. 5; Machin, *Politics and the Churches*, pp. 366–7; Newman Hall to

were particularly anxious to maintain securities for the presence of the bible in elementary school teaching: they argued that it could not legitimately be separated from the secular lessons because its influence was properly ubiquitous. A definable *'common* truth' might easily be taught from it:[93] Stoughton, Conder, Newman Hall, the Irish congregationalist William Urwick, and Spurgeon all strongly opposed secular education in the early 1870s.[94] There were many nonconformist laymen of considerable social standing who did not wish to play up sectarian differences, and who regarded themselves as liberal evangelical Protestants: men like the poet Browning, for instance, who was raised as a congregationalist but was uninterested in theological speculation. He retained a simple faith in God and in the moral example of Christ's life, and held sturdy anti-Catholic views – as noticeable in *The ring and the book* as in his later vehement unionism – which were a passport to popularity with the middle classes.[95]

It is important, nonetheless, not to paint such men as too conservative. It was difficult for any nonconformist not to feel a quickened sympathy for the tone of the Liberal party under Gladstone: Browning, for all his doubts, was more of a democrat than, say, the whig-liberal Tennyson.[96] It is easy to define a class of upwardly mobile, rich, nonconformist MPs whose radicalism appeared to be only skin-deep: Samuel Morley, for instance, or Charles Reed, the London businessman and, later, chairman of the London school board. Morley was a philanthropic hosiery manufacturer, the influential proprietor of the *Daily News* (a middle-class newspaper selling 150,000 copies in 1869),[97] and a squire in the village of Leigh near Tonbridge. He was delighted that his children chose variously to be Anglicans and nonconformists.[98] He himself was not concerned with the speculative and abstract side of religion, contenting himself with the 'old simple sturdy patriotism of his fathers'.[99] He resigned from the executive committee of the Liberation Society in November 1868 when it began to look as if its purely abstract support for disestablishment might be translated into something more alarming: he maintained that the policy was impracticable in the near future.[100] In the early

Gladstone, 25 November 1868, Gladstone papers, 44188, fo. 87. MacColl realised in 1885 how many nonconformists opposed disestablishment: Russell, *MacColl*, p. 117.

[93] (Conder) *National Education League 1870*, pp. 36–8; Stoughton, *Recollections*, p. 194; Lewis, *Stoughton*, pp. 119–20.

[94] See list in *Nonconformist*, 8 May 1872, p. 494; (Spurgeon) Rogers, *Autobiography*, p. 201.

[95] See Dowden, *Browning*, pp. 6, 110, 124–37, 337, 364–8, 389–97; Phipps, *Browning's clerical characters*, pp. 293–5; and for a caustic high-church judgment, G. W. E. Russell, *Portraits of the seventies*, pp. 287–90.

[96] Shannon, *Bulgarian agitation*, p. 218.

[97] Koss, *Political press in the nineteenth century*, p. 96.

[98] Hodder, *Morley*, pp. 372–9.   [99] *Ibid.*, p. 493.

[100] *Ibid.*, pp. 276–81; *Nonconformist*, 9 December 1868, pp. 1195–6.

1870s, he strongly supported bible-reading in the schools,[101] and was very influential, as a member of the London school board, in securing it in 1871. He was also a warm supporter of Brereton's undenominational middle-class schools and his Cambridge college, hoping that they would diminish sectarian and class bitterness, and that they would integrate the sons of respectable Church and dissenting families into the social establishment. In 1876, he attacked radical high churchmen for wishing to abolish all religious teaching in schools, merely out of a selfish regard for their 'own personal sectarianism'.[102] He disliked the sacerdotal element in the Church and in 1864 urged parliament to 'sweep away' those Church formularies that emphasised 'priestly power';[103] in 1871 he called for churchmen and nonconformists to work together against ritualism and Romanism, rationalism and infidelity;[104] he became worried that, under Knowles, the *Contemporary*, whose joint proprietor he became in 1877, was encouraging atheism;[105] and he opposed the atheist Bradlaugh's entry to parliament in the 1880s. Like so many whig-liberals and philanthropists, he urged that the state should tackle constructive rather than destructive measures – the payment of MPs, provision of freeholdings for the poor, purchase of the railways, county boards, the nine-hour day and trade-union reform.[106]

But despite all this, Morley voted for motions for disestablishment in the House, as did Reed and like-minded men like Colman and Edward Baines, MP for Leeds – who was so anti-secularist that he joined the National Education Union in order to defend religious teaching (Reed was Baines' brother-in-law; Conder his son-in-law and his minister in Leeds). Such men did not think that the agitation for disestablishment was politically wise, but they could not refrain from supporting it when asked;[107] indeed, fifteen of the seventeen baptist and congregationalist MPs in the survey supported disestablishment, and the other two abstained. Morley was no less anxious than radical nonconformists to follow Gladstone; indeed in some ways he was more appreciative, on account of Gladstone's refusal to spur on the disestablishment movement. In the 1880s, Morley's praise of Gladstone – 'the greatest, purest, and ablest Statesman . . . of any age' – was unstinting, and carried him into support of home rule.[108]

In short, these men, just as much as the radicals, were happy to join the crusade for evangelism and a moral politics which Gladstone promised for the party. The essence of his relationship with nonconformity was a

---

101 *Nonconformist*, 18 February 1874, p. 147.
102 Hodder, *Morley*, p. 371.   103 *Ibid.*, pp. 236–8.
104 *Nonconformist*, 15 November 1871, p. 1119.
105 Metcalf, *Knowles*, p. 271.   106 Armytage, *Mundella*, p. 117.
107 Colman, *Colman*, p. 260.   108 Hodder, *Morley*, p. 447.

joint commitment to spiritual arousal – and, as Rogers testified in 1898, to anti-erastianism.[109]

However, it must also be said that radical nonconformists, just as much as the less radical, were at times capable of adopting an anti-clerical perspective, much to Gladstone's distaste. Adherents of evangelical nonconformist sects inevitably disliked sacerdotalism; and, despite the radicals' proclaimed belief in the principle of denominational freedom from parliamentary interference, they did not always stand by it in practice. The Liberation Society had disliked Gladstone's request, in dealing with church rates in the mid 1860s, that nonconformists who chose not to pay the rate, once compulsion to pay had been abolished, should be barred from vestry politics.[110] No nonconformist in our survey voted with Gladstone against Holt's amendment to the 1874 Public Worship Regulation Bill (p. 416), despite declarations of sympathy with his aims. Moreover, twelve of the seventeen baptist and congregationalist MPs opposed the mention of Convocation in the 1872 Act of Uniformity Amendment Bill (together with nine of the eleven presbyterians) – but they were joined by only six of the twenty-nine unitarians, quakers and jews (and none of the three Wesleyans). Since the Church was subjugated to parliamentary whims, evangelical nonconformists had the opportunity, indeed the duty, of declaring their disapproval of the tendencies within it – and were happy to do so, especially if their activity hastened calls from within the Church for disestablishment.[111]

However, this anti-clericalism was rarely translated into opposition to equal treatment for Catholics (as can be seen from the figures in the following section detailing MPs' voting records on anti-Catholic motions). In 1886, a few radical nonconformists opposed home rule for Ireland, the most famous being Dale (but he, as it happened, had also always believed, unlike Miall, Colman, Morley and many radical baptists and congregationalists, that Britain might be forced to intervene abroad in order to uphold justice).[112] In the main, Liberal unionism proved attractive only to some of the more 'Protestant', and the less 'populist' and disestablishmentarian, baptists and congregationalists, like Spurgeon and Newman Hall; Gladstone retained the devoted support of most of the radicals.

[109] Rogers, 'Mr Gladstone and the nonconformists', pp. 34, 37; Machin, 'Gladstone and nonconformity', p. 364; Bebbington, 'Gladstone and the nonconformists', p. 369.
[110] Anderson, 'Gladstone's abolition of compulsory church rates', p. 190.
[111] See Illingworth's comment to the Speaker: diary, 13 October 1871, 15th earl of Derby papers. The 1872 debate about Convocation is described on p. 337 below.
[112] Summerton, 'Dissenting attitudes to war and peace', pp. 166–9.

Wesleyans and presbyterians tended to approximate to whig-liberal positions far more than did those discussed above. Like baptists and congregationalists, they were staunchly anti-sacerdotalist; but they were far more disposed to adopt anti-Catholic positions on matters of state, because they did not share the spiritual vision of the radical members of these other sects. Peculiarities in the Wesleyans' position also made them especially hesitant to advocate measures abolishing state guarantees for religious provision. They, consequently, tended to be cool to disestablishment and hostile to secular education; but, in fact, many presbyterians were little warmer.

Wesleyans had traditionally been the most conservative of mainstream nonconformist sects. (Their Primitive Methodist colleagues were more liberal, and had some weight in politics in the West Riding and Durham. However, their strength was especially marked among the rural labouring population of the north and east, and so their political influence was to be most evident after the franchise extension, and redistribution, of 1884–5.) Wesleyans had not renounced support for the *principle* of Establishment; they had been much disturbed by popular unrest early in the century; and in 1847 they accepted state grants in support of their schools, in contrast to the voluntaryist baptists and congregationalists – believing that such grants were valuable aids in the essential task of extending religious belief among the population.[113] After 1843, they sympathised with the Free Church of Scotland, which asserted, just as they did, that, while Churches should be independent from civil interference in their spiritual concerns, this was not incompatible with retention of Established status.[114] In the 1860s, Wesleyans were still comparatively quiescent politically: given their numerical strength, their parliamentary representation, of three atypically radical MPs, was very small.

The leading Wesleyan minister, in the 1870s, was J. H. Rigg, the principal of the Westminster training college. He was a member of the 1870 London school board, and another man who was involved in the Stoughton–Tait interdenominational discussions of 1876. He was a close friend of Stanley, and admired Maurice (while expressing reservations about his theological views).[115] He described himself as a 'liberal and yet evangelical Protestant', disliked the Puseyites who were introducing 'elements of Romanism' into the Church, called for Church reform, and

---

[113] Hempton, *Methodism and politics*, pp. 171–2, 178.
[114] *Ibid.*, p. 187.
[115] Telford, *Rigg*, pp. 251–8; Rigg, *Modern Anglican theology*, p. 551.

anticipated that, under the right conditions, he might be able, as Wesley had hoped, to 'accept the religious hospitality of its communion'.[116]

Some Wesleyans – including their three MPs – were in favour of disestablishment, but, as with the 'Protestant' congregationalists and baptists, this was primarily on anti-sacerdotal grounds: W. S. Allen, MP, feared that, unless the Church were disestablished and allowed to reassert discipline over its own members, ritualist-ridden Anglicanism would 'very soon be Protestant only in name'.[117] A younger generation of ministers, led by Hugh Price Hughes, was to radicalise much of Wesleyanism in the 1880s and 1890s, so that it came increasingly to resemble the other evangelical sects, but even he was opposed to educational secularism.[118] Even Isaac Holden, the atypically radical Wesleyan, ex-MP for Knaresborough and Alfred Illingworth's father-in-law, could not quite bring himself to adopt thoroughgoing secularism when he stood at the West Riding by-election of February 1872 (although he was accused of being a secularist). In the 1870s, not only were most Wesleyans staunchly opposed to secularism;[119] many, like Rigg, did not even wish to merge Wesleyan voluntary schools in the board-school system, on the grounds that the latter gave insufficient securities for religious teaching.[120]

Thus Wesleyans were the most reluctant of all sects to assault the position of the Church of England, although their MPs were to some extent forced to become more anti-clerical in order to keep faith with advanced borough opinion: all three supported the amendments which aimed to prevent dogmatic teaching in schools, and opposed Clause 25 of the 1870 Education Act.

Wesleyanism's 'Protestant' image was strengthened by its high concentration of Ulstermen – notably the celebrated minister William Arthur (author of *Tongue of Fire*), and the MP William McArthur, both of whom had been active in the Evangelical Alliance and the Wesleyan Missionary Society. McArthur, indeed, had been a Conservative, but supported the Liberals in 1865 because he considered Derby's Irish views 'thoroughly anti-Protestant', and admired Palmerston.[121] He advocated Irish and English Church disestablishment in the belief that it would assist the cause of Protestantism. Indeed, his declared aim was to encourage 'the conversion of Roman Catholic Ireland to the Protestant faith'; he would 'rather cut off my right hand than do anything that would injure our common Protestantism'. Methodism, for him, was 'a

[116] Rigg, *Oxford high Anglicanism*, pp. vi–viii, 190–1.
[117] *Nonconformist*, 26 November 1873, p. 1168.
[118] Hughes, *Hughes*, pp. 490, 496, 506.   [119] McCullagh, *McArthur*, p. 164.
[120] Telford, *Rigg*, pp. 172–82, 322.   [121] McCullagh, *McArthur*, p. 91.

breakwater against Popery, Puseyism, and infidelity'.[122] Wesleyans had traditionally been concerned with securing the position of Ulster Protestants in the educational system;[123] and this concern led many to dislike the 1873 Irish University Bill. Later, many more were hostile to home rule: the swing against the Liberals in 1886 was particularly strong in Wesleyan Cornwall.[124]

Calvinistic Methodism, which was strong in Wales, was more aggressively opposed to the Establishment than Wesleyanism; so, increasingly, was Scottish presbyterianism, and this aggressiveness was to ensure that Celtic Liberalism was a particularly forceful constituent of the Liberal alliance in the 1880s. But it was most noticeable from the mid seventies; before then, Scottish presbyterians, especially, had been at odds among themselves on the subject.

There were two major nonconformist presbyterian sects in Scotland, which, between 1863 and 1873, were negotiating the possibility of union. Of these, the Free Church had not formally accepted the principle of disestablishment, although the United Presbyterians had. The section of these Churches which behaved in the most definably whig-liberal way (but whig-liberal in its most evangelical incarnation) was the most Calvinist element in the Free Church – led by James Begg, whose support was concentrated in the Highlands. The success of the union negotiations was prevented by this group's determined resistance, on the grounds of opposition to the United Presbyterians' voluntaryism and to their partial rejection of the Calvinist tradition (the United Presbyterians had become more receptive to new critical ideas than the bulk of Free Churchmen).[125] Begg was accordingly attacked by more radical Free Church leaders, such as Rainy and Buchanan, as an 'evil genius' who was working to throw the Church 'back into the rut of Moderatism and slavish dependence on the Civil power'.[126] Begg opposed the Liberals' Scottish Education Bills of 1871 and 1872, because they did not give sufficient security for religious teaching. Like many Church of Scotland men, he supported a popular agitation in favour of a guarantee that the bible and shorter catechism would be taught in schools, according to 'use and wont'; he was strongly opposed to any hint of the secularist idea. One of his lieutenants, the Highland evangelist Kennedy, blamed Free Church unwillingness to stand firm against United Presbyterian voluntaryist doctrine for the legislature's drift away

[122] *Ibid.*, pp. 106, 118, 69.
[123] Hempton, *Methodism and politics*, pp. 156–7.
[124] Pelling, *Social geography*, p. 163.
[125] Macewen, *Cairns*, pp. 662–80.
[126] Simpson, *Rainy*, ii, 50; Walker, *Buchanan*, p. 462.

from this traditional Scottish educational policy.[127] Begg also disliked the favouritism towards Catholicism which he detected in the Liberal party, especially in connection with Ireland. He opposed Gladstone's Irish Church policy, demanding some pledge from the state that it recognised the position of Protestantism in Ireland; but he was defeated at the Free Church assembly.[128] There were some Free Churchmen in parliament who supported the Establishment, although it is difficult to distinguish them, by behaviour, from Church of Scotland men: R. A. Macfie of Leith, a staunch 'Protestant', was one such.[129] To complicate matters, there were, in addition, a few theological liberals within the Free Church who also defended the idea of Establishment, but on latitudinarian whig-liberal grounds of nationality.[130]

It is less easy to pigeonhole the other Scottish nonconformist presbyterians. Some United Presbyterian ministers, like G. C. Hutton, advocated not only disestablishment but educational secularism;[131] but this was rare, since there was less controversy than in England as to the nature of an undenominational education, given the overwhelming preponderance of presbyterianism in Scotland. For example, Duncan McLaren, a United Presbyterian, the doyen of Scottish radicals, and Bright's brother-in-law, was strongly opposed to the exclusion of the bible from any Scottish school.[132]

Most Scottish nonconformist politicians were able to equate support for disestablishment with anti-Catholicism, by arguing that state Churches lacked the zeal necessary to attack Romanism. This, for example, was the view of the leading Scottish nonconformist in the Gladstone government, the congregationalist Baxter;[133] in addition to him, eight of the eleven nonconformist presbyterian MPs supported disestablishment (and five advocated educational secularism as well).

Until 1874, however, disestablishment was not a major issue, and Free Churchmen and United Presbyterians were able to unite most cordially in opposition to the abolition of patronage. The Begg group again excepted, both sects opposed the movement for patronage abolition which was promoted by the Church of Scotland. They argued that the settlement of the patronage question would not restore enough spiritual independence to the Church to make the sinking of differences with it possible; but also that the proposal itself would interfere with the rights of the non-Established sects. They maintained that the patronage had

[127] Smith, *Begg*, ii, 451; Gordon, *Charteris*, pp. 144, 300–2.
[128] Smith, *Begg*, ii, 430–3.
[129] Macfie, *The Scotch Church question*.
[130] Such as John Stuart Blackie, treated in chapters 1 and 2.
[131] Oliver, *Hutton*, pp. 49–50.
[132] Mackie, *McLaren*, ii, 181–3.   [133] Baxter, *Hints to thinkers*, pp. 169–79.

been given to the national Church, and not to one sect. They contended that parliament, as a mixed assembly, was not competent to judge on the matter, which should be decided by the Churches which were affected;[134] the intervention of the legislature was clearly designed to help the Church of Scotland win back its 'waning and sectional' influence, at the expense of the secessionists.[135] It was thus, they alleged, a blatantly erastian move.

After 1874, when patronage was abolished, pressure for disestablishment grew, and with it the point of view articulated by G. C. Hutton: that, since the state had 'no vocation to propagate theological truth', and 'dares not propagate theological error', the 'true statesman is he who recognises and protects the rights of all men to exercise and propagate their religion on equal terms'.[136] This tolerance of theological error as long as the state did not finance it enabled a number of presbyterians to support home rule. For example, James Bryce, a Belfast-born United Presbyterian, continued to be a fervent Gladstonian after 1886. Bryce was a friend of academic liberals and positivists, a Fellow of Oriel from 1862, regius professor of civil law at Oxford from 1870, and an MP from 1880; he remained a devout presbyterian. He was a strong advocate of disestablishment, of undenominational education for presbyterians, of denominational education for Catholics and jews, and of the Gladstonian plan for Irish university reform.[137] He was atypical of presbyterians, indeed of nonconformists generally until later in the century, in that, as the recipient of a classical and historical education, he had a developed vision of a 'Christian commonwealth' attainable through the 'brotherhood of humanity', and thus had an almost positivist respect for the organisations which historically had done so much to promote this: the Catholic Church and the Holy Roman Empire.[138] But he was less atypical in defending Catholic rights, as long as the state was not asked to contribute financially towards Catholic interests.

Yet many presbyterians were so staunchly anti-Catholic that their view of the Irish problem was inevitably affected. Eight of the eleven presbyterian MPs in the survey voted for at least one of the three motions selected in order to test anti-Catholic feeling, compared with only six of the forty-nine MPs belonging to the other six sects.[139] A suggestive example of the extent to which anti-Catholic feeling could warp a radical

---

[134] Cairns, *Disestablishment of the Church of Scotland*, p. 16.
[135] United Presbyterian resolutions, *Nonconformist*, 25 June 1873, p. 635.
[136] Oliver, *Hutton*, pp. 54–5.
[137] Fisher, *Bryce*, ii, 303–4; i, 324–5, 351–3.
[138] *Ibid.*, i, 70, 82; Bryce, *Holy Roman Empire*, ch. xv.
[139] The three being on a motion of Aytoun's in 1870, on Irish university education; of Newdegate's, in 1870, on convents; and of Bouverie's, in 1873, on the O'Keeffe case.

presbyterian's political perspective is provided by the case of Edward Jenkins. Jenkins was a prominent radical in the early 1870s, a supporter of Chamberlain's National Education League, and MP for Dundee from 1874. He advocated disestablishment – on the grounds that the Church upheld class privilege and bigotry[140] – and a national system of undenominational education.[141] His objection was to denominational education, the assumption that 'religion meant CREED'. In 1870, he published one of the most famous satires of the day, *Ginx's baby*, which in six years went through thirty-six editions. It was partly a call for state intervention in social questions, and partly an attack on the denominational wranglings between the sects, which prevented Ginx's baby from receiving a proper state-directed education. But it was agreement between Protestant sects which he wished to see, sects whose 'petty differences' were preventing the 'impulse of a simple faith' from destroying the 'error' of Catholicism.[142] He was a constant opponent of Gladstone's Irish educational policies and of his high churchmanship, which he saw as a front for the advancement of Catholic interests; he wished to see an unsectarian system maintained in Ireland, and viewed the home-rule agitation of the 1870s as a Catholic attempt to control and suppress Protestantism.[143] Jenkins was in fact an imperialist and a disciple of Carlyle. He founded the Imperial Federation Movement in 1871, which aimed at promoting the emigration of Anglo-Saxon stock and the spread of Protestant values to the less populated parts of the empire. He bitterly attacked Gladstone's imperial policy as well;[144] and in the 1880s he became a Conservative, even before Gladstone's conversion to home rule.

There were three striking differences between the sects mentioned so far, and unitarians, quakers and jews. The political leaders of the last three had less contact with a working-class rank-and-file; indeed, these religious groups all had a comparatively affluent membership. Also, they

---

[140] *Glances at inner England*, pp. 15–23.
[141] See e.g. *Education of the people*, pp. 18–19; *Hansard*, ccxxx, 1210–12, 10 July 1876.
[142] *Ginx's baby*, pp. 127–8.
[143] *Education of the people*, p. 20; *Lord Bantam*, ii, 185, 205; *Barney Geoghegan*.
[144] In 1871, he wrote of his 'ever-saddening experience to live at the heart of this unrivalled Empire and to watch it pulsating with lessening vitality and force . . . Samson shorn of his locks in the lap of faithless luxury were no inapt figure of this majestic State when clipped of its colonial strength by the feminine fingers that might at least have warned it.' But this 'hedging Ministry', with its 'selfish . . . trembling . . . mercenary' supporters, might yet be thwarted in its attempts to sell 'the future glory of a long-ennobled race', by the 'upspringing life and ambition' in the 'heart of the people', and by a 'cleaving sympathy of English heart to English heart all the world over': 'Two solutions', pp. 455–6.

were not evangelical, and so tended to be far less preoccupied by a concern with sinfulness and proselytism. Thirdly, and as a consequence of both these perspectives, they were unable to respond with the same degree of enthusiasm to the development of the Gladstonian Liberal party, since they lacked both evangelical vision for political change, and the commitment infused by mass fervour. Indeed, the religious creed of none of the three sects dictated a particular position, and individual MPs behaved as they did as much because of non-religious considerations as because of religious ones.

The unitarians were the most important of the three groups. Many of their leading spokesmen shared much with the more latitudinarian whig-liberals; indeed, some Anglican Liberal MPs were ex-unitarians, as were some other whig-liberals, like the deist Greg. Unitarian thinkers, like whig-liberals, valued the ethical teaching of Christianity, and tended to dislike ignorant popular agitation. The leading unitarian theologian, Martineau, had been strongly influenced by Maurice's incarnational theology,[145] and shared much political ground with Arnold and Stanley. He was a 'most unwilling Nonconformist', compelled to be so because he could not accept the restrictions of the Thirty-nine Articles, which, like all such theological distinctions, he considered to be stifling and counter-productive. He would be happy to leave definitions of doctrine and belief to the individual, and to achieve unity in a national Establishment on the basis of 'Love to God and Love to Man': this was necessary if 'National Unity' was to be secured.[146] In 1871, he told Matthew Arnold that the Church of England must be reformed, its services and doctrine reconsidered, and all questions of dogma removed to the sphere of private judgment:[147] his only criticism of Arnold and Stanley concerned their willingness to allow sacerdotal principles a part, along with all other views, in the national Establishment – Martineau saw these as unacceptable.[148] He was alarmed at Gladstone's 'old ecclesiastical' view that the Church was the 'Trustee of absolute truth'; it might well encourage him to support 'voluntaryism, rather than acquiesce in any Erastian scheme of comprehension'.[149] He saw non-established religions to be at the mercy of the ignorant; there was, for example, 'nothing more hideous in form, blind in intelligence, and hateful in spirit, than the Free Church religion' in Scotland.[150]

---

[145] Martineau distinguished between Maurice's theology, centred on the moral example of Christ, and the barren sterile impersonal transcendental Idealism of later generations: Drummond and Upton, *Martineau*, ii, 32, 87, 117.
[146] *Ibid.*, ii, 108–9, 117; Martineau, *The new affinities of faith*, pp. 17, 21.
[147] Drummond and Upton, *Martineau*, ii, 6–7.
[148] Martineau, *Why dissent?*, p. 13.
[149] Drummond and Upton, *Martineau*, i, 437, ii, 109.   [150] (1861) *ibid.*, i, 394.

Not all unitarians were as extreme as Martineau, of course, as an examination of the voting record of unitarian MPs makes plain. Twelve of the seventeen unitarian MPs advocated disestablishment, while six supported secular education as well[151] – the latter, probably, because they represented large urban constituencies where such views were usually appreciated. Unitarianism was not a creed which was sufficiently rigid to enforce a particular set of political attitudes: just as some unitarian intellectuals acted much like optimistic latitudinarians or deists, urban MPs who were unitarians behaved much like the average urban radical MP (or, in the case of P. A. Taylor of Leicester, like a Fawcettite Liberal). Furthermore, it is difficult to see the most famous unitarian politician of his day, Joseph Chamberlain, as a man motivated by a particular theological vision.

Chamberlain rose to national prominence in the 1870s, as presiding genius over the National Education League and the instigator of its attack on government educational policy. Far from being a national pressure group of nonconformist sects, the League was an organisation dominated by Birmingham money and Birmingham men – and the prevailing religious tone of Birmingham politics (Dale apart) was unitarian, not evangelical.[152] The League was an attempt to harness the power of nonconformity behind Chamberlain, and away from the politically less antagonistic role which Miall envisaged for it[153] – but it failed in this aim. It was able to establish a presence in local by-election contests in the early 1870s wherever there was little local opposition to it, but it faced difficulty if it had to challenge established Liberal candidates.[154] When, in 1873–4, its continued activity would have posed a direct challenge to the government at a general election, it pulled back from the fight, aware that most nonconformists would not be loyal to it.[155] This was similarly Chamberlain's problem in 1885–6, when his attempt to wrest control of the Liberal party failed because he was unable to woo the nonconformist conscience away from Gladstone.

This failure was rooted in a lack of understanding between Chamberlain and evangelical nonconformity. He had only a limited sense of the spiritual vision which lay behind the call for disestablishment, because he lacked an evangelical perspective.[156] Chamberlain came to realise that his own aim to control and direct mass political activity would be defeated by his incapacity to appeal to the religious mental-

---

[151] Stansfeld, in the government, also supported disestablishment.
[152] Hennock, *Fit and proper persons*, pp. 97–8.   [153] Hamer, *Politics of electoral pressure*, p. 134.
[154] *Ibid.*, p. 135.
[155] Auspos, 'Radicalism, pressure groups, and party politics', pp. 191–5; see also (Leader, 1875) Armytage, *Mundella*, p. 156.
[156] Binfield, *So down to prayers*, p. 123.

ity; in 1884, he told the future Beatrice Webb that he 'always had a grudge against religion for absorbing the passion in man's nature'.[157] In 1883, John Morley accused him of holding 'Whig and Erastian' views on the need to keep (Irish) priests 'under the grip of the State'.[158] Although his religious sense was probably more developed before the death of his second wife in 1875 shook his faith,[159] even then his closest political associates outside Birmingham were not nonconformists but secular radicals like Maxse, Dilke and John Morley.[160] His, indeed, was a secular radicalism, the radicalism that demanded land reform and national education on utilitarian grounds of efficiency. Through the concept of national efficiency, it could later assume an imperialist character – as, of course, it did in Chamberlain's case. Chamberlain's arguments against the Establishment were not, in the main, spiritually elevated: they tended instead to emphasise its political effect (support for Toryism) and its massive wealth (which he wished to see redeployed).[161]

It is difficult, then, to escape the conclusion that unitarians, although warm in comparison with many whig-liberals, were less likely to be sympathetic to the development of the Gladstonian Liberal party than radical nonconformists; they had too many whiggish and intellectual sympathies.[162] Frank Hill, the editor of the *Daily News* from 1869 to 1886, and a unitarian disciple of Martineau, provides a good example of this. He was particularly hostile to Gladstone's Irish education policy, as will become apparent from an examination (p. 362) of the *News*'s views on the Irish University Bill (views which he formulated with the help of the Irishman and Fawcettite academic liberal, J. E. Cairnes). In 1867, Hill had argued that the disestablishment of the Irish Church would remove the grievances of the Catholic laity, distance them from the priests, and thus enable them to accept, and work within, the existing mixed educational system.[163] The *Daily News* was cool to Gladstone in 1874, and similarly in 1879 (for which it was attacked by E. A. Freeman).[164]

Although most nonconformists remained Gladstonians after 1886, defections were most pronounced among Wesleyans, unitarians and

---

[157] Mackenzie, *Diary of Beatrice Webb*, i, 110.
[158] Morley, *Recollections*, i, 158; see Garvin, *Chamberlain*, i, 118.
[159] Mackenzie, *Diary of Beatrice Webb*, i, 266–7; Garvin, *Chamberlain*, i, 209.
[160] Auspos, 'Radicalism, pressure groups, and party politics', p. 192.
[161] *Report of the Manchester conference 1872*, pp. 25–7, 185–6.
[162] See Harvie, *Lights of liberalism*, p. 86, for their links with academic liberalism since the 1840s.
[163] *Questions for a reformed parliament*, pp. 14–16.
[164] Koss, *Political press in the nineteenth century*, pp. 194, 203; see Morley, *Gladstone*, ii, 495, for Gladstone's irritation at its attitude in 1874.

jews.[165] Jews tended to favour the Liberals until the 1870s, as a legacy of the struggle for emancipation – although there had always been a minority jewish Conservative vote.[166] Once emancipation had been achieved, jews wished not to continue to appear as a pressure group, but to be absorbed into the political community; they were thus anxious not to be identified with only one party.[167] The five jewish MPs in the survey kept a low profile, especially on an issue as emotional as disestablishment, on which none voted.[168] As was to be expected, the educational issue brought out their liberal sympathies: all but one supported one or other of the amendments designed to prevent dogmatic teaching in the schools, and none advocated the retention of Clause 25. But they tended to believe strongly that Christian schoolchildren should be given religious education, and none of them supported educational secularism.[169] Such behaviour was typical of propertied and mildly anti-clerical whig-liberals; and of course most jewish MPs – the Goldsmids, the Rothschilds, and Salomans – had immense social standing. Like the jewish MPs, many jewish voters – who were in the main at this time financiers, professional men, shopkeepers or small manufacturers, in London – increasingly swung to the 'right' in the 1870s and 1880s, so that jewish opinion was roughly balanced between the parties for the first time.[170] This drift owed a lot to the same general causes as unsettled the whig-liberals; but, in particular, the Liberals' enthusiasm for the Bulgarian agitation – with its undercurrent of anti-jewish insinuations – led the Rothschilds, and encouraged Sir Francis Goldsmid, to desert Gladstone, and presumably affected many jewish voters similarly.[171] It is significant that the only one of the generation of jewish MPs surveyed who favoured home rule in 1886 was John Simon, the sole MP for a northern industrial town (who had also supported the 1876 agitation); non-jewish considerations probably dictated his behaviour more than specifically jewish ones.

Quakers had a more distinctive set of political opinions than unitarians and jews. Certainly they were, in theory, in favour of disestablishment, since they believed in communal rather than hierarchical religion. However, they distrusted radical nonconformist activity, since

---

[165] Bebbington, *Nonconformist conscience*, pp. 88–94; Koss, *Nonconformity in modern British politics*, p. 26; Wald, *Crosses on the ballot*, pp. 197–8.

[166] Alderman, *Jewish community*, pp. 1–46.

[167] *Ibid.*, pp. 34–5.

[168] Sir Francis Goldsmid paired in its favour. In addition to those jewish MPs in the survey, one (Jessel) was in the government, and two Rothschilds attended too sporadically to merit inclusion.

[169] Goldsmid, *Francis Goldsmid*, pp. 71–2, 97. Julian Goldsmid abstained.

[170] Alderman, *Jewish community*, pp. 31–46; Lipman, *Social history of the jews*, pp. 65–84.

[171] Alderman, *Jewish community*, p. 39.

they were still, in general, more quietist politically than most of the other sects.[172] Although reluctant to adopt militant positions, neither can they properly be described as conservative: rather, their political interests were primarily directed away from all the questions discussed here, towards crusades for peace, humanitarianism and temperance. Their pacifism ensured toleration of the beliefs of others, and many, accordingly, were able to support home rule.

Of seven quaker MPs in the survey,[173] four supported disestablishment, but the prevailing quaker attitude to the subject was that of their most famous politician, John Bright. He distrusted the political influence of the Establishment and viewed its apparently lavish endowments as corrupting, but refused to advocate an attack on it, believing that the Church itself must wish for disestablishment before it was undertaken. The more the Establishment 'shows that it is not a Church merely of monopoly and restriction but [is] in favour of all that beauty and breadth and freedom which belongs to the Christian religion, the more I am perfectly certain it will prolong its existence as an Establishment, and the more useful it will be to the country'.[174] Bright became less radical as he grew older, but his religious radicalism had never been pronounced, and after 1868, when such matters were to the fore, his lack of zeal in discussing them was particularly marked. He had always refused to give a lead to political nonconformity, knowing that, like Chamberlain, his lack of evangelical commitment debarred him from too close a sympathy with its enthusiasms.[175] He also had little time for the populist appeal of high-church Anglicanism: when he attended a service at Hawarden in 1873, with Gladstone 'devout in singing, etc.', he thought that 'much of the service seemed only fitting for a very ignorant people'.[176]

Only one of the seven MPs, E. A. Leatham of Huddersfield – atypical in being a Liberation Society activist – was an educational secularist. Quakers generally held undenominational views on education: six of the seven MPs supported at least one of the amendments designed to prevent dogmatic teaching in schools, five opposed Clause 25, and six favoured the amendments on the University Tests Bill. They thus tended to share the views expressed by the quaker historian and banker Frederic Seebohm, who argued that support for secularism was an abnegation of the state's responsibility for the teaching of ethical behaviour, but that there should be securities against 'proselytizing or sectarian teaching

---

[172] See Robbins, *Bright*, p. 68; Isichei, *Victorian quakers*, p. 199.
[173] John Bright did not attend frequently enough to merit inclusion.
[174] Mills, *John Bright and the quakers*, ii, 94–100, 121, 128.
[175] Vincent, *Formation of the Liberal party*, p. 196; Binfield, *So down to prayers*, p. 123.
[176] Walling, *Diaries of Bright*, p. 356.

during the public school-hours'.[177] (As a historian, Seebohm, significantly, was an opponent of Freeman's historical conceptions.)[178]

Quakers were thus more staunchly anti-clerical than the education minister, W. E. Forster, a convert from quakerism to Anglicanism upon marrying Thomas Arnold's daughter. Forster had also incurred the hostility of quakers for supporting the Crimean War;[179] indeed he was proud of Britain's 'mighty Empire'. She had more duties and responsibilities than any country since 'Rome at the height of its power'; but she could not 'lead the van in the world's march' without a sense of a 'call from above'. This would come only if the nation were agreed in its 'full religious expression', if 'individual wills' were regulated by divine laws.[180] In the 1870s, two questions were of supreme importance for him: the provision of a national system of religious education, and the preservation of a truly national 'State Church':[181] 'we are and mean to remain a Christian people'.[182] By this, of course, he meant a Protestant people: 'I would as little sanction a sacerdotal State Church as I would the reunion of the State with Romanism.'[183]

Forster's political development – which veered markedly rightwards in the 1870s and 1880s, first in defence of religious education, then on Bulgaria, and then on the caucus and Ireland – should not be regarded as typical of quakers. Some quakers, like Bright and Seebohm, also became unionists; but it is probably the case that the views of mainstream quakers were more accurately represented by members of the great quaker families like J. W. Pease in parliament, and Seebohm's brother-in-law Joseph Rowntree outside it, both of whom remained Gladstonians.[184]

---

[177] 'On national compulsory education', pp. 106–7.

[178] He approached *The English village community* with a 'directly political interest': to attack Freeman's assertion that pre-Reformation England understood true liberty. This was won, he contended, only as a result of the struggle against feudalism and Catholicism. The Anglo-Saxon system admired by Freeman was 'communism': a 'settled serfdom' with 'no inherent rights of inheritance'. This system had fortunately been destroyed owing to 'economic evolution', to the great benefit of the stability and prosperity of England. The 'new order of things' was 'individual independence and inequality'; and the English, and the 'new Englands across the oceans', had 'become charged' with the 'vast responsibilities' of spreading this 'new order' to the world – with the aim of imposing '*freedom* and *democracy*', and of securing 'the future happiness of the human race'. *Ibid.*, pp. vii–ix, 438–41.

[179] Reid, *Forster*, i, 302.

[180] *Ibid.*, ii, 100; Forster, 'The university as trainer of politicians', pp. 204–6, 219–20.

[181] *Ibid.*, p. 214.

[182] Reid, *Forster*, i, 463–70.

[183] Speech at Bradford, *Times*, 7 January 1878, p. 11.

[184] See Vernon, *Rowntree*, p. 104.

The radical MPs

It has already been indicated that unitarian and Wesleyan MPs tended to be more radical, in discussing disestablishment and secular education, than average opinion in their denominations; and this tendency is not difficult to explain. The behaviour of borough MPs was necessarily influenced by the climate of opinion in the constituencies; and one of the sub-themes of Part II of this book will be the radicalisation of politics in the large boroughs and the Celtic counties in the decade after 1865, owing primarily to the activity of well-organised pressure groups. It will be argued there that in 1874, whereas many county and southern borough seats moved to the right politically, some large northern boroughs reaffirmed and even intensified their radicalism. The spread of the caucus system in the 1880s further entrenched the radicals' position. One example of an MP who was reluctantly affected by pressures of this sort was William Rathbone, a unitarian philanthropist and nephew of Greg. He was more interested in practical questions – especially in local taxation and education – than in sectarian ones.[185] His religion stressed the ethical example of Christ's personality; he would have liked, rather than to attack the Establishment, to cooperate with it in practical tasks; and he continued to defend Clause 25 of the Education Act, even in 1874.[186] He wrote to Gladstone in March 1874 advocating that the sects should work together against infidelity rather than descend into bitter opposition. But he nonetheless said that if motions for disestablishment were introduced, he would always support them.[187] The exigencies of his parliamentary career forced him, as a Liverpool MP, to support Irish grievances – although he eventually broke with the Liverpool Irish in the late 1870s; then, as MP for Carnarvonshire, he fell in line with his constituents' wishes and supported both disestablishment and (hesitantly) home rule.[188]

The most basic religious question, in the eyes of local constituency activists after 1867, was increasingly disestablishment; and it is thus MPs' opinions on Miall's disestablishment motions which are of most relevance to an analysis of the extent of radicalism within the party. Our survey of MPs' voting habits embraces 62 MPs who it is believed were nonconformists;[189] but, of these, 12 (2 unitarians, 4 quakers, 3 jews and

[185] Rathbone, *Rathbone*, pp. 447–8.
[186] *Ibid.*, pp. 429, 441, 444–5.
[187] Rathbone to Gladstone, 20 March 1874, Gladstone papers, 44443, fo. 105.
[188] Rathbone, *Rathbone*, pp. 291–6, 412–15, 445–7.
[189] As well as those discussed in previous sections, these comprised a Calvinistic Methodist and a member of the Evangelical Union Church. In addition to the 62, 3 nonconformist MPs, John Bright and 2 Rothschilds, sat throughout the parliament but did not attend often enough for inclusion; and 4 more served in the government. There were

3 presbyterians) cannot be categorised as radicals, in that they either voted for the maintenance of the Church Establishment, or abstained on the question while – unlike some other abstainers included with the radicals – voting *against* educational secularism in 1870. In addition to the remaining 50, 68 non-nonconformist MPs either voted for disestablishment (51), or abstained on the disestablishment motions while supporting secularism.[190] Three maverick anti-Catholic evangelicals who voted for disestablishment have been removed from this total and placed with 9 men from outside the 68, whose voting record on disestablishment and education showed some signs of radicalism, to constitute an intermediate group of 12 MPs, already discussed in chapter 2. Excluding these, we can therefore isolate 115 radical MPs.

These 115 MPs formed a remarkably solid voting bloc: 103 voted for at least one of the amendments designed to prevent dogmatic teaching in schools, and 102 opposed the retention of Clause 25, nearly all the others abstaining on both issues. Except that there was a slightly higher number of abstentions (29), radicals were equally united in favour of the university-tests amendments.[191] Twenty-two of the 50 radical nonconformists, and 35 of the 65 other radicals, voted for educational secularism in 1870.

Of the 65 radicals who were not nonconformists, 9 were young men whose radicalism was clearly inspired by university teaching: they are classed as academic liberals, and discussed below; 7 more were radical young whig aristocrats, sitting usually for county or small borough seats, but behaving very much like the urban radicals (4 were members of the Beaumont family, and another was the Irish peer Lord Kensington). As can be seen from Table 1 (p. 145), the other 49 nearly all sat for large borough seats or, in a few cases, for Scottish or Welsh counties; they were usually industrial or commercial men, or lawyers (or, especially in Wales and Scotland, country gentlemen).[192]

    also MPs elected for part of the parliament, who did not vote often enough for inclusion, such as the whiggish quaker, Bassett (Bedfordshire from 1872). Ascriptions of affiliation have been made, in the first place, on the basis of two lists: that in the *Nonconformist* for 16 December 1868, and that in the Gladstone papers, 44612, fo. 138, dated 1869. These lists are not compatible in all cases, and additional research has further modified each, as have helpful communications from many of those named in the preface, especially Dr David Bebbington and Dr Clyde Binfield.

[190] A few in fact abstained on both disestablishment and secularism, but supported Miall's less explicit motion, in 1872, for an investigation into the state of the Establishment.

[191] In these divisions, some 'abstainers' may actually have paired in favour of the amendments.

[192] The preponderance of radicals in large borough seats north of the Severn–Wash line is even more striking than appears from Table 1, since many of the eleven non-radicals who held seats in this category were either local industrial kings whose economic position enabled them to ignore constituency pressures (such as Akroyd, Bass and Bölckow), or whig nominees for seats which, although large, did not, for one reason or

Many of the urban radicals – especially the industrialists and commercial men – were in politics primarily in order to buttress their social standing, and it is difficult to know how many of them had a genuine religious commitment. Many nonconformists, as well as Anglicans, may have had only a limited vision of the spiritual improvement which disestablishment might effect; and it is perhaps safest to assume that the Anglican lace manufacturer and New Model employer Mundella was atypical in possessing such a vision, and in genuinely regarding Gladstone as 'the most wonderful man I ever met' – because of his 'exceedingly simple and modest' manners, and because he constituted a standing reproach to 'excessive wealth and ostentation'.[193]

It is probable that most urban radical MPs supported disestablishment in large part because nonconformists and working-men both pressed for it. Some, indeed, stressed that they did so because they were 'the representative of a large body of Nonconformists';[194] they often supported temperance reform for the same reason.[195] A Church of Scotland radical like Campbell-Bannerman always took nonconformist guidance as a matter of course: he later said, of Illingworth, that he was 'my ecclesiastical leader'.[196] Support for disestablishment was also, often, a way in which to secure support from local working-men. Both for this reason, and because many of them believed what they were saying, radical MPs would often condemn the Establishment on class grounds, depicting it as a repressive and exclusive institution which was unable to sympathise with the position of the average voter, or with his desire for intellectual stimulation.[197] With a view towards understanding why these arguments could cut considerable ice with local working-men, an analysis has been undertaken of the views of some of their most famous spokesmen – views which, if less spiritually intense than those of radical nonconformists, were nonetheless profoundly influenced by ethical aspirations.

another, experience intense mass political activity – such as Foljambe, Grosvenor and Hutt at East Retford, Chester and Gateshead. Where neither of these considerations applied, non-radical MPs were likely to face electoral difficulty – as Forster and Headlam found at Bradford and Newcastle in 1874. In county seats, the reverse applied: the handful of radical MPs sat for industrial areas – for Durham South, Northumberland South, the West Riding South and Gloucestershire West. Representation in the large southern boroughs, and in middle-sized boroughs in both south and north, was often deliberately shared between 'whigs' and 'radicals'.

193 (1874) Armytage, *Mundella*, pp. 152–3.
194 A. W. Young (Helston), *Nonconformist*, 8 October 1873, p. 998.
195 Dingle, *Campaign for prohibition*, pp. 55–6.
196 Illingworth, *Fifty years of politics*, p. 53.   197 Russell, *Lawson*, p. 70.

Working-men

It is, of course, impossible to generalise usefully on the nature of the religion of large classes of men; it is especially important not to begin with stereotyped and unduly radical expectations of working-men's views. Most of them probably accepted the basics of Protestantism, even if they did not attend church.[198] Many would have had no religious or political views. Many would have taken them from their employers. Many, also, would have been unquestioningly religious: John Morley thought that many working-men probably voted Conservative in 1874, believing firmly in their right to choose a religious education for their children.[199]

No set of 'working-class' spokesmen can, therefore, be considered representative of the mass of workmen – especially at a time when workmen's interests were so dissimilar, given that industrialisation was proceeding at such strikingly diverse rates and in such strikingly diverse ways in different trades. It is possible here to elucidate the views of only a few men who, it is frequently assumed, articulated, broadly speaking, the aspirations of the more politically aware and high-minded artisans. Some of the men whose views will be examined here enjoyed a high profile as leaders of working-class opinion; it was from some of these also that sympathetic Liberal politicians derived their perceptions of working-men's political goals. Of course, the nature of these goals had been defined partly by 'middle-class' Liberal orators and writers in the first place; but they also stemmed partly from previous traditions of popular political activity. These goals were not particularly radical, if viewed from the perspective of twentieth-century socialism; but they were more so if seen in an ethical context.

For the working-man's self-appointed spokesmen, the attack on religious exclusiveness was to be undertaken as part of a general assault on vested interests, and a general assertion of independence and dignity – which embraced questions of labour and, less frequently, land. This attack was neither to be explicitly 'socialist', nor explicitly 'laissez-faire': they always saw the most powerful force for good to be the individual conscience, but, like Gladstone, they also believed that the central government had a limited role to play in stimulating it. For them, the state's function was to ensure fair play in the marketplace and on the factory floor;[200] to attempt to ameliorate the operation of the poor laws with-

---

[198] Steele, 'Infidels and churchmen', p. 281; Joyce, *Work, society and politics*, pp. 176–8; Wright, *Our new masters*, pp. 87–90.

[199] Hirst, *Morley*, i, 297.

[200] (Lloyd Jones) *Bee-hive*, 27 July 1872, p. 1.

out promoting pauperism;[201] and to consider other practical questions, like housing reform.[202] This was not interventionism for its own sake. It was demanded in order to advance the sweeping away of privilege – wherever it most blatantly obstructed the pursuit of harmony and efficiency – and to guard against the frequent manifestations of corruption, and the interference of vested interests, in public affairs. To the extent that republicanism and the abolition of the House of Lords were advocated, it was on such grounds.[203] These men requested, most importantly, that the state should encourage the development of a well-rounded educational system: it was argued that, if it did this while checking corruption, the assiduous and self-improving working-man would be able to raise himself in the world. The duty of the state, in short, was to check the spread of 'idleness' and to promote 'industriousness'.[204]

Central to the argument of working-men's spokesmen was, therefore, a criticism of the perceived unfairness with which the traditional governing classes had supervised dealings between sections of the community, and a distrust of authority in all its forms.[205] The practical grievance which was most commonly asserted in the early 1870s was the existence on the statute book of the Master and Servant laws (which made breach of contract, normally a civil offence, a criminal one for employees), and the 1871 Criminal Law Amendment Act (which imposed restraints on peaceful picketing): the Liberals' failure to repeal the latter inspired much irritation with the government. In addition to a demand for reform there, the Labour Representation League's manifesto of 1874 called for a 'complete religious equality', along with 'sound economy', land reform (in order to give 'security to the farmer, and comfort to the labourer'), and 'equitable' electoral reform: all these would enable workmen to effect 'the complete emancipation of labour'.[206]

Demands for disestablishment should therefore be set in this wider context. But this is not to imply that working-men lacked spiritual vision; on the contrary, the Church's formalism was regarded as repressing the expression of genuine Christian sentiment. Many leading working-men were nonconformists: George Potter, founder and editor of the *Bee-hive* newspaper, was a congregationalist; Joseph Arch, founder of the Agricultural Labourers' Union, was a Primitive Methodist; Henry Broadhurst, secretary of the Labour Representation League from 1873, and George

[201] *Bee-hive*, 21 December 1872, p. 9.
[202] *Ibid.*, 5 July 1873, p. 7; Wright, *Our new masters*, p. 227.
[203] See e.g. Wright, *Our new masters*, pp. 179–80, 189–90, 227.
[204] *Ibid.*, pp. 359–92. See e.g. (Applegarth) McCann, 'Trade unionists, artisans and the 1870 Education Act', p. 147.
[205] For the latter, see Morris, 'Whatever happened to the British working class?', p. 15.
[206] *Times*, 29 January 1874, p. 7.

Howell, secretary of the Parliamentary Committee of the TUC between 1872 and 1876 (and member of the executive of the National Education League), were both Wesleyans. Of younger men, Arthur Henderson was also a Wesleyan, and Keir Hardie worshipped with the congregationalists and with the Evangelical Union Church.[207] Even in 1895, all five of the miner MPs were nonconformists.[208] Other spokesmen were more unorthodox in their religious views. Lloyd Jones, leader-writer on the *Bee-hive*, and Broadhurst's predecessor as secretary of the Labour Representation League, was a rationalist; G. J. Holyoake – like Charles Bradlaugh – was a prominent atheist, and his friend Robert Applegarth, the general secretary of the Amalgamated Society of Carpenters and Joiners, also lost his faith. Such men had the same political vision as the nonconformists, but believed that Christianity was unable to effect it, and that ethical teaching must take its place in order to do so.

The nonconformist chapel was one of the major influences in politicising the lives of the Liberal working class, because its religious practice seemed to attest to labour's dignity and independence.[209] Nonconformity was admired, not because of any distinctive creed so much as because it dwelt especially on man's 'common brotherhood' and 'equality before God'. The spiritual aim of most religiously minded working-class politicians was to open the pulpits to 'all good and useful advocates of Christianity' on equal terms, so that a common goodwill could replace exclusiveness and condescension. The 'employer' would 'recognise the workman as a co-worker, the master' would 'recognise the servant as both being children of one Father', and the 'rich and the poor' would 'meet together' and worship their 'Common Saviour'.[210] Working-men's spokesmen perceived the function of Christianity as being to make the rich and strong – whose right to exist was not questioned – 'merciful and unselfish'.[211] They thought the Church unwise to revive notions of sacerdotal authority, because such notions had always been associated with aristocratic exclusiveness, and thus implied that the Church sought to return to the centuries of 'ignorance, poverty, and degradation'.[212] Anglican preachers should also refrain from 'juggling with words over old doctrinal straw that has been thrashed to bits any time during the last three hundred years'.[213] It was claimed that it was Anglican formalism and lack of zeal which kept working-men – who were not at all unsympathetic to the essence of Christianity – away from Church services.[214] It

[207] Morgan, *Hardie*, pp. 8–9.
[208] Bealey and Pelling, *Labour and politics*, p. 15.
[209] Joyce, *Work, society and politics*, pp. 177–8.
[210] (Potter) *Bee-hive*, 26 October 1872, p. 6; see e.g. Morgan, *Hardie*, pp. 9, 13.
[211] Wright, *Our new masters*, p. 104.   [212] *Bee-hive*, 26 July 1873, p. 9.
[213] *Ibid.*, 24 May 1873, pp. 7–8.   [214] Wright, *Our new masters*, pp. 87–90.

was argued that clergymen had a duty to extend their compassion to the poor; and that only disestablishment would impel them to adopt the necessary evangelism.[215]

The movement for disestablishment, which dominated urban politics in the decade after 1867, thus did not stem only from nonconformist enthusiasm; for example, at the conference of the Agricultural Labourers' Union in 1872, it was noted how favourable the members were to the idea.[216] Working-class sympathy for it helped nonconformist and other radical employers, like Samuel Morley and Mundella – who in any case were eager to institutionalise union activity in their own factories – to contribute generously to the support of the candidatures of leading labour activists.[217]

This does not mean that there was not occasionally discord between nonconformists and working-men; the latter's interests were bound to be the more materialistic of the two. When, in 1871, the Liberation Society established a working-men's committee, headed by Howell and Potter, in order to advocate the idea of disestablishment, Miall had to upbraid them for dwelling too much on the financial advantages of the policy, and not enough on the religious and ethical.[218] But the arguments for disestablishment were in fact presented on a number of levels by working-men's spokesmen. It was indeed argued that the revenues of the Establishment, although 'the common property of the whole nation', had been unfairly appropriated for the benefit of a section – and that they should be freed and used for general educational purposes.[219] It was also maintained that the Establishment divided the nation socially and prevented class harmony; that Church leaders were greedy and materialistic;[220] that the Church was 'indifferent to the diversities of doctrine taught by its ministers', and propounded an 'immoral mixture of incongruous beliefs for the sake of personal participation in emoluments';[221] and that parliament was incompetent to govern the Church, which should be allowed self-government.[222] It was also frequently asserted that matters of religion belonged to the 'domain of conscience, in which everything must be left between man and his Maker', and that the existence of the

---

[215] *Bee-hive*, 24 May 1873, pp. 7–8; 15 February 1873, pp. 1–2; 18 October 1873, p. 8.

[216] Horn, *Arch*, pp. 71–2.

[217] See e.g. Harrison, *Before the socialists*, ch. 4. In the same way, Chamberlain, Dixon, Mundella, Jenkins, Hughes, Dilke and Samuel Morley were all sympathetic to the work of the Agricultural Labourers' Union: Horn, *Arch*, pp. 51–5, 63, 75.

[218] Ingham, 'Disestablishment movement', p. 56.

[219] (Liberation Society's working-men's committee) *Bee-hive*, 27 January 1872, p. 8; 18 July 1874, p. 8.

[220] *Ibid.*, 27 January 1872, p. 8; 7 June 1873, p. 7.

[221] Potter, 'Church of England and the people', pp. 179–80.

[222] *Bee-hive*, 26 April 1873, p. 7.

Establishment constituted a 'fatal hindrance' to the attainment of spiritual objects. As soon as man was encouraged to think for himself, Establishments became 'oppressions' attempting to limit individual freedom.[223]

The view that the Churches should be concerned, not with doctrine or sacerdotalism, but with practical ministration, and that religion should teach men to behave considerately was the main determinant of leading working-men's attitudes to educational policy. They desired education for ethical, political and intellectual reasons; they were also instinctively anti-clerical.[224] In practice, in the localities, this issued, as in the case of most nonconformists, in contentment with undenominationalism; in fact, working-men rarely recognised the existence of a 'religious difficulty'.[225] The TUC, in the 1870s, considered unsectarianism to be sufficiently anti-clerical.[226] But many working-men were, nonetheless, keen advocates of secularism: in the 1873 London school-board elections, for example, this was true of Potter in Westminster, Broadhurst in Greenwich, Lloyd Jones in Hackney and Maltman Barry in Marylebone – as it was of Randel Cremer in the Marylebone by-election of 1872. In 1874, the mining MP Thomas Burt was elected on a platform of disestablishment and secular education.[227] In subsequent decades, the Social Democratic Federation and the Independent Labour Party both argued for secularism.[228]

Secular education was advocated partly because some educated working-men were aggressively anxious to display their deliverance from the bondage of superstition: one man, for example, told the 1887 Cross Commission that he had withdrawn his son from the religious instruction given at school, and, while it continued, he had him 'put at one end of the room by himself in front of all the school'.[229] Those who wished to enforce the reading of the bible in the schools were condemned for attempting to use it as 'an instrument for the establishment of priestly power'.[230] Secularism was also defended as the only means by which the masses could be educated out of their 'Pagan darkness', while securing 'equal rights' for 'all classes of the community', and for all sects – 'even

---

[223] (Liberation Society's working-men's committee) *ibid.*, 27 January 1872, p. 8; 25 October 1873, p. 8.
[224] Wright, *Our new masters*, p. 105.
[225] McCann, 'Trade unionists, artisans and the 1870 Education Act', pp. 145–6; *Bee-hive*, 11 May 1872, p. 9.
[226] Griggs, *The TUC*, pp. 83–5.
[227] *Times*, 22 October 1873, p. 12.
[228] Simon, *Studies in the history of education 1870–1920*, pp. 143–4.
[229] *Ibid.*, pp. 124–5.   [230] *Bee-hive*, 20 July 1872, p. 9.

the . . . Jews we are anxious to treat justly'.[231] It was thus seen as the most effective way of spreading both secular knowledge and religious belief.[232] Some of the writers most indebted to positivist thought recommended the policy as likely 'to develop in freedom the individual mind', and to draw minds 'into combined harmonious action'; this would permit the creation of a 'civilization where the highest available human force, mental and moral, may operate in the world on a basis of justice, charity, and freedom'.[233]

Secularism, the *Bee-hive* contended, was also the only policy which would prevent ultramontane influences from dominating the Irish education system.[234] To hand over the 'revenues of the State to any party for the promotion of sectarian objects' would be 'turning back the current of liberal progress', and entrenching that submission to received opinions which the spread of education was supposed to attack.[235] In the early 1870s, it counselled against encouraging the home-rule party, on the grounds that they were dependent on the priests. But it called for the institution of effective local government in Ireland, in order to prevent class legislation, and to defeat oppression, violence and conspiracy.[236] It also argued that Catholic priests should be allowed to exercise their *spiritual* powers – and that, as 'ignorance disappears', their *temporal* powers would weaken of their own accord. (The newspaper condemned attempts by the state to repress ritualism in Britain, on similar grounds, arguing that public opinion would turn against formalistic ritual practices as soon as disestablishment was passed and it was free to do so.)[237] It criticised the Keogh judgment (see p. 349) and the government's subsequent prosecutions of priests who interfered in elections, arguing that it was biassed in acting in this way when landlords were influencing elections just as blatantly – and that it was doubly biassed, given that the priests alone could resist landlord power, and that they alone sympathised with the people.[238]

In other words, there was no lack of sympathy for the political and religious interests of the Irish people. Of course, rank-and-file workingmen, like rank-and-file nonconformists, probably often failed to grasp the distinctions made between temporal and spiritual authority, and many would have been instinctively anti-Catholic. But a number of

---

[231] *Ibid.*, 29 March 1873, pp. 7–8; 27 January 1872, pp. 8–9; 25 January 1873, pp. 10–11.
[232] Wright, *Our new masters*, pp. 136–7.
[233] Leading article, *Bee-hive*, 25 January 1873, pp. 10–11.
[234] *Ibid.*, 3 February 1872, p. 9.   [235] *Ibid.*, 29 March 1873, pp. 7–8.
[236] *Ibid.*, 17 February 1872, pp. 9–10.
[237] *Ibid.*, 11 January 1873, pp. 9–10; 15 November 1873, p. 8; 25 July 1874, p. 2; 8 August 1874, p. 7.
[238] *Ibid.*, 22 February 1873, p. 11.

advanced working-men were nonetheless sympathetic to Irish grievances from an early date. Benjamin Lucraft, a republican and an extremist who moved in Marx's circle, may have been atypical in supporting the Fenians in 1868;[239] and Charles Bradlaugh, the atheist, may also have been unusual in the strength of his commitment, in 1868, to Irish educational and land reform, on the grounds that the poor must be helped.[240] But – for example – Joseph Arch was partially converted to home rule in 1873, when he visited Ireland and appreciated the plight of the Irish labourer. Catholicism, like any sacerdotalist religion, was seen as offensive when it intruded into political life and interfered with individual freedom; or when it controlled all educational channels, secular as well as religious. But, viewed as a creed capable of inspiring men and comforting the poor, it was respected, and so was its right to operate freely. Indeed, Arch invited Cardinal Manning to preside at the Agricultural Labourers' Union meeting at Exeter Hall in December 1872, on account of his sympathy with the poor.[241]

The 'average' Liberal working-man was neither a freethinker, nor a republican, nor a socialist; many working-men were not 'radical' at all. But it was nonetheless common for those whom politicians took to be representative of working-class opinions to support calls for disestablishment, secular education and – when every allowance is made for anti-sacerdotalism – home rule. Whether the *Bee-hive*, Thomas Wright, and the others quoted here *were* representative is, of course, questionable. But, in any case, they argued as they did, not because they were inventing new ideological positions, but because they were acting in an intellectual climate which was heavily influenced by three other schools of thought – the schools which, surely, were most influential in dictating the electoral responses of the politically active Liberal artisan. Of these, the two most important, of course, were nonconformity and Gladstonianism; the third was positivism. Although positivism itself came to be influential in local politics in certain regions – the West Riding, for example – its direct significance was, in general, restricted:[242] for example, most trade-union leaders were far less visionary, more pragmatic, and more loyal to the Liberal party than the positivist intellectuals.[243] But it is still true that positivist conceptions played an important role in defining the 'radical' position in the 1870s and 1880s, and indirectly influenced a large number of working-class politicians. The *Bee-hive* was especially receptive to positivist arguments: Beesly and Harrison, two of the most

---

[239] Harrison, *Before the socialists*, p. 141.
[240] Bradlaugh, *Bradlaugh*, i, 259.   [241] Horn, *Arch*, pp. 90–2, 75.
[242] Joyce, *Work, society and politics*, p. 321; Harrison, *Before the socialists*, pp. 320–4.
[243] Harrison, *Before the socialists*, p. 311.

prolific positivist intellectuals, wrote frequently for it, and Potter and Lloyd Jones of the paper's staff owed much to positivist thought. Perhaps most importantly of all, the *Fortnightly Review*, edited by John Morley between 1867 and 1882, and the most respected of the radical organs (its circulation rose from 1,400 in 1867 to 25,000 in 1872), was also to a great extent in the positivist camp. In order to understand why advanced Liberals warmed to Gladstone as they increasingly did, the political consequences of subscription to positivist thought in its most rigorously defined form must, therefore, be grasped.

Morley, Harrison and positivism

John Morley was the most powerful radical journalist of the 1870s. He also came to be the most definably 'Gladstonian' politician of the 1880s and 1890s, and, of course, Gladstone's biographer – and it was frequently a source of puzzlement that Gladstone and Morley, two characters so diverse theologically, shared so many political aims, and were able to discuss religious subjects with so much sympathy.[244] Morley's father had been a Wesleyan and became an Anglican evangelical. Morley, as a relatively poor Lancashire boy at Oxford in the late 1850s and as a young journalist in London in the early 1860s, reacted against his childhood upbringing into agnosticism and sympathy with the young English admirers of Comte. This school of admirers had been founded by Richard Congreve, a tutor at Wadham, Oxford, but three of its most important spokesmen were three of his pupils there, the contemporaries E. S. Beesly – professor of history at University college London from 1860 – Frederic Harrison, and J. H. Bridges. Of these, Bridges was a physician and only infrequently articulated political views, but Beesly and Harrison were both active friends of the trade unions and of labour representation: both, in addition to contributing frequently to the *Bee-hive*, advised the London Trades Council. Beesly was a friend of Marx, and was committed to the International; but Harrison was more moderate and was Morley's closest associate in the early 1870s, writing regularly for the *Fortnightly*. Morley was never a rigid positivist, and grew progressively less sympathetic to many positivist practices and beliefs; but, in 1872 and 1874, he insisted that he should still be described as one.[245] In fact, Bridges, Beesly and Harrison also rejected some of the explicit ritualism and formalism which Comte and Congreve wished positivism to embrace.[246] But what matters here is not this aspect of the

[244] Rendel, *Personal papers*, p. 79.
[245] Hirst, *Morley*, i, 199–200, 301.
[246] Liveing, *Bridges*, pp. 157–63; (Harrison) Coleridge, *Coleridge*, ii, 343–4; Harrison, 'Beesly', p. 207.

creed, but its view of the relationship between the temporal and spiritual powers, and its recipe for the 'humanisation' of society. We must try to understand why, for Harrison in 1875, 'the vital issues for this generation are plainly laid in the cause of the freedom of thought and religion from the interested wardship of the State'.[247]

To summarise the positivists' view, they believed that the spiritual power must be separated from the temporal, in order to release it from the shackles imposed upon it by the rich and powerful. The deadening materialism of these latter groups, and their conception of religion as a mechanism for social control were thought to have prevented the spiritual power from infusing society with a commitment sufficiently intense to raise the condition of the mass of humanity. A spiritual power separated from the state would, it was argued, be able to do this, but only by casting aside all complacency and by appealing to the poor through the profundity of its spirituality: in which talk of 'morality' in the whig-liberal sense was of no help, and emphasis on 'brotherhood' (which Comte thought could be furthered by means of creeds and ritual) was essential. In other words, the object of worship of a really penetrating religion should be humanity itself.

This was, of course, to some extent, an anti-clerical vision. It replaced traditional conceptions of theology with a faith in the powers of the human brotherhood; it condemned the influence of priests on secular teaching as sectional and divisive; it envisaged the ideal spiritual power as a well-informed 'clerisy' of experts who would channel man's spiritual energies into reverence for science – the agency of the future which would explain the world's underlying harmony. But the positivist vision differed strikingly from that of both whig-liberals and academic liberals (discussed below) in its distrust of authority, even 'expert' authority, and in its unqualified veneration of the popular judgment and of popular enthusiasm.

Positivists disliked all the forms in which whig-liberals expressed their philosophy of life – Carlylean, optimistic latitudinarian, and Benthamite, for example – because all of them appealed to the individual, rather than to the masses, and because their content was unsuitable for anyone outside the intelligentsia or the 'top ten thousand'. The infiltration into nineteenth-century society of whig-liberal corruptions of real religion had led to an 'unmistakable lowering of the level of national life'.[248] Positivists alleged that these thinkers had castrated religion: it was no longer 'that supreme, penetrating, controlling, decisive part of a man's

---

[247] Harrison, *Order and progress*, p. 29.   [248] Morley, *On compromise*, p. 14.

life, which it has been, and will be again' – and this was because the spiritual power had not been left free to articulate agreed truths.[249]

Carlyle, the evolutionists and the optimists alike thought it sufficient to 'leave the mass, and fall down before the individual, and be saved by him'.[250] Morley had little time for German philosophy;[251] he believed that all forms of deism or Idealism allowed man to obscure the distinction between good and evil, truth and falsehood, in vapid and mysterious language. By dehumanising faith and reducing it to a 'vague futility', latitudinarianism and Idealism had secured what they called 'freedom': 'freedom from conviction' and 'emancipation from the duty of settling whether important propositions are true or false'.[252] This was not 'tolerance' but 'indifference'.[253] Rather than contemplate the 'sublime possibilities of the human destiny', they tried to grasp 'that infinite unseen which is in truth beyond contemplation by the limited faculties of man'.[254] Conjecture about such mysteries was fruitless, because man's mind was not capable of defining the 'Unknowable' except in the misleading terminology of the 'Known'.[255]

Nor, the positivists argued, was such an approach even capable of instilling the morality that its advocates claimed for it. It was in any case highly objectionable, they thought, to force people to accept what they believed to be untruths for the sake of maintaining a moral code. But there was no transcendent morality in the Gospels, which merely recorded the axioms prevalent at the time of composition, many of which were 'objectionable'. Moreover, and most importantly, any real religion – as opposed to the 'highly poetised morality' of the deists – had no necessary moral content. The essence of real religion was 'wholly unconnected with principles of conduct; it has its rise in a sphere of feeling . . . absolutely independent of all our moral relations'. Its essence was 'spirituality'.[256] 'Moral' religions were too complacent: they lacked especially an understanding of that 'very real catastrophe in the moral nature of man', that 'horrid burden and impediment on the soul, which the churches call Sin'; they did not see 'the vileness, the cruelty, the utter despicableness' of man.[257]

---

[249] *Ibid.*, p. 29.

[250] Morley (on Carlyle), *Critical miscellanies*, i, 189–91. Harrison thought Carlyle a 'narrow, Bible ridden prejudiced savage, Scotch peasant': *Order and progress*, p. xix. On the evolutionists, see Morley, *Nineteenth-century essays*, pp. 186–7; Harrison, *Politics and a human religion*, p. 15. For a similar view on Benthamism, see Harrison, 'Religion of inhumanity', p. 687.

[251] Gooch, *Under six reigns*, p. 184.

[252] Morley, *Voltaire*, pp. 8, 12.

[253] Morley, *On compromise*, pp. 99–100.

[254] Morley, *Rousseau*, ii, 280.

[255] Morley, *Nineteenth-century essays*, pp. 211–13; *On compromise*, pp. 145–8.

[256] Morley, *Nineteenth-century essays*, pp. 197, 206–14.

[257] Morley, *Critical miscellanies*, i, 344.

Positivists believed that, by pitching their appeal at the individual, these religions made no attempt to 'consolidate and *regulate*' men's individual lives, to bind them together in shared sentiment.[258] A religion of 'humility, gentleness, and love, a body of beautiful maxims' could not bring 'order out of the intellectual anarchy around us',[259] 'sweeten the lives of suffering men', bring succour to those hit by 'wrong and cruelty and despair',[260] and draw out the 'goodness' of the poor from within their coarse exterior.[261]

The 'first and last business of religion', in other words, was to tackle the 'sense of sin in man's heart', to 'inspire men and women with a desire to do their duty, to show what their duty is, to hold out a common end, which harmonises and sanctifies their efforts towards duty, and knits them together in close bonds as they struggle onwards towards it'.[262] Its twin foundations should be 'human enthusiasm and social devotion':[263] the enthusiasm and devotion of the generations of men who had gone before and would come in future, all labouring to shape human destiny. It was this 'great unseen host of our fellows' to whom 'the religious sentiment will more and more attach itself'.[264] The individual's 'moral energy' could be renewed only by 'spiritual contact with the mass of men'.[265]

It was at this point that the stricter positivists and Morley parted company – the former to stress the power of formal doctrine and organisation, the latter to emphasise the role of intellectual discovery. Both, however, were working towards the same end, the manufacture of a religious creed capable of inspiring men to social devotion.

Harrison and Beesly were fond of contrasting the social consequences of Protestantism – which they identified with unbridled capitalism – with the humanising spiritual influence of mediaeval Catholicism. Beesly perceived that, in the middle ages, when the spiritual power was untrammelled by the temporal, it had been able to work for 'liberty, equality, and fraternity'. The Church, 'as every one knows, was the only democratic institution of the Middle Ages'; but 'no Protestant Church has ever taken the side of the poor against the rich'.[266] Harrison also disparaged Protestantism. No spiritual power aiming to educate humanity would rely on anything as individualistic as 'a personal relation with Christ and God': it needed a priesthood and an agreed, secure creed

---

[258] Harrison, 'Religious and conservative aspects', p. 1000.
[259] Harrison, 'Neo-Christianity', p. 330.
[260] Morley, *Voltaire*, pp. 279–80.   [261] Morley, *Rousseau*, i, 68.
[262] Harrison, 'The creeds – old and new', pp. 541–2.
[263] Harrison, *Politics and a human religion*, p. 16.
[264] Morley, *Rousseau*, ii, 278–9.
[265] Morley, *Critical miscellanies*, i, 189–91.   [266] Beesly, *Letters to the working classes*, p. 23.

which would provide an unchallengeable authority.[267] Only a 'body of doctrine and a system of definite axioms', a '*system*' and an '*organization*', could give 'unity and permanence' to a Church, and provide a bond capable of bringing a mass of people into communion with each other.[268] Protestantism worshipped only a book, and once the authority of that book had been destroyed by 'two or three ingenious pedants', Protestantism became only 'a shapeless pile of commentaries on the Hebrew literature'. Catholicism, on the contrary, had a united Church, saints, philosophies, and beautiful traditions;[269] it had ritual and a 'sacerdotal' aspect, encouraging one to 'surrender' one's 'self'.[270] (Harrison had been a contemporary of Liddon's at school, and had been interested in high-church doctrine and ritual before becoming a Comtist.)[271] Catholicism had succeeded, where Protestantism failed, in controlling the 'oppressor', cheering the 'oppressed', and humanising the 'degraded'.[272]

It had become apparent, Harrison argued, that some aspects of Catholic doctrine were illogical and incoherent.[273] He considered that there was no longer certainty in any traditional theology, and that this must be reinfused through an alliance with science. He saw it as the true function of an intelligent, independent spiritual power, a modern priesthood, to work towards this alliance. But the aim was not, as with the latitudinarians, to sublimate 'religion into an emotion' in the hope that science would find nothing offensive in it;[274] it was to re-anchor the mediaeval religion, of duty towards the human brotherhood, on firmer foundations – 'Catholicism became scientific'. The scientific study of society and the natural world would reveal their workings, and show that the pursuit of sympathy between man and man was the necessary basis for right relations within the community.

Morley differed from such thinking, in maintaining that the Reformation had been a beneficial turning-point in European history.[275] Like Harrison, he believed that 'open-minded investigation' was the 'only certain method' of not missing 'the surest and quickest road to the manifold improvements' of which man was capable.[276] But he argued that intelligence could operate effectively only if all 'theological ways of

[267] Harrison, *Positive evolution of religion*, p. 115.
[268] Harrison, 'Religious and conservative aspects', p. 993; 'Neo-Christianity', p. 329.
[269] *Positive evolution of religion*, pp. 178–81; 'The creeds – old and new', pp. 537–8. Harrison was therefore not attracted to nonconformity either.
[270] *Positive evolution of religion*, pp. 121, 125–9; 'The soul and future life', pp. 635–6.
[271] Vogeler, *Harrison*, pp. 13, 33.
[272] Harrison, 'The creeds – old and new', pp. 538–9.
[273] *Positive evolution of religion*, pp. 121–2.
[274] 'Neo-Christianity', p. 332.
[275] Morley to Harrison, 26 October 1872, Harrison papers, 1/79.
[276] Morley, *Voltaire*, p. 179.

regarding life and prescribing right conduct' were destroyed.[277] He believed that the old feudal-monarchical structure which had been toppled by the French Revolution had not allowed this free operation, and so had offered individuals no chance of working to improve the cause of humanity.[278] One element in Morley despised the hypocrisy and repressiveness of priests, and regarded them as an anti-social influence;[279] unlike Harrison, he at first supported the *Kulturkampf*, although he later changed his mind.[280]

But, despite stressing the importance of intellectual free play in order to achieve social and moral progress, and of men like Turgot and Condorcet who had given it such currency, Morley was insistent that the operation of the intelligence alone was not enough: it must be harmonised with emotion for humanity, which the *philosophes* had not sufficiently realised. He thought that, whereas Catholicism had emphasised the latter too much, modern liberals placed too much weight on the former: a perfect harmony must obtain between 'reason and affections'.[281] The 'might' of Christianity as a 'historic force' was owing not so much to its intellectual influence as to the 'high and generous types of character which it inspired', to the 'saint' and 'holy man'. This was because the 'leading of souls to do what is right and humane, is always more urgent than mere instruction of the intelligence as to what exactly is the right and the humane'.[282]

Morley therefore argued that, in order to instil the value of brotherhood and a strong sense of humanity, man's intelligence must be spiritualised. As soon as this was effected, his 'purifying anguish of remorse' at social wrongs, at individual sin and cruelty, would become stronger, because these evils would be viewed as 'weakening and corrupting the future of his brothers'.[283] Voltaire had demanded a spiritual revolution of this sort, and Rousseau a revolution in perception of the poor, the achievement of 'equality of external chance'; but Morley contended that both schemes had failed because they had not appreciated the necessity of the other.[284] Only if the two were combined would there arise once more a sense of 'direction' which, like the Church at its best, would firmly distinguish between right and wrong in social relations –

---

[277] *Critical miscellanies*, ii, 259.
[278] *Voltaire*, pp. 177–80.
[279] Hirst, *Morley*, i, 279; Morley, *Cobden*, i, 200.
[280] Harrison, 'Public affairs' (February 1874), pp. 282–96; Harrison to Morley, 19 August, 3 December 1873, Harrison papers, 1/57, 58; Morley to Harrison, 28 August 1873, *ibid.*, 1/80.
[281] Morley, *Critical miscellanies*, ii, 228–36, iii, 376–7; *Rousseau*, i, 151–2; *Burke*, pp. 283–4.
[282] *Critical miscellanies*, ii, 107–9.
[283] *Voltaire*, pp. 293–4.   [284] *Ibid.*, pp. 180, 345–52.

yet which would also be buttressed by the unchallengeable evidence of science.[285]

Morley agreed with the more rigid positivists, therefore, in asserting the importance of zealous spiritual activity in order to raise the consciousness of the mass of humanity, and in order to enable mankind to endow the state with a more active social conscience than it possessed at present. Both stressed that some authoritative spiritual force must take the lead in regulating and transforming belief: it must govern 'all that relates to thinking, knowing, believing, persuading, and inspiring affection and enthusiasm'.[286] They agreed, moreover, that the triumph of positivist principles could be secured only by separating the spiritual and temporal powers and allowing free play for religious debate unimpeded by force of law: spiritual enlightenment was 'impossible without spiritual freedom'.[287] Unless they were separated, one, it was contended, would dominate the other, and either freedom of conscience, or spirituality, would be destroyed.[288] While disclaiming sympathy with tractarian dogma, Morley pointed out its great merit, that it recognised 'in a very forcible way . . . the doctrine that spiritual matters are not to be settled by the dicta of a political council'.[289] Harrison opposed state direction of spiritual and intellectual life because its morals would be 'unenlightened, formal, average, and official'. Under this dispensation, priests acted as 'mere State police',[290] and were unable to undertake the 'primary duty' of a 'real' Church, which lay in 'protecting the weak and restraining the selfishness of power'.[291] Both maintained that the Established Church had no conception of truth: it stuck unthinkingly by certain catchphrases and refused to pronounce on controversial doctrinal matters. It was, moreover, a Church, some of whose members did not accept its doctrines, but conformed because they considered hell a 'useful fiction for the lower classes', restraining 'anti-social conduct'.[292] But it was thus an engine for maintaining the 'anti-social tendencies' of the privileged themselves,[293] since, acting as a 'moral police in the interest of the rich and powerful', it seldom attempted to 'check the greed of capital'; its spiritual life was 'paralyzed' by 'formalism' and 'privileges', because enthusiasm was regarded as dangerous. It preached 'submission and contentment' to working-men, and promoted class views of political and economic subjects. Disestablishment was necessary in order to

---

285 *On compromise*, p. 110.
286 Harrison, *Positive evolution of religion*, p. 108.
287 Harrison, 'Church and state', p. 666; Beesly, *Letters to the working classes*, p. 24.
288 Morley, *Critical miscellanies*, ii, 337.   289 *On compromise*, p. 91.
290 'Religion of inhumanity', pp. 692–3.   291 *Positive evolution of religion*, p. 113.
292 Morley, *On compromise*, pp. 29–39.
293 Morley, *Voltaire*, p. 351.

strike a blow at the 'Whig indifferentist', at the 'Tory partisan', and at the rich who could not tolerate an 'independent and real Priesthood'.[294]

They maintained, also, that spiritual education must not be controlled by the state. In Prussia and France it was used 'like the army to preserve the *status quo*'.[295] The secular solution to the educational difficulty must, they suggested, be adopted because the roles of the spiritual and temporal powers in education were so different. Morley maintained that the Church should not influence the teaching of non-religious subjects: that it should not corrupt the task of training men for citizenship with its unscientific ideas. The nation could 'only be efficiently instructed through the agency of men who have faith in intelligence, and ample hope of social improvement'; teachers ought to be trained in universities, not selected by clergymen.[296] In his eyes, state-aided education ought to be secular, compulsory and free. But he believed, nonetheless, that all sects should be given the freedom to teach their religion at a fixed time.[297] The 1870 solution, he claimed, was muddled, gave too much power to the Church, reeked of compromise and repressed zeal: it showed the necessity of establishing an 'honest, wholesome, fearless, and independent' spiritual power in order to guide public opinion.[298] Education should not concern itself with individuals, but should increase the '*average* interest, curiosity, capacity', should 'swell that common tide, on the force and the set of whose currents depends the prosperous voyaging of humanity'.[299]

The positivists' ideal of government was thus one in which no class or sect possessed illegitimate authority over any other. Positivists criticised others for displaying, in discussing both Establishment and the franchise, too little 'faith in the self-protective quality of a highly developed and healthy community'.[300] Government would become moral and true to the extent that it was based on 'a complete and unwavering regard to the interests of the majority'.[301] The educated could not be safely entrusted with the 'interests of other classes'; they, like every class except the multitude, might easily become 'anti-social'.[302] Harrison welcomed much of what he saw in the Paris Commune: its working-class leaders were enlightened and practical. He did not endorse the 'mania for democracy' which overcame it, or the battles of the 'crude theorists

[294] Harrison, *Positive evolution of religion*, pp. 150, 153; 'Church and state', pp. 660–2; Beesly, *Bee-hive*, 24 January 1874, p. 1.
[295] Harrison, 'Religion of inhumanity', p. 692.
[296] Morley, *Struggle for national education*, pp. 32–6, 71.
[297] *Ibid.*, p. 97.   [298] *On compromise*, pp. 76, 78.
[299] 'On popular culture', pp. 649–50.   [300] Morley, *On compromise*, p. 194.
[301] Morley, *Burke*, pp. 309–10.
[302] Morley, *Critical miscellanies*, iii, 255; *Burke*, p. 301.

and desperate adventurers', which led it into anarchy. However, he was glad to see a government founded on a belief 'not in god, nor in any man', but on the assumption that capitalists should 'adapt themselves to nobler uses' if they were to continue to be tolerated.[303] Morley had the same belief in government devoid of class bias. He saw free trade as the best safeguard for the maintenance of working-class living standards; he perceived the continuation of international peace to be the most reliable guarantee of the humanitarian and responsible conduct of domestic policy;[304] he regarded as unfair any industrial legislation which discriminated between employer and employee.[305]

Positivists' views on foreign policy were not always those of nonconformists: in February 1871, for example, Harrison demanded British intervention in the Franco-Prussian war, in order to prevent the destruction of the French régime by feudalistic German might.[306] Their reaction to the Bulgarian atrocities was much cooler than that of nonconformists; while their Turcophilism was not very profound, their distrust of Russia's despotic government and imperialist aims knew no bounds. Similarly, Harrison considered the Orthodox Church an 'abject . . . servant' of the czar, which conferred enormous power on him.[307] Most positivists thus displayed an uneasy ambiguity about the merits of the agitation, although Morley was much more Gladstonian than Harrison.[308]

About Ireland, however, there was little positivist ambiguity. In 1868, Morley defended the right of the Irish Catholics to worship 'God after their own manner', and condemned concurrent endowment.[309] Moreover, he defined two more general principles, that the government of a country must 'do its best for the happiness of all the people who come under its influence', and that happiness was not to be measured according to the government's own predilections, but 'simply and solely by the views and actual wishes of a decisive majority of the people of the country'.[310] Four years later, he stressed that Irish Catholics *were* the Irish nation: Protestants and freethinkers were '*such* a minority as not to be worth taking into account by a ruler', except in ensuring civil equality.[311] Protestantism was not a sufficiently spiritual religion anyway: the use of British funds to promote it in Ireland through Establish-

---

[303] Vogeler, *Harrison*, pp. 101–2; 'A "modern symposium" ', pp. 814–22.
[304] See Morley, *Cobden*, ii, 483–4.
[305] Crompton's articles 'Class legislation' and 'The government and class legislation' were published in the *Fortnightly Review* in 1873.
[306] 'Effacement of England'.
[307] *The meaning of history*, p. 376.
[308] Shannon, *Bulgarian agitation*, pp. 216–17, 236–7.
[309] Morley, *Ireland's rights*, pp. 8–9.
[310] *Ibid.*, p. 6.   [311] Hirst, *Morley*, i, 215.

ment or education was absurd, because nothing whatever was to be gained by 'the conversion of an Irish pauper to Protestantism by means of soup-tickets'.[312] It followed that the Irish nation must be given whatever its inhabitants wished. They clearly wished for denominational higher education: it was therefore 'monstrous' to 'thwart' that wish, and they must be allowed Catholic colleges or a Catholic university. Although *endowment* of denominational education was a 'thoroughly bad thing', even that should be considered if it was clearly the wish of the Irish nation, because it was 'emphatically an Irish question'.[313] In 1881, he was still arguing that the prejudices of the English middle classes were keeping alive Irish agitations, because their Protestantism refused to allow the Irish to be given 'the only system of education that they will accept'. Any form of real education would be beneficial: it would create an 'educated middle-class in Ireland', who in turn would be able to govern the country and to promote 'an independent and spontaneous growth of Irish civilisation along its own lines'.[314]

These feelings were even more marked among the other positivists. Harrison and Beesly both singled out the Irish Catholic Church as the only surviving European religious body not to be a class institution, but to be the Church of 'the poor'.[315] The Catholic priest did not preach 'a stale and stupid lecture on some theological topic of no use or interest to any mortal; he deals with right and wrong in the concrete as he sees them in the real life around him'. He was not afraid to rebuke sinners, however rich, whereas the 'middle-class Englishman' was too vain to let clergymen reproach him for his materialism.[316] Positivists formed an Ireland Society, which as early as 1867–8 was arguing not only for the disestablishment and disendowment of the Church, and for extensive land reforms, but also for the treatment of Fenians as political prisoners rather than as criminals, for Irish self-government, and for the withdrawal of all state aid to, and interference with, Irish higher education. They maintained that capital investment and British state control would never be enough to make Ireland satisfied, as long as she was forced to forego 'all the higher objects of the existence of a State':[317] indeed, they perceived such a policy as the concomitant of British capitalist missionary Protestant imperialism abroad – that 'religious commercial form of aggressiveness' for which positivists had 'indignation and contempt'.[318]

---

[312] *On compromise*, p. 189.   [313] *Pall Mall Gazette*, 30 April 1872, p. 3.
[314] 'England and Ireland', p. 425.
[315] Harrison, *Positive evolution of religion*, pp. 156, 170–1; Beesly, *Letters to the working classes*, p. 23.
[316] Beesly, *Letters to the working classes*, p. 23; see also Liveing, *Bridges*, p. 255.
[317] Liveing, *Bridges*, pp. 129–31; Congreve, *Essays*, pp. 186–7, 202–15.
[318] Liveing, *Bridges*, p. 217.

If, therefore, the British parliament would not give the Catholics justice, it should leave Ireland's 'destinies in the hands of the Irish people themselves'.[319]

The relationship between positivists and the Liberal party was far from easy in the 1870s, mainly because of their opposition to government educational policy (Harrison also disliked what he saw as Gladstone's attempt to sever religion from political involvement).[320] Between 1870 and 1874, both Harrison and Morley believed that the Liberal party was so timid and so lacking in spiritual vision that a fundamental radicalisation was necessary.[321] Nonetheless, positivism, like nonconformity, was capable of being moulded by Gladstone into a force which would serve his interests rather than work against them; it was one of his great triumphs that in the twelve years after 1874, he won the support of the bulk of both groups for policies which, while falling short of their highest aspirations, convinced them that his political aims were noble and that he and they shared similar ideals. But the same could not be said of other academic liberals, many of whom showed an increasing tendency to drift with whig-liberal opinion.

Academic liberals

Positivism in its vaguest sense extended widely at this time, appealing to a set of advanced radicals in parliament, to some of the young academic liberals outside it, and to some of the many disciples of Mill. In discussing disestablishment and secular education, rationalist intellectuals, whether strongly influenced by positivist conceptions or not, adopted the standard radical points of view. But, as intellectuals, they found it increasingly easy to share not only the anti-clerical attitudes of those discussed in chapters 1 and 2, but also their anti-populism and anti-sectionalism. In the 1870s and 1880s, it was difficult for men or women convinced of the importance of 'mind', to sustain a whole-hearted confidence in the beneficial workings of democratic politics in England and – especially – in Ireland.

In attempting to group together, as we do now, intellectuals who were not thoroughgoing positivists, yet who at the same time were supporters of disestablishment and, in most cases, freethinkers or only nominal Church members, we are inevitably forced to grapple with some of the most familiar of Victorian minds. We must include Mill, and George Eliot and John Chapman of the *Westminster Review*. There was also Henry Fawcett – the professor of political economy at Cambridge – who was so

---

[319] Harrison, *Order and progress*, p. 239.
[320] McClelland, 'Gladstone and Manning', p. 165.   [321] See e.g. Morley, *On compromise*.

rebellious in parliament that the whip was withdrawn from him in the early 1870s. There was a gaggle of young rich and educated MPs who followed Fawcett's leadership: Charles Dilke, Auberon Herbert, Walter Morrison, Lord Edmond Fitzmaurice (Lansdowne's brother) and, to a lesser extent, G. O. Trevelyan, G. J. Shaw-Lefevre, C. C. Clifford, Sir David Wedderburn and Andrew Johnston.[322] There were a few free-thinking scions of the whig aristocracy, Russell's son Viscount Amberley, and the latter's brother- and sister-in-law, Lyulph Stanley and Rosalind, the future countess of Carlisle. There was James Allanson Picton, the most aggressive of the few advocates of educational secular-ism on the London school board, a future Liberal MP, and at this time an increasingly heterodox congregationalist minister (he resigned his charge in 1879; he was also to be a keener positivist and a more radical politician than most of those discussed). There were journalists like Leslie Stephen, a former Fellow of Trinity Hall, who was (belatedly) to resign his orders in 1875. There were, finally, other academics, such as Goldwin Smith – the former regius professor of modern history at Oxford, but now an emigré, living off his wealth in America – and J. E. Thorold Rogers, the Cobdenite ex-professor of political economy at Oxford, another man who resigned his orders (in 1870) and another future Liberal MP. Because, on the whole, they are so familiar – and too interesting as individuals for procrusteanism to be profitable – no detailed attempt will be made to treat their views about ethical ques-tions, as opposed to their attitudes to matters of practical politics.

The primary point of reference for these intellectuals was opposition to authoritarianism and mental enslavement; many had cut their politi-cal teeth in discussing the issues thrown up by Italian unification and the American civil war. They rejected traditional Christian theology. The central doctrine for them was that which Mill had developed: that com-plete freedom of discussion was necessary in order to advance 'the moral regeneration of mankind', because open competition between different schools of thought, unfettered by state authority, would help man to discern and to isolate the most elevating elements in Christian and non-Christian religions alike, and to create from them the most effective possible ethical and spiritual guide.[323] Any religion which was favoured by unnatural advantages was believed to lose its spiritual freshness and to become stale, dry, formalistic and outdated. Many rationalist Liberals had secularised the evangelicalism in which they had been raised; they

---

[322] Shaw-Lefevre was in the government, and thus is excluded from our survey, which treats the other nine MPs as academic liberals. Like the nonconformist officeholders Baxter and Winterbotham, he abstained on both Miall's disestablishment motions, in 1871 and 1873.

[323] Mill, *On liberty*, pp. 111–18.

retained a belief in each man's responsibility for his salvation, but now saw it to be attained through control of his reason.[324] In most cases, they had little interest in the positivists' explicitly religious message.[325] But they agreed with them that the increase in knowledge about science, nature and society would display more clearly the moral laws by which life should be lived, and which should bind the commonwealth together. They agreed also that this bond could best be developed by sweeping away class and sectional (and even sexist) obstacles to unselfish action, and that, in a rational state, morality would be founded not on theology but on sympathy with other men and women. In the novels of George Eliot, this sympathy for humanity was expressed incandescently. In others, it sometimes seemed clinical and dispassionate, an impression given especially by Fawcett; but in fact even he retained a strong sense of compassion for the poor.

There was, in fact, a constant tension between this sense of sympathy for mankind, and an intellectual distrust of the popular judgment.[326] Mill had wished for safeguards to be instituted against the supremacy of the popular will in politics; John Morley described *On liberty* as 'one of the most aristocratic books ever written'.[327] Morrison, for example, took up Mill's idea of proportional representation, with the same aim of minimising the impact of irrational popular passions, and it is not surprising to find him and Goldwin Smith discussing the question with old whigs like Grey.[328] There was a similar ambivalence about trade-union activity: in 1877, Goldwin Smith considered that unions had redeemed labour 'from that state of semi-serfdom into which when wholly unorganised it is apt to fall';[329] but, in the 1880s and 1890s, he and other individualists like Herbert Spencer were to denounce the 'tyranny' of trade unions themselves.[330] In the same way, these men applauded Gladstone's achievement in dragging the Liberal party away from the clutches of the whig aristocracy: he had 'filled the nation with a spirit of common enthusiasm and hopeful effort for the general good, especially for the good of the masses'.[331] But they did not all continue to admire his devotion to majority opinion, as we shall see.

These tensions did not affect discussion of the Church Establishment, because academic liberals rejected the idea that there was any merit in

---

[324] Harvie, *Lights of liberalism*, pp. 23–7.

[325] For Mill, see Harrison, *Before the socialists*, p. 318.

[326] For Mill, see Knights, *The idea of the clerisy*, pp. 175–6.

[327] Morley, *Nineteenth-century essays*, p. 125.

[328] Morrison to Grey, 26 August 1872, Grey papers; Haultain, *Goldwin Smith's correspondence*, pp. 191–2.

[329] 'The defeat of the Liberal party', p. 13.

[330] Smith, *Essays on questions of the day*, p. xi.

[331] Smith, *My memory of Gladstone*, pp. 87–8; 'The defeat of the Liberal party', pp. 7–8.

retaining an Establishment in order to teach good behaviour to the lower classes: any such institution, if not an 'organ of truth', would be 'an engine of evil'.[332] They believed that the Established Church was a survival of a feudal era, ill-suited to an intellectually liberated society; its interests would always clash with those of the 'progressive party'.[333] Support for disestablishment was, like the advocacy of land and local-government reform, one element in their campaign for a society founded on reason and offering scope for the free exercise of individual responsibility, rather than one littered with anti-social privileges. In the case of some, these aspirations spawned a mild republicanism in the early 1870s: Trevelyan anonymously produced an attack on the queen's utility, *What does she do with it?*, and Dilke and Herbert were the two most prominent republicans in parliament.[334]

A similar perspective led most academic liberals to advocate educational secularism: all but one of the eight MPs who were able to vote on the motion of 1870 supported it. As Auberon Herbert said, the 'freest play' must be allowed to 'all thought and feeling' on religion, in order to 'discover the form of religious teaching best suited to reach and influence the higher parts of men's natures'.[335] It was asserted that the purpose of education – to awaken 'fidelity to conscience' – could not be achieved by taking one religious explanation 'on trust', without comparison and testing.[336] (But, even in discussing education, some academic liberals expressed a fear that to renounce all guarantees for instruction in non-material subjects would not afford a sufficient safeguard that men would be well trained for citizenship. The *Westminster Review* accordingly wanted the principles of natural religion to be taught in schools, as facts – while rejecting undenominationalism as biassed and untrustworthy.)[337]

Where academic liberals differed most fundamentally from nonconformists and the bulk of popular Liberalism was in their distaste for the enthusiasms of the various sections of the party. They could not understand why nearly every discussion of policy towards Establishments and education degenerated into a 'miserable religious squabble'.[338] There was no sympathy at all for Gladstone's own religious vision: Trevelyan complained in 1867 that when he travelled with Gladstone 'he was read-

---

[332] Smith, *Essays on questions of the day*, pp. 96–7.
[333] Haultain, *Goldwin Smith*, p. 53; Smith, 'The defeat of the Liberal party', p. 17.
[334] Goldwin Smith, outside it, was also swayed by the feeling: Wallace, *Goldwin Smith*, pp. 150–1.
[335] *Hansard*, ccix, 1535, 7 March 1872.
[336] Anon., 'The Scotch education settlement of 1872', p. 409.
[337] Anon., 'Religion as a subject of national education', p. 128.
[338] Stephen, *Fawcett*, pp. 238, 263.

ing nothing but a silly little *Church* goody book'.[339] A lot of their hostility to religious education stemmed from an assumption that the religious difficulty, at elementary and university level, had been a fatal obstacle to the achievement of a national system – a system which was necessary in order to secure social stability and to elevate the behaviour of the working-man. But this set of attitudes could dictate conflicting responses to political developments after 1870. Although some radicals continued their work for educational secularism – Lyulph Stanley and Thorold Rogers both stood as radical candidates backed by the League in the early 1870s – others, like Leslie Stephen, were happy to accept the 1870 Act for its practical benefits. He argued that it was not necessary, simply in order to pacify a sectional nonconformist campaign, to tamper with constructive legislation which aimed to instil sound principles into the minds of the potentially threatening lower classes.[340] A similar impatience with religious sectionalism and popular religious enthusiasm, for disrupting the stabilising extension of educational provision, burst forth on a number of occasions in the early 1870s, most famously in Fawcett's attack, in 1873, on the nonconformists' behaviour.[341] Other academic liberals voiced a more general distrust of the unsoundness conveyed by the party's treatment of religious questions: the *Westminster Review* pointed out that, in renouncing secularism in favour of presbyterianism in legislating on Scottish education in 1872, having done the same for Anglicanism in England in 1870, Gladstone had committed a 'second educational blunder'. This arose from 'his fatal fondness for trusting to majorities however motley their description, rather than to principles'; and his third step, logically, would be to hand over Irish education to the priests.[342]

'Ireland' was indeed to be the issue which best demonstrated the ambiguity inherent in the academic liberal mind. Fawcett and Robert Lowe (whom Fawcett resembled, but for the latter's hint of Balliol Idealism), were two of the most strident defenders of mixed education in the Irish university system in the mid 1860s; then, between 1867 and 1873, Fawcett led the parliamentary campaign against the imposition of a denominational education policy in Ireland. He and Herbert opposed the 1873 Irish University Bill, Fitzmaurice abstained, and Morrison was also consistently anxious about the matter. In 1873, the *Westminster Review* criticised the government for teaching Ireland that 'her own will, or the arbitrary . . . resolution of the majority was the standard of right and

---

[339] Trevelyan, *Trevelyan*, p. 69; see also Morrison to Grey, 26 August 1872, Grey papers, and the criticism of the *Westminster Review*, in anon., 'The Gladstone administration', p. 222.

[340] Harvie, *Lights of liberalism*, pp. 189–90.

[341] *Hansard*, ccxvii, 578, 17 July 1873.

[342] Anon., 'The Scotch education settlement of 1872', p. 410.

wrong'.[343] It blamed this tendency, and the government's other failings, on Gladstone's ecclesiastical temperament, his impulsiveness and casuistry, his lack of fixed Liberal principle, and his refusal to give a firm lead.[344] In 1877, Goldwin Smith rejected any possibility of a renewal of the alliance between Liberals and Roman Catholics: it was an 'illusion' to attempt to 'reconcile political liberty with the absolute submission of the soul'.[345]

This is not to say that all academic liberals became unionists; many did not, since other pressures affected them. For example, Dilke and Fawcett both opposed the government's legislation of 1871 imposing coercive legislation on Westmeath. Dilke was one of the earliest academic liberals to decide that priestly power in Ireland must be tolerated, and that some measure of federalism was required.[346] (He had, interestingly, written a satire in late 1873, *The fall of Prince Florestan of Monaco*, in order to show how impossible it was for a man equipped with an Arnoldian liberal education to subvert a monarchical and clerical state.)

In fact, academic liberals divided on the home-rule question (just as they had over the merits of the Bulgarian agitation),[347] precisely because the points at issue were ones on which they were so ambivalent: the religious rights of Roman Catholics, and the rectitude of majority judgment as against the rule of law. Dilke, Herbert, Fitzmaurice and Shaw-Lefevre supported Gladstone – together with many younger academic liberals like A. H. D. Acland; but Morrison and Mrs Fawcett opposed him, and Trevelyan vacillated. Leslie Stephen and Goldwin Smith opposed home rule; Rosalind of Carlisle, Picton and Thorold Rogers supported it. As one would expect, there was a tendency for MPs to be more favourable than non-politicians.

Advocates of home rule believed it to be important to go with Gladstone, and to uphold popular rights and the idea of freedom from oppression by the state. Gladstone's opponents, on the other hand, had a distrust of the religious bond which united his party; a horror of the 'supreme power' which 'ignorant or ill-informed . . . masses of people' were exercising over the political process; and a determination not to allow a Catholic priesthood to secure control of the Irish mind, 'turning the common schools into organs of ecclesiasticism', 'establish[ing] itself'

[343] Anon., 'The Gladstone administration', p. 213.
[344] *Ibid.*, pp. 222–4.
[345] 'The defeat of the Liberal party', p. 14.
[346] Gwynn and Tuckwell, *Dilke*, i, 75–6, 169–70, 293.
[347] Shannon, *Bulgarian agitation*, pp. 202–6.

as the purveyor of the national religion, and attaching Ireland to 'a foreign enemy' of Britain.[348]

*   *   *

When all the qualifications scattered throughout the last two chapters have been made, and all the antagonisms between those discussed within them displayed, it is nonetheless evident that Gladstone's Liberal party continued to attract support from the mass of nonconformists, radicals, and working-men, whereas it did not continue to win the loyalty of most of the 'moderate' Liberals whose interests might at first sight seem more akin to those of a devout Anglican property-owner, such as Gladstone was. Central to understanding this conundrum is the tone of advanced Liberal argument, its veneration of majority opinion. In chapters 3 and 4, we have been dealing with men who believed that the only chance of creating a spiritually and socially well-regulated polity was by offering each man and each religious sect free play to develop their potential. They all expected that the resulting competition would be resolved according to the relative zeal of different groups of free men – but for most this meant, fundamentally, that it would be resolved in the way which was most satisfactory to the Creator of the mass of individuals who constituted the body politic. They saw no better way of ensuring that political and social change was channelled according to God's will. They believed that man should possess no authority to impress his views on other men, since there were no grounds for believing his ambitions to be divinely inspired, and since those in a position to impose authority were inherently more likely than other men to lack unselfishness and sympathy for humanity.

This may appear an unrealistically abstract political creed to appeal to large classes of people. What will be striking to twentieth-century minds, which view politics primarily in terms of legislation and the satisfaction of material wants, is the vagueness with which radicals and Gladstonians approached the question of 'sympathy' for the poor: they rarely constructed a detailed policy platform to substantiate their aspiration. It requires a leap of the imagination to appreciate that the problem which they were addressing was not a bureaucratic but a spiritual one. When nonconformists called for disestablishment, or radicals for an assault on the powers of the House of Lords, they did so in order to challenge the influence of selfish vested interests in politics, and the spirit of class exclusiveness in society, and in order to encourage spiritual communion between classes – in the hope of achieving a more harmonious and better-

---

[348] Smith, *Essays on questions of the day*, pp. 95, 322–4; *My memory of Gladstone*, pp. 61–2; Haultain, *Goldwin Smith's correspondence*, p. 192.

regulated polity. Gladstone did not share the desire for their means – the destruction of institutions – but strongly identified with their proposed ends – the attack on obstacles to an unselfish, spiritually aware political order. The last thirty years of his political life – his rhetoric, his crusades, his cultivation of publicity – were dedicated to achieving that goal. It would not therefore be true to see him as bamboozling radicals away from their desired ends; he furthered them as effectively, by his methods, as they wished to by theirs. It would be misleading to see the Liberal party as prevented, by the eccentricity of one man's vision, from following its 'natural' course and implementing a fully fledged secular radical programme. The secular radical programme, for all but a minority, was not seen as central; it appeared as a component part of Liberal aims, only in so far as it coincided with an intense spiritual mission.

In the late nineteenth, and, especially, the twentieth, centuries, this mission lost momentum, as the strength of evangelicalism declined, and as the effects of secularisation impinged on politics. Nonetheless, in 1906, the Liberals won a great victory by recalling three integral elements of the Gladstonian vision: defence of free trade, and opposition to imperialistic brutality abroad and to denominational favouritism in education at home. In the 1890s, this vision had not seemed as relevant to politics as it had before; but it became so again as a result of the Boer War. This can be seen by looking at the lament of an agnostic, a positivist sympathiser, and yet a 'New Liberal', L. T. Hobhouse.

In 1901–2, when the Liberal dawn had not yet broken, and when unionist foreign, financial and educational policy was exciting so much Liberal antagonism, Hobhouse wrote *Democracy and reaction*, published in 1904. In it, he attacked the influence of Idealist philosophy in national life, which he saw to be responsible for the immorality of unionist policy. He argued that, if the state was to concern itself with individual needs and 'social justice', religion had to be appreciated not in abstract metaphysical terms but as the 'collective wisdom' of humanity. Idealism conflated the spiritual and temporal powers in order to ensure that the state saw 'no limits to its authority' and was aware of 'no necessary responsibility' to cater for society's wants.[349] Its vapid rhetoric sapped 'intellectual and moral sincerity' and softened the 'edges of all hard contrasts between right and wrong, truth and falsity'.[350] Idealists could not, logically, 'realise the tragedy of human life and history', or appreciate 'the massive suffering of millions' or 'sound the abysses of woe and despair that ring round the securest life'.[351] Hobhouse wrote that he had

---

[349] *Democracy and reaction*, pp. 80–1, 107–8; see Collini, *Liberalism and sociology*, pp. 51–4, 152, 216, 242–3.
[350] *Democracy and reaction*, pp. 78–9.   [351] *Ibid.*, pp. 274–6.

once mistakenly thought that the work of Gladstonian Liberalism was done; he now realised, however, that its basic principles were constantly applicable, and constantly liable to be forgotten. The most 'fundamental cleavage of political opinion' was between the ideas, on the one hand, of national and personal self-government, of the independence of spiritual agencies, and of progress through the 'free, vigorous growth of divergent types'; and, on the other, of coercive missionary imperialism and of the abandonment of moral politics. The former were the values of Gladstonian Liberalism: 'a crusade against weaknesses and follies of the natural man, in which final victory is never won, but success is to be measured only by the determination with which the war is waged'.[352]

---

[352] *Ibid.*, pp. 47–8, 164–5, 209–11.

PART II

5

Searching for unity:
the Irish Church question, 1867–9

Liberal disunity, 1867–8

Palmerston's coalition was destroyed within months of his death in October 1865; between June 1866 and March 1868, the Liberal party was disunited and intolerant of leadership. In 1866, radical energy, restrained for so long under Palmerston, was unleashed in the shape of a powerful movement for parliamentary reform. Russell and Gladstone, the party leaders, were too friendly to it for the liking of the whig peers, the Adullamites, and a large, albeit mostly silent, section of the parliamentary party.[1] Grey, Bouverie, Ellice, Elcho, Grosvenor, Lowe, Dunkellin and Horsman led the public resistance, while Brand, Halifax, George Grey, Clarendon and Granville tried, in private, to check the speed of the party's leftward movement. The government was finally overthrown in June 1866, and the old guard further irritated Gladstone by thwarting his attempt to call an election. The Conservatives took office; and Bright's provincial reform campaign in the autumn antagonised the Liberal 'right' even more.[2] Relations between the wings of the party were so bad by February 1867 that Gladstone was unable to hold the traditional party dinner. Despite suspicion of, and ultimately revulsion at, Disraeli's own reform proposals, the old whigs and Adullamites remained unsympathetic to Gladstone throughout the 1867 session, distrusting his unpredictability, ecclesiasticism, aloofness and populism. This itself pushed Gladstone further into the hands of the radicals. But some of these latter were also fickle towards him, since they believed that Disraeli's flexibility, and the government's minority position in the House, would permit them to press for policy initiatives in a number of fields, if the Conservatives retained office: when Disraeli

---

[1] See Vincent, *Formation of the Liberal party*, pp. 21, 23.
[2] See Cowling, *1867*, pp. 102–5; Smith, *Making of the second Reform Bill*, pp. 116–20.

succeeded to the premiership in February 1868, one radical claimed to be 'jubilant'.[3] In 1867, one leading old whig thought that the extent of party disunity, and the intensity of the unpopularity of the Commons leader (Gladstone), were both unparalleled in his experience.[4] It is with the attempt to re-establish Liberal unity that this chapter is concerned.

Gladstone was frustrated by Disraeli's successes in 1867,[5] and was intensely anxious to recover office and standing. But, in casting around for issues on which party unity might be restored, he discovered that many of the backbenchers' enthusiasms were not his, and his not theirs. Radicals, for example, advocated further concentration on the Reform question, proposing to introduce the secret ballot, and to press for a radical redistribution of seats. Gladstone was not disposed to promote secret voting,[6] and in early 1868 was disappointed even in his hope of forging a test for party loyalty out of opposition to one aspect of the Conservatives' Scottish Reform Bill. The government proposed simply to give Scotland an extra seven seats, instead of balancing these, as Gladstone wished, by removing seven from small English boroughs: Argyll warned Gladstone that Scottish Liberals would not support him (Gladstone was to gain the point, however, in the better climate of May).[7]

Most striking was the weight of Liberal pressure for educational reform: many maintained, as Brand put it, that national education was 'first to be taken up' of 'new questions'. Bruce and Forster introduced a private member's bill on the subject in both 1867 and 1868; in late 1867, furthermore, Russell proposed educational resolutions, around which he claimed to hope that the party would unite. He professed puzzlement that Gladstone would not adopt them, although he must have known that he was attacking his Achilles' heel: that Gladstone's ecclesiastical views prevented him from being able to unite the party in favour of any detailed measure, and that Russell's whiggish anti-clericalism chimed in better with mainstream Liberal attitudes towards education.[8] Although Gladstone, speaking at Oldham in December 1867, recommended legislation extending the state system, he withstood pressure from Glyn and

---

[3] White to Lennox, 27 February 1868, Disraeli papers, B/XX/Lx/279a; see also Lennox to Corry, 16 March 1868, *ibid.*, 281.

[4] Halifax journal, 12 April 1867, Halifax papers; for this whole paragraph, see Cowling, *1867*, and Smith, *Making of the second Reform Bill.*

[5] 18 August 1867, Ashwell and Wilberforce, *Wilberforce*, iii, 227.

[6] Glyn to Gladstone, 17 September 1868, Gladstone papers, 44347, fo. 170.

[7] Argyll–Gladstone correspondence, January–February 1868, *ibid.*, 44100, fos. 183–209. Gladstone to Russell, 14 January 1868, Russell papers, 30/22/16E, fo. 65.

[8] Fitzmaurice, *Granville*, i, 516–17; Russell papers, October–November 1867, 30/22/16D, fos. 273–309; Cardwell to Gladstone, 5 November 1867, Gladstone papers, 44118, fo. 234; Russell to Gladstone, 30 October, 12 November 1867, *ibid.*, 44293, fos. 315, 324. For Gladstone's annoyance, see Granville to Argyll, 22 November 1867, Granville papers, 30/29/18/1, fo. 72. For Brand, see Brand to Halifax, 12 November 1867, Hickleton papers, A 4 94.

the rank-and-file, in early 1868, to adopt the question as a means of promoting unity.[9] Similarly, Cardwell pleaded with Gladstone that he should overcome his scruples about the abolition of university tests, and the other university reform proposals; he pointed out that Gladstone's reluctance enabled old whigs like Ellice to claim that they were better Liberals than he. Gladstone made vague conciliatory noises early in 1868, but, again, was not to be provoked into precipitate action.[10]

Gladstone's interests, in fact, lay increasingly with the Irish question. Palmerston's governments had been largely inactive in Ireland, a tendency exemplified especially by his appointments of Horsman, Cardwell and Sir Robert Peel as chief secretary. Cardwell was slightly more conscientious than the other two, but even he took few initiatives – and in 1869 was to warn Gladstone against pursuing too 'Irish' a policy, on the grounds that it would cost him support in Britain.[11] Brand, Palmerston's chief whip, considered Irish Catholics to be 'the natural enemies of a Liberal Government';[12] a leading Irish bishop maintained that the Catholics, for their part, saw Palmerston as 'the incarnation of evil'.[13]

In the last few months of Palmerston's life, however, the university question was agitated at Westminster, as a result of the increasing political activity of the National Association. The government toyed with the issue, in order to gain favour at the 1865 election, but only slowly began seriously to consider legislating on it.[14] In December 1865, the bishops requested a Charter and endowment for the Catholic university.[15] But, with exceptions such as Fortescue and Bruce, the government was prepared, at this stage, only to consider issuing a Charter to the Queen's university, allowing any Irish student, from any institution, to be eligible for a Queen's degree. This plan would permit a student taught in a denominational Catholic college to gain an Irish degree from an unsectarian university, but would not give the college concerned any role in the university system. Even Gladstone advised Fortescue against hasty meddling with the Irish education question when other matters pressed, and when agreement on a course of action was bound to prove difficult.[16]

---

[9] 'Speech at Oldham', pp. 114–16; Glyn to Gladstone, 29 December 1867, 23 January 1868, Gladstone papers, 44347, fos. 78, 91.

[10] Cardwell to Gladstone, 15, 25 January 1868, *ibid.*, 44118, fos. 251, 256; see Harvie, *Lights of liberalism*, p. 92, for his inconclusive meeting with Goldwin Smith.

[11] Erickson, 'Cardwell', p. 32; Cardwell to Gladstone, 6 November 1869, Gladstone papers, 44119, fo. 79.

[12] Vincent, *Formation of the Liberal party*, p. 51.

[13] Moriarty to Denbigh, 20 January 1867, 14th earl of Derby papers, 155/3.

[14] Norman, *Catholic Church*, pp. 195–200.

[15] *Ibid.*, pp. 213–17.

[16] Gladstone to Fortescue, 13 February 1866, Strachie papers, 324, CP 1/4.

As if to underline this point, Peel and Lowe asked, in the Commons, for guarantees that the government would propose no alteration in the Irish university system without prior consultation of parliament.[17] Their apprehension focussed not only on the grant of a Charter itself but also on the provisions of the bill which was likely to accompany the Charter, and which would remodel the government of the Queen's university in order to give representation to the increased number of Catholic students – thus endangering, in some eyes, the survival of the national educational system.[18] For example, there had been discussion inside the government about the wisdom of permanently involving the Catholic bishops in the management of Queen's university, by allocating them *ex officio* seats in the university senate; Gladstone feared that this might mean 'breaking prematurely . . . with English public opinion'.[19]

Despite appearing to give the matter little further consideration during the 1866 session, the government was, in fact, maturing its plan, in private, to grant the Charter to the Queen's university; and, embarrassingly, this was announced in the week after the government's defeat in June 1866.[20] Although Fortescue claimed that he had previously announced his intention of making this initiative,[21] there were widespread complaints that he had acted in far too great a hurry to please the Catholics. Critics were apt to allege this, because it was generally expected, in the weeks after the defeat of June, that the Liberals would very shortly come back into office;[22] Fortescue's actions could thus easily be construed as an attempt to buy Catholic votes, in order to encourage them to support a forthcoming radical Liberal Reform Bill, and thus to enable it to pass despite the opposition of whigs and Adullamites.[23]

This storm blew over. More importantly, notwithstanding his initial hesitation, Gladstone's commitment to Irish university reform quickly matured while he was out of office. On at least three occasions in 1866 and 1867, he upheld the validity of the Catholic educational grievance.[24] He took pains to scorn the undenominational solution, which inflicted 'civil disabilities . . . for religious belief' – and through which, moreover, he warned that 'the sacred bulwarks of Trinity College may be

[17] *Hansard*, clxxxi, 811–12, 964–8, 20, 23 February 1866.
[18] (Hill) *Questions for a reformed parliament*, pp. 14–16.
[19] Gladstone to Fortescue, 25 December 1865, Strachie papers, 324 CP 1/3.
[20] Norman, *Catholic Church*, pp. 230–1.
[21] *Hansard*, clxxxiv, 719–20, 5 July 1866.
[22] See Granville to Gladstone, 6 October 1868, Gladstone papers, 44165, fo. 181; Gleig, 'Shall we follow this man?', p. 111; (Cairns) *Hansard*, clxxxiv, 879, 16 July 1866.
[23] (Peel) *Hansard*, clxxxiv, 854; Argyll to Gladstone, 21 December 1867, 4 June 1868, Gladstone papers, 44100, fos. 178, 220.
[24] *Hansard*, clxxxiv, 894–906, 16 July 1866, esp. 902; clxxxvii, 1456–63, 31 May 1867; (Southport speech) *Times*, 20 December 1867, pp. 5–6.

assailed'.[25] He was supported by Fortescue, who declared that, while religious tests 'warped' the true function of a university and should be abolished, parents should be able to choose between denominational and undenominational colleges for their children;[26] and by Acland, who saw the undenominational policy as 'intolerant and tyrannical', and as discriminating against 'the religious principles of any who entertained sincere convictions'.[27]

But this commitment proved extremely divisive within the party, further opening the wounds inflicted by the Adullamites in discussing the Reform question. The debate of May 1867 about Irish education provoked a furious exchange between Lowe and Gladstone, who was riled beyond reason by the prolonged tory cheers for Lowe's onslaught on Acland. Lowe had attacked the Liberal government's willingness to appease the bishops in 1866, had waved a 'Protestant' flag, and had asserted that Acland had no right to address the House as a Liberal – since he refused to 'vindicate what used to be the Liberal idea of comprehensive and tolerant education'.[28] This line was supported by Fawcett – who moved in June 1867, for the first time, for the abolition of tests in Trinity college, Dublin[29] – by the *Daily News*,[30] by Goschen (more ambiguously),[31] and by Argyll (who wished to preserve the Queen's colleges and grant the Catholics only the right to gain degrees from the university's examining board, and who feared Scottish hostility were any more concessionary plan to be proposed).[32]

Divisions within the Liberal party were less obvious on the Irish Church question, because whigs, anti-Catholic Ulstermen and nonconformists could all appreciate the arguments for disestablishment. This increasingly appeared to be the only policy capable of re-establishing party unity. In the Commons, Dillwyn raised the issue in 1865, and Gray in 1866 and 1867; in the Lords, in March 1866, Grey proposed a division of the property of the Irish Church among the sects, and fifteen months later Russell introduced another motion to similar effect.[33] Carvell Williams of the Liberation Society met with the National Association and the Catholic bishops in the summer of 1867.[34] The Conservatives half admitted defeat by appointing the Irish Church Commission in

---

[25] *Hansard*, clxxxvii, 1462, 31 May 1867.   [26] *Ibid.*, 1431.

[27] *Ibid.*, 1449–51.

[28] *Ibid.*, 1451–6. See Vincent, *Journals of Lord Stanley*, pp. 310–11.

[29] *Hansard*, clxxxviii, 55, 18 June 1867.

[30] Fortescue to Gladstone, 14 December 1867, Gladstone papers, 44121, fo. 60.

[31] *Hansard*, clxxxix, 26–7, 24 July 1867.

[32] Argyll to Gladstone, 14 September 1866, 21 December 1867, 4 June 1868, Gladstone papers, 44100, fos. 130, 178, 220.

[33] *Hansard*, clxxxii, 358, 16 March 1866; clxxxviii, 354, 24 June 1867.

[34] Machin, *Politics and the Churches*, p. 356.

1867, and there was even an expectation, in early 1868, that, if Derby retired, Disraeli and Stanley between them would take up the issue, in the hope that it would persuade radical Liberals to continue to tolerate the Conservatives' tenure of power.[35]

In May 1867, Gladstone announced that he agreed with those who condemned the Irish Church Establishment, but that it was not practicable to bring the question forward now; he abstained on Gray's motion.[36] His reluctance to move stemmed from two considerations. On the one hand, he feared that early action might lead the Liberal party to 'martyrdom'. This was partly because of the danger of arousing anti-Catholic opinion in the country, and partly because, although both the Irish bishops and the British nonconformists had come out in favour of disendowment by October 1867, hostility to it in the whig ranks had not abated.[37] On the other, he faced the general problem that, throughout 1867, as he told Dufferin, 'it has hardly been possible for me to open my mouth without giving offence to sections of the Liberal Party'.[38]

Given these circumstances, he was pessimistic, throughout the winter of 1867–8, about the chances of regaining party unity;[39] the short autumn session of 1867 did nothing to facilitate reunion.[40] The Irish MP Maguire gave notice in late November of a motion for the 1868 session, demanding a reform in the position of the Irish Church, and clearly intended Gladstone to take it over: but Gladstone refused to commit himself to doing so.[41] Then, in December, the Fenian attack on Clerkenwell prison killed twelve people, inspiring widespread revulsion in England. A week later, in a speech at Southport, Gladstone condemned the explosion, but maintained that less murderous Fenian acts should be treated more leniently than if the perpetrators were non-political criminals. Responding to the growing public realisation that Ireland was in crisis, he unveiled his argument that she could be governed well only by appreciating 'the traditions, the views, and the ideas' of the Irish. He maintained that coercion, or bribery with public money were not responsible policies: the government should tackle Catholic grievances regarding the Church Establishment, the land (where some strengthening of the tenant-right principle was desired) and, he repeated, the education system.[42] Lowe, however, denounced the speech as 'disgraceful' and

[35] Russell to Gladstone, 3 January 1868, Gladstone papers, 44294, fo. 3.
[36] *Hansard*, clxxxvii, 96, 7 May 1867.
[37] (10 December 1867) Lathbury, i, 154; Norman, *Catholic Church*, p. 332.
[38] 6 September 1867, Dufferin papers.
[39] Gladstone to Russell, 16 October 1867, Russell papers, 30/22/16D, fo. 268; Brand to Halifax, 12 November 1867, Hickleton papers, A 4 94.
[40] Bruce to de Grey, 4 December 1867, Ripon papers, 43534, fo. 189.
[41] Gladstone to Fortescue, 1 December 1867, Strachie papers, 324 CP 1/8.
[42] *Times*, 20 December 1867, pp. 5–6.

wrote an extremely 'Protestant' article for the *Quarterly Review*.[43] In January, perhaps in consequence, Gladstone was still 'strongly against' an official party motion on Ireland: he thought that the government could not be overthrown on it.[44] In early February, Glyn considered the prospects for party unity so bad that the whole session might have to be written off, and Argyll agreed.[45] Clarendon at the same period could not detect either 'a germ of approximation towards Gladstone, or an attempt to discover how he can be done without'.[46]

A fragile unity restored, 1868

This unpromising state of affairs was changed by Derby's retirement and Disraeli's accession to the premiership in mid February, which enabled Gladstone to reunite the party on the Irish Church issue.[47]

Derby had not favoured action on Irish questions, viewing Catholic promises of support as unreliable, and Protestants as easily disaffected.[48] But, given the political exigencies of a minority government, and Derby's own illness, a Conservative strategy was nonetheless being prepared. This planned to offer a Charter to a Catholic university – a policy towards which Derby himself had been lukewarm,[49] but which many Conservatives, especially the chief secretary Mayo, advocated because it secured the preservation of Protestant education in Trinity.[50] But, by offering this concession, Conservatives hoped to be able to retain the Church Establishment – which Conservative opinion in the constituencies saw to be of vital importance for the cause of Establishments and property everywhere.[51] After Derby's retirement, the remaining obstacles to the quick implementation of this policy were removed. Disraeli, the new prime minister, was especially conscious that, with the Reform question all but settled, the chances that radical Liberals would continue to acquiesce in the survival of a Conservative government were remote, and that the Irish Catholic MPs must be wooed instead.

---

[43] Lennox to Corry, 26 December 1867, Disraeli papers, B/XX/Co/35a; Lowe, 'What shall we do for Ireland?'

[44] Gladstone to Russell, 14 January 1868, Russell papers, 30/22/16E, fo. 65.

[45] Glyn to Gladstone, 4 February 1868, Gladstone papers, 44347, fo. 97; Bell, *Disestablishment in Ireland*, p. 70.

[46] 4 February 1868, Fitzmaurice, *Granville*, i, 518–19.

[47] As one Conservative minister recognised: Gathorne-Hardy, *Cranbrook*, i, 263–4.

[48] Jones, *Derby and Victorian Conservatism*, p. 337; Derby to Disraeli, 6 October 1867, Disraeli papers, B/XX/S/451.

[49] Derby to Mayo, 1 January 1868, 14th earl of Derby papers, 195/1; 6 February 1868, Mayo papers, 11164.

[50] *Hansard*, clxxxviii, 66 (Naas/Mayo), clxxxix, 14 (Graves), 20 (Chatterton), 32 (Bentinck).

[51] Whiteside to Cairns, 3 March 1868, Cairns papers, 30/51/13, fo. 100.

The details were finalised at cabinets in early March: it was agreed to make no move on the Church question before the appearance of the Commissioners' report, which it was known would recommend bolstering the Establishment by reforming its temporalities (to the irritation of high-church Conservatives like Hardy).[52] By inaction on the Church question, the government thought that it would also minimise the chances of a successful attack by the Liberals, on the assumption that they would have to propose a specific motion, on which they would encounter internal opposition.[53]

However, the Catholic university plan was politically extremely dangerous for the Conservatives, as Disraeli seems to have been aware. He tried to minimise controversy, both by rejecting Mayo's proposals for endowment – he forced the cabinet to limit to necessary administrative expenses the financial aid which the state would give[54] – and by stipulating that there would be a heavy lay representation on the governing body.[55] In his speech introducing the proposal on 10 March, Mayo followed this brief, but added that further endowment of the university was 'open to future consideration'.[56] Liberals immediately pounced on this statement, especially as Mayo was known to be favourable to a more lavish endowment; and, although Disraeli denied, on 16 March, that it was his intention to endow Catholicism, this disavowal did not save the government.[57]

The ambiguity of the government's plans regarding the endowment of Catholicism was in fact the crucial element in permitting the reunification of the Liberal party. The government's educational policy was savagely condemned in the House by men as unsympathetic to Gladstone as Horsman and Lowe: Horsman described it as one designed to overthrow the mixed system, and to support an institution which 'unfurl[ed] the banner of intolerance against religious freedom';[58] Lowe saw it as 'one of the most retrograde it is possible to conceive', a policy 'sacrificing the Roman Catholic laity' before the 'Ultramontane hierarchy'.[59] Russell was also stridently against the plan,[60] while F. A. Stanley, for the Conservatives, detected a 'strong general feeling against an exclusively Catholic University'.[61]

---

[52] Hardy to Wilberforce, 1 October 1868. Wilberforce papers, c 16, fo. 94. See Vincent, *Journals of Lord Stanley*, p. 331.

[53] Derby to Disraeli, 3, 6 March 1868, Disraeli papers, B/XX/S/483, 484; Buckle, *Letters of Victoria*, i, 509–11.

[54] 'Diary of Lord John Manners', 2 March 1868, p. 16.

[55] Buckle, *Letters of Victoria*, i, 510.

[56] *Hansard*, cxc, 1384–7. [57] *Ibid.*, 1774.

[58] *Ibid.*, 1462, 12 March 1868. [59] *Ibid.*, 1499–1502.

[60] Russell to Gladstone, 13 March 1868, Gladstone papers, 44294, fo. 36.

[61] To Derby, 17 March 1868, 14th earl of Derby papers, 105/10.

Gladstone immediately capitalised on this feeling, and, on 16 March, six days after Mayo's speech, announced that he would be introducing resolutions discussing the future of the Irish Establishment. He, like other Liberals, described Conservative educational policy as retrograde: as a return to the old practice of giving public money directly to 'sectional or denominational interest[s]'.[62] It was also, he contended, debasing to attempt to shore up the Establishment by bribing Catholics with money, since it assumed that the Catholics cared nothing for religious principle.[63] Gladstone, as a high churchman, was also much offended by the Conservatives' intention – through the Commission – to retain a worthless Establishment by castrating the Irish Church itself: in mid February, he had written to Russell that the prospects for the Irish question 'appear to me darker than they have been for many years'.[64] The 'great danger' of such a policy, if successful, was, moreover, that it put the English Church into the 'same category', to be defended merely on erastian grounds. The Conservatives' drift towards this position constituted one more example, incurred in Gladstone's 'long and painful experience . . . that if the Church is to perish it will be from wounds received in the House and at the hands of her "friends" '.[65] On a more general level, Gladstone was horrified by the potential consequences, for religious policy, of Disraeli's lack of principle, and of backbench Conservative stupidity on Church questions. Mixed in with this, of course, was his intense personal loathing and envy of Disraeli, which intensified as the latter attained the premiership; and it is impossible to know whether this was more potent an influence on him than the concern for Church policy, since the two were so closely linked in his mind. At any rate, Argyll told Shaftesbury's mother-in-law, when she asked why the Irish Church issue had suddenly been espoused, that 'there really was no other way of getting Dizzy out of office'.[66]

Even though the Irish Church issue was by far the best one on which to rally the party, Gladstone still faced some difficulties in composing his resolutions, and they were some days late in appearing. As Childers told him, they must placate whigs who wished for concurrent endowment; Forster, on the other hand, advised him not to antagonise radicals by aggressively attempting to overthrow the government from which they still anticipated concessions, since there was still, apparently, a considerable party of MPs who did not want the government to be forced out

[62] *Hansard*, cxc, 1751, 16 March 1868.
[63] Gladstone to Manning, 12 March 1868, Gladstone papers, 44249, fo. 28.
[64] 18 February 1868, Russell papers, 30/22/16E, fo. 128.
[65] Gladstone to Palmer, 4 April 1868, Gladstone papers, 44296, fo. 122; to Lady Laura Palmer, April 1868, Selborne papers, 1863, fo. 80.
[66] Best, *Shaftesbury*, pp. 61–2.

of office. There was also a more general fear among Liberals that Gladstone was impetuously trying to oust the government before the new electoral registers were ready, thus necessitating two expensive general elections within a short period.[67] When the resolutions were eventually published, their scope was, accordingly, limited: one simply mentioned disestablishment, and the others proposed interim arrangements for Church administration until such time as disestablishment was to be passed. A Liberation Society deputation advocating disestablishment had to be prevented from calling on Gladstone, in order to pacify the whigs;[68] and, such precautions taken, Gladstone was able, on 3 April, to win majorities of fifty-six and sixty on motions to 'consider' the acts establishing the Irish Church.

Few Liberals opposed, or abstained on, these resolutions: there were a handful of Peelites, such as Antrobus, H. B. Baring, Ernest Bruce and Palmer; a couple of disaffected radicals; and a number of men whose seats would disappear at a dissolution. Backbench whig-liberals agreed, with varying degrees of coolness, that the broad principles of religious equality must be supported and the details debated later.[69] Indeed, Laing, Torrens, Lloyd, Greville-Nugent and Roebuck all spoke in favour of the resolutions; and Clive and Bernal Osborne also advocated them, while requesting concurrent endowment. Given the history of Liberal antagonism to the privileges of the Irish Church, and the pronouncements of the last few years, the vast bulk of Liberals could not but support Gladstone's proposals. However, there was much complaint in some quarters – from the queen, Tait, the old whigs, Carlyle and conservative high churchmen like Wilberforce – at the *manner* of the move, which they saw as hurried, vindictive, with an eye to the arousal of nonconformist agitation, and, as the queen put it, certain to 'inflame the old sectarian feuds'.[70]

Despite the defeats – and to the irritation of Bright and Gladstone – Disraeli knew that he was free to stay in office until the new electoral registers were ready.[71] The election did not in fact take place until

---

[67] Childers to Gladstone, 22 March 1868, Gladstone papers, 44128, fo. 81; Cardwell to Gladstone, 22 March 1868, *ibid.*, 44118, fo. 261; Forster to Gladstone, [22 March 1868], *ibid.*, 44157, fo. 6.

[68] Glyn to Gladstone, 14 March 1868, *ibid.*, 44347, fo. 109.

[69] Hutt to Grey, 29 March 1868, Grey papers; 7th duke of Devonshire diary, 4 April 1868, Chatsworth papers. For Conservative perceptions of Liberal coolness, see (Disraeli) Buckle, *Letters of Victoria*, i, 517; Stanley diary, 5 May 1868, 15th earl of Derby papers.

[70] Buckle, *Letters of Victoria*, i, 518–19, 578–9; Ashwell and Wilberforce, *Wilberforce*, iii, 241; Fortescue to Brereton, 5 April 1868, Brereton papers, F 12 68; Davidson and Benham, *Tait*, ii, 5–6; (Roebuck) *Hansard*, cxci, 712, 2 April 1868; Greg, 'Ireland once more', p. 257; Froude, *Carlyle*, ii, 365.

[71] Buckle, *Letters of Victoria*, i, 523–7; Monypenny and Buckle, *Disraeli*, v, 28–37; Stanley diary, 5 May 1868, 15th earl of Derby papers.

November; but the campaign began, in effect, in May. During it, both parties proved amenable to anti-Catholic rhetoric. Following pressure from the whips and party leaders, Mayo announced on 28 May that the bishops had not been willing to compromise, and that the government had accordingly withdrawn its offer of a Charter for the Catholic university.[72] The Conservatives concentrated their campaign on the iniquity and impiety of the Liberal proposal to disestablish the Irish Church; political and Church meetings were arranged throughout the country in order to protest at it.[73] Disraeli occasionally banged the Protestant drum, alleging, for example, that the Liberation Society was 'a mere instrument' in the hands of a confederacy of 'High Church Ritualists and the Irish followers of the Pope'.[74] His ecclesiastical policy, moreover, began in crusadingly Protestant style, with the appointment of McNeile as dean of Ripon. However, a combination of the queen's advocacy of broad churchmen, and the need for high-church votes, led him to be more catholic in his later appointments, which included prominent high churchmen William Bright and Robert Gregory.[75]

This shift in ecclesiastical policy was one minor reason why it became more difficult than Disraeli had anticipated to play the Protestant card – the card which he had expected would give him victory in defence of the Church Establishment. But there were many others. For example, he had insufficient religious conviction to be politically successful in exploiting the Church issue; nor, in fact, was his typical rhetoric, in the few speeches which he made, particularly anti-Catholic.[76] Moreover, a division of opinion between Cairns, Hardy and Stanley made it impossible for Conservatives to agree on the details of a positive Irish religious policy; and the resulting party silence suggested to some that, if elected, the Conservatives might, as in 1867, outbid the Liberals – and pass disestablishment.[77] Again and again, Liberal candidates charged the Conservatives either with having no policy, or with being divided about policy. Leading Conservatives like Northcote and Wilson Patten refused to pledge their party to a definite course with regard to the Irish Church; and the *Times*, arguing from the assumption that the Church was doomed, thought that the Conservatives would have to disestablish it if returned to power.[78]

---

[72] Norman, *Catholic Church*, pp. 275–7; Derby to Mayo, 23 March 1868, 14th earl of Derby papers, 197/1; Taylor to Disraeli, 19 April 1868, Disraeli papers, B/XX/T/112.

[73] Bell, *Disestablishment in Ireland*, pp. 90–102; Machin, *Politics and the Churches*, pp. 369–72.

[74] Monypenny and Buckle, *Disraeli*, v, 24–5.

[75] *Ibid.*, v, 57–73.

[76] E.g. at Aylesbury, *Times*, 20 November, pp. 5–6.

[77] Monypenny and Buckle, *Disraeli*, v, 90.

[78] *Times*, 15 September 1868, p. 6; see also the attacks of Liberal candidates Brand, Acland and Collier: *ibid.*, 2, 6, 11 November.

But another major consideration behind the failure of the Conservatives' Church card – except in Lancashire – was Gladstone's ability to present his policy in a Protestant light. The Liberal whips warned him that 'many many seats' would be lost if he appeared to take too 'Catholic' a line.[79] He rejected a request from Dublin Liberals who wished him to attend a great party demonstration in Ireland; he did not think that his presence would help the party's performance in England.[80] In his campaign speeches, he said that he was an 'ardent Protestant': using this designation, apparently, for the first time since 1836.[81] He repeatedly insinuated that Disraeli's Irish policy was to bribe the Catholics with public money: Disraeli, he said, insisted on maintaining the Irish Establishment, and was prepared to do it by giving 'a great deal more to Maynooth and the Roman Catholics'.[82] Gladstone emphasised that he, in contrast, was an 'anti-reformer' of the Irish Church, which would be far 'nobler' disestablished.[83] He proposed 'a general cessation of State endowments for religion in Ireland',[84] and, specifically, of the *Regium donum* and Maynooth grants, which presbyterians and Catholics received annually.[85] The Liberals 'required' the 'cessation' of the 'Maynooth Endowment', while Conservatives required its 'maintenance'.[86] The Conservatives, he alleged, were also willing to endow a Catholic university 'out of the public purse';[87] this was to be 'a new buttress' for the Irish Church, another bribe to Catholics to attempt to make them forego the quest for justice.[88] His own commitment to Irish university reform received limited attention.

Gladstone's allegations of the Conservatives' willingness to endow Catholicism were taken up by many other Liberal candidates.[89] As Tom Hughes said at Frome, 'it was the Conservatives, by their proposal to endow the Roman Catholics, who had thrust the question upon the Liberal party'; Gladstone would have been 'utterly false to his party and to his country' had he not protested against such a policy.[90]

The consequence of this attack was a general tendency, on the part of Liberal candidates, to contrast the Conservatives' policy of 'levelling up', with the far preferable Liberal one of disendowment. The contrast was

[79] Glyn to Gladstone, 8 October 1868, Gladstone papers, 44347, fo. 190.
[80] Fortescue to Gladstone, 16 September 1868, *ibid.*, 44121, fo. 68.
[81] *Speeches 1868*, p. 63; Reid, *Gladstone*, p. 540, fn. 1.
[82] *Times*, 6 August 1868, p. 6.   [83] *Speeches 1868*, pp. 13–15.
[84] *Ibid.*, pp. iv–v.   [85] *Ibid.*, pp. 23–7.
[86] Gladstone to Killick (public letter), 23 November 1868, Melly papers, XIII 3071.
[87] *Speeches 1868*, p. 72, see also p. 60, on Disraeli and the *Osservatore Romano*.
[88] *Ibid.*, pp. 13–15.
[89] See Brassey at Hastings, Potter at Blackburn, Bowring at Exeter; *Times*, 6, 23 October, 17 November.
[90] *Ibid.*, 7 October, p. 4.

made even in the county seats, where whig opinion was dominant – by Dodson and Cavendish in East Sussex, Brand's son in Hertfordshire, Marling in Gloucestershire West, and Milton in the West Riding South. Milton, for example, could not agree, as 'a Protestant of as broad sentiments as any', with Disraeli's policy of 'giving certain privileges to the Catholics'.[91] Only a small number of candidates, like Walter in Berkshire, even dared to hint that, in an ideal world, concurrent endowment would be a good policy.[92] Gladstone himself was explicit in rejecting concurrent endowment – for example at Liverpool;[93] while in the south, the north and Scotland alike, it was roundly condemned, by evangelicals like Chambers in Marylebone, nonconformists like Bright in Birmingham, and radicals like McLaren and Miller in Edinburgh.[94]

This did not please the whigs who were above the electoral battle. Their great fear was that the need to gratify the passions of the new electorate would lead Gladstone into an unstatesmanlike avowal of the voluntary principle, and would force the Liberals to reject the concessions towards concurrent endowment which would be so valuable, not only in Ireland, but – of most importance in their eyes – in bolstering the position of the Church Establishment in England. In late June, Grey had played a major part in leading the Lords to reject, by ninety-five votes, Gladstone's bill suspending appointments to office in the Irish Church: he thought that its implementation would 'impede a fair settlement of the question'.[95] He was only too well aware that the major pressure impelling the Liberal drift towards disendowment was fear of the nonconformists.[96] Like a number of other whigs, he increasingly blamed Gladstone's desire for office, and his 'mischievous' and 'unprincipled' behaviour – in subservience to 'men of more decided will' – for making him accept disendowment, when the question might otherwise have eventually been settled along concurrent endowment lines.[97] Clarendon warned Gladstone that disestablishment would have no good effect upon Ireland unless the people saw themselves as benefiting from it financially.[98] Reeve urged upon Gladstone the wisdom of not committing himself so quickly to disendowment, and alarming many 'moderate' Liberals.[99] In November 1868, Brand thought that the endowment ques-

[91] *Ibid.*, 14, 23, 29 October, 10 November. [92] *Ibid.*, 26 September.
[93] *Speeches 1868*, p. 27. [94] *Times*, e.g. 1 September, 7, 13 October.
[95] Fair, *British interparty conferences*, p. 18. [96] Grey to Tait, 5 May 1868, Grey papers.
[97] Grey journal 1868 retrospect, Grey papers; Grey to Charles Grey, 16 October 1868, *ibid.* See also Charles Grey to Halifax, 9 May 1868, Hickleton papers, A 4 64; Westbury to Gladstone, 20 May 1868, Gladstone papers, 44337, fo. 249.
[98] Clarendon to Gladstone, 18 June 1868, *ibid.*, 44133, fo. 126.
[99] 31 July 1868, *ibid.*, 44415, fo. 331.

tion would divide the party and lead to the overthrow of two or more
governments before it was settled.[100]

Moreover, having avowed at the end of 1867 that he would not take
office again, Russell suddenly re-emerged on the political scene in
October, in order to try to wrest back the political initiative in favour of
concurrent endowment. He planned to propose resolutions in favour of
the disestablishment of the Episcopal Church and the endowment of the
Catholics, leaving a large sum – Granville estimated £250,000 a year – to
the former. He argued that the object of concurrent endowment would
not be to create a 'pedantic' equality between Catholic and Protestant:
'the prescription of 300 years in favour of the Protestant Established
Church', and the hopeless position of a Protestant clergyman in Ireland
'when turned out in the wild pastures of voluntaryism', made it essential
to direct one's 'efforts' towards enabling the Protestant Church, when
disestablished, to 'maintain its ground'.[101] Russell also proposed to
invite the Liberal peers to an eve-of-session dinner, thus clearly staking
his right to be considered as Liberal leader in the Lords. Granville
thought that Russell wished to be sent for by the queen and that, while
recommending her to choose Gladstone, he intended to 'dictate a policy'
on the Irish Church and to have a voice in cabinet selection. Considerable efforts were required in order to draw Russell's sting; but, in the
event, Disraeli was to resign before meeting parliament, thus making the
conclave unnecessary.[102]

Relations within the party were not improved by a further difference of
opinion between Gladstone and the whigs in the 1868 session – about
church rates. Here also Gladstone feared that the whigs' erastianism
would destroy the Church's independence. They planned that, upon the
abolition of compulsory payment of the rate, non-churchmen should
still, if they wished, be able to play a part in the local administration of
the church, through the vestry. Gladstone's proposal, to abolish the
compulsory payment of the rate, and to have the church administered
not by the vestry but by a committee of church rate-payers, was opposed
by latitudinarians like Tait, who thought that it would enable a tractarian
minority to take over the Church: Gladstone thought that, in his opposition, Tait had 'gone stark mad'.[103] Cairns, Tait and Halifax ensured
that Gladstone's clause was omitted in the Lords. When Gladstone complained to Russell and Halifax about the amendment, they replied that
it was vital '*for the sake of the Church*' to allow nonconformists the chance of

[100] Simpson to Acton, November 1868, Acton papers, 8119 (7).
[101] Russell to Gladstone, 6 October 1868, Gladstone papers, 44294, fo. 124.
[102] Fitzmaurice, *Granville*, i, 528–33.
[103] Anderson, 'Abolition of church rates'; Machin, *Politics and the Churches*, pp. 353–4;
     Gladstone to Catherine Gladstone, 24 April 1868, Glynne–Gladstone papers, 29/2.

administering the rate: Halifax's Yorkshire experience taught him, he said, that nonconformists' children often became churchmen if their father was encouraged to involve himself in church affairs and repairs.[104] Gladstone had, reluctantly, to accept the amendment.[105]

Whig apathy undoubtedly had an effect on the elections. Whigs were unwilling to subscribe to the electoral effort;[106] individuals certainly failed to help in the cause, owing to disaffection over the Irish Church issue,[107] and others helped, reluctantly, only because relatives were candidates.[108] In a few county seats, there was a lack of interest in exercising traditional influence: Sutherland's apathy probably cost the Liberals a seat in Shropshire;[109] another in Nottinghamshire was lost because the Newcastle interest was no longer actively Liberal.

But, in fact, whig apathy was on a small scale in comparison with what it would be in 1874, and, on the whole, the Liberal vote held up well in the counties. A great proportion of the apparent reaction to the Conservatives in county seats can be traced to the effect of the redistribution clauses of the 1867–8 Acts.[110] In those counties whose representation was altered by redistribution, the Conservatives gained twenty-five seats and the Liberals two. In the others, where a more reliable comparison with the 1865 results can be made, the Liberals actually made a net gain of three – although these three were in fact gained owing to another innovation after 1867, the operation of the minority clause in three-member counties. Given that the Liberals made a net gain of four seats in Welsh and Scottish counties, the Conservatives thus had overall gains of four seats in English counties unaffected by redistribution or the minority clause (of these seats, the Liberals gained four in the southwest, or in semi-industrial counties, and lost eight, mainly in rural areas). In those counties whose representation *was* altered by redistribution, it is unclear that the Liberals suffered a real drop in support, except, possibly, in Kent and Lancashire. In short, it is likely that the Liberals' performance in county seats was a creditable one, contrary to appearances – and contrary to contemporary perceptions, which attributed the apparently poor showing either to farmers' distrust of dis-

---

[104] Russell–Gladstone correspondence, 20–23 June 1868, Gladstone papers, 44294, fos. 81–5; Halifax to Gladstone, 27 June 1868, *ibid.*, 44184, fo. 200.

[105] Machin, *Politics and the Churches*, p. 354.

[106] Thompson, 'Gladstone's whips', p. 193.

[107] (Overstone) Hanham, *Elections and party management*, p. 18; Wantage, *Wantage*, pp. 169–70.

[108] (Sefton) Searby, 'Gladstone in West Derby Hundred', pp. 148–51.

[109] Thompson, 'Gladstone's whips', p. 193.

[110] Cowling, *1867*, pp. 71–3.

establishment, or to the imposition on the new voters of landlord or clerical influence.[111]

The only limited success of the Conservatives in the counties is not surprising, given the anti-Catholic tinge to the Liberal campaign, and the constant pledges of Gladstone and many other candidates that disestablishment of the Church of Ireland would strengthen the Church Establishment in England, Protestantism in Ireland, and the Union. The Irish Church issue was likely to win the Conservatives a lot of votes only if they could convince electors that the movement against it threatened the English Establishment; but Gladstone was quite unambiguous, throughout his campaign, that he did not wish to see the English Church disestablished.[112] Moreover, the power of nonconformity over the Liberal party, and the fear of its influence, was by no means as developed as it was to be in 1874, and the threat of disestablishment in England was accordingly much less immediate. Consequently, although the Conservatives undoubtedly picked up some votes by defending the 'Constitution of their country', they did not do well enough to offset their losses in borough seats.[113]

In the boroughs, there was not only far less clerical and aristocratic influence; there had also been a much more pronounced extension of the franchise, and the new electorate was much more easily stirred. The Conservative campaign was not particularly meaningful to borough voters who did not identify with the privileges of the Irish Church and who saw no threat to the Constitution in any other sphere. The Liberal programme, on the other hand, was sufficiently broad to appeal to large numbers of electors, and to excite many more with a sense of participation in political activity.

The attack on the Irish Church was, of course, central to the Liberal campaign. Popular enthusiasm was aroused especially by nonconformist energy: the Liberation Society distributed over one million pamphlets on the Irish Church issue in the year before the election, and its paid lecturers gave 515 lectures on the subject.[114] In addition to this issue, and a considerable, but less marked, emphasis on the need for reforms in Irish land tenure (the number of Liberal candidates who paid any attention to the Irish university issue being minimal), three proposals were uppermost in the minds of Liberal candidates. The first was the demand to extend or amend the provisions of the Reform Act: by removing the

---

[111] Glyn to Gladstone, 8 October 1868, Gladstone papers, 44347, fo. 190; Goschen to Gladstone, 15 November [1868], *ibid.*, 44161, fo. 224; Sydney to Granville, 30 October 1868, Granville papers, 30/29/25, box 1, envelope 3; (Brand) Hanham, *Elections and party management*, p. 15; (Gladstone) Buckle, *Letters of Victoria*, i, 563.
[112] *Speeches 1868*, pp. 52–3.
[113] Disraeli, *Times*, 10 November 1868, p. 3.   [114] Hamer, *Politics of electoral pressure*, p. 119.

grievances of ratepayers adversely affected by the abolition of composition for rates in 1867, by altering or abolishing the minority clause, by a further redistribution of seats in favour of large boroughs, by introducing the secret ballot, and (not so common) by equalising the county with the borough franchise. Of these demands, Gladstone, both in his address and in his speeches, emphasised only the need to tackle the rating problem (which the government did by the 1869 Assessed Rates Act). The second was the call for a more thorough economy, sometimes coupled with a plea for the reduction of taxation on items of working-class consumption, or, especially in county areas, for a diminution of local rate burdens. The third was the desire for the establishment of a national system of education – an issue which was often linked with the abolition of university tests and occasionally with demands to reform endowed and public schools. Gladstone's address mentioned the need for educational legislation, but his speeches concentrated far less on education than on the Irish Church and the economy. This, in fact, was typical of Liberals: even Forster and Miall, standing together at Bradford, agreed that there ought to be an education bill, but did not discuss its details.[115] Other issues were mooted by individual candidates: Trevelyan and Hoare led the campaign for the abolition of the purchase system in the army, while the advocates of a local option bill forced a number of candidates to pledge themselves to support it.[116]

In short, as a result of the campaign, the grass-roots of the party became keenly in favour of the introduction of the secret ballot, the abolition of army purchase, and the repeal of university tests. However, the leadership was not committed to support these policies, and neither had there been much discussion of the details of educational legislation. In fact, the Irish Church issue dominated the 1868 campaign; and one of the most active governments of the nineteenth century was elected on that platform nearly alone.

The Liberals' gains between 1865 and 1868 were achieved in three categories of seat in particular: by an increase in the representation of large boroughs, as a result of redistribution (which gave them a net gain of 12 seats); by improving their position in Welsh and Scottish counties and Ireland (giving a net gain of 11); and by victories in British borough seats whose representation was unaltered by redistribution and which had an electorate of over 2,000 in 1868 (giving a net gain of 15). Against this, they suffered a net loss of 2 seats in the category of British boroughs with unaltered representation but with an electorate of under 2,000, and of 4 seats in those boroughs whose representation was reduced or

---

[115] Wright, 'Bradford election', p. 56.   [116] Harrison, *Drink and the Victorians*, p. 260.

abolished.[117] Conservatives thus retained some strength in the smallest borough seats, which were more susceptible to 'influence'; but of 189 British borough seats, outside Lancashire and Cheshire, with an electorate of over 2,000, they held only 31 after the election, and 8 of these were either preponderantly agricultural or were partially controlled by a Conservative interest. When it is considered that the Conservatives *gained* 10 of the other 23 in 1868, owing to local peculiarities or to divisions within the local Liberal forces, the strength of borough Liberalism, in general, can be appreciated.

The specific electoral influence of the Irish Church issue was most apparent, on the one hand, in tory Lancashire, and, on the other, in the Liberal Celtic belt. In those parts of urban Lancashire where Anglicanism was strong, displays of popular Protestantism, whether exploited by local manufacturers or by anti-Catholic orators like the Irish evangelical William Murphy, formed the basis of Conservative gains.[118] In rural Wales and southern Scotland, the extension of the franchise, and the politicisation of new classes, played a part in the Liberal victories; but, given the sharp swing back to the Conservatives in 1874 in most of the counties, the peculiar attraction of the Irish Church issue should not be forgotten. It appealed to nonconformists on account of its anti-episcopalianism as much as its anti-Establishmentarianism.[119] The victorious Liberal candidate in Carnarvonshire called for Ireland to be released from the interference of 'an unsympathizing [Episcopalian] hierarchy'; the victor in Roxburghshire appealed to Ulstermen to trust in the example of the Scottish Free Churches.[120] At the same time, the Liberals gained 7 seats in Ireland. Unlike later Irish policy, the Irish Church issue was so popular because both pro- and anti-Catholics saw it in a reassuring light.

The results of the election, then, were conclusive; the Liberal majority increased from just under 80 to over 110. In these circumstances, Disraeli resigned and Gladstone formed a government, although not without a certain amount of difficulty from the whigs. Clarendon found a 'total want of confidence' and a 'great fear' of Gladstone in his circles: a 'notion that he is not *quite* sane enough for the headship of affairs'.[121] Three men

[117] These calculations have all been made from the results given in Craig, *British parliamentary election results, 1832–1885*.

[118] Greenall, 'Popular Conservatism in Salford', p. 131; Lowe, 'The tory triumph of 1868', p. 742; Joyce, *Work, society and politics*, pp. 257–60; Arnstein, 'The Murphy riots', pp. 51–71.

[119] See e.g. Jones, 'Merioneth politics', p. 324.

[120] *Times*, 22 September, 7 October 1868.

[121] Clarendon to Granville, 26 November 1868, Granville papers, 30/29/29.

were unjustifiably irritated at being omitted;[122] more importantly, Somerset, George Grey and Cowper(-Temple) refused office,[123] as did Russell and Halifax. One element in this calculation, on the part of the latter two, was that they might be better able to press for concurrent endowment in the Lords on the Church question if released from the bonds of office. Russell (who had been offered a cabinet seat without portfolio) hinted at this to the queen:[124] Halifax refused the viceroyalty of Ireland on similar grounds. He complained that, as viceroy resident in Dublin, he would be unable to make the contribution to the Irish Church Bill which he would desire; he refused to be a 'mere instrument to carry out the details of a measure framed without my concurrence'.[125] He also disliked the expense which the office involved, and the insult of being offered it after Hartington had refused;[126] moreover, he knew that he owed the offer only to the queen's insistence that the cabinet should contain at least one reliable man, and a 'check or counterpoise' to Gladstone.[127] On declining the viceroyalty, Halifax was offered, and declined, a cabinet seat without portfolio. Furthermore, Clarendon, to whom Gladstone had virtually pledged the Foreign Office in July 1868, seems only to have accepted office, reluctantly, for 'fear of being thought shabby'.[128]

Gladstone was no revolutionary, but nor is it accurate to depict the composition of the government of 1868–74 as Palmerstonian in all but name. Two of his ministers, Clarendon and Hartington, ought to be classed as whigs. But the tone of the cabinet was set, on the one hand, by Peelites, high churchmen, and friends of the Catholics (Argyll, Cardwell, Bruce, Ripon, Hatherley and Fortescue), and, on the other, by meritocrats (Lowe, Goschen and Childers), and by Bright for the radicals. In addition, there were two minor aristocrats, Granville and Kimberley, who owed political allegiance to no one but Gladstone. Bright's appoint-

---

[122] Stanley of Alderley (the 2nd Baron, who died in 1869), Overstone and Villiers: Stanley of Alderley to Granville, 19 December 1868, *ibid.*, 30/29/22A/4; Overstone to Granville, 10 December 1868, *ibid.*, 30/29/25, box 1, envelope 3; Clarendon to Granville, 11 December 1868, *ibid.*, 30/29/29.

[123] Matthew, vi, 643–4, 648–9. Somerset was offered the Privy Seal or the Postmaster-generalship; Cowper the Duchy of Lancaster (outside the cabinet); George Grey (presumably) the Home Office, thus explaining the last-minute substitution of Bruce.

[124] Buckle, *Letters of Victoria*, i, 567.

[125] Halifax to Grey, 8, 9 December 1868, Grey papers; Charles Grey to Grey, 11 December 1868, *ibid.*; Halifax to Gladstone, 15 December 1868, Gladstone papers, 44184, fo. 241; journal, 8, 9 December 1868, Halifax papers.

[126] Journal, 8, 9 December 1868, Halifax papers; Halifax to Charles Grey, 20 December 1868, Charles Grey papers.

[127] Halifax to Charles Grey, 17 December 1868, Charles Grey papers; see also (Childers) Halifax journal, 8 December 1868, Halifax papers.

[128] Clarendon to Odo Russell, 14 December 1868, Clarendon papers, 475, fo. 196.

ment to the Board of Trade was an innovation, while there were two other decidedly radical nonconformists in prominent junior positions (Baxter and Stansfeld). Forster, who was still viewed as a strong radical in 1868, was the minister with responsibility for education, and three junior ministers were Anglican radicals and avowed supporters of disestablishment: Ayrton, Shaw-Lefevre and Trevelyan. Not all these faces were new, but the overall image was distinctly different from that of Palmerston's governments.

Gladstone's administration took office with a solid and traditional Liberal majority, considerably strengthened by Irish Catholic and British nonconformist enthusiasm, and slightly weakened by whiggish apathy and Lancastrian anti-Catholicism. The balance of forces in the Liberal election campaign ensured that concurrent endowment was a politically dead issue in the Commons: popular Liberalism had pronounced wholeheartedly against it, while the whigs had retired sulking, and perhaps overawed, to their tents. But, although the party was united on the Irish Church question, unity had been attained at the expense of forward planning on other issues. Most importantly, there had been no attempt to reach agreement on the detail of English or Irish educational reform, and thus no preparation for the difficulties to come: in 1873, Forster and Ripon regretted that 'our side . . . had their mouths stopped by the Irish Church' from discussing education.[129] In fact, the Liberals' outward confidence after the 1868 victory was to some extent misleading. A month after the government's formation, one cabinet minister stressed the need for caution in another's re-election campaign: 'there are so many ticklish questions on which the various sections of the party differ'.[130] As Wilberforce put it in 1872: 'Gladstone's Government came in too much on a single cry: with too wide and too ill-connected a support'.[131] When the Irish Church question had been settled, the coalition of whigs and radicals, Anglicans and nonconformists, high and broad churchmen, Protestants and Catholics, would have to come to terms with itself on the religious question, as it had never had to do before.

The apogee of unity: the Irish Church Act, 1869

The Irish Church Bill, introduced by Gladstone on 1 March 1869, and the fruit of two months' work on his part, was a remarkable legislative achievement; the complexity and scope of the undertaking added greatly

---

[129] Forster to Ripon, 29 October 1873, Ripon papers, 43537, fo. 129.
[130] De Grey to Bruce, 11 January 1869, *ibid.*, 43534, fo. 219.
[131] To Gordon, 26 February 1872, Stanmore papers, 49214, fo. 257.

to his administrative reputation. Its progress through the two Houses occupied a large part of the 1869 session, and many amendments to it were discussed. The details of this controversy are available in a number of valuable accounts,[132] and only the most salient points of controversy, as far as the Liberal party was concerned, require coverage here.

From the beginning, Gladstone maintained that the bill must be framed 'with reference to those who support it, and not to those who oppose it', since, if the former 'keep together', they 'are *amply sufficient* to carry it'. It was, he said, almost as if 'Scotch Presbyterians, English and Welsh Nonconformists, Irish Roman Catholics' were his 'three *corps d'armée*'.[133] This was broadly true; and for this reason, in the summer of 1869, he was to prove determined not to concede on major questions of concurrent endowment.[134] (However, the government's policy did involve two small concessions towards the concurrent endowment position. Legislation of 1870 allowed the Catholics and presbyterians to receive loans from the government for the building of glebe-houses for their ministers, in compensation for an agreement whereby the disestablished Church would buy back its own houses at a substantial discount.[135] Secondly, in repealing the state grant to Maynooth and the *Regium donum*, Gladstone offended some nonconformists by giving a lump sum to the first and annuities in place of the second, both from Church funds.)[136]

In early 1869, the most controversial questions concerned not concurrent endowment, but the amount which was to be left to the disestablished Church. The bill proposed that, once certain payments and grants in compensation had been made to the Church's representative body and to her clergy and curates, the rest of the realised assets (which Gladstone estimated would produce £7.8 million within ten years, but which were in fact to generate a much smaller sum) should go not to religious purposes – either Protestant or Catholic – but 'mainly to the relief of unavoidable calamity and suffering'.[137] In February, Archbishop Tait met Gladstone for negotiations, and told him that the compensation due to the Church's representative body, if it was to be equitable, must include all the post-Reformation endowments. Gladstone, however,

[132] Bell, *Disestablishment in Ireland*; Fair, *British interparty conferences*; Macdowell, *Church of Ireland*; Akenson, *Church of Ireland*; and Norman, *Catholic Church*.

[133] Gladstone to Bishop Hinds, 30 December 1868, Gladstone papers, 44417, fo. 287; Gladstone to Wilberforce, 21 January 1869, Wilberforce papers, d 37, fo. 159.

[134] E.g. 26 June, 19 July 1869, Matthew, vii, 88, 100.

[135] Bell, *Disestablishment in Ireland*, pp. 118–20.

[136] For complaints, see Norman, *Catholic Church*, pp. 373–5; Gladstone to Spurgeon, 16 April 1869, Gladstone papers, 44536, fo. 145; Rigg to Gladstone, 30 June 1869, *ibid.*, 44421, fo. 73; Waddy to Spofforth, 11 June 1869, Disraeli papers, B/XXI/S/434.

[137] Bell, *Disestablishment in Ireland*, p. 122.

refused to concede more than those donated after 1660, partly on financial grounds, and partly in order to avoid raising claims on behalf of the Catholics for those given before the Reformation.[138] In fact, Gladstone was already in dispute with Bright and the Liberation Society, and was criticised even by Kimberley, for being too generous to the Church in setting the terms on which the clergy's life interests were to be commuted;[139] and Tait's proposals were politically unacceptable.

Tait was acting, as he did throughout the crisis, in conjunction with the queen, and, through her, with her favourite old whigs. It was this circle which took the lead, throughout the session, in the negotiations to try to resolve the issue (although, of these, Tait was in fact one of the least disposed to compromise). The queen's friends had all been dismayed by Gladstone's impetuosity and the difficulties placed in the way of a rational and generous settlement by his reliance on mass nonconformist enthusiasm in the election campaign – which, by giving a great impulse to the voluntary principle, had, in their eyes, damaged the prospects for the survival of the Church Establishment in England.[140] But most of them accepted that, in the new political climate, disestablishment must be passed and the question settled as quickly and quietly as possible.

All the major provisions of the bill survived the discussions in the Commons; its first major obstacle was the second reading in the Lords. The queen's friends were anxious for the bill to pass there, in order to uphold the principle of disestablishment agreed at the election, and thus to safeguard the political position of the upper House. The queen wrote (unsuccessfully) to Derby, begging him, as a former servant, not to oppose the second reading.[141] Tait, on Disraeli's suggestion, had called a meeting of eight peers (all Conservatives except Grey) in early May, but they had failed to reach agreement on an approach towards the second reading.[142] In early June, the queen sent A. P. Stanley to request Tait to enter into further negotiations with Gladstone, with the aim of securing concessions which would permit wavering peers to accept the second reading. Tait was not warmly received;[143] but Granville told him – on Gladstone's authority – that the Irishman Ball should be encouraged to frame amendments for the Conservatives, since he appreciated the areas in which the government would be able to concede: this suggests

---

[138] Charles Grey memorandum, 11 February, Charles Grey papers; Davidson and Benham, *Tait*, ii, 12–14; Fitzmaurice, *Granville*, ii, 7–8; Tait to Grey, 4 March 1869, Grey papers.

[139] Bell, *Disestablishment in Ireland*, p. 117; 1 March 1869, Drus, *Journal of Kimberley*, p. 3.

[140] (Victoria) Fulford, *Your dear letter*, pp. 228, 230; Guedalla, *Queen and Gladstone*, i, 172; Clarendon to Odo Russell, 12 July 1869, Clarendon papers, 475, fo. 257; Grey to Halifax, 30 January 1869, Hickleton papers, A 4 55.

[141] Buckle, *Letters of Victoria*, i, 603–4, 606–8.

[142] Bell, *Disestablishment in Ireland*, p. 143.

[143] Davidson and Benham, *Tait*, ii, 20–1; Fair, *British interparty conferences*, pp. 23–4.

that Gladstone was willing to help the Church, as long as he could appear to be doing so under political duress.[144] This communication had little political effect, however, and a large meeting of Conservative peers, led by Derby and Cairns, pronounced in favour of rejecting the second reading.[145]

Nonetheless, the second reading was passed by thirty-three votes on 18 June, after four nights' debate. This to some extent was the result of a break in Conservative and clerical ranks. Salisbury and a small band of high-church Conservatives, including Carnarvon, Bath and Devon, supported the second reading. Their strategy was to recognise that the electors had sanctioned the principle of disestablishment, in the hope of protecting the position of the Lords. Their aim was to obtain as much money as possible for the Church, and they therefore gave notice of a series of amendments for the committee stage, concerning the arrangements for commutation, and the allocation of the Church's endowments.[146] Archbishops Tait and Thomson, and Bishop Wilberforce abstained on the second reading, while Thirlwall was the only bishop to vote for the bill; eleven English bishops and four others opposed it.

But the result owed most to the extraordinary response of the whig peers, so many of whom abandoned their apathy in order to travel to Westminster and to pledge support for a long-standing Liberal principle. The dukes of Grafton, Leeds, Norfolk and Sutherland headed the list of sporadic attenders who joined the entire corpus of active whigs – including fierce critics of Gladstone, such as Somerset, Fitzwilliam, Fortescue, Grey, Minto, Russell, Zetland, Ebury, Lyveden and Westbury – in upholding the state's right to alter its relations with religious institutions (even Shaftesbury abstained). This is not to say that such men were warm to the government. Of non-official whig speakers in the debate, Devonshire (reluctantly) rejected concurrent endowment as impracticable, but Grey, Cleveland, Russell and Westbury all made powerful speeches attacking the voluntary principle and demanding amendments in committee as the price of their support; Tait made similar demands. Russell and Cleveland, in particular, spoke of the great boost which the Liberation Society would receive if the bill were not amended and if the voluntary principle were sanctioned unchecked.[147]

Once the second reading had been passed, both the vast body of whigs, and those Conservatives who were willing to negotiate in order to reach a solution, fixed on certain approximations to concurrent endowment as

[144] Ramm, i, 40; Fair, *British interparty conferences*, p. 25.
[145] Bell, *Disestablishment in Ireland*, pp. 143–4.
[146] See Bath to Salisbury, 7, 10, 17 June 1869, Salisbury papers.
[147] *Hansard*, cxcvi, 1713, 1794, cxcvii, 60, 76, 162, 229 (Tait, Grey, Cleveland, Devonshire, Russell, Westbury).

the best means of gaining more of the Church's property for the Protestants (and of giving a material boon to the Catholics). The 'concurrent endowment' policy was proposed in two forms in committee, firstly in motions to grant glebe-houses and land to the three Churches, and secondly, and more vaguely, in discussions about the wording of the preamble to the bill: this referred to the future distribution of the surplus which was expected eventually to accrue from the Church funds, after all claims for compensation had been settled.

The first policy was attempted in early July, in amendments proposed at the committee stage by the whig Cleveland, and on the third reading by the crossbencher Stanhope. The former failed; the latter succeeded. Russell, Grey, Halifax and Westbury had first organised the movement in the Lords for concurrent endowment, and a large number of Conservatives, led by Salisbury, wished to follow it (as did Northcote and Stanley of the leadership).[148] However, the more anti-Catholic element in the party, headed by the Irishman Cairns, the leader in the Lords, was opposed. Disraeli, seeing the welcome prospect of a Liberal split if concurrent endowment were passed – and the unwelcome one of a revolt, planned by Salisbury, against Cairns's leadership, if the Conservative establishment failed to join the movement – tried to force the latter to fall into line in its support.[149] Cairns himself would not cooperate with this strategy, but many Conservatives did. Disraeli's move was good politics: by capitalising on whig feelings about concurrent endowment, he was doing precisely what Gladstone had prophesied 'the leopard' would – and precisely what he was to do in 1873.[150] The government became worried at the 'very large Cave' for concurrent endowment on the Conservative side in the Lords;[151] government whigs like Bessborough and Clarendon were sympathetic to the movement;[152] moreover, the queen appears to have urged the government to accept Cleveland's motion,[153] and the *Times* also warmly supported the principle.[154] The motion was defeated on 5 July by 146 to 113; but Stanhope, Salisbury, Russell and Carnarvon pressed for another amendment,[155] while the queen impressed on the pessimistic Tait, on 11 July, the need to get a

---

[148] Northcote to Disraeli, 7 April 1869, Iddesleigh papers, 50016, fo. 71; 20 June 1869, Vincent, *Journals of Lord Stanley*, p. 341.

[149] 27 June 1869, Monypenny and Buckle, *Disraeli*, v, 107–8.

[150] Gladstone to Russell, 1 January 1869, Russell papers, 30/22/16F, fo. 3.

[151] Sydney to Granville, 30 June 1869, Granville papers, 30/29/76.

[152] Clarendon to Odo Russell, 28 June 1869, Clarendon papers, 475, fo. 253; (Bessborough) Bath to Salisbury, July 1869, Salisbury papers.

[153] Hatherley to Gladstone, 5 July 1869, Gladstone papers, 44205, fo. 29.

[154] *Times*, 12 July 1869, p. 8.

[155] Stanhope to Wilberforce, 9 July 1869, Wilberforce papers, c 16, fo. 208; Carnarvon to Heathcote, 5 July 1869, Carnarvon papers, 61071.

compromise 'on *both* sides', in order to avoid another year of agitation. She also asked Gladstone why more endowment could not be saved for the Church.[156] On 12 July, Stanhope's amendment was passed by 121 to 114. Cairns voted in the minority; but excluding 23 members of the administration (of whom 2 abstained), 34 Liberal peers supported the government, 36 backed Stanhope, and 34 abstained, including many who must have been in London for the 'season', and therefore able to vote. Examining only the ranks above the baronage, whigs who supported Stanhope included Somerset, Grafton, Devonshire, Cleveland, Leinster, Clanricarde, Sligo, Cowper, Fitzwilliam, Fortescue, Grey, Minto, Dunraven, Lichfield, Russell and Halifax: Sutherland, Airlie, Chichester and Durham were the only equivalents to vote with the government. In addition, as Halifax pointed out to Gladstone, almost the entire peerage with Irish connections supported the amendment.[157]

The Lords' threatened action had meanwhile raised an intense countrywide storm. The Liberation Society, the less radical nonconformists like Charles Reed, the evangelical *Record*, and the Catholic hierarchy alike attacked it: the strength of the agitation seemed to threaten the position of the Lords itself.[158] This agitation made the cabinet resolve that concurrent endowment must be opposed at all costs. Clarendon and Lowe explained privately that had the cabinet not 'sold themselves' to the 'Scotch and nonconformist members', they would have been prepared to accept concurrent endowment in some form;[159] while Gladstone contended that for the government to attempt to concede on it would 'break up the Liberal party'.[160] The government whig Bessborough horrified the queen by telling her that he personally supported concurrent endowment, and had thought Gladstone's mode of raising the whole question unfortunate, but that he would not otherwise have attained the premiership.[161]

On 15 and 16 July, the Commons reasserted the main provisions of the original bill, and on the 16th, Tait, Grey, Stanhope, Salisbury, Cairns and Carnarvon decided not to insist on Stanhope's amendment. However, Cairns had always been willing to support the vaguer proposal to

[156] Davidson and Benham, *Tait*, ii, 35–6; Buckle, *Letters of Victoria*, i, 616–17.
[157] 28 July 1869, Gladstone papers, 44184, fo. 257.
[158] Bell, *Disestablishment in Ireland*, p. 151; Williams to Leader, 8 July 1869, Mundella papers; resolutions, Gladstone papers, 44421, fos. 82, 92; Lurgan to Gladstone, 1 July 1869, *ibid.*, fo. 83; Liberation Society memorandum, 28 June 1869, *ibid.*, 44610, fo. 107; Norman, *Catholic Church*, pp. 379–81.
[159] Clarendon to Odo Russell, 28 June 1869, Clarendon papers, 475, fo. 253; (Lowe) Carnarvon to Salisbury, 26 June 1869, Salisbury papers; see also (Halifax) Grey memorandum, 14–15 March 1873, Grey papers.
[160] 26 June 1869, Drus, *Journal of Kimberley*, p. 6.
[161] 8 July 1869, Buckle, *Letters of Victoria*, i, 616.

reserve a decision on the destination of the surplus, and had proposed an amendment to the preamble to that effect. The majority in the Commons in the vote on this had been unusually low, at seventy-two; nine English Liberals had voted for the amendment, and a large number of old whigs had abstained, headed by George Grey (who had spoken in favour of accepting Stanhope's clause).[162] This encouraged the peers, who decided to insist on the amendment,[163] as well as on others concerned with the financial position of the disestablished Church. On the 19th, Cairns, Salisbury and Carnarvon agreed to try to uphold the amendment on the preamble, with various other amendments, while yet more were dropped;[164] this compromise was accepted by a meeting of the Conservative peers on the 20th.

Carnarvon never remembered 'the temper of the House so keen on both sides' as in the debate on the 20th.[165] The amendment to the preamble was retained by seventy-eight votes, and this provoked an emotional reaction from Gladstone. He had already emphasised that to postpone the decision on the mode of appropriating the surplus would be a 'great moral and political evil';[166] when the Lords' decision was known, he resolved to wash his hands of the bill and to let the anti-concurrent endowment (and anti-Lords) clamour in the country take its course, and he appears to have told Granville to announce in the Lords that the government would renounce all responsibility for the question.[167] This decision was supported by no cabinet minister except Cardwell,[168] and was strongly opposed by Granville, Kimberley, Clarendon, Halifax, Bruce, Lowe and the chief whip, Glyn. Kimberley was appalled at Gladstone's lack of 'cool judgment'; Clarendon and Halifax considered it completely unjustifiable to throw up the bill because of difficulties with the preamble, especially since it exposed the Lords to such danger; George Grey maintained that to do so would lose the government 'the confidence of some of the best and staunchest of our friends in the House of Commons'. Only Granville's political finesse saved the situation: he provoked the Conservatives into enabling him to adjourn the House, thus delaying the implementation of Gladstone's order.[169]

At the cabinet meeting on the next day, Granville forced a reluctant Gladstone to continue with the bill, and not to insist on his version of the

---

[162] *Hansard*, cxcvii, 1922, cxcviii, 94, 15, 16 July 1869.
[163] Cairns to Disraeli, 16 July 1869, Disraeli papers, B/XX/Ca/77.
[164] Diary, 19 July 1869, Carnarvon papers.   [165] *Ibid.*, 20 July 1869.
[166] Morley, *Gladstone*, ii, 273–4.   [167] *Ibid.*, ii, 275–6.
[168] Buckle, *Letters of Victoria*, i, 622. Stanley thought that Argyll was also keen: Vincent, *Journals of Lord Stanley*, pp. 341–2.
[169] Drus, *Journal of Kimberley*, p. 7; Ramm, i, 38; Halifax to Granville, 21 July 1869, Granville papers, 30/29/64; Clarendon to Granville, 19 July 1869, *ibid.*, 30/29/55, fo. 22.

preamble.[170] The compromise which resolved the crisis was the work of Granville in the cabinet, and Halifax – behind whom lurked the queen, Tait and Grey – outside it. Their aim was to force Cairns to give up the other amendments (that giving the Church the Ulster glebes, and the Carnarvon amendment improving the terms of commutation) in return for an agreement to leave the controversial part of the preamble vague.[171] At the same time, it was agreed to accept Clause 68, which left open the mode of distribution of the surplus until a later date, but maintained that it was 'expedient' that it be 'appropriated mainly' to secular uses.[172] Once Gladstone had consented to this change, it was necessary only to get Cairns to agree to give up all the financial amendments affecting the disestablished Church alone, and to accept a compromise – slightly improving the terms of compensation for curates, and the commutation plan – which the cabinet had been prepared to concede for four or five days.[173] Cairns did this at the cost of offending his Orange backbenchers, and, in effect, forfeiting his leadership of the Lords. Behind Cairns, however, was Disraeli, who, it appears, pressed for a settlement because, as long as the Church question remained a running sore, the Liberal majority 'could not be broken'.[174]

The mass of the Liberal party was, of course, delighted that the principle of 'religious equality' had been confirmed, and that of the sanctity of Establishments damaged: the passage of the Act was marked by an unparalleled outburst of Liberal praise of the government. The Liberal press was enthusiastic (although the *Daily News* believed that the Lords had gained an extra million pounds for the Irish Church):[175] the *Economist* was typical in hailing disestablishment as a 'triumph' which 'put . . . an end to Protestant ascendancy'.[176] Nonconformists were also much fortified by the strength of the blow struck against Establishments; they now faced the discussion of English education – and the English Establishment – with renewed expectation.

Satisfaction at the outcome of the crisis was, on the whole, shared also by most whig-liberals: the whigs' publicly expressed dislike of the Irish

---

[170] Malmesbury heard that Granville had threatened to resign as leader in the Lords if the bill were given up: *Memoirs*, ii, 409.

[171] Grey to Cairns, 21 July 1869, Cairns papers, 30/51/14, fo. 70; Grey to Halifax, 29 July 1869, Hickleton papers, A 4 55; Halifax to Grey, 30 July 1869, Grey papers; Halifax to Granville, 21 July 1869, Granville papers, 30/29/64; Ramm, i, 37, 40–2; Davidson and Benham, *Tait*, ii, 41–2.

[172] See Bell, *Disestablishment in Ireland*, p. 153.

[173] Morley, *Gladstone*, ii, 273, 278. For the details, see Bell, *Disestablishment in Ireland*, pp. 153–4.

[174] 22 July 1869, Drus, *Journal of Kimberley*, p. 7. See Russell to Clarendon, 11 August 1869, Clarendon papers, 523.

[175] Bell, *Disestablishment in Ireland*, p. 155.   [176] 24 July 1869, p. 865.

Establishment had, after all, stretched back for thirty-six years. On the other hand, they already showed intimations of disquiet. Halifax doubted if, without concurrent endowment, there was much chance of Ireland's permanent pacification. Thirlwall was worried at the mode in which disestablishment had been effected, the triumph gained by the voluntary principle, and the popular excitement which had been aroused against Establishments in general. Lowe, in 1877, was to characterise the refusal of general endowment in 1869 as an 'injury . . . inflicted upon Ireland'. The Irish Protestant, Tyndall, was to say that all his faith in Gladstone's statesmanship disappeared when he settled the future of the Irish Church (whose position Tyndall recognised to be unjust) in such a disastrously unfair manner. The pessimistic Clarendon, late in 1869, claimed that the Act had 'alienated' the Protestants in Ireland, and merely made the Catholics 'more exacting and more insolently hostile to their Protestant fellow-countrymen'.[177] Amidst the Liberal rejoicing, no great weight should be attached to the whistling in the dark of a despondent Conservative journalist; but there was nonetheless a grain of truth in the comment, in *Blackwood's*, that the circumstances surrounding the passage of the Act had begun the 'severance' between 'Mr Gladstone and the old Constitutional Whigs', a severance that 'will go on widening . . . from day to day till a great gulf divides them'.[178]

---

[177] Halifax to Gladstone, 28 July 1869, Gladstone papers, 44184, fo. 257; Thirlwall, *A charge 1869*, pp. 38–40; (Lowe) *Hansard*, ccxxxv, 1890, 26 July 1877; *Professor Tyndall on party politics*, pp. 6–7; Clarendon to Odo Russell, 13 December 1869, Clarendon papers, 475, fo. 262.

[178] Gleig, 'Lords and Commons', p. 255.

6

Education, Establishment and Ireland, 1869–71

Irish disorder and the Vatican council, 1869–70

With the Irish Church question settled, the body of the Liberal party expected that the government would turn its attention to legislation for English education, and that, in doing so, it would attack clerical pretensions and denominational ascendency in as thoroughgoing a way as it had in 1869. Liberals did not anticipate that Gladstone's clericalism and Forster's Establishmentarianism would militate against the pursuit of such a policy. In consequence, the nonconformist optimism and enthusiasm of 1868–9 was, before the end of 1870, to be transformed into resentment, and then into mobilisation for fundamental educational and ecclesiastical reform. In parallel with the progress of this crisis, moreover, was the emergence of another. The peculiar nature of the Irish Church question had enabled pro- and anti-Catholic sentiment to be harnessed in the same cause, and had hidden the strains between them. In the discussion of educational policy, however, the innate anti-clericalism of much of the Liberal party was bound to be bolstered by a hostile consideration of the Irish dimension to the problem. This dimension was in any case apparent to all Liberals, given the Catholic pressure for Irish university reform; but it was further highlighted by two developments in 1869–70, which were anathema to British Liberalism. One was the increase of lawlessness in Ireland; the other was the papacy's attempt to recover its international standing by asserting its supremacy over the individual judgment of Catholics everywhere. Both these developments presented Gladstone's government with difficult problems to resolve; in resolving them, it began, although not yet fatally, to unsettle Liberal opinion in Britain, and to diminish the stock of confidence with which its supporters had invested it.

By late 1869, some resistance to Gladstone's concessionary Irish policy was already apparent within the cabinet. This took three forms.

There was discontent, expressed primarily by Clarendon, Lowe and Argyll, with the radicalism of the proposed Irish Land Bill – covered thoroughly in Steele's *Irish land and British politics*. But there was also a dispute about the proposed release of Fenian prisoners, and hostility to the political activities of the Catholic hierarchy.

To accompany the passage of the Irish Church Act, Fortescue and Gladstone had persuaded the cabinet to adopt a more lenient approach towards Irish disorder. Eighty-one Fenians were held prisoner by the British, and calls for their amnesty had won much popular support in Ireland at the 1868 election; nearly all the Irish Liberal MPs joined the Amnesty Association. In February 1869, the cabinet agreed to the release of forty-nine of the prisoners.[1] The release inspired problems: reports in the *Pall Mall Gazette* of the seditious language used by the liberated men upset Argyll and especially the queen;[2] while the mayor of Cork, in a speech given at a banquet for the freed prisoners, praised the Irishman who had attempted to assassinate the duke of Edinburgh, and was forced to resign.[3]

But the major future problem for the government stemmed from the firmness with which Fortescue ruled out the release of the remaining thirty-two civilian prisoners, who included 'almost all the main founders, leaders, and organizers of the Fenian movement . . . men who were deeply responsible for the attempted revolution of the last two or three years, and men . . . whose freedom would [not] be compatible with the public safety'.[4] It was therefore unfortunate that forty monster meetings demanding the release of these men were held in Ireland, during the next few months.[5] This worried the queen and some of the cabinet, and led to the first discussion of coercive legislation: Spencer, the viceroy, floated the idea of the local suspension of *Habeas Corpus*.[6]

In August 1869, Fortescue rejected the request of the Irish MP Maguire for further releases.[7] But in September, Gladstone, under Maguire's influence, aware of the volume of Irish protest, and eager to smooth the passage of a moderate Land Bill, brought the question forward again.[8] Fortescue once more emphasised that there was 'no

[1] Hoppen, *Elections in Ireland*, p. 465; Thornley, *Butt*, pp. 65–6.
[2] Matthew, vii, 45–6; 1 May 1869, Guedalla, *Queen and Gladstone*, i, 172; O'Hagan to Spencer, 27 March 1869, O'Hagan papers, D2777/8.
[3] MacDonagh, 'Last bill of pains and penalties'.
[4] *Hansard*, cxciv, 159–61, 22 February 1869.
[5] Thornley, *Butt*, p. 67.
[6] Guedalla, *Queen and Gladstone*, i, 172; 1 May 1869, Matthew, vii, 63; Spencer to O'Hagan, 4 May 1869, O'Hagan papers, D2777/8.
[7] Fortescue memorandum, 6 August 1869, Gladstone papers, 44121, fo. 151.
[8] 23 September 1869, Matthew, vii, 136.

possibility' of releasing the prisoners: to do so would further weaken the enfeebled Irish executive, while the decision would be received 'with indignation by all England and Scotland, by all the upper classes here, and by a great many quiet, lawloving people'.[9] Spencer agreed, as did the rest of the Irish executive, especially since crime and agitation were increasing.[10] Granville also considered that all thought of release must be postponed, in order to quieten whig fears already heightened by the prospect of a Land Bill[11] – fears expressed most strongly by Clarendon in a speech at Watford in late September, when he warned of the futility of giving in to mass pressure, and of the urgent need to reinforce the rule of law.[12] The queen raised objections to release of the prisoners, as did Grey – who wished to see the suspension of *Habeas Corpus* – for the old whigs.[13]

The cabinet decisively rejected release, and a number, led by Fortescue and Argyll, recommended the introduction of coercive legislation.[14] Fortescue and Bruce became more convinced of the need for coercion after the Tipperary by-election on 27 November, when the Fenian prisoner O'Donovan Rossa defeated the Liberal candidate, very largely on the prisoner issue.[15] But when, in mid December, Spencer requested the local suspension of *Habeas Corpus* in order to deal with the deteriorating situation, Gladstone would not countenance it, and argued that a conciliatory Land Bill, following on from the Church Act, would kill Fenianism.[16]

At the end of January, Fortescue, supported by the entire Irish executive, asked the cabinet to sanction legislation giving the viceroy the power to arrest and detain men in the affected districts without warrant, increasing the punishment for possession of firearms, and banning processions for three years.[17] But, unimpressive in advocacy, he lost the cabinet debate on the matter in early February: Spencer and Hartington considered a joint resignation in protest, and Clarendon was equally annoyed, believing that the state of Ireland was never 'so desperately bad', and that the release of the Fenian prisoners had weakened the

[9] Fortescue to Gladstone, 25 September 1869, Gladstone papers, 44121, fo. 163.
[10] Spencer to Gladstone, 12 October 1869, *ibid.*, 44306, fo. 158.
[11] 13 October 1869, Ramm, i, 67.
[12] Steele, *Irish land*, pp. 131–6.
[13] Buckle, *Letters of Victoria*, i, 628–9; Grey to Halifax, 2 November 1869, Hickleton papers, A 4 55.
[14] 26 November 1869, Matthew, vii, 180; Argyll to Gladstone, 26, 29 November 1869, Gladstone papers, 44101, fos. 81, 90.
[15] Fortescue to Gladstone, 30 November 1869, *ibid.*, 44122, fo. 30; Bruce to Gladstone, 1 December 1869, *ibid.*, 44086, fo. 58.
[16] 14 December 1869, Matthew, vii, 198; Gladstone to Bruce, 2 December 1869, *ibid.*, pp. 185–6, and 14 December 1869, Gladstone papers, 44538, fo. 18.
[17] Fortescue memorandum, 31 January 1870, *ibid.*, 44613, fo. 65.

government's authority.[18] But Gladstone was not only confident that the Land Act would destroy Fenianism:[19] he even floated the idea of releasing Rossa, to the incredulity of the whigs.[20] Kimberley thought him operating under a 'happy delusion',[21] and, with Fortescue and Spencer, was soon pressing again for coercion, after a severe deterioration in the situation, which resulted in 694 agrarian outrages in January and February and ten murders in February alone.[22] So were Brodrick in the *Times*, and Trollope in *St Paul's*.[23] Gladstone remained reluctant, partly on the grounds that it might prompt Bright's resignation from the cabinet;[24] he went so far as to ask Fortescue for proof that the current 'outrage and terror' was 'due to labourers rather than to occupiers of land'.[25] However, the cabinet finally agreed in March to the introduction of a Peace Preservation Bill, as long as it did not include powers for the local suspension of *Habeas Corpus*.[26] Clarendon still wanted 'stronger measures',[27] and so did much old Liberal opinion outside the cabinet.[28]

The decision to bring in a bill did not, however, please Irish Liberals, whose political plight had clearly helped to dictate Gladstone's conciliatory stance. The Tipperary and Waterford City by-elections in February were both won by Liberals, but only with single-figure majorities over home rulers; and in May 1870, G. E. Browne was to win the first victory for the home rulers when he gained Mayo, unopposed, on Moore's death. One Irish MP, the O'Conor Don, complained that Irish moderates who supported the Land Bill and the Peace Preservation Bill would lose the respect of their constituents until the remaining prisoners were released.[29]

A very similar division of opinion within the cabinet took place in attempting to formulate a response to the developments at Rome between late 1869 and May 1870.[30] Pius IX had summoned the Vatican council in the hope that it would sanction a declaration of papal infalli-

---

[18] Hartington to Devonshire, 3 February 1870, Chatsworth papers, 340, fo. 433; Clarendon to Odo Russell, 7 February 1870, Clarendon papers, 475, fo. 280.

[19] 17 February 1870, Matthew, vii, 239.

[20] 19 February 1870, Drus, *Journal of Kimberley*, p. 11; Matthew, vii, 240, 247; Spencer to Gladstone, 25 February 1870, Gladstone papers, 44306, fo. 219.

[21] 21 February 1870, Drus, *Journal of Kimberley*, pp. 11–12.

[22] 2 March 1870, *ibid.*, p. 12; Matthew, vii, 247–8; Spencer to Gladstone, 9 March 1870, Gladstone papers, 44306, fo. 233.

[23] (Leading article) 5 March 1870; 'What does Ireland want?', p. 294.

[24] 2 March 1870, Matthew, vii, 247.

[25] 9 March 1870, Gladstone papers, 44122, fo. 142.

[26] 5 March 1870, Drus, *Journal of Kimberley*, p. 12; Matthew, vii, 250.

[27] Clarendon to Odo Russell, 7 March 1870, Clarendon papers, FO 361, i, 341.

[28] Diary, 4 April 1870, Trelawny papers, 417, p. 108; Greg, 'Government dealing with Irish crime', pp. 562–76.

[29] O'Hagan to Spencer, 15 March 1870, O'Hagan papers, D2777/8.

[30] Matthew has already traced this well in 'Gladstone, Vaticanism'.

bility, which it finally did in the spring of 1870. This was a course of action which was especially irritating to Gladstone, to whose aspirations for the unity of the Church catholic such a declaration would constitute a severe blow. Pressured by Acton, Gladstone in mid January floated to Clarendon the idea that the government should intervene and protest;[31] but Granville, Clarendon, Bright, Argyll, Lowe and Odo Russell (the minister at the Vatican; brother of Hastings and Arthur, and nephew of Earl Russell) all argued that the declaration would do more good than harm, and Gladstone was decisively outpointed in cabinet.[32] Prussia and Austria did not approve of concerted action: Clarendon opposed Acton's view that France and England could achieve anything alone.[33] Gladstone and Clarendon clashed again in April, in debating how far Britain should go in supporting the French government's rather tame warning to the pope.[34] Gladstone wished to give written support to the French note of remonstrance: Clarendon, whose policy had been to limit interference at the Vatican to an unofficial comment through Odo Russell, strongly objected. To Gladstone's disquiet, Clarendon circulated the cabinet about the matter; they agreed unanimously with Clarendon – as did the queen.[35]

The cause of this division lay in diverging perceptions, not only of Catholicism and the temporal power (discussed in Part I), but also of the way in which to pacify Ireland. Gladstone regarded the declaration of papal infallibility as the 'most portentous . . . of all events in the history of the Christian Church'[36] and wished to 'save the Pope and the Roman Church from themselves'.[37] But he was also aware that the declaration would unleash a storm of anti-Catholic feeling, and would discourage English opinion from assenting to further concessions to the Catholics on many fronts. He thought that the passage of the Glebe Loans Bill (an offshoot of the Irish Church Act), and the repeal of the Ecclesiastical Titles Act, would be threatened (although both were in fact achieved without difficulty). More importantly, as he also predicted, increased

---

[31] 13 January 1870, Matthew, vii, 220; Clarendon to Gladstone, 15 January 1870, Clarendon papers, 501, fo. 125.

[32] 28 January 1870, Matthew, vii, 229; Odo Russell to Clarendon, 24 January 1870, Clarendon papers, 487, fo. 120; Ramm, i, 88.

[33] Matthew, vii, 238, 243, 245; Clarendon to Gladstone, 23 February 1870, Gladstone papers, 44134, fo. 152.

[34] Clarendon to Gladstone, 5 April 1870, *ibid.*, 44134, fo. 174; Matthew, vii, 270; Odo Russell to Clarendon, 17 April 1870, Clarendon papers, 487, fo. 172.

[35] Clarendon to Gladstone, 28 April 1870, Gladstone papers, 44134, fo. 196; Matthew, vii, 284; Clarendon to Odo Russell, 2 May 1870, Clarendon papers, 475, fo. 291; Ponsonby to Clarendon, 1 May 1870, *ibid.*, 509.

[36] Gladstone to Moriarty, 24 May 1872, Gladstone papers, 44434, fo. 146.

[37] Gladstone to Clarendon, 21 May, 24 August, 7, 14 September 1869, Clarendon papers, 497, fo. 190, 498, fos. 22, 42, 46.

resistance to the Irish Land Bill and to any educational legislation was likely.[38] He knew that many Liberals were disposed to welcome the declaration on the grounds that it would rebound on the popularity of the Catholic Church, and make it politically difficult to recognise Catholics' educational rights – and thus would damage securities for all other sects' denominational teaching as well.[39]

The cabinet whigs did not go so far; but they maintained that a protest from a Protestant government would drive lay Catholics to seek the protection of the pope more than ever, thus playing into his hands.[40] Moreover, in discussing the pacification of Ireland, they placed less weight on the importance of recognising the Catholic educational grievance, and more on the need for political management. Rather than protesting against the pope's temporal power, they valued, or at least accepted, his aid in discouraging disorder in the Irish countryside; they argued that he had influence over the clergy and might, if approached with tact, mitigate the latter's hostility.[41] Clarendon had already persuaded Odo Russell to intervene twice at Rome, in June 1869 and January 1870, in order to secure an expression of the pope's goodwill to the government and of his hostility to Irish agitation;[42] again in March and April 1870, Clarendon's persistent concern was for the pacification of Ireland.[43]

By April, the consequences for British politics of the pope's activity were becoming apparent. Gladstone was irritated by the opposition from 'right-wing' Liberals – led by Palmer, with covert support from government whigs like Dufferin – to the Irish Land Bill.[44] This opposition, of course, also had a life of its own, independent of religious considerations; but Gladstone was undoubtedly right to blame the publicity surrounding the Council for the success of the motion of the anti-Catholic Conservative MP Newdegate, which asked for a select committee in order to investigate practices in convents and monasteries. Newdegate's motion was passed by 131 votes to 129, with the support of the *Times* and of 44

[38] 1 December 1869, Matthew, vii, 184; 8 January 1870, Lathbury, ii, 51.

[39] 25 March 1870, Matthew, vii, 263.

[40] (Granville) Ramm, i, 88; Clarendon to Odo Russell, 31 May 1869, Clarendon papers, 475, fo. 246; Odo Russell to Clarendon, 16 June 1869, *ibid.*, 487, fo. 67.

[41] (Granville) Ramm, i, 88; Clarendon to Gladstone, 23 February 1870, Gladstone papers, 44134, fo. 152.

[42] Norman, *Catholic Church*, pp. 358, 395; Clarendon to Odo Russell, 28 June 1869, Clarendon papers, 475, fo. 253; Odo Russell to Clarendon, 7, 13, 24 January 1870, *ibid.*, 487, fos. 112, 114, 120.

[43] Clarendon to Gladstone, 6, 23 March 1870, Gladstone papers, 44134, fos. 162, 169; Clarendon to Odo Russell, 28 March 1870, Clarendon papers, FO 361, i, 344.

[44] Gladstone to Cardwell, 8 April 1870, Gladstone papers, 44119, fo. 108; to Manning, 16 April 1870, Matthew, vii, 277–8. See Palmer to Dufferin, 9 April 1870, Dufferin papers.

Liberal MPs, mainly anti-Catholic Scotsmen, but also including Thomas Chambers, Dodson, Lubbock and Playfair.[45] Gladstone foresaw that the declaration of infallibility might well provoke 'a repetition of the fury of 1850–1' against popery, and would certainly establish enormous 'obstacles to political and social justice' in Ireland – and by implication to his religious scheme for England.[46] The deliberations of the Council therefore not only aroused what Gladstone described as 'crude opinion . . . working blindly about like hot and cold moist and dry in Ovid's Chaos';[47] they also made Gladstone himself particularly anxious about securities for denominational freedoms – and it was in reacting against crude anti-Catholic opinion that Gladstone was pushed into major pledges concerning both English and Irish education.

The crisis over English and Irish education in the 1870 session

The Liberal government was certain to introduce an Elementary Education Bill early in its tenure of office.[48] Although a few radicals hoped that the state would impose a completely new system of schools, the basis of the government bill – which followed the wishes of the great bulk of public opinion – was that existing voluntary schools would form the core of the national system, wherever they satisfied non-denominational government inspectors and operated a conscience clause. School boards would be established in all areas where the education provided by such schools was insufficient, if the insufficiency had not been remedied within one year; the boards would have the power to levy rates to build new schools. From the beginning of the discussion, in October 1869, there was controversy about the degree of religious teaching to be allowed in the new and existing schools. Forster's memorandum of October asserted that, while it would not be fair to tax ratepayers for the education of other denominations, it would be legitimate to tax them for 'the Bible, and the acknowledgment of Christianity' – which he wished to be compulsory – in schools founded by the boards; and legitimate also to tax them for the secular part of the education given in denominational schools already established.[49] But the government bill eventually provided that school boards were to be left free to decide whether they would aid all schools equally, or none – in other words, that schools founded by

---

[45] See *Hansard*, cc, 906–8, 29 March 1870; Arnstein, *Newdegate*, pp. 125–33, and pp. 144–8, 160–2 for the consequences.

[46] Matthew, vii, 261, 263–4, 277–8.

[47] To Manning, 16 April 1870, Matthew, vii, 277–8.

[48] For the most detailed account of the framing of the bill, see Roland, 'Elementary Education Act', Oxford B.Litt.

[49] Forster memorandum, 21 October 1869, Gladstone papers, 44611, fo. 99.

boards would have the option of offering denominational teaching, as well as existing schools. Gladstone forced Forster round to this policy out of a desire to defend the position of denominational teaching – against undenominationalism – in as many areas as possible.[50]

The bill, introduced into parliament in February 1870, thus embodied a compromise between Gladstone's defence of denominationalism, and Forster's opposition to secularism; but it took little account of the anti-clerical opinions of the bulk of the party. It therefore excited considerable criticism, especially from nonconformists, on the grounds that it allowed state aid to 'clericalism' in schools.[51] However, the complaining Liberals were divided about the merits of any alternative solution. The radical- and nonconformist-dominated National Education League had held its first annual meeting in October 1869, and had been forced to compromise between its secularist and undenominationalist wings by demanding that the reading of the bible, 'without note or comment', should be the maximum allowable extent of religious teaching in the new system.[52] Most anti-clerical whig-liberals were fervent undenominationalists.

But, although this division of opinion prevented agreement on alternatives, Liberal critics of the February bill were able to unite in exploiting one damaging aspect of the plan: its implications for the state support of Catholic teaching in Ireland. The most effective mode of attacking the bill's favouritism in existing *English* denominational schools was by alleging that an *Irish* educational settlement was being planned and that the 1870 bill would be a model for it. Concern about the consequences of the measure in Ireland was expressed by men as dissimilar as Mill, Bryce, Fawcett and Froude[53] – and, most devastatingly, in a hard-hitting Commons speech on 16 March by the young nonconformist MP Winterbotham. He pleaded for an end to the Liberals' alliance with ultramontanism, and demanded that, in order to secure the future of Irish Protestantism, the League's compromise on bible-reading should be adopted in the English bill.[54]

In an attempt to rally anti-clerical Liberals in opposition to the bill, the Birmingham MP Dixon tabled an amendment on the second reading, protesting against the local option clause on the grounds that it gave the Church control of education in most rural districts. His amendment was

---

[50] See Roper, 'Forster's memorandum of 21 October 1869'.
[51] Dale, *Dale*, pp. 275–6; Adams, *History of elementary school contest*, pp. 215–17.
[52] Adams, *History of elementary school contest*, pp. xix–xxi.
[53] Mill to Dilke, 23 February 1870, Dilke papers, 43897, fo. 10; Bryce to Freeman, 13 March [1870], Bryce papers (English), 9, fo. 140; Fawcett, in *Hansard*, cc, 281–3, 18 March 1870; (Froude) Derby diary, 15 March 1870, 15th earl of Derby papers.
[54] *Hansard*, cxcix, 1963–80.

supported by Miall, Richard and Winterbotham; it was also defended by Harcourt for the anti-clerical whig-liberals.[55] However, Mundella, Jacob Bright and Cowper-Temple opposed Dixon's amendment, arguing that the religious difficulty was of little significance, compared to the practical need for a national system; but Mundella did advocate a timetable conscience clause, so that the religious teaching would be confined to the beginning and end of the school day.[56] On 18 March, Gladstone announced that the government would accept the timetable conscience clause, and that where the schoolmaster gave religious instruction to the majority, the school would also be available to the minority persuasions;[57] although these concessions did not satisfy the radicals, Dixon withdrew his amendment and the second reading was agreed.

A prolonged debate now developed within the party, forcing the repeated postponement of the committee stage of the bill – which finally took place in mid June. But the bulk of party opinion drifted – just as Harcourt had predicted – towards undenominationalism, as the most effective mode of countering the clericalism threatened by the government scheme.[58] Russell – in what Gladstone called a 'most ill timed' intervention – and Harcourt both strongly advocated undenominationalism in the *Times* and elsewhere.[59] Although Gladstone ridiculed it, as allowing 'a new sort of Pope in the Council Office' to dictate the content of the religion that children would receive,[60] he recognised that its attractiveness was enhanced, in Liberal eyes, by the unfavourable light in which the Vatican council had cast Catholic denominational teaching.[61] Furthermore, the undenominational policy came to attract support as the only one likely to solve both the English and Irish *higher* education dilemmas. By the time of the committee stage on the bill, the government had been severely pressed by Liberal backbenchers on both these latter issues – with the consequence that anti-clerical feeling in the party had markedly intensified.

The 1868 University Tests Bill – a private member's bill introduced by Coleridge and Bouverie – had proposed to abolish all tests for university fellowships, and to remove all the restrictions which the state had formerly imposed on colleges' freedom of action with regard to college

[55] *Ibid.*, cc, 213–27, 18 March.
[56] *Ibid.*, 236–44 (Mundella), 247–50 (Bright), 287–9 (Cowper-Temple), 18 March.
[57] *Ibid.*, 301–2.
[58] Gardiner, *Harcourt*, i, 215–16.
[59] 26 March 1870, Matthew, vii, 265; Roland, 'Elementary Education Act', pp. 341–6; *Times*, 28 March 1870, p. 5.
[60] 24 March 1870, Lathbury, ii, 138.
[61] Gladstone to Acton, 28 March 1870, Gladstone papers, 44093, fo. 133.

fellowships. Gladstone had voted for the second reading, although he had not spoken in its favour.[62] He was now convinced that the present settlement could not be defended against Liberal pressure, and that that pressure must instead be directed into safe channels.[63] He resisted requests from Cardwell and Coleridge that the same bill, when introduced in 1869, should be a government measure, despite Coleridge's argument that the party was united on it as on nothing else;[64] but he supported the bill explicitly because it gave securities for continued denominational religious education at university level.[65] However, the Conservative majority in the Lords defeated it.

By 1870, party pressure for the abolition of university tests had become irresistible. The Lords' action had led to a countrywide agitation, in which provincial nonconformists and academic liberals were prominent;[66] in February 1870, 105 Liberal MPs urged the government to adopt the abolition bill. Gladstone had already agreed to do so, provided that it was no more controversial than that of 1869,[67] and on this basis the government introduced it in April.

Gladstone had abandoned all inclination to maintain the test, and his hesitation had been partly the result of a desire to ensure agreement with the universities about the details, in order to prevent backbench Liberal MPs – who were likely to demand a more anti-clerical bill – from winning general support for their views (a precaution that was to prove only too necessary). But he had hesitated also, because the acceptance of tests abolition in England placed him in a most difficult position in dealing with Irish university education. Here his sense of a grievance had always been more developed than that of most Liberals, even before the Vatican council: in the light of the impending declaration of papal infallibility, and of the failure of two major pieces of concessionary legislation to stem the rising tide of Irish disorder, it was far more difficult to resist Fawcett's annual resolution for the abolition of tests in Trinity, Dublin. Fawcett's proposal was designed to settle the university question by ensuring the victory, throughout the system, of mixed education, to which he argued that Catholics could not justifiably object. He had brought it forward in August 1869, intending it to press the government

[62] 1 July 1868, Matthew, vi, 607.

[63] See Ward, *Victorian Oxford*, pp. 253–4.

[64] Coleridge memorandum, 17 December 1868, Gladstone papers, 44138, fo. 87; Cardwell to Gladstone, 19 December 1868, *ibid.*, 44118, fo. 298.

[65] *Hansard*, cxcvii, 796–8, 29 June 1869.

[66] Ward, *Victorian Oxford*, p. 258.

[67] Matthew, vii, 168, 221, 261–2; Fowler to Gladstone, 5 February 1870, Gladstone papers, 44424, fo. 245.

into action in 1870, as seemed consistent with Gladstone's vociferous opposition to the Conservatives' proposed Charter of 1868.[68]

By 1870, Fawcett's hand had been strengthened, not only by the events at Rome, but by developments in Ireland. The bishops reasserted their opposition to mixed education in August 1869, arguing that if the government's claim to legislate according to the wishes of the Irish was true, it must sanction denominational education. English reaction to their manifesto, from the *Nonconformist*, whigs like Clarendon, and the queen, was alike hostile.[69] Secondly, Trinity herself announced that she now favoured the abolition of tests and the institution of undenominational education throughout the university system. She opposed any move to supplant the Queen's colleges by denominational ones, as a 'retrograde step . . . subversive of true freedom'. This line was taken ostensibly because Irish Church disestablishment had freed Trinity from observing the restrictions on her fellowships, but also because she feared that Gladstone's government might appropriate her endowments in order to implement a far-reaching 'denominational' reform of Irish university education.[70]

Trinity's decision opened up a tactical possibility for the Conservatives, which Derby (the new, 15th, earl) was not slow to see. If they now adopted the undenominational policy in discussing Irish education, they would split the Liberals, dividing Gladstone, Fortescue and the denominationalists from the bulk of the anti-clericals, a move correct 'both in principle and policy'.[71] Liberal coolness towards further concessions to Catholicism, and the Conservatives' drift towards undenominationalism, thus combined to make the government's position extremely uncomfortable. Kimberley expected as early as March 1870 that Irish education would be the 'rock' on which it would, in due course, be 'wrecked'.[72]

Because of these difficulties, the government proposed no measure on the matter in 1870, although it had stood second on the cabinet's list of suggested bills.[73] On 1 April, Fawcett introduced his resolutions, on behalf, he said, of a party strongly in favour of 'united and undenominational education'.[74] The debate was marked by a widely publicised maiden speech by the MP for Dublin university, Plunket, seconding the

---

[68] *Hansard*, cxcviii, 1197, 3 August 1869.
[69] Norman, *Catholic Church*, pp. 436–7; Clarendon to Gladstone, 8 September 1869, Gladstone papers, 44134, fo. 5; Guedalla, *Queen and Gladstone*, i, 201, 203.
[70] Cairns to Gladstone, 19 February 1870, Gladstone papers, 44425, fo. 15: Cairns was Chancellor of the Dublin university.
[71] Diary, 16 March 1870, 15th earl of Derby papers.
[72] 29 March 1870, Drus, *Journal of Kimberley*, pp. 12–13.
[73] Gladstone papers, 44637, fo. 125.   [74] *Hansard*, cc, 1090–7, 1 April 1870.

motion for the Conservatives; he took up Trinity's new line.[75] Gladstone, in reply, launched into another attack on Mayo's 1868 university policy; but he also insisted that Fawcett's plan would not give Catholics adequate influence on the governing body, and that it went no way towards tackling their grievances.

Most importantly, he felt it necessary to emphasise that the question of control of university policy was in fact one of confidence in the government – a fruit of his ill-temper which had lasting consequences.[76] He later argued that, unless he had threatened in this way, the government would have been defeated and his educational policy ruined; Glyn had prophesied 'defeat and disgrace' in any vote on Fawcett's motion.[77] The threat, which made it almost impossible for the government subsequently to avoid legislation on Irish universities, was roundly attacked by Clarendon (who had also been annoyed by the more veiled threat of resignation which Gladstone had made during the discussions on the Irish Land Bill); Gladstone admitted, in reply, that 'this use of neck-or-nothing remedies is a great calamity. It is playing the last card.'[78]

Gladstone's action on the Irish university question naturally alarmed whig-liberals, and created a still stronger anti-clerical feeling on the matter of English university reform. On the second reading of the University Tests Bill on 23 May, Gladstone expressed his hope that colleges of all sects and of none would affiliate to Oxford and Cambridge: he stressed that the bill was not an attempt to stamp out denominational religious teaching.[79] Dissentient Liberals had other ideas.

The attack on the committee stage came from three directions, but they had the common ambition, as Gladstone perceived, of 'destroy[ing] the established system' and 'enthroning . . . undenominationalism'.[80] The amendments aimed to interfere with statutes and the independence of existing colleges, and to impose terms on which future colleges might affiliate to the university. The first attacked the exclusion of college headships from the provisions of the bill: Gladstone thought the matter of no great importance, and the cabinet and Commons agreed to the change (the clause was of little significance, because most headships were also limited to men in Holy Orders by college statute).[81] Secondly, more importantly, Fawcett proposed the abolition of the whole class of clerical fellowships, a change which would interfere with college

---

[75] *Ibid.*, cc, 1097–113.   [76] *Ibid.*, cc, 1128–31.

[77] Matthew, vii, 269–70, 281–2.

[78] Clarendon to Gladstone, 21 April 1870, Gladstone papers, 44134, fo. 188; Matthew, vii, 281–2.

[79] *Hansard*, cci, 1225–34.

[80] 17 June 1870, Matthew, vii, 309–10.

[81] *Ibid.*, pp. 306, 309, 313; *Hansard*, ccii, 1391–3, 4 July 1870; Ward, *Victorian Oxford*, p. 259.

statutes. The government was able to resist this move by citing nonconformist opposition, expressed in a deputation of December, to tampering
with the internal arrangements of colleges; even so, although Miall and
Morgan spoke and voted with the government, seventy-nine MPs
opposed it.[82]

Thirdly, Harcourt instituted a potentially far more damaging attack
on the whole range of government policy, by questioning the wisdom of
allowing the foundation of future denominational colleges: if tests were
to be abolished in existing institutions, he claimed that it was hypocritical to allow exclusiveness to prevail in new ones. He did not fail to point
out the precedent that the acceptance of an amendment of this sort
would create for Irish policy.[83] Gladstone and Coleridge argued that the
endowments of existing colleges had been given in very different circumstances: colleges founded in future for a specifically religious purpose
must therefore be exempted from state interference, at least for the next
few generations.[84]

Having made his point, Harcourt withdrew his amendment and proposed something far milder, that any Charter for the incorporation of a
future college should be open to inspection by parliament for a thirty-day
period. This led to another ill-tempered exchange, which issued in
Gladstone pledging to introduce the proposal as a separate bill, in order
to allay discontent. But the Scot Aytoun, and Morrison, then revived
Harcourt's motion in order to safeguard 'mixed education' in Ireland,
and, in crushing the motion, Gladstone was forced to throw his whole
weight against it: it was a 'question of the greatest importance, for we
cannot consent to interfere with the future freedom of persons who may
wish to found institutions of this kind. I cannot state too plainly or too
strongly why we object to any measure of the kind.' Given such language,
it was no wonder that academic liberals still distrusted his 'ecclesiasticism' and wished that they had the strength to 'push . . . him aside and
go . . . straighter to the mark'.[85]

In the Lords, Salisbury deflected the prospect of a vote on the second
reading by carrying a proposal to establish a select committee, which
would examine possible safeguards for religious instruction: this was
secured by 95 votes to 79, and the bill accordingly failed to pass.

These disputes were occurring contemporaneously with those on
English elementary education. Since March, there had been demon-
strations and counter-demonstrations on the latter subject. A number of

---

[82] *Hansard*, cci, 1968–73.   [83] *Ibid.*, cci, 1961–3.
[84] *Ibid.*, cci, 1964–6, ccii, 1395.
[85] Goldwin Smith to Bryce, 16 July 1870, Bryce papers (English), 16, fo. 15.

nonconformists and radicals were anxious to promote secularism; Illingworth and Holyoake were among those who spoke when deputations called on Gladstone and Forster to advocate the policy.[86] Gladstone was known privately to sympathise with them; he wrote to Dean Hook to ask him to reprint his 'secularist' proposals of 1846.[87] But nonconformists in general proved reluctant to play Gladstone's game, not wishing to divide forces, as the espousal of secularism would have forced them to do. Richard told him in late April that most nonconformists would settle for a policy which allowed no religious instruction more explicit than bible-reading.[88] Opinion in the party more generally was strongly anti-secularist: the defence of religious teaching had brought Shaftesbury, Hughes, Buxton, Cowper-Temple and Akroyd into alliance with Conservative peers like Salisbury and Northumberland, and the Catholic Norfolk, on the platform of the National Education Union on 8 April.

Party pressure for undenominationalism grew steadily.[89] Convinced by the drift of opinion, Forster and de Grey submitted proposed amendments to the cabinet in mid May, which were designed to stem the flow of criticism. Some were relatively uncontroversial, and Gladstone agreed to them: but one forbade the school board to allow teaching from catechisms or formularies in state-founded schools.[90] Gladstone saw this as 'very grave', and told de Grey that it was grossly irresponsible to make such a change unless the cessation of agitation as a result was certain: he issued a muted threat not to consent to the proceedings.[91] Forster and de Grey would not give way: de Grey maintained that Baines, Jacob Bright and Hughes would support it, and Forster forecast that, unless the government agreed to it, the pressure from backbench Liberals in favour of mere bible-reading in all schools, state-aided as well as state-founded, would be irresistible.[92] Gladstone nonetheless won an interim victory in the cabinet.[93]

This, however, did not last long. On 24 May, Brand told Gladstone that public opinion inside and outside the House had moved clearly against both 'secular' and 'dogmatic' teaching, and would be satisfied only by a statute preventing schools from offering 'contentious teaching

---

[86] McCabe, *Holyoake*, ii, 52–3; Illingworth, *Fifty years of politics*, pp. 23–4.

[87] 14 April 1870, Gladstone papers, 44538, fo. 126.

[88] Richard to Gladstone, 23 April 1870, *ibid.*, 44426, fo. 155.

[89] See, for example, the duchess of Argyll to Gladstone, [2?] May 1870, *ibid.*, 44426, fo. 192.

[90] De Grey to Gladstone, 19 May 1870, *ibid.*, 44286, fo. 88; Forster to de Grey, 18 May 1870, *ibid.*, 44157, fo. 20.

[91] 13, 16 May 1870, Matthew, vii, 289, 291–2.

[92] De Grey to Gladstone, 19 May 1870, Gladstone papers, 44286, fo. 88; Forster to de Grey, 18 May 1870, *ibid.*, 44157, fo. 20.

[93] 21 May 1870, Matthew, vii, 293.

for or against specific religious doctrines'; only this, in his view, would secure long-term party unity.[94] Gladstone replied that the proposal to 'include religion and to exclude dogma' had never been achieved by 'any State or Parliament': but Brand stuck to his guns.[95] George Grey was advocating a similar solution to Forster.[96] On 25 May, deputations from the Baines faction, from the Wesleyans, from Shaftesbury – accompanied by headmasters like H. M. Butler and Abbott – and from Mundella, all pressed in that direction.[97]

Gladstone counterattacked on 29 May with a memorandum aiming to pour cold water on bible-reading, exclusion of catechisms, or any other 'undenominational' solution. The first would involve 'the creation of a new State Religion by the method of reduction or excision'; the second asked the Church to surrender a valuable part of her teaching apparatus without demanding a similar concession from nonconformists. Any legislation of this sort '*savours* of interference with the perfect freedom of religious teaching, which is a principle of the utmost consequence to the wellbeing of the State'. It would also discriminate against the Catholics; it was neither practised in Ireland, nor demanded in Scotland; and to centre religious teaching on the bible – the focus of rationalist attack on Christianity – and not on the formularies which gave it 'moral and practical support', endangered securities for the future hold of the religion. He cautiously advocated the separation of religious and secular education, on the grounds that it would prevent ratepayers from contributing to the teaching of another man's religion.[98] But this did not appease George Grey, who insisted that the bulk of the party desired some undenominational solution, and advocated Jacob Bright's amendment – which allowed mere bible-teaching, on condition that it was not 'used or directed in favour of or against the distinctive tenets of any religious denomination' (Jacob was John Bright's brother). George Grey declared the Catholic problem to be irrelevant, since Catholics would not accept that school boards had a right to interfere with their schools; and he criticised Gladstone's preferred scheme for failing to ensure a religious education for 'destitute and neglected children'.[99] Granville supported compulsory bible-reading in school-hours and voluntary denominational instruction outside them.[100]

---

[94] Brand to Gladstone, 24 May 1870, Gladstone papers, 44194, fo. 124.
[95] Gladstone to Brand, 24 May 1870, *ibid.*, 44194, fo. 129; Brand to Gladstone, 26 May, *ibid.*, fo. 131.
[96] George Grey to Gladstone, 7 June 1870, *ibid.*, 44162, fo. 320.
[97] Matthew, vii, 295; Roland, 'Elementary Education Act', pp. 394–6.
[98] Matthew, vii, 297–300.
[99] George Grey to Gladstone, 7 June 1870, Gladstone papers, 44162, fo. 320.
[100] 9 June 1870, Ramm, i, 101.

Gladstone then approached Miall and Winterbotham to see if nonconformists would accept the secular solution. They agreed that Cowper-Temple's amendment, allowing some sectarian teaching, but excluding catechisms and formularies, was 'intolerable'. They preferred secularism to bible-reading – which, they recognised, would discriminate against Catholics in England and Ireland, who would have to pay rates in order to support schools of which they did not approve. But they also admitted that most nonconformists would happily accept bible-reading or bible-teaching, and that these might be more practicable compromises within the party as a whole. Gladstone's negotiations therefore failed to advance the secularist cause.[101] Forster renewed his advocacy of the 'Cowper-Temple' solution, as the most conservative proposal which might satisfy Liberal opinion;[102] and on 14 June, the cabinet forced Gladstone to agree that the government should espouse Cowper-Temple's amendment, as the lesser of two evils, the other being simple bible-reading. He had 'never made a more painful concession to the desire of unity',[103] but he was under no illusion as to the cause of the increased pressure for undenominationalism: the 'shadow' of the Irish education question.[104] In return, he forced the cabinet to agree that school boards should be compelled to raise the level of aid given to denominational schools which accepted the conscience clause, as long as the aid was understood to be for secular instruction only. Lowe and Goschen strongly objected to this, because of the likely outcry from ratepayers; and Lowe, in an attempt to minimise anti-clerical criticism of Gladstone's move, then secured a fundamental alteration in the system. He persuaded the cabinet to agree to remove from the boards – and thus the ratepayers – the burden of supporting denominational schools (but not board schools). The promised increase in aid to denominational schools was to be provided instead by raising the level of the Privy Council grant by 50 per cent.[105]

After this change was made, and as the bill entered the committee stage, the government encountered two further difficulties. Firstly, Richard, pushed by the failure of the radical strategy into a more hostile position, proposed an amendment on behalf of radical nonconformists, including Dale and Crosskey.[106] This condemned the increase in the

---

[101] Dale, *Dale*, pp. 278–80; Matthew, vii, 304, 305, viii, 67–9; Dixon to Harcourt, 4 June 1870, Harcourt papers, 203, fo. 44.
[102] Reid, *Forster*, i, 501–3.
[103] June 1870, Rathbone, *Rathbone*, p. 273; see also Matthew, vii, 310.
[104] To Manning, 22 June 1870, Matthew, vii, 312–13.
[105] *Ibid.*, pp. 307–9; Lowe to Gladstone, 15 June 1870, Gladstone papers, 44301, fo. 146; Sylvester, *Lowe and education*, pp. 129–31.
[106] Dale, *Dale*, p. 278.

grant to denominational schools, recommended the institution of compulsory attendance, and insisted that 'religious instruction should be supplied by voluntary effort'; it was generally taken to be an amendment in favour of secularism.[107] Sixty-two radicals supported it: Morgan and Winterbotham charged that the Cowper-Temple clause would not exclude dogma from the schools, and therefore did not avert the threat that the government would cede control of the Irish education system to Cullen.[108]

Richard's Liberal opponents numbered 242 (there were also 181 Conservatives), and their spokesmen were equally uncompromising. Cowper-Temple saw that the 'two extremes' of Richard and Hook agreed in repudiating 'religious instruction by laymen', but was certain that this was 'not the view of the Liberal party'. Playfair was not prepared to eject the bible from schools, when it was the only means of 'giving poetry to the . . . existence' of children; McArthur asserted that there was a 'common Christianity . . . apart from creeds and sects . . . wide enough to embrace all'. Reed maintained that Richard's scheme would 'tend to train up a nation of infidels'; Baines insisted that undenominational schools could teach the 'full-hearted Christian doctrine of mutual love and duty', as did Mundella and Morley.[109] Mundella, McArthur and Harcourt (but not Playfair) also protested about the 50 per cent increase in the grant to denominational schools.[110] While opposing secularism, Morley and the quaker Pease considered the Cowper-Temple clause to be too conservative, and hoped to see more checks instituted against denominational teaching, for example those included in Jacob Bright's amendment to prevent any dogmatic teaching.[111]

This last viewpoint was widespread: Trevelyan resigned from the government on those grounds, arguing that it had contradicted the policy of religious equality outlined in the 1869 Irish Church Act.[112] The full force of Liberal feeling on the subject was most apparent when Jacob Bright's amendment was discussed on 30 June. It was opposed by Cowper-Temple and Playfair, who asserted that the Cowper-Temple amendment was adequate and that, while Bright's motion was a good one, it would create unnecessary dissension in the localities.[113] But it was advocated by George Grey, on the grounds that the bill as it stood pro-

---

[107] *Ibid.*, p. 280.
[108] Morgan, *Hansard*, ccii, 672, 21 June; Winterbotham, *ibid.*, 842–3, 23 June.
[109] *Ibid.*, 650, 554, 673–6, 819, 834, 896–904, 542–6.
[110] *Ibid.*, 646, 556–7.
[111] *Ibid.*, 1244–6.
[112] To Gladstone, 21 June 1870, Gladstone papers, 44335, fo. 23; Trevelyan, *Trevelyan*, pp. 91–2.
[113] *Hansard*, ccii, 1276–7, 1278–9.

vided insufficient security against denominationalism; Gladstone was very annoyed that Grey supported the 'foolish motion'.[114] It was supported by 132 Liberals in all; 133 more abstained. The amendment was defeated by 251 votes to 130; 132 Conservatives ensured government victory, but they joined only 91 non-government Liberals.[115] Gladstone had attacked the amendment as introducing a 'new kind of State religion', and made it clear that 'I must entirely decline to be responsible' for it. This was a blatant threat to give up the bill;[116] and, given this, the vote was a resounding humiliation for him.

The arousal of provincial Liberalism, 1870–1

'Practical' educationalists were contented with the form of the 1870 Education Act,[117] but radical opponents were not mollified: Dixon, Chamberlain, Harcourt and Miall all protested about it, even if they could agree only on its faults – the lending of state support to denominationalism – and not on the remedy. Miall delivered a famous condemnation on the third reading of the bill, claiming that, although nonconformists were 'the heart, and . . . the hands of the Liberal cause in the country' and a 'fair moiety' of the party, they had had to 'pass through the Valley of Humiliation' in opposition to the bill. Their cry would henceforth be ' "once bit, twice shy" '.[118] Nonconformist displeasure with the Act was intensified by the decision of the National Society to cooperate with the new system, accept the timetable conscience clause, and qualify for building grants: denominational schools made over three thousand applications for the latter by December 1870 (thirteen hundred were later withdrawn).[119] Furthermore, the first school-board elections, held in the autumn, resulted in widespread victories for candidates who favoured the teaching of religion in schools. The Liberals suffered a great setback in Birmingham, owing to bad organisation; at Leeds and Sheffield, boards decided to teach from the bible, and this policy was also adopted in London, on a motion agreed by the Conservative W. H. Smith and the evangelical nonconformist Samuel Morley, with only three contrary votes.[120]

---

[114] *Ibid.*, 1277–8; 4 July 1870, Matthew, vii, 320.

[115] Adams, *History of elementary school contest*, p. 226, slightly recalculated.

[116] *Hansard*, ccii, 1281.

[117] Mundella to Leader, 2, 24 July 1870, Mundella papers.

[118] *Hansard*, cciii, 741–4, 22 July 1870. See also Dixon, *ibid.*, 737–8; Chamberlain to Harcourt, 2 July 1870, Harcourt papers, 59, fo. 2.

[119] Adams, *History of elementary school contest*, pp. 232, 243–5.

[120] *Times*, 9 March 1871, p. 6; Travis, 'Leeds school board', pp. 83–6; Richards, 'Religious controversy and the school boards', pp. 190–3.

Secularism was hardly ever discussed at the 1870 school-board elections, and its unpopularity led Chamberlain to stop the discussion of a secularist motion at the League's annual meeting in October 1870, knowing that, if successful, it would much divide and weaken the radical forces.[121] There was little prospect of any challenge to government educational policy, until a broader plank on which to base opposition could be found – as was to happen in 1871. Meanwhile, radical frustration could be combated and energies dissipated only by an agitation in a related field – against the Church Establishment itself. Spurred on by the disappointments of the 1870 session, and yet eager to follow up the successes of 1869, the Liberation Society held a series of well-attended meetings in Bradford, Manchester, Liverpool and London to promote the cause; Miall had announced that he would raise the question in the Commons in the 1871 session.[122] The Congregational Union unanimously passed a resolution condemning the Education Act and calling for disestablishment (a minority, led by Binney, walked out in protest).[123] In the first five months of 1871, the Liberation Society staged another 150 meetings throughout the country.[124]

This agitation in turn fuelled that for the abolition of university tests in England, which, consequently, led backbenchers to display even more anti-clerical feeling in 1871 than they had on Jacob Bright's motion at the end of the 1870 session. As Coleridge had predicted,[125] the effect of the year's delay in settling the English tests question was that academic liberals and many nonconformists pressed for a clause repealing all those college statutes which established clerical fellowships. Both groups felt that these statutes intensified competition for the remaining fellowships, and made the governing bodies of the colleges unduly reactionary.[126] Coleridge himself thought clerical fellowships doomed.[127] When faced, in December 1870, with a demand from two advanced Cambridge Liberals that the 1871 bill should embrace the abolition of clerical fellowships, Gladstone refused. He threatened on a number of occasions that the inclusion of such a clause might well release the government from all its pledges on the bill: it would be 'beyond anything odious'.[128] By means of similar private threats, he persuaded influential nonconformists to support the introduction of the bill in its old form.[129]

---

[121] Garvin, *Chamberlain*, i, 121; Adams, *History of elementary school contest*, pp. 238–41.
[122] Miall, *Miall*, p. 311.   [123] Ingham, 'Disestablishment movement', p. 44.
[124] *Ibid.*, pp. 44–5.
[125] Coleridge to Gladstone, 2 December 1870, Gladstone papers, 44138, fo. 107.
[126] Ward, *Victorian Oxford*, p. 260; *Report of the Manchester conference*, pp. 72–83.
[127] To Gladstone, 2 December 1870, Gladstone papers, 44138, fo. 107.
[128] Matthew, vii, 411, 412–13, 420, 431–2.
[129] Gladstone to Carvell Williams, 16 January 1871, Gladstone papers, 44539, fo. 136; Carvell Williams to Gladstone, 21 January 1871, *ibid.*, 44429, fo. 74.

Gladstone himself introduced the bill on 10 February 1871, and with all his authority emphasised that he wanted the matter settled quickly and without raising extraneous questions.[130] However, a winter of anti-clerical agitation in the provinces had pushed backbenchers to such lengths that, in committee, there were party rebellions to a degree rare in Liberal history. Stevenson, a presbyterian MP, moved that non-churchmen should be allowed to take degrees in divinity, and was backed by Playfair, Buxton, Samuelson of Banbury and Horsman: Samuelson said that he would rather that the bill did not pass, than that so half-hearted a measure should be enacted. The government defeated Stevenson's amendment, against its own backbenchers, and with a great deal of Conservative help, by 185 votes to 140. Fawcett then moved for the abolition of clerical fellowships and clerical headships. Osborne Morgan and Fitzmaurice supported him: Coleridge and Gladstone had to maintain, for the government, that the fellowships issue must be raised and settled in a more systematic way at a later date (as it transpired, by a Royal Commission). Gladstone, furious at 'another piece of *Fawcettism*', said, later in the evening, that he could not have supported any bill which did not give 'ample securities for religious education in the Universities and Colleges'.[131] Nonetheless, Fawcett was defeated by only 182 votes to 160; as he said, he had never seen a Liberal government opposed by so many Liberals. The 162 Liberals (including tellers) who opposed the government were defeated by 112 Conservatives, 30 office-holding Liberals, 11 Irishmen, and only 31 backbench British Liberals.[132] Gladstone succeeded, later, in forcing the Commons to accept a Lords amendment, stipulating that the governing body of every college should provide sufficient religious instruction for all members of the Church of England *in statu pupillari* (he altered it to make it refer only to existing colleges, so as not to force the clause on future Roman Catholic or non-conformist ones). Again, he won by only 197 votes to 165, with the vast majority of Liberals against him.[133]

The bill was eventually accepted by the Lords, despite Conservative complaints (especially concerning the absence of a new religious test for academics who undertook positions of responsibility). Gladstone noted that the bill had been brought 'to a form more favourable to the Church than I had recently thought possible', but recognised that this had been

---

[130] *Hansard*, cciv, 146.

[131] *Ibid.*, 527; Bailey, *Diary of Lady F. Cavendish*, ii, 95.

[132] For the debates on both amendments, see *Hansard*, cciv, 500–28.

[133] In the survey of MPs' voting behaviour, the results of which are displayed in Part I, attitudes to university policy are assessed on the basis of the first two of these three divisions.

achieved only by his applying great and scarcely tolerable pressure against the party's natural inclinations.[134]

Anti-clerical feeling within the Liberal party spilled over into discussion of other questions. There was relatively little debate about English elementary education in 1871, beyond the ritual opposition of sixty-six Liberal MPs to the New Code implementing the 50 per cent increase in the grant to voluntary schools.[135] However, the government found itself in difficulty over its Scottish Education Bill, which was introduced by the Lord Advocate, Young. This aimed to extend the existing parochial system, and it left local boards free to aid existing denominational schools or not, as they chose. There was, therefore, considerable disquiet at this scheme: the scientist Sir William Thomson, when chairing a large public meeting in Glasgow against it, maintained that, by the bill, Scotland was 'to be made the stepping-stone from the system of mild denominationalism in England, to utter and destructive denominationalism in Ireland'.[136] Thomson favoured compulsory bible-teaching; some other Liberals, like Campbell-Bannerman, were secularists. On the other hand, the General Assembly of the Church of Scotland, and the Begg faction of the Free Church, wished to see a less radical bill, and desired safeguards for teaching according to 'use and wont'. Over two hundred amendments from the various camps were tabled, and the government was probably relieved not to have time to consider the matter further.[137]

There was further Liberal activity in 1871, in reaction to the perceived inadequacies of the 1869 Endowed Schools Act. This had sanctioned the appointment of three commissioners, whose task was to reorganise the government and scope of those schools whose freedom of action was severely limited by restrictive statutes and bequests. The commissioners' activity proved extremely divisive, because in a large majority of cases the original endowments had been given for religious purposes. Clause 17 of the Act specified that a person's religious opinions should not affect his qualification for membership of the governing body of an endowed school, but Clause 19 exempted certain classes of school – cathedral schools and others clearly intended to fulfil a denominational purpose – from this provision, and, more sweepingly, from interference by the commissioners in any aspect of their religious education and worship. It was very difficult to determine which schools should be given 'Clause 19' status.

---

[134] 12 June 1871, Matthew, vii, 507.   [135] *Hansard*, cciv, 1808–12.
[136] Thompson, *Kelvin*, ii, 589–91.
[137] *Hansard*, cciv, 197, 946; Spender, *Campbell-Bannerman*, i, 38; Omond, *Lord Advocates*, p. 276; Smith, *Begg*, ii, 468–70.

In June 1871, Lubbock, with the support of Hughes and Rathbone, introduced a bill to repeal Clauses 19 and 14 of the Act: the latter excluded from its purview schools maintained by the endowments of the Church of England, Oxford and Cambridge universities, the quakers or the Moravians, and schools whose endowments had been bequeathed less than fifty years before 1869. Lubbock based his case for repeal on the importance of releasing education from outdated dogmatic restrictions. He made a distinction between endowments in favour of *religion*, that is, 'endowments which tended to raise the character without fettering the intellect of man', and endowments 'for the maintenance and propagation of particular opinions': the latter were a 'bribe' to inveigle future generations into accepting religious views which progress had disproved, or rendered irrelevant. He also maintained that the fifty-year exemption period should apply, in due course, to all schools established after 1869 – for which the Act had not provided.[138] The bill was attacked by the high churchman Acland, as well as by the Conservatives (and by Pease for the quakers). Forster also opposed it, on the grounds of fairness to the denominations who administered the schools; but Fitzmaurice and Harcourt supported it, the latter accusing the government of once more taking a line contradictory to 'the true principles of the Liberal party'.

The second reading was defeated by 222 votes to 64, but the government then ran into criticism from opposite quarters over its endowed-schools policy. On the one hand, nonconformists began to agitate against the appointment of clerical governors *ex officio* under the commissioners' new schemes, as had happened in thirty-six of the first forty cases. The Law Officers subsequently declared that the *ex officio* appointments were illegal, and the relevant schemes were withdrawn.[139]

This merely intensified opposition from the other flank, the Lords, engineered by Salisbury. He did not accept the Law Officers' ruling (on the grounds that Clause 17 was intended only to prevent the introduction of a religious test for membership, not *ex officio* appointments themselves), and led the Lords to refuse assent to three schemes which complied with the ruling.[140] But he also condemned the commissioners' activities more generally. He concentrated on one test-case, that of Emanuel Hospital, Westminster, which was managed by the Corporation of London. Against the opposition of nearly all the whigs, he persuaded the Lords to defeat a scheme for its reorganisation, and a similar one for the girls' school, the Grey Coat Hospital.[141]

---

[138] *Hansard*, ccvii, 2, 14 June 1871.   [139] Dale, *Dale*, pp. 284–5.
[140] *Hansard*, ccxii, 1857–64, 26 July 1872.
[141] *Ibid.*, ccvii, 862–902, 30 June 1871. For the Grey Coat Hospital, see Fletcher, *Feminists and bureaucrats*, pp. 77–8.

The matter was to return to parliament in 1873. More importantly, the redistribution of endowments inspired criticism of the commissioners throughout the country;[142] in particular, it created great hostility to the Liberals in the City of London. Arthur Hobhouse, one of the commissioners, himself wrote that it excited fears for 'property' in general, and that, both among the London financial establishment and the 'trading classes', this fear swung the balance of voting in 1874 decisively against the Liberals, who had previously been supreme in the City.[143]

Few leading Liberals outside London defended the old endowed schools, although the government's attack on them undoubtedly lost votes throughout the country. There was much more division within the party on the motion proposed by Miall in May 1871 for the disestablishment of the Church of England. Winterbotham had accepted minor government office in March 1871, but this had not pacified the nonconformists, and Miall won eighty-nine votes in favour of the motion. In reporting the debate, both the *Times* and the *Daily News* averred that disestablishment would come before the end of the century.[144] This assumption was bolstered by the ambiguous language used by Bruce and Gladstone during the debate: both of their speeches displayed what critics viewed as unhealthy regard for majority opinion within the party, in whatever direction that might drift. Bruce ventured that 'no Government would be justified in [recommending disestablishment] without the assurance of success'; Gladstone told Miall that if he wished to win a majority in the Commons, he must undertake 'the preliminary work of converting to those opinions the majority of the people of England'.[145] These statements were eagerly exploited by the Conservatives, who used them to depict the Liberals as inconstant on all matters on which public excitement might be aroused.[146] In fact, Gladstone had made a staunch defence of the Establishment in his speech, as he was to in the two succeeding debates in 1872 and 1873. His argument was always that the nation was deeply attached to the Church; that many millions of only occasional churchgoers looked to it for comfort; and that, while the success of the nonconformist sects had deservedly been handsome, this did not suggest that a great national and historic institution, suddenly disestablished, would be able to cope as well. The Church had played such a large part in the history of England that, without it, that history became 'a chaos, without order, without life, and without meaning'; its

---

[142] *Ibid.*, pp. 75–6.
[143] Hobhouse and Hammond, *Hobhouse*, pp. 44–5.
[144] Miall, *Miall*, p. 317.
[145] *Hansard*, ccvi, 504, 571, 9 May 1871.
[146] See e.g. Disraeli at Glasgow in 1873: *Addresses*, p. 23.

disestablishment might have effects as cataclysmic as had the overthrow of political institutions on the continent.[147]

Gladstone had no option, politically, but to oppose disestablishment, even had he wanted to advance it on other grounds, which he did not. But nonconformist pressure nonetheless increased. At the annual conference of the Liberation Society in May 1871, Illingworth suggested that, once further measures of parliamentary reform had been passed, disestablishment should be made 'a *sine qua non* of adhesion' to the party.[148] In July, the Liberation Society formed a sub-committee in order to campaign for disestablishment among working-men.[149]

This assault on the Establishment in England naturally inspired a reaction from its defenders. It led to the foundation of the Church Defence Institution, by the Conservative bishop Ellicott; Tait became honorary president, and all but five (Gladstonian) bishops vice-presidents. But it also excited much whig-liberal interest in Church reform, in the hope of blocking nonconformist calls for disestablishment, and of improving the Church's effectiveness as an antagonist of rationalism. Controversy centred on the prayer-book, and on the role played by the Athanasian Creed in church services. The Ritual Commission in its fourth report, issued in 1870, was nearly unanimous in favouring a reform in the position of the Creed, but it had been unable to agree on a positive recommendation. A minority had advocated the appendage of an explanatory note that the 'damnatory clauses' of the Creed constituted only a 'solemn warning', but a larger number, led by Tait, then petitioned for a more radical treatment, Tait requesting the Creed's discontinuance in public worship.[150] Moreover, backbench Liberals were anxious for legislation to promote revision of the prayer-book in other ways. Gladstone was strongly opposed to all arguments for parliamentary interference in this class of question, but the only principle on which he could hope to withstand their pressure was a refusal to involve the government in controversial ecclesiastical issues, and a determination to adopt only those bills supported by Convocation; this subservience to a clerical parliament, however, displeased some whig-liberals even more.

The problem of checking enthusiasm for Church reform arose in 1870 in discussion of the bill which gave effect to the proposals of the third report of the Commission, aimed at reforming the table of lessons in order to tailor services more to the needs of working-men. This bill had been accepted by Convocation, but, in the Commons, it encountered

[147] *Hansard*, ccvi, 559, 9 May 1871, ccxii, 572, 2 July 1872, ccxvi, 37, 16 May 1873.
[148] Hamer, *Politics of electoral pressure*, p. 119.
[149] Ingham, 'Disestablishment movement', p. 47.
[150] Marsh, *Victorian Church in decline*, pp. 40–3.

opposition from whigs and evangelical Conservatives, led by George Grey, Bouverie, Locke King, W. H. Smith, Sandon and Russell Gurney: most of them wanted a more wide-ranging measure, reforming the prayer-book as well as the table of lessons. The government withdrew the bill; when Smith asked if it would introduce a bill in 1871 in accordance with the recommendations of the *fourth* report, Gladstone considered it unlikely that such reform would be sufficiently uncontroversial to fall within its ambit. This was unlikely, not least, because Gladstone had in 1866 declared himself 'emphatically' against all revision of the prayer-book by parliament.[151]

In January 1871, Tait published a letter to the bishop of London, urging that a change in the rubric regulating the use of the Athanasian Creed should be embodied in legislation.[152] This suggestion affronted Gladstone, since it made the prospect of passing the Table of Lessons Bill without major parliamentary interference very small; he stressed again that the matter was too controversial for adoption by the government, that men were not agreed on the reform of the Creed, and that any 'sharp contest within the walls of Parliament' on ecclesiastical matters 'would inflict heavy wounds upon the Church as a National Establishment'.[153] The matter was complicated by the fact that the fourth report had recommended various uncontroversial reforms, which the leading bishops were eager, and the government prepared, to sanction; but, as Gladstone realised, backbenchers of both parties would force the Creed question into discussion of any such bill if introduced. Even the cabinet followed Gladstone's line of argument only reluctantly. De Grey agreed with him; but Bruce thought that, if the government did not suggest a course, parliament would probably agree to expunge the Creed from the prayer-book, and considered it unlikely that it would hand over its power in the matter to the initiative of the Church. Cardwell and Fortescue were anxious to reform the Creed, as were Kimberley and Forster if (as they conceded was doubtful) it could be done without encouraging pressure for disestablishment.[154]

---

[151] *Ibid.*, pp. 102–3; *Hansard*, ccii, 1602, 7 July 1870, cciii, 99, 1693, 12 July, 8 August; 2 August 1870, Matthew, vii, 337–8; Gladstone to Keble, 8 January 1866, Gladstone papers, 44536, fo. 6.

[152] Davidson and Benham, *Tait*, ii, 129; letter in *Times*, 11 January 1871, p. 4.

[153] To Tait, Matthew, vii, 429–30, 436–7, and 15 November 1870, Gladstone papers, 44539, fo. 74.

[154] Bruce to Gladstone, 28, 30 December 1870, 12, 24 January 1871, Gladstone papers, 44086, fos. 180, 182, 44087, fos. 3, 9; Gladstone to Bruce, 28 December 1870, 11 January 1871, *ibid.*, 44539, fos. 117, 130; de Grey memorandum, 16 January 1871, *ibid.*, 44286, fo. 108; Cardwell to Gladstone, 18 January 1871, *ibid.*, 44119, fo. 210; Fortescue memorandum, 22 January 1871, *ibid.*, 44122, fo. 217; Kimberley to Gladstone, 24 January 1871, *ibid.*, 44224, fo. 109; Forster memorandum, 25 January 1871, *ibid.*, 44157, fo. 34.

As predicted, there were signs, from the beginning of the parliamentary session, of pressure for the inclusion in the Table of Lessons Bill of proposals regarding the Creed, especially from Smith in the Commons, and Stanhope, Portman, Harrowby and Ebury in the Lords.[155] But the government introduced the same bill as in 1870, despite protests at its unadventurousness from Shaftesbury, Ebury and Grey. Cairns led the Lords to omit the reference in the bill to Convocation's approval of it, much to Gladstone's irritation.[156] However, the many obstacles to the passage through the Commons of so limited a bill were all beaten off – although J. D. Lewis, Rylands and Locke King advocated far-reaching amendments, and although nonconformists like Illingworth and Graham sneered at Convocation's claims to represent the Church, and asserted parliament's superior right to legislate for it. Illingworth told the Speaker that he and his friends had adopted this line in order to make churchmen feel that 'their position of dependence on the State' was 'intolerable'. However, some radical speakers, like Mundella, attacked the idea of parliamentary interference in Church affairs.[157]

The Creed controversy intensified; but the activity of Liddon and Pusey, who threatened to secede from the Church if Tait's plan of diminishing the Creed's role in worship was accepted, ensured that the latitudinarian assault was beaten off, for fear of splitting the Church – to the intense irritation of Tait and Stanley.[158]

The climate in which parliamentary discussion of educational and ecclesiastical questions unfolded in 1871 was also, of course, affected by consciousness of Irish Catholic pretensions, especially in education. This had been especially apparent in the debate on the abolition of English university tests; the stridency of backbench behaviour during those discussions can be attributed largely to a determination not to sanction any measure which would encourage clerical control of Irish higher education. At the back of MPs' minds had been the awareness that the government must soon tackle the question of Irish education; and, in 1871, Fawcett once more introduced his motion for the abolition of tests in Trinity, Dublin. Since the declaration of papal infallibility, moreover, the context in which discussion of Irish affairs took place had worsened,

[155] *Hansard*, cciv, 317, 1265, 16 February, 3 March 1871.
[156] *Ibid.*, 1969, 14 March 1871; Gladstone to Bickersteth, 28 March 1871, Gladstone papers, 44539, fo. 184; Hatherley to Gladstone, 14 March 1871, *ibid.*, 44205, fo. 191.
[157] For this paragraph, see *Hansard*, ccv, 1455, 20 April 1871, ccvii, 103, 957, 15, 30 June 1871; Marsh, *Victorian Church in decline*, p. 105; diary, 13 October 1871, 15th earl of Derby papers; Bruce to Gladstone, 25 May, 8 June 1871, Gladstone papers, 44087, fos. 14, 15; Tait–Gladstone correspondence, 24–5 June 1871, *ibid.*, 44330, fos. 192–9; Gladstone to Ady, 30 June 1871, *ibid.*, 44540, fo. 63.
[158] See Liddon, *Pusey*, iv, 228–58; Davidson and Benham, *Tait*, ii, esp. 135–6, 148–9.

partly because Gladstone had become more than usually afflicted by embarrassing allegations of personal favouritism to Catholicism, and partly because of the government's weak response to the growth of lawlessness in Ireland.

Gladstone had faced abuse from extreme Protestants before, in connection with his behaviour on the Ionian islands (see p. 175), and his sister's Roman Catholicism. When Bruce, the home secretary, had prevented the evangelical orator Murphy from speaking in Tynemouth and Birmingham in 1869, men of this stamp accused the government of bias towards the Catholics;[159] its reluctance to repeal the 1869 Party Processions Act (which hit Ulster Protestants particularly hard) inspired similar allegations.[160] Now, the Italian threat to the pope's personal safety created further difficulties in this respect.

Italian troops had entered Rome on 26 October 1870, thus completing the unification of the country; but there was much alarm in Ireland at the loss of the pope's temporal power.[161] In mid November, Edmund Dease, an Irish MP, wrote to Gladstone, in conformity with the wishes of constituents, to ask the government to support the restoration of the pope's temporal power as a necessary bulwark of his spiritual dignity and authority.[162] Gladstone had written an article in the *Edinburgh Review* which, among other things, celebrated the fall of the pope's temporal power;[163] and, although the article was anonymous, it was widely assumed to be his. Bishop Moriarty criticised it, and told Monsell, the leading Irish MP in the government, that the Liberals were in danger of losing Irish support if they did not defend the temporal power.[164] A split between Liberals and Catholics on the papal issue would, as Monsell saw, damage the chances of settling the educational question satisfactorily, and would give a great boost to the newly founded home-rule movement.[165]

Gladstone's proposed reply to Dease was discussed at a cabinet meeting on 25 November. Kimberley, for one, was worried by the tone of his draft, which he thought would create a 'jealous Protestant feeling' among English and especially Scottish Liberals.[166] Nonetheless, Gladstone replied to Dease on 30 November. He stated that the government would not interfere with the civil government of Rome, and trusted

[159] Arnstein, 'Murphy riots', pp. 65–9.   [160] Macknight, *Ulster as it is*, i, 185–6.

[161] Norman, *Catholic Church*, pp. 414–15.

[162] Dease to Gladstone, 15 November 1870, Gladstone papers, 44428, fo. 205.

[163] 'Germany, France, and England'.

[164] Monsell to Granville, 1 December 1870, Granville papers, 30/29/74, fo. 253.

[165] Monsell to O'Hagan, 18 November [1870], Teeling/O'Hagan papers, 17871.

[166] Matthew, vii, 406; Kimberley to Gladstone, 26 November 1870, Gladstone papers, 44224, fo. 98.

the dispositions of the Italian government; but that it had taken steps to afford protection to the pope if necessary (in mid August, Britain had stationed HMS Defence off Civitavecchia in order, partly, to provide such a refuge).[167] The most controversial sentence in his letter, however, maintained that the government considered 'all that relates to the adequate support of the dignity of the Pope, and to his personal freedom and independence in the discharge of his spiritual functions, to be legitimate matter for their notice'.[168] Gladstone told Monsell that any stronger commitment would have overthrown the government;[169] but, as it was, a storm arose when Gladstone published the letter in the *Times* on 8 December. Protest was especially strident in Scotland, where the Dease letter was regarded as one further indication of the government's determination to make concessions to the hierarchy on Irish education.[170] The cabinet twice discouraged Gladstone from publicly clarifying his position, but agitation in Scotland only slowly died down; there were protests from the Scottish Reformation Society and from MPs like Kinnaird. In England, the *Daily News*, and Chambers of Marylebone, were similarly upset.[171] Gladstone's stance was also blamed for the defection of a number of Newry presbyterians from the Liberal party, and the unopposed gain by the Conservatives at the by-election there in January 1871.[172] In Ireland, in fact, there was disaffection not only from Protestants, but, in the other sense, from Catholics: Martin, the nationalist candidate, won the Meath by-election on 17 January.

Allegations that Gladstone was a closet Catholic continued, and MPs occasionally jumped on these bandwagons.[173] Protestant extremists requested Gladstone to confirm or deny allegations that he had been received into the Roman Catholic Church, and his ambiguous replies did not please the evangelical *Rock*.[174] In August 1871, the Scottish Liberal MP Macfie went so far as to ask in parliament if it was true, as a newspaper had suggested, that the government had agreed to allow the pope

---

[167] Matthew, vii, 344, 346, 361–2, 378, 384; Ramm, i, 122.
[168] 30 November 1870, Matthew, vii, 410.
[169] 6 December 1870, Gladstone papers, 44539, fo. 92.
[170] Guthrie to Argyll, 9 December 1870, *ibid.*, 44428, fo. 270.
[171] Lathbury, ii, 54; Gladstone memorandum, 16 December 1870, Gladstone papers, 44759, fo. 241; Candlish to Gladstone, 22 December 1870, *ibid.*, 44428, fo. 294; (Scottish Reformation Society) 6 January 1871, *ibid.*, 44429, fo. 12; Kinnaird to Gladstone, 5 January 1871, *ibid.*, 44230, fo. 73; 10, 25 December 1870, Ramm, i, 183, 192.
[172] Corry to Disraeli, 17 January 1871, Disraeli papers, B/XX/Co/70.
[173] See Gladstone papers, 44431, fos. 100, 112, 146, 275, 277; 44432, fo. 50; 44434, fos. 58, 183, 220; 44436, fos. 64, 77, 104, 247; Charley to *Globe*, letter dated 19 August 1871, in Glynne–Gladstone papers, 100/1; pamphlets of Anti-Papal League, in *ibid.*; *Seventh annual report of the Leicester Anti-Romanist Association*, pp. 18–19.
[174] Aston to Gladstone, 18 December 1870, Gladstone papers, 44428, fo. 286; anon., *Mr Gladstone and the Birmingham Protestant Association*.

to live on a Scottish island.[175] But campaigns of this sort were probably far less damaging to the government than was Gladstone's attitude to Irish crime.

In August 1870, Gladstone asked Spencer and Fortescue to consider releasing the remaining Fenian prisoners, on the grounds that Fenianism would lose its sting after the passage of the beneficial legislation of 1868–70, that the agitation for release was, temporarily, 'absolutely dead', and that it was important to release the men before it revived. The United States Congress was also eager for release, but probably the most important consideration in impelling Gladstone to reopen the issue was his desire to retain Bright in the cabinet, which, in turn, was in order to pacify the nonconformists. Bright, ill, unhappy with the constraints and detail of official life, had announced his intention to resign in protest at the British government's guarantee to Belgium, but had not yet done so.[176] Gladstone gave Motley, the American ambassador, the impression that the release of the prisoners was practically certain: he assumed that Spencer would agree.[177] But Fortescue and Spencer were both opposed, especially given the creation of a potentially 'Red and revolutionary' republic in France, which might arouse sympathy meetings in Ireland.[178] Despite continued pleas from Gladstone, the Irish executive remained firm, and at a cabinet on 30 September a decision was postponed until some experience of agrarian feeling had been gained.[179]

Within a month, however, Gladstone was pressing Fortescue again, in response to a letter from the Irish MP, McCarthy Downing.[180] In early November, he won his case, against the wishes (not in all cases expressed) of at least six cabinet ministers, and the queen.[181] Spencer's fatalism, and unwillingness to continue resisting his leader, greatly weakened the opposition to release.[182] Only eight civilians were to remain in prison, for the Manchester offences of 1867; of these, six were on five-year sentences and due for liberty in 1871. The release, however, was delayed until 15 December, since the Black Sea crisis had now blown up: Bruce did not want the prisoners freed while there was a chance of

---

[175] *Hansard*, ccviii, 782.
[176] Matthew, vii, 352, 353; Walling, *Diaries of Bright*, pp. 343–5.
[177] 4, 18 September 1870, Matthew, vii, 352, 362.
[178] Fortescue to Gladstone, 9 September 1870, Gladstone papers, 44122, fo. 161; Spencer to Gladstone, 13 September 1870, Strachie papers, 325 CP 2/15.
[179] Gladstone to Spencer, 29 September 1870, Gladstone papers, 44539, fo. 38; 14, 30 September 1870, Matthew, vii, 360–1, 372.
[180] Gladstone to Fortescue, 28 October 1870, Strachie papers, 324 CP 1/135; 5 November 1870, Matthew, vii, 392–3.
[181] Kimberley, Lowe, de Grey, Hartington, Argyll and Halifax. Matthew, vii, 396–7; Argyll to Gladstone, 7 November 1870, Gladstone papers, 44101, fo. 312; Halifax to Gladstone, 14 November 1870, *ibid.*, 44185, fo. 86; Buckle, *Letters of Victoria*, ii, 84.
[182] Spencer to Fortescue, 12 November 1870, Strachie papers, 324 CP 1/145.

war with Russia, which would excite Fenian agitation.[183] The liberation inspired criticism inside and outside parliament;[184] nor had Gladstone managed to prevent Bright from resigning, although he did persuade him to announce that his retirement was not the result of any policy quarrels with the government.[185]

Less than one month after the release, Spencer reported that Ribbonism was rampant in Westmeath and that order had broken down. Kimberley, Argyll and Halifax followed him in anticipating the need for a local suspension of *Habeas Corpus*, against Gladstone's opposition.[186] In early February, Spencer and the entire Irish executive formally requested it: remedial legislation was all very well, but the government's primary function was to 'protect life and maintain its own supremacy'.[187] This argument was supported by the new chief secretary, Hartington,[188] whose appointment, in December 1870, to succeed Fortescue (who replaced Bright at the Board of Trade) was of major significance in stiffening the conduct of Irish policy.

Gladstone reacted to the request with 'horror and dismay' and refused to accept it; but only Granville, Hatherley, Lowe and Cardwell were with him.[189] He secured a compromise at the cabinet on 18 February, whereby the government would recommend that a select committee should investigate the state of affairs in Westmeath: local suspension of *Habeas Corpus* would follow if a case were made. Hartington thought this course absurd:[190] furthermore, in his lukewarm speech announcing the appointment of the select committee, Hartington made plain his differences with his leader by calling it 'the height of insanity' to suppose that 'the establishment of religious equality or the passing of a law regulating the tenure of land in Ireland would put a stop to the Ribbon conspiracy'.[191]

Owing to concern at potential opposition from Irish MPs, the government had to renege on the original proposal to make the committee secret.[192] Even so, there was antagonism from two flanks: from Irish Liberals who thought the existing laws sufficient, and from Conserva-

---

[183] Bruce to Gladstone, 25 November 1870, Gladstone papers, 44086, fo. 159; Fortescue to Gladstone, 1 December 1870, *ibid.*, 44122, fo. 175.

[184] Brodrick, *Memories and impressions*, p. 168; (Grey) *Hansard*, cciv, 1604, ccv, 1925–6, 9 March, 1 May 1871. See also Earl Fortescue to Brereton, 19 December 1870, Brereton papers, F 27 70; Corry to Disraeli, 19 December 1870, Disraeli papers, B/XX/Co/69.

[185] Matthew, vii, 398–9, 400, 408–9, 415, 417.

[186] Spencer to Gladstone, 10 January 1871, Gladstone papers, 44307, fo. 1; memorandum, 23 January 1871, *ibid.*, 44760, fo. 4; 12 January 1871, Matthew, vii, 431.

[187] 6 February 1871, Gordon, *Spencer*, i, 89; Spencer to Hartington, 10 February 1871, Chatsworth papers, 354, fo. 14.

[188] Hartington to Gladstone, 6 February 1871, Gladstone papers, 44143, fo. 52.

[189] Holland, *Devonshire*, i, 84–5; 7 February 1871, Matthew, vii, 444–5.

[190] 15, 18 February 1871, Matthew, vii, 449, 450; Holland, *Devonshire*, i, 85.

[191] *Hansard*, cciv, 1002, 27 February 1871.   [192] Drus, *Journal of Kimberley*, p. 21.

tives and some whig-liberals who alleged that to proceed by select committee constituted unpardonable executive weakness. Gladstone argued that the establishment of the committee was necessary in order to prove to justifiably suspicious Irish MPs that the existing law was insufficient: the 'union of sentiment' with men like McCarthy Downing must survive.[193] He alleged again that the alternative policy for Ireland was Disraeli's, of 'all sorts of endowments for all sorts of religions'.[194] The Conservatives, for their part, maintained that the government cut a laughable image in Ireland. Disraeli – whose false teeth fell out during his speech – jibed that Gladstone had persuaded the British people that, as far as Ireland was concerned, he possessed the 'philosopher's stone': but, under his influence, MPs had 'legalized confiscation, consecrated sacrilege, and condoned high treason; we have destroyed churches, we have shaken property to its foundations, and we have emptied gaols; and now he cannot govern a county without coming to a Parliamentary Committee!'[195] The vote to establish the committee was carried by 256 votes to 175; but 19 Irish MPs and 3 English radicals opposed the government from one position, and there were many backbench whig-liberal abstentions from the other. Disraeli – who maintained that the Conservatives could not yet profitably form a government – had to leave the House with 50 Conservatives in order to prevent government defeat.[196] Kimberley thought Liberal backbenchers 'very angry' with the government: so did Trelawny, a representative of the abstainers, who wished to see the immediate suspension of *Habeas Corpus*. Knatchbull-Hugessen, a junior minister, thought the cabinet's policy 'a lamentable exhibition of Cowardice'.[197] The Westmeath committee's report, advocating local suspension, was circulated on 17 April, and the government then introduced and carried the Protection of Life and Property in Certain Parts of Ireland Bill: this empowered the Lord Lieutenant to suspend *Habeas Corpus* locally at any time within the next two years, and to arrest anyone suspected of Ribbonism or involved in a murder in Westmeath, wherever in Ireland they now were. The Peace Preservation Act was also renewed for two years.[198]

The government proved even more reluctant to introduce an Irish University Bill in 1871. Gladstone had set Fortescue to work on the question

---

[193] *Hansard*, cciv, 1195, 2 March 1871; see also *ibid.*, 1008, 1012, 1024, 1205 (Sherlock, G. E. Browne, Downing, O'Reilly).

[194] *Ibid.*, 1185.

[195] *Ibid.*, 1007–8; Hamilton, *Parliamentary reminiscences*, p. 43.

[196] Monypenny and Buckle, *Disraeli*, v, 138–9; see also 2 March 1871, Drus, *Journal of Kimberley*, p. 21.

[197] Kimberley to de Grey, 4 March 1871, Ripon papers, 43522, fo. 186; diary, 2 March 1871, Trelawny papers, d 418, p. 58; diary, 28 February 1871, Brabourne papers, F27/4.

[198] *Hansard*, ccv, 1242, 1548, ccvi, 1.

in August 1870, when he was optimistic as to the effects of the Land Bill, and when he was about to propose the release of the Fenians; but, given the subsequent change of climate, the proposal to introduce a bill was dropped.[199] Nonetheless, Fawcett's motion had to be faced, and faced, moreover, in the light of the displays of party feeling on the University Tests Bill. Controversies over the Army and Ballot Bills ensured its postponement until the very end of the session, but even so, as Gladstone recognised, the debate would be 'difficult and probably ... dangerous ... for the Government, as there is no more doubtful point in the composition and tendencies of the Liberal party than its disposition to extremes in the matter of unsectarianism as it is called'.[200]

Fawcett had, on this occasion, drawn up a bill proposing the abolition of all tests in Trinity, Dublin, and a limited reform of the government both of Trinity, and of the Dublin university to which it was formally attached. The cabinet, on Gladstone's recommendation, decided that the government would move the previous question;[201] Spencer disliked this, thinking it too direct an opposition to the bill, and likely to offend Irish Protestants and to affront English Liberals.[202] In the debate on the second reading, the Conservative Viscount Crichton seconded the bill in the name of the 'vast majority of Irish Protestants' who supported 'the principle of united and unsectarian as opposed to denominational education'. Plunket also supported the bill, on behalf of Trinity. Pim and Blennerhassett claimed that the measure would not satisfy Catholics, who demanded a denominational college. Gladstone supported the abolition of tests, but also maintained that the bill would not satisfy Catholic opinion: that Fawcett's constitution for the university would ensure Protestant and oligarchical domination for decades. Playfair charged Gladstone with displaying excessive zeal for denominational education, and argued that there was no Catholic grievance: any Catholic youth could take a Dublin university degree while studying at his choice of college. He told Gladstone bluntly that he must 'assent to the inevitable, for there is no government in this House, be it Liberal or Conservative, which could remain in power for an hour, if it proposed to us a measure to convert a liberal religious equality into an intolerant religious inequality'.[203]

It became clear to the government – as Hartington subsequently admitted – that it could not carry the previous question against Liberal

---

[199] Matthew, vii, 344, 346, 390.
[200] To Manning, 28 July 1871, *ibid.*, viii, 14.   [201] 29 July 1871, *ibid.*, p. 15.
[202] Spencer to Hartington, 26 July 1871, Chatsworth papers, 354, fo. 68.
[203] *Hansard*, ccviii, 736, 2 August 1871.

and Conservative opposition.[204] Consequently, Dowse, the Irish solicitor-general, had to talk the bill out.

First intimations of mortality, late 1871

The 1871 session was an unpleasant one for the government on many fronts. The Black Sea crisis of late 1870 inspired the first prolonged criticism of its international weakness, led by the *Pall Mall Gazette*; a junior minister, Otway, resigned in sympathy. The agitation was doubly effective because it capitalised on the widespread fear for property and indeed for European civilisation which followed Paris's decline into anarchy after the Prussian war – a fear enhanced by the discountenance of law in Ireland and the republican agitation in England, which was at its height in 1870–1.[205] There was also criticism of the feebleness of the government's conduct in the negotiations with the United States regarding the *Alabama* affair – echoed inside the cabinet, especially by Lowe and Goschen.[206]

The international situation, and the consequent increase in defence expenditure, forced Lowe to increase taxes in his 1871 budget. The extra indirect tax, on matches, prompted a protest from match-girls, while the proposed increase in succession duties aroused hostility from Liberal peers and gentry MPs;[207] both plans were dropped, and the increased burden was placed entirely on the income tax, a decision which led to protests that the government had discriminated in favour of the working-class. On 1 May, W. H. Smith introduced a motion which attacked the extent of the increase in the income tax, pitching his appeal at men on small fixed incomes, who had 'appearances' to keep up and who earned no more than working-men who did not. Whig-liberal backbenchers like Trelawny were irritated at government financial policy, and Gladstone had to threaten the government's resignation again in order to secure a majority against Smith's motion.[208] At the same time, whig-liberal confidence had also been badly shaken by the scope of Goschen's Local Government Bill, which aimed fundamentally to reform the local-government and rating systems: it was so controversial that it was never even granted leave.[209]

[204] Hartington memorandum, 9 November 1871, Gladstone papers, 44143, fo. 114.
[205] See e.g. Salisbury, 'The Commune and the Internationale'.
[206] Granville to de Grey, 18 March 1871, Ripon papers, 43520, fo. 101; Forster to de Grey, 18 March 1871, *ibid.*, 43536, fo. 269.
[207] See e.g. Halifax to Gladstone, 25 April 1871, Gladstone papers, 44185, fo. 153.
[208] Diary, 1, 4 May 1871, Trelawny papers, 418, pp. 79–80; *Hansard*, ccv, 2015.
[209] See Elliot, *Goschen*, i, 126–7; Bouverie to Ellice, 11 April 1871, Ellice papers, 15005, fo. 100; Fortescue to Halifax, 30 January 1872, Hickleton papers, A 4 181, and to Brereton, n.d. 1871, Brereton papers, F 6 71; Torrens, 'Localism and centralism', p. 400; Dodson, 'The session and its lessons', p. 582.

Some landed Liberals were further irritated by the government's attempt to abolish purchase in the army, a proposal which was obstructed by backbench Conservatives and which was finally forced past the Lords in the closing days of the session by Royal Warrant, earning the censure of the Upper House. They were also affronted by Bruce's Licensing Bill, which antagonised licensed victuallers and had to be withdrawn; and by the Ballot Bill, defeated by the Lords – Somerset, Russell, Shaftesbury and Lyveden among them – at the end of the 1871 session, on the grounds that they had been given insufficient time to consider it.[210] Disaffection among metropolitan and suburban lower-middle-class voters was also fanned by Smith's manipulation of two issues: the government's refusal to allow the Metropolitan Board of Works to have land reclaimed from the Thames Embankment for recreational purposes, even though the London ratepayer had funded the reclamation; and its unwillingness to check the spread of enclosures in Epping Forest, which deprived the public of common ground. In April, Cowper-Temple won a majority of 101 in the Commons on a motion critical of government policy in the Forest.

The only silver lining for the government was the rejection of the Ballot Bill. Although the Lords' action incensed Gladstone, Granville regarded it as a godsend. The issue was the last on which the bulk of the party in the Commons would fall into line; its survival thus held party disunity at bay for another year.[211]

This argument cut less ice in the country, however, and it was in reaction to the failures of the 1871 session that the government suffered its first real setbacks in by-elections. The religious issue probably played a less significant part in these losses than it was to do from 1872 onwards, and foreign, financial and licensing policy, in comparison, had a larger role. Three by-elections were lost in the recess, in East Surrey, and at Truro and Plymouth. The East Surrey by-election aroused the most comment because it indicated the swing of opinion in the metropolis and its suburbia. Glyn blamed opposition to the Licensing Bill, irritation at the increase in income tax, and anti-Catholicism, for the loss.

Gladstone blamed the activity of the London press;[212] and in a speech at Whitby, a week after the by-election, he assaulted the class interests which he discerned to be rife in London. He alleged that, by manipulating the London press, 'powerful classes' were able to attack the government on account of its non-class-based legislation; in London,

[210] *Hansard*, ccviii, 1307, 10 August 1871.
[211] Granville to Lowe, 31 August 1871, Granville papers, 30/29/66.
[212] Glyn to Gladstone, 5 September 1871, Gladstone papers, 44348, fo. 123; Gladstone to G. Leveson Gower, 28 August 1871, *ibid.*, 44540, fo. 96.

'wealth was all-powerful' and had been responsible for the campaign against the abolition of army purchase. He went on to criticise the Lords for rejecting the ballot, 'the people's Bill': he warned that the 'people' constituted a force before which the Lords would be wise to yield. Gladstone himself had of course only recently swung round to support this bill, and with a 'lingering reluctance';[213] but the Lords' action had presented him with a valuable rallying-cry which might obscure the party's divisions on educational questions – to which his speech made little reference. He also attacked the 'alarmism' of the press over the recent war scares: he hoped that 'the time had come when the petty, peddling, narrow policy of meddling with the affairs of other nations would not be tolerated'.[214]

This speech attracted considerable hostility for its 'ultra-democratic' language:[215] it contributed one more element to the deepening pessimism of whig-liberals.[216] At Blackheath in late October, Gladstone was vague, and his failure to take a strong line in denouncing the rising tide of republican agitation and the nonconformist pressure to amend the Education Act was much criticised.[217] George Grey wrote that unless Gladstone made a 'firm stand against the extreme views now openly professed by many members below the gangway . . . some of our institutions will be in great danger'.[218] Halifax, a member of the cabinet, told his son, and Earl Grey, that a man like Peel would be a great 'blessing' at this moment: a 'reasonable sensible moderate Conservative leader who had the confidence of his own party and would not provoke the hostility of reasonable Liberals'. Such feelings were widespread;[219] at the turn of the year, for example, Earl Fortescue expressed his dissatisfaction with the foreign, ecclesiastical, financial, local-government and ballot policy of the government. While refusing to join the Conservatives – 'I am not yet Revolutionary enough for that' – he insisted that Gladstone had 'osten-

---

[213] 29 June 1871, Matthew, vii, 517.

[214] *Times*, 4 September 1871, p. 12.

[215] Derby diary, 6 September 1871, 15th earl of Derby papers; (Earl Fortescue) Northcote to Disraeli, 13 September 1871, Iddesleigh papers, 50016, fo. 105.

[216] See e.g., for Devonshire: Gladstone to Hartington, 20 September 1871, Gladstone papers, 44540, fo. 115. See also, for the reaction of the whigs at Brooks's to a similarly inflammatory speech of Glyn's: Barrington to Disraeli, 22 October 1871, Disraeli papers, B/XX/Ba/11.

[217] *Pall Mall Gazette*, 30 October 1871, p. 1; Russell to Granville, 4 November 1871, Granville papers, 30/29/79.

[218] To Denison, 22 November 1871, Ossington papers, C 1035.

[219] Halifax to Grey, 28 November, 3 December 1871, Grey papers; Grey, 'Letter on the alarming state of public affairs', *ibid.*; 'A sound old-fashioned Whig' gave his views to Lyttelton: Lyttelton to Gladstone, 4 December 1871, Gladstone papers, 44240, fo. 183. Others recalled Palmerston with affection: diary, 6 July 1871, Trelawny papers, 418, p. 101.

tatiously paraded his sympathy' with the radicals' 'dangerous domestic and foreign crotchets'. Gladstone was a 'Puseyite Radical', a 'Peelite convert', who lacked Palmerston's 'true wisdom and calm judgment'. The Whitby speech, the *Alabama* affair, Goschen's and Bruce's bills, Lowe's budget, and the League's burgeoning secularism were all to be condemned; it must be stressed that the 'constitutional whigs are not going to be dragged into the abyss of wild democracy merely to keep out the Tories'.[220]

The whiggish reaction of late 1871 embraced the whole range of politically sensitive questions, but among them were two concerns of particular relevance to this account. One was the worsening situation in Ireland; the other, more crucial still, was the increasingly aggressive tone of radical nonconformity in England – whose aggressiveness was itself partly a response to the new difficulties apparent in Ireland.

It was generally accepted that the government would tackle the Irish university question in 1872. However, in addition to the obvious obstacles in the way of their doing so successfully, two others had appeared by late 1871. The first was the rise of the home-rule party.

Butt had created the Home Government Association in May 1870, exploiting the prisoner issue, dissatisfaction with the moderation of the Land Bill, and the reaction of Protestant and Conservative opinion to disestablishment.[221] At first, this Protestant element was very important in the HGA, and John Martin and Mitchell Henry, both of whom were elected to parliament in early 1871, were Protestants. By 1871, however, defence of denominational education was becoming a major election issue, and priests were increasingly being driven by popular enthusiasm to support the candidatures of home rulers – such as Smyth at Westmeath in June 1871 and Butt at Limerick in September, both of whom stressed their support for denominational education, and both of whom won their by-elections.[222] As it became a grass-roots popular Catholic movement, Conservatives accordingly began to drift away from the HGA.[223]

One product of the home rulers' political activity was the revival of pressure for the release of the few remaining Fenian prisoners, and there was an embarrassment for the government in August 1871 when Spencer banned a 'monster meeting' in Phoenix Park, planned in order to petition for release. Gladstone did not approve of Spencer's action, but

[220] Earl Fortescue to Halifax, 30 January, 1 February 1872, Hickleton papers, A 4 181; Halifax to Fortescue, 29 January 1872, Fortescue papers, FC 126; Fortescue to Brereton, n.d. 1871, Brereton papers, F 6, 10 71.
[221] Thornley, *Butt*, pp. 80–91.
[222] *Ibid.*, pp. 118–23.   [223] *Ibid.*, pp. 124–6.

did not publicly criticise him, despite complaints from Irish and some English MPs: the government escaped a crisis in the Commons only by promising an internal investigation into the incident. Spencer hinted broadly that he was finding the tenure of the viceroyalty irritating and depressing;[224] but at least the government stood firm, for the time being, against release of the prisoners.

Gladstone responded to the rise of the home-rule party in two further ways. Firstly, he unsuccessfully pressed upon the queen a plan to involve the prince of Wales in a reconstituted and more independent Irish administration, preferably by replacing the viceroy – whose position, inevitably, had colonial resonances – as the queen's representative in Ireland, and therefore giving the chief secretary more power and perhaps more respect. This would be a 'palpable *contrecoup* to the Home Rule Agitation', as well as defusing English republican criticism of the queen's seclusion and of the prince's inactive and self-indulgent life-style.[225]

Secondly, he tried to reassure the Protestant Scots, still shaken by the Dease letter, with a speech at Aberdeen in September, which made fun of the home-rule agitation. It was not they alone who were alarmed. Many whigs were concerned that Gladstone might be susceptible to any demand for home rule which was expressed by the representatives of Irish public opinion: Bessborough had said after talking to Gladstone in 1870 that he thought him 'capable of repealing the Union'.[226] Just before making his speech, moreover, Gladstone received the news that Dufferin, the most prominent Ulster Liberal politician, wished to resign from the government, partly out of disillusionment with his position at the Duchy of Lancaster, but mainly out of disquiet at the development of Gladstone's Irish policy (he had disliked the 1870 Land Act and the release of the second batch of Fenian prisoners). Gladstone managed to postpone the announcement of the resignation until Dufferin was appointed governor-general of Canada in early 1872, thus avoiding the appearance of government dissension over Irish policy.[227]

Gladstone's robust criticism of the home rulers was cheered by the presbyterian fishermen of Aberdeen, and applauded by whig opinion in England – by Kimberley, Granville, Dufferin and Bessborough, for

[224] *Hansard*, ccviii, 1094, 1492, 1773, 1869; Matthew, viii, 19–27; Spencer to Gladstone, 14, 22 August 1871, Gladstone papers, 44307, fos. 67, 77; Gladstone to Spencer, 15 August 1871, *ibid.*, fo. 71.

[225] Gladstone to Kimberley, 28 June 1871, Gladstone papers, 44540, fo. 62; Magnus, *Gladstone*, pp. 207–17; Macdowell, *Irish administration*, pp. 69–70; Ramm, i, 170–2; Matthew, vii, 358, 512–16, viii, 3.

[226] Lyall, *Dufferin*, ii, 140.

[227] Harrison, 'Dufferin', pp. 130–1, 223–4; Dufferin to Argyll, 21 November 1870, Dufferin papers.

example – for the 'firmness' of its 'attack'.[228] Given the whigs' disquiet at the drift of Irish policy, this saved Gladstone's face politically. But in fact they did not receive an accurate view of what he had said. Beneath the jocular and belittling tone in which he dismissed the home rulers lay some points of substance: that the government's aim was to satisfy all genuine popular Irish needs, and to adhere to 'the principles of justice'; that the supremacy of the imperial parliament, and the 'great capital institutions of this country', must be maintained; and that, if Ireland were given a degree of legislative independence, Scotland and Wales were entitled to the same.[229] He became extremely annoyed when the Irish Liberal MP Pim alleged that he had indulged in 'taunt and sarcasm', and that the Liberal party wished to enforce policies on Ireland with no reference to her own wishes:[230] with typical self-deception, Gladstone considered this treatment of his speech 'invidious and unfair'. He told Pim (who desired a measure of increased Irish self-government in subordination to Westminster) that they were 'agreed' on 'all questions of principle'. He told Bright that few would be prepared to welcome home rule as warmly as he, subject to the conditions stipulated in his speech, that the continued supremacy of the imperial parliament was maintained, and that similar offers were made to Wales and Scotland.[231]

But the home rulers were not at this time seen as posing a real threat to the Union; whig-liberal alarm at their popularity was aroused mainly because of a suspicion that Gladstone's government, which was already viewed both as populist and as denominationalist, would listen with interest to their educational proposals. Merging with the problem created by the rise of the home-rule party was the second shadow cast over the consideration of the Irish university question in late 1871: the general belief – encouraged by Fortescue himself – that the government would act to reform the Irish *elementary* system along denominational lines.

One of the most consistent demands of both the bishops and the home-rule movement was for an alteration in the system of elementary education, and the report of the Powis Commission, in 1870, heightened the expectation of imminent adjustments. The Commission, seven of whose fourteen members were Catholics, recommended a series of con-

[228] Kimberley to Dodson, 27 September 1871, Monk Bretton papers, 37; Granville, 29 September 1871, Ramm, ii, 262; Dufferin to Gladstone, 27 September 1871, Gladstone papers, 44151, fo. 117; Bessborough to Gladstone, 28 September 1871, *ibid.*, 44431, fo. 282.
[229] Vincent, 'Gladstone and Ireland', pp. 232–6.
[230] *Ireland and the imperial parliament.*
[231] Matthew, viii, 65, 68; Pim, *Ireland and the imperial parliament.*

cessions to denominationalism.[232] Anti-clericals in England were quick to criticise the Commission's report,[233] and an Education League for Ireland, an offshoot from the English one, was founded in 1870.[234] Gladstone announced that, despite the Commission's recommendations, it was inexpedient to consider the question in 1870, even though Fortescue had promised in 1869 that reform of the national system would be 'taken in hand' as soon as the commissioners reported.[235] In 1871, despite pressure from the National Association and the bishops,[236] the government realised that it could still not afford to make any reform proposals (although a minor upward adjustment of teachers' low salaries was made, in order to strike at likely sources of disaffection with the Union). Nonetheless, Hartington promised to raise the whole national education question in 1872.[237]

In October 1871, Fortescue, who had always been the cabinet minister most keen to safeguard denominational rights in Irish national education, delivered a controversial speech at Bristol attacking the prevailing obsession with undenominationalism. He argued that parents desired denominational education for their children; he justified state grants to denominational schools, by presenting them as contributing to the cost of merely the secular part of the instruction. It 'amused' him to hear the many voices which urged undenominationalism in English education in order to prevent its opposite in Ireland, because the Irish system was already 'mainly denominational'. He maintained, moreover, that reform at all levels of Irish education must be directed, in future, towards giving 'the greatest consideration for the circumstances, feelings, and rights of the people of Ireland'.[238] Greenwood of the *Pall Mall Gazette* thought that this speech indicated that the government was bent on 'suicide'.[239] Gladstone was not pleased by the speech, because of its effects on backbench feeling;[240] Spencer made clear his opposition, in principle, to any attempt to reform the model schools as Fortescue wished, besides thinking his proposals politically disastrous.[241]

By late September, Gladstone was also certain that the government

[232] See, for the details, Akenson, *Irish education experiment*, pp. 310–15.
[233] H. W. Bellasis to Gladstone, 7 June 1870, Gladstone papers, 44427, fo. 11.
[234] Adams, *History of elementary school contest*, pp. 241, 261.
[235] *Hansard*, ccii, 1206, 30 June 1870, cxcv, 1698, 27 April 1869.
[236] Norman, *Catholic Church*, p. 441.
[237] Lowe to Gladstone, 7 August 1869, Gladstone papers, 44301, fo. 63; Hartington to Gladstone, 23 June 1871, *ibid.*, 44143, fo. 88; Spencer to Hartington, 23 April 1871, Chatsworth papers, 354, fo. 45; *Hansard*, ccvii, 1788, 1922.
[238] *Times*, 19 October 1871, p. 5.
[239] Lennox to Disraeli, 16 November 1871, Disraeli papers, B/XX/Lx/367.
[240] To Glyn, 1 December 1871, Gladstone papers, 44541, fo. 2.
[241] Spencer to Gladstone, 28 November 1871, *ibid.*, 44307, fo. 93.

could not dare to introduce its own bill for Irish university reform in 1872. Accordingly, he reasoned that the only way in which defeat on Fawcett's bill might be avoided was by agreeing to the abolition of tests, while rejecting the clauses concerned with the organisation of the university. Discussion of the reorganisation of the system might then be postponed until such time as a proper initiative might be effected: with no guarantee that this time would ever arrive. The government inquired if this option would be acceptable to Catholic opinion:[242] Spencer replied that, if this course were adopted, he thought that the bishops would 'turn a favourable ear to Home Rule'.[243] Hartington's memorandum of 9 November spelled out the almost impossible situation: the home rulers would oppose any reasonable university proposal in order to embarrass the government and to show their power, and the bishops and many MPs would be forced to support home rule unless some hope were held out of a measure satisfactory to Catholics. On the other hand, many Liberals had 'assumed an attitude of extreme hostility to denominational education in any shape', and had 'an intense aversion to, and dread of, the Roman Catholic religion'. Had the disestablishment of the Irish Church not been attractive on other grounds, the aid furnished to it by Roman Catholics would have driven many to oppose it. The government had no option but to assent to the abolition of tests and to postpone consideration of the organisation of university government; but, whatever its course, there seemed no chance of retaining both English and Irish support.[244]

But there was great uncertainty that even the division of Fawcett's bill into two parts would abate Liberal opposition. Gladstone was annoyed to hear that someone as respectable as George Grey would have voted for Fawcett's bill in 1871, had there been a division – and so would Somerset. Most significantly of all, even a cabinet minister – Halifax – did not understand the crucial distinction drawn by the government between the tests clauses of Fawcett's bill and the others; he was not aware that Fawcett's bill contained anything but the easily comprehensible proposal for tests abolition.[245] Bruce predicted that the government would be defeated on Fawcett's bill, and able to resign.[246] As Gladstone himself

[242] To Hartington, 28 September 1871, Matthew, viii, 40–1.
[243] Spencer to Hartington, 22 October 1871, Chatsworth papers, 354, fo. 79.
[244] Hartington memorandum, 9 November 1871, Gladstone papers, 44143, fo. 114.
[245] George Grey to Halifax, 26 December 1871, Hickleton papers, A 4 58; Gladstone to Halifax, 28 December 1871, *ibid.*, A 4 88; Halifax to Gladstone, 31 December 1871, Gladstone papers, 44185, fo. 245; (Somerset) *Hansard*, ccviii, 1291, 10 August 1871.
[246] *Letters of Aberdare*, i, 319–20.

recognised, the Irish university question constituted the 'best card' in the tory hand.[247]

It was in this climate of suspicion that nonconformist agitation for a radical reform of the English educational settlement intensified. One element in the defeats at Truro and Plymouth was the revolt of 'right-wing' whig-liberal Anglicans, who refused to vote for Liberal candidates whose positions on Church and educational questions were advanced. Jenkins, the candidate at Truro, was a member of the National Education League, who, moreover, had defeated a local whig in order to gain the nomination; Rooker, at Plymouth, was a nonconformist who advocated disestablishment, of which fact his Conservative opponent made much.[248] In 1872, this trend towards nonconformist control of Liberal by-election campaigns was to continue.

Nonconformist protests at the denominational policy of the government, at all educational levels, were also winning the sympathy of a number of anti-clerical whig-liberals. Among them was Russell, who declared his adhesion to the League in mid November, on the grounds that it supported bible-reading: he wished children to affiliate to the 'Church of Christ', not the 'Church of Rome' or the 'Church of England'.[249] He complained both of government weakness on foreign policy, and of its betrayal of Liberal educational principles. He criticised the cabinet for adopting Forster's 'sectarian' line in England, and for attempting to overthrow the national system in Ireland – Derby's 'acorn' – which, he asserted, would not be 'mistaken for a branch of the Upas Tree by the Protestant Interests of Great Britain'. He gave notice of his intention to resign the Liberal whip. Russell, perhaps, was no longer a serious political force, but nonconformists nonetheless considered his membership of the League an event well worth publicising.[250]

As the autumn progressed, one issue in particular was stressed more and more in order to unite nonconformists and many Anglican Liberals in hostility to the 1870 Education Act: the rate support for denominational schools which was allowed by Clause 25 of the Act. Nonconformist pressure against Clause 25 – which made it possible for children of poor parents to attend Church schools at ratepayers' expense, if the parents and the school board wished – had been growing throughout 1871.[251] In August, the Southampton school board had adopted com-

---

[247] Gladstone to Manning, 18 November 1871, Gladstone papers, 44540, fo. 168.
[248] *Times*, 14 September 1871, p. 9, 22 November 1871, p. 5; Hamer, *Politics of electoral pressure*, pp. 123, 127; *Nonconformist*, 29 November 1871, p. 1175.
[249] *Nonconformist*, 22 November 1871, p. 1138.
[250] Russell to Granville, 4 November 1871, Granville papers, 30/29/79; see Dale, *Politics of nonconformity*, pp. 22–3.
[251] See Adams, *History of elementary school contest*, pp. 254–7.

pulsion and remitted fees for poor children in board schools (under
Clause 17) but not in voluntary schools. To Ripon's great irritation, the
cabinet sanctioned this, seeing no alternative.[252] The Education Department wrote to boards who adopted this policy, expressing a hope that, in
the interests of justice, they would sanction the implementation of
Clause 25 if a poor parent might be deprived of choice. Dale and
Crosskey protested at the content of this letter.[253] In his Greenwich
speech of 28 October, Gladstone defended parents' rights, while
minimising the importance of Clause 25 in practice, and emphasising the
need to envisage rate-aid as bestowed only for the secular part of the
teaching given by denominational schools.[254] In November, in an
attempt to counteract this nonconformist pressure, Gladstone asked
Bright to rejoin the cabinet, but the latter adopted delaying tactics.[255]
The third annual meeting of the League, held the previous month, raised
the political temperature by agreeing to seek to force election candidates
to pledge support for the repeal of Clause 25.[256]

In fact, however, Scottish and Irish policy gained almost as much
attention at the League meeting as the Clause 25 problem: the academic
liberal, Walter Morrison, for example, reminded the meeting of the
favour with which some cabinet ministers viewed a denominational
solution to the Irish educational difficulty.[257] Then, in late October, the
crisis was, according to Dale, 'accelerated' by the publication of another
educational manifesto by the Irish bishops. Dale was by now very
worried that the government might prove amenable to the bishops'
demands; indeed, he thought that to give Ireland what had been offered
to Scotland in 1871 would be to 'concede substantially all' that they
demanded.[258] Consequently, on 21 November, he delivered a famous
and electrifying attack on the denominational policy of the government,
published as *The politics of nonconformity*. This concluded with an inspiring
vision of the Christianised polity which would follow after disestablishment. But its cutting edge was educational: he threatened that, unless
policy changes were made, nonconformists would be 'driven into open
hostility, and . . . compelled to form a separate and independent party in
the State'.[259] Clause 25, the Scottish Education Bill, and the retention of
ex officio appointments to the governing bodies of endowed schools were

[252] Wolf, *Ripon*, i, 273–6.
[253] To Gladstone, 9 September 1871, Gladstone papers, 44617, fo. 106.
[254] *Corrected report of the speech at Greenwich*, pp. 18–20.
[255] 15 November 1871, Ramm, ii, 281; Matthew, viii, 63.
[256] Adams, *History of elementary school contest*, pp. 272–3.
[257] *Ibid.*, pp. 266–75.
[258] Dale to Newman Hall, 7, 16 November 1871, Gladstone papers, 44188, fos. 101, 107.
[259] *Politics of nonconformity*, p. 11.

all scorned. He argued that the parent had no right to compel the community to pay for a child's sectarian instruction:[260] the 'true policy' of a Liberal government was 'gradually to dissociate the secular education of the people' from 'all theological teaching'.[261] The alternative, he maintained, was to agree to endow denominational education in Ireland; but he would rather the 'Liberal party be utterly broken in pieces and for ever destroyed' than that it implement such a policy.[262] If a measure to this effect were introduced, the nonconformists must 'try to secure, at the earliest possible moment, such a defeat of the Government . . . as shall render it impossible for them to remain in office'.[263]

This speech roused nonconformist clamour to new heights. There was renewed interest in the campaign for disestablishment – in parallel with a counter-campaign by the Church Defence Institution.[264] The speech also quickened the pace of the League's conversion to educational secularism. The supporters of this policy were claiming, with increasing plausibility, that it was the only consistent solution to the educational difficulties in all three countries.[265] By the end of 1871, a formal commitment by the League to the secular solution appeared imminent. This in turn outraged many whigs: Earl Fortescue wrote a public letter attacking the drift to secularism in early December, and Halifax told him that he would have written similarly, had he not been a member of the cabinet.[266]

Gladstone told Bright that education in England, Scotland or Ireland would probably 'be the death of this Government'.[267] But Bright was not moved by Gladstone's entreaties that he should assume his cabinet place again. Instead, he fired off a criticism of the 1870 Act, for extending the denominational system, and finally refused outright to return to office in early February 1872 – partly on the grounds that 'peculiarly embarrassing' questions would be raised in the House in the coming session.[268] Not only was Bright in an anti-clerical mood: so was Lowe. He floated the idea that, in return for the 50 per cent increase in grants agreed in 1870, voluntary schools should be obliged to take, free, the children of poor parents who desired a Church education; Gladstone and Forster opposed his proposal.[269] Then, in early December, Lowe made a speech

---

[260] *Ibid.*, p. 20.   [261] *Ibid.*, p. 21.

[262] This was met with loud cheers: *ibid.*, pp. 26–7.

[263] *Ibid.*, pp. 28–9.

[264] See e.g. Harrison, *Drink and the Victorians*, pp. 266–7; *Times*, 23 November 1871, p. 8.

[265] Adams, *History of elementary school contest*, pp. 266–75.

[266] Halifax to Grey, 28 November, 3 December 1871, Grey papers.

[267] 25 November 1871, Matthew, viii, 67–9.

[268] Bright to Gladstone, 28 November 1871, 4 February 1872, Gladstone papers, 44112, fo. 119, 44113, fo. 4; Matthew, viii, 70–1.

[269] Lowe to Granville, 29 November 1871, Granville papers, 30/29/66; Gladstone to Lowe, 26 November 1871, Gladstone papers, 44540, fo. 178; Forster to Ripon, 4 December 1871, Ripon papers, 43536, fo. 297.

at Halifax which was critical of voluntary schools and stressed that they could in future 'be dealt with at the pleasure of the Legislature'.[270]

At the close of 1871, therefore, the Liberation Society was on the offensive against the Church Establishment. The League was sharpening its campaign against Clause 25, in order to promote a far-reaching reform of the 1870 educational settlement; it was also preparing to declare in favour of the secular policy for English education, in order to secure a satisfactory solution of the Irish problem. These assaults were too extremist to be politically acceptable to the majority of the electorate, but the government was unable to propose any alternative answer to either the English or Irish educational dilemmas, because of the division of outlook between Gladstone and the undenominationalists. Disaffection was also rife on a broad range of other questions. The widespread distrust of the Conservative party, and the whigs' propensity for apathy rather than open hostility helped the government to retain some dignity. Even so, the ballot was the only unresolved question which was still capable of inspiring most of the party: that apart, the government had already lost its air of competence, while its hold on backbench confidence was extremely insecure. Over the next two years, Gladstone was, in certain ways, to draw politically closer to radical nonconformists, but only in support of policies which did not appeal to a sufficiently large constituency to offer a prospect of election victory – and on which, therefore, in the main, he kept his silence in public. The bulk of the party appeared unlikely to be able to reach agreement in support of any policy of substance – with one exception. It now seemed possible to unite and inspire a broad-based coalition of whig-liberals, nonconformists and radicals only by espousing anti-clerical positions: for example, by amending Clause 25 and extending the educational powers of the state, or by redistributing more religious and educational endowments, or by advocating a strident assault on clerical influence in the universities. For Gladstone, this was not an encouraging prospect.

[270] *Times*, 6 December 1871, p. 3.

7

The religious problem intensified, 1872–3

In 1872, the Liberal party began to fall into a trap which was largely of its own making. The government was committed to introducing an Irish University Bill, but it could not solve the Irish university question in a way which would satisfy all components of the party. Nonconformists rejected state endowment of Catholic education; Catholics demanded it. Most whig-liberals disliked any concession to denominationalism, and wished merely for the abolition of tests in Trinity, Dublin; Gladstone strongly disapproved of their apparent insensitivity to the Catholic grievance. Then again, the provisions of the 1870 Education Act had created expectations regarding the Irish measure which it was politically impossible to realise: whig-liberals, nonconformists and Irish Catholics all now expected that the government would legislate on the university question in a way which they would find unacceptable. Yet neither was it feasible to amend the 1870 Act in a way which would please both the leadership and the grass-roots of the party. There was a dispute about the merits of secularism; cutting across that was a difficulty about Clause 25 of the Act, which most Liberals disliked, but which the government refused to repeal – if, by doing so, poor parents would be deprived of the right to select a denominational education for their children. Moreover, although party agreement was unattainable in discussions of educational policy, this complex combination of problems could not be ignored. It was therefore impossible to adopt rallying-cries on other topics, in the hope of rediscovering unity.

However, the drift into this unenviable predicament had not been inevitable. Gladstone had always had the option not to commit himself – and to renew his commitment – to the introduction of an Irish University Bill. Indeed, his preoccupation with the question was regarded by a large number of Liberals, from most sections of the party, with incomprehension: Jowett, for example, came to see it as the first step in Gladstone's 'ruin' of the party.[1] Gladstone's commitment stemmed not from political calculation, but from a genuine concern to secure safeguards for denominationalism in practice and for the abstract principle of religious freedom. In a sense, so did his commitment to home rule in 1886. In both cases he showed stubbornness and a disregard for short-term party interests. For short-term interests, in 1872–3 and 1885–6, dictated an anti-clerical position; and Gladstone was not unprincipled enough for that.

In January 1872, radical nonconformists held a conference at Manchester. Its purpose was to declare in favour of secularism as an educational policy for England, Scotland and Ireland – and, in doing so, it added materially to the fears of whig-liberals and Anglican Liberal voters, and had a major impact on politics throughout 1872. It also demanded the abolition of clerical fellowships, the diminution of clerical influence on the governing bodies of endowed schools, the unconditional repeal of Clause 25, and alterations in the burial and marriage laws; it further decided to refuse support for a Liberal parliamentary candidate who would not accept the conference recommendations concerning the Education Act, except given 'great national exigencies'.[2] Over eight hundred chapels and organisations sent 1,885 delegates to Manchester, and there was little pretence of debate or division throughout the proceedings: the atmosphere was revivalistic.[3]

Secularism was advocated largely in order to circumvent the possibility of state endowment of Irish Catholic education.[4] Much of the language used by the idea's proponents was therefore anti-Catholic; but it was also repeatedly asserted that the Irish Catholics would have a just grievance if the episcopalians in England and presbyterians in Scotland were allowed to continue to receive public endowment for their religious teaching, while the mixed system remained in force in Ireland.[5] The mixed system, furthermore, was condemned for its bias towards Protestantism: Guinness Rogers, for example, stressed that the bible was a 'Protestant book' and that the state had no right to force it down Catholic throats. It followed, he argued, that the only proper policy, for both Britain and Ireland, was to refuse to endow any religious teaching.[6]

---

[1] (1875) Abbott and Campbell, *Letters of Jowett*, p. 193.
[2] *Report of the Manchester conference*, pp. 8–12.
[3] Miall, *Richard*, p. 186; *Times*, 25 January 1872, p. 9.
[4] (Mellor, Charles Williams) *Report of the Manchester conference*, pp. 57–8, 150–2.
[5] (Landels, Charles Williams, Street) *ibid.*, pp. 45, 151, 230; see also the argument of the *Nonconformist*, 31 January 1872, p. 105.
[6] *Report of the Manchester conference*, p. 134. See also (Crosskey) pp. 128–30, and (Charles Williams) p. 152.

The conference's policy was reaffirmed by other nonconformist bodies. Dale and Rogers secured the overwhelming backing of the Congregational Union for the secular solution (Binney and Stoughton led the dissent).[7] A 'large majority' of baptists were also secularists, according to the *Baptist Magazine*.[8] In early April, the unitarian Stansfeld – now a member of the cabinet – pledged himself, speaking personally and only with regard to the future, as a secularist and a supporter of disestablishment.[9] Opponents of nonconformist extremism in educational matters were further alarmed when, in February 1872, the Birmingham Town Council – which was controlled by the Chamberlainites – refused to give the (Conservative) school board the funds which it needed to pay fees under Clause 25. Although the school board won its case against the Council in the courts, it decided not to press the issue thereafter.[10]

The Manchester resolutions – which, it was well known, would be followed by Miall's annual parliamentary motion in the direction of disestablishment – encountered heavy criticism from whig-liberals. Secular education and disestablishment were condemned by Knatchbull-Hugessen in a speech on 26 January, and by Lubbock in early February: both, moreover, dwelt on the power that the disestablished Church would certainly enjoy, and the intolerance which it was likely to exhibit.[11] Russell realised his mistake in joining the National Education League, and sent a letter criticising the secular scheme as 'fallacious and inadequate' – although he reaffirmed his opposition to the 'unjust and persecuting' Clause 25.[12] (Kingsley had earlier resigned from the League.) The *Times* opposed the secularist solution and saw it as a bid for disestablishment under another guise: in an unusually forceful and strident leading article, it rejected the principles of the nonconformists – that the state could not act in a matter of national concern in a way which any individual or minority disliked – as 'simply disintegrating civil society'. Price in *Blackwood's* argued similarly.[13] Hardcastle in the *Edinburgh* also condemned the nonconformists' assault on the Establishment and their alliance with high churchmen for this purpose. He alleged that the condition of a disestablished Church in England would be comparable to that of the Roman Catholic Church in Ireland: the clergy

---

[7] Peel, *These hundred years*, p. 189; Rogers, *Autobiography*, pp. 175–6.
[8] Bebbington, *Nonconformist conscience*, p. 131.
[9] *Times*, 4 April 1872, p. 12.
[10] Hennock, *Fit and proper persons*, pp. 134–5; Richards, 'Religious controversy and the school boards', pp. 188–9.
[11] Knatchbull-Hugessen, *Speech at Sandwich*, p. 14; (Lubbock) *Spectator*, 10 February 1872, p. 171. Goschen applauded Knatchbull-Hugessen's stand against the secularists: 29 January 1872, diary, Brabourne papers, F27/4, p. 17.
[12] *Times*, 6 February 1872, p. 12.
[13] *Ibid.*, 25 January 1872, p. 9; Price, 'The Manchester nonconformists'.

would be 'poorer, more ignorant and with a lower standard of manners and feelings', but would claim to exercise more 'spiritual power'.[14]

Many nonconformists were no less strident in opposition to the Manchester resolutions. Over eight hundred eventually signed a declaration protesting at the exclusion of the bible from schools, despite the *Nonconformist*'s claim that adherence to the principles of the declaration was inconsistent with support for disestablishment.[15] Signatories included some nonconformist MPs – Samuel Morley, Reed, Baines, Stevenson, the Wesleyans McArthur and Allen, and the quakers Pease and Backhouse; some famous divines – Arthur, Conder, Newman Hall, Rigg, Spurgeon, Stoughton and Urwick; and Mudie, the bookseller and London school-board member.[16] Urwick and Conder argued that education without religion was immoral. They contended that the pursuit of a secularist policy would allow sacerdotalists to teach their dogmas in the hours set aside for voluntary religious education, and, more worryingly, threatened, in the long run, to produce a 'State establishment of Irreligion'.[17] Martineau and Vance Smith were the leading unitarian opponents of secularism,[18] while Wesleyans were, as a sect, the most strongly committed against the secular solution.[19]

Faced with this increasingly virulent internal party debate, the government refused to amend the Education Act. The radicals in parliament did not wish to antagonise anti-clerical whig-liberals by proposing an explicitly secularist motion, and so Dixon – Chamberlain's puppet – moved the resolutions agreed by the League the previous autumn: these condemned the 1870 Act for failing to establish compulsion and universal school boards, and for its Clause 25.[20] Richard threatened that the Liberal party would be 'disorganized and broken up' unless the Act were amended; Herbert supported the resolution, and secularism, on behalf of all those 'who belonged to modern schools of thought, and who united themselves to no Church or sect whatever'.[21] The vote was 355 to 94 against the motion, the 94 including non-secularists Jacob Bright, Harcourt, McArthur and Melly. Men like Mundella, opposed to an extremist attack on the Act but in favour of repealing Clause 25, abstained,[22] as did Morley and Reed. Many Liberals voted for the gov-

---

[14] 'Miall on disestablishment'.   [15] *Nonconformist*, 15 May 1872, p. 505.
[16] For one copy of the list, not final, see *ibid.*, 8 May 1872, p. 494; see Glover, in *ibid.*, 15 May, p. 509.
[17] Conder, *Education and nonconformity*, p. 15; Urwick, *Nonconformists and the Education Act*, pp. 23, 25–7.
[18] For Martineau, see Drummond and Upton, *Martineau*, ii, 82.
[19] Crosskey, 'The nonconformist programme', p. 371; McCullagh, *McArthur*, p. 164.
[20] *Hansard*, ccix, 1395, 5 March 1872.
[21] *Ibid.*, 1417, 1447.
[22] Mundella to Leader, 18 June 1872, Mundella papers.

ernment in order to give the Act a longer trial.[23] Seven weeks later, Candlish's request for leave to introduce his bill to repeal Clause 25 was rejected by 316 votes to 115. Mundella, Pease and Reed were among those who had not supported Dixon's motion but who voted for this bill. The 316 comprised 188 Conservatives, 42 Irish Liberals and only 67 non-official British Liberals. Even moderate Liberal organs like the *Economist* were by now prepared to see Clause 25 abolished, in order to satisfy nonconformists.[24]

Parliamentary discussion of the Church Establishment and Church reform was equally divisive in 1872. This year, instead of introducing a direct motion for disestablishment, Miall proposed the establishment of a Royal Commission, in order to investigate the Church's property and revenues: 96 Liberals supported him. Hughes, in opposing the motion, moved – again without success – for a Commission which would consider a far-reaching organisational reform of the Church, in order to redistribute resources to the areas of most need.[25] In the following months, he made a series of speeches in the country condemning the Liberation Society's campaign.[26] Church reform – although on a less ambitious scale than that planned by Hughes – was by 1872 a common whig-liberal demand. Shaftesbury took the chair at a meeting to promote it in February, and his accession to the 'Liberal Churchmen's movement' was applauded by the *Spectator*.[27] But Gladstone reiterated his refusal to promote controversial Church legislation, when there seemed a danger – in March – that 'extraneous matter' might be forced into the Act of Uniformity Amendment Bill (which aimed to relax the rules specifying the conduct of worship, in accordance with the Commission's recommendations, and with the agreement of Convocation).[28] Shaftesbury complained how little the bill achieved. Most remarkably of all, Gladstone considered, he twice defeated attempts by Bouverie, supported by Horsman, Hughes and Miall, to omit the formal acknowledgment, in the bill's preamble, that Convocation had consented to it. However, 87 Liberals supported Bouverie's amendment; only 25 non-government Liberals opposed it, with 109 Conservatives.[29]

Gladstone's experience with the bill, as with the Table of Lessons Bill in 1871 (see p. 314) – both of which had 'every possible advantage of

[23] Diary, 6 March, 25 April 1872, Trelawny papers, 418, p. 134, 419, p. 22.
[24] 3 February 1872, p. 134.   [25] *Hansard*, ccxii, 527, 2 July 1872.
[26] See e.g. *The old Church*, pp. 23–78.   [27] 3 February 1872, p. 131.
[28] To Wilberforce, 11 March 1872, Matthew, viii, 124; for another warning of the same kind, see (to Tait) *ibid.*, p. 57.
[29] Marsh, *Victorian Church in decline*, pp. 106–9; 3 June 1872, Matthew, viii, 158; *Hansard*, ccx, 888, 1085; Gladstone–Tait correspondence, May–June 1872, Gladstone papers 44331, fos. 66–75.

consent and authority' – only increased his distrust of parliamentary meddling in Church questions. He had had to exert himself 'very hard indeed' to defeat initiatives 'which would have formed most dangerous precedents for the future'.[30] The government gave no encouragement to two of the major proposals of the National Church Reform Union, Sandon's Parochial Councils Bill and Cowper-Temple's Occasional Sermons Bill. Gladstone, who preferred to leave parishes free to form councils according to local need, had damned the former with faint praise in 1871; Sandon did not attempt to reintroduce it in 1872 or 1873.[31] Gladstone considered Cowper-Temple's bill, which permitted ministers to invite non-Anglican lay preachers to give church sermons, to be 'most indiscreet': he believed that men who were not subject to the rules and laws of the Church should not be allowed to teach her congregations. It was defeated in 1872 and 1873, Gladstone speaking against it on both occasions. Nonconformists and radicals were both divided about the merits of the bill: Campbell-Bannerman, Dilke, Illingworth and Leatham voted with Gladstone, while Colman, Dixon, Herbert, Samuel Morley, Morgan and Mundella opposed him. Most whig-liberals also supported the bill, led by Chambers, Forster, Hardcastle, Hartington, Hughes and Torrens; but some of the 'right-wing' whig-liberals, such as Akroyd, Foljambe, Foster and Trelawny, opposed it, disliking the radical change to the nature of church services which it would involve.[32]

By-elections throughout the first half of 1872 strikingly indicated the damage that would be inflicted on the party's electoral prospects by the radicals' new aggressiveness on the religious question. The most sensational result was the first and only Conservative victory in the northern division of the West Riding, a Liberal stronghold, by forty-four votes, on 3 February: the defeated Liberal, Holden, was a radical, a supporter of disestablishment and, it was widely alleged, a secularist. He had been chosen only after a bitter party struggle. The victor, F. S. Powell, was a Smithian Conservative who was active in the Church Defence Institution, a public-health reformer, and a supporter of the ballot. He claimed that the 'two great principles' on which he stood were opposition to secular education and to disestablishment. He was openly supported by Akroyd, who justified his action by arguing that education was the most important political issue of the day, and by Ripley, the moderate Liberal ousted from the candidature. Gladstone noted that the advocacy

[30] 27 July 1873, Lathbury, ii, 91–2.
[31] *Hansard*, ccv, 822, 29 March 1871.
[32] *Hansard*, ccix, 786, 20 February 1872, ccxii, 236, 26 June 1872, ccxv, 1962, 14 May 1873; 5 November 1871, Matthew, viii, 57.

of the full nonconformist platform had lost votes; the *Spectator* considered
that to campaign on such a platform would inevitably lose the Liberals a
general election.[33] On 26 February, the Conservatives gained North
Nottinghamshire by a majority of over a thousand, apparently because
the dukes of Portland and Newcastle defected to them in reaction to the
threat to the Church Establishment. The Liberal candidate was an
Anglican supporter of disestablishment, and the Conservatives cam-
paigned mainly on religious and educational questions.[34] Five months
after losing the northern division of the West Riding, the Liberals also
lost a by-election in the southern division, after Milton's resignation: the
Conservatives gained the seat unopposed, owing to Fitzwilliam's disaffection. In June, the ex-Liberal Cobbett gained Oldham for the
Conservatives over the Liberationist Lyulph Stanley (in April, they also
gained Tamworth, the Peel interest having shifted allegiance). In other
words, constituency Liberal associations were increasingly at the mercy
of radicals who were able to impose candidates who favoured disestablishment and radical educational reform – with unfortunate consequences for the party's electoral fortunes. There were also three by-
elections for places on the London school board, in Marylebone,
Finsbury and Westminster. All of them were fought between advocates
of undenominational and of secular education, and in each case the
former was easily victorious (one winner being Llewelyn Davies).[35]

Given all these divisions in the Liberal party, it was hardly surprising
that Gladstone again implored Bright to return to the government, in
order to help it to tackle Irish education and to solve the English educational *impasse*. It was equally unsurprising that Bright refused.[36]

The Scottish Education Act

The growing impatience of radical Liberals also cast its shadow in discussion of Scottish education. In November 1871, Gladstone complained
that the 'extreme jealousy, susceptibility and irritation' of the contending factions in all parts of Scotland was making it more difficult than ever

---

[33] See *Nonconformist*, 14 February 1872, pp. 171–2; *Times*, 5 February 1872, p. 8; Hamer,
Politics of electoral pressure, p. 127; Akroyd, *On the present attitude of political parties*, pp. 30, 65;
Spectator, 10 February 1872, pp. 169–70. See *Leeds Mercury*, 3 February 1874, p. 7, for
Holden's complaint of the 'foul insinuation' of secularism repeatedly made against him
in 1872.

[34] See *Nonconformist*, 28 February 1872, p. 220; *Spectator*, 24 February 1872, p. 229; *Times*,
21 February 1872, p. 9.

[35] See *Nonconformist*, 3, 10, 24 April 1872, pp. 346, 370, 425.

[36] Gladstone to Bright, 26 March 1872, Gladstone papers, 44113, fo. 15, and 31 July 1872,
Bright papers, 43385, fo. 206.

to find a solution.[37] Nonetheless, the government's 1872 bill remained loyal to the local option scheme which it had advocated in 1871, although Young had at one stage mooted the secularist policy instead.[38] Opposition to the bill came both from those who wanted safeguards for teaching according to 'use and wont', and from the secularists and anti-clericals (in February 1872, Thomson became President of a League which pressed for bible-reading). The controversy was heightened, not only by the proceedings at Manchester, but by Dean Stanley's insensitive lectures in Edinburgh in January.

Stanley's aim was to publicise his ideal of an ethical, national religion: he minimised the historical differences between the various Scottish sects, venerated the Moderates of the eighteenth century, and scorned the separatist tendencies of modern presbyterians and episcopalians alike. He criticised 'English politicians' – that is, Gladstone – who encouraged sectarian attacks on the Scottish Church Establishment, and he implied that this encouragement was motivated by the hatred of state interference in religious affairs which Scottish episcopalians had exhibited ever since the Jacobite risings.[39] Although Stanley's arguments were defended by Tulloch, for the intellectuals within the Church of Scotland,[40] they considerably aggravated leading Scottish nonconformists' hostility to the Establishment. They were roundly condemned by Free Churchmen, most famously by Rainy and Taylor Innes – whose attack was warmly praised by Gladstone.[41] Rainy insisted that the more Established Churches came to resemble Stanley's ideal, the more they would have become 'a moral nuisance not to be tolerated for an hour', since the state would be exerting itself to 'support the principle that the Church of Christ, as such, has no principle and no conscience – has no peremptory assertions to make, no distinct truth and no distinct life to represent and embody to the world'.[42] The lectures also led John Cairns, for the United Presbyterians, to make a wholesale assault on the Scottish Establishment. He accused Stanley of disdaining 'distinctive Christian truth' and 'our time-hallowed evangelism'; he criticised the 'latitudinarian' Church of Scotland, sunk in 'lethargy and passivity', for forgetting the 'essentially exclusive and dogmatic character of Christianity

[37] Gladstone to Ardmillan, 29 November 1871, Gladstone papers, 44540, fo. 183; to Argyll, 22 November 1871, Matthew, viii, 66.
[38] Young memorandum, 30 December 1871, Glynne–Gladstone papers, 84/2 (f).
[39] Stanley, *Church of Scotland*, esp. pp. xi, 47.
[40] 'Dean Stanley'.
[41] For the latter, see Innes, 'Dean Stanley at Edinburgh'; Gladstone to Innes, 11 March 1872, Gladstone papers, 44541, fo. 90.
[42] Simpson, *Rainy*, i, 240.

itself, which makes it impossible to save the souls of men without instruction, or worship God together without agreement'.[43]

The reaction to the lectures encouraged Dale and his friends in the plan which had been hatched at the Manchester conference, to tour Scotland in order to call for the implementation of the secular solution.[44] Not only Rainy, however, but also John Cairns, was against this course. Most United Presbyterians argued, with Cairns, that religious instruction in schools should continue, and that parental contributions should be deemed to cover its cost, while money raised from the rates paid for the secular teaching. Indeed, although Cairns disliked the provision in the government bill which allowed local authorities to continue grants to denominational schools, he was prepared to accept even that; the motion condemning the local option provision was defeated by 310 votes to 125 at the United Presbyterian synod. Cairns also considered that Dale's appearance in Scotland to advocate his views would, by tainting the United Presbyterians with extremist views, hamper prospects for unity with the Free Church.[45] Dale's tour, predictably, was only a limited success.[46]

On the second reading of the bill, it was an English academic liberal MP, Auberon Herbert, who moved the resolution condemning it for employing the school rate to give religious teaching: he argued that it would furnish a precedent for Irish legislation, would divide localities and poison school-board elections, and would impose contestable religious viewpoints on children.[47] Since to vote for this motion would involve opposing the second reading, support for him was minimal. There was much more Liberal interest, however, in limiting religious teaching in board schools to bible-reading or teaching.[48] At the committee stage of the bill, 127 Liberals voted for Anderson's amendment to exclude catechisms and formularies, distinctive of a particular denomination, from teaching in publicly managed schools: only 13 Irishmen and 26 non-official British Liberals joined the Conservatives and the government men to defeat it.[49] The wording of Anderson's proposal was based on that of Cowper-Temple's amendment to the 1870 Education Bill, which the government had accepted. Although its reason for rejecting a similar amendment on this occasion was that circumstances in Scotland

[43] Cairns, *Disestablishment of the Church of Scotland*.
[44] See also *Nonconformist*, 28 February 1872, p. 213.
[45] Macewen, *Cairns*, pp. 533–4, 544–9; Dale, *Dale*, pp. 289–93; *Nonconformist*, 28 February, 5 June 1872, pp. 213, 586.
[46] Omond, *Lord Advocates*, p. 281.
[47] *Hansard*, ccix, 1531, 7 March 1872.
[48] *Ibid.*, 1548–9, 1552, 1563 (Trevelyan, Duncan McLaren and Graham).
[49] *Ibid.*, ccxi, 1934, 18 June 1872.

were different (the acceptance of the presbyterians' shorter catechism by most Scotsmen made the amendment appear more radical), the impression given by the government's action was that it was trying to renege on the small concessions towards anti-clericalism demanded of it in 1870. Dixon pointed out in the debate that this implied a drift towards denominationalism, which boded ill for the government's proposals for Irish education.[50]

While anti-clerical pressure was being exerted by a good half of the parliamentary party, a few Liberals, together with the Conservatives, the Church of Scotland, and the Begg faction of the Free Church, were calling for a stronger commitment than was provided by the local option clause that instruction in 'the grand, substantial verities of Protestantism' would be guaranteed by the state.[51] As the bill was about to enter the committee stage, Gordon, for the Conservatives, moved a resolution supporting the passage of a measure in the 1872 session, but requesting that it should reaffirm support for the traditional practice of bible-reading in schools. In tabling this motion, the Conservatives were exploiting popular sentiment, not resisting a major change: since 1861 there had been no law providing for bible-reading, merely one enforcing an oath on schoolmasters not to teach contrary to the message of the bible and the Shorter Catechism. The *Economist* condemned the Conservatives' move as an attempt to create the impression in the country that the bill was secularist, when it was not.[52] The Conservatives secured what was a major – if temporary – triumph, winning the debate on their motion by 7 votes: Akroyd, 4 Irish Liberals and 7 Scottish Liberals with rural seats voted against the government. However, when, a month later, Gordon moved an amendment compelling all schools to teach from the bible, in order to give effect to this resolution, it was defeated by 160 votes to 204 (the whips had substantially reduced the number of Liberal abstentions).[53] Nonetheless, the publicity surrounding the debate was to have considerable electoral effects: all over rural Scotland, the Liberals became tarred with the secularist brush, and the climate quickly affected even the cabinet minister Argyll, who denounced the secularist threat with great vehemence on two occasions in the Lords.[54]

In the Lords, the leading Conservatives were happy to accept the bill, which they did not see as seriously threatening religious education, given the traditional inclinations of the Scottish people. Neither the Church

[50] *Ibid.*, 1939.
[51] *Nonconformist*, 13 March 1872, p. 272; Smith, *Begg*, ii, 480–2.
[52] 11 May 1872, p. 575.
[53] *Hansard*, ccxi, 1306, 6 June 1872.   [54] *Ibid.*, ccxii, 686, 1237–8, 5, 16 July.

nor the Conservatives wished to see the bill defeated, because of the need to mollify Free Churchmen and to prevent an agitation for disestablishment.[55] Much of the Conservatives' activity in the Lords was concerned with framing a declaration for the bill's preamble, indicating the enduring importance of religious teaching in schools. Finally the government compromised, agreeing to a declaration which recognised that schools would be free to continue their established custom of giving religious instruction, subject to the liberty of the parent.[56] Indeed, in 1873, the United Presbyterian synod was to pronounce disapproval of the preamble, as 'inconsistent with the spirit and even with the enactments of the measure'.[57]

Ireland in the 1872 session

As one backbencher wrote in his diary at the beginning of the session, the 'great danger' to the survival of the government, among domestic questions, lay in the vote to be taken on Fawcett's bill to abolish tests in Trinity, Dublin.[58] The government was trapped by the rising tides of British anti-clericalism on the one hand and Irish home-rule agitation on the other; and the difficulties which it faced were indicated by the reaction to Hartington's speech in his constituency in early January. Attempting to repair the damage done in Britain by Fortescue's advocacy of denominationalism in the previous October, he stressed that the remedial legislation which had already been passed must be given time to work before any new concessions were introduced. He suggested that what was needed in the meantime was 'the greatest possible firmness' in not tolerating 'any propositions which lead to the insecurity or disseverance of this great Empire; and more than this . . . firmness in showing to the people of Ireland' that the government was 'not willing to hand over the control of education entirely to them and to the priests (loud and long-continued cheers) – no more than they were willing to hand it over to the denominationalists in England'.[59]

This speech had a remarkable effect in Ireland: it made the loss of the two by-elections pending in Kerry and Galway quite certain. After unruly campaigns, the home rulers won sensational victories in both on the same day (6 February). In Kerry, the Protestant home ruler R. P. Blennerhassett defeated the Liberal J. A. Dease; in Galway, Nolan beat

[55] Withrington, 'Towards a national system', p. 121.
[56] *Hansard*, ccxii, 1032, ccxiii, 160, 12, 30 July 1872; Richmond to Cairns, 30 June 1872, Cairns papers, 30/51/2, no. 42.
[57] Gordon, *Charteris*, p. 146.
[58] Diary, 5 February 1872, Cartwright papers, 6/9.
[59] *Times*, 6 January 1872, p. 6.

a Conservative who was supported by whig landowners like Clanricarde.[60] The Irish press was incensed by Hartington's speech, and Bishop Moriarty (the local bishop) told him that it had lost the Kerry election.[61]

These developments placed further difficulties in the way of a solution of the Irish university question. On the one hand, the by-election victories increased the home rulers' confidence, and made them likely to press strongly for denominational endowment in any parliamentary discussion of the matter. On the other, British opinion was not mollified by Hartington's speech, because it was more and more alarmed by the growth of what appeared in British eyes to be a mass Irish party, controlled by the priests and demanding endowment for Catholic education. The history of English and Scottish educational legislation, together with Gladstone's evident ecclesiasticism and populism, suggested that he would be only too susceptible to Irish pressure for such endowment.[62] There was, therefore, much Liberal eagerness to support Fawcett's proposals[63] (except, of course, from John Morley and the *Fortnightly*, and from Liddon and the high churchmen).[64]

Fawcett introduced his bill in March, in order, he said, to give the government no chance of forbidding it time, and every opportunity to propose another solution. In his speech, he criticised the alternative to his motion, which he saw as the endowment of denominational colleges either out of the public funds or by 'despoiling' Trinity and Dublin university.[65]

Gladstone's reaction to the outcry at Hartington's speech had been that a satisfactory solution of the educational dilemma in such a climate was almost impossible.[66] On 9 March, the cabinet agreed to support the second reading of Fawcett's bill. It knew that it was almost universally viewed as a measure simply to abolish tests; that resistance to it, either directly or by amendment, was 'impossible'; and that fewer than ninety Liberals, a third of whom would be members of the government, would probably be willing to vote against it.[67] But the cabinet refused to accept

---

[60] Thornley, *Butt*, pp. 123–31.

[61] Spencer to O'Hagan, 10 January 1872, O'Hagan papers, D2777/8; Moriarty to Hartington, 10 January 1872, Chatsworth papers, 340, fo. 482.

[62] See e.g. *Nonconformist*, 27 March 1872, p. 313; diary, 28 June 1872, Cartwright papers, 6/9.

[63] See e.g. the memorial of Charles Reed and London nonconformists, 11 January 1872, Gladstone papers, 44798, fo. 150.

[64] Morley to Harrison, 1 May 1872, Harrison papers, 1/79; *Pall Mall Gazette*, 30 April 1872, p. 3; Hutton, 'Irish university question'; Johnston, *Liddon*, p. 240.

[65] *Hansard*, ccx, 327, 20 March 1872.

[66] Gladstone to Hartington, 14 January 1872, Chatsworth papers, 340, fo. 135; Matthew, viii, 94.

[67] *Ibid.*, p. 122; Hartington to O'Hagan, 10 March 1872, O'Hagan papers, D2777/8.

the clauses in Fawcett's bill concerning the government of Trinity, and of the Dublin university of which Trinity was the only constituent member: it maintained that the clauses were unfair to Catholic students.[68] Fawcett envisaged the provost, senior fellows, junior fellows, professors and graduates of Trinity sending representatives to boards which would direct studies in the university and college, and the provost, the fellows and the Hebdomadal Board controlling the domestic management of the college. Gladstone's long-term aims, on the other hand, were to divide the government of the university completely from that of the college, in order to allow other colleges to be affiliated to the university. Fawcett's scheme maintained the university in a position of subservience to Trinity, and gave almost complete power over both to the Protestants, who would hold most of the senior positions in the college for some generations to come. Gladstone therefore announced that the government would support the second reading because the bill abolished tests, and would then refuse to accept the bill's other clauses.

The first problem for the government was posed by the home rulers, who tabled an amendment condemning the bill for failing to recognise the Catholics' grievance. Irish Liberals of all shades of opinion criticised the government's weakness and its unwillingness to satisfy legitimate Catholic demands for endowment. A moderate, the O'Conor Don, warned that the home rulers would win more and more support unless the government showed some awareness of the demands of the overwhelming majority of the Catholic population of Ireland. He and Butt both rejected the idea of a mere examining board, and came out in favour of an independent Catholic college, operating in Dublin in conjunction with Trinity. Nolan and Smyth defended the notion of a Catholic teaching university. Synan, the O'Donoghue, Digby and Gray also supported the demands for denominational education.[69]

On 13 April, the cabinet agreed that Hartington was to give notice of an Instruction to divide the bill.[70] In the meantime, the government had an extremely bad week, being defeated three times on ballot and local taxation policy, owing to whig-liberal defections: as Bruce said, these defeats damaged its strength, encouraged discontented Liberals, and rallied the Conservatives.[71] The Instruction, furthermore, made a large number of backbench British Liberals suspicious: it seemed to imply that the government was planning to make an unspecified initiative, at some future date, to placate the Catholics – which would involve endowing

---

[68] Gladstone to Hartington, 24 February 1872, Gladstone papers, 44541, fo. 79; Spencer to Hartington, 27 February, 7 March 1872, Chatsworth papers, 354, fos. 109, 112.

[69] *Hansard*, ccx, 352, 359, 367, 372, 374, 700, 711. For Gladstone, see *ibid.*, 343.

[70] Matthew, viii, 137.   [71] 19 April 1872, *Letters of Aberdare*, i, 340.

denominational education. On 20 April, Glyn reported that some Scots and nonconformists would not vote for the Instruction unless they were reassured as to the government's future intentions.[72] The cabinet accordingly 'came to the conclusion that we should be beaten unless we fought it very high and in fact staked our existence upon the subject of higher education in Ireland not being taken out of our hands'.[73] A *Daily News* article on 22 April – inspired by Stansfeld, the junior member of the cabinet – announced that the vote on Hartington's Instruction would be one of confidence in the government. The newspaper advised compliance with the government's wishes, although it would in other circumstances have recommended support for Fawcett.[74] George Grey and Ellice thought the article 'ill-judged' and blamed it for the crisis in the party which quickly arose; the *Times* also disliked it, and considered that for the government to attempt to fight an election on a platform of opposition to Fawcett's bill would split the party and lead to almost certain defeat.[75]

As Ellice pointed out, there was in any case little threat to the government's position, since the Conservatives were not yet seriously interested in taking office. It was true that Conservative opinion generally supported Fawcett; even Hardy, a staunch defender of denominationalism, did so, reluctantly, seeing his bill as the lesser of two evils. The opposition also disliked the Instruction, which hit at the 'only Conservative part of the Bill', that which protected the autonomy of Trinity.[76] But, notwithstanding this, Disraeli, Derby and Hardy knew that the Conservatives must not force a dissolution before the ballot question was settled. They believed it to be the last issue capable of inspiring the Liberals and of winning an election for them (the Conservative candidates in four recent by-elections had all found it expedient to support secret voting).[77] Not only was a dissolution ruled out; Hardy and Derby, from previous experience, did not wish to take office in a minority government,[78] especially since they did not believe the promises, made by Bouverie and others, that the whigs would support them in such a position. They contended that the 'big whigs' could not be trusted, wish-

---

[72] Glyn to Gladstone, 20 April 1872, Gladstone papers, 44348, fo. 158.

[73] Stansfeld to Halifax, 23 April 1872, Hickleton papers, A 4 51.

[74] *Ibid.*; *Daily News*, 22 April 1872, p. 4.

[75] George Grey to Halifax, 26 April 1872, Hickleton papers, A 4 58; Ellice to Lady Halifax, 23 April 1872, *ibid.*, A 4 104; *Times*, 23 April 1872, p. 9.

[76] Johnson, *Diary of Gathorne Hardy*, pp. 154, 156.

[77] Monypenny and Buckle, *Disraeli*, v, 147; Hunt to Disraeli, 18 April 1872, Disraeli papers, B/XX/Hu/51; Hardy to Disraeli, 18 December 1871, *ibid.*, B/XX/Ha/58.

[78] Johnson, *Diary of Gathorne Hardy*, p. 156; Derby to Disraeli, 9 January 1872, Disraeli papers, B/XX/S/874.

ing merely to ditch Gladstone and continue without him: 'they think they are strong enough to weather the storm'.[79]

The Conservatives' strategy thus concentrated on rallying whig-liberal support in the country, preparatory to winning an election at some future date. It was beginning to become apparent that there was a 'real Conservative reaction' for the first time in twenty-five years.[80] Disraeli accordingly assumed a high political profile with two speeches at Manchester and Crystal Palace in April and June, in which he took pains to try to cultivate whig-liberal sentiment. Both speeches, as the *Spectator* saw, were designed to cast him in the role of the safe statesman, and to contrast this image with a picture of Gladstone as a nominal leader, unable to restrain the enthusiasm of his radical 'left'. Disraeli defended the monarchy, the House of Lords and the rule of law in Ireland; he promised that the Conservatives would conduct foreign policy firmly, and would concentrate their domestic political attention, not on constitutional upheaval, but on practical and constructive administrative questions of limited scope, such as sanitary reform. He was also careful both to defend the Church Establishment, taking the whig view that the Church must be 'comprehensive' in order to be national, and that disestablishment would 'strengthen' the Church's power more than was desirable; and to criticise secularism in education, maintaining that 'a national system of education not founded upon the Providential government of the world would lead to national disaster'.[81]

Pursuit of this strategy required Conservatives to take little part in the discussions about Fawcett's bill, and to avoid provoking the government's resignation. Disraeli thus saw the Irish university dispute, while 'very damaging to the Government', as 'a family quarrel' from which Conservatives should stand aloof.[82]

After the publication of the *Daily News* article, the family quarrel naturally intensified. On 24 April, Fawcett asked Gladstone whether he insisted on imposing a vote of confidence, because, if so, he desired more time for discussion. Gladstone replied ill-temperedly that time was too precious to be wasted on long debates on such issues, but that the

[79] Derby diary, 29 April 1872, 15th earl of Derby papers; Northcote to Disraeli, 23 September 1872, Iddesleigh papers, 50016, fo. 135; Hardy to Disraeli, 18 December 1871, Disraeli papers, B/XX/Ha/58; Feuchtwanger, *Disraeli, democracy*, p. 11.

[80] Hunt to Disraeli, 18 April 1872, Disraeli papers, B/XX/Hu/51; see also Church on the Thanksgiving service of early 1872: Church, *Church*, p. 291.

[81] *Spectator*, 6 April 1872, p. 421, 29 June 1872, pp. 808–9; *Speech at Manchester*, esp. pp. 13–14; *Speech at Crystal Palace*.

[82] Disraeli to Corry, 26 April 1872, Disraeli papers, B/XX/D/171.

government would resign if it was defeated over Hartington's Instruction and was thus prevented from controlling Irish university policy.[83]

Fawcett did not want the government to resign, and so, on 25 April, he moved the adjournment of the House instead. He proclaimed that it was well known that three-quarters of Liberal MPs were strongly in favour of his bill: and that, over the last five years, 'twice my proposals have been talked out. Twice they have been counted out. Twice they have been got rid of by threats of Ministerial resignation.' Playfair and Bouverie took Fawcett's side in the debate.[84] Gladstone, however, accused Playfair of 'singularly inaccurate recitals'; he sneered at Fawcett's 'complacent review . . . of the many mishaps which he has met with in his patriotic labours'; and he attacked him for misrepresenting the government's attitude. It was not true, he argued, that the government had ever concealed its strident opposition to his bill. In reply to Fawcett's point that it would have been unreasonable to assume that 'certain clauses' of his bill would be so objectionable to the government as to prompt a vote of confidence, Gladstone, with a certain disingenuousness, 'beg[ged] to observe that the objection taken was not to certain clauses of the Bill; it was to the whole Bill, with the exception of the provisions that relate to tests'. (The bill was called The University Tests (Dublin) Bill.) He accused Bouverie of misrepresentation in alleging that the government had first announced the vote of confidence to the *Daily News*: it had announced it long ago, 'in the midst of our struggles on the Irish Land Bill'.[85] As Morrison pointed out, he thus forgot that the confidence threat *then* had been levied against precisely the proposal, the abolition of tests, which the government was now supporting; and, moreover, that the government was pledged to legislate on the question, despite calling a vote of confidence against a bill which aimed to fulfil that pledge.[86]

While this debate was raging, Gladstone was also outlining, in private, his support for a rating system for Irish elementary education, on the grounds that it would encourage habits of public responsibility and self-government in Ireland. The immediate context of his proposal was another attempt by the government to grapple with the perpetual difficulty of paying for the Irish elementary system; the advantage of Gladstone's scheme was that it made it possible to tax the Irish themselves less leniently than the government had previously dared to do (the economy-minded Lowe therefore supported the scheme). But the institution, throughout Catholic Ireland, of a system by which local opinion

---

[83] *Hansard*, ccx, 1754–7. Matthew, viii, 143, fn. 2, states that Gladstone denied that there would be a vote of confidence, but this was not the impression gained by most Liberals.
[84] *Hansard*, ccx, 1818–19, 1825, 1822.
[85] *Ibid.*, 1835.   [86] *Ibid.*, 1841–2.

would be allowed to determine the nature of religious instruction, would inevitably entrench denominationalism there; and Hartington, not surprisingly, disliked Gladstone's proposal, arguing that neither British Liberal opinion, nor tax-conscious Irishmen, would tolerate it. Gladstone agreed that the party would not accept such a proposal in the present climate; and the shortfall in funding was met, instead, by a temporary increase in state grants in support of the existing system.[87] Hartington was further alarmed by Gladstone's remarks in the Commons on 2 May, in discussing the laws concerning Irish public meetings: he talked of the desirability of strengthening Irish local government.[88] An Irish correspondent of Hartington's told him that his speech had given an 'immense impulse' to the home-rule cry. Hartington himself felt that Gladstone's views on home rule were 'much too Liberal', and that he was prepared to concede anything that the home rulers demanded, as long as they 'profess to maintain the supremacy of the Imperial Parliament'.[89]

As if Liberal antagonism to Gladstone's concessionary Irish policies were not already sufficiently well-developed, there were two more embarrassments during the 1872 session, namely the Keogh judgment and the O'Keeffe case.

On 27 May, Judge Keogh pronounced judgment on the election petition brought against Nolan, the victorious candidate in the Galway by-election. The nine-hour judgment constituted a formidable condemnation of priestly interference in the election, which the judge castigated as the 'most astounding attempt at ecclesiastical tyranny which the whole history of priestly intolerance presents'.[90] This naturally raised the political temperature. On the one hand, the Irish reaction against Keogh was virulent.[91] This view was also taken by the positivists: Beesly argued that the state should 'altogether renounce interference with the free expression of opinion', and should not prevent any form of *'spiritual bribery and intimidation'.* He contended that the priests were not to be condemned: they were acting as an 'independent spiritual power . . . resting . . . on the moral sympathies and intellectual convictions of the public'.[92]

On the other hand, the judgment aroused renewed hostility to the priests in Britain.[93] There was a widespread demand that the govern-

---

[87] Hartington memorandum, 12 April 1872, Gladstone papers, 44640, fo. 78; Hartington to Gladstone, 1 May 1872, *ibid.*, 44143, fo. 160; 1 May 1872, Matthew, viii, 146.

[88] *Hansard*, ccxi, 160.   [89] Holland, *Devonshire*, i, 95–6.

[90] Norman, *Catholic Church*, pp. 423–4.   [91] *Ibid.*, pp. 425–6.

[92] Beesly, 'The Galway judgment'. Harrison strongly approved of this article: to Morley, 5 July [1872], Harrison papers, 1/54.

[93] *Pall Mall Gazette*, 29 May 1872, p. 1. See also Layard to Gregory, 13 June 1872, Layard papers, 38949, fo. 106.

ment should respond to the judgment by prosecuting a number of those whom Keogh had criticised. Gladstone was naturally reluctant to do this: he had been infuriated by Keogh's language and its effect on the political situation.[94] But, as Derby saw, the cabinet would be in great danger of censure by the Commons if it did not prosecute: if Gladstone, whose 'excessive veneration' for priests was already ridiculed by his party, indulged his natural inclinations and did not act, 'we should have against him the justice of the case, the Liberal feeling against priestly power, the English feeling against lawless and violent proceedings'.[95] Disraeli also saw the chance of scoring a major political point; and the prospect both of his intervention, and of a parliamentary attack from Harcourt's ally, the Liberal backbencher Henry James, left the government no option but to prosecute.[96] The Irish attorney-general announced that twenty-four men, including the bishop of Clonfert, were to be charged under the 1854 Corrupt Practices Act.[97] As it was, James made a strident speech on 25 July appealing to the Liberals to rediscover the 'good old cry of "Civil and religious liberty"', and to renounce association with home rulers and with Irish Catholic supporters of 'sacerdotal supremacy'.[98] But, once the decision to prosecute was known, the government had to endure much abuse from the Irish MPs.[99] Moreover, as had been predicted, the prosecutions were ineffectual; the bishop was acquitted in February 1873, and the other proceedings were then dropped.[100] The result of the affair, as Halifax recognised, was that the government lost face with both Irish Catholic and English Protestant opinion.[101]

The O'Keeffe case had meanwhile brought the issue of priestly control over education, and indeed that of papal interference in politics, even more into the public eye. O'Keeffe was parish priest of Callan, in Ireland, and manager of the Callan National Schools. He had been suspended from the former office by the hierarchy, after he had disobeyed two papal Bulls by bringing a (partially successful) action for slander against his bishop and curates in a civil court. O'Keeffe sued Cullen for unfairly suspending him;[102] but, in April 1872, the Commissioners of National Education decided that, since O'Keeffe had been suspended as parish

[94] Gladstone to Hartington, 5 April 1873, Gladstone papers, 44542, fo. 106.
[95] Derby diary, 9, 24 July 1872, 15th earl of Derby papers; Derby to Disraeli, 11 July 1872, Disraeli papers, B/XX/S/884.
[96] (Disraeli) *Hansard*, ccxii, 18 July 1872, 1370; for James, see 17 July 1872, Matthew, viii, 180.
[97] Norman, *Catholic Church*, p. 427; *Hansard*, ccxii, 1626.
[98] *Hansard*, ccxii, 1834.
[99] *Ibid.*, 1763, 1783, 1804, 1807; ccxiii, 797.
[100] Norman, *Catholic Church*, p. 428; *Hansard*, ccxiv, 898.
[101] Halifax to Northbrook, 19 August 1872, Northbrook papers, 144, 20.
[102] Norman, *Catholic Church*, pp. 431–3.

priest, he should also be replaced as manager of the schools by the new priest.

The case was raised in the Lords by the Conservative Harrowby, and in the Commons by Bouverie. The latter asked if the Education Commissioners were to be 'the instruments of a foreign ecclesiastical Power'.[103] Hartington and Gladstone pledged that the government would take no action until O'Keeffe's suit against Cullen had been decided. Both made it clear that they thought that the Commissioners should similarly have waited.[104] Even so, Bouverie's symbolic motion to reduce by £1,000 the sum allocated annually for Irish education was defeated by only 57 votes to 49.

Gladstone also failed in his vigorous attempts, in July and August 1872, to persuade the prince of Wales to go to Ireland for a certain number of months each year. The favoured plan was that the viceroyalty should be abolished, and that the prince should act as the queen's representative in Ireland. Neither the queen nor the prince liked this plan: they felt that he would either have no real administrative role, and would merely consort with Conservative and Protestant Dublin society, or that he would become entangled in all the controversies attending the exercise of British rule in Ireland; in either event, he would antagonise the Catholics. The prince wished instead to observe the work of a succession of government departments in England, a suggestion which Gladstone considered would effect little good, would not discipline him, and would certainly not provide 'a Plan of Life'. In pressing his proposal as strongly as he did – more strongly than the emollient Halifax was prepared to do – Gladstone lost the queen's goodwill permanently.[105]

By the end of the 1872 session, the government had irritated whig-liberal opinion on a number of other fronts. The defeats of April on local taxation and ballot policy – damaging, although not on matters of confidence – had been caused by substantial whiggish defections. Thirty-seven Liberal MPs voted for the Conservative Massey Lopes's motion demanding that ratepayers should be relieved of part of the burden of payment for services which were not subject to local control. Later in the session, a deputation of Liberal county members called on Gladstone and demanded a reform of local taxation, but to no effect.[106] Two days

[103] *Hansard*, ccxiii, 515.
[104] (Hartington) *ibid.*, 528; 14 August 1872, Matthew, viii, 191; see also *ibid.*, pp. 205–6, 209–10.
[105] See Guedalla, *Queen and Gladstone*, i, 340–1, 351–70, 374–81; Matthew, viii, 122–3, 202–3, 204, 209; Gladstone–Halifax correspondence, August–September 1872, Gladstone papers, 44185, fos. 298–318.
[106] Diary, 11 July 1872, Cartwright papers, 6/9.

after this defeat, exactly the same number of Liberals, including George Grey and Harcourt, voted against the 'despotic' amendment in the Ballot Bill which stipulated that an elector who deliberately showed his completed ballot paper in public should receive a prison sentence.[107] The Ballot Bill eventually passed without the amendment; the Licensing Bill passed as well, in a less severe form than its predecessor of 1871. Meanwhile, the scientific fraternity and the metropolitan press were driven to further distrust of Gladstone by the government's behaviour in what became known as the Ayrton–Hooker affair. The junior minister Ayrton, an exuberant and dedicated philistine, had been unreasonably dictatorial to Hooker, the distinguished scientist and director of Kew Gardens (over which Ayrton had nominal authority), and Hooker's parliamentary and academic friends had rallied to his defence. Gladstone, however, did not prove very sympathetic, and his obvious lack of interest in science, and his public and private criticism of scientists' sensitivity and self-importance, irritated them.[108] Finally, and most importantly, the government's apparent submissiveness in its negotiations with the United States, arising from the *Alabama* affair, inspired much whig-liberal criticism – from Lowe, Cardwell, Goschen, Halifax and Kimberley in the cabinet; from Somerset, Grey and Russell in the Lords; and in the country more generally. At one time, the crisis threatened to break up the government, but it was resolved in June 1872. However, the subsequent announcement, by international arbitrators, that Britain would have to pay $15.5 million to the United States in compensation, afforded fresh opportunities for domestic critics of the government.[109]

In response to both religious and secular policy, therefore, 'a large section of moderate Liberals' in the country held – as one disgruntled junior minister put it – a 'growing *distrust* of Gladstone's leaning to the extreme Party', by the end of the 1872 session.[110] At the end of April, the *Spectator* (which also disliked the government's conduct on the ballot question and during the *Alabama* affair) had viewed the political situation with much disquiet, criticising both the growing instability of the Liberal government, and the showy but insubstantial reappearance of Disraeli

---

[107] *Hansard*, ccx, 1404–7, 1508–12; Kinzer, 'The un-Englishness of the secret ballot', pp. 253–6; diary, 15 April 1872, Cartwright papers, 6/9; diary, 18 April 1872, Trelawny papers, d 419, p. 19.

[108] See Macleod, 'Ayrton incident', esp. p. 72, fn. 9; Huxley, *Huxley*, ii, 427; Buckle, *Letters of Victoria*, ii, 225; Morley, *Gladstone*, ii, 420; Layard to Gregory, 22 July, 20 October 1872, Layard papers, 38949, fos. 109, 113.

[109] Halifax to Grey, 30 January 1872, Grey papers; (Lowe) Salisbury to Carnarvon, 5 February 1872, Carnarvon papers; Granville to Ripon, 6 April 1872, Ripon papers, 43521, fo. 87; Elliot, *Goschen*, i, 134–6; 20 June 1872, Drus, *Journal of Kimberley*, p. 32; 13 June 1872, Matthew, viii, 162.

[110] Knatchbull-Hugessen to Dufferin, 7 September 1872, Dufferin papers.

onto the political stage. It dismissed the idea of a Whig–Conservative coalition; but it recognised that public opinion increasingly desired the formation of an administration staffed by moderate men, who would govern on principles acceptable to the responsible elements in both parties, and who would avoid major legislative innovation. This, indeed, was a viewpoint which was often to be repeated in the press during the next two years.[111]

The framing, introduction and defeat of the Irish University Bill, 1872–3

After the 1872 session, with the ballot and *Alabama* affairs settled, the government's position was at least clear: it would not survive if it did not introduce an Irish University Bill – 'like James I "No Bishop no King" it is "No Bill, no Government" '.[112] On the other hand, it was thought to be increasingly likely that the introduction of the bill would itself lead to the government's fall.[113] Although this created a certain reluctance to tackle the question,[114] the internal party criticism of the government during the previous two sessions, and the exhaustion experienced by many ministers, made the chance of failure quite alluring for some. Granville thought that the question 'seems to afford an admirable opportunity for an honorable defeat';[115] in February 1873, Bruce, misled by the false dawn after Gladstone's speech introducing the government bill, wrote: 'Alas! I fear all prospect of ministerial defeat is over.'[116]

In framing the bill, the need to abolish tests in Trinity was, of course, accepted by all. So was the importance of being seen to avoid any endowment of Catholic teaching – the rock on which Disraeli's university proposals of 1868 had foundered. The first battle to be fought was about the organisation of an ideal university system, and was fought between the schools of thought headed by Lowe and by Playfair. Lowe favoured the separation, as far as possible, of universities' examining and teaching functions, and the establishment of a separate examining board for the award of degrees. Playfair, arguing from his experience of the Scottish system, maintained that the colleges, although teaching bodies, were able to set fair examinations, and would not depress standards in order to achieve good results. Lowe's scheme required Trinity to surrender a

---

[111] 27 April 1872, p. 522.
[112] Gladstone to Hartington, 16 January 1873, Gladstone papers, 44144, fo. 25.
[113] Argyll to Northbrook, 7 January 1873, Northbrook papers, 144/9.
[114] Fortescue to Clermont, 3 November 1872, Strachie papers, C3/234b.
[115] Note, n.d., Gladstone papers, 44640, fo. 199.
[116] 15 February 1873, *Letters of Aberdare*, i, 354. Gladstone himself expressed his eagerness to retire on several occasions, e.g. diary, 2 February 1873, Phillimore papers; Gladstone to Manning, 3 January 1873, Gladstone papers, 44542, fo. 64.

considerable portion of her endowments in order to support the work of the examining board (Lowe, indeed, tended to disapprove of the possession of endowments by teaching institutions). Playfair's views were supported by Argyll and Hartington, on the grounds that they preserved Trinity's freedom of action with regard to examinations, as well as her endowments. Hartington, moreover, did not think that one body of examiners could fairly judge between candidates of different denominations.[117]

Gladstone broadly accepted Lowe's view, but he developed it, as Lowe had not, so as to establish a number of safeguards for denominational independence. The basis of Gladstone's plan was the separation of Trinity from the Dublin university, the redundant institution to which it was connected. The university was to be transformed into an examining board, which would serve the needs of a number of colleges to be affiliated to it – including Trinity, the Queen's colleges, and Catholic and presbyterian denominational colleges. None of these colleges were to be endowed by the state; but the examining board would be funded partly from Trinity's excessive endowments, partly from the surplus left after the disestablishment of the Irish Church, and partly by the British government. Gladstone's plan, put before the cabinet on 20 November, did, however, give the colleges some role in the conduct of the examinations: they might propose a syllabus to the university's governing body, and might protest at the content of the examinations (after the event). If it were found necessary, in order to prevent discrimination against candidates of a particular religion, portions of the modern history and moral and mental philosophy syllabuses – where the religious perspectives of candidates and examiners might affect their judgment – were not to be examinable. Gladstone also introduced a teaching element into the central university: professors would be appointed to lecture. But there would be no chairs in those subjects in which differences of interpretation were possible, and the examining board was to be composed in the main of non-professors, so that their influence would be limited. The governing body of the university would be empowered to reprimand or suspend a professor or examiner who offended religious convictions. The governing body would, in the first instance, be named by parliament; but, after the passage of years had evened out the ratio of Protestants to Catholics throughout the university system, it would be chosen instead mainly by university graduates, although the Crown

---

[117] Matthew, viii, 227–30; Hartington to Gladstone, 30 October 1872, Gladstone papers, 44143, fo. 196; Gladstone to Argyll, 2 November 1872, *ibid.*, 44542, fo. 35; Argyll to Gladstone, 30 October, 4 November 1872, *ibid.*, 44102, fos. 184, 186; Lowe to Gladstone, 27 October 1872, Selborne papers, 1865, fo. 150; Gladstone to Selborne, 21 October 1872, *ibid.*, fo. 160.

would still nominate some. The university was not to have a theological faculty: Trinity's faculty was to be separated from it, in order to preserve its independence, now that tests had been abolished.[118]

At the next cabinet, two days later, Hartington criticised Gladstone's scheme, which he saw as likely to alienate Trinity, to give too much power to the examining board, and to leave Catholic education too much in the hands of the priests. He argued that Trinity would be insulted by her lack of influence over the syllabus: she would probably decline to participate in the examinations, would enter candidates for the London university examinations in medicine and law, and would bestow her own arts degrees. He contended that the examining board had too much power over the colleges and over the professors, who would not be able to dictate a course of teaching independent of the examiners (who Hartington expected would be strongly influenced by sectarian feelings and comparatively uninterested in education). He maintained that the clause permitting protests at the conduct of examinations would empower Catholic priests – who would act on behalf of the constituent Catholic colleges – to undermine the whole system. The effect of the scheme, he thought, would be to perpetuate the power of the priests over Catholic youth, because a large number of provincial colleges would be affiliated to the examining board. To counteract this threat, Hartington wished to see only one Catholic college formally affiliated, and that administered by laymen.

He therefore proposed two amendments: the first was the establishment of an unendowed lay Catholic college, and the second – which he considered to be desirable only if the first were adopted – was the representation of the affiliated colleges on the governing body, in order to give them more influence over the examinations. This would satisfy Trinity, would check the power of the priests, and would permit a closer identity between teaching and examining functions than Gladstone and Lowe had intended. The present plan would be 'as unacceptable to the educated lay Roman Catholics as to Trinity College, and the Protestants generally'.[119]

But the cabinet did not favour Hartington's ideas. He therefore threatened to resign, doubting that he could be responsible for the passage through parliament of such an unfair and unpopular bill. Gladstone succeeded in preventing his resignation, helped by Spencer's reluctance to see a new chief secretary; but Hartington's discontent was openly expressed, and continued throughout the cabinet's discussions. (He was also unhappy that the cabinet would not allow him to introduce

---

[118] Memorandum, 20 November 1872, Granville papers, 30/29/69, fo. 210.
[119] Hartington memorandum, 21 November 1872, *ibid.*, fo. 217.

a measure for the purchase of Irish railways by the state, which he
thought would be far more beneficial to Ireland than the University
Bill.)[120] Argyll was so unsympathetic to the bill that he retired to Scotland rather than sit through the winter cabinets,[121] and Kimberley, who
remained, was sceptical and disillusioned about the whole affair.[122]
Halifax wished to see a mixed teaching university in Dublin;[123] neither
he nor Selborne were to experience any 'disappointment' when the bill
was eventually rejected.[124] Spencer agreed with Hartington that Trinity
would not support the bill.[125] The Irish executive (and Halifax) thought
the bill likely to fail, because Catholics would accept nothing less than
the endowment of a Catholic college.[126]

In December and January the bill was drafted, and Gladstone discussed his proposals with J. K. Ingram, a Fellow of Trinity. In the meantime, the press commentary on two events affected the climate of
opinion. Firstly, Gladstone himself delivered a speech at Liverpool
college on 21 December, claiming that the major work of the age was the
repulsion of the rationalist assault on religion. His Butlerian defence of
faith, although admired by Argyll, Newman Hall and Manning, was
widely criticised – especially by the *Daily News* and *Pall Mall Gazette* – for
its clericalism, and its unwillingness to engage in serious intellectual
debate with the new schools of thought.[127] Secondly, the *Times* and the
Pall Mall Gazette were giving much praise to the arguments of Froude's
newly published *English in Ireland* (see p. 128) – to Manning's great displeasure.[128]

The bill as introduced on 13 February 1873 had been altered in several
particulars, but the cabinet, resigned and weary, seems to have made few
objections, and, indeed, taken little interest in the second round of dis-

---

[120] Hartington to Gladstone, 27 November, 27 December 1872, Gladstone papers, 44143,
     fos. 204, 221; Matthew, viii, 243, 251–2, 283; Holland, *Devonshire*, i, 98–104, 109–10;
     Spencer to Hartington, 30 November 1872, Chatsworth papers, 354, fo. 178.
[121] Argyll to Halifax, 2 December 1872, Hickleton papers, A 4 82.
[122] Kimberley to Ripon, 15 December 1872, 29, 31 January 1873, Ripon papers, 43522,
     fos. 225, 228, 237.
[123] Halifax to Gladstone, 25 December 1872, Gladstone papers, 44185, fo. 319.
[124] Selborne, *Memorials II*, i, 318; Halifax to Northbrook, 19 March 1873, Northbrook
     papers, 144, 21, i.
[125] Spencer to Frederick Cavendish, 10 December 1872, Chatsworth papers, 354, fo. 182.
[126] Halifax to Northbrook, 7 December 1872, Northbrook papers, 144, 20; O'Hagan to
     Hartington, 20 December 1872, Hartington to O'Hagan, 1 February 1873, O'Hagan
     papers, D2777/7.
[127] Gladstone, *Address at Liverpool college*; 24 December 1872, Matthew, viii, 262; Manning to
     Gladstone, 26 December 1872, Gladstone papers, 44250, fo. 69; Argyll to Gladstone,
     31 December 1872, *ibid.*, 44102, fo. 197; Newman Hall to Gladstone, 31 December 1872,
     ibid., 44188, fo. 111; *Daily News*, 23 December 1872, p. 4; *Pall Mall Gazette*, 26 December
     1872, p. 1.
[128] Manning to Gladstone, 2 January 1873, Gladstone papers, 44250, fo. 73.

cussions.[129] The main alteration was apparently only one of presentation: that the central provision of the bill, apart from the abolition of tests, was to be the separation of the university from Trinity.[130] Gladstone made it clear in his speech introducing the bill that nothing else was to be considered of the 'essence' of the bill; the significance of this announcement became clear only later.

The details of the bill had also been slightly altered. Gladstone now proposed a complex system whereby the Crown would nominate some members of the governing body, and the university itself others. Most controversially, he had altered his decision on the representation of colleges, but not in the direction requested by Hartington. Now, all colleges with 50 pupils *in statu pupillari* were to be permitted one member on the governing body, and those with 150 might send two. Gladstone specified Maynooth college (the Catholic theological seminary), and the presbyterian Magee college, Londonderry, as immediate candidates for affiliation, and hoped that other voluntary institutions would follow suit – which, as many were to point out in the Commons, raised the prospect that provincial Catholic colleges would dominate the governing body of the university and thus redirect its endowments to denominational purposes. (However, in line with Gladstone's pledge of 1871, parliament was to have power to prevent the affiliation of any new college.) He also announced that Galway college would be abolished, since it was not sufficiently patronised by the local Catholic students; but the other two Queen's colleges were to be reprieved. Half of the property which remained to Trinity, after claims for compensation to fellows had been met, would go to the university. Apart from the abolition of tests, Trinity's internal affairs would be unaffected. The university's professors would be liable to penalties if, in the judgment of the governing body, they offended religious sentiment (these were the 'gagging clauses', which were to be much criticised in parliament).[131]

The most significant reaction to the bill was that of radical nonconformists, who were pleasantly surprised by it, because it upheld the 'secular' principle which they had been advocating (John Morley also liked it).[132] The *Nonconformist* received the bill as one 'which, beyond even our expectation, furnishes materials for the solution of the most difficult and critical question which the present Parliament has been called upon to decide': it was based on 'the only sound and possible principle', giving colleges freedom to teach religion, but no state money. The newspaper

---

[129] On 22 and 31 January and 8 February: Matthew, viii, 273, 280, 283; Kimberley to Ripon, 31 January 1873, Ripon papers, 43522, fo. 237; Forster to Ripon, 31 January 1873, *ibid.*, 43537, fo. 83.

[130] Gladstone to Thring, 18 January 1873, Gladstone papers, 44332, fo. 76.

[131] *Hansard*, ccxiv, 378, 13 February 1873.   [132] Hirst, *Morley*, i, 233.

was happy that denominational colleges were to be represented on the governing body, even if this proposal allowed Catholics eventually to gain control of the system.

It would be misleading, however, to suggest that even radical nonconformists were *enthusiastic* advocates of the bill – the subject was not one which they could tackle with relish, because to do so demanded sympathy with the sacerdotalists' ambitions. Many were critical of specific concessions to the Catholics, such as the 'gagging clauses', the syllabus restrictions, the dissolution of Galway, and even, in some cases, the representation of denominational colleges. Nonetheless, they were anxious to support the bill's general principles.[133] There were also, of course, exceptions, among 'Protestant' nonconformists, to this tendency to support the bill. Arthur, loyal to the Ulster Wesleyans, was shocked by the measure: it played so blatantly into the pope's hands that it would not have been proposed 'by a Liberal statesman, even in a purely Roman Catholic country on the Continent, say in Belgium or Italy' – because papal designs were better understood there.[134] Martineau saw, in the bill, signs that Gladstone was willing to 'truckle to the Ultramontane power' in education.[135] But most nonconformists were uncharacteristically taciturn in discussing the bill: they considered it to be an acceptable measure – unlike previous education bills – but one difficult to praise to the full.

Protestant opinion in Ireland was divided between those who were broadly contented with the safeguards provided for Protestant denominational teaching, and those who were concerned for the future of mixed education. Magee college, Londonderry, which hoped to gain in stature from affiliation to the university system, supported it; but in Belfast, there was much more disquiet at the measure, especially at the Queen's college.[136] The Queen's university, and Queen's college, Cork, also criticised the bill, protesting at the subordination of teaching colleges to an examining board, and at the concessions to the denominational colleges.[137] Opinion in Trinity was split between those who thought Fawcett's bill satisfactory, and those who wished to guarantee the college's heritage, income and religious attachments by supporting the establishment and endowment of a Catholic college. This group

---

[133] *Nonconformist*, 19, 26 February 1873, pp. 177, 201, 5 March 1873, pp. 227–8; resolutions, 27 February 1873, Gladstone papers, 44620, fo. 88.

[134] Arthur, *Shall the loyal be deserted?*, pp. 11–12.

[135] Drummond and Upton, *Martineau*, ii, 90. Both these comments were made after 1873.

[136] Resolutions, 26 February 1873, Gladstone papers, 44437, fo. 251; Smyth to Gladstone, 28 February 1873, *ibid.*, fo. 267; Moody and Beckett, *Queen's, Belfast*, i, 285–6; Macknight, *Ulster as it is*, i, 280.

[137] *Globe*, 27 February 1873, p. 3; *Nonconformist*, 5 March 1873, p. 228; memorial, 22 February 1873, Gladstone papers, 44620, fo. 76.

included Butt, Ball and Samuel Haughton, but they were in a considerable minority; most Trinity men advocated Fawcett's solution, on condition that some of his clauses were more carefully framed. But both camps found much to criticise in the government's bill: the reduction of Trinity's influence and independence, the consequent lowering of standards, the attack on her endowments, and the influence over university administration given to Catholic colleges.[138]

Irish Catholic opinion, however, was also wary of the bill. The home rulers (who had enjoyed two more by-election successes after those at Galway and Kerry) were quick to oppose it, on the grounds that it did not give enough state money to university education in Ireland; that a first-class endowed Catholic institution was required; that the bill despoiled Trinity to no purpose; and that it lowered teaching standards by imposing syllabus restrictions in an attempt to maintain the fiction of a mixed system.[139] They announced their opposition to the second reading a week after the introduction of the measure.[140]

Catholic opinion more generally was soon hardening against the bill. The *Times* correspondent in Dublin reported that the Irish press had largely pronounced against it by 22 February.[141] Russell of Maynooth complained to Spencer of the measure's unfairness.[142] On 25 February, Spencer had a long conversation with Cullen in which the latter was, without committing himself, hostile to the bill, mainly because he considered that the absence of endowment for denominational colleges would prevent them from competing for students on equal terms with the lavishly endowed undenominational ones.[143] Two days later, the bishops met and voiced these criticisms, but Gladstone and Manning (who thought the bill acceptable) both believed that they might yet prove amenable to negotiation and compromise.[144]

Irish Protestant disquiet influenced Conservative party attitudes to the bill: Cairns and Napier, the vice-chancellor of Dublin university, headed the criticism for them. They objected to the same clauses as other Protestants: the power given to provincial priest-ridden colleges to dominate (or wreck) the governing body, and to interfere with the examination system; the suppression of Galway; the limitations to the

---

[138] Petition, 1 March 1873, Gladstone papers, 44620, fo. 91; Poole to *Daily News*, 27 February 1873, p. 2; *Globe*, 27 February 1873, p. 3.

[139] Henry to Butt, 6 January, 17 February 1873, Butt papers, 8695 (2), (6); Edmund Dease (advanced Liberal MP) to Monsell, 22 February 1873, Emly papers, 8318 (3).

[140] Disraeli to Corry, 22 February 1873, Disraeli papers, B/XX/D/198.

[141] *Times*, 24 February, p. 6.

[142] Spencer to Gladstone, 25 February 1873, Gladstone papers, 44307, fo. 159.

[143] Gordon, *Spencer*, i, 104–6.

[144] Norman, *Catholic Church*, p. 451; Matthew, viii, 294; Hartington to O'Hagan, 1 March 1873, O'Hagan papers, D2777/7.

curriculum; and the 'gagging clauses'.[145] But, although Disraeli believed that the bill was 'all humbug', he was depressed after his wife's death and was thinking of retirement.[146] The Conservatives were slow to appreciate the possibilities afforded to them by the affair – indeed, in late February, Derby, Carnarvon and Cairns were all out of the country.[147] On 22 February, a Conservative conclave proposed to carry on a 'great debate' on the second reading, in order to encourage opposition to the measure, but did not commit itself to voting against the second reading, only to moving resolutions on going into committee.[148]

Conservative interest grew as it became apparent that dislike of the bill was intensifying, not only in Ireland, but, more importantly from a political viewpoint, from broad swathes of British Protestant opinion. Whig-liberal opinion in Britain had at first been quite warm towards the bill, because it had expected something worse – the direct endowment of Catholicism – and because Gladstone's scheme was too complicated for its effects to be perceived at immediate acquaintance. The criticism of Harcourt, Horsman and Huxley had therefore been restrained, although Tait and Stanley had been 'sarcastic' about the bill.[149] But, as the details of the scheme were studied, attitudes changed, among both whig-liberals and academic liberals. In late February, two Liberal MPs wrote letters to the *Daily News* which were hostile to the bill. The first, anonymous, attacked the assumption that there was a Catholic grievance at all, arguing that the Queen's colleges were popular, and that the opening of Trinity would give Catholics increased access to a liberal university training. He disliked the affiliation of denominational colleges to the university, and considered that their withdrawal from the governing body, the abandonment of the 'gagging clauses', and the preservation of Galway, should be the '*sine qua non*' of Liberal support for the bill.[150] Four days later, Morrison wrote a letter, which criticised the representation of denominational colleges on the governing body, government control of half the nominations to it, and the 'gagging clauses'; and which expressed some strong views on the subject of government university

---

[145] Derby to Disraeli, 23 February 1873, Disraeli papers, B/XX/S/887; (Cairns and Napier), February 1873, *ibid.*, B/XX/Ca/97–8; Napier to Hardy, n.d. 1873, Cranbrook papers, Ha43 T 501/146.

[146] Disraeli to Corry, 25, 18 February 1873, Disraeli papers, B/XX/D/200, 196.

[147] *Times*, 13 March 1873, p. 9; Disraeli to Corry, 15 February 1873, Disraeli papers, B/XX/D/194.

[148] Disraeli to Corry, 22 February 1873, Disraeli papers, B/XX/D/198.

[149] Harcourt (warm with reservations) to Butler, [February 1873], Harcourt papers, 204, fo. 7; Huxley (critical of the 'gagging clauses' and of the affiliation of small colleges) to Playfair, 23 February 1873, Playfair papers, 365; (Horsman on 15 February) *Hansard*, ccxiv, 1495; Disraeli to Corry, 17 February 1873, Disraeli papers, B/XX/D/195; Baillie and Bolitho, *Later letters of Lady A. Stanley*, p. 152.

[150] *Daily News*, 22 February 1873, p. 6.

policy in general.[151] In private, Thomson and Jowett attacked the bill on very similar grounds,[152] and even Brand, the new Speaker, wrote to Halifax urging that Gladstone must give way regarding the affiliation of denominational colleges to the university.[153]

On 2 March, Hardy could 'never remember so growing an opposition from all quarters';[154] two days later, Gladstone reported 'much coldness' on the Liberal benches and a 'downcast' chief whip.[155] He had to prevent the Catholic Monsell, against the latter's wishes, from speaking in the debate, in case it irritated backbenchers.[156]

The first two days' discussion in parliament, on 3 and 6 March, made it clear that Liberal dislike of the bill was considerable. A Liberal back-bencher considered that the debate had much damaged its prospects;[157] while the Speaker recorded that he had encountered 'a difficulty in calling men to speak for the Bill'.[158] Fawcett and Fitzmaurice made what were recognised to be powerful speeches against it, charging that it would hand education to the priests, on account of the influence given to denominational colleges: in time, this would allow them to secure control of all educational endowments. They also criticised, inevitably, the 'gagging clauses', the syllabus restrictions, and the suppression of Galway. Both advocated the establishment of a number of mixed teaching universities in Ireland, and argued that mixed education was the only cure for Irish disorder.[159] On 6 March, Horsman made another influential hostile speech, defending the existing mixed institutions, reviewing the government's doubtful record on religious and educational matters, and asserting that Catholic priests, to whom the government would hand education, were challenging the authority of temporal government. In his eyes, the bill 'aimed a deadly blow' at 'the greatest blessing that the British Legislature ever conferred upon Ireland'.[160] Had a division been taken after Horsman's speech, the government considered defeat almost certain, given the effectiveness of his attack.[161] On the same day, Playfair made a far less strident speech, accepting the 'essence' of the bill, and emphasising that it extended the undenominational system to embrace Trinity as well as the Queen's colleges; he announced his intention of supporting the second reading. But he

[151] *Ibid.*, 26 February 1873, p. 5.
[152] Thomson to Playfair, 26 February 1873, Playfair papers, 655; diary, 2 March 1873, Cartwright papers, 6/10.
[153] Brand to Halifax, 3 March 1873, Hickleton papers, A 4 94.
[154] Johnson, *Diary of Gathorne Hardy*, p. 172.
[155] To Ripon, Matthew, viii, 296.
[156] Fortescue to Gladstone, 6 March 1873, Gladstone papers, 44123, fo. 37.
[157] Diary, 6 March 1873, Trelawny papers, 419, p. 77.
[158] Diary, 6 March 1873, Brand papers.   [159] *Hansard*, ccxiv, 1202, 1240.
[160] *Ibid.*, ccxiv, 1398.   [161] Holland, *Devonshire*, i, 116.

blamed the measure for trying too hard to please the ultramontane priests, and he repeated the standard Protestant criticisms. He was naturally most concerned at the immense power given to substandard provincial colleges to influence the conduct of university administration, through the examining board.[162]

As Torrens noted from his talks with MPs, there was 'growing dissatisfaction' with the bill among 'old Whigs and earnest Churchmen'; but 'few, if any', of the nonconformists hesitated in declaring in its favour.[163] Osborne Morgan, the only Liberal to speak on behalf of nonconformist opinion on the first day of the debate, strongly supported it: he contended that it combined 'the greatest possible amount of concession to the Roman Catholics with the strict maintenance of the secular principle in State education by combining voluntary denominational Colleges into a State-supported undenominational University'. He argued that Fawcett's scheme would not solve the Catholics' legitimate grievance, and he welcomed any proposal to give Catholics 'their own Colleges ... their own religious instruction, worship, and discipline' – as long as the colleges were not directed by ultramontanes.[164] Later, Miall made a powerful speech in favour of the bill, claiming that he had always upheld Catholic rights, and asserting that the government 'had done in Ireland with regard to University education what the Nonconformists were asking should be done in England with regard to elementary education. It separated the teaching of religion from the teaching of secular knowledge ... the instruction given by the State should be simply secular.'[165]

Criticism of the bill continued, however, from whig-liberals outside parliament. Blackie congratulated Playfair for the services which his arguments had contributed towards 'battering' it, and hoped that it had scared the government away from meddling in Scotland.[166] Carlyle believed that the role of Gladstone, that 'poor Ritualist', in framing it was 'the consummation of contemptibilities and petty trickeries on his part, one of the most transparent bits of thimblerigging to ... smuggle the education violin into the hands of Cullen and the sacred sons of Belial and the scarlet woman', that he had ever witnessed.[167] Earl Fortescue thought many Liberals 'disgusted' by the way in which Gladstone had tried to conciliate the Catholic priests.[168] In a series of editorials, the *Daily News* protested strongly against the bill's ecclesiasticism. Since it did not satisfy Catholic demands, there was no reason whatsoever for its

---

[162] *Hansard*, ccxiv, 1459.   [163] Torrens, *Twenty years*, pp. 162–3.
[164] *Hansard*, ccxiv, 1227.   [165] *Ibid.*, 1685.
[166] Blackie to Playfair, 6 March 1873, Playfair papers, 31.
[167] 7, 23 March 1873, Froude, *Carlyle*, ii, 423.
[168] Fortescue to Northbrook, 9 March 1873, Northbrook papers, 144, 21, i.

introduction: it reversed 'our set principles and system of national education', and was desired by no one. The *News* strongly supported the arguments that Playfair and Horsman were putting in the Commons.[169]

The government's case was not strengthened by the fact that, Monsell having been forbidden to speak, the first three official speakers, Hartington, Fortescue and Lowe, all had to defend a bill which deviated from the views which they were widely known to hold.[170] Both Hartington and Lowe took comfort from emphasising that most of the provisions were not of the 'essence' of the bill: Lowe insisted that the affiliated colleges would enjoy no 'important power' and that Trinity and Queen's would constitute the core of the new university system. Their disavowals of large parts of the bill were so blatant that Hardy replied that he was unable to perceive in quite what its 'essence' consisted; a sharp dig in view of Gladstone's speech in Croydon the day before, when he had announced that the government was prepared to accept more radical changes to the bill than an administration would normally consider compatible with the retention of its authority.[171]

Apparently unaware of the strength of hostility in the Irish constituencies, Gladstone still felt 'much in the dark' about the attitude of Irish MPs towards the measure.[172] However, he saw four representative Irish MPs on 6 March, and they complained that the bill did not remove the 'chief' Catholic grievance of educational inequality, especially in endowment. This seems to have convinced him of the impossibility of securing the support of the bulk of Catholic members for the second reading – although, typically, he blamed the bishops' criticisms, not the more general hostility of Irish public opinion, for the MPs' desertion of the government. (The bishops had, of course, expressed disapproval of parts of the bill, but Cullen did not in fact publicly condemn it until 9 March, and the episode reveals that the hierarchy was no longer making the political running in Ireland.)[173]

It was also becoming obvious that substantial numbers of British Liberals would not vote for the bill, on 'Protestant' grounds, unless some of its provisions were abandoned. Defeat was thus almost certain, since the Conservatives had now decided to oppose the second reading as well (while agreeing not to take office if the government resigned). The cabinet, meeting on 8 March, decided that, given that all hope of secur-

---

[169] See e.g. *Daily News*, 7, 10 March 1873, p. 4.

[170] See Hoey, 'Irish University Bill', p. 453.

[171] *Hansard*, ccxiv, 1255ff (esp. 1256, 1260), 1479ff (esp. 1479, 1492–3), 1496; *Times*, 6 March 1873, p. 5.

[172] Gladstone to O'Hagan, 6 March 1873, Gladstone papers, 44542, fo. 95.

[173] 6, 8 March 1873, Matthew, viii, 297–8; Gray to Gladstone, 7 March 1873, Gladstone papers, 44438, fo. 47; McCarthy, *Ireland since the union*, p. 208.

ing the support of most Irish MPs had been lost, the government must make concessions to British opinion, if it was to survive. It therefore agreed to announce that it would be willing to see the rejection, at the committee stage, of everything except the 'essence' of the bill.[174] Virtually no one in the cabinet would defend Gladstone's bill: Fortescue had always wished for endowment, and most of the rest had no love for the bill's denominational tendencies.[175]

News of the government's intentions leaked out: although the concessions were unveiled in Cardwell's speech on 10 March, the previous speakers on that day seem to have been aware of the decision. In particular, Harcourt was now able to support the second reading, on the grounds that the bill would be altered in committee. He anticipated that the amended bill would provide for one 'teaching university', offering 'combined and mixed education': no denominational colleges would be affiliated, and the 'gagging clauses' would be dropped. As if to emphasise the success of 'Protestant' Liberal pressure against the bill, he reiterated that Ireland was 'an integral fraction of a united Empire', and 'must be governed, not according to Irish, but according to Imperial ideas'.[176] Dodson announced his willingness to vote for the second reading, in the expectation that substantial alterations would later be made: he was especially keen to see the abandonment of the clause affiliating denominational colleges to the university.[177] The *Daily News* argued that the bill must not cause the downfall of the government, which had more constructive work to do; it maintained that, despite the measure's glaring faults – its 'predominating regard . . . for ecclesiastical interests' and for 'virulent' 'sectarianism' – the second reading should be supported and major amendments made later.[178]

Cardwell's speech gave Irish MPs a cast-iron reason for opposing the bill, and six of them spoke against it on 11 March.[179] Disraeli then drew the bill's opponents together, attacking Gladstone for preventing the application of a policy of concurrent endowment – the policy of all the 'great statesmen . . . of Pitt, of Grey, of Russell, of Peel, and of Palmerston' – and for doing so through 'mistaking the clamour of the Nonconformists for the voice of the nation'.[180] Gladstone closed the debate with an acclaimed speech, portraying 'justice to Ireland' as the

---

[174] Morley, *Gladstone*, ii, 441–3; Cardwell to Northbrook, 14 March 1873, Northbrook papers, 144, 21, i.
[175] See e.g. for Argyll and Halifax, diary, 4 March 1873, Cartwright papers, 6/10; Halifax to Gladstone, 9 March 1873, Gladstone papers, 44186, fo. 6.
[176] *Hansard*, ccxiv, 1618–19.   [177] *Ibid.*, 1712, 1785.
[178] *Daily News*, 10, 11 March 1873, p. 4.
[179] *Hansard*, ccxiv, 1748, 1775, 1781, 1791, 1805, 1806.
[180] *Ibid.*, 1824–6.

'work, I will almost say the sacred work' of his government, and incor-
porating a renewed attack on the principle of concurrent endowment,
and on Conservative support for it in 1868.[181]

Despite his oratory, the government was defeated by 287 votes to 284
– even though a small number of Conservative allies of Salisbury
abstained, not wishing to give Disraeli the chance to form a reckless
minority government, and not believing the pledges, given by Hardy,
that the frontbench had rejected this option.[182] Thirty-eight Irish
Liberals voted or paired against the bill, and 16 voted or paired for it:
only 5 of the latter were Catholics. None of the 16 were to be in the 1874
parliament, and all but one of these were defeated by, or 'retired' in the
face of, home-rule opposition. Ten British Liberals opposed the bill and
9 abstained without pair. Four of these 19 were Fawcettites (including
the unitarian P. A. Taylor, who abstained, the only nonconformist not to
support the bill); excluding a couple of mavericks, the other 13 can all be
defined as whig-liberals.[183] As the *Spectator* said, the bill was defeated by
'Irish Members and Whig animalculae'.[184] But those who persevered in
rebelling formed only the tip of a large iceberg floating in the government's path: Dodson, Harcourt and Morrison, and Playfair and many
other Scottish MPs, including McLagan and Ellice, were reconciled to
supporting the bill only by the possibility of amending it substantially in
committee, and out of an antipathy to seeing Disraeli in office.[185] Disraeli
was hardly being unfair when, speaking in 1874 of Liberal feeling
towards the bill, he maintained that those MPs who voted for it 'voted
under protest, and with the announcement that when the Bill went into
committee they would completely alter its character'.[186]

After the defeat, the cabinet met to discuss its course: the choices soon
came to be either resignation or dissolution. Hartington and Spencer
both strongly opposed the idea of dissolution at that moment, on the

---

[181] *Ibid.*, 1856–8, 1863.
[182] See Cartwright, *Knightley*, p. 239; Johnson, *Diary of Gathorne Hardy*, p. 173.
[183] Of the whig-liberals, Akroyd, Aytoun, Bouverie, W. O. Foster, Horsman and Torrens
voted against; Anson, E. H. Burke, Montagu Chambers, Sir Thomas Lloyd, Macfie,
Maxwell and Trelawny abstained. The mavericks were Peel and Whalley (both
against); Fawcett and Herbert (against) and Fitzmaurice (abstained) were the other
Fawcettites. Of course some of these were disappointed and churlish politicians, but
nearly all nonetheless had firm principles. It is worth noting that Bouverie, for example,
one of the most obviously 'disappointed' and anti-Gladstonian of these men, was
described by Hartington a few weeks after the vote as 'a very fair man': Palles to
O'Hagan, 28 April 1873, O'Hagan papers, D2777/7.
[184] 31 May 1873, p. 689.
[185] See above; Reid, *Playfair*, p. 216; diary, 11 March 1873, Cartwright papers, 6/10;
(Scotsmen) *Scotsman*, 31 January 1874, p. 7; (Ellice) *Times*, 24 January 1874, p. 7.
[186] *Ibid.*, 2 February 1874, p. 5.

grounds that it would throw Ireland into the hands of the home rulers.[187] Gladstone was pessimistic about the chances of maintaining party unity if the government continued in office. He believed that the party was divided about education, taxation, franchise and land policy, and that he could not reunite it since, in all cases, he shared the views of 'the advanced party, whom, on other and general grounds, I certainly will never head or lead'. He could see no '*cause*' on which an election might be fought and won: unless a 'special call' appeared, his public life was over. The cabinet decided to resign.[188]

But Disraeli refused the queen's request to form a government. Gladstone insisted that Disraeli be asked three times, before he agreed to return to office.[189] The Conservatives' reasoning was sound: not only was it important to reassure backbenchers nervous at the prospect of another minority government, but it was also advisable to leave the Liberals in power for a few more months in order to expose their divisions more thoroughly. If the Conservatives took office in a minority, the Liberals would have a ready-made excuse to reunite their forces in opposition to them; while Gladstone would also be able, at the election immediately ensuing, to capitalise on the Conservative–Catholic alliance over the University Bill.[190]

The queen was disappointed that the Conservatives did not take office on a 'Protestant cry'. She had decided that Gladstone's 'mission' to Ireland had not only 'signally failed', but had been the cause of his fall.[191] George Eliot, who disliked party factionalism and the new politics, wished that 'there were some solid, philosophical Conservative to take the reins – one who knows the true functions of stability in human affairs, and, as the psalm says, "Would also practise what he knows" '.[192] The *Westminster Review*, speaking for many academic liberals, shed few tears for the bill, and criticised its denominational tendencies.[193] The whig-liberal inquest into the government's policy showed little mercy. Minto and Ellice both thought the bill 'one of the worst bills ever introduced to Parliament by a Liberal Government'.[194] Reeve, writing in the *Edinburgh*, did not grieve at the defeat: England could not 'forget, that the opposition of civil liberty to clericalism is in all parts of Europe the great principle of the age', and that the maintenance of 'the great principles of

---

[187] Holland, *Devonshire*, i, 118–20; Gordon, *Spencer*, i, 108.
[188] Matthew, viii, 299–302.
[189] *Ibid.*, pp. 301–4.
[190] Feuchtwanger, *Disraeli, democracy*, pp. 14–15; Monypenny and Buckle, *Disraeli*, v, 207–20.
[191] (Victoria) Fulford, *Darling child*, pp. 80–2.
[192] Cross, *Eliot*, iii, 179–80, see also *ibid.*, pp. 201, 375.
[193] Anon., 'Irish university education and the ministerial crisis'.
[194] Minto to Wilson, 24 February 1874, Minto papers, 12360, fo. 88; (Ellice) *Times*, 24 January 1874, p. 7.

. . . State authority and civil liberty against clerical domination, is a thousand times more important than any number of votes'.[195] Earl Fortescue hoped that the defeat would alter Gladstone's course, from destruction and unpredictability, to 'positive and constructive measures' and 'Religious and Educational Endowment'.[196] Horsman saw the bill as a 'suicidal . . . attempt to hand over the education of Ireland to the priests' – as did Shaftesbury – and hoped that it had provoked a 'final' quarrel between the British Liberals and the ultramontanes.[197] The *Times*, Gladstone complained in May, had 'virtually been Disraeli's paper' since it 'whipped round [on] the University Bill'.[198] *Fraser's*, which mounted a lengthy and strident criticism of the bill as an indirect attempt to endow denominationalism, argued that the parliamentary debate had displayed 'the hopelessly irreconcilable antagonism between Irish ideas and Imperial ideas . . . the incompatibility of English Liberalism with Irish Ultramontanism'.[199] It maintained that the defeat of the bill had been 'hailed with gladness and a buoyant sense of relief' by a 'large section' of Liberals, as 'severing the fettering and discreditable tie which had so long entangled them with the Roman Catholic hierarchy'.[200] The *Economist* adopted the variant of the whig-liberal line most favourable to the government; that the Irish university question was not sufficiently important to merit the downfall of the administration, and that it should concentrate instead on more constructive legislation.[201]

There were, however, three solaces for the Liberal party after the defeat. The first was that, however critical Liberals – especially whig-liberals – might be, they were nonetheless relieved that Disraeli had not formed a government. Indeed, there was still disbelief that he could ever be a statesmanlike prime minister. Dufferin ('the very thought . . . is hateful to me'), Ellice and the *Westminster Review* were all agreed on this point; Argyll thought that the same was true of the whole House of Commons.[202] The second was that the crisis had diminished the danger that the religious demands of Irish Catholics would interfere with the conduct of Liberal policy in the near future. The introduction of a denominational bill had undoubtedly left a bitter taste in many whiggish

[195] Reeve, 'Claims of whig government', pp. 575–6.
[196] Fortescue to Brereton, 21 April 1873, Brereton papers, F 10 73.
[197] *Times*, 16 December 1873, p. 6; diary, 12 March 1873, Shaftesbury papers.
[198] To Acland, 6 May 1873, Matthew, viii, 324. The *Spectator* agreed: 29 March 1873, p. 397.
[199] Anon., 'Irish university question', pp. 516–22; 'Our Irish policy', pp. 778–9.
[200] Anon., 'Turn of the tide', pp. 271–2.
[201] *Economist*, 15 March 1873, pp. 305–6.
[202] Dufferin to Kimberley, 14 March 1873, Dufferin papers; Argyll to Dufferin, 23 March 1873, *ibid.*; (Ellice) *Times*, 24 January 1874, p. 7; anon., 'Irish university education and the ministerial crisis', p. 550.

mouths, but, since the government was unlikely to try to reimpose such a suicidally pro-Catholic measure, party relations, if hardly relaxed, became slightly less fraught than before. And the third was that, throughout the crisis, nonconformist opinion had remained almost entirely loyal to Gladstone. It had, with exceptions, not been enthusiastic in its support for the bill, but it had detected in it a reassuring approximation to the secular ideal. The introduction of the plan had in fact checked the rising tide of nonconformist hostility to the government. For both the last two reasons, the Liberals' return to office in March marked a turning-point in the relationship between the provincial radicals and the government. Although their pressure for English educational reform did not let up, their fear of the government's capacity for unacceptable legislation lessened, and their tolerance of its difficulties grew. Moreover, radicals were increasingly able to control the party organisation in large constituencies without difficulty, and thus to pursue their policy goals without practising open hostility towards the leadership. What divided the party more and more was the contrast between the enthusiasm of provincial Liberals for disestablishment and radical educational reform, and the staunch rejection of these proposals by whig-liberals. It was the fears of the 'right' which were to destroy the Liberal majority at the forthcoming general election. These fears were inspired primarily by awareness of the sympathy between Gladstone and nonconformity, and, to a lesser extent, by concern about Gladstone's likely behaviour towards the representatives of Irish popular opinion, in the event of a hung parliament. The Irish University Bill crisis had greatly added to whig-liberals' suspicion of Gladstone's ecclesiasticism, his sacerdotalism and his sympathy with radical nonconformists. It had also alienated Irish Catholic opinion. Agreement about the essence of Liberalism seemed to have disappeared.

8

The fall of the government, 1873–4

1873: a wasted session

The Liberals' enforced return to office obliged them to find policies on which unity might be maintained and a sense of purpose rediscovered. It also required them to try to quieten agitation on English and Irish educational questions. The latter was likely to be the less difficult of the two, partly because the defeat of the Irish University Bill had diminished the urgency for a reform of the 1870 Education Act, and partly because of the atmosphere in the House of Commons, which was 'quite demoralised' between March and the end of the session.[1]

Compromise proved most easily attainable on Irish university policy. There was general agreement that the defeat of March had paid the government's dues to the Irish MPs.[2] Maintaining that the Catholic bishops had plotted the defeat of the University Bill, Gladstone considered the government 'no longer hampered by Irish considerations in the direction of our general policy', and thought further action on the matter unlikely.[3] Fawcett intimated his willingness to cooperate closely with the government in altering his own bill to suit Gladstone's wishes. He now proposed, in addition to the abolition of tests, to give powers to Trinity to reform its own government and that of the Dublin university. Hartington wished to agree to this, since it did not preclude the possibility of Trinity's council and the government agreeing to separate the university from the college – the bill admitted that they were not identical – even if no practical change would result from the admission, as long as the affiliation of no other college was planned. For Gladstone, how-

---

[1] Knatchbull-Hugessen to Dufferin, 20 May 1873, Dufferin papers.
[2] Cardwell to Northbrook, 14 March 1873, Cardwell papers, 30/48/21, fo. 54; Brand to Gladstone, 12 March 1873, Gladstone papers, 44194, fo. 154.
[3] 18 November 1873, Figgis and Laurence, *Acton's correspondence*, i, 175–6; 13 March, 9 December 1873, Matthew, viii, 302, 423.

ever, the plan was unacceptable. Accordingly, Fawcett introduced another bill, which he limited to the abolition of tests, and which the government agreed to support – although Gladstone made it clear that he did not regard it as a permanent solution to the problem. The bill passed, despite protests from Irish MPs.[4]

The most controversial Irish business in 1873 was the O'Keeffe case, on which Liberal opinion was much divided. On the one side were those for whom it was important to prevent ultramontane forces from interfering in temporal affairs, and challenging the state's authority. As the *Pall Mall* put it, any Church was

free to do what the law of the land permits it to do, and no more . . . The State and its laws are the unquestioned and unquestionable masters of the Church as they are of other persons . . . The doctrine of free Churches in free States means in short State supremacy exercised for the common good of the whole nation in a moderate and rational way, but still with unmistakable force.[5]

On the other, the *Nonconformist* spoke for those who held that the papal question was irrelevant to the O'Keeffe case, because the pope was no longer a threat to the independence of the temporal government. It believed that the question at issue, instead, was the right of members of a Church to obey its rules and adhere to its practices without interference from the state.

Every citizen should be entirely at liberty not only to adopt whatever views of truth seem to him most probable, but also to acknowledge, and in spiritual matters subject himself to, whatever ecclesiastical authority seems to him most venerable. In addition, he ought to have a right to associate with others of like mind in the observance of any rules, not contrary to public morality, which they may judge best fitted to promote their common aims.[6]

The first view was taken, albeit less stridently, by many otherwise loyal and tolerant whig-liberals who believed that the Commissioners of National Education had acted unreasonably in depriving O'Keeffe of his management of the schools.[7] Bouverie, moreover, planned to propose a motion of censure on the Commissioners in mid May. Hartington considered it important to forestall this, not only because it would probably succeed, but because, if the Commissioners were to resign, he thought the whole national education system likely to collapse. The government

---

[4] Mundella to Leader, 21 March 1873, Mundella papers; Cardwell to Gladstone, 19 March 1873, Gladstone papers, 44120, fo. 100; Gladstone to Hartington, 25 March 1873, *ibid.*, 44144, fo. 44; Hartington to Gladstone, 25 March 1873, *ibid.*, fo. 37; Gladstone notes, [March] 1873, *ibid.*, 44641, fo. 78; Matthew, viii, 305, 310; *Hansard*, ccxv, 300, 727.

[5] Leading article (by J. F. Stephen), 12 May 1873, p. 1.

[6] 4 June 1873, p. 561.

[7] See diary, 11 May 1873, Cartwright papers, 6/10; *Economist*, 24 May 1873, p. 621.

therefore proposed instead a select committee, in order to investigate the Commissioners' conduct. It secured this committee by only 159 votes to 131, even though the vote was taken (as the Speaker vouchsafed) deliberately early, so as to catch Bouverie's forces unprepared, and even though a number of whig-liberals who sympathised with Bouverie, like Harcourt, voted with Hartington – believing, as he did, that to do so offered the only chance of preserving the national education system. Seventeen Liberals voted against the government, and a large number of others abstained: only 99 Liberal backbenchers supported it.[8] Against the government's will, Harcourt then successfully moved to increase the strength of anti-clerical opinion on the committee.[9] The controversy abated when Bouverie withdrew his censure motion, in return for a pledge that a case like that of O'Keeffe would not occur again without an inquiry before removal, and that O'Keeffe's position should be reviewed. (As it was, despite Bouverie's complaints – and those of the *Times* – O'Keeffe never was restored to his post, owing to the practical difficulties that it would have created locally.)[10] In the Lords, meanwhile, Russell had introduced a bill aimed at strengthening the powers of the Irish administration, in order to combat the threat of ultramontane interference. He criticised the Commissioners' bias, and maintained that the government of Ireland was 'conducted entirely according to the orders and inspiration of the Roman Catholic Church'.[11]

One of the reasons why the O'Keeffe case concerned British Liberals was because it seemed analogous to the struggles between the ecclesiastical and civil powers which were, in Harcourt's view, 'now agitating every part of Europe'.[12] The British parliament appeared, like continental legislatures, to be witnessing the growth of a powerful Catholic party; and the home rulers' role in the defeat of the University Bill suggested to British minds, with renewed force, that they were, at bottom, the puppets of the ultramontane hierarchy. Throughout 1873, the expectation was widely shared that they would hold the balance of power in the next parliament.[13] Although there was more and more alarm at the growth of the movement, its increasing popularity in Ireland had the opposite effect on Gladstone, making him doubly unwilling to offend what seemed to be

---

[8] *Hansard*, ccxv, 2023, (Harcourt) ccxvi, 320, 15, 22 May 1873; diary, 15 May 1873, Brand papers; Matthew, viii, 320, 322, 326, 328.

[9] *Hansard*, ccxvi, 320; Norman, *Catholic Church*, pp. 434–5; Matthew, viii, 332.

[10] *Hansard*, ccxvii, 210; Matthew, viii, 340, 343; Hartington memorandum, 15 November 1873, Gladstone papers, 44621, fo. 134; Norman, *Catholic Church*, pp. 435–6; *Times*, 10 October 1873, p. 9.

[11] *Hansard*, ccxvi, 618, 1527, 9, 30 June 1873.

[12] *Ibid.*, 320.

[13] Knatchbull-Hugessen to Dufferin, 20 May 1873, Dufferin papers; and see below, p. 403.

majority Irish opinion. Despite obvious reluctance, he had to sanction
the renewal of the Peace Preservation Act and the Protection of Life and
Property Act, due to expire on 1 June 1873;[14] however, he was keen to
revive discussion about the release of the remaining Fenian prisoners. By
1873, there were only four civilian Fenians still in gaol, and amnesty
meetings were being held to press for their release. Two – Davitt and
John Wilson – had been sentenced in 1870 for buying and distributing
arms; the others, Shore and Melody, were the only prisoners still in
captivity for the Manchester outrage of 1867. Gladstone and Fortescue
would have liked all the civilians, and the sixteen imprisoned Fenian
soldiers, released; but the duke of Cambridge and Sir Robert Airey, on
behalf of the military, would not allow the latter, and the cabinet was
willing to consider the possibility of freeing only one of the civilians,
Melody. Lowe expressed strong opposition even to this, on the grounds
that the Fenian conspiracy was still active, and that the release would
imply that the hanging of three of those arrested at Manchester had been
an error. Hartington believed that many Irish middle-class people were
'disgusted' by the amnesties already effected, and that they had achieved
no purpose; he, Spencer, and many other members of the cabinet were
opposed to Melody's release. However, Bright was in favour, and it was
finally agreed in February 1874.[15]

At the same time as suspicion of the political power of Irish Catholicism
was spreading, fears of ritualist infiltration into the Church of England
were also rife. Both the prosecution of Mackonochie and the judgment
against Purchas had by 1873 been shown to be ineffective in checking the
increase in the offending practices. The irritation of anti-ritualists at this
state of affairs was enhanced by the Bennett judgment of 1872 – which
admitted the validity of a high-church interpretation of the Eucharist –
and by the failure of the campaign against the Athanasian Creed.

The prevailing restlessness on the subject was also affected by
Gladstone's ecclesiastical appointments. Although, for the sake of the
Church, he tried hard to strike a balance between ecclesiastical
parties, his conception of 'faithful allegiance to the Church' necessarily

---

[14] *Hansard*, ccxv, 2054; Gladstone to Hartington, 13 April 1873, Gladstone papers, 44542,
fo. 110.

[15] See Matthew, viii, 415, 421, 430–1; 16 January 1874, Walling, *Diaries of Bright*, p. 361;
Lowe–Gladstone correspondence, November 1873–January 1874, Gladstone papers,
44302, fos. 153–81; Hartington to Gladstone, 11 May 1872, *ibid.*, 44143, fo. 166;
Hartington memorandum, 18 October 1873, *ibid.*, 44144, fo. 129; Fortescue to
Gladstone, 8 January 1874, *ibid.*, 44123, fo. 77; memoranda, 11 October 1873,
3 November 1873, *ibid.*, 44621, fo. 118, 44761, fo. 185.

swayed his judgment.[16] In particular, his appointments to Oxford chairs and to St Paul's cathedral excited criticism.

Gladstone moved Canon Dale of St Paul's to the deanery of Rochester in early 1870 in order to give Liddon the St Paul's canonry.[17] When Dale died three months later, he translated Scott, the Master of Balliol, to the deanery, vacating the chair of the exegesis of Holy Scripture at Oxford for Liddon. Gladstone then 'got rid' of Payne Smith, the regius professor of divinity at Oxford, by giving him Alford's deanery at Canterbury, and made the high churchman J. B. Mozley his successor.[18] In 1873, he appointed King of Cuddesdon to the regius professorship of moral and pastoral theology: this delighted Liddon and E. S. Talbot, but was opposed by Liddell, dean of Christ Church, who wrote of a 'phalanx of High Church Professors' (William Bright and Pusey were already installed). It was also disliked by Tait – who felt that it would 'greatly shake public confidence in the theological school at Oxford', supplanting 'manly faith' by 'womanly defence' – and by many Oxford Liberals.[19]

Gladstone completed a trio of high-church appointments to St Paul's by making Church dean in 1871 (Gregory had been appointed a canon by Disraeli). Bishop Jackson of London protested at Church's appointment, on the grounds that he adopted the eastward position during the prayer of consecration, and that it would thus undermine the authority of the Purchas judgment: Gladstone replied that that was no concern of his.[20] (Gladstone had been annoyed at, and contemptuous of, the judgment, but considered that the government could not get it revoked.)[21] Liddon and Gregory challenged Jackson to prosecute them, because they refused to abide by the judgment; however, he could not act against them unless asked by the Chapter of St Paul's, which they in effect controlled.[22]

The cathedral soon came to be more in the public eye, because of the controversy surrounding an appeal for its renovation, which had been launched in 1870, and which Gladstone himself, like many high church-

[16] Morley, *Gladstone*, ii, 430–3; Chadwick, *Victorian Church*, ii, 337.
[17] Gladstone to Hook, 11 February 1870, Gladstone papers, 44538, fo. 73.
[18] This was the move as described by Phillimore, diary, 27 January 1871, Phillimore papers, after a conversation with Gladstone.
[19] Talbot to Gladstone, 18 February 1873, Gladstone papers, 44437, fo. 171; Liddon to Phillimore, 22, 24 February 1873, Phillimore papers; Liddell to Gladstone, 20 February 1873, Gladstone papers, 44236, fo. 347; Tait–Gladstone correspondence, 24–5 February 1873, Tait papers, 92, fos. 45–8; diary, 2 March 1873, Cartwright papers, 6/10.
[20] Jackson to Gladstone, 19 August 1871, Gladstone papers, 44431, fo. 210; diary, 9 November 1871, Phillimore papers.
[21] 10 March 1871, Matthew, vii, 460–1; to Liddon, 26 February 1871, Gladstone papers, 44237, fo. 51.
[22] Hutton, *Gregory*, pp. 109, 115.

men, strongly supported. Evangelicals and others – such as Derby – opposed the renovation, from the beginning, as an unnecessary extravagance.[23] The three high churchmen became prominent in the reconstruction, and several improvements were effected, including the appointment of Stainer as organist in 1872. Most controversially, the reconstruction committee replaced its original choice of architect with William Burges, already known as a devoted ceremonialist and mediaevalist. This appointment itself was strongly criticised, and opposition grew when Burges started to produce extravagant schemes – suggesting a marble veneer over the original stone, reinstating the screen, and introducing far more colour, complexity and ornamentation.[24] Divisions clearly polarised on ecclesiastical lines. The *Times*, the *Pall Mall*, and individuals from Fergusson to Lightfoot and Cavendish Bentinck opposed the schemes; the most sustained attack on Burges came from the Ruskinian Emmett in the *Quarterly*. Operations were suspended in late 1874, and Burges was dismissed in 1877.[25]

These controversies reinforced the determination of evangelicals and broad churchmen to introduce more stringent legislation against ritualism. But, despite considerable support from Halifax, Portman, Cross and Bishop Jackson, Shaftesbury had been unable to get his bill for the cheapening and acceleration of prosecutions passed: it was blocked by the Salisbury–Carnarvon party in the Lords, and by Gladstone's refusal to assist its progress unless it were made innocuous.[26] Moreover, the raising of the ecclesiastical temperature led Liddon, Pusey and many other high churchmen to moot schemes for the removal of the Judicial Committee's power as a court of appeal for ecclesiastical cases.[27] They now agitated for a purely lay court: if the bishops were removed, it would lessen the court's authority on controversial matters of doctrine and ritual, and confine its real influence to questions involving temporalities.

In 1873, these quarrels became entangled with the discussion of an important government bill, Selborne's Supreme Court of Judicature Bill. Its purpose was to establish a new court of appeal; this was to be purely

---

[23] Prestige, *St Paul's*, p. 112; Matthew, vii, 324; diary, 14 July 1870, 15th earl of Derby papers.

[24] See Crook, *Burges*, pp. 154–69; Prestige, *St Paul's*, pp. 112–53; Hutton, *Gregory*, pp. 164–225.

[25] Crook, *Burges*, pp. 154–69; Bentinck, *Completion of St Paul's*; Fergusson, 'St Paul's cathedral'; Emmett, 'State of English architecture' and 'Completion of St Paul's'.

[26] *Hansard*, cxcv, 808, cc, 62, cciii, 98, ccix, 618, 1124, ccx, 380, ccxiii, 188; Portman to Halifax, 18 November 1870, Hickleton papers, A 4 92; Halifax to Granville, 12 July 1870, Granville papers, 30/29/64; Gladstone to Selborne, 9 January 1873, Gladstone papers, 44542, fo. 69.

[27] See e.g. Liddon to Salisbury, 14 March 1871, Salisbury papers.

legal in composition, but, in order to avoid controversy, the Judicial Committee was to be retained for ecclesiastical appeals.[28] Salisbury moved to transfer ecclesiastical appeals to the new court, when the bill reached its third reading in the Lords; but he withdrew the motion when Tait proved hostile and Selborne unenthusiastic.[29] However, when the bill came down to the Commons, Wilberforce persuaded Hardy to propose the transfer, and Gladstone to support it. Gladstone was cautious, fearing possible uproar; but Hardy secured the support of Disraeli and Harcourt, and prepared the ground so thoroughly that, in debate, it was unanimously supported (at least until after Gladstone had accepted it, when Burke, Whalley and Gordon immediately protested against it). Some whig-liberals supported the move because, by removing the bishops' influence over the court, it appeared to them that the Church was being more directly subordinated to the state.[30] Nonetheless, others were very annoyed by the change – none more so than Tait.

The alteration was agreed so quickly that Gladstone had an excuse not to communicate with Tait (an interesting deviation from his rule on consulting the Church on Church policy) until afterwards.[31] Tait was 'rather petulant',[32] and told Gladstone that it would now be 'impossible' for him to support the Judicature Bill. Stanley, Archbishop Thomson, Thirlwall and Reeve were also opposed to the move, interpreting it as a step towards a purely clerical court of appeal for ecclesiastical causes, towards the 'wreck' of the Church as a 'National Institution', and towards disestablishment.[33] George Grey and Bouverie also opposed the amendment; moreover, Fremantle found Childers quietly hostile to it and fearing a drift towards disestablishment, although he had held his tongue in cabinet, when all who had spoken were in favour.[34] In the Lords, Cairns and Russell were also opposed to it. Since the bill was also controversial in other respects, Selborne (who had in any case, according to Salisbury, always been rather 'cold' about the amendment) negotiated with Tait and reached agreement on a compromise which would transfer

[28] Stevens, *Law and politics*, pp. 47–57; Selborne, *Memorials II*, i, 306.
[29] Marsh, *Victorian Church in decline*, p. 130.
[30] *Hansard*, ccxvi, 1787, 4 July 1873; 3 July 1873, Matthew, viii, 349; Johnson, *Diary of Gathorne Hardy*, p. 185; diary, 4 July 1873, Trelawny papers, 419, p. 120.
[31] Gladstone to Tait, 4 July 1873, Tait papers, 92, fo. 176.
[32] Johnson, *Diary of Gathorne Hardy*, p. 185.
[33] Tait to Gladstone, 5 July 1873, Gladstone papers, 44331, fo. 105; Stanley to Tait, 5 July 1873, Tait papers, 92, fo. 174; Thomson to Tait, 5 July 1873, *ibid.*, fo. 180; Tait to Hardy, 7 July 1873, *ibid.*, fo. 186; Reeve to Tait's secretary, 8 July 1873, *ibid.*, fo. 188; Thirlwall, *Letters literary*, p. 363.
[34] Diary, 11 July 1873, Brand papers; Fremantle to Tait, 21 July 1873, Tait papers, 92, fo. 205.

the appeals and allow bishops to sit as assessors, without votes, on the new court. This satisfied Cairns, and the dispute died away.[35]

Tait's humour during this controversy was influenced by the crisis developing on the ritual question. The Church Association, the low-church, anti-ritualist organisation, had presented a petition from 60,000 laymen protesting at Anglo-catholic practices and ceremonies. Then there was a prolonged outcry in the country against the request, signed by 483 clergymen, for steps to improve the training of confessors. (Although auricular confession was sanctioned in the prayer-book in certain circumstances, low and broad churchmen were implacably opposed to it.) This outcry was joined not only by men of Shaftesbury's stamp, but by normally quiescent liberal evangelicals like Fitzwilliam.[36] The *Times* added its voice to the growing demand for legislation to provide a simple and quick remedy for parishioners tormented by ritual excesses.[37] Tait, affected by this climate of opinion, indulged in an extended attack, in the Lords, on leading high churchmen who challenged the *status quo* within the Church. He criticised the Oxford professors, Liddon, Pusey, William Bright and King, for infringing their duty to teach 'the doctrines of the Reformed Church to young men who are to be her ministers'; he castigated the dean and canons of St Paul's, for their determination to 'violate the law of the Church and of the land'; and he also demanded responsible behaviour from 'those who appoint' such men to 'posts of influence in the Church'.[38] There was further criticism of Gladstone's appointments when two high churchmen were appointed to bishoprics in the summer of 1873. Browne was chosen to succeed Wilberforce at Winchester, and Woodford to follow Browne at Ely: even the *Spectator* considered that Gladstone was being too biassed.[39]

But, more significantly, Wilberforce's death removed the most powerful episcopal opponent of the introduction of legislation intended to check ritualist extravagance; it thus much increased Tait's opportunity to promote such a measure – as was to become apparent in 1874.[40]

Since a state of armistice had been attained on the Irish university question, the nature of the controversy about English education shifted in 1873. Anti-clerical opinion was no longer preoccupied with the fear that immediate concessions would be made to the Irish priests; and, given the

[35] *Hansard*, ccxvii, 866, 24 July 1873; Selborne, *Memorials II*, i, 312; Salisbury to Phillimore, 21 July 1873, Phillimore papers; Russell to Stanley, 16 July 1873, A. P. Stanley papers, 91, fo. 56.
[36] Marsh, *Victorian Church in decline*, pp. 132–3; *Hansard*, ccxvii, 148, 269, 275, 287, 1166. For Fitzwilliam at York, see *Nonconformist*, 24 December 1873, p. 1278.
[37] (Sandon) *Hansard*, ccxvi, 1851, 7 July 1873; Marsh, *Victorian Church in decline*, pp. 133–4.
[38] *Hansard*, ccxvii, 276, 279, 14 July 1873.   [39] 9 August 1873, p. 1001.
[40] Tait to Thomson, 10 Nov. 1873, Tait papers, 101, fo. 169; 27 July 1873, Lathbury, ii, 91.

proximity of a general election, it was eager to search for a compromise on which the bulk of the party might be able to agree. It was for this reason that increasing attention was devoted to the future of the contentious Clause 25 of the 1870 Education Act: repeal of the clause seemed to anti-clerical Liberals – both nonconformist and whig-liberal – to be a policy which would harness the traditional Liberal dislike of denominational privileges, and which would constitute an acceptable compromise between those who desired a radical reform of the whole educational system, and those who thought such a reform unnecessary and counter-productive.

A number of those radical nonconformists who had previously been most stridently opposed to the government's educational policy were already beginning to moderate their language by late 1872. In November, for example, Dale suggested that the package agreed at Manchester in the previous January should not be forced on election candidates except under certain circumstances.[41] In January 1873, moreover, he abandoned his emphasis on secularism, and reached a compromise with Samuel Morley and Mundella on the so-called 'Bristol platform'. This pledged them all to demand a number of practical anti-clerical reforms: the extension of school boards to all areas, the institution of compulsory attendance, and the repeal of Clause 25. They also agreed to support the continuation of parliamentary grants to those existing voluntary schools which provided one-sixth of their total funding through private contributions; but they advocated a campaign for the abolition of grants to any such schools which were yet to be built.

Anti-clerical Liberals appeared likely to reach agreement on these proposals; but they were, of course, unacceptable to the three government ministers with most influence in the discussion of educational questions, Forster, Ripon and Gladstone. Forster also opposed the idea of Lowe and Bright, which had been revived, that denominational schools should be forced to accept poor children free in return for receiving a parliamentary grant. There was further difficulty for the government, in that W. H. Smith for the Conservatives had astutely given notice of a motion to transfer the obligation to pay poor children's fees from the school boards to the Guardians, in the hope of solving the Clause 25 problem.[42]

It was announced that Dixon, on behalf of the National Education League, would introduce a resolution in early 1873 demanding the extension of school boards and of compulsion, and the repeal of Clause

[41] Ingham, 'Disestablishment movement', p. 53.
[42] Forster to Ripon, 18 January 1873, Ripon papers, 43537, fo. 76; Forster memorandum, 22 January 1873, Gladstone papers, 44620, fo. 29.

25. Forster therefore suggested that the government should take up Smith's idea, but avoid the objections inherent in supporting a Conservative proposal on such an inflamed subject by combining it with three other proposals: with direct compulsion up to the age of ten; with the repeal of the provision (in Clause 17) which allowed a school board to remit fees for children attending its own schools; and with further provisions for the election of school boards by ballot.[43] By March, however, Gladstone was convinced that Forster's proposals would close few wounds, a conviction confirmed by a conversation with Winterbotham. Winterbotham argued that compulsion would actually be a source of further irritation unless Clause 25 were completely repealed. He thought that the proposal to transfer payments under Clause 25 to the Guardians would be of no help, and that most nonconformists would not be satisfied with less than the implementation of the 'one-sixth' rule agreed at Bristol, or the repeal of Clauses 17 and 25.[44]

On 5 April, it was agreed to drop most of the compulsion proposals. Since Forster and Ripon were in no mood to compromise with the League, the bill which was introduced to the Commons on 12 June proposed simply the transfer of payments under Clause 25 to the Guardians, in order to pre-empt Smith;[45] the election of school boards by ballot everywhere; and compulsion for the children (under thirteen) of paupers receiving relief, the Guardian to pay whatever fees were necessary to schools of the parent's choice. Apart from that, compulsion was not to be introduced except where local by-laws enforced it: in such cases, if any parent could not pay the fees, the Guardians would, but this was not to be deemed parochial relief.[46]

The government's proposed solution of the Clause 25 problem was widely regarded as inadequate by Liberal MPs, and hostility to the bill accordingly grew. Chamberlain thought it a 'splendid weapon' for nonconformists, and even Mundella considered it markedly unsatisfactory.[47] Nonconformist agitation in the country soon made its passage impracticable. Before the second reading, the National Education League intervened at the Bath by-election, putting pressure on the Liberal candidate, Hayter, to declare against Forster's bill and in favour of Dixon's proposals. When he declined to do so, an unofficial League

---

[43] Adams, *History of elementary school contest*, pp. 289–90; Sutherland, *Policy-making in elementary education*, pp. 123–4; Forster memorandum, 30 November 1872, Gladstone papers, 44619, fo. 109; 7 December 1872, Matthew, viii, 255.
[44] Matthew, viii, 306–7.
[45] 5 April 1873, *ibid.*, p. 313; Forster to Ripon, 20, 22 March 1873, Ripon papers, 43537, fos. 108, 111.
[46] *Hansard*, ccxvi, 900.
[47] Chamberlain to Dilke, 6 July 1873, Dilke papers, 43885, fo. 19; Mundella to Leader, 30 June, 6 July 1873, Mundella papers.

candidate was found, who appeared in Bath and issued an address. Hayter agreed to make the desired statement only a few days before the poll: the League candidate withdrew, and Hayter lost by fifty-one votes.[48] Then, on 1 July, at a conference of the League and nonconformist bodies at the Westminster Palace Hotel, Bright volunteered a denunciation of the 1870 Act as 'the very worst Act which had ever been passed by any Liberal Government' since 1832.[49]

On 17 July, in the second-reading debate, Forster announced that pressure from ten school boards against the transfer of responsibility for payment of fees to the Guardians had forced him to abandon the attempt to solve the Clause 25 difficulty.[50] This was a major concession, which made the bill innocuous. It had been advocated all along by Halifax and by many whigs, who objected to the idea of, in effect, pauperising a man in order to extend compulsory education; Charles Reed and Harcourt both welcomed the change.[51] The concession enabled Trevelyan and Fawcett, among others, to support the second reading. Opposition, in fact, came from only two directions, from a small rump of diehard Leaguers, and from a few score backbench Conservatives who complained at the burdens that the bill imposed on local taxation. But it gained a second reading by 343 votes to 72. Most Liberals did not think it worthwhile to oppose such a harmless bill, and neither did most leading Conservatives.[52] In committee, however, there was an attempt to repeal Clauses 17 and 25, which gained 100 Liberal supporters, and was opposed by 64 non-government Liberals and 113 Conservatives. The proposal, interestingly, was admired by W. H. Smith (who abstained), on the grounds that it would end the controversy, and abolish all free education for non-paupers. Both Clauses 17 and 25 stipulated not only that parents could have their school fees paid for them, but that, if they did, they were not to be classed as paupers; the abolition of the clauses would thus encourage self-sufficiency, and be a great boon, Smith thought, to thrifty lower-middle-class ratepayers who were subsidising the educational system. (Smith had introduced a motion advocating reform of local taxation in May, in an attempt to appeal to the same class.) But Disraeli prevented Conservatives from supporting the abolition of Clause 25, pointing out that it would destroy 'one of our symbols in the

[48] Adams, *History of elementary school contest*, pp. 291–4; Hamer, *Politics of electoral pressure*, pp. 131–3.

[49] *Nonconformist*, 2 July 1873, p. 671.

[50] *Hansard*, ccxvii, 502.

[51] Halifax to Ripon, 9 December 1872, Ripon papers, 43529, fo. 83; *Hansard*, ccxvii, 545, 755.

[52] See Gorst to Disraeli, 21 June 1873, Disraeli papers, B/XX/G/243; 27 June 1873, Johnson, *Diary of Gathorne Hardy*, pp. 183–4.

impending County elections'.[53] The bill was passed, but the Clause 25 problem was left unresolved.

The endowed schools question also proved controversial in 1873. Nine London Liberals and eight others voted with the Conservatives in favour of Crawford's motion of May 1873 defending the existing management of Emanuel Hospital, and opposing the commissioners' second scheme for its reorganisation. Much of the discussion centred on the supposed advantages which the old system offered to the sons of local tradesmen, clerks and widows.[54] There was more internal Liberal party division when the government introduced a bill later in the session to extend the Commission's life for three years (it expired at the end of 1873). Dillwyn and Leatham, on behalf of the radicals, objected anew to the contentious provisions of the 1869 Act, especially to Clause 19, and to the continuing practice of appointing clerical governors *ex officio* where the founder had so stipulated. Leatham complained that, of the 433 governors appointed *ex officio* under schemes proposed by the commissioners, 392 were Anglicans and 41 nonconformists.[55] Dillwyn's amendment to abolish the provision for the continuation of appointments *ex officio* failed in committee by 84 votes to 40. Fifteen more backbench Liberals supported Dillwyn than opposed him. For the 'right' of the party, meanwhile, Torrens had proposed an amendment designed to restrict access to endowed schools to those in the social class and geographical locality intended by the founder. This, however, was also defeated, as were Conservative amendments aimed at strengthening guarantees for religious teaching in the schools. Salisbury came to an agreement with Ripon that the commissioners' activities would be continued for only one year, rather than the three that the bill had originally envisaged; and the Lords passed it on that basis.[56]

The educational debates of 1873 were thus inconclusive, and did nothing to brighten the party's collective frame of mind. As a consequence of this failure to resolve the disputes within the party, increasing numbers of whig-liberal MPs decided, or were forced by constituency activists to decide, during the summer and autumn, that party unity, and the cessation of agitation against the 1870 Act, were both more important than the retention of Clause 25. Clause 25, after all, was not a provision of practical significance in most areas – instead, it was merely a

---

[53] Disraeli to Cairns, [20 July 1873], Cairns papers, 30/51/1, fo. 100; *Hansard*, ccxvii, 767, 22 July 1873; Smith, *Disraelian Conservatism and social reform*, pp. 178–9.
[54] *Hansard*, ccxv, 1875, 13 May 1873; see also (Torrens) ccxvii, 934–5, 24 July 1873.
[55] *Ibid.*, 718, 720.
[56] *Ibid.*, 1309; Ripon–Salisbury correspondence, July 1873, Ripon papers, 43519, fos. 96–100.

symbol of denominational privilege, which many Liberal MPs were happy to reject. However, Gladstone, Forster and others would not consider repealing the clause. This was partly out of sympathy for the plight of voluntary schools, and partly because they were aware of the electoral consequences of doing so: the energy which nonconformists were expending in proposing abolition, combined with the clause's near-irrelevance in practice, made the campaign against it generally comprehensible only if viewed as a campaign for secularism in disguise – which was how Disraeli was to present it in the 1874 campaign.

The 1874 election

Although the disputes of the 1873 session did nothing to lessen nonconformists' dissatisfaction with past government policy, it was clear that they were now happy to follow Miall's electoral strategy – the strategy of gaining sectional objectives through slow and steady infiltration of the constituencies, rather than through confrontation with the leadership. In April, the Liberation Society decided not to force the disestablishment policy on candidates at the forthcoming general election,[57] indicating that it understood the problems faced by the Liberal leadership and would not impose sensitive questions on candidates at such a time. This is not to say that nonconformists did not continue to press for disestablishment. In October 1873, for example, Leatham argued that the party would have to be 'taken to pieces' and reconstructed in order to work for it; Illingworth, later in the year, recapitulated his support for the policy, although counselling against undue aggression on it before the election. Most alarmingly for opponents of disestablishment, Baxter, who had resigned from the government over the Post Office affair (see p. 384), told his constituents that the government would disestablish the Churches of England and Scotland 'as soon as the public mind was ripe for it'.[58] But nonconformists, on the whole, were happy to work with, rather than against, the official Liberal grain.

However, Chamberlain – and thus the National Education League – dissented from this approach, and over the summer of 1873 won much attention by launching an overt attack on the government. Following the League's publicity success at Bath in June, it intervened in a number of constituencies. But the impact of this campaign should not be exaggerated. From the beginning, it was criticised by the *Nonconformist*; moreover, the July issue of the nonconformist magazine the *British Quarterly Review*

[57] Ingham, 'Disestablishment movement', p. 53.
[58] *Spectator*, 4 October 1873, p. 1230; *Nonconformist*, 31 December 1873, p. 1300, 5 November 1873, p. 1106.

carried an article warmly praising the Gladstone administration and its leader for investing politics with an inspiration derived from 'religious faith'.[59] The League, indeed, was out of touch with local nonconformist sentiment: a number of its electoral interventions were fatally handicapped by its limited knowledge of constituency realities.[60] Its tactics had a limited effect, the Bath defeat apart: at Dundee, its intervention kept out Fitzjames Stephen, but a third Liberal won; at Greenwich, it fielded no candidate and recommended abstention, but the *Times* did not consider that this cost the party the seat; at Shaftesbury, it acted as at Bath, but the seat was lost, not because of this, but through one woman's exercise of patronage.[61] Finally, by mid August, it was clear that the League's strategy had failed to rouse local enthusiasm – and it fell back on the excuse of Bright's return to the government to cease its operations.[62] Chamberlain's only partial interest in the religious question was revealed when, in September, he launched his programme of 'Free Church, Free Land, Free Schools, and Free Labour' in the *Fortnightly*, encouraged by secular-minded radicals like John Morley and Harrison. He accused the government of extending the power of the Church of England over the education system, and of aiming to hand 'over the higher education of Ireland to the Romish priesthood'. He attacked the Establishment, because it was 'a great political engine for repressing the freest intellectual life and thought, and for opposing the manifestation and fulfilment of the popular will and aspirations'; and because its 'vast funds' could be used in order to establish a non-denominational national education system. In conjunction with his advocacy of land reform and of the amendment of labour legislation, these proposals formed an extensive catalogue of demands – but it was the catalogue of a secular-minded radical, not of a mainstream nonconformist.[63]

The League's intervention in by-elections, however limited its effect, coincided with a remarkable and extremely powerful swing of opinion against the government: between May 1873 and the dissolution in January 1874, ten Liberal seats were lost, including Gladstone's own (after his colleague died), as well as five others formerly held by ministers. This débâcle destroyed whatever shreds of self-confidence the government had retained after the defeat of March 1873. It demoralised the party, made it extremely difficult to fill government vacancies for fear of losing the subsequent by-election, and suggested, with a force prob-

---

[59] Hamer, *Politics of electoral pressure*, p. 39; anon., 'The Gladstone administration', p. 215.
[60] Auspos, 'Radicalism, pressure groups, and party politics', p. 191.
[61] *Times*, 1, 6, 8 August 1873, p. 8, p. 7, p. 9.
[62] Hamer, *Politics of electoral pressure*, p. 136.   [63] 'Liberal party and its leaders'.

ably without previous parallel in electoral politics, that Gladstone's majority did not represent public opinion – as Gladstone himself was aware.[64]

These losses were caused by a withdrawal of confidence by voters on the 'right' of the party. If the League campaign played a part in the losses, it was primarily in further antagonising whiggish voters who had already been greatly unsettled by the other campaigns for disestablishment and educational reform, and by the Irish imbroglio. In early 1873, Mundella had noted that the 'middle classes are everywhere becoming more and more Ecclesiastical and Conservative'.[65] Voters were particularly upset by the success of Miall's strategy of infiltration, which had radicalised many local constituency parties: the Liberal candidate even for a Conservative county seat like Mid Cheshire had advocated disestablishment during the by-election there in March 1873.[66] In Staffordshire East, one of the Liberal losses, the official Liberal candidate was the treasurer of the League, Jaffray; nor did the Liberal candidates support state Churches at Hull or Stroud, two of the other seats lost. The leading press commentators were agreed that defections from the 'right' of the party on the religious question were the major cause of the various defeats (they also took pains to minimise the influence of the licensing question).[67] At Renfrewshire, Exeter and Stroud, as at Greenwich and Staffordshire East, fears of Liberal extremism in religion were assigned the major role in explanations of the result; while at Shaftesbury, the dowager marchioness of Westminster, claiming to embody the whig tradition, engineered a Conservative victory for the sake of religion and the monarchy.[68]

The stream of by-election gains gave Disraeli a new plausibility as Conservative leader. His henchmen were already exploiting the Liberals' apparent unsoundness on disestablishment, ritual extravagances, secularism, republicanism and property questions;[69] then, in November, he made a rare public speech at Glasgow, and adopted the same stances. He reasserted that his party would govern responsibly and uncontroversially, concentrating on administrative and social questions, and that it would not harass interests or introduce perpetual 'organic change', as had the Liberals;[70] it would, moreover, be firm in Ireland, not making

---

[64] Buckle, *Letters of Victoria*, ii, 303.

[65] To Leader, 29 January 1873, Mundella papers.   [66] *Spectator*, 1 March 1873, p. 263.

[67] (Greenwich) *Times*, 6 August 1873, p. 7; (Staffs. East) *Spectator*, 9 August 1873, pp. 1002–5. See also, for Stroud, Smith, *Disraelian Conservatism and social reform*, p. 187.

[68] *Times*, 5 September 1873, p. 7; *Economist*, 13 September 1873, p. 1106; Newton, *Victorian Exeter*, pp. 195–7; Ellicott to Disraeli, 24 January 1874, Disraeli papers, B/XX/F/1a.

[69] (Pakington) *Nonconformist*, 29 October 1873, p. 1072; Hamley, 'Dragging out a wretched existence', pp. 249–54; Cowell, 'Liberal party and national education', p. 642.

[70] *Addresses*, pp. 26–8.

concessions to the home rulers and to the priests who manipulated them, but developing her material resources.[71] He concluded with a typically Disraelian flourish. If, he said, all the dangers of Liberalism were averted, and a 'national' party were allowed to govern responsibly, Britain might be able to play her deserved noble part in the 'very grave' struggle that was impending in Europe, between the temporal and spiritual powers, between state law and ultramontanism. In this coming struggle, if England only took 'a stand upon the Reformation (cheers), which 300 years ago was the source of our greatness and our glory', then 'it may be our proud destiny to guard civilization alike from the withering blasts of atheism and from the simoom of sacerdotal usurpation (loud cheers)'.[72]

The government's response to the by-election setbacks was to reshuffle its members, and to try to find new rallying-cries, although in neither case was a great deal achieved. Firstly, beginning in August 1873, there was a redistribution of posts. This began out of necessity – the need to remove men from offices which had been thought to bear responsibility for an embarrassing scandal in the administration of the Post Office. As it developed, however, the reshuffle did make the government look a little less 'clerical' and more amenable to compromise on the education issue. Lowe was one scapegoat, but he was made home secretary: this both smoothed the conduct of Treasury policy, and allowed Gladstone to remove Bruce from the Home Office, slightly appeasing the opponents of his licensing measures; Bruce became lord president and a peer. Monsell, the postmaster-general, was ousted from the government altogether. He had certainly been unpopular – Delane, for example, had considered his employment 'as a go-between with Cullen' to be 'an outrage': he had 'put the whole patronage of the Post Office at the disposal of Manning and Cullen and there is not a letter carrier who does not speak with a brogue'. But it is doubtful if his political demise suggested a significant shift in policy: the main consideration was that he could not hope to defeat the home rulers at the by-election which would result from a fresh ministerial appointment. He too received a peerage.[73] Gladstone and Fortescue hoped to be able to appoint an Irishman to a government office in his place, but could not find a suitable candidate who was likely to win a by-election.[74]

Gladstone planned a more far-reaching rearrangement of sensitive posts, in order to allow Bright – who was at last willing – to return to the

---

[71] *Ibid.*, pp. 25, 30.

[72] *Ibid.*, pp. 29–30.

[73] Delane to Ellice, 25 August 1873, Ellice papers, 15011, fo. 134; Monsell to Granville, 11 August 1873, Granville papers, 30/29/74, fo. 290.

[74] See Gladstone to Fortescue, 6 August 1873, Gladstone papers, 44123, fo. 59.

cabinet, and to remove Ripon and Forster from control of educational policy. Since he also tried to recall Hartington and Spencer from Ireland, the reshuffle would have had a distinctly radical look, had it succeeded. Ripon and Spencer had both been unhappy in office for some time, and had made noises signifying their desire to resign. Gladstone now rather brusquely took them at what he had perceived to be their word.[75] Ripon left office, and Bruce replaced him. Bright requested that Forster should also be removed from the education department, in preparation for a policy initiative designed to appease nonconformists.[76] Gladstone attempted to replace Hartington, with whom his relations had become very sour, with Forster as chief secretary for Ireland:[77] he told Hartington that Spencer wished to resign in December, and suggested that, since he had said that he did not wish to serve in Ireland under another viceroy, he should go before then. Hartington was offered the Post Office, an insulting proposal, since he had taken the post in December 1868 – and had regarded that appointment as a demotion from the war secretaryship which he had held under Russell – and since Monsell, the previous holder, had not even been in the cabinet.[78] He refused, and indicated his willingness to resign altogether. Both he and Spencer – who had not intended his complaints at the burdens of Dublin life to be taken as a request to retire – were offended by the offer, by its manner, and by the realisation that the purpose of the move was to appease Bright. Bessborough could not believe that Gladstone intended to make Forster, 'a Gorilla without any rank', chief secretary: Spencer thought that for Hartington to resign as well as Ripon would make the whigs' discontent with the government seethe over. Moreover, Forster showed no inclination to go to Ireland – or to the Post Office. Granville had to be brought in to pacify relations and to persuade Hartington and Spencer to stay; as Granville himself pointed out, Gladstone could not perform with 'sincerity' the task of telling Hartington that his loss to the government would be immense. Consequently, to Bright's displeasure, Forster remained in charge of education.[79]

The subsequent reshuffle of junior appointments, which brought

[75] See Ripon memorandum on resignation, Ripon papers, 43625, fo. 86.
[76] 17 August 1873, Ramm, ii, 394; Bright to Gladstone, 12, 25 August 1873, Gladstone papers, 44113, fos. 59, 64.
[77] Ramm, ii, 394, 397.
[78] Matthew, viii, 369; Holland, *Devonshire*, i, 123, 126–7.
[79] Ramm, ii, 395–402, 409–14; Holland, *Devonshire*, i, 123–9; Matthew, viii, 388; Gordon, *Spencer*, i, 110–13; Spencer to Granville, 17 August, 14 September 1873, Granville papers, 30/29/75, fos. 408, 421; Bessborough to Granville, 16 August 1873, *ibid.*, 30/29/71, fo. 192; Spencer to Hartington, 26 August 1873, Chatsworth papers, 354, fo. 235; Spencer to Gladstone, 20 September 1873, Gladstone papers, 44307, fo. 171; Forster to Gladstone, 17, 21 September 1873, *ibid.*, 44157, fos. 84, 86.

prominent anti-clerical Liberals into government, was, however, interpreted by some as embodying a change in emphasis. Playfair was eventually appointed to the Post Office, James became attorney-general and Harcourt solicitor-general (although in fact Gladstone had not originally considered either Playfair or Harcourt for the offices which they eventually obtained). Lowe also appointed Fitzmaurice to be his private secretary.[80]

The rearrangement of posts was therefore unable to solve the educational problem: the divisions within the party were too deep. There was an unfortunate clash between Bright and Forster soon after the reshuffle, which only intensified Gladstone's belief that the government should not tackle the question. Bright publicly criticised the 1870 Act, and recommended the reform of Clause 25. Forster was, understandably, furious, and Gladstone had to make it clear to Bright that he did not anticipate introducing an amending bill in 1874.[81] Gladstone, while remaining in 'no fear of the secular system', continued to refuse to accept any of the anti-denominational proposals designed to resolve the educational difficulty, because they were 'measures of oppression against voluntary schools'.[82] He told Bright to discourage candidates from concentrating on the question in the election campaign, maintaining that public discussion of it would merely point up party disunity.[83]

Gladstone made two attempts to rally the party in support of a policy less controversial than any of the religious issues. The first, in July 1873, was a declaration in favour of county franchise reform, but this led Ripon to offer his resignation, and disturbed Spencer and many on the 'right' of the party: the issue could not therefore serve its intended purpose.[84] The second was an initiative in favour of fiscal reform, which he was developing in private in December and January.[85] He had appointed himself chancellor of the exchequer in the August reshuffle, in the hope of re-establishing Liberal credentials by reviving memories of his successful budgets of the early 1860s. At first, he had been looking for a policy on which to found a session's effective government. But, by January

[80] (Horsman) *Times*, 16 December 1873, p. 6; Ramm, ii, 415–24, 432–3, 392; Fortescue to Gladstone, 30 November 1873, Gladstone papers, 44123, fo. 65; Gladstone to Wolverton, 1 November 1873, *ibid.*, 44348, fo. 313; Wolverton to Granville, 2 October 1873, Granville papers, 30/29/76.

[81] Reid, *Forster*, i, 559–71; 30 October 1873, Matthew, viii, 405–6.

[82] 3 September 1873, Ramm, ii, 405.

[83] Bright to Gladstone, 12, 25 August 1873, Gladstone papers, 44113, fos. 59, 64; Matthew, viii, 371–2, 377–8, 449–50.

[84] Ripon memorandum, August 1873, Ripon papers, 43625, fo. 86; Spencer to Hartington, 27 July 1873, Chatsworth papers, 354, fo. 230. See also Cardwell to Gladstone, 10 January 1874, Gladstone papers, 44120, fo. 206; and Somerset's attack, in *Times*, 16 January 1874, p. 7.

[85] See Matthew, vii, lxxxvii–xc.

1874, Gladstone had come to see the fiscal issue instead as the only one on which there was still enough public confidence in the party's record to afford a chance of election victory.[86] To universal surprise, he announced the dissolution of parliament in late January (the decision was conveyed to Spencer, through an erroneous cipher, as 'Bunglers have decided to dissolve').[87]

Gladstone published his address on 24 January. In the main, it was a bland document; it anticipated that there would be action, of an unspecified sort, to resolve the outstanding educational disputes, and to tackle the reform of the local-government system in London and the organisation of Oxford and Cambridge (to follow the report of the Royal Commission). Bills would also be forthcoming to deal with liquor, land, game and labour policy. He thought that public opinion had yet to be fully formed on the matter of the county franchise. He made no reference to past Irish policy, except to allege that the 1873 defeat had been caused, 'if not by a combined, yet by a concurrent, effort of the leader of the Opposition and of the Roman Catholic prelacy in Ireland'. He did however include a vague paragraph outlining the possibility that his government would concede powers to local legislatures in the various kingdoms, subject to the continued supremacy of the imperial parliament. This apart, the obvious intention of the address was to set aside religious and educational questions as incapable of securing party unity, and to concentrate on finance. He indicated that, if the situation at the end of the financial year remained promising, he would probably be able to repeal the income tax, to offer some 'marked relief' on items of popular consumption, and to grant some reduction in the rates.[88]

Internal party criticism focussed on three points in the address. Firstly, there were complaints from the Liberation Society and the National Education League that Gladstone had not approximated to their demands. This was to be expected. But these complaints did not, except in a few seats, result in obstruction and disloyal behaviour towards the party – as we shall see. Both organisations were in fact studiously moderate in their election campaigns. The Liberation Society left each constituency party free to decide how far it wished to press its candidates on the disestablishment question. The League's demands – that Liberals should declare in favour of the abolition of Clause 25 and of the extension of school boards – were acceptable to most candidates. As the *Spectator* said, the divisive educational issues were secularism and the future of state aid to denominational schools, and the League did not

---

[86] See also Argyll to Dufferin, 17 March 1874, Dufferin papers.
[87] Gordon, *Spencer*, i, 122.   [88] *Times*, 24 January 1874, p. 8.

adopt an aggressive policy on either.[89] During the campaign, Gladstone declined to pronounce on disestablishment, and touched on education in a reassuring but unconstructive way, calling for the 're-consideration' of Clause 25, as long as parents' liberty to secure a religious education for their children was safeguarded.[90] Nearly all candidates were able to indulge in similar subterfuges, either blithely assuming that an educational policy could be formulated which would satisfy all parties, or accepting the repeal of Clause 25 for the sake of party unity – on the grounds that it subsidised denominational education, a result which they had not foreseen in 1870.[91] For most, indeed, agreeing to the repeal involved very little – although it may have worried voters. But, except in a few atypical constituencies, such compromises satisfied local nonconformists.

Rather more alarm was expressed on the Liberal 'right', because of two passages in Gladstone's address; Reeve thought that it ensured that the party would be 'smashed'.[92] The first was the section on financial policy itself, in which many whigs detected an impending attack on property. They were quick to see that Gladstone's figures did not tally, and that a substantial source of extra revenue would be required (Gladstone himself privately estimated £2 million); they forecast that this would probably be collected by extending the succession duties, or by imposing a land tax, but that, in any event, property would be hit disproportionately hard. Halifax and Lowe from within the cabinet, Bouverie, Ellice, Somerset, George Grey, Earl Fortescue and the *Times* outside it, all reflected the widespread suspicion of Gladstone's ultimate aims.[93] Gladstone's speeches did not help their equanimity: he attacked the Conservatives, as on Smith's motion in 1873, for promising nothing to the working-man, and for concentrating their efforts on bribing the rural and suburban ratepayer.[94]

The second controversial passage was that discussing Irish local government, which was vague enough to raise many fears, especially from those predisposed to them. The controversy was heightened

---

[89] *Ibid.*, 27, 28 January, p. 10, p. 6; *Spectator*, 31 January 1874, pp. 135–6.
[90] *Times*, 2 February, p. 5.
[91] See the responses of men such as Dent, Ramsden and Frederick Cavendish: *Leeds Mercury*, 25 November 1873, p. 8; 2, 7 February 1874, p. 7.
[92] Laughton, *Reeve*, ii, 222.
[93] (19 January 1874) Matthew, viii, 442–3; Hutchinson, *Avebury*, i, 209; (Lowe) diary, 7 February 1874, 15th earl of Derby papers; Bouverie to Ellice, 26 January 1874, Ellice papers, 15005, fo. 142; Ellice to Grey, 28 January 1874, Grey papers; George Grey to Earl Fortescue, 2 February 1874, Fortescue papers, FC 129; (Somerset) *Hansard*, ccxviii, 39, 19 March 1874; Halifax to Dalhousie, 18 February 1874, Dalhousie papers, GD 45/14/689/179; Fortescue to Brereton, 21 February 1874, Brereton papers, F 13 74; *Times*, 29 January 1874, p. 7.
[94] *Times*, 29 January, 3 February 1874, p. 5.

because Irish Liberals, facing the home-rule onslaught, were desperately interpreting Gladstone's words as a generous concession to nationalist sentiment.[95] The subject had been much under discussion, because congestion of the parliamentary timetable had resulted in the loss of many uncontroversial Irish bills. The idea of establishing a local parliament with powers to discuss such matters had in fact been supported by men from all sections of the party, but it now took on a different aspect in the eyes of whigs who distrusted Gladstone's firmness of purpose. For them, the twin dangers were that the local legislature might later assume control of a matter as sensitive as education, and that it might create a precedent for home rule: either was possible if the home rulers held the balance of power in the next parliament. Gladstone refused to condemn the home rulers during the campaign,[96] and the whigs drew their own conclusions. Grey thought that Gladstone would drift into sanctioning home rule; after the election, Somerset attacked him for a vacillation on the subject unforgivable in a prime minister, and Halifax professed puzzlement and alarm at Gladstone's 'very foolish' refusal to declare against home rule.[97]

The Conservative campaign in 1874 was remarkably well orchestrated, at least in southern England. Front- and backbenchers adopted very similar arguments in their addresses and speeches; a number of simple points were made over and over again. Nearly all addresses began with an attack on the restlessness and unpredictability of the government, and its harassing and 'sensational' legislation. The real focus of the Conservatives' attack, however, was less what the government had done, than what its vulnerability to popular agitation threatened to make it do in future. Candidate after candidate highlighted the divisions in the Liberal ranks, and the vacillation in the cabinet, which made it impossible to predict that the leadership would dare staunchly to oppose anything requested of it. As W. H. Smith said, the government could 'not adopt one line of policy and adhere to it. Instead of leading opinion, they were always inviting discussion.'[98] Northcote asked how the party would formulate policy on disestablishment and English and Irish education, now that their supporters so clearly pulled in different directions.[99] For Disraeli, 'the Liberal party is dissevered and disunited because they do

---

[95] Thornley, *Butt*, p. 179.
[96] In a published letter to Fermoy; 28 January 1874, Matthew, viii, 451.
[97] Grey to Halifax, 25 January 1874, Hickleton papers, A 4 55; (Somerset) *Hansard*, ccxviii, 39, 19 March 1874; Halifax to Northbrook, 26 March 1874, Northbrook papers, 144, 22. The *Pall Mall* also criticised Gladstone's ambiguity about the matter: leading article, 4 February 1874, pp. 1–2. See also Bouverie, in *Times*, 2 February, p. 7.
[98] *Times*, 31 January, p. 6. See also Cotton, in the City, *ibid.*, 29 January, p. 6.
[99] *Ibid.*, 31 January, p. 7; Ditto Pakington, *ibid.*, 2 February, p. 7.

not agree upon some of the greatest and deepest principles which influence upon the government of men': national education, the distribution of electoral power, the Church Establishment and the monarchy.[100] At the less sophisticated level, Conservative argument degenerated into allegations that Liberals were 'Atheists, Republicans, and Teetotallers', or at least that Gladstone would be the 'tool' of the extreme radicals; but such arguments were probably none the less effective for being expressed in this way.[101]

The Conservatives' specific electoral pledges were thus designed to furnish a contrast with Liberal unpredictability. By far the most common, appearing in almost every address in the south of England, and in most elsewhere, was their defence of the Church Establishment, and its corollary, the retention of religious education in school-hours, against the threat posed to both by radical Liberals. Sometimes these pledges were accompanied, as with Repton in Warwick, Grantham in East Surrey and Sandon in Liverpool, by an expression in favour of Church reform or of legislation aimed at stamping out clerical lawlessness.[102] Sometimes Gladstone was criticised for his vacillation on the subject of religious education in schools.[103] The *Yorkshire Post*, a Conservative paper, pointed out that voluntary denominational schools saved the ratepayer five times as much as he would pay even if Clause 25 were regularly implemented across the country.[104] Late in the campaign, Disraeli argued that Clause 25 was the symbol of a far greater question, and that no compromise on it was possible. He maintained that, once government ministers had begun to admit the claims of those who attacked the clause, they had sold the pass to the advocates of secular education. 'Those that are in favour of the 25th clause are in favour of religious education, those that are against it are in favour of secular education ... The only question before the country is whether the education of the country should be founded on a basis of religion, or whether it should be simply secular education.'[105]

The Conservatives also exploited other issues. They often suggested that the monarchy was in danger from republican agitation; and that Britain's 'dignity' ought to be upheld more assiduously abroad – although it was unusual for candidates to point to specific examples of government shortcomings in this area. Sometimes, the union of 'Radical and Ultramontane parties' was blamed for making the attempt to uphold

[100] *Ibid.*, 5 February, p. 5.
[101] Colman, *Colman*, p. 270; (Major Lee) *Times*, 5 January 1874, p. 12.
[102] *Times*, 27 January, p. 12, 2 February, p. 9.
[103] E.g. by Richardson-Gardner (Windsor), *ibid.*, 27 January, p. 12.
[104] *Yorkshire Post* leading article, 2 February, p. 5.
[105] At Aylesbury: *Scotsman*, 11 February, p. 7.

the Protestant institutions of the country impossible.[106] There were many references to the danger which the home rulers' influence over the Liberal party posed to 'the Imperial Government of the United Kingdom'.[107] Disraeli found Gladstone's vagueness on home rule 'ominous'. As at Glasgow in the previous November, he pointed out the danger of placing trust in a government that was so dependent on anti-British, anti-Establishment and anti-monarchical supporters, at a time 'when Europe is more deeply stirred than at any period since the Reformation, and when the cause of civil liberty and religious freedom mainly depends upon the strength and stability of England'.[108] Nor could he resist indicating the failure of Gladstone's mission to Ireland, which, he suggested, had aroused undesirable 'political excitement' among the Irish and in Britain, and yet had resulted in government by a stringent Coercion Act, in an attempt to repress widespread discontent.[109]

In discussing finance, Conservatives were generally keen to emphasise that they disliked the income tax as much as the Liberals, and that they had said so far more consistently. They coupled this with two themes: firstly, that a far-reaching readjustment of local taxation was necessary, and that the Liberals were extremely unlikely to act to this effect, since they had done nothing during the last parliament; and secondly, that Gladstone's fiscal plans foreshadowed a class-based policy. Many Conservatives argued that Gladstone would be forced to levy extra taxes (which they estimated at £4½ million) in order to finance his planned measures of tax relief, and that these taxes would almost certainly fall on property.

One extremely common Conservative theme was to contrast the destruction achieved and threatened by the Liberal party – the 'sensational' politics, the agitation of great questions – with the Conservative policy of practical beneficial legislation. Very few candidates committed themselves to supporting specific social and sanitary reforms;[110] most adopted the platform in order to suggest the soundness and constructiveness of their party. When more detail was offered about likely legislation, the most frequently mentioned proposals were in fact not sanitary ones but the reform of local taxation and local government, the revision of the game laws, the introduction of compensation to tenants for their

---

[106] (Lord George Hamilton) *Times*, 27 January.
[107] E.g. W. Bromley Davenport in North Warwickshire, *Times*, 2 February, and C. B. Denison in the West Riding East, *Yorkshire Post*, 27 January.
[108] *Times*, 26 January, p. 8.
[109] *Scotsman*, 11 February 1874, p. 7.
[110] E.g. Sandon, who had also done so in 1868, and Twells in the City, who mentioned dwellings in a list which started with local taxation: *Times*, 2 February 1874, p. 9, 29 January, p. 11.

unexhausted improvements, the adjustment of industrial laws between employer and employee, and the institution of better protection from imported cattle disease.[111] This stress on practical and uncontroversial legislation was shared, as we have seen, by Gladstone's critics on the Liberal 'right'.[112]

Liberal candidates remained very much on the defensive throughout the campaign. In addition to blurring over the education issue, most relied mainly on two ploys. The first was to avoid specific commitments to particular policy proposals, as far as possible. Instead, they offered a recitation of the achievements of the Gladstone government (usually mentioning the Irish Church, Irish Land, Education and Ballot Acts, and the abolition of army purchase), and declared that they themselves would continue to uphold 'Liberal principles', without specifying what these would entail. To adhere to such principles, they suggested, would promote 'progress', in contrast to tory 'reaction' and Disraelian unpredictability.[113] There was a whiff of nostalgia about the Liberal campaign: candidates would pledge themselves to maintain 'civil and religious liberty', or other cries which invoked the heady successes of past crusades. In order to hide the lack of agreement on a future programme, Rothschild, in the City, appealed for a return to the united enthusiasm of the 1840s; Lord Frederick Cavendish talked of Brougham, Morpeth and Cobden.[114] Men on the 'right' of the party would often vary this line by declaring in favour of 'every sound Liberal measure', and against 'every wild or revolutionary proposal'.[115] This approach was especially popular in southern seats: Cartwright in Oxfordshire, Lambert in Buckinghamshire, and Tufton in East Kent volunteered a general support for the party, while recognising that the government had not been infallible. Walter in Berkshire ambiguously proposed that some of the measures at which Gladstone had hinted in his address – reforms of local government, the county franchise and the land laws – should be carefully considered and elucidated.[116]

Secondly, the one specific argument that most candidates were happy to use in order to justify calling for continued support, was that Gladstone was to be trusted in financial matters. Cowper-Temple, Brassey, Evans, Tufton and Lambert all emphasised this (although even

---

[111] See e.g., in addition to Disraeli (*ibid.*, 26 January, p. 8): Manners (Leicestershire North), Baring and Malins (Essex South), Cubitt (West Surrey), Allen and Bright (Somerset East), Lopes (Devon South), Ashbury (Brighton), Pim (Gravesend), Legard (Scarborough), W. Bromley Davenport (North Warwickshire), Sandon (Liverpool), Tennant (Leeds), Woodd (Knaresborough).

[112] *Pall Mall Gazette*, 31 January 1874, p. 1; (*Fraser's*) anon., 'Turn of the tide', p. 280.

[113] See e.g. Cowen at Newcastle-upon-Tyne, Adam in Clackmannan, *Times*, 27 January.

[114] *Ibid.*, 31 January, p. 6; *Leeds Mercury*, 7 February 1874, p. 7.

[115] E.g. Bass: *Times*, 27 January.   [116] *Ibid.*, 27 January.

here, some county MPs, like Brand's son in Hertfordshire, went out of their way to support a reform of the local taxation system, the part of Gladstone's financial programme to which he was obviously least committed).[117] Apart from this, there was little that was aggressive in the Liberal campaign. Of course, individual candidates raised a large number of other issues. County franchise extension, free trade in land, and the introduction of labour legislation devoid of class bias, were the most popular, since the leadership had managed to prevent too many candidates stressing religious radicalism. In contrast with 1868, however, there was no sense that principles were being formulated during the campaign which would form the basis of a successful term of government.

The election results were conclusive. Conservatives made a net gain of 82 seats, and attained a majority over Liberals and home rulers combined of about 50. The results show a considerable swing to the Conservatives across the country, except, understandably, in Ireland. Interpreting the Conservative gains as a percentage of the number of Liberal seats theoretically available to them, they clearly did best in the counties and in southern borough seats (see Table 2).

It ought to be stressed that it was in 1874, rather than in 1868, that they made unambiguous major gains in the counties: the result of a disaffection among Liberal magnates and Anglican voters of a far greater order than that of 1868. The only county seat gained by the Liberals in Britain in 1874 (except for one gained at a void election) was Elgin and Nairn, which was experiencing its first contest since 1841, denied it in the *annus mirabilis* of 1868. It was in fact in Scottish counties that Liberals suffered some of their most spectacular losses. They did especially badly in the Borders, losing four of their 1868 gains, and three more which they had won in 1865; the Conservatives now held every county seat south of the Clyde except for a semi-industrial one, and Kirkcudbrightshire, which they failed to take by four votes. The Liberals also lost two other Scottish county seats. In the Highlands, there was a less marked reaction than in the Borders, because of the power of the Liberal landlords; but the Liberalism of Highland MPs was distinctly unGladstonian. Of the seven far-Highland MPs elected in 1874, only one was a Conservative; but, of the Liberals, one was a son and nominee of the duke of Sutherland, another was an old whig, a third (Laing) condemned the Irish University Bill and pledged himself to oppose disestablishment and any further concessions to the 'Home Rule and Ultramontane parties',[118] while two of the other three had to defeat more radical Liberals in order to win their seats.

---

[117] *Ibid.*, 29, 30 January.   [118] *Scotsman*, 12 February.

Table 2 *Conservative gains at the 1874 election*

	1868		1874		Con. gain	Con. gain as % of Lib. seats, 1868
	Lib.	Con.	Lib.	Con.		
Boroughs						
with electorate 2,000 or less, 1868	63	39	51	51	12	19
with electorate 2–5,000 1868, south[a]	29	7	14	22	15	52
with electorate 2–5,000 1868, north[a]	42	10	33	19	9	21
with electorate 5,000+ 1868, south[a]	39	7	22	24	17	44
with electorate 5,000+ 1868, north[a]	63	24	60	27	3	5
Counties						
England	47	123	27	143	20	43
Wales	9	8	6	11	3	33
Scotland	25	7	17	15	8	32
Universities	3	4	2	5	1	33
Ireland	64	39	[70]	33	−6	
Total	384	268	302	350	82	21

Source: Craig, *British parliamentary election results, 1832–1885.*
[a] South = south of Severn–Wash line; north = north of it, including Wales and Scotland.
Note: Six seats (three Liberal, three Conservative) which were disfranchised in 1870 are removed from the 1868 figures.
Seats won by home rulers in Ireland in 1874 are added to the Liberal total.

In rural Wales the Liberals lost Carnarvonshire and Carmarthenshire from 1868 and Cardiganshire from 1865, although they retained Merioneth. These losses were caused primarily by distrust of the Liberation Society in the farming areas.[119] In the English counties the Liberal rout was so complete that they retained only the 7 seats virtually guaranteed to them by the minority clause, plus 14 northern or semi-urban seats (15 before one was declared void), 4 seats in the far south-west, and, elsewhere in the midlands, south and east, only one in Bedfordshire.

In Ireland, approximately 17 'Liberals' were returned, and over 50

[119] See Jones, 'Cardiganshire politics', p. 34; (Carmarthenshire) Morgan, *Wales in British politics*, p. 35.

'home rulers': this, in effect, marked the end of Liberal unionism in Ireland. A series of spectacular Liberal defeats at the hands of home rulers was headed by the loss of 'Coercion' Fortescue's seat in Louth. Although Thornley rightly questions how deep the commitment of many of the new 'home-rule' MPs was, there is no doubt that it was necessary in almost every non-Protestant constituency to pledge support for denominational education and home rule.[120] Ulster, however, saw a few striking Liberal gains, partly owing to the political emancipation of the tenant-farmers, and partly owing to increased Catholic activity.[121]

As for British borough seats, it is noticeable from Table 2 that in the smallest boroughs (most of which were in the south), the swing tended to be lower than in those southern boroughs with larger electorates, which indicates the continued importance of patronage in the smallest seats. This category apart, it is apparent that the smaller and more southerly the borough the more marked the swing to the Conservatives was likely to be. In only four southern constituencies with electorates of between 2,000 and 5,000 did the Conservatives fail by more than a close margin (as in two cases) to win at least one seat. Southern seats with over 5,000 electors also fell in large numbers – most notably in London, where the Conservatives, who had held just one seat at the beginning of 1870, and 3 at the dissolution, now had 10 to the Liberals' 12. Only in Finsbury, Hackney and Lambeth of London boroughs, and Bristol, Oxford and Stroud of the other big southern boroughs, did the Liberals retain both seats (strongly challenged in Stroud). Elsewhere outside London, they held one seat only in Norwich, Bath, Southampton and Northampton; the Conservatives took the other 14.

The northern seats swung less dramatically. In some individual seats, the Conservatives did well, and in others not, but in no northern area did they strongly improve on their 1868 position. Their failure is especially striking because of two trends which helped them appreciably. The first was the defection from the Liberal party of Roman Catholics who disliked the educational anti-clericalism of Liberals locally and nationally:[122] Gladstone, Childers and Bright all noticed this phenomenon.[123] The second was that conflict between wings of the Liberal party enabled Conservatives to gain several seats. One was at Bradford, where a Liberal-Conservative, Ripley, stood in combination with

---

[120] Thornley, *Butt*, pp. 176–81, 195–204; Norman, *Catholic Church*, pp. 455–7; Spencer to Gladstone, 27 January 1874, Gladstone papers, 44307, fo. 218.

[121] Macknight, *Ulster as it is*, p. 295; Hoppen, *Elections in Ireland*, pp. 266–70.

[122] Wright, 'Bradford election', p. 63; Greenall, 'Popular Conservatism in Salford', p. 137; (Scarborough) *Yorkshire Post*, 30 January; (Bishop of Salford) *Times*, 3 February 1874, p. 7.

[123] Matthew, viii, 456; Childers to Gladstone, 9 February 1874, Gladstone papers, 44128, fo. 256; Bright to Gladstone, 26 January 1874, *ibid.*, 44113, fo. 89.

Forster:[124] they both supported the Establishment and religious education, against two nonconformist candidates, Miall's friend Godwin, and the working-man Hardaker, whose campaign was managed by Illingworth.[125] A second was at Leeds: the intervention of a temperance candidate, who probably also gained votes from radical nonconformists, lost Baines the seat.[126] Another split, caused by the intervention of a working-man candidate, helped the Conservatives to gain a seat at Stoke. (In Sheffield, Chamberlain stood on the principles that he had sketched out in the *Fortnightly* in September 1873, and was opposed by the 'right-wing' Liberal, Roebuck, who upheld the Church Establishment and religious education; the voters were exhorted by publicans to 'stand by your National Religion and your National Beverage', and to vote for 'Roebuck and the Bible'. Roebuck, together with Mundella, defeated Chamberlain.)[127]

Most of the 'Liberal versus Liberal' contests which resulted in Conservative gains were concentrated in this geographical area: Scarborough and perhaps Wigan were gained for the same reason, although hardly any seats in the south were.[128] The publicity given to these internecine quarrels in areas where nonconformist political activity was considerable has led a large number of historians to argue that nonconformist disloyalty to the party establishment hurt the Liberals more generally in the election.[129] Radical nonconformists certainly encouraged this interpretation themselves, hoping that the party would take more notice of them in future.[130] But the validity of this argument may be questioned. To question it with certainty is impossible, since there are no reliable statistics measuring the relationship between nonconformist strength and Liberal performance. Table 3, comparing nonconformist distribution as recorded by the 1851 census, and party gains, is included only as the crudest of guides: the figures are of very limited value, on account of the doubts cast on the accuracy of the census, the change in population distribution between 1851 and 1874, and the possible divergence between nonconformist strength in the electorate and in the population

---

[124] Ripley, who was to become a Conservative during the 1874 parliament, is classed as one *in* 1874 by Craig, *British parliamentary election results, 1832–1885*, and so the Bradford result is represented in the tables here as a Conservative gain.

[125] See Wright, 'Bradford election', p. 66; Reid, *Forster*, ii, 45–56.

[126] Reid, *Reid*, pp. 209–10.

[127] Garvin, *Chamberlain*, i, 164–9; Leader, *Roebuck*, pp. 341–3.

[128] Lloyd estimates that eleven seats in all were lost owing to a superfluity of Liberal candidates: *General election of 1880*, p. 4.

[129] E.g. Rossi, 'Transformation of the Liberal party', pp. 11–12; Harrison, 'A genealogy of reform', pp. 142–3; Clarke, 'Electoral sociology of modern Britain', p. 46; Gilbert, *Religion and society*, p. 195.

[130] Miall, *Richard*, p. 176.

Table 3 *Party gains, 1874, and distribution of nonconformity, 1851*

	Boroughs: electorates over 5,000		All other seats		Nonconformists as % of Protestants, 1851[a]
	No. of seats	Con. gain, 1874	No. of seats	Con. gain, 1874	
London and S. East[b]	24	+10	65	+19	37
E. Anglia/Central	8	+3	49	+4	46
S. West	14	+4	81	+15	45
Total	46	+17	195	+38	42
W. Midlands	14	−1	43	+2	43
E. Midlands	10	0	32	+5	54
Lancastria	25	0	19	+3	48
Yorkshire	16	+2	21	+5	63
North	6	+1	29	−1	55
Total	71	+2	144	+14	52
Wales	4	0	29	+4	80
Scotland	12	+1	48	+10	69

[a] These figures express total attendances at all congregationalist, baptist, unitarian, methodist, United Presbyterian and Free Church services on 30 March 1851, as a percentage of total attendances at these and at Church of England and Church of Scotland services on that day. Very small Protestant denominations have therefore been excluded from the calculations.
[b] Regions are constituted as follows:

S. East Bucks., Essex, Herts., Kent, Surrey, Sussex
E. Anglia/Central Beds., Berks., Cambs., Hunts., Norfolk, Northants., Oxon., Suffolk
S. West Cornwall, Devon, Dorset, Glos., Hants, Somerset, Wilts.
W. Midlands Herefordshire, Shropshire, Staffs., Warwicks., Worcs.
E. Midlands Derbys., Leics., Lincs., Notts., Rutland
Lancastria Lancashire, Cheshire
North Cumberland, Durham, Northumberland, Westmorland

generally. Calculations are made on the basis of seats gained by the Conservatives, not of votes transferred between the parties, because of the difficulty of assessing the number of the latter in two- and three-member seats for which the number of candidates changed between 1868 and 1874. Column 2, listing Conservative gains in large borough seats, probably gives a better indication of the state of opinion among working-men and artisan electors than does column 4, which includes figures for a large number of county and small-borough seats. The results, notwithstanding the necessary qualifications, suggest that the Liberals, on the whole, performed better, in terms of seats retained, where nonconformity was stronger. It would be too crude, of course, to characterise 'southern' seats simply as Anglican, and 'northern' ones simply as nonconformist. But the Liberals' especially bad results in London, for example, surely cannot be unrelated to the weakness of organised nonconformity there.

The Liberals' surprisingly good performance in the north requires us to try to understand nonconformists' behaviour, given their well-publicised discontent with the government's educational policy. In fact, there are a number of reasons why it would have been odd for an unusually large number of nonconformists to abstain in protest at the government's record, rather than to continue – as, in the absence of evidence to the contrary, we may assume that they did – to vote Liberal. Firstly, although some leading nonconformist spokesmen were undeniably apathetic in 1874, it is not clear that their ill-humour would have affected the behaviour of the politically active rank-and-file, especially after the power of the latter over the former had increased with the extension of the franchise in 1867 (as Hanham pointed out).[131] The rank-and-file's attachment to Gladstone must have been largely unquestioning, an attachment founded on emotion and reverence rather than on considerations of policy. Moreover, a large number of nonconformists, being Wesleyans, would not be moved by agitations for radical educational reform, or, probably, for disestablishment.

Another consideration is often forgotten: that in nearly all large northern boroughs, the educational grievance, the most immediate and trying of nonconformist complaints, had largely disappeared by 1874, as a result of Liberal victories in the 1873 school-board elections. By 1873, nearly all Liberal candidates in board elections advocated an unsectarian policy, of bible-reading or teaching, but with no further religious instruction. (The number of boards which followed the example of Birmingham in declaring that they would be satisfied only with the secular system was infinitesimal – by 1888, there were, probably, only seven such boards in England and fifty in Wales.)[132] In 1870, a good many of the boards had had a 'sectarian' majority; but, after the 1873 elections, the Liberals had control – in addition to secularist Birmingham – of Nottingham, Coventry, Leicester, Northampton, Dudley, Walsall, Leeds, Bradford, Sheffield, Huddersfield, Hull, Middlesborough, Darlington, Rochdale and Oldham. Of the large boards in the north and midlands, they had failed to take only Wolverhampton, Derby, Halifax (owing purely to incompetence) and several in Lancashire (and in the north-east, where, as in so many towns in the south, the whole issue seems to have been less

---

[131] *Elections and party management*, pp. 119–21.   [132] Murphy, *Church, state and schools*, p. 69.

contentious). In most large northern boroughs, therefore, sectarian teaching and the implementation of Clause 25 were no longer irritating Liberals by 1874.

Nonetheless, many nonconformists were certainly capable of being goaded into campaigns against individual 'right-wing' Liberals. However, in the great majority of large northern borough seats, this would not have been necessary. This was because most official party candidates had already been radicals, even in 1868 (as is evident from the results of the survey given in chapter 4) – while a radicalisation had taken place in the subsequent six years, as the history of by-elections since 1871 revealed. There was little reason for nonconformists to abstain from voting for candidates who advocated disestablishment and an assault on denominational education.

Furthermore, in many northern constituencies, the 1874 election campaign itself promoted the process of radicalisation, and enabled advanced Liberal voters to elect fellow-radicals rather than moderates, as the result either of an open contest, or of pressure exerted behind the scenes. Many local associations which were strongly influenced by working-class or nonconformist pressure were so aggressively radical that they would not tolerate 'right-wing' dissension from Gladstone's government. This was occasionally the case even in the south: Tom Hughes had to withdraw from the contest at Marylebone because of radical opposition;[133] the *Times* believed that Lucraft, the nonconformist working-man candidate for Finsbury, represented a large body of opinion when he attacked the sitting (and re-elected) MP, Torrens, for his opposition to the Irish University Bill.[134] But this pattern was especially evident in Scotland, Wales and the north. Of the four Scottish Liberal MPs who rebelled on the Irish University Bill, Bouverie was defeated in Kilmarnock by a man who called him a tory and pledged his support, not only for Gladstone, but for an elected parliament for Dublin and for a degree of home rule for Scotland as well; Macfie was defeated in Leith by another Liberal who promised solid support for Gladstone; and Aytoun was persuaded to retire from Kirkcaldy, and Maxwell likewise from Kirkcudbrightshire, both to be replaced by more thoroughgoing Liberals.[135]

The Liberal representation in other large Scottish boroughs also tended to shift to the left: in Glasgow, Dalglish and Graham were replaced by Cameron, a Catholic, Liberationist and home ruler; in Dundee, Yeaman and Jenkins beat the whig Ogilvy (an interesting exception to the rule was Edinburgh, where there was a whig resurgence). In Welsh boroughs, the same shift was even more apparent:

---

[133] *Times*, 3 February, p. 6.   [134] *Ibid.*, 31 January, p. 6.   [135] *Scotsman*, 7 February.

in Beaumaris and in Flint, the whig candidate of the party establishment (in Flint, this was the sitting MP) was beaten by a Liberationist; in Cardigan, Sir Thomas Lloyd, who had abstained on the Irish University Bill, was persuaded to 'retire' in favour of a Liberationist; in Monmouth, the whig Sir John Ramsden was forced out of his seat by a radical Liberal (who then lost to the Conservatives); while the only Liberal gain was in Pembroke, and was achieved by a supporter of disestablishment (who also had claims on the dockyard vote).[136]

Many working-class constituencies in England showed a similar radical spirit. Hull had refused to tolerate Sir Spencer Robinson, a critic of Gladstone's naval policy, as a candidate in the 1873 by-election;[137] the voters of Dudley re-elected the Anglican radical Brogden in 1874, although their leading Liberal landlord, Dudley, ran a Liberal-Conservative against him.[138] A number of moderate Liberals sitting for northern seats were supplanted by radicals and nonconformists. Two of the most famous casualties were George Grey at Morpeth and T. E. Headlam at Newcastle. Grey 'retired' in favour of the miners' candidate and nonconformist Thomas Burt, who had been petitioned to stand by over 3,000 men, apparently all electors (out of a total of less than 5,000 on the electoral roll).[139] Headlam was theoretically fighting the election in alliance with the radical, nonconformist and home ruler Joseph Cowen, but local radical activists would not work with him, and encouraged voters to plump for Cowen.[140] Earp, a supporter of disestablishment, replaced the moderate Hodgkinson at Newark.

A further explanation of the Conservatives' failure to make extensive gains in northern borough seats was the willingness of groups which advocated radical initiatives in other policy areas to work for the official Liberal candidates. For example, although Liberal seats were occasionally lost owing to the intervention of temperance candidates, these were very few and far between, and most temperance campaigners were loyal to the party.[141] The Labour Representation League ran thirteen independent candidates in the election. It pressed for the repeal of the 1871 Criminal Law Amendment Act; for the amendment of the Master and Servant Act and of the law of conspiracy, in order to give unions equal rights with employers before the law; and for other factory and labour

[136] See the *Times*, the *Daily News* and the *Scotsman*, 26 January to 10 February.
[137] *Spectator*, 13 September 1873, p. 1142.
[138] Trainor, 'Peers on an industrial frontier', p. 98.
[139] *Times*, 20 October 1873, p. 10.
[140] See *Nonconformist*, 11 February 1874, pp. 129–30; *Manchester Guardian*, 13 February 1874, p. 3; Duncan, *Cowen*, p. 84.
[141] Dingle, *Campaign for prohibition*, pp. 45–6.

legislation, such as Mundella's bill for the nine-hour day. But in those seats in which no LRL candidate stood, few discontented working-men seem to have deviated from the party line – although there are infrequent reports of abstentions.[142] They were loyal, on the whole, because, at least in the north, many Liberal candidates (and some Conservatives as well) supported the trade unions' demands for further legislation. Furthermore, a number of leading government ministers, including Forster, Stansfeld and Harcourt, were prominent in pledging that the Liberals would reform the labour laws – and these pledges convinced, for example, Frederic Harrison (who in 1873 had wanted a third party to be founded in order to unite nonconformists and working-men in pursuit of radical change) that the Liberals were in earnest. Beesly, while condemning the failures of the government, still told the readers of the *Bee-hive* to vote Liberal – and most other *Bee-hive* writers were far more conciliatory than he.[143] Certainly, the agricultural labourers' leader, Joseph Arch, was a committed and enthusiastic Liberal in 1874.[144]

In the main, then, nonconformists and working-class activists succeeded both in ensuring Liberal victories in their own constituencies in 1874, and, simultaneously, in protesting against 'moderate' tendencies within the party. It is also noticeable that most radicals who were engaged in intraparty fights against moderates were at pains to affirm their loyalty to Gladstone.[145] In addition, many, as we have seen, were hostile to Liberal critics of the Irish University Bill, and some were even sympathetic to the demands of home rulers. Both these tendencies were interesting pointers to future trends in the history of radicalism.

Abstentions on the 'left' of the party therefore probably bear relatively little responsibility for the election defeat – which must rest squarely on those from the 'right' who retracted their support. Cardwell, Argyll, Halifax and the *Spectator* all blamed 'fear' of the Liberals' burgeoning radicalism as the basic reason for the débâcle: fear of the nonconformists, the home rulers, the trade unions and the republicans, fear for the domestic and international future.[146] The *Economist*, Kimberley and Cartwright blamed the rebuff on the widespread feeling that Gladstone

[142] Fisher and Smethurst, ' "War on the law of supply and demand" ', pp. 134–7.
[143] Smith, *Disraelian Conservatism and social reform*, pp. 188–9; McCready, 'British election of 1874', pp. 173–4; *Bee-hive*, 31 January 1874, pp. 1–2, 8.
[144] Horn, *Arch*, pp. 122–5.
[145] See Fortescue Harrison, against Bouverie at Kilmarnock (above, p. 399); and Godwin and Hardaker at Bradford, in Temmel, 'Liberal versus Liberal', p. 619.
[146] Cardwell to Northbrook, 19 February 1874, Halifax to Northbrook, 12 March 1874, Northbrook papers, 144, 22; Argyll to Halifax, 7 February 1874, Hickleton papers, A 4 82; Halifax to Dalhousie, 18 February 1874, Dalhousie papers, GD 45/14/689/179; *Spectator*, 14 February 1874, p. 197.

would 'accept any measure which the extreme Liberals require as the price of their support'.[147]

In the country, the withdrawal of confidence, on the part of 'right-wing' Liberals, was obvious. One would expect landowning whigs to overcome their apathy when fighting elections, which were seen as contests with local opponents as much as a means of choosing a government – and, in most cases, they did so. Even so, there was no doubt as to the lack of enthusiasm for the cause. Several prominent aristocrats did little to prevent defeats in their constituencies, such as Fitzwilliam in the southern division of the West Riding (although he did campaign, unsuccessfully, against the home rulers in his Irish seat, Wicklow county),[148] Yarborough in Lincolnshire North,[149] and Minto in Roxburghshire. Other whig landowners used their influence to elect moderate Liberals rather than radicals.[150] In several areas – in Lincolnshire, Essex and Norwich, for example – there were not enough whigs of sufficient weight to sustain an effective contest.[151] In Lincolnshire Mid, Lincolnshire North, Nottinghamshire North, Staffordshire North, Surrey West and Sussex East, where there had previously been a contest or an agreement to share the representation, two Conservatives were returned unopposed in 1874. Moreover, the Conservatives retained unopposed three county seats which they had gained only at recent by-elections. There was thus more than a grain of truth in Goldwin Smith's comment that the whigs from families not represented in the government 'for the most part withdrew their support', and that 'some of them broke into open hostility'.[152]

The *Times*'s attitude was typical of that of many of the less hostile 'right-wing' Liberals. It eventually decided to advocate a Liberal victory, although with considerable equivocation – and mainly because of great dislike of Disraeli, and because of the trust engendered by the government's past record. But it expressed reservations about the future, both

---

[147] *Economist*, 14 February 1874, p. 190; Kimberley to Dufferin, 19 February 1874, Dufferin papers; diary, 6 February 1874, Cartwright papers, 6/10.

[148] Hoppen, *Elections in Ireland*, p. 169.

[149] Hanham, *Elections and party management*, p. 27.

[150] Sutherland helped to ensure Pender's victory over Bryce at Wick: Harvie, *Lights of liberalism*, p. 185. Isaac Holden and Alfred Illingworth were removed as the candidates for the northern division of the West Riding, and the small borough of Knaresborough, respectively; the local party leaders replaced them with the moderates Sir Matthew Wilson and Sir Andrew Fairbairn (the latter was opposed to the repeal of Clause 25). The assumption was that a moderate candidate would be more likely to withstand the Conservative assault. Wilson won, Fairbairn lost. Illingworth, although occupied in managing the campaign against Forster in Bradford, was still looking for a seat of his own on 29 January: Hamer, *Politics of electoral pressure*, p. 194. For Fairbairn, see *Leeds Mercury*, 28 January, p. 8; for Holden, see *Holden–Illingworth letters*, pp. 487–8.

[151] Olney, *Lincolnshire politics*, pp. 176–9; *Spectator*, 7 February 1874, p. 163; Colman, *Colman*, pp. 268–9.

[152] 'The defeat of the Liberal party', p. 8.

on account of Gladstone's financial plans, and in view of the likely pressure from radicals for extreme policies. It found Gladstone unconvincing in his attempts to unite the party and invigorate it with a sense of purpose.[153]

But many Liberal voters went further than this, and either abstained, or voted Conservative. In any attempt to explain this development, a number of considerations must be borne in mind: the foreign, financial, local government, military and ballot policies of the government had all made enemies, while Conservative organisation had improved markedly. The hostility of some publicans to the Licensing Act certainly lost the Liberals some votes – although Hanham and Harrison have both forcefully warned against exaggerating the shift of support generated by the Act, since, before and after 1872, there was much divergence of opinion in the drink trade about both politics and the merits of licensing reform.[154] One component in the general middle-class 'fear' to which commentators accorded considerable importance was dislike of the activity of trade unions: there had been a large number of well-publicised strikes since 1871, including those of the Fulham gas stokers, the Newcastle engineers, and the South Wales colliers, while the agitations of Arch's Agricultural Labourers' Union had caused great ill-feeling in the countryside.[155]

Nonetheless, fears for the Church Establishment and for religious education – and, to a lesser extent, for the union with Ireland and for the survival of Protestantism in England – undoubtedly had a seminal impact on the results in the county and southern borough seats.

It is unclear how many voters were worried by the danger of home rule, but three leading Liberals, Argyll, Kimberley and Spencer, all rejoiced at the conclusive nature of the Conservative victory, because their great fear had been that the home rulers would hold the balance of power – a result that throughout 1873 had looked very likely – and that they would try to force concessions from Gladstone or Disraeli.[156] In the Scottish counties, fear of Catholicism played a considerable part in the victory. This was evident, for example, in Perthshire, where the Conservative candidate believed that many ex-Liberals were upset at the aggressive attitude of the papacy, and that the disestablishment of the Irish Church had lost votes by appearing to play into the pope's hands. The candidate himself exploited this feeling by accusing Gladstone, and his Liberal

---

[153] *Times*, 26, 28, 31 January, 2 February, p. 9, 29 January, p. 7.
[154] Hanham, *Elections and party management*, pp. 222–7; Harrison, *Drink and the Victorians*, pp. 279–85.
[155] For Mundella's view, see Armytage, *Mundella*, pp. 135–6.
[156] Argyll to Dufferin, 17 March 1874, Kimberley to Dufferin, 19 February, Spencer to Dufferin, 19 March, Dufferin papers.

opponent, C. S. Parker, of closet Catholicism.[157] More importantly, the heavy swing against the Liberals in the Borders was almost certainly connected with presbyterians' sympathy for the plight of their fellow Protestants across the water in Ulster.[158] Gladstone himself received letters from Liberals announcing their defection on account of his alleged sympathy with the 'Anglo-Catholic as against the Protestant cause'.[159]

But it was fear of disestablishment and of radical educational reform which constituted the most effective Conservative weapon throughout Britain as a whole – as their candidates, in concentrating on the issues, were aware. It was these policies which, in the eyes of the average voter, would have the most obvious and severe consequences. The education question was doubly controversial, because it could be exploited in tandem with another issue, voters' dislike of high rates. To suggest adding to the ratepayer's load in order to fund the building of board schools was unpopular not only in rural areas but in many small towns. Cambridge, for example, rejected calls for a school board in late 1873, on the grounds of expense;[160] in Lincoln, there was no school board until 1902, despite a recorded deficiency, in 1873, of 1,330 school places.[161] In August 1875, it was announced that the average attendance at voluntary elementary schools was 1.6 million, whereas that at board schools was only 227,000.[162] Another embarrassment for the Liberals was the victory of the secularists in the Birmingham school-board elections in the previous autumn: Conservatives portrayed this as an indication of future Liberal policy. There was, moreover, much concern that the use of the bible was declining, and that biblical teaching was being lethargically given in schools controlled by 'unsectarian' boards.[163] It was thus easy for Conservatives to harness all these fears, and to charge that the Liberals wished not only to secularise education but to make the ratepayers pay more for it: to 'maintain at the public expense a system of irreligious education which is opposed to . . . the opinions and wishes of the ratepayers'.[164] The aggressiveness of school boards was also often reproached; they were alleged to be erecting too many well-equipped

[157] Stirling-Maxwell to Dufferin, 17 January–17 February 1874, *ibid.*; *Scotsman*, 7 February.
[158] For the influence of the Orange Lodge campaign in Wigtown and Ayr, see *Scotsman*, 4, 11 February.
[159] Buchanan to Gladstone, 25 November 1873, Gladstone papers, 44441, fo. 98; Williams to Gladstone, 25 November 1873, *ibid.*, fo. 106.
[160] *Cambridge Independent Press*, 8, 29 November 1873, p. 7, p. 8.
[161] Hill, *Victorian Lincoln*, pp. 272–3.
[162] Smith, *Disraelian Conservatism and social reform*, p. 242.
[163] See also *ibid.*, p. 250.
[164] (Martin) *Cambridge Independent Press*, 17 January, p. 6.

schools in close proximity to, and in obvious competition with, voluntary schools.[165]

The education and rating issues were widely exploited in Scotland, and probably provide, together with anti-Catholicism, the major explanation for the large swing to the Conservatives in the Borders (especially since candidates were agreed on so many other issues – supporting the abolition of hypothec, legislation to grant tenants equal access to ground game, and even, in some seats, the extension of the county franchise). The Conservatives' major ploys were to stress the lack of securities for religious teaching afforded by the 1872 Scottish Education Act, and the significance of the Birmingham school board's secularist policy as a guide to the Liberals' real aims. Although the Liberal lord advocate (who narrowly lost his seat) argued that only one out of a thousand Scottish school boards had taken advantage of the provisions of the 1872 Act to institute the secular system, Conservatives suggested that, under Liberal control, Protestant teaching in board schools would become steadily less pronounced.[166] The Conservative Anstruther in Lanarkshire South was one of the few openly to make capital from the discontent at the extra burdens imposed on the ratepayers by the 1872 Act; others were reluctant to mention it publicly, for fear of sounding irresponsibly mean. Nonetheless, the *Scotsman* was in no doubt that voters' dislike of the educational rate was one of the most important reasons for the Liberal defeats.[167] One elector in Midlothian, where Dalkeith, the son of the duke of Buccleuch, was the Conservative candidate, charged the Liberals with increasing the rates in order to pay for schools, whereas Buccleuch was happy to provide the churches and schools at his own expense.[168]

In England, the Liberals also found it impossible to evade the educational issue – as a result of their own policy. When, in 1870, they had introduced machinery for the election of school boards, they had considerably heightened the temperature of local political activity. In London, there was a ratepayer franchise; in other boroughs, a burgess one; in both cases, single women and widows could vote. In order to win, it was, therefore, necessary to mobilise large numbers of voters, and to coordinate the efforts of a variety of local political organisations. The consequence was that school-board elections in large towns became central political events, especially when held, as in late 1873, only weeks before a general election. Where, as in many northern boroughs, the results of the 1873 board election removed a grievance, they helped the

[165] Travis, 'Leeds school board', p. 87; (Abel Smith in Hertfordshire) *Times*, 27 January.
[166] See *Scotsman*, leading article, 16 February, p. 4; (Birmingham) Stewart and Dalkeith, *ibid.*, 2 February; Young, *ibid.*, 30 January; Gordon, *Charteris*, p. 228.
[167] 16 February, p. 4. See (Anstruther) *ibid.*, 30 January.
[168] *Ibid.*, 9 February.

Liberals at the general election; but in the south, in the areas where clerical feeling against the government's education policy was most developed, the timing of the board elections assisted the Conservatives in the 1874 campaign. And in no town was this more obvious than in London, the scene not only of a considerable Conservative revival in 1874, but of marked educational dissension in late 1873: dissension which is all the more striking when it is remembered that the London board had always pursued a relatively conservative religious policy.

The second London school-board elections, which took place on 27 November 1873, were characterised by the intervention of an organised 'Church' party. This party was pledged to defend the place of voluntary schools in the London educational system, and to attack the board for its alleged extravagance in spending ratepayers' money on the building of too many unwanted schools – in what was claimed to be a campaign of harassment against existing voluntary institutions. Robert Gregory, canon of St Paul's, treasurer of the National Society, and leader of the Church party, maintained that there were already over 200,000 empty places in London schools. His party also demanded that the board should give as good a religious instruction in all its schools as was allowed by the law.[169] The party put up seventeen candidates for election in 1873. In addition, a number of candidates standing for re-election from the old board half-associated with its aims, and attacked the radicals, while defending the board's past policy: they included Macgregor in Greenwich, Canon Cromwell in Chelsea, and W. H. Smith, Alfred Barry and J. H. Rigg in Westminster. The Church campaign was promoted at meetings patronised by Shaftesbury, Beauchamp, the bishops of London and of Winchester, and a number of Conservative MPs.

Many unsectarian members of the board who did not associate with the 'Churchmen's' grievances were forced, as was Samuel Morley, for example, to stress that they had not intended to harm voluntary schools and would continue to value their educational services. A small number of secularists also stood, including a number of working-men candidates. The London Nonconformist Committee, on which Guinness Rogers sat, was more radical than in 1870, regretting that the board had not accepted secularism, and strongly opposing any return to 'sectarianism' in educational policy.[170]

The results were startling. Of the 30 members of the former board who sought re-election, 6 were defeated, all of them unsectarians and most of them nonconformists; of the 25 new members, 16 were Churchmen (that

---

[169] *Times*, 7, 12, 21 November, p. 7, p. 6, p. 10.
[170] *Nonconformist*, 5 November 1873, p. 1101.

is, only one Church candidate, in Southwark, failed to win election), one more was associated with the Church ticket, 7 were unsectarians, and one, George Potter, was a secularist.[171] All the other working-men secularists – Broadhurst in Greenwich, Lloyd Jones in Hackney, and Maltman Barry in Marylebone – were defeated, although the 3 board members who had supported the secular solution in 1871 were re-elected. The totals of votes cast – 19,764 for the Churchman who topped the poll in Greenwich, 17,022 for his counterpart in Lambeth, 25,999 in Marylebone, 40,264 in Tower Hamlets – indicate the degree of enthusiasm which the Church campaign was able to evoke, and the extent of the reaction against the radicals' apparent threat to the continuation of religious teaching in schools.[172]

The cry of the 'Church in danger', therefore, almost certainly inflicted immense damage on the Liberals in 1874. The loss of votes from this cause was undoubtedly most apparent among the 'middle classes'. But this should not blind us to the fact that the same arguments also alienated considerable numbers of working-men – and not just in Protestant Lancashire.[173] Nor were nonconformists – especially Wesleyans – immune from it;[174] Chamberlain himself, in analysing the 1874 results, thought that many nonconformists had been 'carried over to the enemy by the "Bible" cry'.[175]

After the election was over, criticism of the party's spinelessness in the face of radical pressure flowed freely from whig-liberals. Reeve wrote a forceful article in the *Edinburgh* for April, which Gladstone thought was 'distinctly aimed at me', and designed to promote a coup by the 'younger men' (Hartington and Harcourt).[176] Reeve advocated the staunch government of Ireland, and an end to concessionary legislation; he supported the cause of religious education (and welcomed Forster's re-election at Bradford); he attacked the 'parsimony' of the Treasury; he asserted that the government's foreign policy had been weak, and 'entirely opposed to that of Lord Russell, Lord Palmerston, and Lord Clarendon'. Gladstone had 'lost the confidence of the country' because he had deviated from whig principles, towards supporting the 'avowed enemies of the Church of England, Ultramontane priests, and Home Rulers'. The foundation of British strength since 1688 had been whig

---

[171] Three other newly elected candidates were described as secularists in some of the newspaper accounts, but these accounts are contradicted by others.
[172] The sources for the above account are *Times*, late November and early December 1870, November 1873; and *Bee-hive*, 6 December 1873, p. 10.
[173] So John Morley thought: Hirst, *Morley*, i, 297.
[174] Hempton's description of Wesleyan voting habits in the 1830s is surely also, albeit to a lesser extent, applicable in 1874: *Methodism and politics*, p. 207.
[175] Peel, *Letters to Allon*, p. 43.
[176] Gladstone to Allon, 29 April 1874, Gladstone papers, 44095, fo. 330.

principles, the principles of 'liberty, toleration, improvement, and reform', principles that placed sound administration before exciting legislation, and that supported the National Church as 'a great organ of education' and as 'a barrier against the fanaticism and spirit of the Church of Rome'. He argued that the Liberals must reassert those principles, slough off the home rulers and the ultramontanes, and keep the radicals in order; until they did so, the Conservatives – who were now responsible and practical – might be relied upon to form a successful government.[177]

This line of criticism was upheld by many others. Argyll told Gladstone that he had almost no 'tie of attachment to the Liberal Party' except personal regard for him as an old friend; and that he would not tolerate radicalism on educational, ecclesiastical or land questions.[178] Somerset launched into a wickedly amusing satire on Gladstone in the Lords, forecasting the permanent alienation of moderate Liberals from his party: Halifax noted that, while few would declare publicly, 'a great number of people *think* the same'.[179] Minto argued that the party had been too subservient to Gladstone, whose Liberalism was not genuine, rested on 'no sound basis of education or character', and was of 'accidental growth'.[180] Bedford suggested to Earl Fortescue that neither of them should exert themselves to install Gladstone in Downing Street again – he had tried to supplant whig principles. George Grey apparently thought similarly.[181] Russell told Halifax that 'one of the favourite objects of the Gladstone ministry was to throw discredit on Charles Fox, Charles Grey and the Whig party'.[182] The queen welcomed the Conservative victory – it showed the 'healthy state of the country'. Gladstone had altered everything and 'in many cases ruined' things; he had upset 'real Liberals'; he had no wisdom or judgment, but was 'arrogant, tyrannical and obstinate', and a 'fanatic in religion'.[183] Matthew Arnold was not 'sorry at the change': the party possessed no sound Liberal principles.[184] Thirlwall could not regret the Liberal defeats in Wales, because 'the Churchman in me has . . . got the better of the Liberal'.[185] Layard contended that the party under Gladstone had lost the broad central platform and the elevation of moral tone that it had had before: it was a

[177] Reeve, 'Past and future of the whig party'.
[178] Argyll to Dufferin, 17 March 1874, Dufferin papers.
[179] *Hansard*, ccxviii, 39, 19 March 1874; Halifax to Northbrook, 26 March 1874, Northbrook papers, 144, 22.
[180] To Wilson, 24 February 1874, Minto papers, 12360, fo. 88.
[181] Bedford to Fortescue, 15 February 1874, Fortescue papers, FC 129; Stanhope to Disraeli, 15 February 1874, Disraeli papers, B/XXI/S/506.
[182] 11 March 1874, Hickleton papers, A 4 56.
[183] (Victoria) Fulford, *Darling child*, pp. 128, 130.
[184] Russell, *Letters of Arnold*, ii, 112.   [185] Thirlwall, *Thirlwall*, p. 214.

collection of disparate groups, often 'of extreme opinions and of crazy crotchets'. This, he thought, was partly owing to Gladstone's lack of 'judgment and prudence' in matters theological and otherwise, but also because of the strains inherent in a sectional party in a democracy.[186] Both he and Froude were content for the Conservatives to retain power for the time being, as long as they pursued a responsible policy.[187] Froude's magazine, *Fraser's*, still looked to the Liberal party for 'progress, prosperity, and the stability as well as the amendment of our institutions', but regretted the religious, Irish and financial policies of Gladstone's government, and its inability to prevent strikes. These traits, it maintained, had alienated Liberal supporters and dissolved party coherence: the Liberal party as a 'homogeneous political body . . . united by common principles of action . . . has now ceased to exist'.[188] The *Pall Mall* also claimed still to stand for the principles of 'true Liberalism', but argued that the government had 'divided, shattered, and shamed the Liberal party'.[189]

Gladstone was shaken by the result. Almost immediately, he started to discuss his retirement, at least until such time as the party had 'settled its differences and . . . acquired as keen a sense of the duties of followers as of those of leaders'. Although he eventually agreed to remain as leader until the beginning of the 1875 session (but attending parliament only occasionally) he voiced his resentments: at the 'insults and outrages' to which the party had subjected him in 1866–8, and at the determination, since 1870, of independent backbenchers like Fawcett, Torrens, Bouverie, Horsman, Harcourt, and the class of men 'represented by the *Daily News*', to flout his leadership. He also appreciated the obstacles in the way of future unity: he saw no cause on which the party might unite. Education in particular was a subject on which he considered that his position was 'irreconcileable' [*sic*] with that of many liberals.[190] He attached no value to Clause 25, but to concede on it would encourage those Liberals whose views were anathema to him. He would 'never be a party' to undenominationalism, despite its popularity on the backbenches.[191] As long as MPs considered their primary bond of unity

---

[186] Layard to Gregory, 26 February 1874, Layard papers, 38949, fo. 132.
[187] Layard to Gregory, 22 August, 2 December 1875, *ibid.*, fos. 144, 148; Froude, 'Party politics', pp. 17–18.
[188] Anon., 'Turn of the tide'.
[189] 6 February 1874, p. 1.
[190] Aberdare to Ripon, 17 February 1874, Ripon papers, 43535, fo. 82; Morley, *Gladstone*, ii, 495–6; Bessborough to Granville, 25 February 1874, Granville papers, 30/29/71, fo. 214; 5, 7 March 1874, Matthew, viii, 471–2; Fitzmaurice, *Granville*, ii, 138; *Letters of Aberdare*, i, 361.
[191] To Bright, 27 January 1874, Matthew, viii, 449–50; diary, 10 March 1874, Cartwright papers, 6/10.

to be an anti-clerical one, his leadership was bound to be both unsuccess-ful, and counter-productive to the Church's interests. Only if he could inspire nonconformists and the Liberal masses with a crusading moral cry could he reassert his control over the party, and, in his view, render useful public service.

9

Disunity explicit, 1874–5

The 1874 session: ritualism and Scottish patronage

Disraeli's intention at the start of his 1874 government was to exploit the fears for political stability which Gladstone's government had provoked. The Conservatives determined to present a more 'constructive' face to the electorate to dispel their former image – of incompetence and irresponsibility – and expressed an intention to concentrate on uncontroversial but useful reforms in the social sphere. Social legislation dominated their domestic programme between 1874 and 1876 – and it was designed not to pander to 'Tory democracy', but to lower the political temperature. As one Conservative MP said in 1875, it was 'suet-pudding legislation; it was flat, insipid, dull, but it was very wise and very wholesome'.[1]

Stress on this class of question was intended to imply a spurning of the larger and more intractable issues, in dealing with which Gladstone had alienated so many. For example, Disraeli set out with the determination to 'keep Ireland in the background': he did not even give his chief secretary a cabinet seat.[2] His outlook on the Irish question was appreciably different from Gladstone's: he considered that the ideal candidate for the chief secretaryship would be 'rather a fine [gentleman]' and 'a capital rider', with 'the gift of the gab'.[3] In March 1874, he refused to receive a deputation of Irish MPs demanding the release of the remaining Fenian prisoners.[4] As early as 1872, he had spurned Catholic requests for concessionary legislation on the grounds that he had learned the lesson of 1868: as an adviser said, 'a burnt child dread[s] the fire'. (However, these

---

[1] (Salt) Smith, *Disraelian Conservatism and social reform*, p. 203.
[2] Disraeli to Richmond, 5 March 1874, Richmond papers, 865, W 22.
[3] Disraeli to Cairns, 6 August 1875, Cairns papers, 30/51/1, fo. 123.
[4] Notes, Disraeli papers, B/XII/D/22–7.

intentions inevitably had to be modified later, in accordance with political exigencies.)[5]

Only one major issue raised by the Conservatives in the 1874 session gave the Liberal party a chance to exhibit solidarity: their attempt to amend the Endowed Schools Act. They proposed not only to transfer the functions of the commissioners to the Charity Commission, but to extend exemption from the operation of the Act to cover all schools whose original trust funds had linked them even indirectly with ecclesiastical purposes. Forster and Gladstone were at one with the bulk of the party in opposition to the exemption clause, and many Conservatives were also aware that it was unwise to insist upon it; it was eventually dropped, to the irritation of Salisbury and Carnarvon.[6]

But this apart, the indications throughout the 1874 session were, as leading party figures remarked, that the Liberals were 'more disunited than ever'.[7] This was apparent in the vote on Trevelyan's County Franchise Bill, which Lowe opposed and on which Hartington abstained: Gladstone was persuaded, against his will, to stay away from the division, in order not to point up the extent of disunity.[8] There was more embarrassment when Richard, Samuel Morley and McArthur introduced a bill to abolish Clause 25 of the 1870 Education Act. It was defeated by 373 votes to 128; but constituency pressures, and the desire for a compromise, had produced a substantial shift of opinion among Liberal MPs. Lowe, Hartington, Goschen, Stansfeld, Baxter, Grant Duff, Adam and Frederick Cavendish from the ex-government supported the bill; so, even, did Acland. Forster opposed it – with Cowper-Temple, Knatchbull-Hugessen and the sons of Argyll and Ripon – but there were only forty British Liberals in his lobby, together with thirty-seven Irish MPs. Gladstone again did not vote.[9] There was a further difficulty when Butt raised the home-rule question. Again Gladstone stayed away, and Hartington took the opportunity afforded by his absence to make a staunch defence of unionism. He pledged that 'no motive of personal

[5] Barrington to Disraeli, 2 May 1872, *ibid.*, B/XX/Ba/15. For subsequent proposals for Irish educational reforms, see e.g. Foster, *Churchill*, pp. 37–8, 48, 55; Hicks Beach, *St Aldwyn*, i, 52–8.

[6] Cecil, *Salisbury*, ii, 62–4; Gardiner, *Harcourt*, i, 279; Richmond to Disraeli, 18 July 1874, Disraeli papers, B/XII/F/59; Cross to Disraeli, 24 July 1874, *ibid.*, B/XX/Cr/6; Sandon to Disraeli, 18 July 1874, *ibid.*, B/XXI/S/38; diary, 20, 24, 25 July 1874, Carnarvon papers. See Fletcher, *Feminists and bureaucrats*, pp. 126–7.

[7] Granville to Gladstone, 25 June 1874, Ramm, ii, 455; Cardwell to Northbrook, 27 June 1874, Northbrook papers, 144, 22.

[8] Ramm, ii, 450–1; Wolverton to Gladstone, 30 April, 4 May 1874, Gladstone papers, 44349, fos. 13, 19; Zetland, *Letters of Disraeli to Lady Bradford*, p. 84.

[9] *Hansard*, ccxix, 1355–8, 10 June 1874; Reid, *Forster*, ii, 58–63.

ambition, no consideration of party advantage, could ever induce' either him or 'those who sat round him . . . to purchase the support of hon. Members representing Irish constituencies by any sacrifice which, in their opinion, would endanger the union between the two countries'. He also expressed 'his firm conviction that if any [Liberal MPs] were so reckless as to show a symptom on their part of a disposition to coquet with this question, there would instantly be such a disruption and disorganization of parties, that they would find that they had lost more support from England and Scotland than they could ever hope to obtain from Ireland'. There was little doubt for whom this warning was primarily intended.[10]

Division within the Liberal party, and whig-liberals' approximation to the position of most Conservatives, were both especially noticeable during the major political controversy of the 1874 session: this concerned the Public Worship Regulation Bill. Since there are already two full accounts of this crisis, what follows will concentrate on internal Liberal politics during the debate on the bill.[11]

The Church's inability to check ritualism had inspired considerable pressure for such a bill from broad and low churchmen, and the queen and Tait were both anxious to see a measure passed. Tait introduced it, as a private member's bill, early in the session; but its scope was limited, in the hope of diminishing controversy. After amendment by the Lords, it provided that, on receipt of a complaint from parishioners against their clergyman, his bishop should have the discretion to proceed with the complaint: if the bishop was unable to settle the dispute himself by agreement with the parties, it would be decided by a lay judge – unless the bishop exercised his right of veto, and halted the proceedings. Appeals against the judge's decision would be determined by the Judicial Committee. Evangelicals wished to amend the bill in order to define more rigorously what practices were to be illegal, but they were not successful. The aim of the Act remained, instead, to enforce the existing codes of practice more efficiently; and the virulence of the political conflict over the bill and Act was, as so often, remarkably disproportionate to its practical importance.

High churchmen were quick to condemn the bill. Convocation expressed itself as strongly as it was allowed, given the questions that Tait had restricted it to discussing; Pusey, Liddon and Phillimore led a campaign against it in the country, urging that it would exacerbate conflict and repress zeal. Hook, Church, Moberly and Mackarness were very hostile to it (although Blachford and Acland were too anti-ritualist to

[10] *Hansard*, ccxx, 771–2, 30 June 1874.
[11] Bentley, *Ritualism and politics*, pp. 46–79; Marsh, *Victorian Church in decline*, pp. 158–92.

follow them).[12] By the time of the Commons debate, a mass of petitions had been drawn up, not only by high churchmen on the one hand, but by Tait's supporters on the other. Discussion of the bill roused sectional antagonism within the Church to fever-pitch; by the end of the crisis, one hostile high churchman viewed Tait as riding 'on the crest of the wave of lay frenzy'.[13]

Gladstone considered this public acrimony between churchmen to be very damaging to the Church's reputation; his dislike of it was one of the considerations which prompted his politically mistaken attack on the bill in the debate on the second reading on 9 July. He objected that it was inadvisable for parliament to enforce too rigid a policy of dealing with ritual questions, when local customs and expectations differed so greatly; that the bill had been framed without the consent of Convocation; that it gave too much power to men who might be irresponsible in using it; and that its passage would promote ill-feeling and lead to an agitation for disestablishment.[14] He laid six rather vague resolutions on the table of the Commons, which embodied his criticisms, and which were intended to replace the bill.[15]

Throughout the debates about the bill, Gladstone was to receive a certain amount of support from Liberals; these were mostly nonconformists such as Richard and Leatham, and others who did not object to disestablishment, such as Dillwyn, Mundella, Fawcett and Fitzmaurice. Richard and Leatham supported Gladstone because he had defended the principle of Christian freedom, and the 'Congregational theory', against the threats of uniformity and erastianism.[16] (Illingworth, however, had no sympathy for Gladstone's stand.)[17] A few whig-liberals were able to follow Gladstone as well, on the grounds that variety in the Church was beneficial, and that the principle of toleration should extend to ritualist practices as well as to disputed doctrine.[18] But, as Fawcett told Gladstone, there was little support for his resolutions even among those who opposed the bill;[19] while they were roundly condemned by majority opinion on both sides of the House. They were immediately criticised by

---

[12] Bentley, *Ritualism and politics*, pp. 49–52; Marsh, *Victorian Church in decline*, pp. 173–5; Stephens, *Hook*, ii, 498; Church, *Church*, pp. 245–6, (Blachford) 252; Moberly, *Moberly*, pp. 247–8; Mackarness, *Mackarness*, pp. 72–3; Acland, *Acland*, p. 315.

[13] Moberly, *Moberly*, p. 248.

[14] *Hansard*, ccxx, 1372; notes, 1874, Gladstone papers, 44762, fo. 142.

[15] They were reprinted in *Church of England and ritualism*, pp. 48–9.

[16] *Hansard*, ccxx, 1431–7, ccxxi, 61.

[17] *Holden–Illingworth letters*, p. 497.

[18] *Economist*, 18 July 1874, pp. 866–7; *Spectator*, 18 July 1874, pp. 904–5. Bentley (*Ritualism and politics*, pp. 77–8) is mistaken in arguing that Childers and Horsman also opposed the bill: see *Hansard*, ccxxi, 1170–1, 878.

[19] Fawcett to Gladstone, 15 July 1874, Gladstone papers, 44156, fo. 26.

Harcourt, who accused Gladstone, 'the great enchanter', of undermining the principles of uniformity in the Church, and the 'supremacy of the law', the 'only guarantee of the liberty of the clergy and of the rights of the people'.[20] Perhaps the most remarkable attack on the resolutions came from Hussey Vivian, a 'representative' Liberal backbencher rebelling from his party for only the second time in twenty-two years.[21] As Thomson Hankey, another old whig, pointed out, 'not one man' was prepared to second them.[22] Even Spencer, one of the more radical whigs on the Church question, thought the resolutions impractical, vague and almost certain to lead to disestablishment.[23]

Many Liberals, in fact, were warm supporters of the bill. Forster and Goschen declared in its favour on the grounds that the supremacy of parliament over the Church must be upheld.[24] Childers thought that Gladstone's opposition to this bill and to the abolition of Scottish patronage (see below) was losing the Liberals much support in the country.[25] Nonconformists like Samuel Morley and Colman also supported the measure, because of the 'frightful evils of Ritualism'.[26] Outside the Commons, Hughes, Stanley, Thirlwall, H. M. Butler and Northbrook all welcomed it as a necessary attempt to check the alarming growth of sacerdotalism in the Church.[27] The whig-liberal viewpoint was articulated caustically by the *Times*: both Delane and the proprietor Walter strongly approved of the bill, which Delane saw as 'one of the most important ... of our times'.[28] In three leading articles in four days, the newspaper charged Gladstone with attempting to subvert the Act of Uniformity. It predicted that his defence of the right of each congregation to freedom of practice would subsequently allow him to argue that the nonconformists still had a claim to a share of Church property; and, therefore, that the Church should be disestablished and partially disendowed. (This was not fanciful, since Gladstone's attack on the Scottish Patronage Bill, a few days before, had in fact employed similar logic.) It argued that Gladstone's aim appeared to be to encourage the growth of a large number of clearly defined sects within the Church – a policy which threatened schism and, again, disestablishment. It maintained that his speech against Tait's bill had associated him with those who

[20] *Hansard*, ccxx, 1414–23.
[21] *Ibid.*, ccxxi, 82; Goldney to Disraeli, 12 July 1874, Disraeli papers, B/XII/F/63.
[22] To Northbrook, 8 August 1874, Northbrook papers, 144, 22.
[23] Gordon, *Spencer*, i, 124.   [24] *Hansard*, ccxxi, 38, 67.
[25] Childers, *Childers*, i, 229–30.
[26] *Times*, 22 October 1874, p. 7; Colman, *Colman*, p. 282.
[27] Hughes, *The old Church*, pp. 98–100; Prothero, *Stanley*, ii, 212–14; Thirlwall, *Letters literary*, pp. 380–1; Graham, *H. M. Butler*, p. 348; Northbrook to Dufferin, 17 May 1874, Dufferin papers.
[28] *Hansard*, ccxxi, 22; Delane to Tait, 9 August 1874, Tait papers, 93, fo. 278.

insisted that the state had 'no place at all in spiritual questions'; he advocated 'confusion and disorder', his proposals were 'intolerable', and his speech 'about the most destructive ever made' by an important politician.[29]

Disraeli now exploited the Liberal rift. He had forced the cabinet to agree to adopt the bill as a government measure, backbench pressure for it being overwhelming. On 14 July, his speech on the second reading did more than anything to inflate its political significance. Not only did he famously describe it as a bill to 'put down Ritualism', not only did he denounce 'Mass in masquerade'; he made a blatant set at Gladstone's ecclesiastical unsoundness, on the same lines as at Glasgow in 1873. He claimed that, whenever he had spoken in the country since 1871, he had warned the nation 'that a great change was occurring in the politics of the world . . . that . . . the great struggle between the Temporal and Spiritual power . . . was reviving in our own time'. As a result, 'disturbance and possible disasters' gravely threatened Europe; and Britain could surmount them only by rallying around 'the broad platform of the Reformation' and 'the institution of the Church of England, based upon those principles of the Reformation which that Church was called into being to represent'.[30] Artful as ever, he offered Gladstone, as an act of courtesy, time in which to debate his resolutions: Gladstone '*ran away*', as Disraeli put it, and the second reading was passed without a division.[31] Two days later, after conferring with Hartington, Forster, Cowper-Temple and Knatchbull-Hugessen, Gladstone withdrew his resolutions.[32] Disraeli had scored a major triumph: as one whig backbencher put it, he had attained 'the position of a Protestant statesman'.[33]

The Commons was certainly now in a staunchly Protestant mood, and two significant amendments were passed. One, carried by 238 votes to 57, made it far easier to institute proceedings against ritualists who worked in cathedrals: this was aimed directly at the trio at St Paul's. The other, proposed by the evangelical Holt, removed the bishop's right to veto the assignment of a case to a lay judge – against Gladstone's express opposition.[34] This was a much more controversial amendment, which was debated twice. It passed by 118 votes to 95; 42 Liberals supported it, and 26 voted with Gladstone against it. It split the Conservatives just as severely, a large body of high churchmen opposing it.

Gladstone considered this amendment to cut 'at the root of the Episcopal office'. He conveyed to the archbishops the threat that if it was

---

[29] *Times*, 10, 11, 13 July, p. 9, p. 9, p. 11.

[30] *Hansard*, ccxxi, 78–80.   [31] Bentley, *Ritualism and politics*, p. 69.

[32] *Hansard*, ccxxi, 118–19; notes, 15 July 1874, Gladstone papers, 44762, fo. 129.

[33] Diary, 15–16 July 1874, Cartwright papers, 6/10.

[34] *Hansard*, ccxi, 1066–71, 1080–1.

carried, he felt 'altogether discharged from maintaining any longer the Establishment of the Church' – and Browne, the bishop of Winchester, agreed to support this announcement.[35] This threat frightened Tait, who foresaw a move in the Commons for disestablishment.[36] A severe crisis was averted when Salisbury and Carnarvon led the Lords to reject the amendment, and when Harcourt, in the Commons, agreed not to challenge the rejection.[37]

The bill passed in this form, but not before Harcourt had delivered a remarkable speech, vehemently hostile to Gladstone. He paid tribute to Disraeli's 'dignified decency' and 'talents'; he claimed that Disraeli had become prime minister because 'he had long had the sagacity to divine the sentiments and to execute the will of the English people'; he asked him now to rouse the nation to continue the work begun by the bill. The controversy between the temporal and spiritual powers was by 'far the largest business which has occupied Parliament or the public mind in my life-time', since Europe was divided into two camps: on the one side stood 'Ultramontanism and Sacerdotalism', and on the other 'Freedom and the Reformation'. It was Disraeli's task, he argued, to save the Church by Protestantising it. (In fact, of course, Disraeli could not afford to go very far down this track, since his party included so many high churchmen.)[38] The speech outraged Gladstone: 'even his slimy, fulsome, loathsome eulogies upon Dizzy were aimed at me'. Harcourt 'meant business, namely my political extinction'.[39] But Fremantle, in the *Edinburgh*, supported Harcourt's line, welcoming the 'refreshing and unexpected' spirit and resolution displayed in the debates. They had revealed a determination that 'the National Church must be upheld, and, secondly, that this could only be done by maintaining its Protestant character'. He hoped that Disraeli would introduce further Church reform, neutralise the power of Convocation, and remove the bishop's veto on proceedings against ritualists. Under Gladstone's influence, parliament, the 'only body which could maintain the national as opposed to the clerical organisation', had apparently 'abdicated its functions': it had made the mistaken calculation that the 'theories' of the 'sacerdotal party' had a 'serious hold upon the national conscience', and had given the 'Church system the aspect of a mere engine for the promotion of Romanism'.[40]

---

[35] Bassett, *Gladstone to his wife*, pp. 203–4; Browne to Tait, 5 August 1874, Tait papers, 93, fo. 270.
[36] Tait to dean of Wells, 7 August 1874, enclosed in diary, Tait papers, 54.
[37] Marsh, *Victorian Church in decline*, pp. 189–91.
[38] *Hansard*, ccxxi, 1341–54, esp. 1352–3.
[39] Gladstone to Granville, 7 August 1874, Ramm, ii, 457.
[40] Fremantle, 'Convocation, parliament and the prayer-book'.

Almost simultaneously with the passage of the Public Worship Regulation Act, the government promoted another ecclesiastical bill which similarly divided the Liberals; that which proposed to abolish patronage in the Church of Scotland. By now, the Scottish Establishment almost unanimously favoured abolition. There had been a strong cross-party move in its favour since 1869, led by Gordon and Richmond for the Conservatives, and Argyll, Rosebery and the MP Anstruther for the Liberals. Argyll had pressed it on the cabinet in 1871–2;[41] in 1873, Anstruther and Airlie introduced parliamentary resolutions pointing towards abolition. They were opposed by Dalhousie in the Lords and by McLaren and Gladstone in the Commons – the latter on the grounds that the motion was vague, and that Scotland was divided about the matter.[42] Gladstone's coolness towards abolition was manifest: in 1869, he had replied to a petition for patronage abolition signed by thirty-seven MPs, by requesting that the views of the seceding sects should be taken into account before the question was tackled, since they might be considered to have some claim on the property involved.[43] The General Assembly of the Free Church was known to be opposed to abolition; indeed, the growing pressure for it from the Church of Scotland was driving increasing numbers of Free Churchmen to view the possibility of disestablishment more favourably.[44]

Given the support for it in the Church of Scotland, it was not surprising that the Conservatives introduced a bill to abolish patronage during their first session in power. Richmond, in advocating it, hoped that it would 'extend and perpetuate' the Church of Scotland.[45] Argyll warmly supported it, arguing that only those who wished to promote disestablishment could justifiably oppose the measure.[46]

There was no doubt that the bill was popular among defenders of Establishments, in Scotland and England; it was widely seen as checking an agitation for disestablishment and as removing the grievance of 1843. Taylor Innes, the Free Churchman who was so helpful in supplying Gladstone with material against the bill, recognised that it was 'a most skilfully planned measure to restore the balance in Scotland in favour of Conservatism', and reported that it was very difficult to find dignified justifications for opposition to the bill.[47] The Conservatives had once more driven a wedge between Gladstone and many Liberal supporters of

---

[41] Argyll memorandum, 1871, Gladstone papers, 44102, fo. 89.
[42] *Hansard*, ccxvi, 1032, 1090, 17 June 1873.
[43] Gordon, *Charteris*, p. 210.
[44] *Ibid.*, pp. 395–6; Walker, *Buchanan*, pp. 489–90.
[45] *Hansard*, ccxix, 368, 18 May 1874.
[46] Argyll to Richmond, 22 June 1874, Disraeli papers, B/XX/Le/51a; *Hansard*, ccxix, 815.
[47] Taylor Innes to Gladstone, 3 June 1874, Gladstone papers, 44443, fo. 260.

Establishments; Gladstone himself later admitted that the introduction of the Patronage Bill was 'the cleverest move that I have known in my whole Parliamentary life'.[48]

The measure left many whig-liberals in a quandary. They would favour it if they thought that it would strengthen the Establishment in Scotland. But in addition to doubts about its capacity to do this on general grounds – since the tempers of many Free Churchmen were rising in opposition to the bill – there was another consideration. They thought it unfair that the constituent body for the election of ministers should be limited, as it was in the bill, to those who were defined by the Church as communicants in each parish: it seemed to contradict the claims of the Church to nationality, and the duty of the state to protect that nationality. They thought that, if Free Church laymen were given a voice in the decision, they might be less inclined to participate in a campaign for disestablishment. Many whig-liberals therefore called for a wider electoral body: Anstruther, Playfair, Horsman, Camperdown, Airlie, Huntly, Grey and Dean Stanley all suggested either that each parish ratepayer should be allowed to participate in the election, or that some other means of embracing large numbers of nonconformist presbyterians should be found.[49] But amendments to this effect were forthrightly opposed, not only by many Conservatives, but by Argyll, who ridiculed them as 'Hyper-Erastian'. While, he averred, no high churchman, he could 'hardly conceive' such a proposal 'being deliberately made by any sane man'; to suggest allowing the 'avowed enemies' of the Church to help to elect its ministers was a product of the 'modern slip-shod Liberalism', as opposed to the 'historical Liberalism' of Scotland.[50]

In neither the Lords nor the Commons, as it transpired, was there sufficient agreement on the proper nature of an alternative constituency for any of the proposed amendments to be successful. This failure to alter the bill relieved many whig-liberals from having to support it: Camperdown, for example, was able to argue that in its present form it would not induce the seceders to make peace with the Establishment.[51] Laing thought that the retention of a limited electoral body would promote the agitation for disestablishment: the bill as it stood emphasised the 'glaring injustice' of the situation in the Highlands, where a respectable electorate could be assembled only by including seceders.[52] Playfair also

[48] Gordon, *Charteris*, p. 248.
[49] *Hansard*, ccxix, 1227, 1233, 1251, 1252, ccxx, 1151, ccxxi, 694; Anstruther to Gladstone, 26 June 1874, Gladstone papers, 44443, fo. 310; Baillie and Bolitho, *Later letters of Lady A. Stanley*, pp. 247–8.
[50] *Hansard*, ccxix, 815, 1239.
[51] *Ibid.*, 834, 1257.
[52] Laing to Gladstone, 17 June 1874, Gladstone papers, 44443, fo. 298.

decided that the bill was 'fatal to the Establishment' if it excluded the non-communicant parishioners.[53]

Free Churchmen and their supporters argued that the bill discriminated in favour of the Church of Scotland, and that it would therefore encourage a campaign for disestablishment by the other Scottish sects. This was the line taken by Dalhousie for the Free Churchmen in the Lords, by Taylor Innes, by the *Nonconformist* and by Gladstone. Gladstone's argument, in his speech of 6 July – three days before that on the Public Worship Regulation Bill – was that the real heirs of the spirit of the Scottish Reformation had been the seceders of 1843 who had refused to bow to temporal dictation; they had fired the imagination of many with their zeal in creating a successful Church. He claimed that the Patronage Bill betrayed the nonconformist sects by awarding control of all those endowments which had been granted to the whole presbyterian Church, to a sect which now ministered to a minority of the Scottish people. (As G. C. Hutton put it for the United Presbyterians, they were faced with a 'legalised policy of kidnapping'.) Gladstone maintained that the measure was also intended, by attracting laymen back to the Establishment, to dry up the supply of lay donations to the nonconformist Churches.[54]

Despite the opposing positions from which the 'differing parties' within the Liberal ranks, the whig-liberals and nonconformists, were arguing, enough common ground was discernible to make unity a possibility: after much manoeuvring and difficulty, a delaying motion was framed which maintained that it was inexpedient to legislate without further inquiry into, and information about, the ecclesiastical situation in Scotland.[55] But the amendment was defeated by 307 votes to 109, the whig-liberal vote in fact dividing. Although 110 Liberals, including Dodson, Goschen, Hartington, Playfair and Samuel Morley, supported the amendment, the Basses, Harcourt, Horsman, Lorne, Lowe, Matheson, A. W. Peel, Cowper-Temple, Torrens, Walter, Whalley and 53 others voted for the bill.[56] It passed; and the way was open either, as the Conservatives predicted, for the diminution of sectarian hostility, or, as many Liberals forecast, for radical Free Churchmen to give effect to their threats of a campaign against the Establishment.

[53] Playfair to Gladstone, 6, 23 June 1874, *ibid.*, 44280, fos. 165, 167.
[54] *Hansard*, ccxx, 1113; Oliver, *Hutton*, pp. 81–3. See also Spender, *Campbell-Bannerman*, i, 47; (Dalhousie) *Hansard*, ccxix, 382, 835, (Campbell-Bannerman) ccxx, 1553; Innes, *Church of Scotland crisis*; *Nonconformist*, 20 May 1874, p. 469.
[55] Williams to Gladstone, 13 June 1874, Gladstone papers, 44443, fo. 294. On the difficulty involved in the venture, see Innes to Gladstone, 23 June 1874, *ibid.*, fo. 304, and Playfair to Gladstone, 6 June 1874, *ibid.*, 44280, fo. 165.
[56] *Hansard*, ccxx, 1601–4, 13 July 1874.

Vaticanism and Gladstone's resignation, 1874–5

At the end of the 1874 session, speculation about the future course of politics was rife. Gladstone himself feared the introduction of further ecclesiastical legislation (presumably expecting the Conservatives to capitalise on his own political discomfort when such topics were discussed).[57] He anticipated that low churchmen might move to revise the prayer-book in order to outlaw ritualism, which would 'at once seal the doom' of the Establishment.[58]

Many nonconformists, on the other hand, were encouraged by the events of the session. They praised Gladstone's 'nobly maintained' position against the Public Worship Regulation Act, and perceived that 'the decks are being cleared, and that the two antagonistic principles, Erastianism and spiritual freedom, are being brought face to face'.[59] They enjoyed renewed hope that the increasing pressure for legislation to reform the Church would lead him to advocate disestablishment – a work which 'no man . . . can do . . . so well as he'.[60] The *Nonconformist* had opposed the Public Worship Regulation Act, because Convocation had 'almost with one voice' rejected it;[61] in August, it perceived that Gladstone's course on the disestablishment question in England, Wales and Scotland would be determined by 'time, events, and reflection'. His mind

is evidently in a state of transition . . . towards the inevitable conclusion . . . He believes in the right of the Church – may we not say of all the Churches of Christendom? – to spiritual independence. He cannot hold that principle as a fixed point in his creed without being eventually driven by the force of logic and by the pressure of events to perceive the impossibility of regulating, or even of supporting *by law*, a body claiming and occupying any such position. His instincts naturally recoil from the coarseness of Erastianism.[62]

The *British Quarterly Review* was even more explicit: it argued that the Liberal party could be restored to office only by adopting the rallying-cry of disestablishment, 'that great enterprise to which all the achievements of [Gladstone's] career have led up'.[63]

In this climate, mass nonconformist enthusiasm for disestablishment naturally intensified. The Liberation Society announced a campaign, projected to cost £100,000, to agitate the question in the south of

---

[57] 22 October 1874, Lathbury, i, 397–9.

[58] *Ibid.*, pp. 395–9.

[59] Rogers to Gladstone, 13 August 1874, Gladstone papers, 44444, fo. 204; Anon., 'The Established Church and its defenders', p. 512.

[60] Potter to Gladstone, 20 August 1874, Gladstone papers, 44282, fo. 45; Anon., 'The tory administration and its whig admirers', p. 191.

[61] *Nonconformist*, 27 May 1874, p. 498.

[62] *Ibid.*, 12 August 1874, p. 761.

[63] Anon., 'Tory administration and its whig admirers', p. 191.

England; Rogers and Dale embarked on a great lecture tour in 1875–6.[64] In Scotland, Free Church hostility to the abolition of patronage inspired a similar movement. In May 1874, for the first time, the Free Church Assembly passed an explicit motion in favour of disestablishment, and, in December, Rainy began to advocate it in a series of speeches.[65] In the *Fortnightly Review*, Chamberlain and John Morley also launched a campaign for disestablishment, as the 'next page of the Liberal programme'. Chamberlain now considered that the party in the provinces could not yet be united in support of the reform of the land laws or of the county franchise, and that the working-man could be led to join an agitation for disestablishment – as long as the Liberals promised to employ the immense wealth of the Church which disestablishment would release (estimated at £90 million) in establishing a free national-education system.[66] Morley supported the campaign and criticised Harcourt for attempting to reorganise the party on Establishmentarian lines: there was no future for a non-Conservative party on that ticket.[67] Throughout 1875 and 1876, the 'Church question' (with its corollary, education) was the 'only one' for which Morley cared.[68]

This radical enthusiasm encouraged whig-liberal fears of Gladstone's own proclivities. Selborne and Argyll both discussed them with great alarm: Selborne pointed to Gladstone's enthusiasm and lack of balance; Argyll perceived that disestablishment might be, for Gladstone, 'the best card to play, both for the leadership of the Liberal party in politics and for the resistance of Liberalism in ecclesiastical affairs'. He refused any longer to accept Gladstone's leadership, especially in ecclesiastical matters.[69] These views were widely shared.[70] Halifax found Gladstone's conduct on the two ecclesiastical bills of 1874 most mysterious: 'What on earth he means on Church matters puzzles us all.'[71] Kimberley and Brand thought that parties were likely to be broken up and recast on religious questions, since they were at the forefront of politics: Northbrook could not see how Gladstone could remain as Liberal leader, since he was opposed to the great mass of the party on these issues, and commanded 'no confidence' on them.[72] Conservatives encouraged this whig-

---

[64] Temmel, 'Liberal versus Liberal', pp. 621–2; Hamer, *Politics of electoral pressure*, p. 141.
[65] Fleming, *Church of Scotland*, p. 238.
[66] Chamberlain, 'Next page of the Liberal programme'.
[67] 'The Liberal eclipse', pp. 297–8.
[68] Hirst, *Morley*, ii, 1–12; Hamer, *Morley*, pp. 107–9.
[69] Selborne, *Memorials II*, i, 353–7; Argyll, *Argyll*, ii, 319–20.
[70] Tulloch to Playfair, 13 June 1874, Playfair papers, 667; Earl Fortescue to Brereton, 6 October, 28 December 1874, Brereton papers, F 32, 33 74; Jowett, 27 July [1874], Abbott and Campbell, *Jowett*, ii, 95–6.
[71] Halifax to Northbrook, 12 August 1874, Northbrook papers, 144, 22.
[72] Kimberley to Northbrook, 9 August 1874, *ibid.*; Northbrook to Kimberley, 8 September 1874, *ibid.*; Brand diary, résumé of 1874 session, Brand papers.

liberal concern, arguing that the impending movement of the high-church Liberal leader into the radical camp on the disestablishment question would be merely one manifestation of the 'impending struggle' in 'half Europe' between 'the principles of freedom and well-ordered religion on the one hand, against the combined forces of sacerdotal pre-tension and degrading infidelity on the other'.[73]

Gladstone's course became more perplexing to whig-liberals after he published two controversial pieces in late 1874. First, he wrote an article for the October issue of the *Contemporary Review*, the aim of which was to place ritualism in its proper perspective, as neither a valuable aid to wor-ship – unless it accompanied devout spiritual feeling – nor a serious threat to the survival of Anglicanism. Moreover, in challenging the view that a ritualist need be any more susceptible to conversion to Roman Catholicism than any other man, he defined, at one point in the article, the errors which a convert made. These errors, he maintained, were unconnected with posture or vestment; they were errors of the intellect. A convert surrendered his 'moral and mental freedom' and was prepared to place his 'civil loyalty and duty at the mercy of another'.[74] When criticised for this apparently off-hand remark, he published *The Vatican decrees in their bearing on civil allegiance* in November, in order to develop it. In this pamphlet, he maintained that the papacy aimed to involve Europe in bloodshed in an attempt to restore its own temporal powers.[75] He delivered a lengthy condemnation of ultramontanism,[76] but he also took the opportunity to criticise the interference of the temporal power in the legitimate concerns of spiritual authorities.[77]

One motive for his outburst was a desire to advance the cause of the continental Old Catholics in their struggle against the papacy – and hence, he thought, the prospects of the ultimate reunion of the Churches. Another was resentment at the defeat of his Irish University Bill by Irish denominationalists, acting, he believed, under pressure from the ultramontane hierarchy.[78] He may also have been influenced by the announcement, in August, of Ripon's conversion to Romanism. This tarred the ex-government with the clericalist brush even more than before, and did little for the cause of denominational education, which Ripon had so publicly advocated. Gladstone may have been trying to stress the difference between his mind and Ripon's, and Ripon was cer-

---

[73] Cowell, 'Review of the session', pp. 255–62.
[74] Gladstone, *Church of England and ritualism*, p. 30.
[75] 2 November 1874, Ramm, ii, 458.
[76] See above, pp. 156–7.
[77] *Vatican decrees*, pp. 19, 29; these phrases were picked up by the *Nonconformist*, 11 November 1874, p. 1078.
[78] Gladstone to Ripon, 4 October 1874, Gladstone papers, 44286, fo. 200.

tainly hurt by the publication, believing that Gladstone must have realised that public opinion would assume him to be the 'convert' criticised.[79]

Gladstone also told Granville that he hoped that the pamphlet would help to regain party unity.[80] But this particular argument may have been merely a public justification of his course. A party united simply on an anti-Romanist ticket would hardly be amenable to Gladstone's educational and ecclesiastical goals; nor would he wish to lead such a force. In January 1875, he recognised that the popularity of his pamphlet had tended to 'strengthen, and *hearten*' the party generally; but he went on to say that he personally was unable to unite it on religious questions, on which politics might well focus in 1875.[81] That party considerations were not uppermost in his mind is indicated by his contemptuous reaction to a suggestion that he ought to show the pamphlet to his senior parliamentary colleagues before publication.[82]

By the end of 1874, 145,000 copies of the *Vatican decrees* pamphlet had been printed; provincial nonconformists were especially enthusiastic about it. But Gladstone's publications did not convince whig-liberal critics of his religious soundness: indeed, in some quarters they exacerbated the reluctance to see him continue as party leader.[83]

Criticism of him was led publicly by the *Times* and the *Pall Mall Gazette*. The *Times* argued that Gladstone had ignored the telling point against ritualism, which was precisely that it did approximate so closely to Roman Catholicism. The important contemporary religious conflict, it maintained, was between those who defended freedom and toleration, and those who insisted that men should submit to particular ecclesiastical doctrines and laws – and the men in the second camp who most obviously threatened the liberties of Englishmen were not Roman Catholics, but Anglo-catholics. It claimed that these men were especially dangerous because they upheld objectionable *doctrines*; nonetheless, their ritualism was also to be condemned, because its purpose was to give expression to these doctrines, and to inveigle laymen into accepting them. The *Times* also pointed out that Gladstone's belief that all local variations in practices should be tolerated – his apparent renunciation of

---

[79] Ripon to Gladstone, 1, 14 October 1874, *ibid.*, fos. 196, 206. For the Conservative tendency to smear Gladstone with complicity in Ripon's conversion, see Arnstein, *Newdegate*, p. 186.

[80] As others also thought: Wolverton to Gladstone, 28 November 1874, Gladstone papers, 44349, fo. 43; (Cardwell) Gordon diary, [November] 1874, Stanmore papers, 49262. This argument has been highlighted in Steele, 'Gladstone and Ireland', pp. 75–6.

[81] Gladstone to Granville, 7 December 1874, Ramm, ii, 461.

[82] Gordon diary, [30 October] 1874, Stanmore papers, 49262.

[83] Notes, 9 January 1875, Gladstone papers, 44762, fo. 155.

the Act of Uniformity – gave congregations no liberty to protest against the imposition of unpopular practices by their clergymen.[84]

This response was more generally shared. Halifax, Harcourt, Lowe, Layard and Houghton, and probably many other whig-liberals, all opposed Gladstone's arguments on much the same grounds (Halifax, in fact, thought that Gladstone had 'lost his reason'). Firstly, they disliked Gladstone's attempt to pass off 'Old Catholicism' as 'Protestantism'. They rejected the arguments in favour of Old Catholicism, seeing it, indeed, as retaining some of the most objectionable characteristics of the Catholic religion, particularly its stress on the 'sacramental claims of the priesthood'. Gladstone would not 'find a panacea for modern ills in the decisions of the First Six Councils', nor did the path to Christian reunion lie there. They insisted that priestly attempts to dominate the Church must never be encouraged, and that the Public Worship Act had been so necessary for that reason. Ritualism, they contended, was too dangerous to be belittled: unless repressed, it would probably break up the Establishment and the Church.

Secondly, they perceived that Gladstone's increasing interest in freedom of local ecclesiastical practice might portend a declaration in favour of disestablishment (a suspicion enhanced by the support given to his publications by high churchmen, nonconformists and secularists). They argued that disestablishment would not only destroy the national Church, but would split the party irrevocably. The Church could be strengthened, they alleged, only by enforcing the law, driving out the extremists, and opening her gates to those Protestant nonconformists of 'common faith', who had been alienated by a sacerdotalist Church.

Thirdly, they disagreed that the pope's behaviour since 1870 required Britain to demand any more of Catholics than she had previously. They considered that, in practice, Catholics would remain as loyal to the Crown as before. Gladstone's effusion appeared to them to be extremely stupid politics since it was bound to offend Catholics, to discourage them from voting Liberal, and to drive them into the hands of the ultramontanes. It also seemed to strengthen the case for home rule, because it suggested that there was a potential incompatibility between Irish Catholicism and British nationality. However, this particular set of arguments was not universally adopted: some whig-liberal critics of Gladstone's behaviour, like George Grey, found his apparent intention of breaking his alliance with the Irish Catholics the only praiseworthy aim of his publications.[85]

[84] *Times*, 28, 29 September, 10 November 1874, p. 9, p. 7, p. 9. See George Grey (agreeing with the newspaper) to Ellice, 2 October 1874, Ellice papers, 15024, fo. 29.
[85] George Grey to Halifax, 9 November 1874, A 4 58. For these three paragraphs, see: Harcourt, *Speech December 1874*; Houghton to Harcourt, 24 December 1874, Harcourt

These arguments were most eloquently expressed in a speech delivered by Harcourt in Oxford in December 1874 – a speech which was designed to reveal him as the bearer of the whig tradition of stability, progress and tolerance,[86] and which was warmly applauded by Westminster, Bedford, Cowper-Temple and Houghton.[87] Thirlwall, Jowett and the *Economist* were similarly critical of the publications;[88] the queen considered the *Contemporary* article to be 'disingenuous';[89] and Villiers maintained that Liberals now hoped that Palmerston's fabled last words had been proved true, and that Gladstone – 'ever a Roman Catholic at heart' – was mad enough to be 'put under restraint'.[90]

The sections of the party therefore entered 1875 in a state not only of disunity and mutual recrimination, but of apprehension at the political and religious future. A minority, such as Harcourt and those in Jowett's circles, did not want Gladstone to lead the party any more, and the *Times* was also decidedly cool towards him.[91] When another attack on the pope appeared from Gladstone's pen, in the January issue of the *Quarterly Review*, Coleridge, one of the most Gladstonian of Liberals, thought that his obsession with the subject 'plainly disqualified [him] from leading the Party'. Gladstone's new nickname, apparently, was 'Charles V'.[92]

Gladstone did in fact resign the leadership in January 1875. It would be wrong, however, to suggest that he was forced out by internal party criticism. Despite the difficulties of the past year, the prevailing response from within the party to his decision was one of regret, although hardly of surprise. It was thought that the party would be even more divided without his services in imposing authority and in inspiring the Liberal troops. It was frequently emphasised that only he could unite the party – whenever the party evinced a disposition to be united. Many whig-liberals feared that the radicals would gain even more power over the

papers, 205, fo. 97; Layard to Gregory, 17 December 1874, Layard papers, 38949, fo. 137; Lowe to Ellice, 13 December 1874, Ellice papers, 15036, fo. 86; Halifax to Grey, 14 November 1874, Grey papers; Halifax to Northbrook, 6 October, 16 December 1874, Northbrook papers, 144, 22; Anon, 'Papal Rome and Catholic reform'.

[86] See *Speech December 1874*, esp. p. 12.
[87] Houghton to Harcourt, 24 December 1874, Harcourt papers, 205, fo. 97; Westminster to Harcourt, 8 January 1875, *ibid.*, 206, fo. 10; Bedford to Harcourt, 11 January 1875, *ibid.*; Cowper-Temple to Harcourt, 28 January 1875, *ibid.*, fo. 51.
[88] Thirlwall, *Letters literary*, p. 383; Abbott and Campbell, *Letters of Jowett*, pp. 76, 78; *Economist*, 3 October 1874, p. 1186.
[89] Derby diary, 3 October 1874, 15th earl of Derby papers.
[90] Hewett, *Waldegrave*, p. 243; Burghclere, *Derby*, p. 404.
[91] Gardiner, *Harcourt*, i, 285–8; Abbott and Campbell, *Letters of Jowett*, p. 77; *Times*, 14 January 1875, p. 9.
[92] Coleridge, *Coleridge*, ii, 248; *Times*, 18 January 1875, p. 9. See Gladstone, 'Speeches of Pope Pius IX'.

party once they were released from his restraining influence – and, indeed, neither Chamberlain nor Harrison regretted the resignation.[93]

But most Liberals nonetheless appreciated the wisdom of Gladstone's decision, and in particular the impossibility of his position while religious questions were to the political forefront.[94] Gladstone considered the party to be as disunited and unwilling to accept leadership as in 1867; he thought that the position of any leader would be weaker than at any time, perhaps, since 1830.[95] He argued that only time would heal party divisions and create new issues on which unity might be reforged. It was impossible, he believed, for the party at present to agree on a course of action towards the franchise, disestablishment, education, Ireland, the land laws, retrenchment, colonial policy or local-government reform. The subject on which he saw Liberals to be nearest to unity was undenominational education, the one issue on which he would find it most difficult to 'follow them with honour'.[96] If the Conservatives proposed an education bill, he would not be able to 'concur' in the anti-clerical policy that his backbenchers would adopt in opposition to it; if the government introduced further legislation to reform the Church, he would be forced to attempt to hold the Church together according to arguments and principles which were 'intensely unpopular with the constituents of Liberal members'.[97]

In resigning, Gladstone was also astute enough to realise that there was little danger of the party cooperating cordially under his successor; indeed, a number of people held the view that he was only biding his time until a new set of issues came to the fore.[98] Hartington, a reluctant contender for the leadership, would have liked a frank recognition of the fact that there were now three separate groups in the party: whigs, radicals and home rulers.[99] Men like Mundella, Trevelyan, Fawcett and Playfair wished Forster to become leader, because he supported the extension of the county franchise, and was interested in a number of other social questions, which they hoped would replace religious ones in the minds

---

[93] Fitzmaurice, *Granville*, ii, 138–41; Halifax to Northbrook, 21 January 1875, Northbrook papers, 144, 23; diary, 14–15 January 1875, Cartwright papers, 6/10; Garvin, *Chamberlain*, i, 222; Vogeler, *Harrison*, p. 133.

[94] *Economist*, 16 January 1875, p. 58; Halifax to Northbrook, 21 January 1875, Northbrook papers, 144, 23; (Houghton) Fitzmaurice, *Granville*, ii, 143–4.

[95] 9 January 1875, Lathbury, ii, 312; Gladstone to Hartington, 2 February 1875, Gladstone papers, 44144, fo. 174. See also (for the importance of the religious consideration in his resignation): Wolverton to Granville, 21 December 1874, Granville papers, 30/29/25, box 1, envelope 2; Gladstone notes, 9 January 1875, Gladstone papers, 44762, fo. 155. The point has been amplified in Temmel, 'Gladstone's resignation', esp. pp. 166–8.

[96] Draft of Gladstone to Granville, 13 January 1875, Gladstone papers, 44762, fo. 149.

[97] Memoranda, 14 January 1875, Gladstone papers, 44762, fo. 162.

[98] Hewett, *Waldegrave*, pp. 241–3; Acland, *Acland*, p. 319.

[99] Gardiner, *Harcourt*, i, 289; Fitzmaurice, *Granville*, ii, 150–1.

of most Liberals and thus promote unity. But radical nonconformists would not tolerate the architect of the 1870 Act, and its stubborn defender, as their leader; nor would large numbers of anti-clerical whig-liberals, led by Harcourt, Lowe and Torrens. It was increasingly obvious, as discussion continued, that these two camps were likely to provide Hartington with a clear – if less than enthusiastic – majority within the parliamentary party. Forster accordingly withdrew from the contest – thus allowing the representatives of provincial radicalism to indulge their anti-clericalism by electing the son of a duke as their parliamentary standard-bearer.[100]

[100] Ramm, ii, 467–9; Fitzmaurice, *Granville*, ii, 146–50; Gwynn and Tuckwell, *Dilke*, i, 186; Armytage, *Mundella*, pp. 153–4.

Conclusion

In Part II of this book, we have seen how the Liberal party spectacularly lost its sense of direction between 1870 and 1875, and how, in 1874, it suffered an election defeat which was almost unprecedented in scale. Throughout, mention has been made of the non-religious considerations which accelerated that process – which were, primarily, the government's low-key supervision of foreign affairs, and its licensing, taxation and local-government policies. But it was in discussing religious questions that division within the party was most embarrassingly explicit; and it was mainly because of radical agitation about these same questions that many Liberal voters increasingly doubted the future soundness of the party.

The opportunities for internal party conflict about religion had been obvious from early in the period under discussion. The reunification of 1868 was achieved by securing agreement on the principle of Irish Church disestablishment, and by shared dislike of the Conservatives' Irish university policy. The Irish Church issue was so powerful a cohesive force that, by the time of the 1868 election, little else had been agreed to be party policy (despite the large amount of legislation concerning non-religious subjects which was to be passed by the 1868–74 government). In particular, there had been no attempt to reach consensus within the party about the educational policy to be followed in England, Scotland and Ireland; and it was discord in discussion of these issues which disrupted Liberal unity so markedly from 1870 onwards. One element which inflamed the discussions was the heated anti-Catholicism which was expressed in reaction to the Vatican council, the rise of the home-rule party, and the O'Keeffe case. This highlighted the political dangers which would result from a denominationalist reform of Irish education (which would hand control to the Catholic bishops). Another difficulty was the increasing zeal and aggressiveness of radical nonconformists, who were anxious, once the Irish Church had been disestablished, to

429

promote disestablishment in England as well. Their agitation for this
was fuelled by their resentment at the provisions of the 1870 Education
Act, which they considered to be unduly sympathetic to existing denominational schools. After 1870, therefore, the disestablishment campaign
ran parallel with the movement for radical educational reform.
Moreover, both nonconformists and anti-clerical whig-liberals attacked
the denominational bias of the 1870 Act primarily by exploiting its
ramifications for the forthcoming legislation on Irish education. Opposition to any concession to the Irish Catholics on the educational issue
became so strong within the party that only a man with Gladstone's
appreciation of religious rights would have persisted with the idea of
introducing a measure designed to accord them full educational
equality. But, when he introduced his Irish University Bill in 1873, it won
few friends. On the one hand, Protestant opinion in Britain, especially
whig-liberal opinion, was alarmed at many of the provisions; on the
other, the Irish Catholic MPs – bolstered in their opposition by mass
Irish interest in the religious question – rejected it because of the lack of
state endowment.

After March 1873, very few Irish MPs were still active members of the
Liberal coalition – a state of affairs which many anti-clerical British
Liberals had desired for a long time. The fear grew, however, that the
home rulers might hold the balance of power in the next parliament, and
that Gladstone or Disraeli might then be eager to approximate to a
number of their demands in an attempt to win their votes. Nonetheless,
of more central concern to most British voters in 1873–4 was the future
of the Church Establishment in England and Scotland, and of religious
education in the schools. Some anti-clerical whig-liberals were happy to
support nonconformists in criticising the 1870 Act, and to declare for the
repeal of its Clause 25; but they were no more prepared than most 'right-
wing' whig-liberals to countenance disestablishment or secular education. Nonconformists continued to advocate disestablishment, and,
although after 1873 they placed less emphasis on secularism, they still
pressed for a series of radical educational reforms, which in the eyes of
many Anglican Liberal electors would eventually abolish all effective
religious teaching in school hours. Moreover, borough constituency
parties, especially in the north, Scotland and Wales, were becoming
steadily more radical, whether as a result of genuine popular enthusiasm
for disestablishment, or of the machinations of local nonconformist
leaders. The effect, by 1874, was that the Liberal party did appear, at
grass-roots level, to be increasingly favourable to disestablishment and
against bible-teaching in schools; and whiggish voters rebelled in large
numbers. Many abstained; many voted Conservative, because Disraeli's
emphasis on social and administrative measures appealed to them.

Conservatives adopted this emphasis, not in an attempt to pander to the 'working classes', but from a desire to appear more responsible and competent, and less dangerous, than the Liberals. In 1874, the most controversial issue was the Liberals' past and future religious policy; Disraeli, instead, offered sound, constructive but uncontentious administration.

Gladstone's position during these crises was paradoxical. His refusal to tolerate anti-clerical legislation, whether it was designed to amend the 1870 Act, to reform the Church, or to modernise the English universities, bracketed him with a handful of Liberals on the far 'right', and disquieted the centre of the party as much as it did the radicals. On the other hand, both the 'right' and the centre had little confidence in his ability to resist radical nonconformist demands in the long run – partly because he was a devout high churchman and thus was assumed to wish for disestablishment in order to prevent the suppression of extreme sacerdotalist practices, and partly because of his populist streak. In one sense, this ambiguity was an immense asset to Gladstone (together with his oratorical skill and remarkable capacity for administration): it was impossible to imagine other Liberals holding the party together as well as he did as leader. But in another, it handicapped him. Throughout the 1870–5 period, he had to fight so many battles on so many fronts within his own party in order to get his way that he became demoralised. His extraordinary powers carried him through, except for the occasional defeat; but the task of repressing the Liberals' innate anti-clericalism was almost sisyphean. He retired in 1875, in the hope that once his own presence was removed, religious questions would become less controversial, and Liberal energies would be diverted to more wholesome projects. If this happened, he might, or might not, return as leader. But he knew that it would take a long time for the Liberals' anxiety about clericalism to die down: even in 1877, he was still complaining that the party could be 'muster[ed] . . . for votes of religious liberalism (so to call it) and for little else'.[1]

In the same letter in which he delivered this complaint, he made his well-known assertion that the 'vital principle of the Liberal party', the only way of reinvigorating it and fitting it for government, was *'action'*. The two statements were intimately linked. The Liberal party, he considered, was the only agency by which Britain could be governed responsibly, without class bias, and without pandering to sectional vested interests. He saw it to be essential to restore the party to power, and then to occupy it constructively – or it would fall apart. But he also hoped that both these goals would be achieved by elevating rallying-cries, not by agreement on anti-clericalism. In the decade after 1876,

---

[1] 19 May 1877, Ramm, *Gladstone–Granville correspondence 1876–1886*, i, 40.

Gladstone therefore had two hopes for the Liberal party: the first was to regain unity and office in pursuit of a policy which was as devoid of class bias as possible, while the second was to lead mass opinion in a spiritually elevating direction, by the use of what are usually called his 'moral crusades'. His vision came to be that, as a result of the arousal of popular enthusiasm in defence of abstract or religious issues, politics could be impregnated with a strict moral code.

It was the 'virtuous passion' engendered by the Bulgarian atrocities which did most to convince Gladstone that this endeavour might succeed: the Bulgarian agitation of 1876 thus marked a turning-point in his career. His behaviour in and after 1876 confronted whig-liberals, more bluntly than ever before, with the problem of how to respond to popular political 'enthusiasm'; and their reaction, in most cases, was cool. Shannon has convincingly demonstrated the preponderance of nonconformist and Anglo-catholic support for the agitation – both sects being keen to defend the Eastern Christians' liberty of spiritual expression from oppression by the 'immoral' Ottoman temporal power – and the apathy or hostility of most of the whig and latitudinarian establishment, and of the leaders of metropolitan opinion. The latter groups tended to distrust the zeal and earnestness propagated by the agitation, to regret its influence on the sober consideration of British national interests, and to depict Orthodox Russia as an aggressive power.[2] The party's disagreement about the Eastern question was only too evident between 1876 and 1878, but perhaps the most embarrassing indication of it came in May 1877, when the moderates forced Gladstone to emasculate his proposed resolutions concerning the future treatment of Turkey. Within weeks, Gladstone, probably in reaction, was addressing the inaugural meeting of Chamberlain's National Liberal Federation; his appearance inspired widespread hostile whiggish comment, because of the Federation's association with caucus politics, and with the policy of disestablishment.[3]

However, by the time of the 1880 election, divisions within the party had become much less marked. This was for two main reasons. Firstly, the Liberals were able to exploit the Conservatives' conduct of foreign and financial policy, and to contrast the government's shortcomings with their own record in both these areas. The party was first able to

---

[2] Shannon, *Bulgarian agitation*, esp. pp. 42, 161, 165. Of course there were exceptions to these generalisations: see *ibid.*, and above p. 123. See also Rossi, 'Transformation of the British Liberal party', pp. 33–8.

[3] Villiers to Lady Waldegrave, 28 May [1877], Strachie papers, 291 WW 61/4; Granville to Gladstone, 21 May 1877, Ramm, *Gladstone–Granville correspondence 1876–1886*, i, 41, and the stronger draft version, including two extra paragraphs, in Granville papers, 30/29/25, box 1, envelope 3.

unite, in late 1878, in criticism of the outbreak of the Afghan war. Whigs with Indian experience condemned the British advance as a showy departure from the policy of wise restraint practised by administrations for forty years, and forecast that it would prove counter-productive: the massacre of the British garrison in Kabul in September 1879 seemed to confirm their viewpoint. Disraeli's manner of conducting foreign affairs irritated moderate Liberals more generally: they disliked its glitter, and charged that, while shamelessly rousing the worst passions of a jingoistic electorate, he had failed to impose a sound long-term policy.[4] They were also incensed by his flunkeyism and apparent disdain for the supremacy of parliament in the constitutional process.[5] At Midlothian, Gladstone emphasised all these complaints, and, in particular, repeatedly condemned the government for its financial extravagance in pursuing its Afghan and South African policy – a condemnation which was all the more effective because the policy seemed to have failed. Income tax, which he would have abolished had he been returned in 1874, stood at sixpence in the pound in 1880. He further criticised the government for irresponsibly issuing Exchequer bonds in order to spread the cost of its extra defence expenditure over a number of years. Most Liberals agreed with his arguments, and took pride in believing that their claim to be more efficient than the Conservatives in the administration of domestic and foreign affairs had been borne out.

The Liberals were also able to regroup in relative harmony in 1880 because the various religious questions were far less prominent than in 1874. Even in 1877–8, the threat of disestablishment had still been prominent in the minds of whig-liberals, and they had delivered a series of blistering attacks on the policy. These included a famous speech by Forster at Bradford, which intensified the local radicals' campaign against his re-election; and a series of periodical articles, clearly inspired in part by distrust of Gladstone, which traded on the benefits that the sacerdotalists would gain from disestablishment.[6] But the nonconformists' campaign for disestablishment had petered out after 1877, and Gladstone constantly refused to pronounce on the issue. By 1880, there-

---

[4] Lowe, 'Imperialism'; 'The docility of an "imperial" parliament'; (Carlyle) Froude, *Carlyle*, ii, 439–40, 448; Reid, *Forster*, ii, 217; Halifax to Ellice, 12 October 1878, Ellice papers, 15061, fo. 134; (Halifax, Grey) *Hansard*, ccxliii, 245, 406; Greg, *Enigmas of life*, pp. xxxviii–xxxix; Dunn, *Froude*, ii, 501.

[5] Holland, *Devonshire*, i, 249–54; see also (Gladstone) *PMP*, iv, 35–6; (Ripon) Esher, *Cloud-capp'd towers*, p. 146. Fears of this revival were inflamed by the Conservative journalist Courthope's article 'The Crown and the Constitution', as well as by the Royal Titles Act and by the government's failure always to gain parliamentary sanction for military expenditure during the Eastern crisis.

[6] See Brodrick, *Political studies*, esp. p. 239; Davies, 'Erastianism *versus* ecclesiasticism', p. 148; Tulloch, 'Liberal party and the Church of Scotland'.

fore, the danger of Conservative unsoundness in the conduct of foreign and financial policy seemed much more immediate to whig-liberals than the threat of Liberal irresponsibility in religious affairs. Having reunited, the Liberals were accordingly able to win the 1880 election with a majority even bigger than that of 1868.

In fact, religious questions as such were of much less concern throughout the 1880s than they had been in the 1870s. The peculiar combination of circumstances which had given them prominence – the widespread perception of a need for substantial educational legislation, the nonconformists' attempts to agitate the new voters in favour of disestablishment, and Gladstone's concern with the ultramontane threat – did not recur. There were, of course, controversies about specific problems – for example, Gladstone's determination to champion the right of the atheist Bradlaugh to sit in parliament offended a dozen whig-liberals and Samuel Morley, and probably a large number of Liberal voters.[7] But only at one point did religious controversy divide the Liberal party as fundamentally as it had done in the previous decade: when the Liberation Society, and then Chamberlain, advocated disestablishment at the 1885 general election. This inspired a virulent counter-agitation, headed by the Church and the Conservatives, but also affecting many whig-liberals: Grey, Westminster, Earl Fortescue, Bedford, Somerset, Fitzwilliam, Ebury, Selborne, Hughes, Bouverie, Cowper-Temple (now Lord Mount-Temple) and others signed a joint letter to the *Times* suggesting that Anglicans should demand that their Liberal candidates declare against disestablishment. Gladstone endured much whig-liberal criticism for maintaining an ambiguous silence on the issue, but political exigencies finally forced him to state, at Edinburgh, that he did not see disestablishment becoming a major question in the near future, and that those who were agitating for it were doing a disservice to party unity.

Chamberlain's campaign undoubtedly lost the Liberals seats in metropolitan and suburban areas.[8] But its stridency also displeased considerable numbers of nonconformists. From the 1880s onwards, it was evident that the intense evangelical impulse for moral regeneration which had driven the nonconformist political juggernaut since the 1840s was diminishing. This lessened nonconformists' pressure for disestablishment, and led them to concentrate increasingly on humanitarian questions – such as temperance, the immoral consequences of urban

---

[7] Foster, 'Tory democracy', p. 156; *Hansard*, cclxvi, 92–6, cclxxviii, 1859–62.
[8] For the disestablishment campaign and the election, see Simon, 'Church disestablishment'; Barker, *Gladstone and radicalism*, pp. 31–4; *Times*, 4 November 1885, pp. 9–10; Morley, *Gladstone*, iii, 248; Lathbury, i, 184–5; Bosworth Smith, *Reasons of a layman*.

housing conditions, and human rights abroad.[9] To recommend the disestablishment of the Church of England appeared less noble than it had when evangelical nonconformists had popularised the notion that a Christianised polity would result from it. In the 1870s, disestablishment had also seemed the logical culmination to a series of advances towards religious equality, and the most rational solution to the difficulties which had preoccupied evangelical nonconformists – the difficulty of safeguarding denominational independence, and of salving the conscience of the taxpayer who objected to subsidising the teaching of other sects. But it now took on the aspect, more and more, of a destructive attack on the Church's endowments, with the aim of allowing the state to spend more on other programmes. Although many nonconformists still believed in the abstract rectitude of disestablishment, it was not, therefore, so possible to inspire a mass crusade in its favour. Disestablishment in Wales and to some extent in Scotland continued to be advocated, but this was less for the spiritual benefits which it was anticipated would follow from it, than for the fillip which its achievement would give to the burgeoning awareness of national identity in those countries. (Even so, the Welsh Church was not disestablished until 1920, and the Scottish Church not at all.) The disestablishment policy was also much less attractive to high churchmen by the 1880s, partly because of the shift in the campaign's emphasis, towards stripping the Church of her endowments, and partly because parliament and the lay courts were by this time interfering far less with the Church's doctrinal and ritual practices.

But, if religious issues themselves were not as controversial in the 1880s as before, there are many indications that the component parts of the Liberal coalition still expressed diverging views about the issues which were presented in Part I of this book as underlying the specific religious quarrels discussed there. Any attempt to sum this divergence up in one phrase would be to simplify and vulgarise it, but probably the most basic point at issue was the distribution of political virtue in the nation. By the 1870s and 1880s, most Liberals appreciated the potential respectability and spirituality of the common man. However, those who have been characterised throughout as whig-liberals tended to be more convinced than those discussed in chapters 3 and 4, that the judgment of the common man was not, by itself, reliable; they tended to argue that those with experience of government, and superior wisdom, should be allowed to use the power of the state in order to provide moral guidance. Nonconformists, radicals and other Gladstonians, on the other hand, placed more value on the virtue, rectitude and responsibility of the aver-

[9] Bebbington, *Nonconformist conscience*, pp. 27–8; Helmstadter, 'Nonconformist conscience', p. 139.

age elector. Their emphases thus won the respect of many self-improving working-men who were anxious to discover a sense of dignity through participation in politics.

A distinction along such lines cannot, of course, be simply equated with the divisions about religious Establishments which were analysed in the body of the book. In particular, a group of young intellectuals who became politically active in the 1880s were latitudinarian defenders of a reformed Establishment (they often had extremely hazy theological views), but admired the popular judgment wholeheartedly, and were fervent Gladstonians: many of them were disciples of T. H. Green. By this time, there were also a number of other 'whig-liberals' who revered Gladstone's moral vision, and considered his influence on public opinion to be uplifting and civilising. Moreover, the whole tone of politics changed in the 1880s, and, in reacting to it, active politicians were bound to cultivate techniques of public address which would previously have been condemned as 'populist'. This change was to some extent prompted by the rise of the caucus system within the Liberal party. But of more general significance was the growth, over the previous twenty years, of the mass market, of a more efficient communications network, and of the publishing industry. In the 1880s, it seemed, quite suddenly, to become easier to perceive, and address, a national electorate than it had previously been; political programmes were developed, and advertised with panache, in well-publicised speeches; politicians themselves became marketable commodities, to be celebrated in the cheap press, in hagiographies, and on mass-produced porcelain. From the late 1870s, some whig-liberals participated in this shift in political behaviour: most prominent among them was Harcourt. While retaining his latitudinarian religious views, he became convinced that the future of the party lay with the 'sections' in the provinces, and assiduously cultivated them: by 1879, Fitzjames Stephen saw him as a 'mere noisy mouthpiece of ignorant popular views'.[10]

But such men were exceptions to the rule: most whig-liberals were alarmed by the change in political tone in the five years after 1876, and, especially, watched with increasing foreboding the metamorphosis of Gladstone into a popular hero. For Gladstone was undoubtedly the politician who was most successful in exploiting the available opportunities for publicity. He began to cultivate it, on a continuous basis, in the late 1870s, admitting parties to watch him felling trees at Hawarden (they were allowed to collect the chips). From then on, he was the subject of an apparently ceaseless flow of popular commemorative

---

[10] Dingle, *Campaign for prohibition*, p. 83; Hamer, *Politics of electoral pressure*, p. 6; Roach, 'Liberalism and the Victorian intelligentsia', pp. 70–1.

literature.[11] The popular clamour which surrounded the Midlothian campaign added to the disquiet with which unfriendly whig-liberals viewed this transformation: they saw him increasingly as the servant of 'King Mob'.[12] Many of them disliked the prospect of his return to the premiership in 1880, and would have preferred to see Hartington or Granville as prime minister.[13]

Concern about 'populism' was therefore widespread in the 1880s, and, with exceptions, affected Liberals in ways very similar to the overtly religious controversies of the early 1870s. But did this concern have any major political effect? In order to determine its relevance as a divisive force on the party, we must look ahead to the crisis of 1885–6.

In late 1885, Gladstone announced that he had become convinced of the need to grant Ireland home rule: over the next six months, while he brought forward his Home Rule Bill, the party split permanently. One widely held interpretation of the secession of the Liberal unionists in response to Gladstone's move explains it in terms of an underlying preoccupation with the defence of property in general, in opposition to 'socialist' legislation. In other words, the argument goes that the Irish problem itself was not of primary concern to the unionists, and that they seceded because they disliked the class-based politics which some radicals, especially Chamberlain, appeared to be preaching in the mid 1880s.[14]

This interpretation is, however, questionable. It is certainly true that the major domestic questions during the 1880–5 government were related to property, especially land. A number of government measures affecting property rights irritated a great many Liberals on the 'right' – many of whom joined the Liberty and Property Defence League, which was founded in 1882 in order to campaign against all examples of 'socialist' legislation. Chamberlain's rise in the party was of especial concern to these men. Nonetheless, the issues raised by home rule cannot be compared directly with those thrown up by the 'interventionist' initiatives of 1880–5, and they divided Liberals on different lines – a point which Hartington himself explicitly made.[15] It would, of course, be

---

[11] Hamer, 'Gladstone'.

[12] Colaiaco, *Stephen*, p. 194; see also Selborne, *Memorials II*, i, 470; Reeve, 'Plain whig principles', p. 279.

[13] Jenkins, 'Gladstone, the whigs and the Liberal party'.

[14] See e.g. I. Jennings, *Party politics: volume II: the growth of parties* (Cambridge, 1961), p. 184; and, for a suggestion that the importance of the home-rule issue has been exaggerated in accounting for the swing of propertied voters to the Conservatives: Alderman, *The railway interest*, p. 11.

[15] Southgate, *Passing of the whigs*, p. 414.

a strange 'socialism' which divided Gladstone from Argyll, Dilke from Chamberlain, or Freeman from Tom Hughes. Most revealingly, detailed statistical analysis has now borne out the view that the Liberal unionists and Gladstonians had very similar voting records, after 1886, on nearly all classes of 'secular' questions, including land.[16] This is not to say that fears for the future of property played no part at all in encouraging Liberals to secede from the party; they, in conjunction with other considerations, did have a role. But that role should not be overstressed. Moreover, the consequence of the division was not to establish the Liberal party as the party of 'interventionism'. Indeed, the long-term consequences of Chamberlain's activity in stressing such questions were very different from his expectations. From the mid 1880s, land, housing and labour reform became recognised functions of government, whichever party was in power. By familiarising both Liberal and Conservative politicians with such issues, Chamberlain unwittingly opened a door through which he might, and in fact did, pass into the Conservative party. What he failed to do was – as he had hoped – to make himself indispensable to the radical wing of the Liberals.

On the contrary, the introduction of home rule marked Chamberlain's nemesis as a radical: it showed that Gladstone's hold on the nonconformist and provincial conscience was far greater than his own. When Chamberlain challenged Gladstone's home-rule policy and left the party, the constituency organisations overwhelmingly supported Gladstone: outside Birmingham, no caucus rejected a candidate because he was a Gladstonian, and the Gladstonians regained control of even the Birmingham organisation in 1888.[17] Chamberlain's radical unionist bloc in the Commons never numbered more than twenty after 1886; by 1892, it was reduced to eleven.[18]

If this interpretation of the home-rule division has begun to lose favour recently, it has been at the expense of a new consensus view which does not seek to explain the split in ideological terms at all.[19] As more detail about the parliamentary crisis of 1885–6 becomes available, MPs' behaviour appears more and more devious, hesitant and compromising, and less and less dictated by allegiance to simple principles. But this is not surprising. The home-rule debate required MPs to make very hard

---

[16] Phillips, 'The whig lords and Liberalism'; Lubenow, 'Irish home rule: the dimensions of parliamentary Liberalism'.
[17] Griffiths, 'The caucus and the Liberal party'.
[18] Heyck, 'Home rule, radicalism', p. 70.
[19] Cooke and Vincent, *The governing passion*; Harvie, 'Ideology and home rule', p. 300. Harvie's evidence for his statement that Liberals' opinions about the Irish, the 'people', democracy and the Empire were 'no guide' to the division of sentiment does not conflict with any which I present below: his examples are two anti-*imperialist* unionists, and Freeman, whose preoccupation with self-determination he fails to record.

decisions. The issue itself demanded of parliament 'the most momentous judgement . . . since the Revolution of 1688';[20] in addition, Liberals faced the choice of breaking formally with their party – and often the party of their ancestors. Many would be confused, keen to do 'justice' to Ireland, and yet to defend 'the rule of law' and the 'security of the Protestants'. There was an understandable expectation that delay might enable reconciliation, and perhaps the withdrawal of Gladstone's proposal. It was to be expected, therefore, that some Liberals would display inconsistency during the crisis. However, this does not in itself invalidate the importance of ideological considerations, as long as it can be shown that, once it became obvious that a decision had to be taken, most Liberals acted consistently with the views which they had previously expressed in discussing related questions. But to which questions did the participants in the debate consider home rule to be related?

It is, in fact, striking how far the party divided, in 1886, along lines which will be familiar to readers of Part I of this book. On the one hand, Gladstone won support from the younger generation of Liberal high churchmen, and from, for example, Acland, Coleridge, Freeman, MacColl, E. C. Lowe, C. S. Parker and Lady Frederick Cavendish. Those high churchmen who were unable to follow him were usually either increasingly 'Protestant' in sympathy, like Selborne, or were semi-theocrats (or at least profoundly distrusted the Liberals' soundness in discussing Establishments), such as Blachford, Browne, and the *Guardian* newspaper. (But Church was also hostile, with regret, and Liddon was hesitant and doubtful.) Some of the high-church supporters of home rule voted for it only because of their respect for Gladstone: this was probably true of Acland and Coleridge, but was clearly so in the case of Aberdeen's son, Sir Arthur Gordon.[21] Gladstone also, of course, won Acton's enthusiastic support.

The vast majority of nonconformists supported the bill. Exceptions were: most jews; a substantial section of Wesleyans; some anti-Catholic presbyterians, unitarian intellectuals, and Chamberlainites from Birmingham (including the congregationalist Dale); a small but respectable minority of quakers (including Bright and Leatham) and congregationalists (including Newman Hall, Allon and Stoughton); and very few baptists (including Spurgeon).[22] This support was given, in the main, out of loyalty to Gladstone: as Henry Richard said, 'come what may, I

---

[20] Diary, 7 June 1886, Cartwright papers, 6/16.

[21] See e.g. Johnston, *Liddon*, p. 337; Acland, *Acland*, pp. 334, 357–9; Church, *Church*, p. 321; Kitchin, *Browne*, p. 473; Coleridge, *Coleridge*, ii, 349; (*Guardian*) Bell, *Disestablishment in Ireland*, p. 262; Chapman, *Stanmore*, pp. 349–64.

[22] See above, pp. 216, 219, 224–5, 228. The best summary of nonconformist attitudes towards home rule is Bebbington, *Nonconformist conscience*, pp. 85–92.

shall stand by the Grand Old Man'.[23] In many ways, the crisis resembled a much more significant replay of the 1873 university dispute: few nonconformists were instinctively enthusiastic for the Home Rule Bill, because it seemed to grant so many boons to Catholic opinion, but they could not but sympathise with the abstract principles on which it was based. Neither did they feel any loyalty to Chamberlain, who was frequently charged with behaviour unbecoming in a Christian statesman: with opportunism and with a love of confrontation.[24] Morley, Harrison, Beesly and Picton were also, of course, keen home rulers;[25] so were Bradlaugh, Broadhurst, Burt and Randal Cremer in parliament, and young leaders of working-class opinion like Keir Hardie outside it. Moreover, as has recently been pointed out, the swing against the Liberals between the 1885 and 1886 general elections does not necessarily imply that among rank-and-file nonconformist and working-class voters the issue was more than marginally unpopular: losses of seats which had been Liberal in 1885 usually occurred where the sitting (unionist) MP had a strong political base.[26]

Whig-liberals provided the great majority of defections in 1886. Recent work on Liberal and unionist voting patterns after 1886 has shown that, while there was no correlation between voting on secular questions and attitudes to home rule, there was a marked correlation between views about the latter and about disestablishment: opponents of home rule strongly tended to oppose disestablishment as well.[27] One of Aberdare's (Bruce's) friends explicitly commented on the oddity of his Gladstonianism, given that the latitudinarian views which he held dictated a unionist position in nearly all other cases.[28] Almost the entire whig peerage declared against home rule when the Lords discussed the bill in 1893. Just 41 peers voted for it, against 419 Conservatives and Liberals: only 17 of these 41 held peerages which had not been created by Gladstone, and 4 of those 17 were Catholics. (Many of Gladstone's own creations after 1886 cast little glory on the Lords, and at least 3 had considerable reputations for immorality.) Moreover, all but a score of the 93 Liberal MPs who opposed the Home Rule Bill in the Commons in 1886 were Hartingtonian, rather than Chamberlainite, unionists. Of the leading whig-liberal MPs and non-official peers mentioned in the body of this book, only Harcourt, Childers, Aberdare, Playfair and Whitbread

---

[23] Miall, *Richard*, p. 358.

[24] Colman, *Colman*, pp. 308–9; Illingworth, *Fifty years of politics*, p. 30.

[25] See Vogeler, *Harrison*, pp. 200–2.

[26] Pugh, *Modern British politics*, pp. 35–6.

[27] Lubenow, 'Irish home rule: the dimensions of parliamentary Liberalism', pp. 165, 168–9; see also Kellas, 'Liberal party and Scottish Church disestablishment', p. 40.

[28] (Grant Duff) *Letters of Aberdare*, i, 14.

remained with Gladstone. But it would, of course, be odd if a number of MPs and peers – whig-liberals in the context of the 1870s – had *not* supported home rule, either because of calculations of personal advantage, or force of circumstances – or because they could see, in practice, no alternative once the question had been posed. Several whiggish office-holders, Gladstone's associates for years, adhered to his policy;[29] other MPs did not defect, out of reluctance to offend constituency feeling; yet others remained loyal to Gladstone through comparative indifference to the Irish question.[30] It was far harder for whig-liberals who were still in parliament to defect than it was for like minds – like Lowe (now Viscount Sherbrooke) and Grant Duff – who were now ex-MPs. But those whig-liberals who remained with Gladstone were often not happy with a continuing commitment to home rule, and were especially disposed to identify with 'Liberal Imperialism' in the 1890s. It is no coincidence that the leaders of this group were classic whig-liberal types: a Scottish whig, a Northumberland whig, a Balliol man converting to Anglicanism from congregationalism, an Idealist philosopher, a very wealthy Anglican, and two Wesleyans.[31]

The latitudinarian intellectuals and churchmen mentioned in chapters 1 and 2 tended almost to a man to follow the example of parliamentary sympathisers like Goschen and Lubbock, and to defect: so did evangelicals and Carlyleans. Llewelyn Davies and Grove, Tennyson and Thomson, Brodrick and Huxley, Hutton and Blackie, Macgregor and Hughes – to name but a few – all became unionists, as did most adherents of the 'Balliol school'.[32] As for the queen, she hoped, from late 1885 onwards, that Goschen and Hartington would organise a secession from the party and a coalition with the Conservatives.[33] Also, as pointed out in chapter 4, a large number of secularist academic liberals joined the whig-liberals in objecting to home rule – an alliance which had first been apparent on the 1873 University Bill. But why was opinion so clearly divided in this way?

When whig-liberals objected to home rule, they were objecting, above all, to Gladstone's manner of conducting government. For them, the

---

[29] When, temperamentally, they were probably averse to it. See, for Spencer and Kimberley: Ribblesdale, *Impressions and memories*, pp. 185–6.

[30] For example Playfair: Reid, *Playfair*, pp. 349–53, 367.

[31] Rosebery, Sir Edward Grey, Asquith, Haldane, Brassey, Fowler and Perks.

[32] The radical disciples of T. H. Green who contributed to the formulation of the 'New Liberalism' were not typical of Balliol men: A. L. Illingworth, *The life and work of John Richardson Illingworth* (London, 1917), p. 90; Freeden, *New Liberalism*, p. 56. Famous Balliol graduates who were unionists included Milner, St Loe Strachey, Prothero, Sir Henry Craik, J. A. Godley, Sir Robert Mowbray, George Coates, Sir Thomas Raleigh, the duke of Bedford, Canon Rawnsley, W. P. Ker and Reginald Lane Poole.

[33] Ponsonby, *Ponsonby*, p. 201.

essence of government was administration, the preservation of order and balance through the firm but impartial and respected rule of law. They believed that politicians should be responsible and should not exploit issues in order to enhance their own popularity; that they should take their line from the matured public opinion of those who thought about politics, rather than from the passing whims of a mass electorate which had been excited by unprincipled demagogues. Whig-liberals had no intention of imposing policies which would be perpetually resisted by a permanent majority of the population, because civil disorder would result. But neither would they bow to the shallow enthusiasm of the ignorant and impassioned.

It was the abundant evidence that the Home Rule Bill offered of Gladstone's apparent subservience to mass opinion, rather than any consideration of the details of the legislation, which was most influential in encouraging whig-liberals to secede from the Liberal party. In fact, by 1885, there was a tendency for many of those who were to be staunch unionists to accept that it was politically unwise, if not impossible, to refuse to grant Ireland a substantial measure of local government (while ensuring that Britain retained some power over her development).[34] Northbrook, for example, did not deny that in the climate of early 1886, political exigencies forced some consideration of a measure of Irish self-rule: but the reason why he refused office in the home-rule ministry was because he 'had never any intention of joining another administration of which Mr Gladstone was the head'. Later in the summer, after the 1886 election, he condemned Gladstone's 'unscrupulous appeal to class prejudices', but rejoiced that the electorate had rejected it in favour of the 'educated men'.[35] Knatchbull-Hugessen (now Lord Brabourne) similarly condemned Gladstone's sarcasms at the expense of the 'upper ten thousand', and his appeal to 'the people', in the 1886 election campaign.[36] Argyll refused to follow Gladstone because the latter would not lead the party but weakly supported every new impassioned clamour. Huxley did the same, because Gladstone 'slavishly follow[ed] ... average opinion [when] government by average opinion is merely a circuitous method of going to the devil'.[37]

One of Gladstone's greatest offences, in whig-liberal eyes, was that, as

---

[34] See Brabourne, *Facts and fictions*, p. 58; Arnold, 'Nadir of Liberalism', pp. 68–9; Elliot, *Goschen*, i, 311.

[35] Mallet, *Northbrook*, pp. 229, 232–3.

[36] Diary, 28 June 1886, Brabourne papers, F27/10, p. 33.

[37] Argyll, *Argyll*, ii, 399–401, 454, 458; Huxley, *Huxley*, ii, 440; see also Prothero, 'National party of the future', p. 559; Stodart-Walker, *Letters of Blackie*, p. 351; Seeley, 'Ethics and religion', p. 507.

a result of his conversion to home rule, he had been able to form a government after the 1885 election – because he had won round the eighty-six Irish MPs who held the balance of power at Westminster. Whig-liberals alleged that he had bargained away a country's future for the sake of a parliamentary majority.[38] Nor was this all: he had entered into 'an open alliance with men who receive their instructions and draw their pay from the foreign enemies of Great Britain'; and men, moreover, 'who defy the supremacy of the law'.[39] The Gladstonians were accused of asserting that 'law-makers are more responsible for crime than law-breakers, that only self-imposed laws are sacred, that the masses are the sole source of authority, justice, and right'.[40]

Whig-liberals were naturally worried about the guarantees for order and for property, and the prospects for economic progress if home rule were granted. Tyndall charged that practically all the country's 'intellect' opposed home rule, because it would repress 'enlightenment and energy' in Ireland and substitute for them 'bigotry and ignorance'.[41] Others thought it dangerous, and a 'positive crime', to give Ireland self-government, because there was no 'stable or substantial middle class', and insufficient 'political virtue'.[42] The 'flower of industrial Ireland' would be 'placed at the mercy of the indolent – her intellect at the mercy of her ignorance'.[43] The distinction between intellect and ignorance was often used as a euphemism for that between Protestant and Catholic; but many whig-liberals were not slow to make the point more directly. The measure was frequently described as 'a Bill for the political annihilation of the Protestants of Ireland' – one which would hand control of Irish education to the Catholics, and direction of parliament to the priests.[44]

For whig-liberals, therefore, home rule threatened their most cherished political principles: the rule of law, the defence of property, the superiority of the judgment of the educated, the might of British power, and the probability of the eventual defeat of a superstitious

---

[38] Honan, *Arnold*, p. 336; Prothero, 'Disestablishment', p. 286; Bosworth Smith, 'Liberal party and home rule', p. 2; Butler, *H. M. Butler*, p. 96.

[39] Brodrick, *Unionism*, p. 6.

[40] Prothero, 'National party of the future', p. 558. See also Brabourne, 'Mr Gladstone', p. 410; Dicey, *Why England maintains the union*, p. 64.

[41] *PMP*, iv, 85, 87.

[42] (James) Russell, *MacColl*, pp. 375–6; Brodrick, *Home rule and justice*, pp. 6–7; Butler, *H. M. Butler*, p. 98; Arnold, 'The political crisis'. See also Goschen, *Disruption bill*, p. 18; (Raleigh) Froude (with others), *Lights on home rule*, p. 22.

[43] (Tyndall) Froude (with others), *Lights on home rule*, p. 6.

[44] Dowden, 'Irish opinion on the Home Rule Bill', p. 601; Bosworth Smith, 'Liberal party and home rule'; Huxley, *Huxley*, iii, 39; Goschen, *Disruption bill*, p. 18; Tyndall, *Perverted politics*, pp. 8, 13; (Chamberlain) Steele, 'Gladstone and Ireland', p. 85; (Bright) Morley, *Gladstone*, iii, 327. See also Holland, *Devonshire*, i, 403; Hutton, 'Mr Gladstone', p. 623; Mack and Armytage, *Hughes*, p. 259.

religion by a rational and ethical one. But at the heart of their objection was distaste for Gladstone's renunciation of the responsibilities of leadership. The unionists considered that, in failing to give a lead, he was acting immorally, and was denying the duty imposed upon Britain by God. In his speech on the first reading of the 1886 Home Rule Bill, Hartington warned against making the mistake of trying to 'escape' from 'our legislative responsibility', which was to uphold 'the undisputed supremacy of the law' (which the Protestant minority in Ireland relied upon Britain to do).[45] To refuse to act in this way was, whig-liberals maintained, to renounce all the sentiments and principles upon which Liberal politics had once been based.[46] The proper function of politics was to give 'guidance' and to teach 'principles' to the people: to 'tell them what is the nature of human society, what are the limits in which it can be modified by any causes external to the individuals who comprise it'. Gladstone, however, offered not intellectual superiority, but emotional communion.[47]

Gladstone and his followers saw home rule in a very different light from whig-liberals: as granting self-government to a nation whose capacity to rule herself had been unfairly doubted on social and religious grounds – because she was poor and small, and because she was primarily Catholic. As Hammond pointed out many years ago, the Gladstonians' view was thus founded upon an identification with popular rights, and a 'mystical' reverence for public opinion.[48] This is not to say that Gladstone raised the issue only in order to uphold such principles: there were many other reasons for his move. He was certainly a vain old man who wished to retain control of the party against the threats of challengers, and thought that most Liberals would follow him wherever he sounded the cry of 'justice'.[49] He undoubtedly wished to try to preserve the union of the 'classes and the masses', and to prevent the whigs and radicals from breaking up the party on property questions. He was unquestionably influenced by electoral arithmetic, and knew that only by wooing the Parnellites could the Liberals form a government. He probably desired to divert nonconformist attention away from disestablishment, as had happened in 1876 as a result of the Bulgarian agitation.[50] Acceptance of these arguments does not, however, imply that Gladstone was not genuinely concerned to solve the Irish problem. Moreover, advocacy of home rule was an effective rallying-cry precisely because the policy was founded on abstract principles: principles which

---

[45] *Hansard*, ccciv, 1261–3, 9 April 1886.
[46] Wormell, *Seeley*, p. 173; Grant Duff, *Out of the past*, i, 217–18; Colaiaco, *Stephen*, p. 191.
[47] Creighton, *Creighton*, p. 348.
[48] Hammond, *Gladstone and the Irish nation*, pp. 532–54.
[49] Cooke and Vincent, *The governing passion*, pp. 55–6.   [50] (Rogers) Dale, *Dale*, p. 736.

Gladstone held in common with most Liberal activists, and to which he himself had approximated in public declarations for so long that it would be churlish to suggest that any hypocrisy was required in enabling him to broach the question.

The basis of the Gladstonians' argument was that the 'people' of Ireland had a right to rule themselves. This, they maintained, was both a historic right,[51] and a moral one. They asserted that it was unethical to refuse the Irish self-government when it was so consistently demanded; they saw the home-rule measure to be based on the 'principle of liberty'.[52] Beesly considered that Ireland was 'not a whit behind our own in political knowledge, public spirit, or morality'.[53] Cowen contended that in the 'principle' of the bill – 'the liberty for a nation to work faithfully after the type of its own individuality – will be found the political gospel of the future'. It was 'contrary to the whole spirit of the law' to 'put a man above the law, and entrust him with discretionary power over the liberty and fortunes of his fellow-subjects, upon the presumption that it will not be abused'. He claimed that what Gladstone was offering was not only liberty, but also the chance for the common man to elevate himself through political participation, on a basis of equality, in a joint enterprise: to 'dress the labourer's face with smiles', to 'educate and enrich him'.[54]

Although the specific problems of the 1870s – problems about ultramontanism and Catholic religious freedom – were not so much at issue in 1886, Gladstone was nonetheless aware that his scheme would advance the religious ends which he had been concerned with in the previous decade. His scheme would ensure, for example, that Catholics were ceded full liberty in matters in which the British had been reluctant to see it granted, such as education. Indeed, one of the reasons why Gladstonians advocated home rule was because the policy was founded on the 'first principles of religion'.[55] Guinness Rogers was astonished by the hypocrisy of opponents of home rule, who upheld 'great principles of religious liberty', and yet shrank 'from applying them when they favour creeds which are obnoxious to themselves'.[56] But, at the same time, the home-rule plan imposed safeguards in order to check the rampant ambition of the unscrupulous leaders of Catholic opinion. Gladstone and his supporters in fact argued that the granting of self-government

---

[51] Gladstone, 'Further notes and queries', p. 321; Stephens, *Freeman*, ii, 175, 292–4.
[52] Russell, *Lawson*, p. 185; *Letters of Acton to Mary Gladstone*, p. 216.
[53] *Socialists against the grain*, p. 11.
[54] Duncan, *Cowen*, pp. 156–8.
[55] (E. C. Lowe) Heeney, *Mission to the middle classes*, pp. 147–8; (Scott Holland) Ollard, *A forty years' friendship*, pp. 116–17; Fisher, *Bryce*, i, 203.
[56] *Ulster problem*, p. 22; *Autobiography*, p. 55.

provided the best means of defeating ultramontane pretensions to exercise temporal power. They considered that the Irish looked to the pope for leadership only because they were denied power themselves: the achievement of home rule would lead to the 'government of the people by the people', and not by 'undue' ecclesiastical influence. They believed that, if the bill were passed, the lay Catholic ratepayer would be able, for the first time, to control the provision of education; he would wish for denominational teaching, but not in thraldom to the priests.[57] Moreover, Gladstone envisaged that the concession of home rule would restore the position of the natural leaders of Irish society, the large landowners, and that these would be able to wrest some influence away from the less elevated class of men from which Irish MPs were increasingly drawn: his bill therefore proposed that the Irish parliament should have two 'orders', one comprised of peers.

In short, the Liberal party was bound together after 1886 by a recognition of the dignity and virtue of the common man. Support for the policy of home rule was one way in which to indicate that recognition; but the policy itself was less important, in the minds of most Liberals, than the principles which underlay it. Perhaps political parties are always united by emotional sympathy rather than by reasoned adherence to a legislative programme. At any rate, the real unifying cry for the Liberals after 1886 was less home rule – with all its attendant difficulties – than 'Gladstone'; it was Gladstone who articulated the Liberals' creed in the most inspiring way, and retained the devotion of the great majority of both nonconformists and aspiring working-men. His performance was inspiring enough, for example, to lead Hardie, Henderson and Lansbury, all devout Christians, to revere him.[58] There were many reasons for the defection of men like these to an independent working-class political movement in the 1890s, and for the eventual success of that movement in attracting most of the Liberals' working-class support; but it would be difficult to identify among them a sense of failure of sympathy between Gladstone and the interests of the politically active late Victorian working-man. The Labour movement in fact inherited many of its ethical aspirations from Gladstonianism – aspirations which, arguably, were to restrain it from many of the enthusiasms of its continental counterparts between 1900 and 1940.

*   *   *

[57] (Gladstone) Rendel, *Personal papers*, pp. 57–8, 65; Rogers, *Ulster problem*, pp. 19–21; MacColl, *Reasons for home rule*, pp. 68–9.

[58] Morgan, *Hardie*, p. 20; Hamilton, *Henderson*, pp. 17, 36; Postgate, *Lansbury*, pp. 20–1 (on 1876–80).

It has been suggested in these pages that it is helpful to interpret the division in the Liberal party in 1886, and politics in the 1870s and 1880s in general, in the light of a difference of opinion about the power of the state, and about the political virtue of the common man. But it would be misleading to imply that the contentious matters were purely abstract, or that the dispute was only one-dimensional. It could be perceived in one or more of a number of ways. For some, the most important questions involved the relationship, on specific points, between the temporal power and religious sects. Others were more concerned with the same problems in a more general way, and would ask how far it was proper for the state to offer moral advice to its citizens. Some would consider that the debate concerned the average elector's capacity to pronounce upon affairs of state; others, while interested in much the same question, would view it more bluntly in class terms.

Practical interests, of a number of kinds, were affected by the dispute. As we have seen throughout the book, some of these were religious interests: the defence of one's freedom to worship as one wished; one's right not to be taxed in order to support the teaching of other sects; the need to reform Church and educational endowments, in order to put them to good use. No less real were a series of economic considerations. On the one hand, propertied Anglican Liberals refused to rely completely on the popular judgment, partly because they feared that it would lead to a new fiscal policy founded on discrimination between classes, and that legislation would be passed which restricted the rights of property. They were also alarmed for the preservation of social stability if all securities for religious instruction in schools were removed, or if the Church were disestablished. On the other hand, when working-men, and indeed nonconformist small businessmen, participated in politics, they did not do so merely because it confirmed their 'dignity' or secured their 'independence': it also reflected their social status and gave them the confidence to assert their power against other economic groups, especially in their own localities. The dislike of the Established Church entertained by nonconformists was affected by their awareness of unsatisfied grievances, those touching burial laws, for example; by the memory of recently satisfied ones, such as the requirement to pay church rates; and by their hostility to the privileged social life which they believed was enjoyed by bishops and country clergymen. In short, it would be wrong to depict the controversies discussed here as either essentially religious or essentially secular: in the minds of most of the participants, the two were intimately intermixed.

But if the dispute between the sections of the party which has been analysed in this book touched on a number of concerns, there is one on which it did not touch, except peripherally, and yet on which it would be easy, at first acquaintance, to assume that it did. This was the controversy about the *legislative* role of the state – the controversy between 'laissez-faire' and 'interventionism'. The points at issue were, rather, concerned with the propriety of the state giving *moral* guidance. Those, like the Gladstonians, who wished it to refrain from doing so, were eager for the executive government to interfere in many other contexts, in order to prevent the operation of vested interests – just as many whig-liberals who saw the state as an organism shunned 'socialist' legislation, believing that it would interfere with the rule of 'natural' or 'Providential' law. All those in both camps, except for a few doctrinaires, were able to define areas in which 'intervention' would promote their ends, as well as areas in which it would retard them.

The research which has recently been undertaken in the politics of other primarily Protestant countries in the nineteenth century has tended to reach much the same conclusion: that, while 'interventionism' as such cannot be assigned the importance, as a divisive issue, which it was once accorded, the power of the state in the lives of its citizens was controversial in other ways, apparently more abstract, but in fact just as real. This was partly because of the importance of the denominational (especially the Catholic) question, and partly because denominations which considered themselves to be at risk of oppression by the state tended to work in formal or informal political alliance with social groups which also wished to assert their dignity and social status. Both these bodies of men were increasingly unsympathetic to 'liberals' who, while usually radical in the sense of being anti-clerical, wished to use the power of the state to check the influence not only of religious sects, but also, for example, of labour organisations. In the 1870s and 1880s – although inevitably in different contexts – the same pattern was apparent in both Germany and the Netherlands. In Germany, this was because Windthorst, the leader of the Catholic Centre party (aided occasionally by the Progressive, Richter), was Bismarck's most formidable parliamentary opponent, not only in resisting the *Kulturkampf*, but also in assisting Social Democrats and racial minorities to fight for the right to participate fully in politics.[59] In the Netherlands, it was because a Calvinist party, led by Kuyper, was able to associate with the Catholics in challenging the anti-clerical education policy of Kappeyne's liberals. Both parties were then able greatly to improve their parliamentary representation by mobilising large numbers of the new voters enfranchised in 1887; this quickly bore legislative fruit in the 1889 Education Act, which secured

[59] M. L. Anderson, *Windthorst: a political biography* (Oxford, 1981).

the position of the voluntary schools.[60] Much the same issues had been to the fore in politics in the United States between the 1830s and 1860. In these decades, the Democrats' political platform emphasised their opposition to the manipulation of the economy by publicly sanctioned banks and corporations; their loyalty to the farmer (including the slave-owner) and their defence of his right to manage his own concerns; their support for the rights of minority sects to enjoy full religious freedom; and their antagonism to any policy which raised the spectre of a Church–state connection. In opposition to them, the Whigs' electoral appeal stemmed partly from a popular desire for the state to further economic progress (by the building, for example, of roads and canals), and partly from mass evangelical fervour, which inspired political crusades in favour of temperance and sabbatarianism – and, more importantly, made anti-Catholicism and, eventually, abolitionism into central political issues. The strains imposed by these crusades broke the old Whig party apart; in the 1850s, much the same forces regrouped, in a more 'populist' format, as the Republican party. The Republicans' emphasis on the sanctity of the rule of law made the Southern secession of 1860 as intolerable to them as Gladstone's call for Irish home rule was to the whig-liberals in 1886.[61]

One consequence of analysing politics in the terms utilised here is that less emphasis has been placed on the occasional squabbles between different radical groups within the British Liberal party in the 1870s and 1880s. In that sense, this book adopts a different perspective from that of many of the historians who have written about the development of the party after 1867. Some of these, indeed, have identified 'sectionalism' among the various radical pressure-groups as the disease which attenuated the party's sense of 'common purpose', and prevented it from working towards a programme of social policy which was sufficiently 'coheren[t]' and 'constructive' to continue to arouse mass electoral enthusiasm.[62] The present author, however, does not believe that parties, in order to prosper, required constantly to be confronting the *status quo*; their need, instead, was to evoke grass-roots loyalty through exploiting emotional rapport, while reassuring mainstream public opinion by appearing competent and responsible in administration. (Even the Liberals' eventual loss of most of their working-class electorate

---

[60] E. H. Kossmann, *The Low Countries 1780–1940* (Oxford, 1978), esp. pp. 301–7, 348–54.

[61] These arguments have been developed by, among others, Ronald Formisano, *The birth of mass political parties: Michigan, 1827–1861* (Princeton, 1971), and Lee Benson, *The concept of Jacksonian democracy: New York as a test case* (Princeton, 1961). A good synthesis of the considerable amount of related work is available in Robert Kelley, *The cultural pattern in American politics: the first century* (New York, 1979).

[62] Hamer, *Liberal politics in the age of Gladstone and Rosebery*, esp. pp. 322–9.

to the Labour party occurred, it is arguable, not because of any inadequacy in the Liberals' legislative programme, but because, by the 1920s, trade unions offered a more effective emotional bond than did the Liberals, who were by then bereft of the fervour which Gladstonianism had supplied. Religion was no longer so important in the political perceptions of most voters; as a result, manifestations of class sentiment, especially in the factory, became more politically significant.) Nor does the present author believe that disputes about legislative priorities between the radical sections – whose membership, of course, overlapped considerably[63] – were as damaging to the party in the 1880s as the opposition of a fair half of the party in the Commons, and most of the peerage, to the activities of nearly all the sections. In the 1880s, there remained a substantial fund of radical enthusiasm for the Liberal cause at grassroots level; the problem was the antagonism to this enthusiasm, and to Gladstone's receptivity to it, in the upper reaches of the party, and among many propertied Anglican voters.[64] As one whig-liberal wrote, in a remarkable attack on the party in 1878, Gladstone had turned the party of '*reason*' and 'enlighten[ment]' into one of 'agitation' and 'sectarianism'. 'Every coterie – from the anti-Vaccinators to the anti-State-Churchmen – which believes itself better than its neighbours, and has its *nostrum* for the cure of society, or the advance of its own dogmas at the expense of common interests, finds in [Gladstone] some measure of sympathy.' And why was this? Because, he argued, of Gladstone's insistence on the sanctity of each individual's judgment, however irresponsible; the necessity of allowing him to find his own 'truth'. This 'sort of talk about "the truth" ', when applied to religious affairs, had made Gladstone 'the idol at once of the High Church bigot and the Dissenting dogmatist, and even of the omniscient Positivist'.[65] When applied to general politics, it seemed to herald instability and possible anarchy.

In the two decades after 1867, most public figures were primarily concerned to ensure that society was well-regulated, and that its citizens worked, as far as their talents allowed, to promote the nation's progress in the directions desired by God. A public figure's approval or disapproval of the Gladstonian Liberal party depended on his assessment of Gladstone and the leaders of provincial political opinion – on his percep-

---

[63] As Professor Hamer himself recognises: *Politics of electoral pressure*, p. 57.

[64] Professor Hamer perceives that his treatment is bound to be affected by his decision to concentrate on *organisations* within the party; since the whig-liberal half of the party was unorganised, it is omitted from his account: *ibid.*, pp. xii–xiv, 76–80. There is some – not total – identity between my argument here and the criticism of Professor Hamer advanced by Dr Barker and Dr Morgan in the *Times Literary Supplement*, 26 September, 14 November 1975, pp. 1094, 1361.

[65] Tulloch, 'Liberal party and the Church of Scotland', p. 260.

tion of their ability to achieve these ends. Whig-liberals increasingly questioned that ability, because their outlook came to differ markedly from that of the Gladstonians. Whig-liberals maintained that affairs of state should be conducted by wise and responsible politicians, not demagogues, sectionalists and ecclesiastics who would indulge the 'materialist' foibles of the people: that, in particular, given man's anti-social nature, the state should not refuse to provide moral guidance for its citizens, unless it wished to endanger the social fabric. Their ideal was for rational, highminded and unselfish politicians to cooperate, in order to promote, not divisive and 'populist' legislation which would foment class and sectional hatred, but practical, sober measures. They called for government, not so much by the *properties*, as by the *educated*.

The Gladstonians, on the other hand, had an immeasurable distrust of human authority, because of the power of evil and sin in the human condition, and the particular susceptibility to temptation of the richest and most powerful. They maintained that moral and spiritual progress was most probable if the state determined to leave religious agencies free to evangelise. (A number of advanced secular radicals, who allied with the 'religious' Gladstonians in the 1880s and 1890s, also believed that freedom from state dictation would promote progress, but in their case this was because they took an optimistic view of human nature.) The Gladstonians envisaged that, from this competition of zealous men, there would arise a genuinely popular morality, representative of the national sentiment. As with any human undertaking, the product would be flawed; but such a policy constituted, in their eyes, the best guarantee that society would always be regulated along lines acceptable to God – a God who, they stressed, spoke with equal force to all mankind, rather than primarily to the 'thinking classes'. They thus saw the politician who wished to dictate a position to God's creatures as being in error: in the words of the proverb which Gladstone recalled, so appropriately, in 1876, '*Vox populi Vox Dei*'.[66] The purpose of the politician, they argued, was not to direct but to inspire. If he succeeded in maintaining the public mind in a state of alertness against manifestations of evil, those manifestations might be checked; if not, prospects were dark. The connection between politics and religion was thus vital; and Gladstone's perspective was nowhere better summarised than when, writing in 1874, he looked forward to the operation of mass democracy in Britain with qualified optimism: 'as to its politics, this country has much less, I think, to fear than to hope; unless through a corruption of its religion – against which, as Conservative or as Liberal, I can perhaps say I have striven all my life long'.[67] The Liberal party was a valuable aid in the mission to arouse

---

[66] Shannon, *Bulgarian agitation*, p. 112.   [67] Purcell, *De Lisle*, ii, 79.

popular political awareness, but Gladstone was only intermittently interested in satisfying mundane party aspirations. His Liberalism developed because he decided to tame and ride the popular radical movement of the 1860s – which had been founded upon the desire to challenge the aristocracy's tenure of debilitating material privileges, and to diminish the legislative and financial impediments to the dignity, comfort and spiritual progress of the working-man. As an Anglican high churchman, Gladstone saw in this movement – once its aggressiveness had been blunted – the means of reinvigorating government, of attacking corruption, of defending denominationalism, of promoting evangelism, and thus of forestalling pressure for fundamental constitutional or fiscal change. His success in promoting these aims was considerable; and, even if they were not all fully realised, his achievement in securing zealous and devoted popular commitment to them was unparalleled. In that – admittedly restricted – sense, Gladstone was surely one of the most influential spiritual leaders of the British people.

Bibliography

The bibliography is divided into the following sections:

A. Manuscript sources .... *page* 453
B. Printed sources 456
   1. Official and semi-official publications 456
   2. Newspapers and periodicals consulted extensively ... 456
   3. Principal works of reference 456
   4. Contemporary writings 457
   5. Biographies, collections of letters, and diaries 474
C. Printed secondary works 485

Volumes in sections B4, B5 and C are listed alphabetically by author. Works by the same author are listed alphabetically by title in section B4, and by date of publication in sections B5 and C.

The following abbreviations of periodical titles have been used throughout the bibliography:

BM	*Blackwood's Magazine*
BQR	*British Quarterly Review*
CR	*Contemporary Review*
EHR	*English Historical Review*
ER	*Edinburgh Review*
FM	*Fraser's Magazine*, new series
FR	*Fortnightly Review*, new series
HJ	*Historical Journal*
MM	*Macmillan's Magazine*
NC	*Nineteenth Century*
QR	*Quarterly Review*
TR	*Theological Review*
VS	*Victorian Studies*
WR	*Westminster Review*

A. MANUSCRIPT SOURCES

Acland papers: papers of Sir Thomas Acland, Devon record office, Exeter.
Acton papers: papers of 1st Baron Acton, University library, Cambridge.
Avebury papers: papers of Sir John Lubbock, 1st Baron Avebury, British library, Add. MSS.

Brabourne papers: papers of Edward Knatchbull-Hugessen, 1st Baron Brabourne, Kent Archives Office, Maidstone (by permission of Baron Brabourne).

Brand papers: papers of Henry Brand, 1st Viscount Hampden, House of Lords record office.

Brereton papers: papers of J. L. Brereton, Homerton college, Cambridge (by permission of the Trustees of Homerton).

Bright papers: papers of John Bright (including the Bright–Northy papers), British library, Add. MSS.

Brodrick papers: papers of G. C. Brodrick (including cuttings of his *Times* leading articles), Merton college, Oxford.

Bryce papers: papers of 1st Viscount Bryce, Bodleian library, Oxford.

Butt papers: papers of Isaac Butt, National library of Ireland.

Cairns papers: papers of 1st Earl Cairns, Public record office, Kew.

Cardwell papers: papers of 1st Viscount Cardwell, Public record office, Kew.

Carnarvon papers: papers of 4th earl of Carnarvon, British library.

Cartwright papers: papers of W. C. Cartwright, Northamptonshire record office, Northampton.

Chamberlain papers: papers of Joseph Chamberlain, University library, Birmingham.

Chatsworth papers: papers of 7th and 8th dukes of Devonshire, Chatsworth (by permission of the Trustees of the Chatsworth settlement).

Clarendon papers: papers of the 4th earl of Clarendon, Bodleian library, Oxford (MSS Clar 474–561), and Public record office, Kew (FO 361 i) (by permission of the earl of Clarendon).

Cranbrook papers: papers of Gathorne Hardy, 1st earl of Cranbrook, Ipswich and East Suffolk record office.

Cross papers: papers of 1st Viscount Cross, British library, Add. MSS.

Dalhousie papers: papers of 11th earl of Dalhousie, Scottish record office.

Daunt papers: papers of W. J. O'Neill Daunt, National library of Ireland.

Derby papers: papers of 14th earl of Derby, in the possession of Lord Blake, Queen's college, Oxford.
    Papers of 15th earl of Derby, Liverpool record office (by permission of the earl of Derby).

Dilke papers: papers of Sir Charles Dilke, British library, Add. MSS.

Disraeli papers: papers of Benjamin Disraeli, 1st earl of Beaconsfield, consulted at the University library, Cambridge (microfilm).

Dufferin papers: papers of 1st marquess of Dufferin and Ava, Public record office of Northern Ireland, Belfast.

Ellice papers: papers of Edward Ellice, National library of Scotland.

Emly papers: papers of William Monsell, 1st Baron Emly, National library of Ireland.

Fortescue papers: papers of 3rd Earl Fortescue, Devon record office, Exeter.

Gladstone papers: papers of W. E. Gladstone, British library, Add. MSS.

Glynne–Gladstone papers: papers of W. E. Gladstone and family, Clwyd record office, Hawarden (by permission of Sir William Gladstone).

Granville papers: papers of 2nd Earl Granville, Public record office, Kew.

Grey papers: papers of 3rd Earl Grey, Department of paleography and diplomatic, University of Durham.

Charles Grey papers: papers of General Charles Grey, Department of paleography and diplomatic, University of Durham.

Halifax papers: journal of Charles Wood, 1st Viscount Halifax, consulted at the Borthwick Institute, York (by permission of the earl of Halifax). [See also Hickleton]

Harcourt papers: papers of Sir William Harcourt, Bodleian library, Oxford.

Harrison papers: papers of Frederic Harrison, British library of political and economic science, London.

Harrowby papers: papers of 2nd and 3rd earls of Harrowby, Sandon Hall, Stafford.

Hickleton papers: papers of Charles Wood, 1st Viscount Halifax, consulted on microfilm, University library, Cambridge.

Iddesleigh papers: papers of Sir Stafford Northcote, 1st earl of Iddesleigh, British library, Add. MSS.

Layard papers: papers of Sir Austen Henry Layard, British library, Add. MSS.

Mayo papers: papers of 6th earl of Mayo, National library of Ireland.

Melly papers: papers of George Melly, Liverpool record office.

Minto papers: papers of 3rd earl of Minto, National library of Scotland.

Monk Bretton papers: papers of J. G. Dodson, 1st Baron Monk Bretton, Bodleian library, Oxford.

Mundella papers: papers of A. J. Mundella, University library, Sheffield.

Northbrook papers: papers of 1st earl of Northbrook, India Office library.

O'Hagan papers: papers of 1st Baron O'Hagan, Public record office of Northern Ireland, Belfast.

Ossington papers: papers of J. E. Denison, 1st Viscount Ossington, Department of manuscripts, University of Nottingham.

Phillimore papers: papers of Sir Robert Phillimore, Christ Church, Oxford.

Pim papers: papers of Jonathan Pim, Trinity college, Dublin.

Playfair papers: papers of 1st Baron Playfair, Imperial college, London.

Richmond papers: papers of 6th duke of Richmond, West Sussex county record office, Chichester.

Ripon papers: papers of 1st marquess of Ripon, British library, Add. MSS.

Rosebery papers: papers of 5th earl of Rosebery, National library of Scotland.

Russell papers: papers of 1st Earl Russell, Public record office, Kew.

Salisbury papers: papers of 3rd marquess of Salisbury, Hatfield House.

Selborne papers: papers of Roundell Palmer, 1st earl of Selborne, Lambeth Palace library.

Shaftesbury papers: papers of 7th earl of Shaftesbury, Broadlands (consulted at the National register of archives, Chancery Lane).

Stanley papers: papers of A. P. Stanley, Bodleian library, Oxford.

Stanmore papers: papers of Arthur Gordon, 1st Baron Stanmore, British library, Add. MSS.

Strachie papers: papers of Chichester Fortescue, 1st Baron Carlingford, and his family, Somerset county record office, Taunton.

Tait papers: papers of A. C. Tait, Lambeth Palace library.

Teeling/O'Hagan papers: papers of 1st Baron O'Hagan, National library of Ireland.

Trelawny papers: diary of Sir John Trelawny, Bodleian library, Oxford.

Trinity college, Dublin papers: correspondence of H. A. Bruce and of Lord Wodehouse, 1865, on the Irish university question (2161).

Wilberforce papers: papers of Samuel Wilberforce, Bodleian library, Oxford.

B. PRINTED SOURCES

1. Official and semi-official publications

Census of Great Britain 1851: religious worship, England and Wales: reports and tables, HC (1852–3), lxxxix, 1.

Census of Great Britain 1851: religious worship, Scotland: reports and tables, HC (1854), lix, 301.

Hansard's *Parliamentary debates*, 3rd series.

2. Newspapers and periodicals consulted extensively

Bee-hive
Daily News
Economist
Manchester Guardian
Nonconformist
Pall Mall Gazette
Scotsman
Spectator
Times
Vanity Fair Album

3. Principal works of reference

The annual register, 1869–74.
The Balliol college register: second edition: 1833–1933, ed. Sir I. Elliott, Oxford, 1934.
Bateman's great landowners of Great Britain and Ireland, London, 1879 edn.
British historical facts 1830–1900, ed. C. Cook and B. Keith, London, 1975.
British parliamentary election results 1832–1885, ed. F. W. S. Craig, London, 1977.
Burke's peerage.
The Catholic directory, 1869–70, 1873.
The complete peerage.
A concise dictionary of Irish biography, ed. J. S. Crone, Dublin, 1937.
Congregational year book, 1869–73.
Dictionary of labour biography, ed. J. M. Bellamy and J. Saville, 7 vols., London, 1972–84.
Dictionary of national biography.
Dod's parliamentary companion, 1869–75.
Journals of the House of Lords, 1857–95.
Modern English biography, ed. F. Boase, 6 vols., Truro, 1892–1921.
Parliamentary buff book: being an analysis of the divisions of the House of Commons, ed. T. N. Roberts, London, 1870–2.
Parliamentary election results in Ireland, 1801–1922, ed. B. M. Walker, Dublin, 1978.
Rugby school register: volume I: from April 1675 to October 1857, ed. G. A. Solly, Rugby, 1933.
The Wellesley index to Victorian periodicals 1824–1900, ed. W. E. Houghton, 3 vols., Toronto, 1966–79.

4. Contemporary writings

Abbott, E. A., 'The Church and the congregation', in *Essays on Church policy*, ed. W. L. Clay, London, 1868, pp. 158–91.

Aberdare, 1st Baron, *Lectures and addresses*, privately printed, 1900?

Abram, W. A., 'Social condition and political prospects of the Lancashire workmen', *FR*, iv (Oct. 1868), 426–41.

Acton, 1st Baron, *Essays on Church and state*, ed. D. Woodruff, London, 1952.

'The history of freedom in antiquity', in *Essays on the liberal interpretation of history: selected papers by Lord Acton*, ed. W. H. McNeill, Chicago, 1967, pp. 243–70 (1877).

Adams, F., *History of the elementary school contest in England*, together with Morley, J., *The struggle for national education*, ed. A. Briggs, Brighton, 1972 (1882; 1873).

Address of the Home Government Association to the people of Ireland, Dublin, 1871.

Akroyd, E., *The Church, in its relation to the state and nonconformists*, Leeds, 1872.

On the present attitude of political parties, London, 1874.

Allon, H., *Religious reasons for disestablishment*, Bolton, 1872.

'Why nonconformists desire disestablishment', *CR*, xvii (June 1871), 365–98.

'The worship of the Church', in *Ecclesia: Church problems considered, in a series of essays*, ed. H. R. Reynolds, London, 1870, pp. 393–462.

Anon., 'Catholicism and papal infallibility', *BQR*, lviii (July 1873), 60–103.

'The conference of nonconformists at Manchester', *BQR*, lv (Apr. 1872), 505–29.

'The Eastern question', *FM*, iii (Feb. 1871), 174–83.

'The Established Church and its defenders', *BQR*, lx (Oct. 1874), 476–514.

'The genius of nonconformity and the progress of society', *BQR*, liv (July 1871), 127–55.

'The Gladstone administration', *WR*, xliii (Jan. 1873), 208–41.

'The Gladstone administration', *BQR*, lviii (July 1873), 189–215.

'Home government for Ireland', *FM*, iv (July 1871), 1–12.

'Irish university education and the ministerial crisis', *WR*, xliii (Apr. 1873), 529–51.

'The Irish university question – attempts at legislation', *FM*, vii (Apr. 1873), 514–24.

Mr Gladstone and the Birmingham Protestant Association, Birmingham, 1871.

'Mr Gladstone's retirement from the Liberal leadership', *BQR*, lxi (Apr. 1875), 478–99.

'Mr Matthew Arnold and puritanism', *BQR*, lii (July, Oct. 1870), 170–99, 386–419.

'Our Irish policy', *FM*, vii (June 1873), 778–89.

'Papal Rome and Catholic reform', *ER*, cxli (Apr. 1875), 554–84.

'Parties in the Episcopal Church', *BQR*, liii (Apr. 1871), 352–91.

'A policy for Ireland', *FM*, viii (Sept. 1873), 273–83.

Political portraits: characters of some of our public men, London, 1873.

'Political prospects', *FM*, v (Jan. 1872), 1–16.

'Religion as a subject of national education', *WR*, xliii (Jan. 1873), 111–46.

'Russia and Turkey', *FM*, ix (June 1874), 671–87.

'The Scotch education settlement of 1872', *WR*, xlii (Oct. 1872), 401–14.

'The tory administration and its whig admirers', *BQR*, lx (July 1874), 171–94.

'The turn of the tide: what does it mean?', *FM*, ix (Mar. 1874), 269–80.

'Ultramontanism and civil allegiance', *BQR*, lxi (Apr. 1875), 442–78.

Argyll, 8th duke of, 'Christian socialism', *NC*, xxxvi (Nov. 1894), 690–707.
'Disestablishment', *CR*, xxxi (Jan. 1878), 217–55.
Irish nationalism: an appeal to history, London, 1893.
'Morality and politics', *CR*, xxx (July 1877), 319–33.
The philosophy of belief or law in Christian theology, London, 1896.
'Presbytery examined': an essay, critical and historical, on the ecclesiastical history of Scotland since the Reformation, London, 2nd edn, 1849.
The reign of law, London, 1867.
Some words of warning to the presbyterians of Scotland, Edinburgh, 1890.
The unity of nature, London, 1884.
The unseen foundations of society: an examination of the fallacies and failures of economic science due to neglected elements, London, 1893.
Arnold, M., 'The Church of England: an address delivered at Sion college', *MM*, xxxiii (Apr. 1876), 481–94.
The complete prose works of Matthew Arnold, ed. R. H. Super, 11 vols., Ann Arbor (Mich.), 1960–77.
Culture and anarchy, ed. J. Dover Wilson, Cambridge, 1932 edn (1869).
'The future of Liberalism' (1880), in Super, *Prose works*, ix, 136–60.
'Higher schools and universities in Germany: preface to the second edition' (1874), in Super, *ibid.*, vii, 90–130.
'Irish Catholicism and British Liberalism' (1878), in Super, *ibid.*, viii, 321–47.
'Literature and dogma: an essay towards a better apprehension of the bible' (1873), in Super, *ibid.*, vi, 139–411.
'The nadir of Liberalism' (1886), in Super, *ibid.*, xi, 54–77.
'On the study of Celtic literature' (1867), in Super, *ibid.*, iii, 291–395.
'Pagan and medieval religious sentiment' (1864), in Super, *ibid.*, iii, 212–31.
'The political crisis' (1886), in Super, *ibid.*, xi, 78–81.
The popular education of France with notices of that of Holland and Switzerland, London, 1861.
'Preface to *Irish essays*' (1882), in Super, *Prose works*, ix, 312–17.
'St Paul and Protestantism' (1870), in Super, *ibid.*, vi, 1–127.
'An unregarded Irish grievance' (1881), in Super, *ibid.*, ix, 295–311.
Arthur, W., *Shall the loyal be deserted and the disloyal set over them? An appeal to Liberals and nonconformists*, London, 1886.
Avebury, 1st Baron, *Addresses, political and educational*, London, 1879.
Peace and happiness, London, 1909.
The pleasures of life, parts I and II in one volume, London, 1891.
Prehistoric times, as illustrated by ancient remains, and the manners and customs of modern savages, London, 1865.
Bagehot, W., *The English constitution*, London, 1963 edn (1867 and 1872).
Barry, A., 'The new school boards', *QR*, cxxxi (July 1871), 263–300.
True education: 'the truth shall make you free', London, 1870.
Baxter, W. E., *Hints to thinkers; or, lectures for the times*, London, 1860.
Beaconsfield, 1st earl of, *Addresses on education, finances, and politics*, London, 1873.
Speech . . . at the banquet of the National Union of Conservative and Constitutional Associations. At the Crystal Palace, on Monday, June 24th, 1872, London, 1872.
Speech of the right hon. B. Disraeli MP at the Free Trade Hall, Manchester, April 3, 1872, London, 1872.
Beesly, E. S., 'The Galway judgment', *FR*, xii (July 1872), 39–50.
Home Rule, London, 1886.
Letters to the working classes, London, 1870.
Socialists against the grain: or, the price of holding Ireland, London, 1887.

Begg, J., *The Duke of Argyll's bill on national education considered: with some remarks on Scotch legislation and the statement of the United Presbyterian committee*, Edinburgh, 1869.

Bentinck, G. C., *The completion of St Paul's: a letter*, London, 1874.

Blackie, J. S., *Democracy: a debate between Professor Blackie, of Edinburgh; and the late Ernest Jones, of Manchester. Held at Edinburgh, January, 1867*, London, 2nd edn, 1885.

Essays on subjects of moral and social interest, Edinburgh, 1890.

What does history teach? Two Edinburgh lectures, London, 1886.

Blackley, M. J. J., with W. L. Blackley, *Thrift and national insurance as a security against pauperism [by W. L. Blackley]; with a memoir of the late Rev. Canon Blackley and reprint of his essays*, London, 1906.

Brabourne, 1st Baron, *Facts and fictions in Irish history: a reply to Mr Gladstone*, Edinburgh, 1886.

'Mr Gladstone on "The Irish demand" ', *NC*, xxi (Mar. 1887), 397–414.

Mr Knatchbull-Hugessen's speech upon education, spoken at Sandwich, London, 1872.

'The session and the ministry', *ER*, cxl (Oct. 1874), 549–89.

Brereton, J. L., 'Cavendish college: an experiment in university education', *CR*, xxxiii (Sept. 1878), 361–75.

County education: lecture, London, 1873.

'Middle schools', *CR*, xliv (Dec. 1883), 872–6.

Newness of life and its pledges: two sermons, London, 1867.

School boards: an address, London, 1871.

Bridges, J. H., *Essays and addresses*, London, 1907.

Bright, J., *Disestablishment: speech*, London, 1875.

Brodrick, G. C., *Home rule and justice to Ireland: a letter to the editor of 'The Times'*, Oxford, 1886.

The influence of the older English universities on national education: a paper, London 1875 (Gladstone's copy).

Political studies, London, 1879.

'The progress of democracy in England', *NC*, xiv (Nov. 1883), 907–24.

Unionism: the basis of a national party: an address, Oxford, 1888.

Brodrick, G. C., with W. H. Fremantle, *A collection of the judgments of the Judicial Committee of the Privy Council in ecclesiastical cases relating to doctrine and discipline: with a preface by the lord bishop of London [A. C. Tait] and an historical introduction*, London, 1865.

Browne, E. H., *The position and parties of the English Church: a pastoral letter*, London, 1875.

A speech not spoken: being a letter . . . on the Irish Church Bill, London, 1869.

Bruce, H. A., see Aberdare, 1st Baron.

Bryce, J., *The Holy Roman Empire*, London, 1907 edn.

Butler, H. M., *Public schools: the conditions of their permanence. A sermon*, London, 1867.

Butt, I., *Home government for Ireland. Irish federalism! Its meaning, its objects, and its hopes*, Dublin, 3rd edn, 1871.

The liberty of teaching vindicated: reflections and proposals on the subject of Irish national education, Dublin, 1865.

The parliamentary policy of home rule: an address, Dublin, 1875.

The problem of Irish education: an attempt at its solution, London, 1875.

Caird, J., *Christian manliness: a sermon*, Glasgow, 1871.

The universal religion: a lecture, Glasgow, 1874.

Cairnes, J. E., 'University education in Ireland', *TR*, iii (Jan. 1866), 116–49.

University education in Ireland: a letter to J. S. Mill, Esq., MP, London, 1866.

Cairns, J., *On the disestablishment of the Church of Scotland*, Edinburgh, 1872.

Carlingford, 1st Baron, *Christian profession not the test of citizenship: an essay for the day*, London, 1849.

Carlyle, T., 'Shooting Niagara: and after?', *MM*, xvi (Aug. 1867), 319–36.

Carter, L. M., *Lord Beaconsfield and the Irish Catholic University scheme; or, an alliance between Conservatism and ultramontanism considered as a party move and an imperial policy: a letter*, Dublin, 1879 (Gladstone's copy, British library).

Cartwright, W. C., *To the electors of Oxfordshire*, 1868.

Catholic education: report of a meeting of the Catholics of the diocese of Dublin, held at the cathedral, Marlborough-Street, January 17th, 1872, Dublin, 1872.

Chamberlain, J., 'The Liberal party and its leaders', *FR*, xiv (Sept. 1873), 287–302.

'The next page of the Liberal programme', *FR*, xvi (Oct. 1874), 405–29.

Church, R. W., *The beginning of the middle ages*, London, 1895.

'The Church and nonconformity', *QR*, cxxx (Apr. 1871), 432–62.

Dante and other essays, London, 1888.

The gifts of civilisation and other sermons and lectures delivered at Oxford and at St Paul's, London, new edn, 1880.

Occasional papers selected from the Guardian, the Times, and the Saturday Review 1846–90, 2 vols., London, 1897.

The Oxford movement: twelve years 1833–1845, London, 1900 edn (1891).

'Ritualism', *NC*, ix (Feb. 1881), 201–10.

Saint Anselm, London, 1888 edn (1870).

Clifford, J., *The future of Christianity; or Jesus Christ, the eternal king of men*, London, 1876.

Jesus Christ and modern social life, London, 1872.

A New Testament Church in its relation to the needs and tendencies of the age: a statement, London, 1876.

Coleridge, 1st Baron, 'Convocation', *ER*, cv (Jan. 1857), 78–111.

'The freedom of opinion necessary in an Established Church in a free country', *MM*, xxi (Mar. 1870), 369–76.

Inaugural address delivered to the members of the Philosophical Institution Edinburgh at the opening of the session 1870–71, Edinburgh, 1870.

Conder, E. R., *Education and nonconformity: a lecture*, London, 1872.

Congreve, R., *Essays political, social and religious*, London, 1874.

Corrigan, D. J., *University education in Ireland*, Dublin, 1865 (Gladstone's copy, British library).

Courthope, W. J., 'The Crown and the Constitution', *QR*, cxlv (Apr. 1878), 277–328.

'Whigs, Radicals, and Conservatives', *QR*, cl (July 1880), 269–304.

Cowell, H., 'The Conservative party and national education', *BM*, cxiv (Dec. 1873), 739–51.

'The Liberal party and national education', *BM*, cxiv (Nov. 1873), 627–42.

'Liberty, equality, fraternity: Mr John Stuart Mill', *BM*, cxiv (Sept. 1873), 347–62.

'The political situation', *BM*, cxv (Apr. 1874), 504–18.

'The prospects of the session', *BM*, cxvii (Mar. 1875), 396–406.

'Review of the session', *BM*, cxvi (Sept. 1874), 249–66.

Cowper, 7th Earl, 'Desultory reflections of a whig', *NC*, xiii (May 1883), 729–39.

Crompton, H., 'Class legislation', *FR*, xiii (Feb. 1873), 205–17.

'The government and class legislation', *FR*, xiv (July 1873), 25–40.

Croskerry, T., 'Drunkenness, abstinence, and restraint', *ER*, cxxxvii (Apr. 1873), 398–421.

'Froude's *English in Ireland*', *ER*, cxxxvii (Jan. 1873), 122–53.

'Froude's "Irish parliament and Irish rebellion"', *ER*, cxxxix (Apr. 1874), 468–506.

'The Irish Roman Catholic laity', *FM*, vi (Oct. 1872), 491–6.

'Irish university education', *ER*, cxxxv (Jan. 1872), 166–96.

'Trench's "Ierne"; Irish federalism', *ER*, cxxxiii (Apr. 1871), 501–29.

Crosskey, H. W., 'The nonconformist programme and policy', *TR*, ix (July 1872), 356–72.

Dale, R. W., 'Anglicanism and Romanism', *BQR*, xliii (Apr. 1866), 281–338.

The doctrine of the Real Presence and of the Lord's Supper', in *Ecclesia: Church problems considered, in a series of essays*, ed. H. R. Reynolds, London, 1870, pp. 315–90.

The evangelical revival and other sermons: with an address on the work of the Christian ministry in a period of theological decay and transition, London, 1880.

The Holy Spirit in relation to the ministry, the worship, and the work of the Church, London, 2nd edn, 1869.

'Mr Matthew Arnold and the nonconformists', *CR*, xiv (July 1870), 540–71.

'The nonconformists and the educational policy of the government', *CR*, xxii (Sept. 1873), 643–62.

The politics of nonconformity: a lecture, Manchester, 1871.

Protestantism: its ultimate principle, London, 1874.

The Scotch Education Bill: a speech, Birmingham, 1872.

Davies, J. Llewelyn, 'Congregationalism and the Church of England', *CR*, xvii (Apr. 1871), 15–31.

'Erastianism *versus* ecclesiasticism', *CR*, xxx (June 1877), 142–64.

'Introduction' to *The national Church: essays on its history and constitution and criticism of its present administration*, by H. Hensley Henson, London, 1908.

The Irish Church question: a parochial system, London, 1868.

'Mr Matthew Arnold's new religion of the bible', *CR*, xxi (May 1873), 842–66.

Order and growth: as involved in the spiritual constitution of human society, London, 1891.

'Secularism and Mr Maurice's theology', *CR*, xxiv (June 1874), 23–39.

Social questions: from the point of view of Christian theology, London, 1885.

The things above in relation to education and science: a sermon, London, 1877.

'The voluntary principle', in *Essays on Church policy*, ed. W. L. Clay, London, 1868, pp. 47–90.

Warnings against superstition: in four sermons for the day, London, 1874.

Derby, 15th earl of, 'University education and teaching' (1875), in *Rectorial addresses delivered before the university of Edinburgh 1859–1899*, ed. A. Stodart-Walker, London, 1900, pp. 171–84.

Devonshire, 8th duke of, *An address delivered before the university of Edinburgh, on his inauguration as lord rector*, London, 1879.

Dicey, A. V., *Why England maintains the union: a popular reading of 'England's case against home rule'*, prepared by C. E. S., London, 1887.

Dilke, C., *The fall of Prince Florestan of Monaco*, London, 1874.

Disraeli, B., see Beaconsfield, 1st earl of.

Dodson, J. G., see Monk Bretton, 1st Baron.

Dowden, E., 'Irish opinion on the Home Rule Bill', *FR*, liii (May 1893), 593–609.

'True Conservatism – what it is', *CR*, xii (Oct. 1869), 267–81.

Duff, M. E. Grant, 'British interests in the East', *NC*, vii (Apr. 1880), 658–76.
  'The changes most wanted in Aberdeen university' (1870), in *Rectorial addresses delivered in the universities of Aberdeen 1835–1900*, ed. P. J. Anderson, Aberdeen, 1902, pp. 153–69.
  'Must we then believe Cassandra?', *FR*, xvi (Nov. 1874), 581–604.
  'Russia', *NC*, i (Mar., Apr. 1877), 72–96, 298–314.
  'The situation', *NC*, iii (Mar. 1878), 571–90.
Emly, 1st Baron, 'University education in Ireland', *Home and Foreign Review*, ii (Jan. 1863), 32–58.
Emmett, J. T., 'The completion of St Paul's', *QR*, cxxxiii (Oct. 1872), 342–86.
  'The state of English architecture', *QR*, cxxxii (Apr. 1872), 295–335.
Ernle, 1st Baron, 'Disestablishment', *QR*, clxxv (July 1892), 258–86.
  'The national party of the future', *QR*, clxix (Oct. 1889), 543–72.
Essays on reform, London, 1867.
Farrar, F. W., *The English clergy, their claims and their position: a sermon*, London, 1875.
Fawcett, H., 'The present position of the government', *FR*, x (Nov. 1871), 544–58.
  Speeches on some current political questions, London, 1873.
Fergusson, J., 'St Paul's cathedral', *CR*, xxiv (Oct. 1874), 750–71.
Fitzmaurice, 1st Baron, *Home rule for Ireland: speech delivered by the Lord Edmond Fitzmaurice, and letter from the right hon. W. E. Gladstone, MP*, Trowbridge, 1887?
Forster, W. E., *Speech of the right hon. W. E. Forster, on November 25, 1873, delivered after laying the memorial stone of the first school built by the Liverpool school board*, London, 1873.
  'The university a trainer of politicians' (1876), in *Rectorial addresses delivered in the universities of Aberdeen 1835–1900*, ed. P. J. Anderson, Aberdeen, 1902, pp. 199–222.
Fortescue, 3rd Earl, *Our next leap in the dark, with postscript on the Corrupt Practices Bill*, London, 1884.
  Public schools for the middle classes, London, 1880.
  Rate-and-tax-aided education: why I joined the Liberty and Property Defence League, London, 3rd edn, 1883.
Fortescue, C. P., see Carlingford, 1st Baron.
Fottrell, G., *Letter containing a scheme of Irish university reform, addressed to the most noble the marquis of Hartington*, Dublin, 1873.
Fraser, J., *Charge delivered at his primary visitation, at the cathedral, Manchester, and St Mary's, Lancaster*, Manchester, 1872.
  National education: a sermon, London, 1868.
  National Education Union: a great demonstration in favour of religious education was held April 14th, 1873, in the Free Trade Hall, Manchester. Speech, Manchester, 1873.
Freeman, E. A., *The chief periods of European history: six lectures . . . with an essay on Greek cities under Roman rule*, London, 1886.
  Disestablishment and disendowment, what are they?, London, 1874.
  'The Eastern Church', *ER*, cvii (Apr. 1858), 322–57.
  'Froude's *History of England – Vol. XII*', *Saturday Review*, xxix (Feb. 1870), 187–8, 221–3.
  'Froude's *Reign of Elizabeth*', *Saturday Review*, xvii (Jan. 1864), 80–2, 142–4; xxii (Oct., Nov. 1866), 519–20, 550–1, 642–4, 677–8.
  The growth of the English constitution from the earliest times, London, 1872.
  Historical essays, 4 vols., I: 3rd edn, 1875; II: 2nd edn, 1880; III: 1879; IV: 1892.
  History of federal government in Greece and Italy, ed. J. B. Bury, London, 1893.

The history of the Norman conquest of England, its causes and its results, 6 vols., Oxford, 1867–79.

'Mahomet', *BQR*, lv (Jan. 1872), 100–35.

'Mr Froude's final volumes', *Saturday Review*, xxix (Jan. 1870), 116–18, 153–5.

'Mr Froude's "Life and times of Thomas Becket, parts I–VI" ', *CR*, xxxi (Mar. 1878), 821–42; xxxii (Apr., June 1878), 116–39, 474–500; xxxiii (Sept. 1878), 213–41.

The Ottoman power in Europe, its nature, its growth, and its decline, London, 1877.

'Prospects of home rule', *FR*, xl (Sept. 1886), 317–33.

The unity of history: the Rede lectures, London, 1872.

Fremantle, W. H., *Christian authority and Christian liberty: a sermon*, London, 1866.

'Convocation, parliament and the prayer-book', *ER*, cxl (Oct. 1874), 427–61.

Lay power in parishes: the most needed Church reform, London, 1869.

'Progress': a sermon, Oxford, 1871.

Fremantle, W. H., ed., with A. Grey, *Church reform*, London, 1888.

Froude, J. A., *Calvinism: an address delivered at St Andrew's*, London, 1871.

The English in Ireland in the eighteenth century, 3 vols., London, 1881 edn, with supplementary chapter (1872–4).

The English in the West Indies or the bow of Ulysses, London, 1888.

History of England from the fall of Wolsey to the defeat of the Spanish Armada, 12 vols., London, 1856–70.

Is Russia wrong? A series of letters by a Russian lady, with a preface by J. A. Froude, London, 2nd edn, 1878.

Life and letters of Erasmus: lectures delivered at Oxford 1893–4, London, 1894.

'Life and times of Thomas Becket, parts I–VI', *NC*, i (June, July 1877), 548–62, 843–56; ii (Aug., Sept., Oct., Nov. 1877), 15–27, 217–29, 389–410, 669–91.

'Party politics', *FM*, x (July 1874), 1–18.

Russia and England from 1876 to 1880: a protest and an appeal by O.K. with a preface by James Anthony Froude, London, 1880.

Short studies on great subjects, 4 vols., London, vols. I–III, 1878 edn, vol. IV, 1883.

Froude, J. A. (with others), *Lights on home rule*, London, 1893.

Gladstone, W. E., *Address delivered at the distribution of prizes in the Liverpool Collegiate Institution, December 21, 1872*, London, 1873.

'Address, 1860', and 'Valedictory address . . . "On the place of ancient Greece in the providential order of the world", 1865', in *Rectorial addresses delivered before the university of Edinburgh 1859–1899*, ed. A. Stodart-Walker, London, 1900, pp. 3–24, 27–76.

'Aggression on Egypt and freedom in the East', *NC*, ii (Aug. 1877), 149–66.

The Church of England and ritualism, London, 1875.

Church principles considered in their results, London, 1840.

A corrected report of the speech of the right hon. W. E. Gladstone, MP at Greenwich, October 28, 1871, London, 1871.

'Count Montalembert on Catholic interests in the nineteenth century', *QR*, xcii (Dec. 1852), 137–56.

'The county franchise and Mr Lowe thereon', *NC*, ii (Nov. 1877), 537–60.

'The declining efficiency of parliament', *QR*, xcix (Sept. 1856), 521–70.

'The duke of Argyll on presbytery', *QR*, lxxxiv (Dec. 1848), 78–105.

'Ecce Homo', London, 1868.

'Further notes and queries on the Irish demand', *CR*, liii (Mar. 1888), 321–39.

'Germany, France, and England', *ER*, cxxxii (Oct. 1870), 554–93.

Gleanings of past years 1843–78, 7 vols., London, 1879.

Later gleanings: a new series of gleanings of past years: theological and ecclesiastical, London, 2nd edn, 1898.
A letter to the right rev. William Skinner, DD, bishop of Aberdeen, and Primus, on the functions of laymen in the Church, ed. M. MacColl, London, 1869 edn (1852).
'Liberty in the East and West', *NC*, iii (June 1878), 1154–74.
'Mr Forster and Ireland', *NC*, xxiv (Sept. 1888), 451–64.
'The new parliament and its work', *QR*, ci (Apr. 1857), 541–84.
'Notes and queries on the Irish demand', *NC*, xxi (Feb. 1887), 165–90.
'On the influence of authority in matters of opinion', *NC*, i (Mar. 1877), 2–22.
'The past and present administrations', *QR*, civ (Oct. 1858), 515–60.
'The paths of honour and of shame', *NC*, iii (Mar. 1878), 591–604.
Proceedings at the opening of Farnworth Park . . . with a report of the oration delivered by the chancellor of the exchequer, Bolton, 1865.
'Prospects political and financial', *QR*, ci (Jan. 1857), 243–84.
'Rejoinder on authority in matters of opinion', *NC*, i (July 1877), 902–26.
Remarks on the royal supremacy as it is defined by reason, history, and the constitution: a letter to the lord bishop of London, London, 1850.
'Russia and England', *NC*, vii (Mar. 1880), 538–56.
'Speech at the Science and Art school, Oldham, 18 Dec. 1867', *The Educational Record, with the proceedings of the British and Foreign Schools Society,* vii (n.s.) (Jan. 1868), 114–16.
'Speeches of Pope Pius IX', *QR*, cxxxviii (Jan. 1875), 266–304.
Speeches of the right honourable William Ewart Gladstone, MP in South-west Lancashire, October 1868, Liverpool, 1868.
The state in its relations with the Church, 2 vols. in 1, London, 4th edn, 1841.
Substance of a speech on the motion of Lord John Russell for a committee of the whole House, with a view to the removal of the remaining Jewish disabilities, London, 1848.
The Vatican decrees in their bearing on civil allegiance: a political expostulation, London, 1874.
'The war and the peace', *Gentleman's Magazine,* i (n.s.) (Aug. 1856), 140–55.
Wedgwood: an address, London, 1863.
Gleig, G. R., 'The Church bill in the Lords', *BM*, cvi (July 1869), 111–24.
'The coming elections', *BM*, civ (Nov. 1868), 622–44.
'The great problem: can it be solved?', *BM*, cxvii (Jan. 1875), 132–44.
'The Lords and the Commons', *BM*, cvi (Aug. 1869), 240–56.
'Mr Gladstone and the state in its relations with the Church', *BM*, ciii (May 1868), 626–47.
'Shall we follow this man?', *BM*, civ (July 1868), 109–28.
Gore, C., *Christianity applied to the life of men and of nations,* ed. R. H. Tawney, London, 2nd edn, 1940 (1920).
ed., *Essays in aid of the reform of the Church,* London, 1898.
Goschen, 1st Viscount, *The cultivation of the imagination: an address,* London, 1878.
The disruption bill: speeches of the right hon. G. J. Goschen, MP, and the right hon. the marquis of Hartington, MP, in the House of Commons, April 13th 1886, London, 1886.
'Intellectual interest' (1888), in *Rectorial addresses delivered in the universities of Aberdeen 1835–1900,* ed. P. J. Anderson, Aberdeen, 1902, pp. 259–79.
Mental training and useful knowledge: an address, London, 1879.
Greg, W. R., 'Cost of party government', *QR*, cxxvi (Apr. 1869), 394–413.
Enigmas of life: with a prefatory memoir edited by his wife, London, 18th edn, 1891.
'Froude's *English in Ireland*', *QR*, cxxxiv (Jan. 1873), 169–85.

'Government dealing with Irish crime', *QR*, cxxviii (Apr. 1870), 560–76.

The great duel; its true meaning and uses, London, 1871.

'Ireland once more', *QR*, cxxv (July 1868), 254–86.

'Is a Christian life feasible?', *CR*, xxi (Apr. 1873), 680–700.

Literary and social judgments, London, 2nd edn, 1869.

Miscellaneous essays, London, 1882.

'Mr Gladstone's *Apologia*', *QR*, cxxvi (Jan. 1869), 121–34.

Political problems for our age and country, London, 1870.

'Priests, parliaments, and electors', *QR*, cxxxiii (July 1872), 276–92.

'The proletariat on a false scent', *QR*, cxxxii (Jan. 1872), 251–94.

'Realities of Irish life', *QR*, cxxvi (Jan. 1869), 61–80.

'Rocks ahead; or, the warnings of Cassandra. Part III', *CR*, xxiv (Aug. 1874), 339–59.

'Scientific *versus* amateur administration', *QR*, cxxvii (July 1869), 41–68.

'The truth about Ireland', *QR*, cxxvii (July 1869), 270–92.

Grey, 3rd Earl, 'The armed peace of Europe', *QR*, cxli (Jan. 1876), 81–103.

Parliamentary government considered with reference to reform: a new edition, containing suggestions for the improvement of our representative system, and an examination of the Reform Bills of 1859 and 1861, London, 1864.

'South Africa', *NC*, viii (Nov. 1880), 933–53.

Hall, C. Newman, *Atonement: the fundamental fact of Christianity*, London, 1893.

Hamley, W. G., 'Dragging out a wretched existence', *BM*, cxiv (Aug. 1873), 244–64.

'The late attempt at suicide', *BM*, cxiii (Apr. 1873), 484–504.

'Mr Gladstone's night attack and its results', *BM*, cxv (Mar. 1874), 379–96.

'Our fair wind – setting sail', *BM*, cxv (May 1874), 643–54.

'The second Gladstone administration', *BM*, cxiii (June 1873), 740–60.

Harcourt, W. V., *The Irish Church*, London, 1868.

A speech, addressed to his constituents, in the Corn Exchange, at Oxford, on December 21, 1874, London, 1875.

Hardcastle, J. A., 'Mr Disraeli's "Glasgow speeches"', *ER*, cxxxix (Jan. 1874), 271–88.

'Mr Miall on disestablishment', *ER*, cxxxv (Apr. 1872), 366–93.

Harrison, F., 'Church and state', *FR*, xxi (May 1877), 653–75.

'The creeds – old and new', *NC*, viii (Nov. 1880), 526–49.

'The effacement of England', *FR*, ix (Feb. 1871), 145–66.

'The future of agnosticism', *FR*, xlv (Jan. 1889), 144–56.

The meaning of history and other historical pieces, London, 1894.

'Neo-Christianity', *WR*, xviii (Oct. 1860), 293–332.

Order and progress: thoughts on government: studies of political crises, ed. M. S. Vogeler, Hassocks, 1975 (1875).

'Politics and a human religion': a discourse, London, 1885.

The positive evolution of religion: its moral and social reaction, London, 1913.

The present and the future: a positivist address, London, 1880.

'Public affairs', *FR*, xiv (Oct. 1873), 548–56.

'Public affairs', *FR*, xv (Feb. 1874), 282–96.

'The religion of inhumanity', *FR*, xiii (June 1873), 677–99.

'The religious and conservative aspects of positivism. Part I', *CR*, xxvi (Nov. 1875), 992–1012.

'The soul and future life', *NC*, i (June 1877), 623–36.

Hartington, marquess of, see Devonshire, 8th duke of.

Headlam, S., *The place of the bible in secular education: an open letter to the teachers under the London school board*, London, 1903.
    Priestcraft and progress; being sermons and lectures, London, 1878.
Hobhouse, L. T., *Democracy and reaction*, ed. P. F. Clarke, Brighton, 1972 edn (1904).
Hoey, J. C., 'The Irish University Bill', *Dublin Review*, xxii (Apr. 1874), 448–69.
Home Government Association, Dublin, 1871.
Hook, W. F., *The disestablishment of the theocracy: a sermon*, Oxford, 1868.
    On the means of rendering more efficient the education of the people: a letter, London, 8th edn, 1846.
Horsman, E., *Five speeches on ecclesiastical affairs*, London, 1849.
    Speech . . . at the public dinner given to him at Stroud, January 31st, 1867, London, 1867.
Hughes, T., *A layman's faith*, London, 1868 edn (1861).
    The manliness of Christ, London, 1879.
    'National education: more practical aims for the guidance of Liberal policy', *MM*, xxxv (Jan. 1877), 230–8.
    The old Church; what shall we do with it?, London, 1878.
    Tom Brown at Oxford, London, 1903 edn (1861).
    Tom Brown's schooldays, London, 1966 edn (1857).
Hutton, H. D., 'The Irish university question', *FR*, x (Dec. 1871), 748–62.
Huxley, T. H., 'Administrative nihilism', *FR*, x (Nov. 1871), 525–43.
    'A liberal education; and where to find it: an inaugural address', *MM*, xvii (Mar. 1868), 367–78.
    'The school boards: what they can do and what they may do', in *T. H. Huxley on education: a selection from his writings with an introductory essay and notes*, ed. C. Bibby, Cambridge, 1971, pp. 108–17.
Innes, A. Taylor, *The Church of Scotland crisis 1843 and 1874: and the duke of Argyll*, Edinburgh, 1874 (Gladstone's copy, British library).
    'Dean Stanley at Edinburgh', *CR*, xix (Mar. 1872), 443–60.
Jelf, W. E., *Supremacy of scripture: an examination into the principles and statements advanced in the essay on the Education of the World: in a letter to the Rev. Dr Temple*, London, 1861 (Hawarden copy).
Jenkins, J. E., *Barney Geoghegan, MP; and home rule at St Stephen's*, London, 1872.
    The education of the people: an address, London, 1870.
    Ginx's baby: his birth and other misfortunes, London, 6th edn, 1871 (1870).
    Glances at inner England: a lecture, London, 1874.
    Lord Bantam, 2 vols., London, 1872.
    'Two solutions', *FM*, iii (Apr. 1871), 451–6.
Jennings, L. J., 'Mr Gladstone and Ireland', *QR*, clxiii (July 1886), 257–88.
    'The public questions at issue', *QR*, cxxv (Oct. 1868), 540–72.
Jex-Blake, T. W., 'Church reform by comprehension, AD 1689 and 1873', *MM*, xxvii (Mar. 1873), 417–23.
Jowett, B., *The dialogues of Plato: translated into English with analyses and introductions*, 4 vols., Oxford, 4th edn, 1953.
    Sermons on faith and doctrine, ed. W. H. Fremantle, London, 1901.
Kingsley, C., *Alexandria and her schools: four lectures*, Cambridge, 1854.
    Alton Locke tailor and poet: an autobiography, ed. E. A. Cripps, Oxford, 1983 edn (1850).
    'God's feast': a sermon*, London, 1869.
    Hypatia, London, 1907 edn (1853).
    The limits of exact science as applied to history: an inaugural lecture delivered before the university of Cambridge, Cambridge, 1860.

'Science: a lecture delivered at the Royal Institution', *FM*, lxxiv (July 1866), 15–28.

Knatchbull-Hugessen, E. H., see Brabourne, 1st Baron.

Layard, A. H., 'Architecture', *QR*, cvi (Oct. 1859), 285–330.

Discoveries in the ruins of Nineveh and Babylon; with travels in Armenia, Kurdistan and the desert: being the result of a second expedition undertaken for the trustees of the British Museum, London, 1853.

'Fresco-painting', *QR*, civ (Oct. 1858), 277–325.

'German, Flemish, and Dutch art', *QR*, cix (Apr. 1861), 463–96.

'The influence of education upon character' (1855), in *Rectorial addresses delivered in the universities of Aberdeen 1835–1900*, ed. P. J. Anderson, Aberdeen, 1902, pp. 73–91.

'Italian painting', *QR*, cxxxiii (July 1872), 119–47.

Nineveh and its remains: with an account of a visit to the Chaldaean Christians of Kurdistan, and the Yezidis, or devil-worshippers; and an enquiry into the manners and arts of the ancient Assyrians, 2 vols., London, 1849.

'Objects of the war', *QR*, xcvii (June 1855), 245–90.

Savonarola and Italy, London, 1866.

'The Turks and the Greeks', *QR*, xciv (Mar. 1854), 509–58.

Lewis, J. D., 'Clergy and laity', *FR*, xvi (Dec. 1874), 782–97.

Liddon, H. P., *The life of faith and the Athanasian Creed: a sermon*, London, 1872.

Some elements of religion: Lent lectures 1870, London, 4th edn, 1883.

Lowe, R., see Sherbrooke, 1st Viscount.

Lubbock, Sir J., see Avebury, 1st Baron.

MacColl, M., *The 'damnatory clauses' of the Athanasian Creed rationally explained in a letter to the right hon. W. E. Gladstone, MP*, London, 1872.

The education question and the Liberal party, London, 1902.

Is there not a cause? A letter to Colonel Greville-Nugent, MP, on the disestablishment of the Irish Church: with a vindication of Mr Gladstone's consistency, London, 1868.

Lawlessness, sacerdotalism, and ritualism discussed in six letters addressed, by his permission to the right hon. Lord Selborne, London, 3rd edn, 1875.

Papal infallibility and its limitations, London, 1873.

'The rationale of ritualism', *CR*, xvii (May 1871), 176–91.

Reasons for home rule, London, 4th edn, 1886.

'Some current fallacies about Turks, Bulgarians, and Russians', *NC*, ii (Dec. 1877), 831–42.

Macfie, R. A., *The Scotch Church question: a letter of an heritor in a country parish*, Edinburgh, 1885.

Macgregor, J., *The Rob Roy on the Jordan, Nile, Red Sea, and Gennesareth etc.: a canoe cruise in Palestine and Egypt, and the waters of Damascus*, London, 2nd edn, 1870.

Mackarness, J. F., *A charge delivered to the diocese of Oxford, at his primary visitation, April 16, 1872*, Oxford, 1872.

Macknight, T., *Ulster as it is: or twenty-eight years' experience as an Irish editor*, 2 vols., London, 1896.

Mackonochie, A. H., 'Disestablishment and disendowment', *NC*, i (June 1877), 686–706.

'A suggested act for the separation of Church and state', *NC*, iv (Oct. 1878), 627–42.

Maclaren, A., *Religious equality, in its connection with national and religious life: a lecture*, Manchester, 1871.

'Time for thee to work': the annual sermon for the National Bible Society of Scotland*, Edinburgh, 1874.

Week-day evening addresses delivered in Manchester, London, new edn, 1879 (Hawarden copy).

Maguire, J. F., *Home government for Ireland*, Dublin, 1872.

Mallock, W. H., *The new republic: culture, faith, and philosophy in an English country house*, ed. J. Lucas, Leicester, 1975 edn (1877).

Manning, H. E., *Caesarism and ultramontanism*, London, 2nd edn, 1874.

Ireland: a letter to Earl Grey, London, 1868.

Martineau, J., *The national Church as a federal union*, London, 1887.

The new affinities of faith: a plea for free Christian union, London, 1869.

Why dissent? An address, London, 1871.

Maurice, F. D., 'The Irish Church Establishment', *CR*, vii (Jan. 1868), 54–65.

Memorial of rector, professors, officers, and students, present, and past, of the Catholic university of Ireland, 1872.

Miall, E., *Bases of belief: an examination of Christianity as a divine revelation by the light of recognised facts and principles: in four parts*, London, 1853 (Hawarden copy).

The bearing of religious equality on the rights of individuals and spiritual communities: a lecture, Manchester, 1873.

Mill, J. S., *On liberty*, ed. G. Himmelfarb, Harmondsworth, 1974 edn (1859).

Moberly, G., *Charge delivered to the clergy and churchwardens of the diocese of Salisbury, at his second visitation*, Salisbury, 1873.

Primary charge to the clergy and churchwardens of the diocese of Salisbury, in August 1870, Salisbury, 1870.

'A modern "symposium": is the popular judgment in politics more just than that of the higher orders?', *NC*, iii, iv (May, July 1878), 797–822, 174–92.

Monk Bretton, 1st Baron, 'The Church, the land, and the Liberals', *ER*, cxxxv (Jan. 1872), 250–92.

'The session and its lessons', *ER*, cxxxiv (Oct. 1871), 564–90.

Monsell, W., see Emly, 1st Baron.

Morley, John, 1st Viscount, *Critical miscellanies*, 3 vols., London, 1908, 1905, 1904 edns.

Edmund Burke: a historical study, London, 1867.

'England and Ireland', *FR*, xxix (Apr. 1881), 407–25.

Ireland's rights and England's duties: a lecture, Blackburn, 1868.

'Irish revolution and English Liberalism', *NC*, xiii (Nov. 1882), 647–66.

'The Liberal eclipse', *FR*, xvii (Feb. 1875), 295–304.

Miscellanies, fourth series, London, 1908.

Nineteenth-century essays, ed. P. Stansky, Chicago, 1970.

On compromise, London, 1874.

'On popular culture: an address', *FR*, xx (Nov. 1876), 632–50.

The Radical programme, by J. Chamberlain and others, ed. D. A. Hamer, Brighton, 1971 edn.

Rousseau, 2 vols., London, 1873.

The struggle for national education (see Adams, F.).

Voltaire, London, 1886 edn (1872).

Morley, John, 1st Viscount (with others), *Handbook of home rule being articles on the Irish question*, London, 2nd edn, 1887.

Mozley, J. B., 'The education of the people', *QR*, cxxviii (Apr. 1870), 473–506.

National Education League: report of a conference of nonconformist ministers, held at Leeds, on Tuesday, January 18, 1870, London, 1870.

National Education Union: authorised report of the educational congress, held in the Town Hall, Manchester, on November 3 and 4, 1869, London, 1869.

O'Reilly, M. W., *Two articles on education*, London, 1863.
Palgrave, W. G., *Essays on Eastern questions*, London, 1872.
Picton, J. A., *The bible in school: a question of ethics*, London, 1901.
  The conflict of oligarchy and democracy: six lectures, London, 2nd edn, 1885.
  'Denominational education from a national point of view', *MM*, xxix (Apr. 1874), 542–6.
  'Moral aspects of the religious difficulty', *FR*, xvi (Sept. 1874), 308–22.
  The transfiguration of religion: a discourse, London, 1878.
Pim, J., *Ireland and the imperial parliament*, Dublin, 1871.
Playfair, 1st Baron, *On primary and technical education: two lectures*, Edinburgh, 1870.
  On teaching universities and examining boards, Edinburgh, 1872.
  'Universities and universities', *MM*, xxxv (Jan. 1877), 205–11.
  Universities in their relation to professional education, Edinburgh, 1873.
Playfair, 1st Baron (with others), *Aspects of modern study being university extension addresses*, London, 1894.
Plunket, D. R., 'The Irish University Bill and the defeat of the ministry', *QR*, cxxxiv (Apr. 1873), 552–79.
Potter, G., 'The Church of England and the people', *FR*, xi (Feb. 1872), 176–90.
  'Working men and the Eastern question', *CR*, xxxviii (Oct. 1876), 851–65.
Price, B., 'Catholicity', *CR*, xii (Oct. 1869), 161–85.
  'The Church of England', *CR*, x (Feb. 1869), 161–77.
  'Disestablishment, and Dean Alford on the Church of the future', *BM*, civ (Nov. 1868), 576–88.
  'The Manchester nonconformists and political philosophy', *BM*, cxi (Mar. 1872), 334–47.
  'Mr Gladstone and disestablishment', *BM*, cv (Feb. 1869), 238–52.
  'The political temper of the nation', *FM*, lxix (Feb. 1864), 135–59.
  'Religious equality and unlimited formulas', *BM*, civ (Oct. 1868), 466–78.
  'University tests', *BM*, cvii (Feb. 1870), 139–60.
  What is education?, London, 1884.
Prothero, R. E., see Ernle, 1st Baron.
Pusey, E. B., *'Blessed are the meek': a sermon*, Oxford, 1876.
  The Church the converter of the heathen: two sermons, Oxford, 1838.
  The Councils of the Church, London, 1857.
  The doctrine of the Real Presence, Oxford, 1855.
  Is healthful reunion impossible? A second letter to the very rev. J. H. Newman, Oxford, 1870.
  The Presence of Christ in the Holy Eucharist, Oxford, 1853.
  The Purchas judgment: a letter of acknowledgment to the rt. hon. Sir J. T. Coleridge by H. P. Liddon together with a letter to the writer by the Rev. E. B. Pusey, London, 1871.
  The responsibility of intellect in matters of faith: a sermon, Oxford, 1873.
Questions for a reformed parliament, London, 1867.
Raleigh, T., *Annals of the Church of Scotland: together with his own autobiographical notes and some reminiscences*, ed. Sir H. R. Reichel, Oxford, 1921.
Reeve, H., 'Autobiography of John Stuart Mill', *ER*, cxxxix (Jan. 1874), 91–129.
  'The claims of whig government', *ER*, cxxxvii (Apr. 1873), 569–86.
  'Communal France', *ER*, cxxxiv (July 1871), 250–90.
  'England and Ireland', *ER*, cliii (Jan. 1881), 274–304.
  'France', *ER*, cxxxiii (Jan. 1871), 1–32.
  'Plain whig principles', *ER*, cli (Jan. 1880), 257–80.
  'Popular education in England', *ER*, cxiv (July 1861), 1–38.

'Reminiscences of Thomas Carlyle', *ER*, cliii (Apr. 1881), 469–97.

'The national Church', *ER*, cxxviii (July 1868), 251–87.

'The past and future of the whig party', *ER*, cxxxix (Apr. 1874), 544–73.

'A whig retort', *ER*, clv (Jan. 1882), 279–90.

Reeve, H., with F. H. Geffcken, 'Prince Bismarck and the Church of Rome', *ER*, cxxxix (Apr. 1874), 360–83.

Report of the general conference of nonconformists, held in Manchester, January 23, 24, and 25, 1872, Manchester, 1872.

Richard, H., 'Nonconformists and Church reform', *CR*, xliv (Aug. 1883), 237–48.

On the application of Christianity to politics: an address, London, 1877.

Richard, H., with J. Carvell Williams, *Disestablishment*, London, 1885.

Rigg, J. H., 'Government education: thirty years past, and thirty years to come', *CR*, xxxi (Jan. 1878), 322–43.

Modern Anglican theology: chapters on Coleridge, Hare, Maurice, Kingsley, and Jowett, and on the doctrine of sacrifice and atonement: to which is prefixed a memoir of Canon Kingsley, with personal reminiscences, London, 1880 edn (1857).

National education in its social conditions and aspects, and public elementary school education English and foreign, London, 1873.

Oxford high Anglicanism and its chief leaders, London, 1895.

Rogers, J. Guinness, *The Bennett judgment and recent episcopal charges: a lecture*, Manchester, 1873.

'The congregationalism of the future', in *Ecclesia: Church problems considered, in a series of essays*, ed. H. R. Reynolds, London, 1870, pp. 462–531.

'The middle class and the new Liberalism', *NC*, xxvi (Oct. 1889), 710–20.

'Mr Forster's defence of the Church', *NC*, iii (Mar. 1878), 509–30.

'A nonconformist's view of the election', *NC*, vii (Apr. 1880), 628–37.

Priests and sacraments; being the substance of a series of sermons on the 'errors of ritualism', London, 1867.

The ritualistic movement in the Church of England, a reason for disestablishment, London, 1868.

'Social aspects of disestablishment', *NC*, i (May 1877), 436–57.

The Ulster problem: 'Trust in God and do the right!': addressed to nonconformists and Liberals in reply to Rev. W. Arthur, London, 1886 (Gladstone's copy, British library).

Why ought not the state to give religious education? An argument addressed to nonconformists, London, 1872.

Russell, 1st Earl, *Essays on the rise and progress of the Christian religion in the West of Europe from the reign of Tiberius to the end of the Council of Trent*, London, 1873.

'The general aspect of the world: does it teach us to hope or to despond?' (1864), in *Rectorial addresses delivered in the universities of Aberdeen 1835–1900*, ed. P. J. Anderson, Aberdeen, 1902, pp. 138–52.

A letter to the right hon. Chichester Fortescue, MP, on the state of Ireland, London, 1868.

A second letter to the right hon. Chichester Fortescue, MP, on the state of Ireland, London, 1868.

Some thoughts on national education for the United Kingdom, London, 1875.

A third letter to the right hon. Chichester Fortescue, MP, on the state of Ireland, London, 1869.

Russell, G. W. E., *The household of faith: portraits and essays*, London, 1902.

'The new Liberalism: a response', *NC*, xxvi (Sept. 1889), 492–9.

'A protest against whiggery', *NC*, xiii (June 1883), 920–7.

Salisbury, 3rd marquess of, 'The Church in her relations to political parties', *QR*, cxviii (July 1865), 193–224.

'The Commune and the Internationale', *QR*, cxxxi (Oct. 1871), 549–80.

'Political lessons of the war', *QR*, cxxx (Jan. 1871), 256–86.

Seebohm, F., 'The education difficulty', *CR*, xix (Feb. 1872), 281–300.

The English village community examined in its relations to the manorial and tribal systems and to the common or open field system of husbandry: an essay in economic history, Port Washington, 1971 edn (1883).

'On national compulsory education', *FR*, viii (July 1870), 103–13.

'The savings of the people', *ER*, cxxxviii (July 1873), 94–119.

Seeley, J. R., 'The Church as a teacher of morality', in *Essays on Church policy*, ed. W. L. Clay, London, 1868, pp. 247–91.

Ecce Homo: a survey of the life and work of Jesus Christ, London, 1866.

'Ethics and religion', *FR*, xlv (Apr. 1889), 501–14.

'The impartial study of politics', *CR*, liv (July 1888), 52–65.

Seventh annual report of the Leicester Anti-Romanist Association, for 1871–72, with a list of subscribers, Leicester, 1872.

Shaftesbury, 7th earl of, *The National Education Union and the denominational system: speech*, London, 1870.

Sherbrooke, 1st Viscount, 'The docility of an "imperial" parliament', *NC*, vii (Apr. 1880), 556–66.

'Imperialism', *FR*, xxiv (Oct. 1878), 453–65.

'Legislation for Ireland', *NC*, viii (Nov. 1880), 677–89.

Middle class and primary education: two speeches, Liverpool, 1868.

Middle class education: endowment or free trade, London, 1868.

'A new Reform Bill', *FR*, xxii (Oct. 1877), 437–52.

Primary and classical education: an address, Edinburgh, 1867.

'Recent attacks on political economy', *NC*, iv (Nov. 1878), 858–68.

Speech . . . on the occasion of his being presented with the Freedom of the City of Glasgow, on Tuesday 26th September, 1872, Glasgow, 1872.

Speeches and letters on Reform; with a preface, London, 1867.

'What shall we do for Ireland?', *QR*, cxxiv (Jan. 1868), 255–86.

Simpkinson, J. N., 'Arnold on Puritanism and national Churches', *ER*, cxxxiii (Apr. 1871), 399–425.

Smith, G., 'The defeat of the Liberal party', *FR*, xxii (July 1877), 1–24.

Essays on questions of the day: political and social, 2nd edn, New York, 1894.

'The Irish question', *CR*, xxi (Mar. 1873), 503–28.

'Whigs and Liberals', *FR*, xxiii (Mar. 1878), 404–16.

Smith, R. Bosworth, 'The Eastern question: Turkey and Russia', *CR*, xxix (Dec. 1876), 147–68.

'The Liberal party and home rule', *National Review*, vii (Mar. 1886), 1–6.

Mohammed and Mohammedanism: lectures delivered at the Royal Institution of Great Britain, London, 1874.

The reasons of a layman and a Liberal for opposing disestablishment: three letters to 'The Times' and one to Mr Gladstone, London, 1885.

Somerset, 12th duke of, *Christian theology and modern scepticism*, London, 1872.

Monarchy and democracy: phases of modern politics, London, 1880.

Stanley of Alderley, 3rd Baron, ed., *The East and the West: our dealings with our neighbours: essays by different hands*, London, 1865.

Stanley, A. P., *An address on the connection of Church and state delivered at Sion college on February 15, 1868*, London, 1868.

The Athanasian Creed: with a preface on the general recommendations of the Ritual Commission, London, 1871.

'The Bennett judgment', *ER*, cxxxvi (July 1872), 270–98.

'Christianity and ultramontanism', *CR*, xxiv (Aug. 1874), 494–502.

'The Church and dissent', *ER*, cxxxvii (Jan. 1873), 196–224.

England and India: a sermon, London, 1875.

Essays chiefly on questions of Church and state from 1850 to 1870, London, 1870.

'The hopes of theology' (1876), in *Rectorial addresses delivered at the university of St Andrews 1863–1893*, ed. W. Knight, London, 1894, pp. 210–34.

An Indian statesman, London, 1879.

'Introduction', in *The recovery of Jerusalem: a narrative of exploration and discovery in the city and the Holy Land*, by C. W. Wilson and C. Warren, ed. W. Morrison, London, 1871, pp. xiii–xxvii.

Lectures on the history of the Church of Scotland: delivered in Edinburgh in 1872, London, 2nd edn, 1879.

Lectures on the history of the Eastern Church: with an introduction on the study of ecclesiastical history, London, 3rd edn, 1864.

'The Old Catholics and the ultramontanes', *CR*, xxi (Apr. 1873), 763–78.

'The Oxford school', *ER*, cliii (Apr. 1881), 305–35.

'The reconstruction of the Irish Church', *QR*, cxxvii (Oct. 1869), 493–514.

The three Irish Churches: an historical address, London, 1869.

'The Vatican Council', *ER*, cxxxiv (July 1871), 131–61.

'What is "disestablishment"?', *CR*, xvii (May 1871), 282–98.

Stephen, J. F., 'Caesarism and ultramontanism', *CR*, xxiii (Mar. 1874), 497–527.

'Liberalism', *Cornhill Magazine*, v (Jan. 1862), 70–83.

Liberty, equality, fraternity, ed. R. J. White, Cambridge, 1967 edn (1873).

'Mr Carlyle', *FM*, lxxii (Dec. 1865), 778–810.

'Mr Gladstone and Sir George Lewis on authority', *NC*, i (Apr. 1877), 270–97.

'Parliamentary government', *CR*, xxiii (Dec. 1873, Jan. 1874), 1–19, 165–81.

Stephen, L., *Essays on freethinking and plainspeaking*, London, 1873.

'Mr Matthew Arnold and the Church of England', *FM*, ii (Oct. 1870), 414–31.

'Mr Voysey and Mr Purchas', *FM*, iii (Apr. 1871), 457–68.

'Religion as a fine art', *FM*, v (Feb. 1872), 158–68.

'The religious difficulty', *FM*, i (May 1870), 623–34.

Stephens, W. R. W., *Christianity and Islam: the bible and the Koran: four lectures*, London, 1877.

Saint Chrysostom: his life and times: a sketch of the Church and the Empire in the fourth century, London, 1872.

Stoughton, J., *History of religion in England: from the opening of the Long Parliament to the end of the eighteenth century: volume VI: the Church in the Georgian era*, London, new edn, 1881.

Religion in England from 1800 to 1850: a history, with a postscript on subsequent events, 2 vols., London, 1884.

Strachey, Sir E., *Jewish history and politics in the times of Sargon and Sennacherib: an inquiry into the historical meaning and purpose of the prophecies of Isaiah*, London, 2nd edn, 1874.

Tait, A. C., *Middle class education: a speech*, London, 1865.

The present position of the Church of England: seven addresses delivered to the clergy and churchwardens of his diocese, London, 3rd edn, 1873.

Some thoughts on the duties of the Established Church of England as a national Church, London, 1876.

Some thoughts on the mission of the Church of England to this age: a sermon, London, 1866.

Temple, F., 'The education of the world', in *Essays and reviews*, London, 5th edn, 1861 (Hawarden copy).

'National education', in *Oxford essays, contributed by members of the university*, London, 1856, pp. 218–70.

Thirlwall, C., *A charge delivered to the clergy of the diocese of St David's, at his tenth visitation, October and November 1869*, London, 1869.

The Irish Church: a speech delivered in the House of Lords on June the 15th, 1869, London, 1869.

Torrens, W. T. M., *Imperial and colonial partnership in emigration*, London, 1881.

'Localism and centralism', *CR*, xvii (June 1871), 399–413.

'The London school board', *CR*, xvi (Feb. 1871), 374–89.

(as W. T. McCullagh), *A remonstrance against the cry of no-popery*, London, 2nd edn, 1836.

Trollope, A., *Lord Palmerston*, London, 1882.

'The new cabinet, and what it will do for us', *St Paul's*, iii (Feb. 1869), 538–51.

'What does Ireland want?', *St Paul's*, v (Dec. 1869), 286–301.

Tulloch, J., 'Arnold's "Literature and dogma" ', *BM*, cxiii (June 1873), 678–92.

'Dean Stanley and the Scotch "Moderates" ', *CR*, xx (Oct. 1872), 698–717.

'Dogmatic extremes', *CR*, xxvii (Jan. 1874), 182–96.

'The Liberal party and the Church of Scotland', *BM*, cxxiv (Sept. 1878), 259–72.

National Churches and the national good, London, 1883.

'On dogma and dogmatic Christianity', *CR*, xxiii (May 1874), 919–33.

Position and prospects of the Church of Scotland: address, Edinburgh, 1878.

Tyndall, J., *Address delivered before the British Association assembled at Belfast with additions*, London, 1874.

Fragments of science: a series of detached essays, addresses, and reviews, volume II, London, 1899 edn.

'Personal recollections of Thomas Carlyle', *FR*, xlvii (Jan. 1890), 5–32.

Perverted politics: a few thoughts for the time, Edinburgh, 1887.

Principal Forbes and his biographers, London, 1873.

Professor Tyndall on party politics: a letter, Edinburgh, 2nd edn, 1885.

The Sabbath: presidential address, London, 1880.

Scientific use of the imagination and other essays, London, 3rd edn, 1872.

Urwick, W., *The nonconformists and the Education Act, a protest and a plea; being the substance of a paper*, London, 1872.

Vickers, J., 'The future of Turkey', *FM*, i (Apr. 1870), 531–9.

Tinker Aesop and his little lessons for the age, London, 1869.

Ward, W. G., 'Caesarism and ultramontanism – Mr Fitzjames Stephen', *Dublin Review*, xxii (Apr. 1874), 402–23.

'Liberalism religious and ecclesiastical', *Dublin Review*, xviii (Jan. 1872), 1–24.

'The priesthood in Irish politics', *Dublin Review*, xix (Oct. 1872), 257–93.

Warren, C., *The land of promise; or, Turkey's guarantee*, London, 1875.

Williams, J. Carvell, *Protestant nonconformists and the general election: a paper*, London, 1868.

Winterbotham, H. S. P., *Letter to my constituents on popular education*, Stroud, 1869.

Woodlock, B., *Catholic university education in Ireland: a letter*, Dublin, 1868 (Gladstone's copy, British library).

Wright, T., *Our new masters*, London, 1873.

5. Biographies, collections of letters, and diaries

Aberdare *Letters of the rt. hon. Henry Austin Bruce, Lord Aberdare of Duffryn*, 2 vols., Oxford, 1902.

Acland *Memoir and letters of the right honourable Sir Thomas Dyke Acland*, by A. H. D. Acland, London, 1902.

Acton *Letters of Lord Acton to Mary, daughter of the right honourable W. E. Gladstone*, ed. H. Paul, London, 1904.

Selections from the correspondence of the first Lord Acton, ed. J. N. Figgis and R. V. Laurence, volume I, London, 1917.

Lord Acton: a study in conscience and politics, by G. Himmelfarb, London, 1952.

Allon *Henry Allon, pastor and teacher: the story of his ministry with selected sermons and addresses*, by W. H. Harwood, London, 1894.

Letters to a Victorian editor: Henry Allon editor of the 'British Quarterly Review', ed. A. Peel, London, 1929.

Amberley *The Amberley papers: the letters and diaries of Lord and Lady Amberley*, ed. B. and P. Russell, 2 vols., London, 1937.

Arch *Joseph Arch (1826–1919): the farm workers' leader*, by P. Horn, Kineton, 1971.

Argyll *George Douglas eighth duke of Argyll: autobiography and memoirs*, ed. dowager duchess of Argyll, 2 vols., London, 1906.

Passages from the past, by the 9th duke of Argyll, 2 vols., London, 1907.

Arnold, Matthew *Letters of Matthew Arnold 1848–1888*, ed. G. W. E. Russell, 2 vols., London, 1895.

Matthew Arnold: a life, by P. Honan, London, 1981.

Arnold, Thomas *Life of Thomas Arnold, headmaster of Rugby*, by A. P. Stanley, London, 1904 edn.

Avebury *Life of Sir John Lubbock Lord Avebury*, by H. G. Hutchinson, 2 vols., London, 1914.

Bagehot *Biographical studies*, by W. Bagehot, ed. R. H. Hutton, London, 1881.

Life of Walter Bagehot, by Mrs R. Barrington, London, 1914.

'The political genius of Walter Bagehot', by N. St John Stevas, in *The collected works of Walter Bagehot*, London, 1974, v, 35–159.

Beaconsfield *Lord Beaconsfield*, by J. A. Froude, London, 1890.

Lord Beaconsfield and other tory memories, by T. E. Kebbel, London, 1907.

The life of Benjamin Disraeli, earl of Beaconsfield, by W. F. Monypenny and G. E. Buckle, 6 vols., London, 1910–20.

The letters of Disraeli to Lady Bradford and Lady Chesterfield, ed. marquis of Zetland, 2 vols., London, 1929.

Disraeli, by R. Blake, London, 1966.

Disraeli's reminiscences, by H. M. and M. Swartz, London, 1975.

Bedford (Hastings Russell) *The late duke of Bedford*, London, 1891.

Beesly 'Professor Beesly and the working-class movement', by R. Harrison, in *Essays in labour history: in memory of G. D. H. Cole*, ed. A. Briggs and J. Saville, London, 1960, pp. 205–41.

Begg *Memoirs of James Begg*, by T. Smith, 2 vols., Edinburgh, 1888.

Blachford *Letters of Frederic Lord Blachford under-secretary of state for the colonies 1860–71*, ed. G. E. Marindin, London, 1896.

Blackie *John Stuart Blackie: a biography*, by A. M. Stoddart, 2 vols., Edinburgh, 3rd edn, 1895.

The letters of John Stuart Blackie to his wife: with a few earlier ones to his parents, ed. A. Stodart-Walker, London, 1909.

Bradlaugh *Charles Bradlaugh: a record of his life and work*, by H. B. Bradlaugh, 2 vols., London, 1895.

Bridges *A nineteenth-century teacher: John Henry Bridges*, by S. Liveing, London, 1926.

Bright, John *The life of John Bright*, by G. M. Trevelyan, London, 1913.
The diaries of John Bright, ed. R. A. J. Walling, London, 1930.
John Bright and the quakers, by J. T. Mills, 2 vols., London, 1935.
John Bright, by K. Robbins, London, 1979.

Bright, William *Selected letters of William Bright*, ed. B. J. Kidd, London, 1903.

Brodrick *Memories and impressions 1831–1900*, by G. C. Brodrick, London, 1900.

Browne *Edward Harold Browne: a memoir*, by G. W. Kitchin, London, 1895.

Browning *Robert Browning*, by E. Dowden, Port Washington, 1970 edn.
Browning's clerical characters, by C. T. Phipps, Salzburg, 1976.

Bryce *Studies in contemporary biography*, by J. Bryce, London, 1903.
James Bryce (Viscount Bryce of Dechmont), by H. A. L. Fisher, 2 vols., London, 1927.

Buchanan *Robert Buchanan: an ecclesiastical biography*, by N. L. Walker, London, 1877.

Burges *William Burges and the high Victorian dream*, by J. M. Crook, London, 1981.

Butler, A. J. *Memoir of Arthur John Butler*, by Sir A. Quiller-Couch, London, 1917.

Butler, H. M. *The Harrow life of Henry Montagu Butler*, by E. Graham, London, 1920.
Henry Montagu Butler: Master of Trinity College, Cambridge, 1886–1918: a memoir, by J. R. M. Butler, London, 1925.

Butt *Isaac Butt and home rule*, by D. Thornley, London, 1964.

Butterfield *William Butterfield*, by P. Thompson, London, 1971.

Cairns, Earl *Brief memories of Hugh McCalmont, first Earl Cairns*, London, 1885.

Cairns, John *Life and letters of John Cairns*, by A. R. Macewen, London, 1895.

Calderwood *The life of Henry Calderwood*, by W. L. Calderwood and D. Woodside, London, 1900.

Campbell-Bannerman *The life of the right hon. Sir Henry Campbell-Bannerman*, by J. A. Spender, 2 vols., London, 1923.

Candlish, R. S. *Memorials of Robert Smith Candlish*, by W. Wilson, Edinburgh, 1880.

Cardwell 'Edward T. Cardwell: Peelite', by A. B. Erickson, *Transactions of the American Philosophical Society*, xlix (1959), part II.

Carlingford ' . . . and Mr Fortescue': a selection from the diaries from 1851 to 1862 of Chichester Fortescue, Lord Carlingford*, by O. Hewett, London, 1958.
Lord Carlingford's journal: reflections of a cabinet minister 1885, ed. A. B. Cooke and J. R. Vincent, Oxford, 1971.

Carlisle *Extracts from journals kept by George Howard, earl of Carlisle*, ed. Lady C. Lascelles, London, [1871].

Carlyle *Thomas Carlyle: a history of his life in London 1834–1881*, by J. A. Froude, 2 vols., London, 1884.
Carlyle in old age (1865–1881), by D. A. Wilson and D. W. MacArthur, London, 1934.

Carnarvon *The life of Henry Howard Molyneux Herbert, fourth earl of Carnarvon, 1831–1890*, by Sir A. H. Hardinge, 3 vols., Oxford, 1925.

Cavendish, Lady Frederick *The diary of Lady Frederick Cavendish*, ed. J. Bailey, 2 vols., London, 1927.

Chamberlain *The life of Joseph Chamberlain: volume I, 1836–1885*, by J. L. Garvin, London, 1932.

Charteris *The life of Archibald Hamilton Charteris*, by A. Gordon, London, 1912.

Childers *The life and correspondence of the right hon. Hugh C. E. Childers 1827–1896*, by S. Childers, 2 vols., London, 1901.

Church *Life and letters of Dean Church*, by M. C. Church, London, 1895.

Churchill *Lord Randolph Churchill: a political life*, by R. F. Foster, Oxford, 1981.

Clarendon *The life and letters of George William Frederick fourth earl of Clarendon*, by Sir H. Maxwell, 2 vols., London, 1913.

Clifford *Dr John Clifford: life, letters and reminiscences*, by Sir J. Marchant, London, 1924.

Cobden *The life of Richard Cobden*, by J. Morley, 2 vols., London, 1881.

Coleridge, Arthur *Arthur Coleridge: reminiscences*, ed. J. A. Fuller-Maitland, London, 1921.

Coleridge, J. D. *Life and correspondence of John Duke Lord Coleridge Lord Chief Justice of England*, by E. H. Coleridge, 2 vols., London, 1904.

 Forty years of friendship as recorded in the correspondence of John Duke, Lord Coleridge and Ellis Yarnell during the years 1856 to 1895, ed. C. Yarnell, London, 1911.

Colman *Jeremiah James Colman: a memoir*, by H. C. Colman, London, 1905.

Cowen *Life of Joseph Cowen (MP for Newcastle, 1874–86)*, by W. Duncan, London and Newcastle, 1904.

Cranbrook *Gathorne Hardy, first earl of Cranbrook: a memoir, with extracts from his diary and correspondence*, by A. E. Gathorne-Hardy, 2 vols., London, 1910.

 The diary of Gathorne Hardy, later Lord Cranbrook, 1866–1892: political selections, ed. N. Johnson, Oxford, 1981.

Creighton *Life and letters of Mandell Creighton*, by L. Creighton, 2 vols., London, 1904.

Cross *A political history*, by Viscount Cross, privately printed, 1903.

Dale *The life of R. W. Dale of Birmingham*, by A. W. W. Dale, London, 1898.

 'R. W. Dale and Christian worldliness', by J. Kenyon, in *The view from the pulpit: Victorian ministers and society*, ed. P. T. Phillips, Toronto, 1978, pp. 187–209.

Dalhousie *The Panmure papers being a selection from the correspondence of Fox Maule, second Baron Panmure, afterwards eleventh earl of Dalhousie*, by Sir G. Douglas and Sir G. D. Ramsay, 2 vols., London, 1908.

Davies, Llewelyn *From a Victorian post-bag: being letters addressed to the Rev. J. Llewelyn Davies by Thomas Carlyle and others*, London, 1926.

Dawson *The life of George Dawson*, by W. Wilson, Birmingham, 1905.

Delane *John Thadeus Delane editor of 'The Times': his life and correspondence*, by A. I. Dasent, 2 vols., London, 1908.

 Delane of the Times, by Sir E. Cook, London, 1915.

Derby, 14th earl of *The earl of Derby*, by G. Saintsbury, London, 1892.

 Lord Derby and Victorian Conservatism, by W. D. Jones, Oxford, 1956.

Derby, 15th earl of *Speeches and addresses of Edward Henry, xvth earl of Derby*, ed. E. S. Roscoe and Sir T. H. Sanderson, 2 vols., London, 1894.

 Disraeli, Derby and the Conservative party: journals and memoirs of Edward Henry, Lord Stanley 1849–69, ed. J. R. Vincent, Hassocks, 1978.

Derby, countess of *A great lady's friendships: letters to Mary, marchioness of Salisbury, countess of Derby 1862–90*, ed. Lady Burghclere, London, 1933.

Devonshire *The life of Spencer Compton eighth duke of Devonshire*, by B. Holland, 2 vols., London, 1911.

Dicey *Memorials of Albert Venn Dicey: being chiefly letters and diaries*, ed. R. S. Rait, London, 1925.

Dilke   *The life of the right honourable Sir Charles W. Dilke*, by S. Gwynn and G. M. Tuckwell, 2 vols., London, 1918.

Disraeli   see Beaconsfield.

Dowden   *Fragments from old letters E.D. to E.D.W. 1869–1892*, London, 1914.

Edward Dowden 1843–1913: an address, by H. O. White, Dublin, 1943.

Duff, Grant   *Some brief comments on passing events, made between February 4th, 1858, and October 5th, 1881*, by Sir M. E. Grant Duff, Madras, 1884.

Notes from a diary 1851–72, by Sir M. E. Grant Duff, 2 vols., London, 1897.

Out of the past: some biographical essays, by M. E. Grant Duff, 2 vols., London, 1903.

Dufferin   *The life of the marquis of Dufferin and Ava*, by Sir A. Lyall, 2 vols., London, 1905.

'The first marquess of Dufferin and Ava: whig, Ulster landlord and imperial statesman', by A. T. Harrison, 2 vols., New University of Ulster D.Phil., 1983.

Durnford   *A memoir of Richard Durnford . . . with selections from his correspondence*, by W. R. W. Stephens, London, 1899.

Edward VII   *King Edward VII: a biography*, by Sir S. Lee, 2 vols., London, 1925–7.

Eliot   *George Eliot's life: as related in her letters and journals*, by J. W. Cross, 3 vols., Edinburgh, 1886 edn.

Ernle   *Whippingham to Westminster*, by Lord Ernle, London, 1938.

Esher   *Cloud-capp'd towers*, by Reginald, Viscount Esher, London, 1927.

Journals and letters of Reginald Viscount Esher, I, 1870–1903, ed. M. V. Brett, London, 1934.

Fawcett   *Life of Henry Fawcett*, by L. Stephen, London, 3rd edn, 1886.

Forbes   *Alexander Penrose Forbes bishop of Brechin: the Scottish Pusey*, by W. Perry, London, 1939.

Forster   *Life of the right honourable William Edward Forster*, by T. Wemyss Reid, 2 vols., London, 4th edn, 1888.

Fortescue   see Carlingford.

Fraser   *James Fraser second bishop of Manchester: a memoir 1818–1885*, by T. Hughes, London, 1887.

'James Fraser, "bishop of all the denominations" ', by P. T. Phillips, in *The view from the pulpit: Victorian ministers and society*, ed. P. T. Phillips, Toronto, 1978, pp. 87–115.

Freeman   *The life and letters of Edward A. Freeman*, by W. R. W. Stephens, 2 vols., London, 1895.

Fremantle   *Recollections of Dean Fremantle*, by W. H. D[raper], London, 1921.

'William Fremantle, Samuel Barnett and the broad church origins of Toynbee Hall', by L. E. Nettleship, *Journal of Ecclesiastical History*, xxxiii (1982), 564–79.

Froude   *The life of Froude*, by H. Paul, London, 1905.

James Anthony Froude: a biography, by W. H. Dunn, 2 vols., Oxford, 1961–3.

Gladstone   *The right honourable William Ewart Gladstone*, by G. W. E. Russell, London, 1891.

'Mr Gladstone', by R. H. Hutton, *CR*, lxv (May 1894), 616–34.

'Mr Gladstone', by M. MacColl, *FR*, lxiii (June 1898), 1008–19.

'Mr Gladstone', by W. G. F. Phillimore, *FR*, lxiii (June 1898), 1020–8.

'Mr Gladstone's theology', by G. W. E. Russell, *CR*, lxxiii (June 1898), 778–94.

'Mr Gladstone and the nonconformists', by J. G. Rogers, *NC*, xliv (July 1898), 30–45.

Mr Gladstone: a monograph, by Sir E. W. Hamilton, London, 1898.

The life of William Ewart Gladstone, ed. T. Wemyss Reid, London, 1899.

The life of William Ewart Gladstone, by J. Morley, 3 vols., London, 1903.

Talks with Mr Gladstone, by L. A. Tollemache, London, 3rd edn, 1903.
Correspondence on Church and religion of William Ewart Gladstone, ed. D. C. Lathbury, 2 vols., London, 1910.
After thirty years, by H. Gladstone, London, 1928.
Gladstone of Hawarden: a memoir of Henry Neville, Lord Gladstone of Hawarden, by I. Thomas, London, 1936.
Gladstone to his wife, ed. A. T. Bassett, London, 1936.
The orb and the cross: a normative study in the relations of Church and state with reference to Gladstone's early writings, by A. R. Vidler, London, 1945.
The political correspondence of Mr Gladstone and Lord Granville 1868–1876, ed. A. Ramm, Camden third series, lxxxi, 2 vols., London, 1952.
The political correspondence of Mr Gladstone and Lord Granville 1876–1886, ed. A. Ramm, 2 vols., Oxford, 1962.
Gladstone: a biography, by P. Magnus, London, 1963 edn.
The Gladstone diaries, ed. M. R. D. Foot and H. C. G. Matthew, 8 vols., Oxford, 1968–82.
'Gladstone's review of "Robert Elsmere": some unpublished correspondence', by W. S. Peterson, *Review of English Studies*, xxi (1970), 442–61.
The prime ministers' papers series: W. E. Gladstone, ed. J. Brooke and M. Sorensen, 4 vols., London, 1971–81.
Gladstone, by E. J. Feuchtwanger, London, 1975.
'Gladstone: the making of a political myth', by D. A. Hamer, *VS*, xxii (1978–9), 29–50.
'Gladstone and the conscience of the state', by D. Schreuder, in *The conscience of the Victorian state*, ed. P. T. Marsh, Hassocks, 1979, pp. 73–134.
Gladstone: Church, state, and tractarianism: a study of his religious ideas and attitudes, 1809–1859, by P. Butler, Oxford, 1982.
Gladstone: I: 1809–1865, by R. Shannon, London, 1982.
Goldsmid   *Memoir of Sir Francis Henry Goldsmid*, by L. S. Goldsmid, London, 1879.
Gooch   *Under six reigns*, by G. P. Gooch, London, 1958.
Gore   *The life of Charles Gore*, by G. L. Prestige, London, 1935.
Goschen   *The life of George Joachim Goschen first Viscount Goschen 1831–1907*, by A. R. D. Elliot, 2 vols., London, 1911.
Goulburn   *Edward Meyrick Goulburn dean of Norwich: a memoir*, by B. Compton, London, 1899.
Gower   *My reminiscences*, by Lord Ronald Gower, 2 vols., London, 1883.
Graham   *Life and letters of Sir James Graham 1792–1861*, by C. S. Parker, 2 vols., London, 1907.
Granville   *The life of Granville George Leveson Gower second Earl Granville 1815–1891*, by Lord Edmond Fitzmaurice, 2 vols., London, 1905.
Green, J. R.   *Letters of John Richard Green*, ed. L. Stephen, London, 1902.
Gregory, R.   *Robert Gregory 1819–1911 being the autobiography of Robert Gregory, dean of St Paul's*, ed. W. H. Hutton, London, 1912.
Gregory, Sir W.   *Sir William Gregory . . . an autobiography*, ed. Lady A. Gregory, London, 1894.
Greville   *The Greville memoirs: a journal of the reigns of King George IV King William IV and Queen Victoria*, ed. H. Reeve, 8 vols., London, 1896 edn.
Grey, 4th Earl   *Albert 4th Earl Grey: a last word*, by H. Begbie, London, 1917.
Grey, Sir G.   *Memoir of Sir George Grey*, by M. Creighton, London, 1901 edn.
Grove   *The life and letters of Sir George Grove*, by C. L. Graves, London, 1903.
Guthrie   *Autobiography of Thomas Guthrie, and memoir*, ed. D. K. and C. J. Guthrie, 2 vols., London, 1875.

Life of Thomas Guthrie, by J. L. Watson, Edinburgh, 1880.

Hall, C. Newman *An autobiography*, by Newman Hall, London, 1898.

Hamilton, Lord George *Parliamentary reminiscences and reflections 1868 to 1885*, by Lord George Hamilton, London, 1917.

Harcourt *The life of Sir William Harcourt*, by A. G. Gardiner, 2 vols., London, 1923.

Hardie *J. Keir Hardie: a biography*, by W. Stewart, London, 1921.
Keir Hardie: radical and socialist, by K. O. Morgan, London, 1975.

Hardy see Cranbrook.

Harrison *Frederic Harrison: the vocations of a positivist*, by M. Vogeler, Oxford, 1984.

Hatherley *A memoir of the right honourable William Page Wood, Baron Hatherley*, by W. R. W. Stephens, 2 vols., London, 1883.

Headlam *Stewart Headlam: a biography*, by F. G. Bettany, London, 1926.

Heathcote *A country gentleman of the nineteenth century: being a short memoir of the right honourable Sir William Heathcote 1801–1881*, by F. Awdry, London, 1906.

Henderson *Arthur Henderson: a biography*, by M. A. Hamilton, London, 1938.

Herbert *Sidney Herbert Lord Herbert of Lea: a memoir*, by Lord Stanmore, 2 vols., London, 1906.

Hobhouse, A. *Lord Hobhouse: a memoir*, by L. T. Hobhouse and J. L. Hammond, London, 1905.

Holden *The Holden–Illingworth letters*, Bradford, 1927.
'Sir Isaac Holden, Bart. (1807–97): his place in the Wesleyan Connexion', by E. Jennings, *Proceedings of the Wesley Historical Society*, xliii (1982), 117–26, 150–8.

Holland, Scott *Personal studies*, by H. Scott Holland, London, 1905.
A bundle of memories, by H. Scott Holland, London, 1915.
A forty years' friendship: letters from the late Henry Scott Holland to Mrs Drew, ed. S. L. Ollard, London, 1919.
Henry Scott Holland: memoir and letters, by S. Paget, London, 1921.
The mind and character of Henry Scott Holland, by E. Lyttelton, Oxford, 1926.

Holyoake *Life and letters of George Jacob Holyoake*, by J. McCabe, 2 vols., London, 1908.

Hook *The life and letters of Walter Farquhar Hook*, by W. R. W. Stephens, 2 vols., London, 1878.

Hooker *Life and letters of Sir Joseph Dalton Hooker*, by L. Huxley, 2 vols., London, 1918.

Houghton *The life, letters, and friendships of Richard Monckton Milnes first Lord Houghton*, by T. Wemyss Reid, 2 vols., New York, 1981 edn.
Monckton Milnes: the flight of youth 1851–1885, by J. Pope-Hennessy, London, 1951.

Howell *Respectable radical: George Howell and Victorian working-class politics*, by F. M. Leventhal, London, 1971.

Hughes, H. P. *The life of Hugh Price Hughes*, by D. P. Hughes, London, 1904.

Hughes, T. *Thomas Hughes: the life of the author of 'Tom Brown's schooldays'*, by E. C. Mack and W. H. G. Armytage, London, 1952.

Hutton, G. C. *Life of George Clark Hutton*, by A. Oliver, Paisley, 1910.

Huxley *Life and letters of Thomas Henry Huxley*, by L. Huxley, 3 vols., London, 1903 edn.

Iddesleigh *Life, letters, and diaries of Sir Stafford Northcote first earl of Iddesleigh*, by A. Lang, 2 vols., London, 2nd edn, 1890.

Illingworth *Fifty years of politics: Mr Alfred Illingworth's retrospect: recollections and anecdotes*, Bradford, 1905.

Innes, Taylor *Chapters of reminiscence*, by A. Taylor Innes, London, 1913.

Jowett *The life and letters of Benjamin Jowett*, by E. Abbott and L. Campbell, 2 vols., London, 1897.

Letters of Benjamin Jowett, ed. E. Abbott and L. Campbell, London, 1899.

Jowett's correspondence on education with Earl Russell in 1867, ed. J. M. Prest, Oxford, 1965.

Kelvin *The life of William Thomson Baron Kelvin of Largs*, by S. P. Thompson, 2 vols., London, 1910.

Kimberley *John, first earl of Kimberley: a journal of events during the Gladstone ministry, 1868–74*, ed. E. Drus, Camden miscellany, xxi, London, 1958.

Kingsley *Charles Kingsley: his letters and memories of his life*, by F. E. Kingsley, 2 vols., London, 1877.

'Alton Locke: tailor and poet: an autobiography', by C. Kingsley, with a prefatory memoir by Thomas Hughes, 2 vols., London, 1881.

Knightley *The journals of Lady Knightley of Fawsley 1856–1884*, ed. J. Cartwright, London, 1915.

Knowles *James Knowles: Victorian editor and architect*, by P. Metcalf, Oxford, 1980.

Lake *Memorials of William Charles Lake dean of Durham 1869–1894*, by K. Lake, London, 1901.

Lansbury *The life of George Lansbury*, by R. Postgate, London, 1951.

Lawrence *Life of Lord Lawrence*, by R. Bosworth Smith, 2 vols., London, 1883.

Lawson *Sir Wilfrid Lawson: a memoir*, by G. W. E. Russell, London, 1909.

Layard *Sir A. Henry Layard: autobiography and letters from his childhood until his appointment as HM ambassador at Madrid*, ed. W. N. Bruce, 2 vols., London, 1903.

Layard of Nineveh, by G. Waterfield, London, 1963.

Leveson-Gower *Bygone years: recollections*, by F. Leveson Gower, London, 1905.

'Freddy Leveson', by G. W. E. Russell, *Cornhill Magazine*, xxiii (Aug. 1907), 169–78.

Years of content 1858–1886, by G. Leveson Gower, London, 1940.

Lewis *Letters of the right hon. Sir George Cornewall Lewis to various friends*, ed. Sir G. F. Lewis, London, 1870.

Liddon *Life and letters of Henry Parry Liddon*, by J. O. Johnston, London, 1904.

Lisle, De *Life and letters of Ambrose Phillips de Lisle*, by E. S. Purcell, 2 vols., London, 1900.

Lowe see Sherbrooke.

Lytteltons *Memories and hopes*, by E. Lyttelton, London, 1925.

The Lytteltons: a family chronicle of the nineteenth century, by B. Askwith, London, 1975

McArthur *Sir William McArthur: a biography, religious, parliamentary, municipal, commercial*, by T. McCullagh, London, 1891.

MacColl *Malcolm MacColl: memoirs and correspondence*, by G. W. E. Russell, London, 1914.

Macgregor *John Macgregor ('Rob Roy')*, by E. Hodder, London, 1894.

Mackarness *Memorials of the episcopate of John Fielder Mackarness, bishop of Oxford from 1870 to 1888*, by C. C. Mackarness, Oxford, 1892.

Mackonochie *Alexander Heriot Mackonochie: a memoir by E.A.T.*, ed. E. F. Russell, London, 1890.

Maclaren, A. *The life of Alexander Maclaren preacher and expositor*, by D. Williamson, London, 1910.

McLaren, D.   *The life and work of Duncan McLaren*, by J. B. Mackie, 2 vols., London, 1888.

Macleod   *Memoir of Norman Macleod*, by D. Macleod, 2 vols., London, 1876.

MacNeill   *What I have seen and heard*, by J. G. Swift MacNeill, London, 1925.

Magee   *The life and correspondence of William Connor Magee, archbishop of York*, by J. C. MacDonnell, 2 vols., London, 1896.

Malmesbury   *Memoirs of an ex-minister: an autobiography*, by the earl of Malmesbury, 2 vols., London, 3rd edn, 1884.

Manchester   *'My dear duchess': social and political letters to the duchess of Manchester 1858–1869*, ed. A. L. Kennedy, London, 1956.

Manners   see Rutland.

Manning   *Life of Cardinal Manning, archbishop of Westminster*, by E. S. Purcell, 2 vols., London, 2nd edn, 1896.

Martin   *The life and letters of John Martin*, by P. A. Sillard, Dublin, 2nd edn, 1901.

Martineau   *The life and letters of James Martineau*, by J. Drummond and C. B. Upton, 2 vols., London, 1902.

Melly   *Recollections of sixty years (1833–1893): political, social and sportive*, by G. Melly, Coventry, 1893.

Miall   *Life of Edward Miall*, by A. Miall, London, 1884.

Mill   *The letters of John Stuart Mill*, ed. H. S. R. Elliot, 2 vols., London, 1910.

Milnes   see Houghton.

Moberly   *Dulce Domum: George Moberly: his family and friends*, by C. A. E. Moberly, London, 1911.

Morley, J.   *Recollections*, by John, Viscount Morley, 2 vols., London, 1917.
Early life and letters of John Morley, by F. W. Hirst, 2 vols., London, 1927.
John Morley: Liberal intellectual in politics, by D. A. Hamer, Oxford, 1968.

Morley, S.   *The life of Samuel Morley*, by E. Hodder, London, 3rd edn, 1887.

Morrison   *Walter Morrison*, by G. Dawson, London, 1922.
Portrait of a merchant prince: James Morrison 1789–1857, by R. Gatty, Northallerton, 1977.

Mount-Temple   *Memorials*, by Baroness Mount-Temple, privately printed, 1890.

Mowbray   *Seventy years at Westminster, with other letters and notes of the late right honourable Sir John Mowbray*, ed. E. M. Mowbray, London, 1900.

Mundella   *A. J. Mundella 1825–1897: the Liberal background to the Labour movement*, by W. II. G. Armytage, London, 1951.

Napier   *The life of Sir Joseph Napier ex-lord chancellor of Ireland from his private correspondence: a political biography*, by A. C. Ewald, London, 1887.

Newdegate   *Protestant versus Catholic in mid-Victorian England: Mr Newdegate and the nuns*, by W. L. Arnstein, Columbia, 1982.

Northbrook   *Thomas George earl of Northbrook: a memoir*, by B. Mallet, London, 1908.

Ossington   *Notes from my journal when Speaker of the House of Commons*, by Viscount Ossington, London, 1900.

Palmerston   *The life and correspondence of Henry John Temple, Viscount Palmerston*, by E. Ashley, 2 vols., London, 1879 edn.

Pell   *The reminiscences of Albert Pell, sometime MP for South Leicestershire*, ed. T. Mackay, London, 1908.

Playfair   *Memoirs and correspondence of Lyon Playfair, first Lord Playfair of St Andrews*, by T. Wemyss Reid, London, 1899.

Ponsonby   *Henry Ponsonby Queen Victoria's private secretary: his life from his letters*, by A. Ponsonby, London, 1942.

Powell   *Sir Francis Sharp Powell: a memoir*, by H. L. P. Hulbert, Leeds, 1914.

Pusey   *Life of Edward Bouverie Pusey*, by H. P. Liddon, 4 vols., London, 1897.

Raikes   *The life and letters of Henry Cecil Raikes*, by H. St J. Raikes, London, 1898.

Rainy   *The life of Principal Rainy*, by P. C. Simpson, 2 vols., London, 1909.

Rathbone   *William Rathbone: a memoir*, by E. F. Rathbone, London, 1905.

Reed   *Memoir of Sir Charles Reed*, by C. E. B. Reed, London, 1883.

Reeve   *Memoirs of the life and correspondence of Henry Reeve*, by J. K. Laughton, 2 vols., London, 1898.

Reid, Wemyss   *Cabinet portraits: sketches of statesmen*, by T. Wemyss Reid, London, 1872.

Memoirs of Sir Wemyss Reid 1842–1885, ed. S. J. Reid, London, 1905.

Rendel   *The personal papers of Lord Rendel containing his unpublished conversations with Mr Gladstone (1888 to 1898) and other famous statesmen; selections from letters and papers reflecting the thought and manners of the period; and intimate pictures of parliament, politics, and society*, London, 1931.

Ribblesdale   *Impressions and memories*, by Lord Ribblesdale, London, 1927.

Richard   *Henry Richard: a biography*, by C. S. Miall, London, 1889.

Rigg   *The life of James Harrison Rigg 1821–1909*, by J. Telford, London, 1909.

Ripon   *Life of the first marquess of Ripon*, by L. Wolf, 2 vols., London, 1921.

Roebuck   *Life and letters of John Arthur Roebuck, with chapters of autobiography*, by R. E. Leader, London, 1897.

Rogers, J. G.   *An autobiography*, by J. Guinness Rogers, London, 1903.

Rogers, W.   *Reminiscences of William Rogers*, by R. H. Hadden, London, 1888.

Rosebery   *Lord Rosebery*, by the marquess of Crewe, 2 vols., London, 1931.

Rothschilds   *The English Rothschilds*, by R. W. Davis, London, 1983.

Rowntree   *A quaker business man: the life of Joseph Rowntree 1836–1925*, by A. Vernon, London, 1958.

Russell, Earl   *Recollections and suggestions 1813–1873*, by John, Earl Russell, London, 1875.

The life of Lord John Russell, by S. Walpole, 2 vols., London, 1889.

The later correspondence of Lord John Russell 1840–78, ed. G. P. Gooch, 2 vols., London, 1925.

Russell, G. W. E.   *Collections and recollections by one who has kept a diary*, by G. W. E. Russell, London, 1898.

Social silhouettes, by G. W. E. Russell, London, 1906.

One look back, by G. W. E. Russell, London, 1912.

Portraits of the seventies, by G. W. E. Russell, London, 1916.

Prime ministers and some others: a book of reminiscences, by G. W. E. Russell, London, 1918.

Rutland   *Lord John Manners and his friends*, by C. Whibley, 2 vols., London, 1925.

'The diary of Lord John Manners – Part III', *Salisbury Review*, vi (Winter 1984), 14–17.

St Aldwyn   *Life of Sir Michael Hicks Beach (Earl St Aldwyn)*, by Lady V. Hicks Beach, 2 vols., London, 1893.

Sala   *The life and adventures of George Augustus Sala*, by G. A. Sala, 2 vols., London, 2nd edn, 1895.

Salisbury   *Life of Robert marquis of Salisbury*, by Lady G. Cecil, 4 vols., London, 1921–32.

Seeley   'John Robert Seeley and the idea of a national Church', by R. Shannon, in *Ideas and institutions of Victorian Britain: essays in honour of George Kitson Clark*, ed. R. Robson, London, 1967, pp. 236–67.

Sir John Seeley and the uses of history, by D. Wormell, Cambridge, 1980.

Selborne *Memorials part I: family and personal 1766–1865*, by the earl of Selborne, 2 vols., London, 1896.

Memorials part II: personal and political 1865–1895, by the earl of Selborne, 2 vols., London, 1898.

Shaftesbury *The life and work of the seventh earl of Shaftesbury*, by E. Hodder, 3 vols., London, 1886.

Shaftesbury, by G. F. A. Best, London, 1964.

The seventh earl of Shaftesbury 1801–1885, by G. B. A. M. Finlayson, London, 1981.

Sherbrooke *Life and letters of the right honourable Robert Lowe Viscount Sherbrooke*, by A. P. Martin, 2 vols., London, 1893.

Robert Lowe and education, by D. W. Sylvester, Cambridge, 1974.

Robert Lowe, by J. Winter, Toronto, 1976.

Smith, Bosworth *Reginald Bosworth Smith: a memoir*, by E. F. Grogan, London, 1909.

Smith, Goldwin *My memory of Gladstone*, by Goldwin Smith, London, 1904.

A selection from Goldwin Smith's correspondence . . . 1846–1910, ed. A. Haultain, London, 1913.

Goldwin Smith: his life and opinions, by A. Haultain, London, 1914.

Goldwin Smith: Victorian Liberal, by E. Wallace, Toronto, 1957.

Smith, W. H. *Life and times of the right honourable William Henry Smith*, by Sir H. Maxwell, 2 vols., Edinburgh, 1893.

Somerset *Letters, remains and memoirs of Edward Adolphus Seymour, twelfth duke of Somerset*, by W. H. Mallock and Lady G. Ramsden, London, 1893.

Strange inheritance, by J. Colville, Wilton, 1983.

Spencer *The red earl: the papers of the fifth Earl Spencer, 1835–1910*, ed. P. Gordon, volume I, Northampton, 1981.

Spurgeon *C. H. Spurgeon's autobiography: compiled from his diary, letters, and records*, ed. S. Spurgeon, 4 vols., London, 1897–1900.

The life of Charles Haddon Spurgeon, by C. Ray, London, 1903.

Stanley *The life and correspondence of Arthur Penrhyn Stanley*, by R. E. Prothero, 2 vols., London, 1893.

Later letters of Lady Augusta Stanley 1864–1876, ed A. V. Baillie and H. Bolitho, London, 1929.

Stanley, Lord see Derby, 15th earl of.

Stanley of Alderley *The Stanleys of Alderley: their letters between the years 1851–1865*, ed. N. Mitford, London, 1939.

Stanmore *The career of Arthur Hamilton Gordon first Lord Stanmore 1829–1912*, by J. K. Chapman, Toronto, 1964.

Stansfeld *James Stansfeld: a Victorian champion of sex equality*, by J. L. and B. Hammond, London, 1932.

Stanton *Arthur Stanton: a memoir*, by G. W. E. Russell, London, 1917.

Stephen, J. F. *The life of Sir James Fitzjames Stephen*, by L. Stephen, London, 1895.

'The religious creed and criticism of Sir James Fitzjames Stephen', by J. C. Livingston, *VS*, xvii (1974), 279–300.

James Fitzjames Stephen and the crisis of Victorian thought, by J. A. Colaiaco, London, 1983.

Stephen, L. *The life and letters of Leslie Stephen*, by F. W. Maitland, London, 1906.

Stoughton   *Recollections of a long life*, by J. Stoughton, London, 2nd edn, 1894.
John Stoughton: a short record of a long life, by G. K. Lewis, London, 1898.
Strachey   *The adventure of living: a subjective autobiography*, by J. St Loe Strachey, London, 1922.
Tait   *Life of Archibald Campbell Tait archbishop of Canterbury*, by R. T. Davidson and W. Benham, 2 vols., London, 1891.
Talbot   *Edward Stuart Talbot 1844–1934*, by G. Stephenson, London, 1936.
Temple   *The Exeter episcopate of Archbishop Temple*, by E. G. Sandford, London, 1907.
Rugby memoir of Archbishop Temple 1857–1869, by F. E. Kitchener, London, 1907.
Tennyson   *Alfred Lord Tennyson: a memoir*, by H. Tennyson, 2 vols., London, 1897.
Thirlwall   *Letters literary and theological of Connop Thirlwall*, ed. J. J. S. Perowne and L. Stokes, London, 1881.
Letters to a friend, by Connop Thirlwall, ed. A. P. Stanley, London, 1881.
Connop Thirlwall: historian and theologian, by J. C. Thirlwall, London, 1936.
Thorold   *The life and work of Bishop Thorold*, by C. H. Simpkinson, London, 1896.
Torrens   *Twenty years in parliament*, by W. T. M. Torrens, London, 1893.
Trevelyan   *Sir George Otto Trevelyan: a memoir*, by G. M. Trevelyan, London, 1932.
Tulloch   *A memoir of the life of John Tulloch*, by M. O. W. Oliphant, Edinburgh, 3rd edn, 1887.
Tyndall   *Life and work of John Tyndall*, by A. S. Eve and C. H. Creasey, London, 1945.
Victoria   *The letters of Queen Victoria second series: a selection from Her Majesty's correspondence and journal between the years 1862 and 1885*, ed. G. E. Buckle, 3 vols., London, 1926–8.
The queen and Mr Gladstone, ed. P. Guedalla, 2 vols., London, 1933.
Your dear letter: private correspondence of Queen Victoria and the crown princess of Prussia 1865–1871, ed. R. Fulford, London, 1971.
Darling child: private correspondence of Queen Victoria and the crown princess of Prussia 1871–1878, ed. R. Fulford, London, 1976.
Waldegrave   *Strawberry Fair: a biography of Frances, Countess Waldegrave 1821–1879*, by O. W. Hewett, London, 1956.
Wantage   *Lord Wantage: a memoir*, by Lady [H. S.] Wantage, London, 1907.
Ward   *A writer's recollections*, by Mrs H. Ward, London, 1918.
Waugh   *The life of Benjamin Waugh*, by R. Waugh, London, 1913.
Webb   *My apprenticeship*, by B. Webb, Cambridge, 1979 edn.
The diary of Beatrice Webb: volume one 1873–1892: glitter around and darkness within, ed. N. and J. Mackenzie, London, 1982.
West   *Recollections 1832 to 1886*, by Sir A. West, 2 vols., London, 2nd edn, 1899.
Westbury   *The life of Richard Lord Westbury*, by T. A. Nash, 2 vols., London, 1888.
Westminster   *Victorian duke: the life of Hugh Lupus Grosvenor first duke of Westminster*, by G. Huxley, London, 1967.
White   *The inner life of the House of Commons*, by W. White, 2 vols., London, 1897.
Wilberforce   *Life of the right reverend Samuel Wilberforce, with selections from his diaries and correspondence*, by A. R. Ashwell and R. G. Wilberforce, 3 vols., London, 2nd edn, 1883.
Lord bishop: the life of Samuel Wilberforce 1805–1873, by S. Meacham, Cambridge, Mass., 1970.
Woodard   *Nathaniel Woodard: a memoir of his life*, by Sir J. Otter, London, 1925.
Wordsworth   *Christopher Wordsworth, bishop of Lincoln 1807–1885*, by J. H. Overton and E. Wordsworth, London, 1888.

C. PRINTED SECONDARY WORKS

Akenson, D. H., *The Irish education experiment: the national system of education in the nineteenth century*, London, 1970.

The Church of Ireland: ecclesiastical reform and revolution, 1800–1885, New Haven, 1971.

Alderman, G., *The railway interest*, Leicester, 1973.

The jewish community in British politics, Oxford, 1983.

Altholz, J. L., *The liberal catholic movement in England: the 'Rambler' and its contributors 1848–1864*, London, 1962.

Anderson, O., 'Gladstone's abolition of compulsory church rates: a minor myth and its historiographical career', *Journal of Ecclesiastical History*, xxv (1974), 185–98.

Arnstein, W. L., *The Bradlaugh case: a study in late Victorian opinion and politics*, Oxford, 1965.

'The religious issue in mid-Victorian politics: a note on a neglected source', *Albion*, vi (1974), 134–43.

'The Murphy riots: a Victorian dilemma', *Victorian studies*, xix (1975–6), 51–71.

Auspos, P., 'Radicalism, pressure groups, and party politics: from the National Education League to the National Liberal Federation', *Journal of British Studies*, xx (1980), 184–204.

Baer, M. B., 'Social structure, voting behaviour and political change in Victorian London', *Albion*, ix (1977), 227–41.

Bahlman, D. W. R., 'The queen, Mr Gladstone, and church patronage', *VS*, iii (1959–60), 349–80.

Barker, M., *Gladstone and radicalism: the reconstruction of Liberal policy in Britain 1885–94*, Hassocks, 1975.

Beales, D. E. D., 'Gladstone and his diary: "myself, the worst of all interlocutors"', *HJ*, xxv (1982), 463–9.

'Gladstone and his first ministry', *HJ*, xxvi (1983), 987–98.

Bealey, F., and Pelling, H., *Labour and politics 1900–1906: a history of the Labour Representation Committee*, London, 1958.

Bebbington, D. W., 'Gladstone and the nonconformists: a religious affinity in politics', *Studies in Church History*, xii (1975), 369–82.

'Gladstone and the baptists', *Baptist Quarterly*, xxvi (1976), 224–39.

'Baptist MPs in the nineteenth century', *Baptist Quarterly*, xxix (1981), 3–24.

The nonconformist conscience: chapel and politics, 1870–1914, London, 1982.

Bell, P. M. H., *Disestablishment in Ireland and Wales*, London, 1969.

Bentley, J., *Ritualism and politics in Victorian Britain: the attempt to legislate for belief*, Oxford, 1978.

Best, G. F. A., 'The religious difficulties of national education in England, 1800–70', *Cambridge Historical Journal*, xii (1956), 155–73.

Binfield, C., *So down to prayers: studies in English nonconformity 1780–1920*, London, 1977.

Brent, C. E., 'The immediate impact of the second Reform Act on a southern county town: voting patterns at Lewes borough in 1865 and 1868', *Southern History*, ii (1980), 129–77.

Briggs, A., *Victorian people: a reassessment of persons and themes 1851–67*, Harmondsworth, 1982 edn.

Bristow, E., 'The Liberty and Property Defence League and individualism', *HJ*, xviii (1975), 761–89.

Brown, A. W., *The Metaphysical Society: Victorian minds in crisis, 1869–1880*, New York, 1947.

Cannadine, D., *Lords and landlords: the aristocracy and the towns 1774–1967*, Leicester, 1980.

Chadwick, O., *The Victorian Church*, 2 vols., London, 1966–70.

Clarke, P. F., 'Electoral sociology of modern Britain', *History*, lvii (1972), 31–55.

Clayton, J. D., 'Mr Gladstone's leadership of the parliamentary Liberal party 1868–74', Oxford D.Phil., 1960.

Collini, S., *Liberalism and sociology: L. T. Hobhouse and political argument in England 1880–1914*, Cambridge, 1979.

Cooke, A. B., and J. R. Vincent, *The governing passion: cabinet government and party politics in Britain 1885–86*, Brighton, 1974.

Cowling, M., *1867: Disraeli, Gladstone and revolution: the passing of the second Reform Bill*, Cambridge, 1967.

Cruickshank, M., *Church and state in English education: 1870 to the present day*, London, 1963.

Davis, R. W., *Political change and continuity 1760–1885: a Buckinghamshire study*, Newton Abbot, 1972.

Dingle, A. E., *The campaign for prohibition in Victorian England: the United Kingdom Alliance, 1872–1895*, London, 1980.

Drummond, A. L., and Bulloch, J., *The Church in Victorian Scotland 1843–1874*, Edinburgh, 1975.

Fair, J. D., *British interparty conferences: a study of the procedure of conciliation in British politics, 1867–1921*, Oxford, 1980.

Feuchtwanger, E. J., *Disraeli, democracy and the tory party: Conservative leadership and organization after the second Reform Bill*, Oxford, 1968.

Fisher, C., and Smethurst, J., ' "War on the law of supply and demand": the Amalgamated Association of Miners and the Forest of Dean colliers, 1869–1875', in *Independent collier: the coal miner as archetypal proletarian reconsidered*, ed. R. Harrison, Hassocks, 1978, pp. 114–55.

Fleming, J. R., *A history of the Church of Scotland 1843–1874*, Edinburgh, 1927.

Fletcher, S., *Feminists and bureaucrats: a study in the development of girls' education in the nineteenth century*, Cambridge, 1980.

Forbes, D., *The Liberal Anglican idea of history*, Cambridge, 1952.

Foster, R. F., 'Tory democracy and political elitism: provincial Conservatism and parliamentary tories in the early 1880s', in *Parliament and community: Historical Studies XIV*, ed. A. Cosgrove and J. I. McGuire, Dublin, 1983, pp. 147–75.

Fraser, D., *Urban politics in Victorian England: the structure of politics in Victorian cities*, Leicester, 1976.

Freeden, M., *The new Liberalism: an ideology of social reform*, Oxford, 1978.

Gash, N., *Reaction and reconstruction in English politics 1832–1852*, Oxford, 1965.

Ghosh, P., 'Disraelian Conservatism: a financial approach', *EHR*, xcix (1984), 268–96.

Gilbert, A. D., *Religion and society in industrial England: Church, chapel and social change, 1740–1914*, London, 1976.

Gooch, G. P., *History and historians in the nineteenth century*, London, 1952 edn.

Greenall, R. L., 'Popular Conservatism in Salford 1868–1886', *Northern History*, ix (1974), 123–38.

Griffiths, P. C., 'The caucus and the Liberal party in 1886', *History*, lxi (1976), 183–97.

Griggs, C., *The Trades Union Congress and the struggle for education 1868–1925*, Barcombe, 1983.

Gurowich, P., 'The continuation of war by other means: party and politics, 1855–1865', *HJ*, xxvii (1984), 603–31.

Hamer, D. A., *Liberal politics in the age of Gladstone and Rosebery: a study in leadership and policy*, Oxford, 1972.

The politics of electoral pressure: a study in the history of Victorian reform agitations, Hassocks, 1977.

Hammond, J. L., *Gladstone and the Irish nation*, London, 1938.

Hanham, H. J., *Elections and party management: politics in the time of Disraeli and Gladstone*, Hassocks, 1978 edn.

Hargest, L., 'The Welsh Educational Alliance and the 1870 Elementary Education Act', *Welsh History Review*, x (1980), 172–206.

Harrison, B., *Drink and the Victorians: the temperance question in England 1815–1872*, London, 1971.

'A genealogy of reform in modern Britain', in *Anti-slavery, religion, and reform: essays in memory of Roger Anstey*, ed. C. Bolt and S. Drescher, Folkestone, 1980, pp. 119–48.

Harrison, F. M. W., 'The Nottinghamshire baptists and education', *Baptist Quarterly*, xxvii (1977), 94–109.

Harrison, R., *Before the socialists: studies in labour and politics 1861–1881*, London, 1965.

Harvie, C., 'Ideology and home rule: James Bryce, A. V. Dicey and Ireland, 1880–1887', *EHR*, xci (1976), 298–314.

The lights of liberalism: university liberals and the challenge of democracy 1860–86, London, 1976.

Heeney, B., *Mission to the middle classes: the Woodard schools 1848–1891*, London, 1969.

Helmstadter, R., 'The nonconformist conscience', in *The conscience of the Victorian state*, ed. P. T. Marsh, Hassocks, 1979, pp. 135–72.

Hempton, D., *Methodism and politics in British society 1750–1850*, London, 1984.

Hennock, E. P., *Fit and proper persons: ideal and reality in nineteenth-century urban government*, London, 1973.

Heyck, T. W., 'Home rule, radicalism, and the Liberal party, 1886–1895', *Journal of British Studies*, xiii (1973–4), 66–91.

The dimensions of British radicalism: the case of Ireland 1874–95, Urbana, 1974.

Hill, Sir F., *Victorian Lincoln*, Cambridge, 1974.

Honey, J. R. de S., *Tom Brown's universe: the development of the Victorian public school*, London, 1977.

Hoppen, K. T., 'Tories, Catholics, and the general election of 1859', *HJ*, xiii (1970), 48–67.

Elections, politics, and society in Ireland 1832–1885, Oxford, 1984.

Hurst, M. C., 'Liberal versus Liberal: the general election of 1874 in Bradford and Sheffield', *HJ*, xv (1972), 669–713.

Ingham, S. M., 'The disestablishment movement in England, 1868–74', *Journal of Religious History*, iii (1964–5), 38–60.

Isichei, E., *Victorian quakers*, Oxford, 1970.

Jenkins, T. A., 'Gladstone, the whigs and the leadership of the Liberal party, 1879–1880', *HJ*, xxvii (1984), 337–60.

Jones, A., *The politics of Reform 1884*, Cambridge, 1972.

Jones, G. S., *Languages of class: studies in working class history 1832–1982*, Cambridge, 1983.

Jones, I. G., 'The Liberation Society and Welsh politics, 1844 to 1868', *Welsh History Review*, i (1961), 193–224.

'Cardiganshire politics in the mid-nineteenth century: a study of the elections of 1865 and 1868', *Ceredigion*, v (1964), 14–41.

'The elections of 1865 and 1868 in Wales, with special reference to Cardiganshire and Merthyr Tydfil', *Transactions of the Honourable Society of Cymmrodorion* (1964), 41–68.

'Merioneth politics in mid-nineteenth century: the politics of a rural economy', *Journal of the Merioneth Historical and Record Society*, v (1968), 273–334.

Joyce, P., *Work, society and politics: the culture of the factory in later Victorian England*, London, 1982 edn.

Kellas, J. G., 'The Liberal party and the Scottish Church disestablishment crisis', *EHR*, lxxix (1964), 31–46.

Kent, C., *Brains and numbers: elitism, Comtism and democracy in mid-Victorian England*, Toronto, 1978.

Kinzer, B. L., 'The un-Englishness of the secret ballot', *Albion*, x (1978), 237–56.

Knights, B., *The idea of the clerisy in the nineteenth century*, Cambridge, 1978.

Koss, S., *Nonconformity in modern British politics*, London, 1975.

The rise and fall of the political press in Britain: volume I: the nineteenth century, London, 1981.

Laqueur, T. W., *Religion and respectability: Sunday schools and working class culture 1780–1850*, New Haven, 1976.

Lipman, V. D., *Social history of the jews in England 1850–1950*, London, 1954.

Lloyd, T., *The general election of 1880*, Oxford, 1968.

Lowe, J. C., 'The tory triumph of 1868 in Blackburn and Lancashire', *HJ*, xvi (1973), 733–48.

Lubenow, W. C., 'Irish home rule and the great separation in the Liberal party in 1886: the dimensions of parliamentary Liberalism', *VS*, xxvi (1982–3), 161–80.

'Irish home rule and the social basis of the great separation in the Liberal party in 1886', *HJ*, xxviii (1985), 125–42.

McCann, W. P., 'Trade unionists, artisans and the 1870 Education Act', *British Journal of Educational Studies*, xviii (1970), 134–50.

McCarthy, J. H., *Ireland since the union: sketches of Irish history from 1798 to 1886*, London, 1887.

McClelland, K., 'A politics of the labour aristocracy? Skilled workers and radical politics in Tyneside, c. 1850–74', *Bulletin of the Society for the Study of Labour History*, xl (1980), 8–9.

McClelland, V. A., 'Gladstone and Manning: a question of authority', in *Gladstone, politics and religion: a collection of Founder's Day Lectures delivered at St Deiniol's Library, Hawarden, 1967–83*, ed. P. J. Jagger, London, 1985, pp. 148–70.

McCord, N., *North east England: an economic and social history*, London, 1979.

McCready, H. W., 'The British election of 1874: Frederic Harrison and the Liberal–Labour dilemma', *Canadian Journal of Economics and Political Science*, xx (1954), 166–75.

MacDonagh, O., 'The last bill of pains and penalties: the case of Daniel O'Sullivan, 1869', *Irish Historical Studies*, xix (1974), 136–55.

McDonald, T. A., 'Religion and voting in an English borough: Poole in 1859', *Southern History*, v (1983), 221–37.

McDowell, R. B., *The Irish administration 1801–1914*, London, 1964.

The Church of Ireland 1869–1969, London, 1975.

Machin, G. I. T., 'The Maynooth grant, the dissenters and disestablishment, 1845–7', *EHR*, lxxxii (1967), 61–85.

'Gladstone and nonconformity in the 1860s: the formation of an alliance', *HJ*, xvii (1974), 347–64.

Politics and the Churches in Great Britain 1832 to 1868, Oxford, 1977.

McIntire, C. T., *England against the papacy 1858–1861: Tories, Liberals, and the overthrow of papal temporal power during the Italian Risorgimento*, Cambridge, 1983.

Mackintosh, W. H., *Disestablishment and liberation: the movement for the separation of the Anglican Church from state control*, London, 1972.

McLeod, H., *Class and religion in the late Victorian city*, London, 1974.

Macleod, R. M., 'The X-club: a social network of science in late-Victorian England', *Notes and records of the Royal Society of London*, xxiii (1968), 305–23.

'The Ayrton incident: a commentary on the relations of science and government in England, 1870–1873', in *Science and values: patterns of tradition and change*, ed. A. Thackray and E. Mendelsohn, New York, 1974, pp. 45–78.

Maehl, W. H., 'Gladstone, the Liberals, and the election of 1874', *Bulletin of the Institute of Historical Research*, xxxvi (1963), 53–69.

Mandler, P., 'Cain and Abel: two aristocrats and the early Victorian Factory Acts', *HJ*, xxvii (1984), 83–109.

Marcham, A. J., 'Educating our masters: political parties and elementary education 1867 to 1870', *British Journal of Educational Studies*, xxi (1973), 180–91.

Marsh, P. T., *The Victorian Church in decline: Archbishop Tait and the Church of England 1868–1882*, London, 1969.

Matthew, H. C. G., 'Gladstone, Vaticanism, and the question of the East', *Studies in Church History*, xv (1978), 417–42.

'Disraeli, Gladstone, and the politics of mid-Victorian budgets', *HJ*, xxii (1979), 615–43.

Mitchell, L., *Holland House*, London, 1980.

Moody, T. W., and J. C. Beckett, *Queen's, Belfast, 1845–1949: the history of a university*, 2 vols., London, 1959.

Morgan, K. O., *Wales in British politics 1868–1922*, Cardiff, 1980 edn.

Morris, R. J., 'Whatever happened to the British working class, 1750–1850?', *Bulletin of the Society for the Study of Labour History*, xli (1980), 13–15.

Murphy, J., *Church, state and schools in Britain, 1800–1970*, London, 1971.

Newsome, D., *Godliness and good learning: four studies on a Victorian ideal*, London, 1961.

Newton, R., *Victorian Exeter 1837–1914*, Leicester, 1968.

Norman, E. R., *The Catholic Church and Ireland in the age of rebellion 1859–1873*, London, 1965.

Anti-Catholicism in Victorian England, London, 1968.

Church and society in England 1770–1970: a historical study, Oxford, 1976.

Nossiter, T. J., *Influence, opinion and political idioms in Reformed England: case studies from the North-east 1832–74*, Hassocks, 1975.

'The middle class and nineteenth century politics: notes on the literature', in *The middle class in politics*, ed. J. Garrard, D. Jary, M. Goldsmith and A. Oldfield, Farnborough, 1978, pp. 67–84.

Offer, A., *Property and politics, 1870–1914: landownership, law, ideology and urban develop-ment in England*, Cambridge, 1981.

Olney, R. J., *Lincolnshire politics 1832–1885*, Oxford, 1973.

Omond, G. W. T., *The Lord Advocates of Scotland: second series, 1834–1880*, London, 1914.

Owen, D., *The government of Victorian London 1855–1889: the metropolitan board of works, the vestries, and the city corporation*, Harvard, 1982.

Peel, A., *These hundred years: a history of the Congregational Union of England and Wales, 1831–1931*, London, 1931.

Pelling, H., *Social geography of British elections 1885–1910*, London, 1967.

Perkin, H., *The structured crowd: essays in English social history*, Brighton, 1981.

Phillips, G. D., 'The whig lords and Liberalism, 1886–1893', *HJ*, xxiv (1981), 167–73.

Phillips, P. T., 'Religion and society in the cloth region of Wiltshire, c. 1830–70', *Journal of Religious History*, xi (1980), 95–110.

Philpott, H. B., *London at school: the story of the school board, 1870–1904*, London, 1904.

Port, M. H., 'A contrast in styles at the Office of Works: Layard and Ayrton: aesthete and economist', *HJ*, xxvii (1984), 151–76.

Prestige, G. L., *St Paul's in its glory: a candid history of the cathedral 1831–1911*, London, 1955.

Pugh, M., *The making of modern British politics 1867–1939*, Oxford, 1982.

Ramm, A., 'The parliamentary context of cabinet government, 1868–1874', *EHR*, xcix (1984), 739–69.

'Gladstone as politician', in *Gladstone, politics and religion: a collection of Founder's Day Lectures delivered at St Deiniol's Library, Hawarden, 1967–83*, ed. P. J. Jagger, London, 1985, pp. 104–16.

Read, D., *The English provinces c. 1760–1960: a study in influence*, London, 1964.

Reardon, B. M. G., *Religious thought in the Victorian age: a survey from Coleridge to Gore*, London, 1980.

Richards, N. J., 'Religious controversy and the school boards 1870–1902', *British Journal of Educational Studies*, xviii (1970), 180–96.

Roach, J., 'Liberalism and the Victorian intelligentsia', *Cambridge Historical Journal*, xiii (1957), 58–81.

Roland, D., 'The struggle for the Elementary Education Act and its implemen-tation, 1870–73', Oxford B.Litt., 1957.

Roper, H., 'W. E. Forster's memorandum of 21 October, 1869: a re-examination', *British Journal of Educational Studies*, xxi (1973), 64–75.

'Towards an Education Act for England and Wales, 1865–68', *British Journal of Educational Studies*, xxiii (1975), 181–208.

Rossi, J. P., 'The transformation of the British Liberal party: a study of the tactics of the Liberal opposition, 1874–1880', *Transactions of the American Philosophical Society*, lxviii (1978), part VIII.

Royle, E., *Radicals, secularists and republicans: popular freethought in Britain, 1866–1915*, Manchester, 1980.

St Quintin, G., *The history of Glenalmond: the story of a hundred years*, Edinburgh, 1956.

Searby, P., 'Gladstone in West Derby Hundred: the Liberal campaign in South-west Lancashire in 1868', *Transactions of the Historic Society of Lancashire and Cheshire*, cxi (1959), 139–66.

Selby, D. E., 'Henry Edward Manning and the Education Bill of 1870', *British Journal of Educational Studies*, xviii (1970), 197–212.

Semmel, B., *The Governor Eyre controversy*, London, 1962.

Shannon, R. T., *Gladstone and the Bulgarian agitation 1876*, Hassocks, 2nd edn, 1975.

Simon, A., 'Church disestablishment as a factor in the general election of 1885', *HJ*, xviii (1975), 791–820.

Simon, B., *Studies in the history of education: education and the labour movement 1870–1920*, London, 1965.

Studies in the history of education: the two nations and the educational structure 1780–1870, London, 1974.

Simpson, J. B. H., *Rugby since Arnold: a history of Rugby school from 1842*, London, 1967.

Skeats, H. S., and Miall, C. S., *History of the Free Churches of England 1688–1891*, London, 1894.

Smith, F. B., *The making of the second Reform Bill*, Cambridge, 1966.

Smith, P., *Disraelian Conservatism and social reform*, London, 1967.

Southgate, D., *The passing of the whigs, 1832–86*, London, 1962.

Spring, D., 'Aristocracy, social structure, and religion in the early Victorian period', *VS*, vi (1962–3), 263–80.

'English landowners and nineteenth-century industrialism', in *Land and industry: the landed estate and the industrial revolution*, ed. J. T. Ward and R. G. Wilson, Newton Abbot, 1971, pp. 16–62.

Steele, E. D., 'Gladstone and Ireland', *Irish Historical Studies*, xvii (1970), 58–88.

Irish land and British politics: tenant-right and nationality 1865–1870, Cambridge, 1974.

'Infidels and churchmen', *Northern History*, xiii (1977), 280–2.

'Gladstone, Irish violence, and conciliation', in *Studies in Irish history presented to R. Dudley Edwards*, ed. A. Cosgrove and D. McCartney, Dublin, 1979, pp. 257–78.

'Gladstone and Palmerston, 1855–65', in *Gladstone, politics and religion: a collection of Founder's Day Lectures delivered at St Deiniol's Library, Hawarden, 1967–83*, ed. P. J. Jagger, London, 1985, pp. 117–47.

Stevens, R., *Law and politics: the House of Lords as a judicial body, 1800–1976*, London, 1979.

Summerton, N. W., 'Dissenting attitudes to foreign relations, peace and war, 1840–1890', *Journal of Ecclesiastical History*, xxviii (1977), 151–78.

Sutherland, G., *Policy-making in elementary education 1870–1895*, Oxford, 1973.

Temmel, M. R., 'Liberal versus Liberal, 1874: W. E. Forster, Bradford and education', *HJ*, xviii (1975), 611–22.

'Gladstone's resignation of the Liberal leadership, 1874–1875', *Journal of British Studies*, xvi (1976–7), 153–77.

Thompson, A. F., 'Gladstone's whips and the general election of 1868', *EHR*, lxiii (1948), 189–200.

Thompson, D., 'The Liberation Society, 1844–1868', in *Pressure from without in early Victorian England*, ed. P. Hollis, London, 1974, pp. 210–38.

'The making of the English religious classes', *HJ*, xxii (1979), 477–91.

Tibawi, A. L., *British interests in Palestine 1800–1901: a study of religious and educational enterprise*, Oxford, 1961.

Trainor, R., 'Peers on an industrial frontier: the earls of Dartmouth and of Dudley in the Black Country, *c.* 1810 to 1914', in *Patricians, power and politics in nineteenth-century towns*, ed. D. N. Cannadine, Leicester, 1982, pp. 69–132.

Travis, M. A., 'The work of the Leeds school board 1870–1902', *Researches and Studies (The University of Leeds Institute of Education)*, viii (1953).

Turner, F. M., 'Rainfall, plagues, and the prince of Wales: a chapter in the conflict of religion and science', *Journal of British Studies*, xiii (1974), 46–65.

'Victorian scientific naturalism and Thomas Carlyle', *VS*, xviii (1974–5), 325–43.

The Greek heritage in Victorian Britain, New Haven, 1981.

Vincent, J. R., *The formation of the Liberal party 1857–1868*, London, 1966.

'The effect of the second Reform Act in Lancashire', *HJ*, xi (1968), 84–94.

Pollbooks: how Victorians voted, Cambridge, 1968.

'Gladstone and Ireland', *Proceedings of the British Academy*, lxiii (1977), 193–238.

Wald, K. D., *Crosses on the ballot: patterns of British voter alignment since 1885*, Princeton, 1983.

Waller, P. J., *Democracy and sectarianism: a political and social history of Liverpool 1868–1939*, Liverpool, 1981.

Ward, W. R., *Victorian Oxford*, London, 1965.

Whyte, J. H., *The independent Irish party 1850–9*, Oxford, 1958.

Withrington, D. J., 'Towards a national system, 1867–72: the last years in the struggle for a Scottish Education Act', *Scottish Educational Studies*, iv (1972), 107–24.

Wohl, A. S., *The eternal slum: housing and social policy in Victorian London*, London, 1977.

Wright, D. G., 'Liberal versus Liberal, 1874: some comments', *HJ*, xvi (1973), 597–603.

'The Bradford election of 1874', in *Nineteenth century Bradford elections*, ed. J. A. Jowitt and R. K. S. Taylor, Bradford, 1979, pp. 50–73.

Index

Abbott, E. A. (headmaster, City of London school 1865–89; Church reform enthusiast), 303
Aberdeen, 4th earl of, 36, 37, 38
academic liberals, 249–55; and education, 252–3; and Ireland, 253–5, 441; and populism, 252–3; and religion, 250–2
Acland, A. H. D., 254
Acland, Sir T. D. (baronet 1871) (1809–98), 183n, 184, 189n, 190, 191n, 192, 265, 310, 412, 413, 439
Acton, J. E. E. D. (cr. Baron 1869) (1834–1902), 193–5, 198, 293–4
Adam, W. P. (Liberal chief whip 1873–80), 412
Adderley, Sir C. B., 138
Agar-Ellis, Hon. L. G. F., 197
Airlie, 7th earl of (1826–81), 64, 285, 419
Akroyd, E. (1810–87), 93, 109n, 146, 148n, 302, 338, 342, 365n
Alabama affair, 122, 321, 352
Allen, W. S., 218, 336
Allon, H., 38, 209, 439
Althorp, Viscount, 17
Amberley, Viscount, 27, 76, 250
Amory, J. H., 146
Anderson, G., 341
Anson, A. H. A. (brother of Lichfield), 365n
Anstruther, Sir R., 405, 418, 419
Antrobus, Sir E., 191n, 192, 270
Applegarth, R., 234
Arch, J., 206, 233–4, 238, 401
Argyll, duchess of, 61
Argyll, 8th duke of (1823–1900), 31, **75**, 87, 98, 262, 267, 269, 279, 367, 401; and Catholicism, 125, 137, 293; and democratic politics, 31, 81–2, 119, 123, 408, 422, 442; and Ireland, 132, 137, 290, 291, 318, 403, 442, education, 135, 265, 354,

356; and Scottish Church, 102, 103, 342, 418, 419, 442
army purchase question, 119, 277, 322
Arnold, E., 124
Arnold, M. (1822–88), 58, **69**, 72, 73, 87, 127, 223; and education, 106, 110; and Ireland, 134; and Liberal party, 120, 408; and nonconformity, 31, 93, 99, 120
Arnold, T., 17, 68–71, 77
Arthur, W., 218, 336, 358
Ashley, Hon. A. E. M., 66
Asquith, H. H., 441n
Athanasian Creed, 44–5, 99–100, 155, 312–14
Ayrton, A. S., 121, 280, 352
Aytoun, R. S., 301, 365n, 399

Backhouse, E., 336
Bagehot, W. (1826–77), 76, 77, 117, 118, 121, 142
Baines, E. (1800–90), 22, 40, **215**, 302, 303, 305, 336, 396
Ball, J. T., 282, 359
ballot question, 117, 322, 345, 346, 351–2
Baptist, The, 206
Baptist Magazine, 335
baptists, 22–3, 24, 200–16; and anti-clericalism, 216; and disestablishment, 204–6, 213–15; and education, 210–11, 214; and foreign policy, 208; and high churchmen, 208–9; and Ireland, 211–12, 216, 439; and the poor, 207; and religion, 202–16
Baring, C. T., 62
Baring, H. B., 270
Barry, Alfred (1826–1910), **79**, 80, 100, 107, 406
Barry, Maltman, 236, 407
Bass, M. A., 146, 420

493

Bass, M. T., 146, 420
Bath, 4th marquess of, 283
Baxter, W. E. (1825–90), 220, 250n, 280, 381, 412
Beauchamp, 6th Earl, 406
Beaumont family, 230
Bedford, Hastings Russell, 9th duke of (1819–91), 61, 64, 72, 408, 426, 434
Bee-hive, 233–9, 401
Beesly, E. S. (1831–1915), 238, **239–49**, 349, 401, 440, 445
Begg, J. (1808–83), 219–20, 309, 342
Bennett judgment, 44, 372
Bentinck, G. A. F. C. (Conservative MP), 374
Bessborough, 5th earl of (government whip in Lords 1868–74) (1809–80), 284, 285, 325, 385
Bickersteth, R., 24
Binney, T., 38, 212, 307, 335
Birmingham Town Council, 335
Blachford, 1st Baron (cr. 1871) (1811–89), **182**, 186, 190, 413, 439
Blackie, J. S. (professor of Greek, Edinburgh university 1852–72) (1809–95), 74, 220n, 362, 441
Blackley, W., 115n
Black Sea crisis, 122, 321
Blackwood's Magazine, 288, 335
Blennerhassett, Sir R., 193, 198, 320
Blennerhassett, R. P., 343
Bölckow, H. W. F., 146
Bonham-Carter, J., 146
Bouverie, E. P. (cabinet office 1855–8, ecclesiastical commissioner 1869) (1818–89), **26, 64**, 365; and Church of England, 313, 337, 375, 434; and Gladstone, or the Liberal party, 141, 142, 346, 388, 399, 409, 434; and Irish education, 348, 351, 365n, 370–1, 399; and parliamentary reform, 10, 261; and university tests, 26, 297
Bowring, E. A., 146
Bradlaugh, C., 159, 215, 234, 238, 434, 440
Bradley, G. G., 69, 70, 72
Brand, H. B. W. (Liberal chief whip 1859–67, Speaker 1872–84) (1814–92), **61**, 136, 261, 262, 273–4, 302–3, 361, 422
Brand, H. R. (son of H. B. W. Brand), 273, 393
Brassey, T., 392, 441n
Brereton, J. L. (1822–1901), 68, 69, 72, 110, 112n, 215
Bridges, J. H., 239
Bright, Jacob (1821–99), 297, 302, 303, 305–6, 336
Bright, John (1811–89), 207, 220, **227**, 279,

293, 330, 331, 339, 384–5; and education, 331, 379, 386; and foreign policy, 317; and Ireland, 228, 273, 282, 292, 372, 439; and parliamentary reform, 28, 261; and religion, 25, 227
Bright, William (1824–1901), 185, 190, 271, 376
British and Foreign Schools Society, 18, 211
British Quarterly Review, 209, 210, 381–2, 421
Broadhurst, H., 233–4, 236, 440
Brocklehurst, W. C., 148n
Brodrick, G. C. (1831–1903), 58, **70**, 101, 111, 118, 120, 143, 149, 165, 292, 441
Brogden, A., 400
Brougham and Vaux, 1st Baron, 18
Brown, Baldwin, 38
Browne, E. H. (1811–91), **182**, 190n, 376, 406, 417, 439
Browne, G. E., 292
Browning, R., 214
Bruce, Lord **Charles** W. B., 192
Bruce, Lord **Ernest** A. C. B., 191, 192, 270
Bruce, H. A. (cr. Baron Aberdare 1873) (1815–95), 15, **76**, 279, 315, 322, 345, 384; and Church of England, 311, 313; and education, 41, 262; and Ireland, 263, 286, 291, 317, 328, 353, 440
Bryce, J., 221, 296, 402n
Buchanan, R., 219
Bunting, J., 24
Burges, W., 374
Burials Bill, 37, 147
Burke, E. H., 365n, 375
Burt, T., 236, 400, 440
Butler, A. G., 69
Butler, A. J., 183
Butler, H. M., 69, 303, 415
Butt, I. (1813–79), 196, 197, 324, 345, 359
Buxton, C., 302, 308
By-elections: Bath, 378–9; Cheshire Mid, 383; Dundee, 382; Exeter, 383; Galway, 343–4, 349; Greenwich, 382, 383; Hull, 383; Kerry, 343–4; Limerick, 324; Mayo, 292; Meath, 316; Newry, 316; Notts N., 339; Oldham, 339; Plymouth, 322, 329; Renfrewshire, 383; Shaftesbury, 382, 383; Staffs E., 383; Stroud, 383; Surrey E., 322; Tamworth, 339; Tipperary, 291, 292; Truro, 322, 329; Waterford city, 292; Westmeath, 324; Yorks. West Riding N., 218, 338–9; Yorks. West Riding S., 339

Caird, J., 71
Cairnes, J. E., 225
Cairns, 1st Baron (cr. 1867) (1819–85), 271, 274, 283–7, 314, 359–60, 375

Cairns, J., 340–1
Calvinistic Methodism, 219
Cambridge, 2nd duke of, 372
Cameron, C., 399
Camoys, 3rd Baron, 198
Campbell-Bannerman, H., 231, 309, 338
Camperdown, 3rd earl of, 66, 67, 419
Candlish, J., 337
Cardwell, E. (cr. Viscount Cardwell 1874)
  (1813–86), 47, 191, 263, 279, 286, 298,
  313, 318, 352, 364, 401
Carlisle, countess of, 76, 250, 254
Carlisle, 7th earl of (Viscount Morpeth,
  1825–48), 15, 33, 142
Carlyle, T. (1795–1881), 73–6, 80, 118, 123,
  222, 270, 362
Carnarvon, 4th earl of (1831–90), 283–6,
  360, 374, 417
Carter, T. T., 182
Cartwright, W. C., 392, 401
Catholic bishops, 20, 42, 263, 265, 285, 299,
  326–7, 330, 349–50, 359, 363
Catholicism, *see* Catholics; Vatican council;
  and Gladstone, high churchmen, noncon-
  formity, positivism, whig-liberals *for*
  attitudes to
Catholics: English, voting characteristics,
  196, 395; Irish, *see* Catholic bishops,
  Fenianism, home rule party, liberal
  Catholics, National Association,
  Ribbonism
Cavendish, Lord E., 273
Cavendish, Lady F. C. (daughter of 4th
  Baron Lyttelton), 439
Cavendish, Lord F. C. (1836–82), 76, 149,
  392, 412
Chamberlain, J. (1836–1914), 50, **224–5**,
  235n, 407; and education, 145, 306, 336,
  378, 381–2; and home rule, 438, 440; and
  Liberal party, 396, 422, 427, 432
Chambers, M., 365n
Chambers, T. (knight 1872) (1814–91), 66,
  146, 273, 295, 316, 338
Chapman, J., 249
Charteris, A. H., 71
Chichester, 3rd earl of, 285
Childers, H. C. E. (1827–96), 47, 59, **61**,
  269, 279, 375, 415, 440
Christian socialism, 30, 72–3, 114, 118
Church, R. W. (1815–90), **184**, 186–7,
  189n, 190, 373, 413, 439
Church Association, 43, 376
Church Defence Institution, 100, 312, 331,
  338
Church of England, *see also* Court of Arches,
  Judicial Committee of the Privy Council,
  ritualism; *and see* Gladstone, high

churchmen, nonconformity,
  Peelites, positivism, whig-liberals,
  working-men, *for attitudes to*; appointments, 372–3; in parliament, 311–14,
  337–8, 374–6, 413–17; rates, 21–2, 25–6,
  37, 216, 274–5
Church of Scotland, 45–6, 102–4, 309, 342,
  418–20
Clanricarde, 1st marquess of (cabinet
  office 1846–52, 1858) (1802–74), 60, 285,
  344
Clarendon, 4th earl of (1800–70), 58, **60**,
  65, 127; and Ireland, 135–6, 273, 284–6,
  288, 290–1, 299, 300; and Liberal party,
  261, 267, 278, 279; and Vatican council,
  292–4
Clarke, C., 80n
Clay, Sir W., 25
Cleveland, 4th duke of (1803–91), **61**, 62,
  126n, 283–5
Clifford, J. (1836–1923), 201, 207, 210
Clive, G., 270
Cobbett, J. M., 339
Cobden, R., 25
Colenso, J. W., 44
Coleridge, J. D. (knight 1868; cr. Baron
  Coleridge 1874) (1820–94), 26, **184–5**,
  189, 190, 192, 297–8, 301, 307, 308, 426,
  439
Colman, J. J. (1830–98), 201, **215**, 216, 338,
  415
Conder, E., 212, 214, 215, 336
Congreve, R., 239
congregationalists, *see all references under*
  baptists
Congregational Union, 307, 335
Conservative party, 137–8, 346–7, 366,
  383–4; and Church of England, 413–17,
  422–3; and education, 379–80, 412; and
  elections, 271–2, 276, 389–92, 403–5; and
  foreign policy, 433; and Ireland, 267–9,
  299, 319, 359–60, 364–5, 411; and Scotland,
  342–3, 418–20; and social questions, 411
Contemporary Review, 27, 215, 423
Cork, mayor of, 290
Corrigan, Sir D. J., 193
Courthope, W. J., 433n
Court of Arches, 35, 43, 44, 184
Cowen, J., 400, 445
Cowper, 7th Earl, 66, 67, 285
Cowper, H. F., 66
Cowper (-Temple added 1869), W. F.
  (1811–88), 15, 59, **66**, **72**, 116, 322; and
  education, 109 and n, 297, 302, 304, 305,
  412; and Liberal party, 279, 392, 416,
  426, 434; and religion, 59, 90, 213, 338,
  420, 426, 434

Crawford, R. W. (MP, City of London
  1857–74; director, Bank of England), 380
Creighton, M., 70
Cremer, R., 236, 440
Crichton, Viscount, 320
Cromwell, J. G., 406
Cross, R. A., 137, 374
Crosskey, H. W. (unitarian minister in
  Birmingham, follower of Chamberlain),
  304, 330
Cullen, P. (1803–78), 39, 42, 43, 350–1, 359,
  363

Daily News, 214, 225, 265, 287, 311, 316, 346,
  356, 360–1, 362–3, 364, 409
Daily Telegraph, 124, 163–4
Dale, R. W. (1829–95), 28, 93, **201–5**,
  207–10, 216, 304, 330–1, 335, 341, 377,
  422, 439
Dale, T., 373
Dalglish, R., 399
Dalhousie, 11th earl of (cabinet office
  1855–8), 418, 420
Dalkeith, earl of, 405
Daunt, O'Neill, 38
Davies, J. Llewelyn (1826–1916), 27, 71, 73,
  97n, 339, 441
Dawson, G., 28, 201
Dease, E., 315
Dease, J. A., 195, 343
de Grey, *see* Ripon, marquess of
Delane, J. T., 65, 384, 415
de Mauley, 2nd Baron, 31
Denison, G. A., 182
Denison, J. E. (cr. Viscount Ossington
  1872) (Speaker 1857–72), 100n, 142n
Derby, 14th earl of (Lord Stanley 1834–51)
  (1799–1869), 19, 266, 267, 282, 283
Derby, 15th earl of (Lord Stanley 1851–69)
  (1826–93), 137, 143, 266, 271, 284, 299,
  346, 350, 360, 373–4
Devon, 4th earl of, 283
Devonshire, 7th duke of (1808–91), **61**, 62,
  63, **67**, **69**, 75, 283, 285
Dicey, A. V. (1835–1922), 58, 70, 149
Dickinson, S. S., 146
Digby, K. T., 345
Dilke, Sir C. W. (1843–1911), 225, 235n,
  250, 252, 254, 338
Dillwyn, L. L. (1814–92), 265, 380, 414
Disraeli, B. (1804–81), 9–10, 21, 50, 139;
  and ecclesiastical legislation, 375,
  416–17; and education, 52, 379–80; and
  Ireland, 266, 267–8, 284, 287, 319, 346,
  350, 360, 364–5, 411; public speeches,
  271, 347, 383–4, 389–91
Divorce Act, 37, 158

Dixon, G. (1820–98), 235n, 296, 297, 306,
  336, 338, 377
Dodson, J. G. (deputy Speaker, 1865–72)
  (1825–97), 26, **67**, 273, 295, 364, 365, 420
Döllinger, J. J. I. von, 165, 193
Dowden, E. (professor of English literature,
  Trinity college, Dublin) (1867–1913),
  87n
Downing, McC., 317, 319
Dowse, R., 321
Dublin university, *see* Trinity college,
  Dublin
Dudley, 1st earl of, 185, 400
Duff, M. E. Grant (1829–1906), 30, 59, **70**,
  72, 87, 119, 121, 412, 441
Dufferin, 4th Baron (cr. 1st earl of 1871)
  (1826–1902), **66**, **67**, 121, 124, 130, 131,
  139–40, 325, 367
Dundas, F., 61
Dunkellin, Lord (son of Clanricarde), 261
Dunraven and Mount-Earl, 3rd earl of, 285
Durham, 2nd earl of, 285
Durham letter, 33, 36
Durnford, R. (1802–95), 182, 186n

Earp, T., 400
Eastern question, 25, 122–5, 175–6, 432
Ebury, 1st Baron (1801–93), 66, 283, 314,
  434
Ecclesiastical Titles Act, 33, 293
Economist, **76**, 131, 287, 337, 342, 367, 401,
  426
Edinburgh Review, **65**, 113, 115, 119, 128, 335,
  366, 407, 417
Education, *see also* academic liberals,
  Gladstone, high churchmen, noncon-
  formity, Peelites, positivism, whig-
  liberals, working-men, *for attitudes to*;
  elementary, 18, 39–41, 262–3, 277,
  294–7, 301–6, 309, 334–6, 376–80, Clause
  25 of 1870 Act, 52, 211, 218, 226, 227,
  329–30, 377–80, 380–1, 390, 412;
  endowed, 110, 309–11, 380, 412; *see also*
  Emanuel Hospital
Education League, *see* National Education
  League
Egerton, Hon. A.F., 41
Elcho, Lord (Adullamite; later 9th earl of
  Wemyss and March, and founder of
  Liberty and Property Defence League),
  261
election results: *1868*, 275–8; *1874*, 393–6
Eliot, G. (1819–80), 27, 31, **249**, 251, 366
Ellice, E. (1810–80), **61**, 64, 261, 263, 346,
  365, 366, 367, 388
Elliot, A. R. D., 61
Elliot, H. G., 61, 124

Emanuel Hospital, 146, 148, 310, 380
Emmeitt, J. T., 374
Enfield, Viscount (son of Strafford), 79
Epping Forest, 116, 146, 322
Essays and reviews, 27, 44
Essays on Reform, 58
Evangelical Alliance, 213, 218
Evans, T. W., 392
Eversley, 1st Viscount (Speaker, 1839–57), 64

Fairbairn, Sir A., 402n
Farrar, F. W., 69, 72
Fawcett, H. (1833–84), 27, 29, 116, **249–50**, 251, 409, 414; and education, 253, 296, 379; and Ireland, 253, 254, 265, 296, 298–300, 314, 320, 328, 343–8, 361, 365n, 369–70; and university tests, 300–1, 308
Fawcett, M. G., 254
Fenianism, 42–3, 266
Fenian prisoners, 290–2, 317–18, 324–5, 372
Fergusson, J. (writer on architecture), 374
financial policy, 37, 119, 167–8, 172, 321, 386–8
Fitzmaurice, Lord E. G. P. (1845–1935), **250**, 253, 308, 310, 361, 365n, 386, 414
Fitzwilliam, 6th Earl (1815–1902), 10, **61**, **62**, 63, 283, 285, 339, 376, 402, 434
Fitzwilliam, Hon. C. W. W., 61
Foljambe, F. J. S., 338
Forbes, A. P., 183n, 185
Forster, J., 74
Forster, W. E. (1818–86), 15, **108**, **169**, **228**, 269, 280, 385, 401; and Church of England, 313, 338, 415, 416, 433; and education, 41, 109, 262, 277, 295–7, 302–5, 377–9, 385, 386, 427–8, endowed schools, 310, 412; and Liberal party, 396, 427–8
Fortescue, C. S. P. (cr. Baron Carlingford 1874) (1823–98), **67**, 72, 279, 395; and Church of England, 67, 96n, 313; and Irish disorder, 290–2, 317–18, 395; and Irish education, 134, 135, 263, 264–5, 299, 319, 327, 363, 364
Fortescue, 3rd **Earl** (1818–1905), **61**, **64**, 112n, 283, 285, 323–4, 331, 362, 367, 388, 408, 434
Fortnightly Review, 27, 239, 344
Foster, W. H., 338, 365n
Fowler, H. H., 441n
Fraser, J. (1818–85), **69**, 72, 73, 107, 149
Fraser's Magazine, 27, 71, 74, 367, 409
Free Church, Scottish, 45–6, 104, 217, 219–22, 309, 418–20, 422

Freeman, E. A. (1823–92), **184**, 186–8, 225, 228, 439
Fremantle, W. H. (1831–1916), 61, **70**, 73, 101, 149, 417
Froude, J. A. (1818–94), 27, 58, 72, **74**, 113, 123, 187, 356, 409; and education, 106, 108; and Ireland, 128, 132, 296; and religion, 83, 89, 95, 98, 108, 126

Garrett, E., 80
Gladstone, W. E. (1809–98), **153–81**; and Bradlaugh, 159, 434; and Catholicism/ ultramontanism, 156–7, 176, 177, 292–5, 315–17, 404, 423–4, 426, 445; and Church of England, appointments, 372–3, Establishment, 160–2, 311–12, 388, 434, in parliament, 311–14, 337–8, 375–6, 414–17, Purchas judgment, 373, rates, 37, 216, 274–5; and democratic politics, 50, 167–74, 436–7, 451–2; and Eastern question, 175–6, 432; and education, elementary, 40, 164–7, 262–3, 296–7, 302–6, 330, 377–9, 386, 388, 409, 427, endowed, 412, university, 164–7, 263, 298, 300–1, 307–9; and finance, 37, 167–8, 172, 386–7; and foreign policy, 174–5, 432–3; and Ireland, 276–81, Church question, 38, 178–9, 180, 266, 268–70, 280–7, disorder, 290–2, 317–19, 324–5, 372, education, national, 327, 348–9, education, university, 179–81, 263–6, 298–300, 319–20, 328–9, 333–41, 344–8, 353–7, 361, 363–5, 369–70, home rule, 181, 325–6, 349, 371–2, 389, 412, 437, 444–6, Keogh judgment, 350, O'Keeffe case, 351, 371, royal residence, 325, 351; and Liberal party, 171–4, 255–6, 261–2, 269, 272–3, 276, 409–10, 426–7, 431–3; and nonconformists, 162–4, 167, 211; and Palmerston, 36, 37, 168, 174–5; and parliamentary reform, 159, 167–73, 261–2, 323, 386; and religion, 31, 36–8, 153–67, 203, 352, 356; and Scotland, 164, 340, 418–20
Glyn, G. G. (2nd Baron Wolverton 1873; Liberal chief whip 1867–73) (1824–87), 262, 267, 286, 300, 322, 346, 361
Godwin, J. V., 396
Goldney, G., 138
Goldsmid, Sir F. H., 226
Goldsmid, J., 226
Gordon, Sir A. H., 192–3, 439
Gordon, E. S., 342, 375, 418
Gore, C., 184, 189, 190
Gorham judgment, 35, 158

Goschen, G. J. (1831–1907), 26, 30, **69–70**, 75, 112, 119, 279, 321; and ecclesiastical legislation, 415, 420; and education, 304, 412; and foreign policy, 122, 352; and Ireland, 265, 441

Grafton, 6th duke of, 283, 285

Graham, Sir J., 19, 36

Graham, W., 314, 399

Grantham, W., 390

Granville, 2nd Earl (1815–91), 47, **65**, 72, 261, 279, 303, 322, 385; and Ireland, 286, 287, 291, 318, 325, 353; and Vatican council, 293–4

Graves, S. R., 137

Gray, Sir J. (advanced Irish Liberal MP; proprietor, *Freeman's Journal*), 265, 266, 345

Green, T. H., 49, 436, 441n

Greenwood, F., 79, 327

Greg, W. R. (1809–81), 27, 59, **76–7**, 87, 92, 113, 114, 128, 133, 223, 229

Gregory, R. (1819–1911), **185**, 271, 373, 406

Gregory, W. H. (1817–92), 72, 121, 125, 191n

Greville-Nugent, F. S., 270

Grey, Albert, 61, 63

Grey, Charles, 61, 64, 136n

Grey, Sir Edward, 441n

Grey, Sir **George** (1799–1882), 15, **61**, **62**, 63, **67**, 70, 261, 279, 400; and Church of England, 313, 375; and education, 303, 305–6; and Ireland, 133, 286, 328, 346, 425; and Liberal party, 323, 352, 388, 400, 425

Grey, Henry, 3rd Earl (Viscount Howick, 1807–45) (1802–94), 10, 17, **61**, **63–4**, 119, 251, 261, 352; and Church of England, 33, 96, 99–100, 314, 419, 434; and Ireland, 131, 134, 265, 273, 283, 284, 285, 287, 291, 389

Grey Coat Hospital, 310

Grosvenor, Earl, *see* Westminster, 3rd marquess of

Grove, G., 70, 123, 441

Guardian, 439

Gurney, R., 138, 313

Haldane, R. B., 441n

Halifax, 1st Viscount (Charles Wood, cr. 1866) (1800–85), 24, **61**, **62**, 63, 64, **65**, 67, 351, 352; and Church of England, 274–5, 374, 425–6; and education, 331, 379; and Ireland, 284–8, 318, 328, 350, 356, 389, 425–6; and Liberal party, 119, 261, 279, 323, 331, 388, 389, 401, 422, 425–6

Hall, C. Newman (1816–1902), 38, 212,

213, 214, 216, 336, 356, 439

Hamilton, W. K. (1808–69), 37, 184, 190

Hampden, R. D., 35

Hankey, T., 415

Hanmer, Sir J., 191n

Harcourt, W. G. G. V. (knight 1873) (1827–1904), 30, 50, **62**, 66, 146, 301, 386; and church questions, 91, 375, 415–17, 420; and education, 297, 305, 306, 310, 336, 379, 428; and Gladstone, 409, 415–17, 425–6; and Ireland, 91, 136, 301, 360, 364, 365, 371, 425–6, 440; and Liberal party, 116, 136, 352, 401, 436

Hardaker, J., 396

Hardcastle, J. A., 335, 338

Hardie, J. K., 234, 440, 446

Hardy, G. (1814–1906), 268, 271, 346, 361, 363, 375

Harrison, F. (1831–1923), 27, 238, **239–49**, 382, 401, 427, 440

Harrowby, 2nd earl of, 314, 351

Hartington, marquess of (1833–1908), **61**, **66**, **67**, 148, 279, 385, 416, 427–8; and church questions, 338, 420; and democratic politics, 117–18, 120; and education, 412, 427–8; and Ireland, 135, 291, 318–19, 327, 351, 370–1, 372, 385, 412–13, 437, 444, university question, 148, 320, 328, 343–9, 354, 355–6, 363, 365, 369–70

Hatherley, 1st Baron (W. P. Wood, cr. 1868) (1801–81), 183, **184–5**, 186n, 189, 191, 279, 318

Haughton, S., 359

Hayter, A. D., 378

Headlam, S., 184, 188–9

Headlam, T. E., 400

Henderson, A., 234, 446

Henderson, J., 146

Henley, Lord, 108

Henry, M., 196, 324

Herbert, Hon. A. E. W. M. (1838–1906), 36, **250**, 252, 253, 254, 336, 338, 341, 365n

Herschel, Sir J. F. W., 27

high churchmen, 151–2, 181–91; and church questions, 186, 189, 191, 413–14, 435; and Eastern question, 187–8, 432; and education, 190–1, 192; and Ireland, 190–1, 192–3, 439, 444–6; and politics, 186–91, 451–2

Hill, F. H., 225

Hoare, Sir H. A., 277

Hobhouse, A., 311

Hobhouse, L. T., 256–7

Hodgkinson, G., 400

Holden, I., 218, 338, 402n

Holland, H. S., 183n, 184

Holt, J. M., 416
Holyoake, G. J., 234, 302
home rule party, 43, 196–7, 292, 315, 324, 326, 328, 343–4, 345, 359, 363, 371–2, 394–5, 412–13
Hook, W. F. (dean of Chichester 1859–75) (1798–1875), **182–3**, 186n, 190n, 191, 302, 413
Hooker, Sir J. D., 75, 352
Horsman, E. (1807–76), **61**, **72**, **78**, 109, 308; and church questions, 78, 337, 419, 420; and Ireland, 136, 263, 268, 360, 361, 365n, 367; and Liberal party, 261, 409
Houghton, 1st Baron, 31, 425–6
Howard, Hon. C. W. G., 61
Howell, G., 233–4, 235
Howick, Viscount, *see* Grey, Henry, 3rd Earl
Hughes, H. P., 218
Hughes, T. (1822–96), **69**, 72, 79, 86, 122n, 146, 399; and democratic politics, 31, 58, 235n, 399, 434; and education, 109, 302, 310; and Ireland, 272, 441; and religion, 86, 93, 100, 337, 338, 415, 434
Hughes, W. B., 191n
Huntly, 11th marquess of, 419
Hutton, G. C., 220, 221, 420
Hutton, R. H. (1826–97), 58, 72, **76**, 135, 149, 441
Huxley, T. H. (1825–95), 27, 30, 53, 58, **74**, 80, 87, 94n, 97, 106, 108, 360, 441, 442

Illingworth, A. (1827–1907), **201**, 206, 207, 212, **218**, 231, 396, 402n; and Church of England, 312, 314, 338, 381, 414; and education, 302, 396, 402n
Independent Labour Party, 236
Ingram, J. K., 356
Innes, A. T., 340; 418, 420
Ireland, *see also* Fenian prisoners, *and see* academic liberals, Gladstone, high churchmen, home rule party, liberal Catholics, nonconformity, Peelites, positivism, whig-liberals, working-men, *for attitudes to*; Church question, 9–10, 18–19, 32–3, 38–9, 265–70, 280–8, 293; coercion legislation, 291–2, 318–19, 372; land question, 290, 294; national education question 19–20, 326–7, 348–9; university question, 4, 20, 38–9, 41–2, 263–5, 298–300, 319–21, 328–9, 344–8, 353–68, 369–70
Italian unification, 11, 25

Jackson, J., 373, 374, 406
Jaffray, J., 383
James, H. (knight 1873) (1828–1911), 79, 146, 350, 386

Jardine, R., 148n
Jenkins, J. E. (1838–1910), 222, 235n, 329, 399
Jessel, G. (knight 1871), 226n
jews, 21, 222–3, 226, 439
Jex-Blake, T. W., 69
Johnston, A., 250
Jones, P. Lloyd (1811–86), 234, 236, 239, 407
Jowett, B. (1817–93), 27, **67**, 68, 72, 92, 112, 114, 127, 361, 426
Judicial Committee of the Privy Council, 35, 43, 44, 60, 101, 158, 372, 374–6, 413

Kennedy, J., 219
Kensington, Lord, 230
Keogh, W. N., 38, 237, 349–50
Kew Gardens, 352
Kimberley, 1st earl of (Baron Wodehouse 1846–66) (1826–1902), 47, **66**, **67**, 119, 279, 352, 401; and church questions, 313, 422; and democratic politics, 119, 422; and Ireland, 67, 136, 282, 286, 292, 299, 315, 318, 319, 325, 356, 403, 441n
King, E. (1829–1910), 183, 185, 373, 376
King, Hon. P. J. Locke, 313–14
Kingsley, C. (1819–75), **71**, **72**, 84–5, 106, 109, 123, 124, 335
Kinnaird, Hon. A. F., 146, 316
Knatchbull-Hugessen, E. H. (1829–93), **79**, 121, **192**, 319, 335, 352, 412, 416, 442
Knowles, J., 215

Labouchère, H., 33
Labour Representation League, 233–4, 400–1
Laing, S. (1812–97), 10, 220, 393, 419
Lambert, N. G., 392
Lancaster, J., 146
Lansbury, G., 446
Lansdowne, 5th marquess of, 66, 67
Lawrence, J. (cr. Baron 1869), 80, 109n
Lawson, Sir W., 208n
Layard, A. H. (1817–94), **72–3**, 84, 121, 123, 124, 126, 127, 408–9, 425–6
League, *see* National Education League
Leatham, E. A. (1828–1900), 227, 338, 380, 381, 414, 439
Leeds, 8th duke of, 283
Leicester, 2nd earl of, 64n
Leinster, duchess of, 61
Leinster, 3rd duke of, 64, 285
Leveson-Gower, Hon. E. F., 72
Lewes, G. H., 27
Lewis, Sir G. C., 15, 142
Lewis, J. D., 314
liberal Catholics, 193–8

Liberal party: and 1868 election, 276–7; and 1874 election, 392–3
Liberation Society, 23, 25, 26, 28, 38–9, 93, 213, 214, 227, 235, 265, 270, 276, 282, 285, 307, 312, 381, 387–8, 421–2, 434
Liberty and Property Defence League, 112, 437
licensing question, 115–16, 322, 352, 400, 403
Lichfield, 2nd earl of, 61, 66, 285
Liddell, H. G., 68, 373
Liddon, H. P. (1829–90), 44, 151, **183**, 186n, 190, 243, 314, 344, 373, 374, 376, 413, 439
Lightfoot, J. B., 374
Lloyd, Sir T. D. (1820–77), 270, 365n, 400
local government question, 321
local taxation question, 115, 345, 351–2, 404–7
Locke, J., 78
London school board, 79–80, 108–9, 217, 236, 306, 339, 406–7
Lopes, Sir L. M., 351
Lorne, marquess of (son of Argyll), 75, 412, 420
Lowder, C. F., 34
Lowe, E. C. (1823–1912), 183–4, 190, 439
Lowe, R. (1811–92), 10, 15, 47, **75**, **76–7**, 253, 279, 293, 352, 384, 386, 420; and democratic politics, 117, 119, 120, 261, 388, 412; and education, 109, 110–11, 304, 331–2, 412, 428; and Gladstone, 425–6; and Ireland, 133, 135, 136, 253, 264, 265, 266–7, 268, 285, 286, 288, 290, 318, 348, 353–4, 363, 372, 441
Lubbock, Sir J. (1834–1913), 30, **70**, 77, 88, 97, 112, 149, 295, 310, 335, 441
Lucas, F., 22
Lucraft, B., 238, 399
Lyttelton, 4th Baron, 191
Lyttelton, Hon. A. T., 184
Lyttelton, Hon. C. G., 191, 192
Lyveden, 1st Baron (cabinet office 1855–8), 64, 283, 322

McArthur, W. (1809–87), 80, 218–19, 305, 336, 412
Macaulay, T. B., 77
McClure, T., 197
MacColl, M. (1831–1907), 183, 184, 186n, 190, 439
McCombie, W., 148n
Macfie, R. A. (1811–93), 220, 316–17, 365n, 399
Macgregor, J. (1825–92), **80**, 122, 123, 124, 406, 441
Mackarness, J. F. (1820–89), 184, 413

Mackonochie, A. H. (1825–97), 34, 43, 184, 189, 372
McLagan, P., 365
Maclaren, A. (1826–1910), 28, 163, **201**, 208, 210
McLaren, D. (1800–86), 220, 273, 418
Macleod, N., 71, 102
Macmillan's Magazine, 27, 70
McNeile, H., 271
Magee college, Londonderry, 42, 357, 358
Maguire, J. F., 266, 290
Maitland, Sir A. C. R. G., 148n
Manchester conference, 334–5
Manning, H. E. (1808–92), 35, 196, 238, 356, 359
Marling, S. S., 273
Martin, J., 196, 316, 324
Martineau, J. (1805–1900), 223, 336, 358
Matheson, A., 420
Maurice, F. D., 27, 130, 201, 217, 223
Maxse, F. A., 225
Maxwell, W. H., 148n, 365n, 399
Maynooth, 42, 179, 272, 281, 357, 359
Mayo, 6th earl of (Lord Naas 1849–67), 267, 268, 271
Melly, G., 336
Miall, E. (1809–81), 22, **23**, **201**, 206, 216, 301, 362; and church questions, 45, 229, 235, 307, 311, 337; and education, 40, 277, 297, 304, 306; and Liberal party, 224, 381, 396
Mill, J. S. (1806–73), 5, 27, 29, **249–50**, 251, 296
Miller, J., 273
Milton, Viscount, 273, 339
Minto, 3rd earl of (1814–91), **61**, 63, 64, 283, 285, 366, 402, 408
Minto, 4th earl of, 61
Moberly, G. (1803–85), 182, 186n, 413
Monk, C. J., 146
Monsell, W. (cr. Baron Emly 1874) (1812–94), 38, 193, 198, 315, 361, 384
Moore, G. H., 22
Morgan, G. O. (1826–97), 301, 305, 308, 338, 362
Moriarty, D. (1814–77), 195, 263, 315, 344
Morley, 3rd earl of, 66, 67
Morley, J. (1838–1923), 225, 232, **239–49**, 251, 344, 357, 382, 422, 440
Morley, S. (1809–86), 202, 206, 208, **214–15**, 216, 235, 434; and church questions, 338, 415, 420; and education, 305, 306, 336, 377, 406, 412
Morpeth, Viscount, *see* Carlisle, 7th earl of
Morrison, W. (1836–1921), **250**, 251, 253, 254, 301, 330, 348, 360–1, 365
Motley, J. L., 317

Mozley, J. B., 185, 373
Mudie, C. E., 336
Mundella, A. J. (1825–97), **231**, 235, 297, 303, 305, 314, 336–7, 338, 377, 378, 383, 396, 414, 427
Murphy, W., 278, 315

Napier, Sir J., 359–60
National Association, 38–9, 263, 265
National Church Reform Union, 73, 100, 338
National Education League, 41, 109, 145, 222, 224, 253, 296, 307, 329, 330–1, 336, 377–9, 381–2, 383, 387–8
National Education Union, 109, 215, 302
National Society, 18, 40, 306
Newcastle, 5th duke of, 36
Newcastle, 6th duke of, 31, 275, 339
Newdegate, C. N., 294
Newman, F. W., 27
Nicholson, W., 148n
Nolan, J. P., 343, 345, 349
Nonconformist, 23, 209, 299, 336, 357, 370, 381, 420, 421
nonconformity, 145–6, 200–28, 397; and Catholicism, 205, 209–10, 212, 213–14, 216, 218–19, 220–2; and Church of England, 45, 202–9, 213, 214–16, 217, 218, 223, 224, 226, 227, 307, 331, 414–17, 421–2, 433–4, 434–5; and education, 40, 41, 210–11, 214–15, 218, 224–5, 226, 227–8, 296–7, 302–6, 306–7, 329–31, 334–5, 336, 377, endowed schools, 310, 380; and foreign policy, 207–8, 228, 432; and high churchmen, 35, 205, 208–9, 215–16, 217–18, 414–17; and Ireland, education, 211–12, 218–19, 225, 330–1, 334–5, 345–6, 357–8, 362, home rule, 212, 216, 218–19, 228, 438, 439–40, 444–6; and politics, 6–7, 11–13, 23–4, 28–9, 39, 144–5, 202, 205–8, 214, 229–30, 287, 368, 381–2, 396–401, 451–2; and Scottish Church patronage, 419–20
Norfolk, 15th duke of, 64, 283, 302
Normanby, 2nd marquess of (junior office 1853–8, 1868–71; governor of Queensland, 1871–4), 121
Northbrook, 2nd Baron (1826–1904), 61, 66, 67, 415, 422, 442
Northcote, Sir S. H. (1818–87), 138, 271, 284, 389
Northumberland, 6th duke of, 302

O'Connell, D., 22
O'Conor Don, The, 292, 345
O'Donoghue, The, 345
Ogilvy, Sir J., 399

O'Hagan, T. (cr. Baron 1870) (1812–85), 193, 198
O'Keeffe case, 350–1, 370–1
Osborne, R. B., 270
Overstone, 1st Baron, 64, 279n
Oxford movement, 30, 34, 71–2; *see also* high churchmen
Oxford professors, 185, 373

Palestine Exploration Fund, 123
Palgrave, W. G., 124n
Pall Mall Gazette, 74, **79**, 122, 327, 356, 370, 374, 409, 424–5
Palmer, Sir R., *see* Selborne, Baron
Palmerston, Viscount, 24–5, 26, 60, 124, 130; and Gladstone, 36, 37, 142, 426
parliamentary reform: *1866–8*, 10, 28–9, 30, 39, 261–2, 276–7; *1873–4*, 119, 386, 412
Parker, C. S., 191, 192, 404, 439
Party Processions Act, 315
Patten, J. Wilson, 271
Pease, J. W. (1828–1903), 228, 305, 310, 336, 337
Peel, A. W. (youngest son of the prime minister), 420
Peel, Sir R. (1822–95), 191n, 263, 264, 365n
Peelites, 15, 36, 141, 185, 191–3
Pelham, J. T., 24
Pender, J., 148n, 402n
Perks, R. W., 441n
Phillimore, Sir R. J. (1810–85), 76, 184, 190, 413
Phillimore, W. G. F., 184
Picton, J. A. (1832–1910), 80n, 250, 254, 440
Pim, J. (1806–85), 193, 320, 326
Pius IX, 43, 292
Playfair, L. (1818–98), **71**, **75**, 149, 305, 386, 427; and Ireland, 135, 320, 348, 353–4, 361–2, 365, 440; and religion, 91, 295, 419, 420; and university reform, 111–12, 308
Plunket, Hon. D. R., 299–300, 320
Portland, 5th duke of, 339
Portman, 1st Baron (cr. Viscount 1873), 314, 374
Portsmouth, 5th earl of, 64, 66
positivism, 238, 239–49; and education, 246; and foreign policy, 247; and Ireland, 247–9; and Liberal party, 249; and religion, 240–6; and the state, 246–7
Potter, G. (1832–93), **233–4**, 235, 236, 239, 407
Powell, F. S., 338
Price, B. (1807–88), 69, 142, 335
Primitive Methodism, 217
Prothero, R. E., 70, 92

Public Worship Regulation Act, 192, 216, 413–17
Purchas, J., 43, 372, 373
Pusey, E. B. (1800–82), 34, 44, **182–3**, 186n, 187, 190, 314, 374, 376, 413

quakers, 222–3, 226–8, 439
Queen's university and colleges, 20, 42, 263–4, 354–7, 358

Rainy, R. (1826–1906), 219, 340, 341
Ramsden, Sir J. W., 61, 400
Rathbone, W., 229, 310
Record, 285
Reed, C. (1819–81), 80n, 214, 215, 285, 305, 336, 337, 379
Reeve, H. (1813–95), **65**, 70, **101**, 123, 127–8; and church questions, 92, 126, 143, 375, 407; and Gladstone, 143, 407; and Ireland, 132, 133–4, 273, 366, 407–8; and Liberal party, 118–19, 120, 273, 407–8
Regium donum, 272, 281
Repton, G. W. J., 390
Ribbonism, 43, 318
Rice, T. Spring, 17
Richard, H. (1812–88), 28, **201**, 210–11, 212, 297, 302, 304–5, 336, 412, 414, 439–40
Richmond, 6th duke of, 418
Rigg, J. H. (1821–1909), 80n, 217–18, 336, 406
Ripley, H. W., 338, 395
Ripon, marquess of (cr. 1871; Earl de Grey and Ripon, 1859–71) (1827–1909), **184**, 279, 302, 313, 330, 377–9, 385, 386, 412, 423–4
Ritual Commission, 44, 312–14
ritualism, 30, 34–5, 43–4, 374, 376; *see also* Church of England, high churchmen, Public Worship Regulation Act, Ritual Commission
Robinson, Sir S., 400
Rock, 316
Roebuck, J. A. (1801–79), 77–8, 270, 396
Rogers, J. E. **Thorold** (1823–90), 250, 253, 254
Rogers, J. Guinness (1822–1911), 28, **201**, 210, 211, 212, 334, 335, 406, 422, 445
Rogers, W., 80
Rosebery, 5th earl of, 418, 441n
Rossa, O'Donovan, 291, 292
Rothschild, Baron L. de, 392
Rothschild, Baron L. N. de, 21
Rothschild family, 226
Rowntree, J., 228
Russell, Lord Arthur, 76, 149

Russell, C. W., 359
Russell, F. C. Hastings, *see* Bedford, 9th duke of
Russell, G. W. E., 184, 188, 190
Russell, John, 1st Earl (1792–1878), 21, **63**, **76**, 116, 123; and education, 18, 109, 262, 297, 329, 335; and Ireland, 33, 38, 132, 134, 265, 268, 274, 283–5, 329, 371; and Liberal party, 279, 322, 329, 352, 408; and parliamentary reform, 261; and religion, 26, 33, 35–6, 83, 84, 101, 127, 274–5, 375
Russell, Lord Odo, 293–4
Russell, Sir W., 148n
Rylands, P., 314

Sadleir, J., 38
St Albans, 10th duke of, 61, 66
St Paul's, 292
St Paul's cathedral, 185, 373–4, 416
Sala, G. A., 124
Salisbury, 3rd marquess of (1830–1903), 283–6, 301, 302, 310, 365, 374, 375, 380, 417
Salomans, Sir D., 226
Samuelson, B., 308
Sandon, Viscount (1831–1900), 80, 100–1, 137, 313, 338, 390
school boards, 306–7, 398–9, 404–7; *see also* London school board
Scotland: Church Establishment and patronage questions, 23, 102–3, 164, 220–1, 418–20; education, 39, 103–4, 219–20, 309, 339–43
Scott, R., 373
Scottish Reformation Society, 316
Seebohm, F., 227–8
Seeley, J. R. (1834–95), 27, 30, 72, 73
Selborne, Baron (Sir Roundell Palmer, cr. 1872) (1812–95), **184–5**, 186, 191, 192, 270, 294, 356, 374–6, 422, 434, 439
Shaftesbury, 7th earl of (1801–85), 58, **65**, 68, 115, 123, 322; and church questions, 45, 89, 92, 100, 314, 337, 374, 376; and democratic politics, 81, 142; and education, 108, 109, 302, 303, 406; and Ireland, 132, 283, 367
Shaw-Lefevre, G. J., 250, 254, 280
Simon, J., 226
Sligo, 3rd marquess of, 285
Smith, Goldwin (1823–1910), 27, 29, 250–5, 402
Smith, G. Vance (unitarian minister in York), 336
Smith, R. Bosworth (1839–1908), 69, 124
Smith, R. Payne, 373
Smith, W., 22–3

Smith, W. H. (1825–91), 80, 137–8, 146, 306, 313–14, 321, 322, 377–80, 389, 406
Smyth, P. J., 345
Social Democratic Federation, 236
Somerset, 12th duke of (1804–85), **60**, 61, **64**, 123–4; and church questions, 26, 434; and Ireland, 283, 285, 328, 389; and Liberal party, 141n, 279, 322, 352, 388, 408; and religion, 84, 141n
Spectator, 31, 72, **76**, 135n, 337, 352–3, 376, 401
Spencer, 5th Earl (1835–1910), **66**, **67**; and church questions, 98, 415; and Ireland, 290–2, 317–19, 320, 324–5, 327, 328, 355, 356, 359, 365, 372, 403, 441n; and Liberal party, 385, 386
Spencer, H., 27, 251
Spurgeon, C. (1834–92), 28, 93, **212**, 213, 214, 216, 336, 439
Stanhope, 5th Earl, 284–5, 314
Stanley, Lord, *see* Derby, 14th *and* 15th earls of
Stanley, A. P. (1815–81), **68–9**, 71, 72, 123; and church questions, 100, 101, 314, 375, 415, 419; and Ireland, 131n, 282, 360; and nonconformity, 91, 99, 209, 210; and religion, 27, 58, 73, 83, 87, 88, 91, 99, 102, 125, 127, 217, 223, 340–1
Stanley, Hon. E. Lyulph (1839–1925), 76, 250, 253, 339
Stanley, Hon. F. A., 268
Stanley of Alderley, 2nd Baron (cabinet office 1855–8, 1860–6) (1802–69), 60, 279n
Stanley of Alderley, 3rd Baron (1827–1903), 66, 76, 123
Stansfeld, J. (1820–98), 224n, 280, 335, 346, 401, 412
Stanton, A. (1839–1913), 184, 189
Stephen, J. F. (1829–94), 27, 58, **74**, 76–7, 87, 117, 382
Stephen, L. (1832–1904), 250, 253, 254
Stephens, W. R. W. (1839–1902), 182, 183
Stevenson, J. C., 308, 336
Stoughton, J. (1807–97), **212**, 213, 214, 217, 335, 336, 439
Strachey, Sir E. (1812–1901), 65, 123
Strachey, J. St Loe, 65n
Strafford, 2nd earl of, 64
strikes, 31–2, 403
Supreme Court of Judicature Act, 374–6
Sutherland, duchess of, 64
Sutherland, 3rd duke of (1828–92), **61**, 62, 275, 283, 285, 402n
Synan, E. J., 345

Table of Lessons Bill, 313

Tait, A. C. (1811–82), **68–9**, **70**, 71, 111n; and Church of England, 36, 213, 217, 274, 312, 313, 373, 375–6, 413–17; and Ireland, 131n, 270, 281–5, 287, 360
Talbot, C. R. M., 148n
Talbot, E. S. (1844–1934), 183, 184, 373
Taylor, P. A. (1819–1901), 224, 365
Temple, F. (1821–1902), 68, 72, 73, 100, 107, 131n, 149, 161
Tennyson, A., 214, 441
Thames Embankment, 116, 146, 322
Thirlwall, C. (1797–1875), 17, 22, **68**, 82, 130, 131, 133, 283, 288, 325, 408, 415, 426
Thomson, W. (**archbishop** of York 1862–90) (1819–90), 123, 283, 375
Thomson, Sir W. (1824–1907), **75–6**, 309, 340, 361, 441
Thorold, A. W., 80
Times, 65, 70, 77, 191; and church questions, 311, 335, 374, 376, 415; and education, 297, 335; and Ireland, 284, 292, 346, 356, 367, 371; and politics, 271, 388, 402–3, 415, 424–5; and religion, 294, 415, 424–5
Tollemache, Hon. F. J., 191n
Tomline, G., 191n
Torrens, W. T. M. (1813–94), **78**, 80, 112n, 148n, 270, 338, 365n, 380, 399, 409, 420, 428
Townsend, M. (joint editor and proprietor, *Spectator*), 72
Trades Union Congress, 236
Trelawny, Sir J. S. (1816–85), 25, 126n, 319, 321, 338, 365n
Trevelyan, G. O. (1838–1928), **250**, 252–3, 254, 277, 280, 305, 379, 412, 427
Trinity college, Dublin, 20, 42, 265, 298, 299, 314, 320, 345, 354–7, 358–9
Trollope, A. (editor, *St Paul's*, 1867–70) (1815–82), 31, 48, 139, 292; *see also St Paul's*
Tufton, Sir H. J., 392
Tulloch, J. (Principal and professor of theology, St Andrews) (1823–86), 27, **71**, 102, 103, 143, 340, 450
Tyndall, J. (1820–93), 74–5, 94n, 288, 443

ultramontanism, *see* Catholicism
United Presbyterians, 45–6, 104, 219–22, 341, 343, 418–20
unitarians, 22–3, 222–5, 439
university tests, 26–7, 111, 147, 190, 192, 227, 230, 297–8, 300–1, 307–9
Urwick, W., 214, 336

Vatican council, 43, 125–6, 156–7, 209–10, 292–5, 423–6

Vaughan, C. J., 69

Vickers, J., 149n

Victoria, Queen (1819–1901), 31, **63–4**, **75**, 413; and Gladstone, 270, 279, 325, 351, 366, 408, 426; and Ireland, 129n, 132, 270, 282, 284–5, 287, 290, 291, 299, 317, 325, 351, 366, 441; and religion, 59, 102, 127, 426

Villiers, C. P. (cabinet office 1859–66; brother of Clarendon; veteran anti-corn law campaigner) (1802–98), 279n, 426

Villiers, H. M. (brother of Clarendon), 24

Vivian, H. H., 415

Waldegrave, F. E. A., Countess (1821–79), 67, 141n

Wales, prince of, 31, 71, 325, 351

Walter, J. (1818–94), 191, 192, 273, 392, 415, 420

Wedderburn, Sir D., 250

Wellesley, G. V., 71

Wesleyans, 18, 24, 28, 217–19, 225, 303, 336, 439

Westbury, 1st Baron (Lord Chancellor 1861–5) (1800–73), **60**, 101, 132, 283, 284

Westminster, dowager marchioness of, 383

Westminster, duchess of, 61

Westminster, 3rd marquess of (cr. duke 1874; Earl Grosvenor 1845–69) (1825–99), 10, **61**, 62, 63, 64n, **66**, 67, 109n, 116, 123, 261, 426, 434

Westminster Review, 249, 252, 253, 366, 367

Wetherell, T. F., 193n

Whalley, G. H. (1813–78), **66**, 146, 365n, 375, 420

whig-liberals: and Catholicism, 125–6, 146–7, 403–4, 424–6; and Church of England, 96–102, 274–5, 404, 414–17; and Church of Scotland, 102–4, 419–20; and Conservative party, 120, 137–40; and democratic politics, 29–32, 116–20; and Eastern question, 122–5, 432; and

education, 103–4, 105–10, 147, 296–7, 302–6, 329, 335–6, 377–9, 380–1, 388, 404–7, endowed schools, 110, 146, 147–8, 380; and finance, 388, 423; and foreign policy, 121–2, 126–8, 433; and Gladstone, 35–6, 94–6, 140–3, 325–6, 407–9, 422–3, 424–6, 426–8, 450–1; and Ireland, 32–4, 128–37, Church, 32–4, 130–3, 147, 270, 273–4, 283–8, education, 133–5, 146–7, 328, 333–4, 345–6, 348, 360–5, 366–8, home rule, 325–6, 388–9, 403, 440–4; and Liberal party, 82–3, 275–6, 323–4, 401–9, 422–3, 426–8, 450–1; and religion, 16–17, 21, 80–102; and the state, 112–16

Whitbread, S. (1830–1915), 76, 149, 440

Wilberforce, S. (1805–73), 34, 182, 186n, 270, 283, 375

Williams, J. Carvell, 265

Wilson, Sir M., 402n

Winterbotham, H. S. P. (1837–73), 251n, 296, 297, 304, 305, 311, 378

Wodehouse, Baron, *see* Kimberley, 1st earl of

Wood, Charles, *see* Halifax, 1st Viscount

Wood, W. P., *see* Hatherley, 1st Baron

Woodard, N., 183–4

Woodford, J. R., 184, 376

Wordsworth, Christopher, 182

working-men, 29, 232–9; and education, 40–1, 236–7; and Ireland, 237–8, 440; and religion, 232–6; and the state, 232–3

Wright, T., 238

Yarborough, 3rd earl of, 402

Yeaman, J., 399

Yorkshire Post, 390

Young, G., 309, 340

Zetland, 2nd earl of (1795–1873), 61, 62, 63, 64, 109n, 192, 283

Zetland, 3rd earl of, 61, 62

Cambridge Studies in the History and Theory of Politics

Editors: Maurice Cowling, G. R. Elton and J. R. Pole

A series in two parts, studies and original texts. The studies are original works on political history and political philosophy while the texts are modern, critical editions of major texts in political thought. The titles include:

TEXTS

Vladimir Akimov on the Dilemmas of Russian Marxism 1895–1903. An English edition of 'A Short History of the Social Democratic Movement in Russia' and 'The Second Congress of the Russian Social Democratic Labour Party', with an introduction and notes by Jonathan Frankel

J. G. Herder on Social and Political Culture, translated, edited and with an introduction by F. M. Barnard

Kant's Political Writings, edited with an introduction and notes by Hans Reiss; translated by H. B. Nisbet

Karl Marx's Critique of Hegel's 'Philosophy of Right', edited with an introduction and notes by Joseph O'Malley; translated by Annette Jolin and Joseph O'Malley

The Political Writings of Leibniz, edited and translated by Patrick Riley

Turgot on Progress, Sociology and Economics: A Philosophical Review of the Successive Advances of the Human Mind. On Universal History. Reflections on the Formation and Distribution of Wealth, edited, translated and introduced by Ronald L. Meek

Georg Wilhelm Friedrich Hegel: Lectures on the Philosophy of World History: Reason in History, translated from the German edition of Johannes Hoffmeister by H. B. Nisbet and with an introduction by Duncan Forbes

A Machiavellian Treatise by Stephen Gardiner, edited and translated by Peter S. Donaldson

The Political Works of James Harrington, edited by J. G. A. Pocock

Selected Writings of August Cieszkowski, edited and translated with an introductory essay by André Liebich

De Republica Anglorum by Sir Thomas Smith, edited by Mary Dewar

Sister Peg: A Pamphlet Hitherto Unknown by David Hume, edited with an introduction and notes by David R. Raynor

STUDIES

1867: Disraeli, Gladstone and Revolution: The Passing of the Second Reform Bill, by Maurice Cowling

The Social and Political Thought of Karl Marx, by Shlomo Avineri

Idealism, Politics and History: Sources of Hegelian Thought, by George Armstrong Kelly

Alienation: Marx's Conception of Man in Capitalist Society, by Bertell Ollman

Hegel's Theory of the Modern State, by Shlomo Avineri

The Impact of Hitler: British Politics and British Policy 1933–1940, by Maurice Cowling

The Liberal Mind 1914–1929, by Michael Bentley

Revolution Principles: The Politics of Party 1689–1720, by J. P. Kenyon

John Locke and the Theory of Sovereignty: Mixed Monarchy and the Right of Resistance in the Political Thought of the English Revolution, by Julian H. Franklin

Adam Smith's Politics: An Essay in Historiographic Revision, by Donald Winch

Lloyd George's Secretariat, by John Turner

The Tragedy of Enlightenment: An Essay on the Frankfurt School, by Paul Connerton
Religion and Public Doctrine in Modern England, by Maurice Cowling
Bentham and Bureaucracy, by L. J. Hume
A Critique of Freedom and Equality, by John Charvet
The Dynamics of Change: The Crisis of the 1750s and English Party Systems, by J. C. D. Clark
Resistance and Compromise: The Political Thought of the Elizabethan Catholics, by P. J. Holmes
Nationalism, Positivism and Catholicism: The Politics of Charles Maurras and French Catholics, 1890–1914, by Michael Sutton
The Christian Polity of John Calvin, by Harro Höpfl
Sir John Davis and the Conquest of Ireland: A Study in Legal Imperialism, by Hans S. Pawlisch
Religion and Public Doctrine in Modern England, Volume 2: 'Assaults', by Maurice Cowling
English Society 1688–1832: Ideology, Social Structure and Political Practice during the Ancien Regime, by J. C. D. Clark